Top 100

Computer and Technical

CAREERS™

Your Complete Guidebook to Major Jobs in
Many Fields at All Training Levels

THIRD EDITION

Michael Farr

JIST
Works
America's Career Publisher

Top 100 Computer and Technical Careers, Third Edition
Your Complete Guidebook to Major Jobs in Many Fields at All Training Levels

Previous edition was titled *America's Top 101 Computer and Technical Jobs.*

© 2007 by JIST Publishing, Inc.

Published by JIST Works, an imprint of JIST Publishing, Inc.
8902 Otis Avenue
Indianapolis, IN 46216-1033
Phone: 1-800-648-JIST   Fax: 1-800-JIST-FAX
E-mail: info@jist.com   Web site: www.jist.com

Some books by Michael Farr:
Best Jobs for the 21st Century
Overnight Career Choice
Same-Day Resume
Next-Day Job Interview
The Quick Resume & Cover Letter Book
The Very Quick Job Search

JIST's Top Careers™ Series:
Top 300 Careers
Top 100 Health-Care Careers
100 Fastest-Growing Jobs
Top 100 Careers Without a Four-Year Degree
Top 100 Careers for College Graduates
Top 100 Computer and Technical Careers

Visit www.jist.com for free job search information, book excerpts, and ordering information on our many products. For free information on 14,000 job titles, visit www.careeroink.com.

Quantity discounts are available for JIST products. Have future editions of JIST books automatically delivered to you on publication through our convenient standing order program. Please call 1-800-648-JIST or visit www.jist.com for a free catalog and more information.

Acquisitions Editor: Susan Pines
Development Editors: Stephanie Koutek, Jill Mazurczyk
Database Work: Laurence Shatkin
Cover Layout: Trudy Coler
Interior Design and Layout: Marie Kristine Parial-Leonardo
Proofreader: Jeanne Clark

Printed in the United States of America

08 07 06   9 8 7 6 5 4 3 2 1

Library of Congress Cataloging-in-Publication Data

Farr, J. Michael.
   Top 100 computer and technical careers : your complete guidebook to major jobs in many fields at all training levels /
Michael Farr. -- 3rd ed.
      p. cm. -- (Top career series)
   "Previous edition was titled America's Top 101 Computer and Technical Jobs."
   Includes bibliographical references and index.
   ISBN-13: 978-1-59357-320-1 (alk. paper)
   ISBN-10: 1-59357-320-0 (alk. paper)
   1. Computer science--Vocational guidance--United States. 2. Technology--Vocational guidance--United States. 3. Occupations--United
States. 4. Labor market--United States. 5. Job hunting--United States. I. America's top 101 computer and technical jobs. II. Title.
   QA76.25.F37 2007
   004.023--dc22
                                                                                            2006028739

ISBN-13: 978-1-59357-320-1
ISBN-10: 1-59357-320-0

Relax. You Don't Have to Read This Whole Book!

You don't need to read this entire book. I've organized it into easy-to-use sections so you can get just the information you want. You will find everything you need to

★ Learn about the 100 top computer and technical careers, including their daily tasks, pay, outlook, and required education and skills.

★ Match your personal skills to the careers.

★ Take seven steps to land a good job in less time.

To get started, simply scan the table of contents to learn more about these sections and to see a list of the jobs described in this book. Really, this book is easy to use, and I hope it helps you.

Who Should Use This Book?

This is more than a book of job descriptions. I've spent quite a bit of time thinking about how to make its contents useful for a variety of situations, including

★ **Exploring career options.** The job descriptions in Part II give a wealth of information on many of the most desirable jobs in the labor market. The assessment in Part I can help you focus your career options.

★ **Considering more education or training.** The information helps you avoid costly mistakes in choosing a career or deciding on additional training or education—and it increases your chances of planning a bright future.

★ **Job seeking.** This book helps you identify new job targets, prepare for interviews, and write targeted resumes. The advice in Part III has been proven to cut job search time in half.

* **Career planning.** The job descriptions help you explore your options, and Parts III and IV provide career planning advice and other useful information.

Source of Information

The job descriptions come from the good people at the U.S. Department of Labor, as published in the most recent edition of the *Occupational Outlook Handbook*. The *OOH* is the best source of career information available, and the descriptions include the most current, accurate data on jobs. Thank you to all the people at the Department of Labor who gather, compile, analyze, and make sense of this information. It's good stuff, and I hope you can make good use of it.

Mike Farr

Mike Farr

Contents

Summary of Major Sections

Introduction. Provides an explanation of the job descriptions, how best to use the book, and other details. *Begins on page 1.*

Part I: Using the Job-Match Grid to Choose a Career. Match your skills and preferences to the jobs in this book. *Begins on page 13.*

Part II: Descriptions of the Top 100 Computer and Technical Careers. Presents thorough descriptions of the top 100 computer and technical jobs. Education and training requirements for these jobs vary from on-the-job training to a four-year college degree or more. Each description gives information on the nature of the work, working conditions, employment, training, other qualifications, advancement, job outlook, earnings, related occupations, and sources of additional information. The jobs are presented in alphabetical order. The page numbers where specific descriptions begin are listed in the detailed contents. *Begins on page 29.*

Part III: Quick Job Search—Seven Steps to Getting a Good Job in Less Time. This relatively brief but important section offers results-oriented career planning and job search techniques. It includes tips on identifying your key skills, defining your ideal job, using effective job search methods, writing resumes, organizing your time, improving your interviewing skills, and following up on leads. The last part of this section features professionally written and designed resumes for some of the top computer and technical jobs. *Begins on page 287.*

Part IV: Important Trends in Jobs and Industries. This section includes three well-written articles on labor market trends. The articles are worth your time. Titles of the articles are "Tomorrow's Jobs," "Employment Trends in Major Industries," and "Training for Techies: Career Preparation in Information Technology." *Begins on page 347.*

Detailed Contents

iv

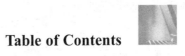

Part III: Quick Job Search—Seven Steps to Getting a Good Job in Less Time 287

Part IV: Important Trends in Jobs and Industries 347

Index 377

Introduction

This book is about improving your life, not just about selecting a job. The career you choose will have an enormous impact on how you live your life.

A huge amount of information is available on occupations, but most people don't know where to find accurate, reliable facts to help them make good career decisions—or they don't take the time to look. Important choices such as what to do with your career and whether to get additional training or education deserve your time.

If you are considering more training or education—whether additional course work, a college degree, or an advanced degree—this book will help with solid information. Training or education beyond high school is now typically required to get better jobs, but many good jobs can be learned through on-the-job experience, informal training, and technical training or education lasting from several months to two years. The education and training needed for the jobs described in *Top 100 Computer and Technical Careers* vary enormously. This book provides descriptions for major jobs requiring computer and technical skills and gives you the facts you need for exploring your options.

A certain type of work or workplace may interest you as much as a certain type of job. If your interests and values lead you to work in healthcare, for example, you can do this in a variety of work environments, in a variety of industries, and in a variety of jobs. For this reason, I suggest you begin exploring alternatives by following your interests and finding a career path that allows you to use your talents doing something you enjoy.

Also, remember that money is not everything. The time you spend in career planning can pay off in higher earnings, but being satisfied with your work—and your life—is often more important than how much you earn. This book can help you find the work that suits you best.

Keep in Mind That Your Situation Is Not "Average"

Projected employment growth and earnings trends are quite positive for many occupations and industries. Keep in mind, however, that the averages in this book will not be true for many individuals. Within any field, many people earn more and many earn less than the average.

My point is that your situation is probably not average. Some people do better than others, and some are willing to accept less pay for a more desirable work environment. Earnings vary enormously in different parts of the country, in different occupations, and in different industries. But this book's solid information is a great place to start. Good information will give you a strong foundation for good decisions.

Four Important Labor Market Trends That Will Affect Your Career

Our economy has changed in dramatic ways over the past 10 years, with profound effects on how we work and live. Part IV of this book provides more information on labor market trends, but in case you don't read it, here are four trends that you simply *must* consider.

1. Education Pays

I'm sure you won't be surprised to learn that people with higher levels of education and training have higher average earnings. The data that follows comes from the U.S. Department of Labor. I've selected data to show you the median earnings for people with various levels of education. (The median is the point where half earn more and half earn less.) Based on this information, I computed the earnings advantage of people at various education levels over those who did not graduate from high school. I've also included information showing the average percentage of people at that educational level who are unemployed.

Earnings for Year-Round, Full-Time Workers Age 25 and Over, by Educational Attainment

Level of Education	Median Annual Earnings	Premium Over High School Dropouts	Unemployment Rate
Master's degree	$53,200	$33,400	2.9
Bachelor's degree	45,000	25,200	3.3
Associate degree	33,600	13,800	4.0
Some college, no degree	31,100	11,300	5.2
High school graduate	27,700	7,900	5.5
High school dropout	19,800	—	8.8

Source: Bureau of Labor Statistics

As you can see in the table, the more education and training you have, the more you are likely to earn—and the less likely you are to be unemployed. These two factors can make an enormous difference in long-term earnings. For example, the earnings gap between a college graduate and someone with a high school education is now $17,300 a year. That's enough to buy a nice car, make a down payment on a house, or even take a month's vacation for two to Europe. As you see, over a lifetime, these additional earnings can make an enormous difference in the college graduate's lifestyle.

And there's more. Jobs that require education and training beyond high school are projected to grow significantly faster than jobs that do not. Research shows that people with higher educational levels are less likely to be unemployed and that they remain unemployed for shorter periods of time. Overall, the data on earnings and other criteria indicate that people with more education and training do better than those with less. There are exceptions, of course, but for most people, more education and training results in higher earnings and lower rates of unemployment.

Many jobs can be obtained without a college degree, but most better-paying jobs now require either training beyond high school or substantial work experience.

2. Knowledge of Computer and Other Technologies Is Increasingly Important

Jobs requiring computer and technical skills are projected to be among the fastest-growing jobs in America. As you look over the list of jobs in the table of contents for *Top 100 Computer and Technical Careers,* you will notice the enormous variety of technical jobs. The education and training requirements for these jobs range from on-the-job experience to a four-year college degree and more. But even jobs that do not appear to be technical often call for computer literacy or technical skills. Managers, for example, are often expected to understand and use spreadsheet, word-processing, and database software.

In all fields, people without job-related technical and computer skills will have a more difficult time finding good opportunities than people who have these skills. Employers tend to hire people with the skills they need, and people without these abilities won't get the best jobs. So consider upgrading your job-related computer and technology skills if you need to—and plan to stay up to date on your current and future jobs.

3. Ongoing Education and Training Are Essential

School and work once were separate activities, and most people did not go back to school after they began working. But with rapid changes in technology, most people are now required to learn throughout their work lives. Jobs are constantly upgraded, and today's jobs often cannot be handled by people who have only the knowledge and skills that were adequate for workers a few years ago. To remain competitive, people without technical or computer skills must get them. Those who do not will face increasingly limited job options.

What this means is that you should upgrade your job skills throughout your working life. This may include taking formal courses, reading work-related magazines at home, signing up for on-the-job training, or participating in other forms of education. Upgrading your work-related skills on an ongoing basis is no longer optional for most jobs, and you ignore doing so at your peril.

4. Good Career Planning Has Increased in Importance

Most people spend more time watching TV in a week than they spend on career planning during an entire year. Yet most people will change their jobs many times and make major career changes five to seven times.

While you probably picked up this book for its information on jobs, it also provides a great deal of information on career planning. For example, Part III gives good career and job search advice, and Part IV has useful information on labor market trends. I urge you to read these and related materials because career-planning and job-seeking skills are the keys to survival in this new economy.

Tips on Using This Book

This book is based on information from a variety of government sources and includes the most up-to-date and accurate data available. The entries are well written and pack a lot of information into short descriptions. *Top 100 Computer and Technical Careers* can be used in many ways, and I've provided tips for these four major uses:

★ For people exploring career, education, or training alternatives

★ For job seekers

★ For employers and business people

★ For counselors, instructors, and other career specialists

Tips for People Exploring Career, Education, or Training Alternatives

Top 100 Computer and Technical Careers is an excellent resource for anyone exploring career, education, or training alternatives. Many people do not have a good idea of what they want to do in their careers. They may be considering additional training or education but may not know what sort they should get. If you are one of these people, *Top 100 Computer and Technical Careers* can help in several ways. Here are a few pointers.

Review the list of jobs. Trust yourself. Research studies indicate that most people have a good sense of their interests. Your interests can be used to guide you to career options you should consider in more detail.

Begin by looking over the occupations listed in the table of contents. Look at all the jobs, because you may identify previously overlooked possibilities. If other people will be using this book, please don't mark in it. Instead, on a separate sheet of paper, list the jobs that interest you. Or make a photocopy of the table of contents and mark the jobs that interest you.

Next, carefully read the descriptions of the jobs that most interest you. A quick review will often eliminate one or more of these jobs based on pay, working conditions, education required, or other considerations. After you have identified the three or four jobs that seem most interesting, research each one more thoroughly before making any important decisions.

Study the jobs and their training and education requirements. Too many people decide to obtain additional training or education without knowing much about the jobs the training will lead to. Reviewing the descriptions in this book is one way to learn more about an occupation before you enroll in an education or training program. If you are currently a student, the job descriptions in this book can also help you decide on a major course of study or learn more about the jobs for which your studies are preparing you.

Do not be too quick to eliminate a job that interests you. If a job requires more education or training than you currently have, you can obtain this training in many ways.

Don't abandon your past experience and education too quickly. If you have significant work experience, training, or education, these should not be abandoned too quickly. Many skills you have learned and used in previous jobs or other settings can apply to related jobs. Many times, after people carefully consider what they want to do, they change careers and find that the skills they have can still be used.

Top 100 Computer and Technical Careers can help you explore career options in several ways. First, carefully review descriptions for jobs you have held in the past. On a separate sheet of paper, list the skills needed in those jobs. Then do the same for jobs that interest you now. By comparing the lists, you will be able to identify skills you used in previous jobs that you could also use in jobs that interest you for the future. These "transferable" skills form the basis for moving to a new career.

You can also identify skills you have developed or used in nonwork activities, such as hobbies, family responsibilities, volunteer work, school, military, and extracurricular interests. The descriptions can be used even if you want to stay with the same employer. For example, you may identify jobs within your organization that offer more rewarding work, higher pay, or other advantages over your present job. Read the descriptions related to these jobs, as you may be able to transfer into another job rather than leave the organization.

Tips for Job Seekers

You can use the descriptions in this book to give you an edge in finding job openings and in getting job offers—even when you are competing with people who have better credentials. Here are some ways *Top 100 Computer and Technical Careers* can help you in the job search.

Identify related job targets. You may be limiting your job search to a small number of jobs for which you feel qualified, but by doing so you eliminate many jobs you could do and enjoy. Your search for a new job should be broadened to include more possibilities.

Go through the entire list of jobs in the table of contents and check any that require skills similar to those you have. Look at all the jobs, as doing so sometimes helps you identify targets you would otherwise overlook.

Many people are not aware of the many specialized jobs related to their training or experience. The descriptions in *Top 100 Computer and Technical Careers* are for major job titles, but a variety of more-specialized jobs may require similar skills. The "Other Major Career Information Sources" section later in this introduction lists sources you can use to find out about more-specialized jobs.

The descriptions can also point out jobs that interest you but have higher responsibility or compensation levels. Although you may not consider yourself qualified for such jobs now, you should think about seeking jobs that are above your previous levels but within your ability to handle.

Prepare for interviews. This book's job descriptions are an essential source of information to help you prepare for interviews. If you carefully review the description of a job before an interview, you will be much better prepared to emphasize your key skills. You should also review descriptions for past jobs and identify skills needed in the new job.

Negotiate pay. The job descriptions in this book will help you know what pay range to expect. Note that local pay and other details can differ substantially from the national averages in the descriptions.

Tips for Employers and Business People

Employers, human resource professionals, and other business users can use this book's information to write job descriptions, study pay ranges, and set criteria for new employees. The information can also help you conduct more-effective interviews by providing a list of key skills needed by new hires.

Tips for Counselors, Instructors, and Other Career Specialists

Counselors, instructors, and other career specialists will find this book helpful for their clients or students exploring career options or job targets. My best suggestion to professionals is to get this book off the shelf and into the hands of the people who need it. Leave it on a table or desk and show people how the information can help them. Wear this book out—its real value is as a tool used often and well.

Additional Information About the Projections

For more information about employment change, job openings, earnings, unemployment rates, and training requirements by occupation, consult *Occupational Projections and Training Data*, published by the Bureau of Labor Statistics. For occupational information from an industry perspective, including some occupations and career paths that *Top 100 Computer and Technical Careers* does not cover, consult another BLS publication, *Career Guide to Industries*. This book is also available from JIST with enhanced content under the title *40 Best Fields for Your Career*.

Information on the Major Parts of This Book

This book was designed to be easy to use. The table of contents provides brief comments on each part, and that may be all you need. If not, here are some additional details you may find useful in getting the most out of this book.

Part I: Using the Job-Match Grid to Choose a Career

Part I features an assessment with checklists and questions to match your skills and preferences to the jobs in this book. The seven skills covered in the assessment are artistic, communication, interpersonal, managerial, mathematics, mechanical, and science. The five job characteristics covered in the assessment are economically sensitive, geographically concentrated, hazardous conditions, outdoor work, and physically demanding.

Part II: Descriptions of the Top 100 Computer and Technical Careers

Part II is the main part of this book and is probably the reason you picked it up. It contains brief, well-written descriptions for 100 major jobs that require computer and other technical skills. The content for these job descriptions comes from the U.S. Department of Labor and is considered by many people to be the most accurate and up-to-date data available. The jobs are presented in alphabetical order. The table of contents provides a page number that shows where each description begins.

Together, the jobs in Part II provide enormous variety at all levels of earnings, training, and education. One way to explore career options is to go through the table of contents and identify those jobs that seem interesting. If you are interested in medical jobs, for example, you can quickly spot those you want to learn more about. You may also see other jobs that look interesting, and you should consider those as well.

Next, read the descriptions for the jobs that interest you and, based on what you learn, identify those that *most* interest you. These are the jobs you should consider. Parts III and IV give you additional information on how best to do so.

How the 100 Jobs Were Selected

The jobs included in this book are selected from the nearly 270 jobs covered in detail by the *Occupational Outlook Handbook,* published by the U.S. Department of Labor. They are jobs that require considerable use of computers, science, or technology. In recent years, technology has not only created many new jobs; it is playing an increasing role in many formerly low-tech jobs. For example, urban and regional planners starting out nowadays are expected to be proficient in use of geographic information system (GIS) technology. Drafters sometimes spend the whole day manipulating data at a computer terminal rather than holding a pencil at an old-fashioned drafting table.

The size of the workforce for these jobs varies from a high of 2.4 million (registered nurses) to a low of 2,500 (mathematicians). Most of the jobs have a workforce over 100,000 and therefore account for a lot of job openings. Even if overall employment in such a job is shrinking, the large workforce guarantees many job opportunities because of retirements and turnover, so such jobs are worth your consideration for that reason alone. Jobs in this book that have a small workforce generally have high entry requirements (for example, mathematicians need at least a master's degree), so there is usually less competition for the limited number of openings.

Details on Each Section of the Job Descriptions

Each occupational description in this book follows a standard format, making it easier for you to compare jobs. The following overview describes the kinds of information found in each part of a description and offers tips on how to interpret the information.

Job Title

This is the title used for the job in the *Occupational Outlook Handbook.*

O*NET Codes

This section of each job description lists one or more code numbers (for example: 11-9031.00, 11-9032.00) for related jobs in a major occupational information system used by the U.S. Department of Labor. This system, named the Occupational Information Network (or O*NET), is used by a variety of state and federal programs to classify applicants and job openings and by a variety of career information systems. You can use the O*NET code numbers to get additional information on the related O*NET titles on the Internet at www.onetcenter.org or at www.careeroink.com. Reference books that provide O*NET descriptions include the *O*NET Dictionary of*

Occupational Titles and the *Enhanced Occupational Outlook Handbook,* both published by JIST Publishing. Your librarian can help you find these books.

Significant Points

The bullet points in this part of a description highlight key characteristics for each job, such as recent trends or education and training requirements.

Nature of the Work

This part of the description discusses what workers typically do in a particular job. Individual job duties may vary by industry or employer. For instance, workers in larger firms tend to be more specialized, whereas those in smaller firms often have a wider variety of duties. Most occupations have several levels of skills and responsibilities through which workers may progress. Beginners may start as trainees performing routine tasks under close supervision. Experienced workers usually undertake more difficult tasks and are expected to perform with less supervision.

In this part of a description, you will also find information about the influence of technological advancements on the way work is done. For example, because of the Internet, reporters are now able to submit stories from remote locations with just a click of the mouse.

This part also discusses emerging specialties. For instance, Webmasters—who are responsible for all the technical aspects involved in operating a Web site—comprise a specialty within computer scientists and database administrators.

Working Conditions

This part of the description identifies the typical hours worked, the workplace environment, physical activities, risk of injury, special equipment, and the extent of travel required. For example, stationary engineers and boiler operators are susceptible to injury, while paralegals and legal assistants have high job-related stress. Radiologic technologists and technicians may wear protective clothing or equipment, machinists do physically demanding work, and some engineers travel frequently.

In many occupations, people work regular business hours—40 hours a week, Monday through Friday. In other occupations, they do not. For example, licensed practical nurses often work evenings and weekends. The work setting can range from a hospital to a mall to an off-shore oil rig.

Information on various worker characteristics, such as the average number of hours worked per week, is obtained from the Current Population Survey (CPS), a survey of households conducted by the U.S. Census Bureau for the Bureau of Labor Statistics (BLS).

Training, Other Qualifications, and Advancement

After finding out what a job is all about, you probably want to understand how to train for it. This section describes the most significant sources of education and training, including the education or training preferred by employers, the typical length of training, and the possibilities for advancement. Job skills sometimes are acquired through high school, informal on-the-job training, formal training (including apprenticeships), the U.S. Armed Forces, home study, hobbies, or previous work experience. For example, sales experience is particularly important for many sales jobs. Many professional and technical jobs, on the other hand, require formal postsecondary education— postsecondary vocational or technical training or college, postgraduate, or professional education.

This section also mentions desirable skills, aptitudes, and personal characteristics. For some entry-level jobs, personal characteristics are more important than formal training. Employers generally seek people who read, write, and speak well; compute accurately; think logically; learn quickly; get along with others; and demonstrate dependability.

Some occupations require certification or licensing to enter the field, to advance in the occupation, or to practice independently. Certification or licensing generally involves completing courses and passing examinations. Many occupations increasingly are requiring workers to participate in continuing education or training in relevant skills, either to keep up with the changes in their jobs or to improve their advancement opportunities.

Employment

This section reports the number of jobs the occupation recently provided, the key industries where these jobs are found, and the number or proportion of self-employed workers in the occupation, if significant. Self-employed workers accounted for about 8 percent of the workforce in 2004; however, they were concentrated in a small number of occupations, such as farmers and ranchers, childcare workers, lawyers, health practitioners, and the construction trades.

When significant, the geographic distribution of jobs and the proportion of part-time (less than 35 hours a week) workers in the occupation are mentioned.

Job Outlook

In planning for the future, you need to consider potential job opportunities. This section describes the factors that will result in employment growth or decline. A number of factors are examined in developing employment projections. One factor is job growth or decline in industries that employ a significant percentage of workers in the occupation. If workers are concentrated in a rapidly growing industry, their employment will likely also grow quickly. For example, the growing need for business expertise is fueling demand for consulting services. Hence, management, scientific, and technical consulting services are projected to be among the fastest-growing industries through 2014.

Demographic changes, which affect what services are required, can influence occupational growth or decline. For example, an aging population demands more healthcare workers, from registered nurses to pharmacists. Technological change is another key factor. New technology can either create new job opportunities or eliminate jobs by making workers obsolete. The Internet has increased the demand for workers in the computer and information technology fields, such as computer support specialists and systems administrators. However, the Internet also has adversely affected travel agents, because many people now book tickets, hotels, and rental cars online.

Another factor affecting job growth or decline is changes in business practices, such as the outsourcing of work or the restructuring of businesses. In the past few years, insurance carriers have been outsourcing sales and claims adjuster jobs to large 24-hour call centers, sometimes in foreign countries, in order to reduce costs. Corporate restructuring also has made many organizations "flatter," resulting in fewer middle management positions.

The substitution of one product or service for another can affect employment projections. For example, consumption of plastic products has grown as they have been substituted for metal goods in many consumer and manufactured products in recent years. The process is likely to continue and should result in stronger demand for machine operators in plastics than in metal.

Competition from foreign trade usually has a negative impact on employment. Often, foreign manufacturers can produce goods more cheaply than they can be produced in the United States, and the cost savings can be passed on in the form of lower prices with which U.S. manufacturers cannot compete. Increased international competition is a major reason for the decline in employment among textile, apparel, and furnishings workers.

In some cases, this book mentions that an occupation is likely to provide numerous job openings or, in others, that an occupation likely will afford relatively few openings. This information reflects the projected change in employment as well as replacement needs. Large occupations that have high turnover, such as food and beverage serving occupations, generally provide the most job openings, reflecting the need to replace workers who transfer to other occupations or who stop working.

Some job descriptions discuss the relationship between the number of job seekers and the number of job openings. In some occupations, there is a rough balance between job seekers and job openings, resulting in good opportunities. In other occupations, employers may report difficulty finding qualified applicants, resulting in excellent job opportunities. Still other occupations are characterized by a surplus of applicants, leading to keen competition for jobs. On the one hand, limited training facilities, salary regulations, or undesirable aspects of the work—as in the case of private household workers—can result in an insufficient number of entrants to fill all job openings. On the other hand, glamorous or potentially high-paying occupations, such as actors or musicians, generally have surpluses of job seekers. Variation in job opportunities by industry, educational attainment, size of firm, or geographic location also may be discussed. Even in crowded fields, job openings do exist. Good students or highly qualified individuals should not be deterred from undertaking training for, or seeking entry into, those occupations.

Key Phrases Used in the Job Descriptions

This table explains how to interpret the key phrases that describe projected changes in employment. It also explains the terms for the relationship between the number of job openings and the number of job seekers.

Changing Employment Between 2004 and 2014

If the statement reads	Employment is projected to
Grow much faster than average	Increase 27 percent or more
Grow faster than average	Increase 18 to 26 percent
Grow about as fast as average	Increase 9 to 17 percent
Grow more slowly than average	Increase 0 to 8 percent
Decline	Decrease any amount

Opportunities and Competition for Jobs

If the statement reads	Job openings compared to job seekers may be
Very good to excellent opportunities	More numerous
Good or favorable opportunities	In rough balance
May face or can expect keen competition	Fewer

Earnings

This section discusses typical earnings and how workers are compensated—by means of annual salaries, hourly wages, commissions, piece rates, tips, or bonuses. Within every occupation, earnings vary by experience, responsibility, performance, tenure, and geographic area. Information on earnings in the major industries in which the occupation is employed may be given. Some statements contain additional earnings data from non-BLS sources. Starting and average salaries of federal workers are based on 2005 data from the U.S. Office of Personnel Management. The National Association of Colleges and Employers supplies information on average salary offers in 2005 for students graduating with a bachelor's, master's, or Ph.D. degree in certain fields. A few statements contain additional earnings information from other sources, such as unions, professional associations, and private companies. These data sources are cited in the text.

Benefits account for a significant portion of total compensation costs to employers. Benefits such as paid vacation, health insurance, and sick leave may not be mentioned because they are so widespread. Although not as common as traditional benefits, flexible hours and profit-sharing plans may be offered to attract and retain highly qualified workers. Less common benefits also include childcare, tuition for dependents, housing assistance, summers off, and free or discounted merchandise or services. For certain occupations, the percentage of workers affiliated with a union is listed.

Related Occupations

Occupations involving similar duties, skills, interests, education, and training are listed here. This allows you to look up these jobs if they also interest you.

Sources of Additional Information

No single publication can describe all aspects of an occupation. Thus, this section lists the mailing addresses of associations, government agencies, unions, and other organizations that can provide occupational information. In some cases, toll-free telephone numbers and Internet addresses also are listed. Free or relatively inexpensive publications offering more information may be mentioned; some of these publications also may be available in libraries, in school career centers, in guidance offices, or on the Internet.

Part III: Quick Job Search—Seven Steps to Getting a Good Job in Less Time

For more than 25 years, I've been helping people find better jobs in less time. If you have ever experienced unemployment, you know it is not pleasant. Unemployment is something most people want to get over quickly—in fact, the quicker the better. Part III will give you some techniques to help.

I know that most of you who read this book want to improve yourselves. You want to consider career and training options that lead to a better job and life in whatever way you define this—better pay, more flexibility, more-enjoyable or more-meaningful work, proving to your mom that you really can do anything you set your mind to, and other reasons. That is why I include advice on career planning and job search in Part III. It's a short part, but it includes the basics that are most important in planning your career and in reducing the time it takes to get a job. I hope it will make you think about what is important to you in the long run.

The second section of Part III showcases professionally written resumes for some of America's top computer and technical jobs. Use these as examples when creating your own resume. I know you will resist completing the activities in Part III, but consider this: It is often not the best person who gets the job, but the best job seeker. People who do their career planning and job search homework often get jobs over those with better credentials because they have these distinct advantages:

1. **They get more interviews,** including many for jobs that will never be advertised.

2. **They do better in interviews.**

People who understand what they want and what they have to offer employers present their skills more convincingly and are much better at answering problem questions. And, because they have learned more about job search techniques, they are likely to get more interviews with employers who need the skills they have.

Doing better in interviews often makes the difference between getting a job offer and sitting at home. And spending time planning your career can make an enormous difference to your happiness and lifestyle over time. So please consider reading Part III and completing its activities. I suggest you schedule a time right now to at least read Part III. An hour or so spent there can help you do just enough better in your career planning, job seeking, and interviewing to make the difference.

One other thing: If you work through Part III and it helps you in some significant way, I'd like to hear from you. Please write or e-mail me via the publisher, whose contact information appears elsewhere in this book.

Part IV: Important Trends in Jobs and Industries

This section is made up of three very good articles on labor market trends. These articles come directly from U.S. Department of Labor sources and are interesting, well written, and short. One is on overall trends, with an emphasis on occupational groups; another is on trends in major industry groups; and the third is on training in computer-related fields. I know they sound boring, but the articles are quick reads and will give you a good idea of factors that will impact your career in the years to come.

The first article is titled "Tomorrow's Jobs." It highlights many important trends in employment and includes information on the fastest-growing jobs, jobs with high pay at various levels of education, and other details.

The second article is titled "Employment Trends in Major Industries." I included this information because you may find that you can use your skills or training in industries you have not considered. The article provides a good review of major trends with an emphasis on helping you make good employment decisions. This information can help you seek jobs in industries that offer higher pay or that are more likely to interest you. Many people overlook one important fact—the industry you work in is as important as the occupation you choose.

The third article, "Training for Techies," describes several kinds of certification and various degrees that are applicable for people interested in a career in the fields of computer science or information technology.

Some Additional Jobs to Consider

This book includes only 100 jobs, but many other occupations have aspects that can be considered computer-oriented or technical in nature. For example, in the following list you'll find news analysts, reporters, and correspondents—an occupation that includes people who write about science and technology. You can look up the jobs that interest you in one of the references mentioned in the following section, "Other Major Career Information Sources."

- ★ Accountants and auditors
- ★ Actors, producers, and directors
- ★ Agricultural engineers
- ★ Barbers, cosmetologists, and other personal appearance workers
- ★ Biomedical engineers
- ★ Boilermakers
- ★ Bookbinders and bindery workers
- ★ Budget analysts
- ★ Chemical engineers
- ★ Coin, vending, and amusement machine servicers and repairers
- ★ Cost estimators
- ★ Electricians
- ★ Financial analysts and personal financial advisors
- ★ Home appliance repairers
- ★ Jewelers and precious stone and metal workers

★ Landscape architects

★ Market and survey researchers

★ News analysts, reporters, and correspondents

★ Petroleum engineers

★ Writers and editors

Other Major Career Information Sources

The information in this book will be very useful, but you may want or need additional information. Keep in mind that the job descriptions here cover major jobs and not the many more-specialized jobs that are often related to them. Each job description in this book provides some sources of information related to that job, but here are additional resources to consider.

The *Occupational Outlook Handbook* (or the *OOH*): Updated every two years by the U.S. Department of Labor, this book provides descriptions for almost 270 major jobs covering more than 85 percent of the workforce. The *OOH* is the source of the job descriptions used in this book, and the book *Top 300 Jobs* includes all the *OOH* content plus additional information.

The *Enhanced Occupational Outlook Handbook:* Includes all descriptions in the *OOH* plus descriptions of more than 6,300 more-specialized jobs related to them.

The *O*NET Dictionary of Occupational Titles:* The only printed source of the more than 900 jobs described in the U.S. Department of Labor's Occupational Information Network database.

The *New Guide for Occupational Exploration:* An important career reference that allows you to explore all major O*NET jobs based on your interests.

www.careeroink.com: This Web site provides more than 14,000 job descriptions, including those mentioned in the previous books, and a variety of useful ways to explore them.

Best Jobs for the 21st Century: Includes descriptions for the 500 jobs (out of more than 900) with the best combination of earnings, growth, and number of openings. Useful lists make jobs easy to explore (examples: highest-paying jobs by level of education or training; best jobs overall; and best jobs for different ages, personality types, interests, and many more).

Exploring Careers—A Young Person's Guide to 1,000 Jobs: For youth exploring career and education opportunities, this book covers 1,000 job options.

Using the Job-Match Grid to Choose a Career

By the Editors at JIST

This book describes so many occupations—how can you choose the best job for you? This section is your answer! It can help you to identify the jobs where your abilities will be valued, and you can rule out jobs that have certain characteristics you'd rather avoid. You will respond to a series of statements and use the Job-Match Grid to match your skills and preferences to the most appropriate jobs in this book.

So grab a pencil and get ready to mark up the following sections. Or, if someone else will be using this book, find a sheet of paper and get ready to take notes.

Thinking About Your Skills

Everybody knows that skills are important for getting and keeping a job. Employers expect you to list relevant skills on your resume. They ask about your skills in interviews. And they expect you to develop skills on the job so that you will remain productive as new technologies and new work situations emerge.

But maybe you haven't thought about how closely skills are related to job satisfaction. For example, let's say you have enough communication skills to hold a certain job where these skills are used heavily, but you wouldn't really *enjoy* using them. In that case, this job probably would be a bad choice for you. You need to identify a job that will use the skills that you *do* enjoy using.

That's why you need to take a few minutes to think about your skills: the ones you're good at and the ones you like using. The checklists that follow can help you do this. On each of the seven skills checklists that follow, use numbers to indicate how much you agree with each statement:

3 = I strongly agree

2 = I agree

1 = There's some truth to this

0 = This doesn't apply to me

Artistic Skills

_____ I am an amateur artist.

_____ I have musical talent.

(continued)

(continued)

_____ I enjoy planning home makeovers.

_____ I am good at performing onstage.

_____ I enjoy taking photos or shooting videos.

_____ I am good at writing stories, poems, articles, or essays.

_____ I have enjoyed taking ballet or other dance lessons.

_____ I like to cook and plan meals.

_____ I can sketch a good likeness of something or somebody.

_____ Playing music or singing is a hobby of mine.

_____ I have a good sense of visual style.

_____ I have participated in amateur theater.

_____ I like to express myself through writing.

_____ I can prepare tasty meals better than most people.

_____ I have a flair for creating attractive designs.

_____ I learn new dance steps or routines easily.

_____ **Total for Artistic Skills**

A note for those determined to work in the arts: Before you move on to the next skill, take a moment to decide whether working in some form of art is essential to you. Some people have exceptional talent and interest in a certain art form and are unhappy unless they are working in that art form—or until they have given their best shot at trying to break into it. If you are that kind of person, the total score shown above doesn't really matter. In fact, you may have given a 3 to just *one* of the statements above, but if you care passionately about your art form, you should toss out ordinary arithmetic and change the total to 100.

Communication Skills

_____ I am good at explaining complicated things to people.

_____ I like to take notes and write up minutes for meetings.

_____ I have a flair for public speaking.

_____ I am good at writing directions for using a computer or machine.

_____ I enjoy investigating facts and showing other people what they indicate.

_____ People consider me a good listener.

_____ I like to write letters to newspaper editors or political representatives.

_____ I have been an effective debater.

_____ I like developing publicity fliers for a school or community event.

_____ I am good at making diagrams that break down complex processes.

_____ I like teaching people how to drive a car or play a sport.

_____ I have been successful as the secretary of a club.

_____ I enjoy speaking at group meetings or worship services.

_____ I have a knack for choosing the most effective word.

_____ I enjoy tutoring young people.

_____ Technical manuals are not hard for me to understand.

_____ **Total for Communication Skills**

Interpersonal Skills

_____ I am able to make people feel that I understand their point of view.

_____ I enjoy working collaboratively.

_____ I often can make suggestions to people without sounding critical of them.

_____ I enjoy soliciting clothes, food, and other supplies for needy people.

_____ I am good at "reading" people to tell what's on their minds.

_____ I have a lot of patience with people who are doing something for the first time.

_____ People consider me outgoing.

_____ I enjoy taking care of sick relatives, friends, or neighbors.

_____ I am good at working out conflicts between friends or family members.

_____ I enjoy serving as a host or hostess for houseguests.

_____ People consider me a team player.

_____ I enjoy meeting new people and finding common interests.

_____ I am good at fundraising for school groups, teams, or community organizations.

_____ I like to train or care for animals.

_____ I often know what to say to defuse a tense situation.

_____ I have enjoyed being an officer or advisor for a youth group.

_____ **Total for Interpersonal Skills**

Managerial Skills

_____ I am good at inspiring people to work together toward a goal.

_____ I tend to use time wisely and not procrastinate.

_____ I usually know when I have enough information to make a decision.

_____ I enjoy planning and arranging programs for school or a community organization.

_____ I am not reluctant to take responsibility when things turn out wrong.

_____ I have enjoyed being a leader of a scout troop or other such group.

_____ I often can figure out what motivates somebody.

_____ People trust me to speak on their behalf and represent them fairly.

_____ I like to help organize things at home, such as shopping lists and budgets.

(continued)

(continued)

_____ I have been successful at recruiting members for a club or other organization.

_____ I have enjoyed helping run a school or community fair or carnival.

_____ People find me persuasive.

_____ I enjoy buying large quantities of food or other products for an organization.

_____ I have a knack for identifying abilities in other people.

_____ I am able to get past details and look at the big picture.

_____ I am good at delegating authority rather than trying to do everything myself.

_____ **Total for Managerial Skills**

Mathematics Skills

_____ I have always done well in math classes.

_____ I enjoy balancing checkbooks for family members.

_____ I can make mental calculations quickly.

_____ I enjoy calculating sports statistics or keeping score.

_____ Preparing family income tax returns is not hard for me.

_____ I like to tutor young people in math.

_____ I have taken or plan to take courses in statistics or calculus.

_____ I enjoy budgeting the family expenditures.

_____ **Subtotal for Mathematics Skills**

x 2   **Multiply by 2**

_____ **Total for Mathematics Skills**

Mechanical Skills

_____ I have a good sense of how mechanical devices work.

_____ I like to tinker with my car or motorcycle.

_____ I can understand diagrams of machinery or electrical wiring.

_____ I enjoy installing and repairing home stereo or computer equipment.

_____ I like looking at the merchandise in a building-supply warehouse store.

_____ I can sometimes fix household appliances when they break down.

_____ I have enjoyed building model airplanes, automobiles, or boats.

_____ I can do minor plumbing and electrical installations in the home.

_____ **Subtotal for Mechanical Skills**

x 2   **Multiply by 2**

_____ **Total for Mechanical Skills**

Science Skills

_____ Some of my best grades have been in science classes.

_____ I enjoy tweaking my computer's settings to make it run better.

_____ I have a good understanding of the systems and organs of the human body.

_____ I have enjoyed performing experiments for a science fair.

_____ I have taken or plan to take college-level courses in science.

_____ I like to read about new breakthroughs in science and technology.

_____ I know how to write programs in a computer language.

_____ I enjoy reading medical or scientific magazines.

_____ **Subtotal for Science Skills**

x 2   **Multiply by 2**

_____ **Total for Science Skills**

Finding Your Skills on the Job-Match Grid

Okay, you've made a lot of progress so far. Now it's time to review what you've said about skills so you can use these insights to sort through the jobs listed on the Job-Match Grid.

Look at your totals for the seven skills listed previously. Enter your totals in the left column on this scorecard:

Total	Skill	Rank
_____	Artistic	_____
_____	Communication	_____
_____	Interpersonal	_____
_____	Managerial	_____
_____	Mathematics	_____
_____	Mechanical	_____
_____	Science	_____

Next, enter the rank of each skill in the right column—that is, the highest-scored skill gets ranked #1, the next-highest #2, and so forth. **Important:** Keep in mind that *the numbers in the Total column are only a rough guideline*. If you feel that a skill should be ranked higher or lower than its numerical total would suggest, *go by your impressions rather than just by the numbers*.

Now turn to the Job-Match Grid and find the columns for your #1-ranked and #2-ranked skills. Move down through the grid, going from page to page, and notice what symbols appear in those columns. If a row of the grid has a black circle (●) in *both* columns, circle the occupation name—or, if someone else will be using this book, jot down the name on a piece of paper. These occupations use a high level of both skills, or the skills are essential to these jobs.

Go through the Job-Match Grid a second time, looking at the column for your #3-ranked skill. If a *job you have already circled* has a black circle (●) or a bull's-eye (◉) in the column for your #3-ranked skill, put a check mark next to the occupation name. If none of your selected jobs has a black circle or a bull's-eye in this column, look for a white circle (○) and mark these jobs with check marks.

A second note for those determined to work in the arts: If a *particular* art form is essential for you to work in, you almost certainly know which occupations involve that art form and which don't. So not every job that has a black circle (●) in the "Artistic" column is going to interest you. Circle only the jobs that have a black circle in this column that *are* related to your art form (if you're not sure, look at the description of the occupation in this book) and that also have a symbol of some kind (●, ◉, or ○) in the column for your #2-ranked skill. As you circle each job, also give it a check mark, because there will be so few of them that you won't need to go through the Job-Match Grid a second time. If you have a more general interest in the arts, follow the general instructions.

Your Hot List of Possible Career Matches

Now that you have made a first and second cut of the jobs on the Job-Match Grid, you can focus on the occupations that look most promising at this point. Write the names of the occupations that are both *circled* and *checked:*

_____   _____

_____   _____

_____   _____

_____   _____

_____   _____

This is your Hot List of occupations that you are going to explore in detail *if* they are not eliminated by certain important job-related factors that you'll consider next.

Thinking About Other Job-Related Factors

Next, you need to consider four other job-related factors:

★ Economic sensitivity   ★ Physically demanding work

★ Outdoor work   ★ Hazardous conditions

Economic Sensitivity

You've read about how our nation's economy has gone up and down over the years. When the economy is on an upswing, there are more job openings, but when it veers downward toward recession, jobs are harder to find.

Are you aware that these trends affect some occupations more than others? For example, during an economic upswing, people do more vacation traveling and businesses send more workers on business trips. This keeps travel agencies very busy, so they need to hire more travel agents. When the economy is going down, people cut back on their vacation travel, businesses tell their workers to use teleconferencing instead of business trips, and travel agents are not in demand. Some may be laid off, and people who want to enter this field may find very few openings. By contrast, most jobs in the health-care field are not sensitive to the economy, and automotive mechanics are just as busy as ever during economic slowdowns because people want to keep their old cars running.

So this issue of economic sensitivity (and its opposite, job security) is one that may affect which occupation you choose. Some people want to avoid economically sensitive occupations because they don't want to risk losing their job (or having difficulty finding a job) during times of recession. Other people are willing to risk being in an economically sensitive occupation because they want to profit from the periods when both the economy and the occupation are booming.

> How important is it to you to be in an occupation that *doesn't* go through periods of boom and bust along with the nation's economy? Check one:
>
> _____ It doesn't matter to me.
>
> _____ It's not important, but I'd consider it.
>
> _____ It's somewhat important to me.
>
> _____ It's very important to me.

If you answered "It doesn't matter to me," skip to the next section, "Outdoor Work." Otherwise, turn back to the Job-Match Grid and find the column for "Economically Sensitive."

If you answered "It's not important, but I'd consider it," see whether any of the jobs on your Hot List have a black circle (●) in this column. If so, cross them off and write an "E" next to them.

If you answered "It's somewhat important to me," see whether any of the jobs on your Hot List have a black circle (●) or a bull's-eye (◉) in this column. If so, cross them off and write an "E" next to them.

If you answered "It's very important to me," see whether any of the jobs on your Hot List have *any* symbol (●, ◉, or ○) in this column. If so, cross them off and write an "E" next to them.

Outdoor Work

Some people prefer to work indoors in a climate-controlled setting, such as an office, a classroom, a factory floor, a laboratory, or a hospital room. Other people would rather work primarily in an outdoor setting, such as a forest, an athletic field, or a city street. And some would enjoy a job that alternates between indoor and outdoor activities.

> What is *your* preference for working indoors or outdoors? Check one:
>
> _____ It's very important to me to work **indoors.**
>
> _____ I'd prefer to work mostly **indoors.**
>
> _____ Either indoors or outdoors is okay with me.
>
> _____ I'd prefer to work mostly **outdoors.**
>
> _____ It's very important to me to work **outdoors.**

If you answered "Either indoors or outdoors is okay with me," skip to the next section, "Physically Demanding Work." Otherwise, turn to the Job-Match Grid and find the column for "Outdoor Work."

If you answered "It's very important to me to work **indoors**," see whether any of the jobs on your Hot List have *any* symbol (●, ◉, or ○) in this column. If so, cross them off and write an "O" next to them.

If you answered "I'd prefer to work mostly **indoors**," see whether any of the jobs on your Hot List have a black circle (●) in this column. If so, cross them off and write an "O" next to them.

If you answered "I'd prefer to work mostly **outdoors**," see whether any of the jobs on your Hot List have *no* symbol—just a blank—in this column. If so, cross them off and write an "O" next to them. All the jobs remaining on your Hot List should have some kind of symbol (●, ◉, or ○) in this column.

If you answered "It's very important to me to work **outdoors,**" see whether any of the jobs on your Hot List have either *no* symbol or just a white circle (○) in this column. If so, cross them off and write an "O" next to them. All the jobs remaining on your Hot List should have either a black circle (●) or a bull's-eye (◉) in this column.

Physically Demanding Work

Jobs vary by how much muscle power they require you to use. Some jobs require a lot of lifting heavy loads, standing for long times, climbing, or stooping. On other jobs, the heaviest thing you lift is a notebook or telephone handset, and most of the time you are sitting. Still other jobs require only a moderate amount of physical exertion.

> What is *your* preference for the physical demands of work? Check one:
>
> _____ I don't care whether my work requires heavy or light physical exertion.
>
> _____ I want my work to require only light physical exertion.
>
> _____ I want my work to require no more than occasional moderate physical exertion.
>
> _____ I want my work to require moderate physical exertion, with occasional heavy exertion.
>
> _____ I want my work to require a lot of heavy physical exertion.

If you answered "I don't care whether my work requires heavy or light physical exertion," skip to the next section, "Hazardous Conditions." Otherwise, turn to the Job-Match Grid and find the column for "Physically Demanding Work."

If you answered "I want my work to require only light physical exertion," see whether any of the jobs on your Hot List have *any* symbol (●, ◉, or ○) in this column. If so, cross them off and write a "P" next to them.

If you answered "I want my work to require no more than occasional moderate physical exertion," see whether any of the jobs on your Hot List have either a black circle (●) or a bull's-eye (◉) in this column. If so, cross them off and write a "P" next to them.

If you answered "I want my work to require moderate physical exertion, with occasional heavy exertion," see whether any of the jobs on your Hot List have either a black circle (●), a white circle (○), or *no* symbol in this column. If so, cross them off and write a "P" next to them. All the jobs remaining on your Hot List should have a bull's-eye (◉) in this column.

If you answered "I want my work to require a lot of heavy physical exertion," see whether any of the jobs on your Hot List have either *no* symbol or just a white circle (○) or a bull's-eye (◉) in this column. If so, cross them off and write a "P" next to them. All the jobs remaining on your Hot List should have a black circle (●) in this column.

Hazardous Conditions

Every day about 9,000 Americans sustain a disabling injury on the job. Many workers have jobs that require them to deal with hazardous conditions, such as heat, noise, radiation, germs, toxins, or dangerous machinery. These workers need to wear protective clothing or follow safety procedures to avoid injury.

> What is *your* preference regarding hazardous conditions on the job? Check one:
>
> _____ I want hazardous workplace conditions to be very unlikely.
>
> _____ I want hazardous conditions to be unlikely or minor.
>
> _____ I am willing to accept some major workplace hazards.

If you answered "I am willing to accept some major workplace hazards," skip to the section "Geographically Concentrated Jobs." Otherwise, turn to the Job-Match Grid and find the column for "Hazardous Conditions."

If you answered "I want hazardous workplace conditions to be very unlikely," see whether any of the jobs on your Hot List have *any* symbol (●, ◉, or ○) in this column. If so, cross them off and write an "H" next to them.

If you answered "I want hazardous conditions to be unlikely or minor," see whether any of the jobs on your Hot List have a black circle (●) in this column. If so, cross them off and write an "H" next to them.

If Every Job on Your Hot List Is Now Crossed Off

It's possible that you have crossed off *all* the occupations on your Hot List. If so, consider these two options:

★ You may want to relax some of your requirements. Maybe you were too hasty in crossing off some of the jobs. Take another look at the four job-related factors and decide whether you could accept work that doesn't meet the requirements you set previously—for example, work that is not as much indoors or outdoors as you specified. If you change your mind now, you can tell by the letters in the margin which jobs you crossed off for which reasons.

★ You may want to add to your Hot List by considering additional skills. So far you have considered only occupations that involve your top three skills. You may want to add jobs that have a black circle (●) or a bull's-eye (◉) in the column for your #4-ranked skill and possibly for your #5-ranked skill. If you do add any jobs, be sure to repeat your review of the four job-related factors.

Evaluating Occupations Described in This Book

You are now ready to make the jump from the checklists to the detailed information about jobs in this book. The first detailed issue you need to consider is whether you will be able to find work in your area or have to relocate.

Geographically Concentrated Jobs

Turn to the Job-Match Grid one more time and find the column for "Geographically Concentrated." Look at all the occupations on your Hot List that haven't been crossed off. If there is a symbol in this column, especially a bull's-eye (◉) or a black circle (●), it means that employment for this occupation tends to be concentrated in certain geographic areas. For example, most acting jobs are found in big cities because that's where you'll find most theaters, TV studios, and movie studios. Most water transportation jobs are found on the coasts and beside major lakes and rivers.

If a symbol shows that a Hot List occupation *is* geographically concentrated, the location of the jobs may be obvious, as in the examples of acting and water transportation. If it's not clear to you where the jobs may be found, find the occupation in "The Job Descriptions" section and look for the facts under the heading "Employment" in the description. Once you understand where most of the jobs are, you have to make some decisions:

★ **Are most of the job openings in a geographic location where I am now or would enjoy living?** If you answered "yes" to this question, repeat this exercise for all the other occupations still on your Hot List. Then jump to the next heading, "Nature of the Work." If you answered "no," proceed to the next bulleted question.

★ **If most of the job openings are in a distant place where I don't want to relocate, am I willing to take a chance and hope to be one of the few workers who get hired in an *uncommon* location?** If you answered "yes," take a good look at the Job Outlook information in the job description. If the outlook for the occupation is very good and if you expect to have some of the advantages mentioned there (such as the right degree, in some cases), taking a chance on being hired in an unusual location may be a reasonable decision. On the other hand, if the outlook is only so-so or not good and if you have no special qualifications, you probably are setting yourself up for disappointment. You should seriously consider changing your mind about this decision. At least speak to people in your area who are knowledgeable about the occupation to determine whether you have any chance of success. If you answered "no"—you are not willing to take a chance—cross off this occupation and write a "G" next to it. (If you now have no jobs left on your Hot List, see the previous section titled "If Every Job on Your Hot List Is Now Crossed Off.")

Nature of the Work

When you read the job description for an occupation on your Hot List, you will see that the "Nature of the Work" section discusses what workers do on the job, what tools and equipment they use, and how closely they are supervised. Keep in mind that this is an overview of a diverse collection of workers, and in fact few workers perform the full set of tasks itemized here. In fact, in many cases the work force covered by the job description is so diverse that it actually divides into several occupational specialties, which are italicized.

Here are some things to think about as you read this section:

★ Note the kinds of problems, materials, and tools you will encounter on the job. Are these are a good match for your interests?

★ Also note the work activities mentioned here. Do you think they will be rewarding? Are there many that stand out as unpleasant or boring?

Working Conditions

This section in each job description identifies the typical hours worked, the workplace environment (both physical and psychological), physical activities and susceptibility to injury, special equipment, and the extent of travel required. If conditions vary between the occupational specialties, that is mentioned here. Here are some things to look for in the Working Conditions section:

★ If you have a disability, note the physical requirements that are mentioned here and consider whether you can meet these requirements with or without suitable accommodations.

★ If you're bothered by conditions such as heights, stress, or a cramped workspace, see whether this section mentions any conditions that would discourage you.

★ Note what this section says about the work schedule and the need for travel, if any. This information may be good to know if you have pressing family responsibilities or, on the other hand, a desire for unusual hours or travel.

★ If you find a working condition that bothers you, be sure to check the wording to see whether it *always* applies to the occupation or whether it only *may* apply. Even if it seems to be a condition that you cannot avoid, find out for sure by talking to people in the occupation or educators who teach related courses. Maybe you can carve out a niche that avoids the unappealing working condition.

Training, Other Qualifications, and Advancement

In the "Training, Other Qualifications, and Advancement" section, you can see how to prepare for the occupation and how to advance in it. It identifies the significant entry routes—those that are most popular and that are preferred by employers. It mentions any licensure or certification that may be necessary for entry or advancement. It also identifies the particular skills, aptitudes, and work habits that employers value. Look for these topics in this section:

★ Compare the entry requirements to your background and to the educational and training opportunities that are available to you. Be sure to consider nontraditional and informal entry routes, if any are possible, as well as the formal routes. Ask yourself, Am I willing to get the additional education or training that will be necessary? Do I have the time, money, ability, interest, and commitment?

★ Maybe you're already partway down the road to job entry. In general, you should try to use your previous education, training, and work experience rather than abandon it. Look for specifics that are already on your resume—educational accomplishments, skills, work habits—that will meet employers' expectations. If you have some of these qualifications already, this occupation may be a better career choice than some others.

Employment

The "Employment" section in the job description reports how many jobs the occupation currently provides, the industries that provide the most jobs, and the number or proportion of self-employed or part-time workers in the occupation, if significant. In this section, you'll want to pay attention to these facts:

★ Note the industries that provide most of the employment for the occupation. This knowledge can help you identify contacts who can tell you more about the work, and later it can help in your job hunting.

★ If you're interested in self-employment or part-time work, see whether these work arrangements are mentioned here.

Job Outlook

The "Job Outlook" section describes the economic forces that will affect future employment in the occupation. Here are some things to look for in this section:

★ The information here can help you identify occupations with a good job outlook so that you will have a better-than-average chance of finding work. Be alert for any mention of an advantage that you may have over other job seekers (for example, a college degree) or any other factor that might make your chances better or worse.

★ If you are highly motivated and highly qualified for a particular occupation, don't be discouraged by a bad employment outlook. Job openings occur even in shrinking or overcrowded occupations, and with exceptional talent or good personal connections, you may go on to great success.

★ These projections are the most definitive ones available, but they are not foolproof and apply only to a 10-year time span. No matter what occupation you choose, you will need to adapt to changes.

Earnings

The "Earnings" section discusses the wages for the occupation. Here are some things to keep in mind:

★ The wage figures are national averages. Actual wages in your geographic region may be considerably higher or lower. Also, an average figure means that half of the workers earn more and half earn less, and the actual salary any one worker earns can vary greatly from that average.

★ Remember to consider *all* the pluses and minuses of the job. Not every day of the work week is payday, so make your choice based on the whole occupation, not just the paycheck.

Related Occupations

The "Related Occupations" section identifies occupations that are similar to the one featured in the job description in terms of tasks, interests, skills, education, or training. You may find this section interesting for these reasons:

★ If you're interested in an occupation but not strongly committed to pursuing it, this section may suggest another occupation with similar rewards that may turn out to be a better fit. Try to research these related occupations, but keep in mind that they may not all be included in this book.

★ You may want to choose one of these occupations as your Plan B goal if your original goal should not work out. In that case, it helps to identify an occupation that involves similar kinds of problems and work settings but requires *less* education or training.

Sources of Additional Information

This section in each job description lists several sources and resources you can turn to for more information about the occupation. Try to consult at least some of these sources. This book should be only the beginning of your career decision-making process. You need more detailed information from several viewpoints to make an informed decision.

Don't rely entirely on the Web sites listed here. You especially need to talk to and observe individual workers to learn what their workdays are like, what the workers enjoy and dislike about the job, how they got hired, and what effects the job has had on other aspects of their lives. Maybe you can make contact with local workers through the local chapter of an organization listed here.

Narrowing Down Your Choices

The information in the job descriptions should help you cross more jobs off your Hot List. And what you learn by turning to other resources should help you narrow down your Hot List jobs to a few promising choices and maybe one best bet. Here are some final considerations: Have I talked to people who are actually doing this work? Am I fully aware of the pluses and minuses of this job? If there are aspects of the job that I don't like, how do I expect to avoid them or overcome them? If the odds of finding a job opening are not good, why do I expect to beat the odds? What is my Plan B goal if I lose interest in my original goal or don't succeed at it?

The Job-Match Grid

The grid on the following pages provides information about the personal skills and job characteristics for occupations covered in this book. Use the directions and questions that start at the beginning of this section to help you get the most from this grid.

Below is what the symbols on the grid represent. If a job has no symbol in a column, it means that the skill or job characteristic is not important or relevant to the job.

Personal Skills

● Essential or high skill level

◉ Somewhat essential or moderate skill level

○ Basic skill level

Job Characteristics

● Highly likely

◉ Somewhat likely

○ A little likely

Job-Match Grid

	Personal Skills							Job Characteristics				
	Artistic	Communication	Interpersonal	Managerial	Mathematics	Mechanical	Science	Economically Sensitive	Outdoor Work	Physically Demanding Work	Hazardous Conditions	Geographically Concentrated
Actuaries		○	○	○	●		◉					
Agricultural and food scientists		◉	○	◉	●	●	●		◉	○	○	
Aircraft and avionics equipment mechanics and service technicians		○	○		◉	●	◉	◉	●	◉	○	◉
Aircraft pilots and flight engineers		●	●	●	●	◉	●	●	○	◉	●	○
Architects, except landscape and naval	●	◉	◉	◉	●	●	◉	◉	◉	○		
Archivists, curators, and museum technicians	●	◉	○	○	◉	●	●			○		◉
Armed forces		◉	◉	◉	○	○	○		◉	●	◉	◉
Atmospheric scientists		◉	○	◉	●	●	●	○	◉			
Audiologists		●	◉	●	◉	○	●					
Automotive body and related repairers	○	○	○		○	●	○		○	◉	○	
Automotive service technicians and mechanics		○	○		○	●	◉		○	◉	○	
Biological scientists		◉	○	◉	●	●	●	○	◉	○	○	
Broadcast and sound engineering technicians and radio operators		○	◉		◉	●	◉		○			○
Cardiovascular technologists and technicians		◉	○	○	●	●	●			○		
Chemists and materials scientists	○	◉	○	◉	●	●	●	◉			○	
Chiropractors		●	◉	●	◉	○	●			○		
Clinical laboratory technologists and technicians		◉	○		●	●	●			○	○	
Computer control programmers and operators		○			◉	◉	○	○				
Computer programmers		◉	○	○	●	◉	●	○				
Computer scientists and database administrators		◉	○	○	●		●	○				
Computer software engineers		◉	◉	◉	●	●	●	○				
Computer support specialists and systems administrators		◉	◉	○	◉	●	◉	○				
Computer systems analysts		◉	○	○	●		●	○				
Computer, automated teller, and office machine repairers		○	○		○	●	○		○	○		
Conservation scientists and foresters		◉	○	◉	●	●	●	○	●	◉	○	●
Dental assistants		◉	◉	○	○	●	◉			◉	◉	
Dental hygienists		◉	◉	○	◉	●	◉			○	◉	
Dentists	○	●	●	●	◉	●	●			○	◉	
Desktop publishers	●	○	○		○	◉	○	○				
Diagnostic medical sonographers		◉	○	○	●	●	●					
Diesel service technicians and mechanics		○	○		○	●	◉	◉	○	◉	○	

(continued)

Personal Skills: ●—Essential or high skill level; ◉—Somewhat essential or moderate skill level; ○—Basic skill level
Job Characteristics: ●—Highly likely; ◉—Somewhat likely; ○—A little likely

(continued)

	Personal Skills							Job Characteristics				
	Artistic	Communication	Interpersonal	Managerial	Mathematics	Mechanical	Science	Economically Sensitive	Outdoor Work	Physically Demanding Work	Hazardous Conditions	Geographically Concentrated
Dietitians and nutritionists		●	●	○	◉	○	●					
Drafters	●	◉	○		◉	●	○	◉				
Economists		◉	○	◉	●							
Electrical and electronics installers and repairers		○	○		◉	●	○				○	◉
Electronic home entertainment equipment installers and repairers	◉	○	○		◉	●	○	●		◉		
Elevator installers and repairers		○	○		○	●	○	●	○	●	●	
Engineering and natural sciences managers		●	●	●	●	●	●	◉				
Engineering technicians	○	◉	○		●	●	●	○	○	○	○	
Engineers	◉	◉	○	◉	●	●	●	◉	○	○	○	◉
Environmental scientists and hydrologists	○	◉	○	◉	●	●	●	○	●	○		
Geoscientists	○	◉	○	◉	●	●	●	○	●	○		
Heating, air conditioning, and refrigeration mechanics and installers		○	○		○	●	○	◉	○	◉	○	
Heavy vehicle and mobile equipment service technicians and mechanics		○	○		○	●	◉	●	○	◉	○	
Industrial machinery mechanics and maintenance workers		○			○	●	○	○		◉	◉	○
Licensed practical and licensed vocational nurses		◉	●	○	○	●	●			◉	◉	
Machinists	◉	○			●	●	◉	○		◉	◉	
Mathematicians		○	○	○	●		◉					
Medical records and health information technicians		◉	○	○	◉		◉					
Medical scientists		◉	○	◉	●	●	●	○			○	
Medical transcriptionists		●	○	○	○	○	●					
Medical, dental, and ophthalmic laboratory technicians	◉	○	◉		○	●	◉				○	
Millwrights		○	○		◉	●	○	●	○	◉	◉	◉
Nuclear medicine technologists		◉	○	○	●	●	●				◉	
Nursing, psychiatric, and home health aides		◉	◉	○	○	◉	○			●	●	
Occupational health and safety specialists and technicians		◉	○	◉	◉	◉	◉		○	◉	◉	
Occupational therapist assistants and aides		◉	●	○	○	●	◉			◉	◉	
Occupational therapists		●	●	◉	◉	◉	◉			○	◉	
Operations research analysts		○	○	○	●		◉	○				
Opticians, dispensing	◉	◉	◉	○	◉	◉	○	○		○		
Optometrists	○	●	◉	●	◉	◉	●				◉	
Paralegals and legal assistants		●	●	◉	○		○	◉				
Pharmacists		●	◉	◉	●	○	●				○	

Personal Skills: ●—Essential or high skill level; ◉—Somewhat essential or moderate skill level; ○—Basic skill level
Job Characteristics: ●—Highly likely; ◉—Somewhat likely; ○—A little likely

	Personal Skills							Job Characteristics				
	Artistic	Communication	Interpersonal	Managerial	Mathematics	Mechanical	Science	Economically Sensitive	Outdoor Work	Physically Demanding Work	Hazardous Conditions	Geographically Concentrated
Pharmacy aides		◉	◉	○	○		○			○		
Pharmacy technicians		◉	◉	○	◉	◉	◉			○		
Photographers	●	○	○	○	○	●	○	◉	◉	◉		
Photographic process workers and processing machine operators	○	○			○	●	○	○		○	◉	
Physical therapist assistants and aides		◉	◉	○	○	◉	◉			●	◉	
Physical therapists		●	●	○	◉	○	●			●	◉	
Physician assistants		●	●	○	◉	◉	●			◉	◉	
Physicians and surgeons	◉	●	●	●	◉	◉	●			◉	◉	
Physicists and astronomers	○	◉	○	○	●	●	●	○	○			○
Podiatrists	○	●	●	●	◉	◉	●					
Power plant operators, distributors, and dispatchers		○	◉	○	●	○	●				◉	
Precision instrument and equipment repairers	○	○			◉	●	○			◉		
Prepress technicians and workers	◉	◉	○		◉	◉	○	○		○		
Printing machine operators		○			○	●	○	○		●	◉	
Psychologists		●	●	○	◉		◉					
Radiation therapists		●	◉	●	◉	◉	●			●		
Radio and telecommunications equipment installers and repairers		○	○		◉	●	◉	○	●	◉		◉
Radiologic technologists and technicians		◉	◉	○	●	●	◉			◉	◉	
Registered nurses		●	●	◉	●	●	●			◉	◉	
Respiratory therapists		●	●	○	●	●	●			○	◉	
Sales engineers	○	●	●		◉	○	◉	●				
Science technicians	○	◉	○		●	●	●	◉	○	○	○	
Semiconductor processors		○			●	◉	●	◉		○		●
Small engine mechanics		○	○		○	●	◉	◉	○	◉	○	
Social scientists, other		◉	◉	○	◉	○	○					
Speech-language pathologists	○	●	●	○	●	○	●					
Stationary engineers and boiler operators		○	○	○	○	●	○				◉	
Statisticians		○	○	○	●		◉					
Surgical technologists		◉	◉	○	◉	●	◉			◉	◉	
Surveyors, cartographers, photogrammetrists, and surveying technicians	◉	◉	◉	○	◉	◉	◉	◉	◉	◉		
Teachers—postsecondary	◉	●	●	●			◉					
Television, video, and motion picture camera operators and editors	●	○	○	○	○	●	○		◉	●		●
Tool and die makers	○	○			●	●	◉	○		◉	◉	
Urban and regional planners	◉	◉	◉	◉	●	○	○	○	○			

(continued)

Personal Skills: ●—Essential or high skill level; ◉—Somewhat essential or moderate skill level; ○—Basic skill level
Job Characteristics: ●—Highly likely; ◉—Somewhat likely; ○—A little likely

(continued)

	Personal Skills							Job Characteristics				
	Artistic	Communication	Interpersonal	Managerial	Mathematics	Mechanical	Science	Economically Sensitive	Outdoor Work	Physically Demanding Work	Hazardous Conditions	Geographically Concentrated
Veterinarians	○	●	●	●	●	●	●		○	●	●	
Veterinary technologists and technicians		◉	◉	◉	◉	●	◉	○	○	●	●	
Water and liquid waste treatment plant and system operators		○	○	○	◉	●	◉		◉	◉	●	

Personal Skills: ●—Essential or high skill level; ◉—Somewhat essential or moderate skill level; ○—Basic skill level
Job Characteristics: ●—Highly likely; ◉—Somewhat likely; ○—A little likely

Descriptions of the Top 100 Computer and Technical Careers

This is the book's major section. It contains descriptions for 100 major occupations that require computer and technical skills. The jobs are arranged in alphabetical order. Refer to the table of contents for a list of the jobs and the page numbers where their descriptions begin.

Review the table of contents to discover occupations that interest you, and then find where their descriptions begin. If you are interested in medical jobs, for example, you can go through the list and quickly pinpoint those you want to learn more about. Or use the assessment in Part I to identify several possible career matches.

While the descriptions in this section are easy to understand, the introduction to this book provides additional information for interpreting them. Keep in mind that the descriptions present information that is average for the country. Conditions in your area and with specific employers may be quite different.

Also, you may come across jobs that sound interesting but require more education and training than you have or are considering. Don't eliminate them too soon. There are many ways to obtain education and training, and most people change jobs and careers many times. You probably have more skills than you realize that can transfer to new jobs, so consider taking some chances. You often have more opportunities than barriers, but you have to go out and find the opportunities. Use the descriptions to learn more about possible jobs and look into the suggested resources to help you take the next step.

Actuaries

(O*NET 15-2011.00)

Significant Points

■ A strong background in mathematics is essential; actuaries must pass a series of examinations to gain full professional status.

■ About 6 out of 10 actuaries are employed in the insurance industry.

■ Employment opportunities should remain good for those who qualify because the stringent qualifying examination system restricts the number of candidates.

Nature of the Work

One of the main functions of actuaries is to help businesses assess the risk of certain events occurring and to formulate policies that minimize the cost of that risk. For this reason, actuaries are essential to the insurance industry. Actuaries assemble and analyze data to estimate the probability and likely cost of the occurrence of an event such as death, sickness, injury, disability, or loss of property. Actuaries also address financial questions, including those involving the level of pension contributions required to produce a certain retirement income and the way in which a company should invest resources to maximize its return on investments in light of potential risk. Using their broad knowledge of statistics, finance, and business, actuaries help design insurance policies, pension plans, and other financial strategies in a manner that will help ensure that the plans are maintained on a sound financial basis.

Most actuaries are employed in the insurance industry, specializing in life and health insurance or property and casualty insurance. They produce probability tables that determine the likelihood that a potential future event will generate a claim. From these tables, they estimate the amount a company can expect to pay in claims. For example, property and casualty actuaries calculate the expected amount payable in claims resulting from automobile accidents, an amount that varies with the insured person's age, sex, driving history, type of car, and other factors. Actuaries ensure that the price, or premium, charged for such insurance will enable the company to cover claims and other expenses. The premium must be profitable yet competitive with other insurance companies. Within the life and health insurance fields, actuaries are helping to develop long-term-care insurance and annuity policies, the latter a growing investment tool for many individuals.

Actuaries in other financial services industries manage credit and price corporate security offerings. They also devise new investment tools to help their firms compete with other financial services companies. Pension actuaries working under the provisions of the Employee Retirement Income Security Act (ERISA) of 1974 evaluate pension plans covered by that act and report on the plans' financial soundness to participants, sponsors, and federal regulators. Actuaries working in government help manage social programs such as Social Security and Medicare.

Actuaries may play a role in determining company policy and may need to explain complex technical matters to company executives, government officials, shareholders, policyholders, or the public in general. They may testify before public agencies on proposed legislation affecting their businesses or explain changes in contract provisions to customers. They also may help companies develop plans to enter new lines of business or new geographic markets with existing lines of business by forecasting demand in competitive settings.

Both staff actuaries employed by businesses and consulting actuaries provide advice to clients on a contract basis. The duties of most consulting actuaries are similar to those of other actuaries. For example, some may evaluate company pension plans by calculating the future value of employee and employer contributions and determining whether the amounts are sufficient to meet the future needs of retirees. Others help companies reduce their insurance costs by lowering the level of risk the companies assume. For instance, they may provide advice on how to lessen the risk of injury on the job, which will lower worker's compensation costs. Consulting actuaries sometimes testify in court regarding the value of the potential lifetime earnings of a person who is disabled or killed in an accident, the current value of future pension benefits (in divorce cases), or other values arrived at by complex calculations. Many consulting actuaries work in reinsurance, a field in which one insurance company arranges to share a large prospective liability policy with another insurance company in exchange for a percentage of the premium.

Working Conditions

Actuaries have desk jobs, and their offices usually are comfortable and pleasant. They often work at least 40 hours a week. Some actuaries—particularly consulting actuaries—may travel to meet with clients. Consulting actuaries also may experience more erratic employment and be expected to work more than 40 hours per week.

Training, Other Qualifications, and Advancement

Actuaries need a strong background in mathematics. Applicants for beginning actuarial jobs usually have a bachelor's degree in mathematics; actuarial science; statistics; or a business-related discipline such as economics, finance, or accounting. About 100 colleges and universities offer an actuarial science program, and most offer a degree in mathematics, statistics, economics, or finance. Some companies hire applicants without specifying a major, provided that the applicant has a working knowledge of mathematics, including calculus, probability, and statistics, and has demonstrated this knowledge by passing one or two actuarial exams required for professional designation. Courses in economics, accounting, finance, and insurance also are useful. Companies increasingly prefer well-rounded individuals who, in addition to having acquired a strong technical background, have some training in liberal arts and business and possess strong communication skills.

In addition to knowledge of mathematics, computer skills are becoming increasingly important. Actuaries should be able to develop and use spreadsheets and databases as well as standard statistical analysis software. Knowledge of computer programming languages, such as Visual Basic, also is useful.

Two professional societies sponsor programs leading to full professional status in their specialty. The Society of Actuaries (SOA) administers a series of actuarial examinations in the life insurance, health benefits systems, retirement systems, and finance and investment fields. The Casualty Actuarial Society (CAS) gives a series of examinations in the property and casualty field, which includes fire, accident, medical malpractice, worker's compensation, and personal injury liability.

The first four exams in the SOA and CAS examination series are jointly sponsored by the two societies and cover the same material. For this reason, students do not need to commit themselves to a specialty until they have taken the initial examinations, which test an individual's competence in probability, calculus, statistics, and other branches of mathematics. The first few examinations help students evaluate their potential as actuaries. Many prospective actuaries begin taking the exams in college with the help of self-study guides and courses. Those who pass one or more examinations have better opportunities for employment at higher starting salaries than those who do not.

After graduating from college, most prospective actuaries gain on-the-job experience at an insurance company or consulting firm while at the same time working to complete the examination process. Actuaries are encouraged to finish the entire series of examinations as soon as possible, advancing first to the Associate level (with an ASA or ACAS designation) and then to the Fellowship level (FSA or FCAS designation). Advanced topics in the casualty field include investment and assets, dynamic financial analysis, and valuation of insurance. Candidates in the SOA examination series must choose a specialty—group and health benefits, individual life and annuities, pensions, investments, or finance. Examinations are given twice a year, in the spring and the fall. Although many companies allot time to their employees for study, home study is required to pass the examinations, and many actuaries study for months to prepare for each examination. It is likewise common for employers to pay the hundreds of dollars for examination fees and study materials. Most actuaries reach the Associate level within 4 to 6 years and the Fellowship level a few years later.

Specific requirements apply to pension actuaries, who verify the financial status of defined benefit pension plans for the federal government. These actuaries must be enrolled by the Joint Board of the U.S. Treasury Department and the U.S. Department of Labor for the Enrollment of Actuaries. To qualify for enrollment, applicants must meet certain experience and examination requirements, as stipulated by the Board.

To perform their duties effectively, actuaries must keep up with current economic and social trends and legislation, as well as with health, business, finance, and economic developments that could affect insurance or investment practices. Good communication and interpersonal skills also are important, particularly for prospective consulting actuaries.

Beginning actuaries often rotate among different jobs in an organization to learn various actuarial operations and phases of insurance work, such as marketing, underwriting, and product development. At first, they prepare data for actuarial projects or perform other simple tasks. As they gain experience, actuaries may supervise clerks, prepare correspondence, draft reports, and conduct research. They may move from one company to another early in their careers as they advance to higher positions.

Advancement depends largely on job performance and the number of actuarial examinations passed. Actuaries with a broad knowledge of the insurance, pension, investment, or employee benefits fields can rise to administrative and executive positions in their companies. Actuaries with supervisory ability may advance to management positions in other areas, such as underwriting, accounting, data processing, marketing, and advertising. Some actuaries assume college and university faculty positions. (See the description of teachers—postsecondary elsewhere in this book.)

Employment

Actuaries held about 18,000 jobs in 2004, with 6 out of 10 employed in the insurance industry. A growing number of actuaries work for firms providing a variety of corporate services, especially management and public relations, or for firms offering consulting services. A relatively small number of actuaries are employed by security and commodity brokers or by government agencies.

Job Outlook

Employment of actuaries is expected to grow faster than average for all occupations through 2014. Employment opportunities should remain good for those who qualify because the stringent qualifying examination system restricts the number of candidates. Employment growth in the insurance industry is expected to continue at a stable pace, while more significant job growth is likely in some other industries. In addition, a small number of jobs will open up each year to replace actuaries who leave the occupation to retire or who find new jobs.

Steady demand by the insurance industry—the largest employer of actuaries—should ensure the creation of new actuary jobs in this key industry over the projection period. Actuaries will continue to be needed to develop, price, and evaluate a variety of insurance products and calculate the costs of new risks. Although employment of actuaries in life insurance had begun to decline recently, the growing popularity of annuities, a financial product offered primarily by life insurance companies, has resulted in some job growth in this specialty. Also, new actuarial positions have been created in property-casualty insurance to analyze evolving risks, such as terrorism.

Some new employment opportunities for actuaries should also become available in the health care field as health care issues and Medicare reform continue to receive growing attention. Increased regulation of managed health care companies and the desire to contain health care costs will continue to provide job opportunities for actuaries, who will also be needed to evaluate the risks associated with new medical issues, such as genetic testing and the impact of new diseases. Others in this field are involved in drafting health care legislation.

A significant proportion of new actuaries will find employment with consulting firms. Companies that may not find it cost-effective to hire their own actuaries are increasingly hiring consulting actuaries to analyze various risks. Other areas with notable growth prospects are information services and accounting services. Also, because actuarial skills are increasingly seen as useful to other industries that deal with risk, such as the airline and the banking industries, additional job openings may be created in these industries.

The best job prospects for entry-level positions will be for those candidates who have passed at least one or two of the initial actuarial exams. Candidates with additional knowledge or experience, such as those who possess computer programming skills, will be particularly attractive to employers. Most jobs in this occupation are located in urban areas, but opportunities vary by geographic location. States in which actuary jobs are concentrated include Illinois, New Jersey, New York, and Connecticut.

Earnings

Median annual earnings of actuaries were $76,340 in May 2004. The middle 50 percent earned between $54,770 and $107,650. According to the National Association of Colleges and Employers, annual starting salaries for graduates with a bachelor's degree in actuarial science averaged $52,741 in 2005. Insurance companies and consulting firms give merit increases to actuaries as they gain experience and pass examinations. Some companies also offer cash bonuses for each professional designation achieved.

Related Occupations

Actuaries need a strong background in mathematics, statistics, and related fields. Other workers whose jobs involve related skills include accountants and auditors, budget analysts, economists, market and survey researchers, financial analysts and personal financial advisors, insurance underwriters, mathematicians, and statisticians.

Sources of Additional Information

Career information on actuaries specializing in pensions is available from

▸ American Society of Pension Actuaries, 4245 N. Fairfax Dr., Suite 750, Arlington, VA 22203. Internet: http://www.aspa.org

For information about actuarial careers in life and health insurance, employee benefits and pensions, and finance and investments, contact

▸ Society of Actuaries (SOA), 475 N. Martingale Rd., Suite 600, Schaumburg, IL 60173-2226. Internet: http://www.soa.org

For information about actuarial careers in property and casualty insurance, contact

▸ Casualty Actuarial Society (CAS), 1100 N. Glebe Rd., Suite 600, Arlington, VA 22201-0425. Internet: http://www.casact.org

The SOA and CAS jointly sponsor a Web site for those interested in pursuing an actuarial career. Internet: http://www.BeAnActuary.org

For general information on a career as an actuary, contact

▸ American Academy of Actuaries, 1100 17th St. NW, 7th Floor, Washington, DC 20036. Internet: http://www.actuary.org

Agricultural and Food Scientists

(O*NET 19-1011.00, 19-1012.00, 19-1013.01, and 19-1013.02)

Significant Points

■ About 1 in 4 agricultural and food scientists work for federal, state, or local governments.

■ A bachelor's degree in agricultural science is sufficient for some jobs in applied research; a master's or Ph.D. degree is required for basic research or teaching.

■ Over 1 in 3 agricultural and food scientists are self-employed.

Nature of the Work

The work of agricultural and food scientists plays an important part in maintaining the nation's food supply by ensuring agricultural productivity and the safety of the food supply. Agricultural scientists study farm crops and animals and develop ways of improving their quantity and quality. They look for ways to improve crop yield with less labor, control pests and weeds more safely and effectively, and conserve soil and water. They research methods of converting raw agricultural commodities into attractive and healthy food products for consumers.

Agricultural science is closely related to biological science, and agricultural scientists use the principles of biology, chemistry, physics, mathematics, and other sciences to solve problems in agriculture. They often work with biological scientists on basic biological research and on applying to agriculture the advances in knowledge brought about by biotechnology.

In the past two decades, rapid advances in basic biological knowledge related to genetics spurred growth in the field of biotechnology. Some agricultural and food scientists use this technology to manipulate the genetic material of plants and crops, attempting to make organisms more productive or resistant to disease. These advances in biotechnology have opened up research opportunities in many areas of agricultural and food science, including commercial applications in agriculture, environmental remediation, and the food industry. Another emerging technology expected to affect agriculture is nanotechnology—a future molecular manufacturing technology which promises to revolutionize methods of manufacturing and distribution in many industries.

Many agricultural scientists work in basic or applied research and development. Others manage or administer research and development programs or manage marketing or production operations in companies that produce food products or agricultural chemicals, supplies, and machinery. Some agricultural scientists are consultants to business firms, private clients, or government.

Depending on the agricultural or food scientist's area of specialization, the nature of the work performed varies.

Food science. Food scientists and technologists usually work in the food processing industry, universities, or the federal government and help to meet consumer demand for food products that are healthful, safe, palatable, and convenient. To do this, they use their knowledge of chemistry, physics, engineering, microbiology, biotechnology, and other sciences to develop new or better ways of preserving, processing, packaging, storing, and delivering foods. Some food scientists engage in basic research, discovering new food sources; analyzing food content to determine levels of vitamins, fat, sugar, or protein; or searching for substitutes for harmful or undesirable additives, such as nitrites. They also develop ways to process, preserve, package, or store food according to industry and government regulations. Traditional food processing research into functions involving baking, blanching, canning, drying, evaporation, and pasteurization will continue to be conducted and will find new applications. Other food scientists enforce government regulations, inspecting food processing areas and ensuring that sanitation, safety, quality, and waste management standards are met. Food technologists generally work in product development, applying the findings from food science research to the selection, preservation, processing, packaging, distribution, and use of safe, nutritious, and wholesome food.

Plant science. Agronomy, crop science, entomology, and plant breeding are included in plant science. Scientists in these disciplines study plants and their growth in soils, helping producers of food, feed, and fiber crops to continue to feed a growing population while conserving natural resources and maintaining the environment. Agronomists and crop scientists not only help increase productivity, but also study ways to improve the nutritional value of crops and the quality of seed, often through biotechnology. Some crop scientists study the breeding, physiology, and management of crops and use genetic engineering to develop crops resistant to pests and drought. Entomologists conduct research to develop new technologies to control or eliminate pests in infested areas and to prevent the spread of harmful pests to new areas, as well as technologies that are compatible with the environment. They also conduct research or engage in oversight activities aimed at halting the spread of insect-borne disease.

Soil science. Soil scientists study the chemical, physical, biological, and mineralogical composition of soils as they relate to plant or crop growth. They also study the responses of various soil types to fertilizers, tillage practices, and crop rotation. Many soil scientists who work for the federal government conduct soil surveys, classifying and mapping soils. They provide information and recommendations to farmers and other landowners regarding the best use of land, plant growth, and methods to avoid or correct problems such as erosion. They may also consult with engineers and other technical personnel working on construction projects about the effects of, and solutions to, soil problems. Because soil science is closely related to environmental science, persons trained in soil science also apply their knowledge to ensure environmental quality and effective land use.

Animal science. Animal scientists work to develop better, more efficient ways of producing and processing meat, poultry, eggs, and milk. Dairy scientists, poultry scientists, animal breeders, and other scientists in related fields study the genetics, nutrition, reproduction, growth, and development of domestic farm animals. Some animal scientists inspect and grade livestock food products, purchase livestock, or work in technical sales or marketing. As extension agents or consultants, animal scientists advise agricultural

producers on how to upgrade animal housing facilities properly, lower mortality rates, handle waste matter, or increase production of animal products such as milk or eggs.

Working Conditions

Agricultural scientists involved in management or basic research tend to work regular hours in offices and laboratories. The work environment for those engaged in applied research or product development varies, depending on the discipline of agricultural science and on the type of employer. For example, food scientists in private industry may work in test kitchens while investigating new processing techniques. Animal scientists working for federal, state, or university research stations may spend part of their time at dairies, farrowing houses, feedlots, or farm animal facilities or outdoors conducting research associated with livestock. Soil and crop scientists also spend time outdoors conducting research on farms and agricultural research stations. Entomologists work in laboratories, insectories, or agricultural research stations and also may spend time outdoors studying or collecting insects in their natural habitat.

Training, Other Qualifications, and Advancement

Training requirements for agricultural scientists depend on their specialty and on the type of work they perform. A bachelor's degree in agricultural science is sufficient for some jobs in applied research or for assisting in basic research, but a master's or doctoral degree is required for basic research. A Ph.D. in agricultural science usually is needed for college teaching and for advancement to administrative research positions. Degrees in related sciences such as biology, chemistry, or physics or in related engineering specialties also may qualify persons for some agricultural science jobs.

All states have a land-grant college that offers agricultural science degrees. Many other colleges and universities also offer agricultural science degrees or some agricultural science courses. However, not every school offers all specialties. A typical undergraduate agricultural science curriculum includes communications, mathematics, economics, business, and physical and life sciences courses in addition to a wide variety of technical agricultural science courses. For prospective animal scientists, these technical agricultural science courses might include animal breeding, reproductive physiology, nutrition, and meats and muscle biology. Graduate students typically specialize in a subfield of agricultural science, such as animal breeding and genetics, crop science, or horticulture science, depending on their interest and the kind of work they wish to do. For example, those interested in doing genetic and biotechnological research in the food industry need to develop a strong background in life and physical sciences, such as cell and molecular biology, microbiology, and inorganic and organic chemistry. However, students normally need not specialize at the undergraduate level. In fact, undergraduates who are broadly trained have greater flexibility when changing jobs than if they had narrowly defined their interests.

Students preparing as food scientists take courses such as food chemistry, food analysis, food microbiology, food engineering, and food processing operations. Those preparing as crop or soil scientists take courses in plant pathology, soil chemistry, entomology, plant physiology, and biochemistry, among others. Advanced degree programs include classroom and fieldwork, laboratory research, and a thesis or dissertation based on independent research.

Agricultural and food scientists should be able to work independently or as part of a team and be able to communicate clearly and concisely, both orally and in writing. Most of these scientists also need an understanding of basic business principles and the ability to apply basic statistical techniques. Employers increasingly prefer job applicants who are able to apply computer skills to determine solutions to problems, to collect and analyze data, and to control various processes.

The American Society of Agronomy offers certification programs in crop science, agronomy, crop advising, soil science, plant pathology, and weed science. To become certified, applicants must pass designated examinations and have at least 2 years of experience with at least a bachelor's degree in agriculture or 4 years of experience with no degree. To become a certified crop advisor, however, candidates do not need a degree.

Agricultural scientists who have advanced degrees usually begin in research or teaching. With experience, they may advance to jobs such as supervisors of research programs or managers of other agriculture-related activities.

Employment

Agricultural and food scientists held about 30,000 jobs in 2004. In addition, several thousand persons held agricultural science faculty positions in colleges and universities. (See the description of teachers—postsecondary elsewhere in this book.)

About 1 in 4 salaried agricultural and food scientists work for federal, state, or local governments. One out of 7 worked for state governments at state agricultural colleges or agricultural research stations. Another one out of 10 worked for the federal government in 2004, mostly in the U.S. Department of Agriculture. Some worked for agricultural service companies; others worked for commercial research and development laboratories, seed companies, pharmaceutical companies, wholesale distributors, and food products companies. About 10,000 agricultural scientists were self-employed in 2004, mainly as consultants.

Job Outlook

Employment of agricultural and food scientists is expected to grow about as fast as average for all occupations through 2014. Past agricultural research has resulted in the development of higher-yielding crops, crops with better resistance to pests and plant pathogens, and chemically based fertilizers and pesticides. Research is still necessary, particularly as insects and diseases continue to adapt to pesticides and as soil fertility and water quality continue to need improvement, resulting in job opportunities in biotechnology. Agricultural scientists are using new avenues of research in biotechnology to develop plants and food crops that require less fertilizer, fewer pesticides and herbicides, and even less water for growth. Emerging biotechnologies and nanotechnologies will play an increasingly larger role in creating more plentiful global food supplies.

Biotechnological research will continue to offer possibilities for the development of new food products. This research will allow agricultural and food scientists to develop techniques to detect and control food pathogens and should lead to better understanding of other infectious agents in foods.

Agricultural scientists will be needed to balance increased agricultural output with protection and preservation of soil, water, and ecosystems. They will increasingly encourage the practice of "sustainable agriculture" by developing and implementing plans to manage pests, crops, soil fertility and erosion, and animal waste in ways that reduce the use of harmful chemicals and do little damage to farms and the natural environment.

Further studies at scientific research and development services firms will result in more job opportunities for food scientists and technologists. This research will be stimulated by a heightened public focus on diet, health, changes in food safety, and biosecurity—preventing the introduction of infectious agents such as foot-and-mouth disease into a herd of animals. Increasing demand for these workers also will stem from issues such as a growing world population; availability and cost of usable water; shrinking natural resources, including the loss of arable land; and deforestation, environmental pollution, and climate change.

Graduates with a bachelor's degree should find work in a variety of fields, mostly in the private sector, although many of the positions may be related to agricultural or food science rather than as an agricultural or food scientist. A bachelor's degree in agricultural science is useful for managerial jobs in businesses that deal with ranchers and farmers, such as feed, fertilizer, seed, and farm equipment manufacturers; retailers or wholesalers; and farm credit institutions. In some cases, persons with a 4-year degree can provide consulting services or work in sales and marketing—promoting high-demand products such as organic foods. Bachelor's degree holders also can work in some applied research and product development positions under the guidance of a Ph.D. scientist, but usually only in certain subfields, such as food science and technology. The federal government hires bachelor's degree holders to work as soil scientists. Four-year degrees also may help persons enter occupations such as farmer or farm or ranch manager, cooperative extension service agent, agricultural products inspector, or purchasing or sales agent for agricultural commodity or farm supply companies.

Opportunities may be better for those with a master's degree, particularly for graduates seeking applied research positions in a laboratory. Master's degree candidates also can seek to become a certified crop advisor, helping farmers better manage their crops. Those with a Ph.D. in agricultural and food science will experience the best opportunities, especially in basic research and teaching positions at colleges and universities as retirements of faculty are expected to accelerate during the projection period.

Fewer opportunities for agricultural and food scientists are expected in the federal government, mostly because of budgetary cutbacks at the U.S. Department of Agriculture.

Employment of agricultural and food scientists is relatively stable during periods of economic recession. Layoffs are less likely among agricultural and food scientists than in some other occupations because food is a staple item and its demand fluctuates very little with economic activity.

Earnings

Median annual earnings of food scientists and technologists were $50,840 in May 2004. The middle 50 percent earned between $36,450 and $72,510. The lowest 10 percent earned less than $28,410, and the highest 10 percent earned more than $91,300. Median annual earnings of soil and plant scientists were $51,200 in May 2004. The middle 50 percent earned between $37,890 and $69,120. The lowest 10 percent earned less than $30,660, and the highest 10 percent earned more than $88,840. In May 2004, median annual earnings of animal scientists were $49,920.

The average federal salary for employees in nonsupervisory, supervisory, and managerial positions in 2005 was $87,025 in animal science and $73,573 in agronomy.

According to the National Association of Colleges and Employers, beginning salary offers in 2005 for graduates with a bachelor's degree in animal sciences averaged $30,614 a year; plant sciences, $31,649 a year; and in other agricultural sciences, $36,189 a year.

Related Occupations

The work of agricultural scientists is closely related to that of other scientists, including biological scientists, chemists, and conservation scientists and foresters. It also is related to the work of managers of agricultural production, such as farmers, ranchers, and agricultural managers. Certain specialties of agricultural science also are related to other occupations. For example, the work of animal scientists is related to the work of veterinarians, and horticulturists perform duties similar to duties of landscape architects.

Sources of Additional Information

Agricultural career brochures are available from

▸ American Society of Agronomy, Crop Science Society of America, Soil Science Society of America, 677 S. Segoe Rd., Madison, WI 53711-1086. Internet: http://www.agronomy.org

Information on careers in agricultural science is available from

▸ Food and Agricultural Careers for Tomorrow, Purdue University, 1140 Agricultural Administration Bldg., West Lafayette, IN 47907-1140.

Information on acquiring a job as an agricultural scientist with the federal government is available from the Office of Personnel Management through USAJOBS, the federal government's official employment information system. This resource for locating and applying for job opportunities can be accessed through the Internet at http://www.usajobs.opm.gov or through an interactive voice response telephone system at (703) 724-1850 or TDD (978) 461-8404. These numbers are not toll free, and charges may result.

Aircraft and Avionics Equipment Mechanics and Service Technicians

(O*NET 49-2091.00, 49-3011.01, 49-3011.02, and 49-3011.03)

Significant Points

■ Most workers learn their job in 1 of about 170 schools certified by the Federal Aviation Administration (FAA).

■ Job opportunities should be excellent for persons who have completed an aircraft mechanic training program, but keen competition is likely for the best-paying airline jobs.

■ Job opportunities are likely to be the best at small commuter and regional airlines, at FAA repair stations, and in general aviation.

Nature of the Work

To keep aircraft in peak operating condition, aircraft and avionics equipment mechanics and service technicians perform scheduled maintenance, make repairs, and complete inspections required by the Federal Aviation Administration (FAA).

Many aircraft mechanics, also called airframe mechanics, power plant mechanics, and avionics technicians, specialize in preventive maintenance. They inspect aircraft engines; landing gear; instruments; pressurized sections; accessories—brakes, valves, pumps, and air-conditioning systems, for example—and other parts of the aircraft and do the necessary maintenance and replacement of parts. They also maintain records related to the maintenance performed on the aircraft. Mechanics and technicians conduct inspections following a schedule based on the number of hours the aircraft has flown, calendar days since the last inspection, cycles of operation, or a combination of these factors. In large, sophisticated planes equipped with aircraft monitoring systems, mechanics can gather valuable diagnostic information from electronic boxes and consoles that monitor the aircraft's basic operations. In planes of all sorts, aircraft mechanics examine engines by working through specially designed openings while standing on ladders or scaffolds or by using hoists or lifts to remove the entire engine from the craft. After taking an engine apart, mechanics use precision instruments to measure parts for wear and use X-ray and magnetic inspection equipment to check for invisible cracks. They repair or replace worn or defective parts. Mechanics also may repair sheet metal or composite surfaces; measure the tension of control cables; and check for corrosion, distortion, and cracks in the fuselage, wings, and tail. After completing all repairs, they must test the equipment to ensure that it works properly.

Mechanics specializing in repair work rely on the pilot's description of a problem to find and fix faulty equipment. For example, during a preflight check, a pilot may discover that the aircraft's fuel gauge does not work. To solve the problem, mechanics may troubleshoot the electrical system, using electrical test equipment to make sure that no wires are broken or shorted out, and replace any defective electrical or electronic components. Mechanics work as fast as safety permits so that the aircraft can be put back into service quickly.

Some mechanics work on one or many different types of aircraft, such as jets, propeller-driven airplanes, and helicopters. Others specialize in one section of a particular type of aircraft, such as the engine, hydraulics, or electrical system. *Airframe mechanics* are authorized to work on any part of the aircraft except the instruments, power plants, and propellers. *Powerplant mechanics* are authorized to work on engines and do limited work on propellers. *Combination airframe-and-powerplant mechanics*—called A&P mechanics— work on all parts of the plane except the instruments. Most mechanics working on civilian aircraft today are A&P mechanics. In small, independent repair shops, mechanics usually inspect and repair many different types of aircraft.

Avionics systems are now an integral part of aircraft design and have vastly increased aircraft capability. *Avionics technicians* repair and maintain components used for aircraft navigation and radio communications; weather radar systems; and other instruments and computers that control flight, engine, and other primary functions. These duties may require additional licenses, such as a radiotelephone license issued by the U.S. Federal Communications Commission (FCC). Because of the increasing use of technology, more time is spent repairing electronic systems, such as computerized controls. Technicians also may be required to analyze and develop solutions to complex electronic problems.

Working Conditions

Mechanics usually work in hangars or in other indoor areas. When hangars are full or when repairs must be made quickly, they can work outdoors, sometimes in unpleasant weather. Mechanics often work under time pressure to maintain flight schedules or, in general aviation, to keep from inconveniencing customers. At the same time, mechanics have a tremendous responsibility to maintain safety standards, and this can cause the job to be stressful.

Frequently, mechanics must lift or pull objects weighing more than 70 pounds. They often stand, lie, or kneel in awkward positions and occasionally must work in precarious positions, such as on scaffolds or ladders. Noise and vibration are common when engines are being tested, so ear protection is necessary. Aircraft mechanics usually work 40 hours a week on 8-hour shifts around the clock. Overtime work is frequent.

Training, Other Qualifications, and Advancement

Most mechanics who work on civilian aircraft are certified by the FAA as an "airframe mechanic" or a "powerplant mechanic." Mechanics who also have an inspector's authorization can certify work completed by other mechanics and perform required inspections. Uncertified mechanics are supervised by those with certificates.

The FAA requires at least 18 months of work experience for an airframe or powerplant certificate. For a combined A&P certificate, at least 30 months of experience working with both engines and airframes is required. Completion of a program at an FAA-certified mechanic school can substitute for the work experience requirement. Applicants for all certificates also must pass written and oral tests and demonstrate that they can do the work authorized by the certificate. To obtain an inspector's authorization, a mechanic must have held an A&P certificate for at least 3 years, with 24 months of hands-on experience. Most airlines require that mechanics have a high school diploma and an A&P certificate.

Although a few people become mechanics through on-the-job training, most learn their job in 1 of about 170 trade schools certified by the FAA. About one-third of these schools award 2-year and 4-year degrees in avionics, aviation technology, or aviation maintenance management.

FAA standards established by law require that certified mechanic schools offer students a minimum of 1,900 actual class hours. Coursework in schools normally lasts from 18 to 24 months and provides training with the tools and equipment used on the job. Aircraft trade schools are placing more emphasis on technologies such as turbine engines, composite materials—including graphite, fiberglass, and boron—and aviation electronics, which are increasingly being used in the construction of new aircraft. Additionally, employers prefer mechanics who can perform a variety of tasks.

Some aircraft mechanics in the Armed Forces acquire enough general experience to satisfy the work experience requirements for the FAA certificate. With additional study, they may pass the certifying exam. In general, however, jobs in the military services are too specialized to provide the broad experience required by the FAA. Most Armed Forces mechanics have to complete the entire training program, although a few receive some credit for the material they learned in the service. In any case, military experience is a great advantage when seeking employment; employers consider applicants with formal training to be the most desirable applicants.

Courses in mathematics, physics, chemistry, electronics, computer science, and mechanical drawing are helpful because they demonstrate many of the principles involved in the operation of aircraft, and knowledge of these principles is often necessary to make repairs. Courses that develop writing skills also are important because mechanics are often required to submit reports.

FAA regulations require current work experience to keep the A&P certificate valid. Applicants must have at least 1,000 hours of work experience in the previous 24 months or take a refresher course. As new and more complex aircraft are designed, more employers are requiring mechanics to take ongoing training to update their skills. Recent technological advances in aircraft maintenance necessitate a strong background in electronics—both for acquiring and for retaining jobs in this field. FAA certification standards also make ongoing training mandatory. Every 24 months, mechanics are required to take at least 16 hours of training to keep their certificate. Many mechanics take courses offered by manufacturers or employers, usually through outside contractors.

Aircraft mechanics must do careful and thorough work that requires a high degree of mechanical aptitude. Employers seek applicants who are self-motivated, hard working, enthusiastic, and able to diagnose and solve complex mechanical problems. Agility is important for the reaching and climbing necessary to do the job. Because they may work on the tops of wings and fuselages on large jet planes, aircraft mechanics must not be afraid of heights.

Advances in computer technology, aircraft systems, and the materials used to manufacture airplanes have made mechanics' jobs more highly technical. Aircraft mechanics must possess the skills necessary to troubleshoot and diagnose complex aircraft systems. They also must continually update their skills with, and knowledge of, new technology and advances in aircraft technology.

As aircraft mechanics gain experience, they may advance to lead mechanic (or crew chief), inspector, lead inspector, or shop supervisor positions. Opportunities are best for those who have an aircraft inspector's authorization. In the airlines, where promotion often is determined by examination, supervisors sometimes advance to executive positions. Those with broad experience in maintenance and overhaul might become inspectors with the FAA. With additional business and management training, some open their own aircraft maintenance facilities. Mechanics learn many different skills in their training that can be applied to other jobs, and some transfer to other skilled repairer occupations or electronics technician jobs. Mechanics with the necessary pilot licenses and flying experience may take the FAA examination for the position of flight engineer, with opportunities to become pilots.

Employment

Aircraft and avionics equipment mechanics and service technicians held about 142,000 jobs in 2004; about 5 in 6 of these workers were aircraft mechanic and service technicians. More than half of aircraft and avionics equipment mechanics and service technicians worked for air transportation companies. About 18 percent worked for the federal government, and about 14 percent worked for aerospace products and parts manufacturing firms. Most of the rest worked for companies that operate their own planes to transport executives and cargo. Few mechanics and technicians were self-employed.

Most airline mechanics and service technicians work at major airports near large cities. Civilian mechanics employed by the U.S. Armed Forces work at military installations. Mechanics who work for aerospace manufacturing firms typically are located in California or in Washington State. Others work for the FAA, many at the facilities in Oklahoma City, Atlantic City, Wichita, or Washington, DC. Mechanics for independent repair shops work at airports in every part of the country.

Job Outlook

Opportunities for aircraft and avionics equipment mechanics and service technicians should be excellent for who have completed aircraft mechanic training programs. Employment is expected to increase about as fast as the average for all occupations through the year 2014, and large numbers of additional job openings should arise from the need to replace experienced mechanics who retire.

Reduced passenger traffic—resulting from a weak economy and the events of September 11, 2001—forced airlines to cut back flights and take aircraft out of service. However, over the next decade, pas-

senger traffic is expected to increase as the result of an expanding economy and a growing population, and the need for aircraft mechanics and service technicians will grow accordingly. Furthermore, if the number of graduates from aircraft mechanic training programs continues to fall short of employer needs, opportunities for graduates of mechanic training programs should be excellent.

Most job openings for aircraft mechanics through the year 2014 will stem from replacement needs. Many mechanics are expected to retire over the next decade and create several thousand job openings per year. In addition, others will leave to work in related fields, such as automobile repair, as their skills are largely transferable to other maintenance and repair occupations. Also contributing to favorable future job opportunities for mechanics is the long-term trend toward fewer students entering technical schools to learn skilled maintenance and repair trades. Many of the students who have the ability and aptitude to work on planes are choosing to go to college, work in computer-related fields, or go into other repair and maintenance occupations with better working conditions. If the trend continues, the supply of trained aviation mechanics will not be able to keep up with the needs of the air transportation industry.

Job opportunities are likely to be the best at small commuter and regional airlines, at FAA repair stations, and in general aviation. Commuter and regional airlines are the fastest-growing segment of the air transportation industry, but wages in these companies tend to be lower than those in the major airlines, so they attract fewer job applicants. Also, some jobs will become available as experienced mechanics leave for higher-paying jobs with the major airlines or transfer to another occupation. At the same time, general aviation aircraft are becoming increasingly sophisticated, boosting the demand for qualified mechanics. Mechanics will face more competition for jobs with large airlines because the high wages and travel benefits that these jobs offer generally attract more qualified applicants than there are openings. Also, there is an increasing trend for large airlines to outsource aircraft and avionics equipment mechanic jobs overseas; however, most airline companies prefer that maintenance work done on aircraft be performed in the U.S. because of safety and regulation issues of overseas contractors.

In spite of these factors, job opportunities with the airlines are expected to be better than they have been in the past. But, in general, prospects will be best for applicants with experience. Mechanics who keep abreast of technological advances in electronics, composite materials, and other areas will be in greatest demand. Also, mechanics who are mobile and willing to relocate to smaller rural areas will have better job opportunities. The number of job openings for aircraft mechanics in the federal government should decline as the government increasingly contracts out service and repair functions to private repair companies.

Job opportunities for avionics technicians who are prepared to master the intricacies of the aircraft and work with A&P mechanics are expected to be good. Technicians who are cross-trained and able to work with complex aircraft systems should have the best job prospects. Additionally, technicians with licensing that enables them to work on the airplane, either removing or reinstalling equipment, are expected to be in especially high demand.

Earnings

Median hourly earnings of aircraft mechanics and service technicians were about $21.77 in May 2004. The middle 50 percent earned between $17.82 and $27.18. The lowest 10 percent earned less than $13.99, and the highest 10 percent earned more than $33.84. Median hourly earnings in the industries employing the largest numbers of aircraft mechanics and service technicians in May 2004 were

Scheduled air transportation $27.37
Federal government 21.67
Nonscheduled air transportation 20.88
Aerospace product and parts manufacturing 20.60
Support activities for air transportation 18.70

Median hourly earnings of avionics technicians were about $21.30 in May 2004. The middle 50 percent earned between $18.12 and $25.12. The lowest 10 percent earned less than $14.63, and the highest 10 percent earned more than $27.85.

Mechanics who work on jets for the major airlines generally earn more than those working on other aircraft. Airline mechanics and their immediate families receive reduced-fare transportation on their own and most other airlines.

About 4 in 10 aircraft and avionics equipment mechanics and service technicians are members of unions or covered by union agreements. The principal unions are the International Association of Machinists and Aerospace Workers and the Transport Workers Union of America. Some mechanics are represented by the International Brotherhood of Teamsters.

Related Occupations

Workers in some other occupations that involve similar mechanical and electrical work are electricians, electrical and electronics installers and repairers, and elevator installers and repairers.

Sources of Additional Information

Information about jobs with a particular airline can be obtained by writing to the personnel manager of the company.

For general information about aircraft and avionics equipment mechanics and service technicians, contact

▸ Professional Aviation Maintenance Association, 717 Princess St., Alexandria, VA 22314. Internet: http://www.pama.org

For information on jobs in a particular area, contact employers at local airports or local offices of the state employment service.

Information on obtaining positions as aircraft and avionics equipment mechanics and service technicians with the federal government is available from the Office of Personnel Management through USAJOBS, the federal government's official employment information system. This resource for locating and applying for job opportunities can be accessed through the Internet at http://www.usajobs.opm.gov or through an interactive voice response telephone system at (703) 724-1850 or TDD (978) 461-8404. These numbers are not toll free, and charges may result.

Aircraft Pilots and Flight Engineers

(O*NET 53-2011.00 and 53-2012.00)

Significant Points

■ Regional and low-fare airlines offer the best opportunities; pilots attempting to get jobs at the major airlines will face strong competition.

■ Pilots usually start with smaller commuter and regional airlines to acquire the experience needed to qualify for higher-paying jobs with national or major airlines.

■ Many pilots have learned to fly in the military, but growing numbers have college degrees with flight training from civilian flying schools that are certified by the Federal Aviation Administration (FAA).

■ Earnings of airline pilots are among the highest in the nation.

Nature of the Work

Pilots are highly trained professionals who either fly airplanes or helicopters to carry out a wide variety of tasks. Most are *airline pilots*, *copilots*, and *flight engineers* who transport passengers and cargo, but 1 out of 5 pilots is a commercial pilot involved in tasks such as dusting crops, spreading seed for reforestation, testing aircraft, flying passengers and cargo to areas not served by regular airlines, directing fire fighting efforts, tracking criminals, monitoring traffic, and rescuing and evacuating injured persons.

Except on small aircraft, two pilots usually make up the cockpit crew. Generally, the most experienced pilot, the *captain*, is in command and supervises all other crew members. The pilot and the copilot, often called the first officer, share flying and other duties, such as communicating with air traffic controllers and monitoring the instruments. Some large aircraft have a third pilot, the flight engineer, who assists the other pilots by monitoring and operating many of the instruments and systems, making minor in-flight repairs, and watching for other aircraft. The flight engineer also assists the pilots with the company, air traffic control, and cabin crew communications. New technology can perform many flight tasks, however, and virtually all new aircraft now fly with only two pilots, who rely more heavily on computerized controls.

Before departure, pilots plan their flights carefully. They thoroughly check their aircraft to make sure that the engines, controls, instruments, and other systems are functioning properly. They also make sure that baggage or cargo has been loaded correctly. They confer with flight dispatchers and aviation weather forecasters to find out about weather conditions en route and at their destination. Based on this information, they choose a route, altitude, and speed that will provide the safest, most economical, and smoothest flight. When flying under instrument flight rules—procedures governing the operation of the aircraft when there is poor visibility—the pilot in command, or the company dispatcher, normally files an instrument flight plan with air traffic control so that the flight can be coordinated with other air traffic.

Takeoff and landing are the most difficult parts of the flight and require close coordination between the pilot and first officer. For example, as the plane accelerates for takeoff, the pilot concentrates on the runway while the first officer scans the instrument panel. To calculate the speed they must attain to become airborne, pilots consider the altitude of the airport, outside temperature, weight of the plane, and speed and direction of the wind. The moment the plane reaches takeoff speed, the first officer informs the pilot, who then pulls back on the controls to raise the nose of the plane. Pilots and first officers usually alternate flying each leg from takeoff to landing.

Unless the weather is bad, the flight itself is relatively routine. Airplane pilots, with the assistance of autopilot and the flight management computer, steer the plane along their planned route and are monitored by the air traffic control stations they pass along the way. They regularly scan the instrument panel to check their fuel supply; the condition of their engines; and the air-conditioning, hydraulic, and other systems. Pilots may request a change in altitude or route if circumstances dictate. For example, if the ride is rougher than expected, pilots may ask air traffic control if pilots flying at other altitudes have reported better conditions; if so, they may request an altitude change. This procedure also may be used to find a stronger tailwind or a weaker headwind to save fuel and increase speed. In contrast, because helicopters are used for short trips at relatively low altitude, helicopter pilots must be constantly on the lookout for trees, bridges, power lines, transmission towers, and other dangerous obstacles. Regardless of the type of aircraft, all pilots must monitor warning devices designed to help detect sudden shifts in wind conditions that can cause crashes.

Pilots must rely completely on their instruments when visibility is poor. On the basis of altimeter readings, they know how high above ground they are and whether they can fly safely over mountains and other obstacles. Special navigation radios give pilots precise information that, with the help of special maps, tells them their exact position. Other very sophisticated equipment provides directions to a point just above the end of a runway and enables pilots to land completely without an outside visual reference. Once on the ground, pilots must complete records on their flight and the aircraft maintenance status for their company and the FAA.

The number of nonflying duties that pilots have depends on the employment setting. Airline pilots have the services of large support staffs and, consequently, perform few nonflying duties. However, because of the large numbers of passengers, airline pilots may be called upon to coordinate handling of disgruntled or disruptive passengers. Pilots employed by other organizations, such as charter operators or businesses, have many other duties. They may load the aircraft, handle all passenger luggage to ensure a balanced load, and supervise refueling; other nonflying responsibilities include keeping records, scheduling flights, arranging for major maintenance, and performing minor aircraft maintenance and repairs.

Some pilots are flight instructors. They teach their students in ground-school classes, in simulators, and in dual-controlled planes and helicopters. A few specially trained pilots are examiners or check pilots. They periodically fly with other pilots or pilot's license applicants to make sure that they are proficient.

Working Conditions

Because of FAA regulations, airline pilots flying large aircraft cannot fly more than 100 hours a month or more than 1,000 hours a year. Most airline pilots fly an average of 75 hours a month and work an additional 75 hours a month performing nonflying duties. Most pilots have a variable work schedule, working several days on, then several days off. Most spend a considerable amount of time away from home because the majority of flights involve overnight layovers. When pilots are away from home, the airlines provide hotel accommodations, transportation between the hotel and airport, and an allowance for meals and other expenses. Airlines operate flights at all hours of the day and night, so work schedules often are irregular. Flight assignments are based on seniority. An airline seniority number is normally assigned to a pilot on completion of training. The sooner pilots are hired, the lower their seniority number and the stronger their bidding power.

Commercial pilots also may have irregular schedules, flying 30 hours one month and 90 hours the next. Because these pilots frequently have many nonflying responsibilities, they have much less free time than do airline pilots. Except for corporate flight department pilots, most commercial pilots do not remain away from home overnight, but they may work odd hours. However, if the company owns a fleet of planes, pilots may fly a regular schedule. Flight instructors may have irregular and seasonal work schedules, depending on their students' available time and the weather. Instructors frequently work in the evening or on weekends.

Airline pilots, especially those on international routes, often experience jet lag—fatigue caused by many hours of flying through different time zones. To guard against pilot fatigue, which could result in unsafe flying conditions, the FAA requires airlines to allow pilots at least 8 hours of uninterrupted rest in the 24 hours before finishing their flight duty.

Commercial pilots face other types of job hazards. The work of test pilots, who check the flight performance of new and experimental planes, may be dangerous. Pilots who are crop-dusters may be exposed to toxic chemicals and seldom have the benefit of a regular landing strip. Helicopter pilots involved in rescue and police work may be subject to personal injury.

Although flying does not involve much physical effort, the mental stress of being responsible for a safe flight, regardless of the weather, can be tiring. Pilots must be alert and quick to react if something goes wrong, particularly during takeoff and landing.

Training, Other Qualifications, and Advancement

All pilots who are paid to transport passengers or cargo must have a commercial pilot's license with an instrument rating issued by the FAA. Helicopter pilots must hold a commercial pilot's certificate with a helicopter rating. To qualify for these licenses, applicants must be at least 18 years old and have at least 250 hours of flight experience. The experience required can be reduced through participation in certain flight school curricula approved by the FAA.

Applicants also must pass a strict physical examination to make sure that they are in good health and have 20/20 vision with or without glasses, good hearing, and no physical handicaps that could impair their performance. They must pass a written test that includes questions on the principles of safe flight, navigation techniques, and FAA regulations, and they must demonstrate their flying ability to FAA or designated examiners.

To fly during periods of low visibility, pilots must be rated by the FAA to fly by instruments. Pilots may qualify for this rating by having the required hours of flight experience, including 40 hours of experience in flying by instruments; they also must pass a written examination on procedures and FAA regulations covering instrument flying and demonstrate to an examiner their ability to fly by instruments. Requirements for the instrument rating vary depending on the certification level of flight school.

Airline pilots must fulfill additional requirements. Pilots must have an airline transport pilot's license. Applicants for this license must be at least 23 years old and have a minimum of 1,500 hours of flying experience, including night and instrument flying, and must pass FAA written and flight examinations. Usually, they also have one or more advanced ratings depending on the requirements of their particular job. Because pilots must be able to make quick decisions and accurate judgments under pressure, many airline companies reject applicants who do not pass required psychological and aptitude tests. All licenses are valid so long as a pilot can pass the periodic physical and eye examinations and tests of flying skills required by the FAA and company regulations.

The U.S. Armed Forces have always been an important source of trained pilots for civilian jobs. Military pilots gain valuable experience on jet aircraft and helicopters, and persons with this experience—because of the extensive flying time military pilots receive—usually are preferred for civilian pilot jobs. Those without Armed Forces training may become pilots by attending flight schools or by taking lessons from FAA-certified flight instructors. The FAA has certified about 600 civilian flying schools, including some colleges and universities that offer degree credit for pilot training. Until 2014 , trained pilots leaving the military are not expected to increase very much in number as the need for pilots grows in civilian aviation. As a result, FAA-certified schools will train a larger share of pilots than in the past.

Although some small airlines hire high school graduates, most airlines require at least 2 years of college and prefer to hire college graduates. In fact, most entrants to this occupation have a college degree. Because the number of college-educated applicants continues to increase, many employers are making a college degree an educational requirement.

Depending on the type of aircraft, new airline pilots start as first officers or flight engineers. Although some airlines favor applicants who already have a flight engineer's license, they may provide flight engineer training for those who have only the commercial license. Many pilots begin with smaller regional or commuter airlines, where they obtain experience flying passengers on scheduled flights into busy airports in all weather conditions. These jobs often lead to higher-paying jobs with bigger, national, or major airlines.

Initial training for airline pilots includes a week of company indoctrination; 3 to 6 weeks of ground school and simulator training; and 25 hours of initial operating experience, including a check-ride with an FAA aviation safety inspector. Once trained, pilots are required to attend recurrent training and simulator checks once or twice a year throughout their career.

Companies other than airlines usually require less flying experience. However, a commercial pilot's license is a minimum requirement, and employers prefer applicants who have experience in the type of craft they will be flying. New employees usually start as first officers or fly less-sophisticated equipment. Test pilots often are required to have an engineering degree.

Advancement for all pilots usually is limited to other flying jobs. Many pilots start as flight instructors, building up their flying hours while they earn money teaching. As they become more experienced, these pilots occasionally fly charter planes or perhaps get jobs with small air transportation firms, such as air-taxi companies. Some advance to flying corporate planes. A small number get flight engineer jobs with the airlines.

In the airlines, advancement usually depends on seniority provisions of union contracts. After 1 to 5 years, flight engineers advance according to seniority to first officer and, after 5 to 15 years, to captain. Seniority also determines which pilots get the more desirable routes. In a nonairline job, a first officer may advance to pilot and, in large companies, to chief pilot or director of aviation in charge of aircraft scheduling, maintenance, and flight procedures.

Employment

Civilian aircraft pilots and flight engineers held about 106,000 jobs in 2004. About 84,000 worked as airline pilots, copilots, and flight engineers. The remainder were commercial pilots who worked as flight instructors at local airports or for large businesses that fly company cargo and executives in their own airplanes or helicopters. Some commercial pilots flew small planes for air-taxi companies, usually to or from lightly traveled airports not served by major airlines. Others worked for a variety of businesses, performing tasks such as dusting crops, inspecting pipelines, or conducting sightseeing trips. Federal, state, and local governments also employed pilots. A few pilots were self-employed.

Pilots are located across the country, but airline pilots usually are based near major metropolitan airports or airports operating as hubs for the major airlines.

Job Outlook

The passenger airline industry is undergoing many changes, with some airlines posting increases in passenger traffic and adding routes while others are cutting back. Overall, the employment of aircraft pilots is projected to increase about as fast as the average for all occupations through 2014. In the long run, demand for air travel is expected to grow along with the population and the economy. In the short run, however, employment of pilots is generally sensitive to cyclical swings in the economy. During recessions, when a decline in the demand for air travel forces airlines to curtail the number of flights, airlines may temporarily furlough some pilots.

After September 11, 2001, air travel was severely depressed. A number of the major airlines were forced to reduce schedules, lay off pilots, and even declare bankruptcy. At the same time, hiring continued at regional and low-fare airlines. Job opportunities are expected to continue to be better with the regional airlines and low-fare carriers, which are growing faster than the more well-known major airlines. Opportunities with air cargo carriers also should arise because of increasing security requirements for shipping freight on passenger airlines and growth in electronic commerce. Business and corporate travel also should provide some new jobs for pilots.

Pilots attempting to get jobs at the major airlines will face strong competition, as those firms tend to attract many more applicants than they have jobs. They also will have to compete with laid-off pilots for any available jobs. Pilots who have logged the greatest number of flying hours using sophisticated equipment typically have the best prospects. For this reason, military pilots often have an advantage over other applicants. However, prior to September 11, 2001, some airlines reported a shortage of qualified pilots to operate the most sophisticated aircraft. Thus, when hiring improves, jobseekers with the most FAA licenses will have a competitive advantage.

Fewer flight engineers will be needed as new planes requiring only two pilots replace older planes that required flight engineers. Pilots also will experience some productivity improvements as airlines switch to larger planes and adopt the low-fare carrier model that emphasizes faster turnaround times for flights, keeping more pilots in the air rather than waiting on the ground.

Earnings

Earnings of aircraft pilots and flight engineers vary greatly depending whether they work as airline or commercial pilots. Earnings of airline pilots are among the highest in the nation and depend on factors such as the type, size, and maximum speed of the plane and the number of hours and miles flown. For example, pilots who fly jet aircraft usually earn higher salaries than do pilots who fly turboprops. Airline pilots and flight engineers may earn extra pay for night and international flights. In May 2004, median annual earnings of airline pilots, copilots, and flight engineers were $129,250.

Median annual earnings of commercial pilots were $53,870 in May 2004. The middle 50 percent earned between $37,170 and $79,390. The lowest 10 percent earned less than $26,300, and the highest 10 percent earned more than $110,070.

Airline pilots usually are eligible for life and health insurance plans. They also receive retirement benefits and, if they fail the FAA physical examination at some point in their careers, they get disability payments. In addition, pilots receive an expense allowance, or "per diem," for every hour they are away from home. Some airlines also provide allowances to pilots for purchasing and cleaning their uniforms. As an additional benefit, pilots and their immediate families usually are entitled to free or reduced-fare transportation on their own and other airlines.

More than half of all aircraft pilots are members of unions. Most of the pilots who fly for the major airlines are members of the Airline Pilots Association, International, but those employed by one major airline are members of the Allied Pilots Association. Some flight engineers are members of the Flight Engineers' International Association.

Related Occupations

Although they are not in the cockpit, air traffic controllers and airfield operation specialists also play an important role in making sure flights are safe and on schedule and participate in many of the decisions that pilots must make.

Sources of Additional Information

Information about job opportunities, salaries for a particular airline, and qualifications required may be obtained by writing to the personnel manager of the airline.

For information on airline pilots, contact

▸ Air Line Pilots Association, International, 1625 Massachusetts Ave. NW, Washington, DC 20036.

▸ Air Transport Association of America, Inc., 1301 Pennsylvania Ave. NW, Suite 1100, Washington, DC 20004.

▸ Federal Aviation Administration, 800 Independence Ave. SW, Washington, DC 20591. Internet: http://www.faa.gov

For information on helicopter pilots, contact

▸ Helicopter Association International, 1635 Prince St., Alexandria, VA 22314.

For information about job opportunities in companies other than airlines, consult the classified section of aviation trade magazines and apply to companies that operate aircraft at local airports.

Architects, Except Landscape and Naval

(O*NET 17-1011.00)

Significant Points

■ About 1 in 4 architects is self-employed—more than three times the proportion for all professional and related occupations.

■ Licensing requirements include a professional degree in architecture, 3 years of practical work training, and passing all divisions of the Architect Registration Examination.

■ Architecture graduates may face competition, especially for jobs in the most prestigious firms; opportunities will be best for those with experience working for a firm while still in school and for those with knowledge of computer-aided design and drafting technology.

Nature of the Work

People need places in which to live, work, play, learn, worship, meet, govern, shop, and eat. These places may be private or public; indoors or outdoors; or rooms, buildings, or complexes, and together, they make up neighborhoods, towns, suburbs, and cities. *Architects*—licensed professionals trained in the art and science of building design—transform these needs into concepts and then develop the concepts into images and plans of buildings that can be constructed by others.

Architects design the overall aesthetic and look of buildings and other structures, but the design of a building involves far more than its appearance. Buildings also must be functional, safe, and economical and must suit the needs of the people who use them. Architects consider all these factors when they design buildings and other structures.

Architects provide professional services to individuals and organizations planning a construction project. They may be involved in all phases of development, from the initial discussion with the client through the entire construction process. Their duties require specific skills—designing, engineering, managing, supervising, and communicating with clients and builders. Architects spend a great deal of time explaining their ideas to clients, construction contractors, and others. Successful architects must be able to communicate their unique vision persuasively.

The architect and client discuss the objectives, requirements, and budget of a project. In some cases, architects provide various pre-design services—conducting feasibility and environmental impact studies, selecting a site, or specifying the requirements the design must meet. For example, they may determine space requirements by researching the numbers and types of potential users of a building. The architect then prepares drawings and a report presenting ideas for the client to review.

After discussing and agreeing on the initial proposal, architects develop final construction plans that show the building's appearance and details for its construction. Accompanying these plans are drawings of the structural system; air-conditioning, heating, and ventilating systems; electrical systems; communications systems; plumbing; and, possibly, site and landscape plans. The plans also specify the building materials and, in some cases, the interior furnishings. In developing designs, architects follow building codes; zoning laws; fire regulations; and other ordinances, such as those requiring easy access by disabled persons. Throughout the planning stage, they make necessary changes. Computer-aided design and drafting (CADD) technology has replaced traditional paper and pencil as the most common method for creating design and construction drawings. Continual revision of plans on the basis of client needs and budget constraints is often necessary.

Architects may also assist clients in obtaining construction bids, selecting contractors, and negotiating construction contracts. As construction proceeds, they may visit building sites to make sure that contractors follow the design, adhere to the schedule, use the specified materials, and meet work quality standards. The job is not complete until all construction is finished, required tests are conducted, and construction costs are paid. Sometimes, architects also provide postconstruction services, such as facilities management. They advise on energy efficiency measures, evaluate how well the building design adapts to the needs of occupants, and make necessary improvements.

Architects design a wide variety of buildings, such as office and apartment buildings, schools, churches, factories, hospitals, houses, and airport terminals. They also design complexes such as urban centers, college campuses, industrial parks, and entire communities. In addition, they may advise on the selection of building sites, prepare cost analysis and land-use studies, and do long-range planning for land development.

Architects sometimes specialize in one phase of work. Some specialize in the design of one type of building—for example, hospitals, schools, or housing. Others focus on planning and predesign services or construction management and do minimal design work. They often work with engineers, urban planners, interior designers, landscape architects, and other professionals. In fact, architects spend a great deal of their time coordinating information from, and the work of, others engaged in the same project. Many architects—particularly at larger firms—use the Internet and e-mail to update designs and communicate changes efficiently. Architects also use the Internet to research product specifications and government regulations.

Working Conditions

Architects usually work in a comfortable environment. Most of their time is spent in offices consulting with clients, developing reports and drawings, and working with other architects and engineers. However, they often visit construction sites to review the progress of projects. Although most architects work approximately 40 hours per week, they often have to work nights and weekends to meet deadlines.

Training, Other Qualifications, and Advancement

All states and the District of Columbia require individuals to be licensed (registered) before they may call themselves architects and contract to provide architectural services. During this time between graduation and becoming licensed, architecture school graduates generally work in the field under supervision of a licensed architect who takes legal responsibility for all work. Licensing requirements include a professional degree in architecture, a period of practical training or internship, and a passing score on all divisions of the Architect Registration Examination (ARE).

In most states, the professional degree in architecture must be from one of the 113 schools of architecture that have degree programs accredited by the National Architectural Accrediting Board (NAAB). However, state architectural registration boards set their own standards, so graduation from a non-NAAB-accredited program may meet the educational requirement for licensing in a few states. Three types of professional degrees in architecture are available through colleges and universities. The majority of all architectural degrees are from 5-year Bachelor of Architecture programs, intended for students entering university-level studies from high school or with no previous architectural training. In addition, a number of schools offer a 2-year Master of Architecture program for students with a preprofessional undergraduate degree in architecture or a related area or a 3- or 4-year Master of Architecture program for students with a degree in another discipline.

The choice of degree depends upon each individual's preference and educational background. Prospective architecture students should consider the available options before committing to a program. For example, although the 5-year Bachelor of Architecture program offers the fastest route to the professional degree, courses are specialized, and if the student does not complete the program, transferring to a program offered by another discipline may be difficult. A typical program includes courses in architectural history and theory, building design, structures, technology, construction methods, professional practice, math, physical sciences, and liberal arts. Central to most architectural programs is the design studio, where students put into practice the skills and concepts learned in the classroom. During the final semester of many programs, students devote their studio time to creating an architectural project from beginning to end, culminating in a three-dimensional model of their design.

Many schools of architecture also offer postprofessional degrees for those who already have a bachelor's or master's degree in architecture or other areas. Although graduate education beyond the professional degree is not required for practicing architects, it may be for research, teaching, and certain specialties.

Architects must be able to communicate their ideas visually to their clients. Artistic and drawing ability is helpful, but not essential, to such communication. More important are a visual orientation and the ability to conceptualize and understand spatial relationships. Good communication skills, the ability to work independently or as part of a team, and creativity are important qualities for anyone interested in becoming an architect. Computer literacy also is required for writing specifications, for two- and three-dimensional drafting, and for financial management. Knowledge of CADD is essential and has become a critical tool for architects. Most schools now teach students CADD programs and methods that adhere to the National CAD Standards.

All state architectural registration boards require architecture graduates to complete a training period—usually 3 years—before they may sit for the ARE, the third and final requirement for becoming licensed. Every state, with the exception of Arizona, has adopted the training standards established by the Intern Development Program, a branch of the American Institute of Architects and the National Council of Architectural Registration Boards (NCARB). These standards stipulate broad and diversified training under the supervision of a licensed architect over a 3-year period. Most new graduates complete their training period by working as interns at architectural firms. Some states allow a portion of the training to occur in the offices of related professionals, such as engineers or general contractors. Architecture students who complete internships in architectural firms while still in school can count some of that time toward the required 3-year training period.

Interns in architectural firms may assist in the design of one part of a project, help prepare architectural documents or drawings, build models, or prepare construction drawings on CADD. Interns also may research building codes and materials or write specifications for building materials, installation criteria, the quality of finishes, and other related details.

After completing their on-the-job training period, interns are eligible to sit for the ARE. The examination tests a candidate's knowledge, skills, and ability to provide the various services required in the design and construction of buildings. The test is broken down into 9 divisions consisting of either multiple-choice or graphical questions; states give candidates an eligibility period for completion of all divisions of the exam that varies by state. Candidates who pass the ARE and meet all standards established by their state board become licensed to practice in that state.

Most states require some form of continuing education to maintain a license, and many others are expected to adopt mandatory continuing education. Requirements vary by state, but usually involve the completion of a certain number of credits annually or biennially through workshops, formal university classes, conferences, self-study courses, or other sources.

A growing number of architects voluntarily seek certification by the NCARB, which can facilitate an individual's becoming licensed to practice in additional states. This practice is known as "reciprocity." Certification is awarded after independent verification of the candidate's educational transcripts, employment record, and professional references. Certification is the primary requirement for reciprocity of licensing among state boards that are NCARB members. In 2004, approximately one-third of all licensed architects had NCARB certification.

After becoming licensed and gaining experience, architects take on increasingly responsible duties, eventually managing entire projects. In large firms, architects may advance to supervisory or managerial positions. Some architects become partners in established firms, while others set up their own practices. Graduates with degrees in architecture also enter related fields, such as graphic, interior, or industrial design; urban planning; real estate development; civil engineering; and construction management.

Employment

Architects held about 129,000 jobs in 2004. Approximately 3 out of 5 jobs were in the architectural, engineering, and related services industry—mostly in architectural firms with fewer than five workers. A small number worked for residential and nonresidential building construction firms and for government agencies responsible for housing, community planning, or construction of government buildings, such as the U.S. Departments of Defense and Interior and the General Services Administration. About 1 in 4 architects was self-employed.

Job Outlook

Employment of architects is expected to grow about as fast as the average for all occupations through 2014. Besides employment growth, additional job openings will arise from the need to replace the many architects who are nearing retirement and others who transfer to other occupations or stop working for other reasons. Internship opportunities for new architectural students are expected to be good over the next decade, but more students are graduating with architectural degrees and some competition for entry-level jobs can be anticipated. Competition will be especially keen for jobs at the most prestigious architectural firms as prospective architects try to build their reputation. Prospective architects who have had internships while in school will have an advantage in obtaining intern positions after graduation.

Employment of architects is strongly tied to the activity of the construction industry. Strong growth is expected to come from nonresidential construction as demand for commercial space increases. Residential construction, buoyed by low interest rates, is also expected to grow as more and more people become homeowners. If interest rates rise significantly, this sector may see a falloff in home building.

Current demographic trends also support an increase in demand for architects. As the population of Sunbelt states continues to grow, the people living there will need new places to live and work. As the population continues to live longer and baby boomers begin to retire, there will be a need for more health care facilities, nursing homes, and retirement communities. In education, buildings at all levels are getting older and class sizes are getting larger. This will require many school districts and universities to build new facilities and renovate existing ones.

Some types of construction are sensitive to cyclical changes in the economy. Architects seeking design projects for office and retail construction will face especially strong competition for jobs or clients during recessions, and layoffs may ensue in less successful firms. Those involved in the design of institutional buildings, such as schools, hospitals, nursing homes, and correctional facilities, will be less affected by fluctuations in the economy. Residential construction makes up a small portion of work for architects, so major changes in the housing market would not be as significant as fluctuations in the nonresidential market.

Despite good overall job opportunities, some architects may not fare as well as others. The profession is geographically sensitive, and some parts of the nation may have fewer new building projects than others. Also, many firms specialize in specific buildings, such as hospitals or office towers, and demand for these buildings may vary by region. Architects may find it increasingly necessary to gain reciprocity in order to compete for the best jobs and projects in other states.

In recent years, some architecture firms have outsourced to architecture firms overseas the drafting of construction documents for large-scale commercial and residential projects. This trend is expected to continue and may have a negative impact on employment growth for lower-level architects and interns who would normally gain experience by producing these drawings. However, most firms will keep design services in-house, and opportunities will be best for those architects that are able to distinguish themselves from others with their creativity.

Earnings

Median annual earnings of wage and salary architects were $60,300 in May 2004. The middle 50 percent earned between $46,690 and $79,230. The lowest 10 percent earned less than $38,060, and the highest 10 percent earned more than $99,800. Those just starting their internships can expect to earn considerably less.

Earnings of partners in established architectural firms may fluctuate because of changing business conditions. Some architects may have difficulty establishing their own practices and may go through a period when their expenses are greater than their income, requiring substantial financial resources.

Related Occupations

Architects design buildings and related structures. Construction managers, like architects, also plan and coordinate activities concerned with the construction and maintenance of buildings and facilities. Others who engage in similar work are landscape architects; civil engineers; urban and regional planners; and designers, including interior designers, commercial and industrial designers, and graphic designers.

Sources of Additional Information

Information about education and careers in architecture can be obtained from

▸ The American Institute of Architects, 1735 New York Ave. NW, Washington, DC 20006. Internet: http://www.aia.org

▸ Intern Development Program, National Council of Architectural Registration Boards, Suite 1100K, 1801 K Street NW, Washington, DC 20006-1310. Internet: http://www.ncarb.org

Archivists, Curators, and Museum Technicians

(O*NET 25-4011.00, 25-4012.00, and 25-4013.00)

Significant Points

■ Most work in museums, historical sites, and similar institutions; educational institutions; or in federal, state, or local government.

■ A graduate degree and related work experience generally are required.

■ Keen competition is expected for most jobs because qualified applicants generally outnumber job openings.

Nature of the Work

Archivists, curators, and museum technicians acquire and preserve important documents and other valuable items for permanent storage or display. They work for museums, governments, zoos, colleges and universities, corporations, and other institutions that require experts to preserve important records. They also describe, catalogue, analyze, exhibit, and maintain valuable objects and collections for the benefit of researchers and the public. These documents and collections may include works of art; transcripts of meetings; coins and stamps; living and preserved plants and animals; and historic objects, buildings, and sites.

Archivists and curators plan and oversee the arrangement, cataloguing, and exhibition of collections and, along with technicians and conservators, maintain collections. Archivists and curators may coordinate educational and public outreach programs, such as tours, workshops, lectures, and classes, and may work with the boards of institutions to administer plans and policies. They also may research topics or items relevant to their collections. Although some duties of archivists and curators are similar, the types of items they deal with differ: Curators usually handle objects with cultural, biological, or historical significance, such as sculptures, textiles, and paintings, while archivists handle mainly records and documents that are retained because of their importance and potential value in the future.

Archivists collect, organize, and maintain control over a wide range of information deemed important enough for permanent safekeeping. This information takes many forms: photographs, films, video and sound recordings, computer tapes, and video and optical disks, as well as more traditional paper records, letters, and documents. Archivists work for a variety of organizations, including government agencies, museums, historical societies, corporations, and educational institutions that use or generate records of great potential value to researchers, exhibitors, genealogists, and others who would benefit from having access to original source material.

Archivists maintain records in accordance with accepted standards and practices that ensure the long-term preservation and easy retrieval of the documents. Records may be saved on any medium, including paper, film, videotape, audiotape, electronic disk, or computer. They also may be copied onto some other format to protect the original and to make the records more accessible to researchers who use them. As various storage media evolve, archivists must keep abreast of technological advances in electronic information storage.

Archivists often specialize in an area of history or technology so they can more accurately determine which records in that area qualify for retention and should become part of the archives. Archivists also may work with specialized forms of records, such as manuscripts, electronic records, photographs, cartographic records, motion pictures, and sound recordings.

Computers are increasingly being used to generate and maintain archival records. Professional standards for the use of computers in handling archival records are still evolving. Expanding computer capabilities that allow more records to be stored and exhibited electronically have transformed, and are expected to continue to transform, many aspects of archival collections.

Curators administer the affairs of museums, zoos, aquariums, botanical gardens, nature centers, and historic sites. The head curator of the museum is usually called the *museum director*. Curators direct the acquisition, storage, and exhibition of collections, including negotiating and authorizing the purchase, sale, exchange, or loan of collections. They are also responsible for authenticating, evaluating, and categorizing the specimens in a collection. Curators oversee and help conduct the institution's research projects and related educational programs. Today, an increasing part of a curator's duties involves fundraising and promotion, which may include the writing and reviewing of grant proposals, journal articles, and publicity materials, as well as attendance at meetings, conventions, and civic events.

Most curators specialize in a particular field, such as botany, art, paleontology, or history. Those working in large institutions may be highly specialized. A large natural-history museum, for example, would employ separate curators for its collections of birds, fishes, insects, and mammals. Some curators maintain their collections, others do research, and others perform administrative tasks. In small institutions with only one or a few curators, one curator may be responsible for a number of tasks, from maintaining collections to directing the affairs of the museum.

Conservators manage, care for, preserve, treat, and document works of art, artifacts, and specimens—work that may require substantial historical, scientific, and archaeological research. They use X rays, chemical testing, microscopes, special lights, and other laboratory equipment and techniques to examine objects and determine their condition, their need for treatment or restoration, and the appropriate method for preserving them. Conservators

document their findings and treat items to minimize their deterioration or to restore them to their original state. Conservators usually specialize in a particular material or group of objects, such as documents and books, paintings, decorative arts, textiles, metals, or architectural material.

Museum technicians assist curators by performing various preparatory and maintenance tasks on museum items. Some museum technicians also may assist curators with research. Archives technicians help archivists organize, maintain, and provide access to historical documentary materials.

Working Conditions

The working conditions of archivists and curators vary. Some spend most of their time working with the public, providing reference assistance and educational services. Others perform research or process records, which often means working alone or in offices with only a few people. Those who restore and install exhibits or work with bulky, heavy record containers may lift objects, climb, or stretch. Those in zoos, botanical gardens, and other outdoor museums and historic sites frequently walk great distances.

Curators who work in large institutions may travel extensively to evaluate potential additions to the collection, organize exhibitions, and conduct research in their area of expertise. However, travel is rare for curators employed in small institutions.

Training, Other Qualifications, and Advancement

Employment as an archivist, conservator, or curator usually requires graduate education and related work experience. While completing their formal education, many archivists and curators work in archives or museums to gain the "hands-on" experience that many employers seek.

Although archivists earn a variety of undergraduate degrees, a graduate degree in history or library science, with courses in archival science, is preferred by most employers. Also, a few institutions now offer master's degrees in archival studies. Some positions may require knowledge of the discipline related to the collection, such as business or medicine. Many colleges and universities offer courses or practical training in archival science as part of their history, library science, or other curriculum. The Academy of Certified Archivists offers voluntary certification for archivists. The designation "Certified Archivist" is obtained by those with at least a master's degree and a year of appropriate archival experience. The certification process requires candidates to pass a written examination, and they must renew their certification periodically.

Archivists need research and analytical ability to understand the content of documents and the context in which they were created and to decipher deteriorated or poor-quality printed matter, handwritten manuscripts, photographs, or films. A background in preservation management is often required of archivists because they are responsible for taking proper care of their records. Archivists also must be able to organize large amounts of information and write clear instructions for its retrieval and use. In addition, computer skills and the ability to work with electronic records and databases are very important. Because electronic records are becoming the prevalent form of recordkeeping and archivists must create searchable databases, a knowledge of Web technology is increasingly being required.

Many archives, including one-person shops, are very small and have limited opportunities for promotion. Archivists typically advance by transferring to a larger unit that has supervisory positions. A doctorate in history, library science, or a related field may be needed for some advanced positions, such as director of a state archive.

For employment as a curator, most museums require a master's degree in an appropriate discipline of the museum's specialty—art, history, or archaeology—or in museum studies. Many employers prefer a doctoral degree, particularly for curators in natural history or science museums. Earning two graduate degrees—in museum studies (museology) and a specialized subject—gives a candidate a distinct advantage in this competitive job market. In small museums, curatorial positions may be available to individuals with a bachelor's degree. For some positions, an internship of full-time museum work supplemented by courses in museum practices is needed.

Curatorial positions often require knowledge in a number of fields. For historic and artistic conservation, courses in chemistry, physics, and art are desirable. Because curators—particularly those in small museums—may have administrative and managerial responsibilities, courses in business administration, public relations, marketing, and fundraising also are recommended. Like archivists, curators need computer skills and the ability to work with electronic databases. Many curators are responsible for posting information on the Internet, so they also need to be familiar with digital imaging, scanning technology, and copyright law.

Curators must be flexible because of their wide variety of duties, among which are the design and presentation of exhibits. In small museums, curators need manual dexterity to build exhibits or restore objects. Leadership ability and business skills are important for museum directors, while marketing skills are valuable in increasing museum attendance and fundraising.

In large museums, curators may advance through several levels of responsibility, eventually becoming the museum director. Curators in smaller museums often advance to larger ones. Individual research and publications are important for advancement in larger institutions.

When hiring conservators, employers look for a master's degree in conservation or in a closely related field together with substantial experience. There are only a few graduate programs in museum conservation techniques in the United States. Competition for entry to these programs is keen; to qualify, a student must have a background in chemistry, archaeology or studio art, and art history, as well as work experience. For some programs, knowledge of a foreign language also is helpful. Conservation apprenticeships or internships as an undergraduate can enhance one's admission prospects. Graduate programs last 2 to 4 years, the latter years of which include internship training. A few individuals enter conservation through apprenticeships with museums, nonprofit organizations, and conservators in private practice. Apprenticeships should be supplemented with courses in chemistry, studio art, and history. Apprenticeship training, although accepted, is a more difficult route into the conservation profession.

Museum technicians usually need a bachelor's degree in an appropriate discipline of the museum's specialty; training in museum studies; or previous experience working in museums, particularly in the design of exhibits. Similarly, archives technicians usually need a bachelor's degree in library science or history or relevant work experience. Technician positions often serve as a stepping-stone for individuals interested in archival and curatorial work. Except in small museums, a master's degree is needed for advancement.

Relatively few schools grant a bachelor's degree in museum studies. More common are undergraduate minors or tracks of study that are part of an undergraduate degree in a related field, such as art history, history, or archaeology. Students interested in further study may obtain a master's degree in museum studies, offered in colleges and universities throughout the country. However, many employers feel that, while museum studies are helpful, a thorough knowledge of the museum's specialty and museum work experience are more important.

Continuing education, which enables archivists, curators, and museum technicians to keep up with developments in the field, is available through meetings, conferences, and workshops sponsored by archival, historical, and museum associations. Some larger organizations, such as the National Archives, offer such training in-house.

Employment

Archivists, curators, and museum technicians held about 27,000 jobs in 2004. About 34 percent were employed in museums, historical sites, and similar institutions, and 16 percent worked for state and private educational institutions, mainly college and university libraries. Nearly 28 percent worked in federal, state, and local government, excluding educational institutions. Most federal archivists work for the National Archives and Records Administration; others manage military archives in the U.S. Department of Defense. Most federal government curators work at the Smithsonian Institution, in the military museums of the Department of Defense, and in archaeological and other museums and historic sites managed by the U.S. Department of the Interior. All state governments have archival or historical-record sections employing archivists. State and local governments also have numerous historical museums, parks, libraries, and zoos employing curators.

Some large corporations that have archives or record centers employ archivists to manage the growing volume of records created or maintained as required by law or necessary to the firms' operations. Religious and fraternal organizations, professional associations, conservation organizations, major private collectors, and research firms also employ archivists and curators.

Conservators may work under contract to treat particular items rather than as regular employees of a museum or other institution. These conservators may work on their own as private contractors, or they may work as an employee of a conservation laboratory or regional conservation center that contracts their services to museums.

Job Outlook

Keen competition is expected for most jobs as archivists, curators, and museum technicians because qualified applicants generally outnumber job openings. Graduates with highly specialized training, such as master's degrees in both library science and history with a concentration in archives or records management and extensive computer skills, should have the best opportunities for jobs as archivists. A curator job also is attractive to many people, and many applicants have the necessary training and knowledge of the subject, but there are only a few openings. Consequently, candidates may have to work part time, as interns, or even as volunteer assistant curators or research associates after completing their formal education. Substantial work experience in collection management, research, exhibit design, or restoration, as well as database management skills, will be necessary for permanent status.

The job outlook for conservators may be more favorable, particularly for graduates of conservation programs. However, competition is stiff for the limited number of openings in these programs, and applicants need a technical background. Conservation program graduates with knowledge of a foreign language and a willingness to relocate will have an advantage over less-qualified candidates.

Employment of archivists, curators, and museum technicians is expected to increase about as fast as the average for all occupations through 2014. Jobs are expected to grow as public and private organizations emphasize establishing archives and organizing records and information and as public interest in science, art, history, and technology increases. Museum and zoo attendance has experienced a drop in recent years because of a weak economy, but the long-term trend has been a rise in attendance, and this trend is expected to continue. There is healthy public and private support for and interest in museums, which will generate demand for archivists, curators, and museum technicians. However, museums and other cultural institutions can be subject to cuts in funding during recessions or periods of budget tightening, reducing demand for these workers. Although the rate of turnover among archivists and curators is relatively low, the need to replace workers who leave the occupation or stop working will create some additional job openings.

Earnings

Median annual earnings of archivists in May 2004 were $36,470. The middle 50 percent earned between $28,900 and $46,480. The lowest 10 percent earned less than $21,780, and the highest 10 percent earned more than $61,260. Median annual earnings of curators in May 2004 were $43,620. The middle 50 percent earned between $32,790 and $58,280. The lowest 10 percent earned less than $25,360, and the highest 10 percent earned more than $77,490. Median annual earnings of museum technicians and conservators in May 2004 were $31,820. The middle 50 percent earned between $23,770 and $43,020. The lowest 10 percent earned less than $18,210, and the highest 10 percent earned more than $58,260.

In 2005, the average annual salary for archivists in the federal government in nonsupervisory, supervisory, and managerial positions was $75,876; for museum curators, $76,126; for museum specialists and technicians, $55,291; and for archives technicians, $41,347.

Related Occupations

The skills that archivists, curators, and museum technicians use in preserving, organizing, and displaying objects or information of historical interest are shared by artists and related workers; librarians; and anthropologists and archeologists, historians, and other social scientists.

Sources of Additional Information

For information on archivists and on schools offering courses in archival studies, contact

▸ Society of American Archivists, 527 South Wells St., 5th Floor, Chicago, IL 60607-3922. Internet: http://www.archivists.org

For general information about careers as a curator and schools offering courses in museum studies, contact

▸ American Association of Museums, 1575 Eye St. NW, Suite 400, Washington, DC 20005. Internet: http://www.aam-us.org

For information about careers and education programs in conservation and preservation, contact

▸ American Institute for Conservation of Historic and Artistic Works, 1717 K St. NW, Suite 200, Washington, DC 20006. Internet: http://aic.stanford.edu

For information about archivists and archivist certification, contact

▸ Academy of Certified Archivists, 48 Howard St., Albany, NY 12207. Internet: http://www.certifiedarchivists.org

For information about government archivists, contact

▸ National Association of Government Archivists and Records Administrators, 48 Howard St., Albany, NY 12207. Internet: http://www.nagara.org

Information on obtaining positions as archivists, curators, and museum technicians with the federal government is available from the Office of Personnel Management through USAJOBS, the federal government's official employment information system. This resource for locating and applying for job opportunities can be accessed through the Internet at http://www.usajobs.opm.gov or through an interactive voice response telephone system at (703) 724-1850 or TDD (978) 461-8404. These numbers are not toll free, and charges may result.

Job Opportunities in the Armed Forces

(O*NET 55-1011.00, 55-1012.00, 55-1013.00, 55-1014.00, 55-1015.00, 55-1016.00, 55-1017.00, 55-1019.99, 55-2011.00, 55-2012.00, 55-2013.00, 55-3011.00, 55-3012.00, 55-3013.00, 55-3014.00, 55-3015.00, 55-3016.00, 55-3017.00, 55-3018.00, and 55-3019.99)

Significant Points

■ Some training and duty assignments are hazardous, even in peacetime; hours and working conditions can be arduous and vary substantially.

■ Enlisted personnel need at least a high school diploma or its equivalent, while officers need a bachelor's or an advanced degree.

■ Opportunities should be good in all branches of the Armed Forces for applicants who meet designated standards.

Nature of the Work

Maintaining a strong national defense encompasses such diverse activities as running a hospital, commanding a tank, programming computers, operating a nuclear reactor, or repairing and maintaining a helicopter. The military provides training and work experience in these and many other fields for more than 2.6 million people. More than 1.4 million people serve in the active Army, Navy, Marine Corps, and Air Force, and more than 1.2 million serve in their Reserve components and the Air and Army National Guard. The Coast Guard, which is also discussed in this description, is now part of the U.S. Department of Homeland Security.

The military distinguishes between enlisted and officer careers. Enlisted personnel, who make up about 85 percent of the Armed Forces, carry out the fundamental operations of the military in areas such as combat, administration, construction, engineering, health care, and human services. Officers, who make up the remaining 15 percent of the Armed Forces, are the leaders of the military, supervising and managing activities in every occupational specialty of the Armed Forces.

The sections that follow discuss the major occupational groups for enlisted personnel and officers.

Enlisted occupational groups

Administrative careers include a wide variety of positions. The military must keep accurate information for planning and managing its operations. Both paper and electronic records are kept on personnel and on equipment, funds, supplies, and all other aspects of the military. Administrative personnel record information, type reports, maintain files, and review information to assist military officers. Personnel may work in a specialized area such as finance, accounting, legal affairs, maintenance, supply, or transportation.

Combat specialty occupations refer to enlisted specialties, such as infantry, artillery, and special forces, whose members operate weapons or 2execute special missions during combat. Persons in these occupations normally specialize by the type of weapon system or combat operation. These personnel maneuver against enemy forces and position and fire artillery, guns, and missiles to destroy enemy positions. They also may operate tanks and amphibious assault vehicles in combat or scouting missions. When the military has difficult and dangerous missions to perform, they call upon special forces teams. These elite combat forces maintain a constant state of readiness to strike anywhere in the world on a moment's notice. Team members from the special forces conduct offensive raids, demolitions, intelligence, search-and-rescue missions, and other operations from aboard aircraft, helicopters, ships, or submarines.

Construction occupations in the military include personnel who build or repair buildings, airfields, bridges, foundations, dams, bunkers, and the electrical and plumbing components of these structures. Personnel in construction occupations operate bulldozers, cranes, graders, and other heavy equipment. Construction specialists also may work with engineers and other building specialists as part of military construction teams. Some personnel specialize in areas such as plumbing or electrical wiring. Plumbers and pipefitters install and repair the plumbing and pipe systems needed in buildings and on aircraft and ships. Building electricians install and repair electrical-wiring systems in offices, airplane hangars, and other buildings on military bases.

Electronic and electrical equipment repair personnel repair and maintain electronic and electrical equipment used in the military. Repairers normally specialize by type of equipment, such as avionics, computer, optical, communications, or weapons systems. For example, electronic instrument repairers install, test, maintain, and repair a wide variety of electronic systems, including navigational controls and biomedical instruments. Weapons maintenance technicians maintain and repair weapons used by combat forces; most of these weapons have electronic components and systems that assist in locating targets and in aiming and firing the weapon.

Engineering, science, and technical personnel in the military require specific knowledge to operate technical equipment, solve complex problems, or provide and interpret information. Personnel normally specialize in one area, such as space operations, information technology, environmental health and safety, or intelligence. Space operations specialists use and repair ground-control command equipment having to do with spacecraft, including electronic systems that track the location and operation of a craft. Information technology specialists develop software programs and operate computer systems. Environmental health and safety specialists inspect military facilities and food supplies for the presence of disease, germs, or other conditions hazardous to health and the environment. Intelligence specialists gather and study information by means of aerial photographs and various types of radar and surveillance systems.

Health care personnel assist medical professionals in treating and providing services for men and women in the military. They may work as part of a patient-service team in close contact with doctors, dentists, nurses, and physical therapists to provide the necessary support functions within a hospital or clinic. Health care specialists normally specialize in a particular area—emergency medical treatment, the operation of diagnostic tools such as X-ray and ultrasound equipment, laboratory testing of tissue and blood samples, or maintaining pharmacy supplies or patients' records, among others. Dental and optical laboratory technicians construct and repair dental equipment and eyeglasses for military personnel.

Human resources development specialists recruit and place qualified personnel and provide the training programs necessary to help people perform their jobs effectively. Personnel in this career area normally specialize by activity. For example, recruiting specialists provide information about military careers to young people, parents, schools, and local communities and explain the Armed Service's employment and training opportunities, pay and benefits, and service life. Personnel specialists collect and store information about the people in the military, including information on their previous and current training, job assignments, promotions, and health. Training specialists and instructors teach classes and give demonstrations to provide military personnel with the knowledge they need to perform their jobs.

Machine operator and production personnel operate industrial equipment, machinery, and tools to fabricate and repair parts for a variety of items and structures. They may operate engines, turbines, nuclear reactors, and water pumps. Often, they specialize by type of work performed. Welders and metalworkers, for instance, work with various types of metals to repair or form the structural parts of ships, submarines, buildings, or other equipment. Survival equipment specialists inspect, maintain, and repair survival equipment such as parachutes and aircraft life support equipment.

Media and public affairs personnel deal with the public presentation and interpretation of military information and events. They take and develop photographs; film, record, and edit audio and video programs; present news and music programs; and produce graphic artwork, drawings, and other visual displays. Other public affairs specialists act as interpreters and translators to convert written or spoken foreign languages into English or other languages.

Protective service personnel include those who enforce military laws and regulations and provide emergency response to natural and human-made disasters. These personnel normally specialize by function. For example, military police control traffic, prevent crime, and respond to emergencies. Other law enforcement and security specialists investigate crimes committed on military property and guard inmates in military correctional facilities. Fire fighters put out, control, and help prevent fires in buildings, on aircraft, and aboard ships.

Support service personnel provide subsistence services and support the morale and well-being of military personnel and their families. Food service specialists prepare all types of food in dining halls, hospitals, and ships. Counselors help military personnel and their families deal with personal issues. They work as part of a team that may include social workers, psychologists, medical officers, chaplains, personnel specialists, and commanders. Religious program specialists assist chaplains with religious services, religious education programs, and related administrative duties.

Transportation and material handling specialists ensure the safe transport of people and cargo. Most personnel within this occupational group are classified according to mode of transportation, such as aircraft, motor vehicle, or ship. Aircrew members operate equipment on board aircraft during operations. Vehicle drivers operate all types of heavy military vehicles, including fuel or water tank trucks, semi-trailers, heavy troop transports, and passenger buses. Quartermasters and boat operators navigate and pilot many types of small watercraft, including tugboats, gunboats, and barges. Cargo specialists load and unload military supplies, using equipment such as forklifts and cranes.

Vehicle and machinery mechanics conduct preventive and corrective maintenance on aircraft, automotive and heavy equipment, heating and cooling systems, marine engines, and powerhouse station equipment. These workers typically specialize by the type of equipment that they maintain. For example, aircraft mechanics inspect, service, and repair helicopters and airplanes. Automotive and heavy equipment mechanics maintain and repair vehicles such as humvees, trucks, tanks, self-propelled missile launchers, and other combat vehicles. They also repair bulldozers, power shovels, and other construction equipment. Heating and cooling mechanics install and repair air-conditioning, refrigeration, and heating equipment. Marine engine mechanics repair and maintain gasoline and diesel engines on ships, boats, and other watercraft. They also repair shipboard mechanical and electrical equipment. Powerhouse mechanics install, maintain, and repair electrical and mechanical equipment in power-generating stations.

Officer occupational groups

Combat specialty officers plan and direct military operations, oversee combat activities, and serve as combat leaders. This category includes officers in charge of tanks and other armored assault vehicles, artillery systems, special forces, and infantry. Combat specialty officers normally specialize by the type of unit that they lead. Within the unit, they may specialize by the type of weapon system. Artillery and missile system officers, for example, direct personnel as they target, launch, test, and maintain various types of missiles and artillery. Special-operations officers lead their units in offensive raids, demolitions, intelligence gathering, and search-and-rescue missions.

Engineering, science, and technical officers have a wide range of responsibilities based on their area of expertise. They lead or perform activities in areas such as space operations, environmental health and safety, and engineering. These officers may direct the operations of communications centers or the development of complex computer systems. Environmental health and safety officers study the air, ground, and water to identify and analyze sources of pollution and its effects. They also direct programs to control safety and health hazards in the workplace. Other personnel work as aerospace engineers to design and direct the development of military aircraft, missiles, and spacecraft.

Executive, administrative, and managerial officers oversee and direct military activities in key functional areas such as finance, accounting, health administration, international relations, and supply. Health services administrators, for instance, are responsible for the overall quality of care provided at the hospitals and clinics they operate. They must ensure that each department works together to provide the highest quality of care. As another example, purchasing and contracting managers negotiate and monitor contracts for the purchase of the billions of dollars worth of equipment, supplies, and services that the military buys from private industry each year.

Health care officers provide health services at military facilities on the basis of their area of specialization. Officers who examine, diagnose, and treat patients with illness, injury, or disease include physicians, registered nurses, and dentists. Other health care officers provide therapy, rehabilitative treatment, and additional services for patients. Physical and occupational therapists plan and administer therapy to help patients adjust to disabilities, regain independence, and return to work. Speech therapists evaluate and treat patients with hearing and speech problems. Dietitians manage food service facilities and plan meals for hospital patients and for outpatients who need special diets. Pharmacists manage the purchase, storage, and dispensation of drugs and medicines. Physicians and surgeons in this occupational group provide the majority of medical services to the military and their families. Dentists treat diseases and disorders of the mouth. Optometrists treat vision problems by prescribing eyeglasses or contact lenses. psychologists provide mental health care and also conduct research on behavior and emotions.

Human resource development officers manage recruitment, placement, and training strategies and programs in the military. They normally specialize by activity. Recruiting managers direct recruiting efforts and provide information about military careers to young people, parents, schools, and local communities. Personnel managers direct military personnel functions such as job assignment, staff promotion, and career counseling. Training and education directors identify training needs and develop and manage educational programs designed to keep military personnel current in the skills they need to perform their jobs.

Media and public affairs officers oversee the development, production, and presentation of information or events for the public. These officers may produce and direct motion pictures, videotapes, and television and radio broadcasts that are used for training, news, and entertainment. Some plan, develop, and direct the activities of military bands. Public information officers respond to inquiries about military activities and prepare news releases and reports to keep the public informed.

Protective service officers are responsible for the safety and protection of individuals and property on military bases and vessels. Emergency management officers plan and prepare for all types of natural and human-made disasters. They develop warning, control, and evacuation plans to be used in the event of a disaster. Law enforcement and security officers enforce all applicable laws on military bases and investigate crimes when the law has been broken.

Support services officers manage food service activities and perform services in support of the morale and well-being of military personnel and their families. Food services managers oversee the preparation and delivery of food services within dining facilities located on military installations and vessels. Social workers focus on improving conditions that cause social problems such as drug and alcohol abuse, racism, and sexism. Chaplains conduct worship services for military personnel and perform other spiritual duties covering the beliefs and practices of all religious faiths.

Transportation officers manage and perform activities related to the safe transport of military personnel and material by air and water. These officers normally specialize by mode of transportation or area of expertise because, in many cases, they must meet licensing and certification requirements. Pilots in the military fly various types of specialized airplanes and helicopters to carry troops and equipment and to execute combat missions. Navigators use radar, radio, and other navigation equipment to determine their position and plan their route of travel. Officers on ships and submarines work as a team to manage the various departments aboard their vessels. Ship engineers direct engineering departments aboard ships and submarines, including engine operations, maintenance, repair, heating, and power generation.

Training, Other Qualifications, and Advancement

Enlisted personnel. In order to join the services, enlisted personnel must sign a legal agreement called an enlistment contract, which usually involves a commitment to 8 years of service. Depending on the terms of the contract, 2 to 6 years are spent on active duty, and the balance is spent in the National Guard or Reserves. The enlistment contract obligates the service to provide the agreed-upon job, rating, pay, cash bonuses for enlistment in certain occupations, medical and other benefits, occupational training, and continuing education. In return, enlisted personnel must serve satisfactorily for the period specified.

Requirements for each service vary, but certain qualifications for enlistment are common to all branches. In order to enlist, one must be between 17 and 35 years old for active service, be a U.S. citizen or an alien holding permanent resident status, not have a felony record, and possess a birth certificate. Applicants who are aged 17 must have the consent of a parent or legal guardian before entering the service. Coast Guard enlisted personnel must enter active duty before their 28th birthday, whereas Marine Corps enlisted personnel must not be over the age of 29. Applicants must both pass a written examination—the Armed Services Vocational Aptitude Battery—and meet certain minimum physical standards, such as height, weight, vision, and overall health. All branches of the Armed Forces require high school graduation or its equivalent. In 2004, more than 9 out of 10 recruits were high school graduates.

People thinking about enlisting in the military should learn as much as they can about military life before making a decision. Doing so is especially important if you are thinking about making the military a career. Speaking to friends and relatives with military experience is a good idea. Find out what the military can offer you and what it will expect in return. Then, talk to a recruiter, who can determine whether you qualify for enlistment, explain the various enlistment options, and tell you which military occupational specialties currently have openings. Bear in mind that the recruiter's job is to recruit promising applicants into his or her branch of military service, so the information that the recruiter gives you is likely to stress the positive aspects of military life in the branch in which he or she serves.

Ask the recruiter for the branch you have chosen to assess your chances of being accepted for training in the occupation of your choice, or, better still, take the aptitude exam to see how well you score. The military uses this exam as a placement exam, and test scores largely determine an individual's chances of being accepted into a particular training program. Selection for a particular type of training depends on the needs of the service, your general and technical aptitudes, and your personal preference. Because all prospective recruits are required to take the exam, those who do so before committing themselves to enlist have the advantage of knowing in advance whether they stand a good chance of being accepted for training in a particular specialty. The recruiter can schedule you for the Armed Services Vocational Aptitude Battery without any obligation. Many high schools offer the exam as an easy way for students to explore the possibility of a military career, and the test also affords an insight into career areas in which the student has demonstrated aptitudes and interests.

If you decide to join the military, the next step is to pass the physical examination and sign an enlistment contract. Negotiating the contract involves choosing, qualifying for, and agreeing on a number of enlistment options, such as the length of active-duty time, which may vary according to the option. Most active-duty programs have first-term enlistments of 4 years, although there are some 2-, 3-, and 6-year programs. The contract also will state the date of enlistment and other options—for example, bonuses and the types of training to be received. If the service is unable to fulfill any of its obligations under the contract, such as providing a certain kind of training, the contract may become null and void.

All branches of the Armed Services offer a delayed entry program (DEP) by which an individual can delay entry into active duty for up to 1 year after enlisting. High school students can enlist during their senior year and enter a service after graduation. Others choose this program because the job training they desire is not currently available, but will be within the coming year, or because they need time to arrange their personal affairs.

Women are eligible to enter most military specialties; for example, they may become mechanics, missile maintenance technicians, heavy-equipment operators, and fighter pilots, or they may enter into medical care, administrative support, and intelligence specialties. Generally, only occupations involving direct exposure to combat are excluded.

People planning to apply the skills gained through military training to a civilian career should first determine how good the prospects are for civilian employment in jobs related to the military specialty that interests them. Second, they should know the prerequisites for the related civilian job. Because many civilian occupations require a license, certification, or minimum level of education, it is important to determine whether military training is sufficient for a person to enter the civilian equivalent or, if not, what additional training will be required. Other descriptions in this book discuss the job outlook, training requirements, and other aspects of civilian occupations for which military training and experience are helpful. Additional information often can be obtained from school counselors.

Following enlistment, new members of the Armed Forces undergo initial-entry training, better known as "basic training" or "boot camp." Through courses in military skills and protocol recruit training provides a 6-week to 13-week introduction to military life. Days and nights are carefully structured and include rigorous physical exercise designed to improve strength and endurance and build each unit's cohesion.

Following basic training, most recruits take additional training at technical schools that prepare them for a particular military occupational specialty. The formal training period generally lasts from 10 to 20 weeks, although training for certain occupations—nuclear power plant operator, for example—may take as long as a year. Recruits not assigned to classroom instruction receive on-the-job training at their first duty assignment.

Many service people get college credit for the technical training they receive on duty, which, combined with off-duty courses, can lead to an associate degree through programs in community colleges such as the Community College of the Air Force. In addition to on-duty training, military personnel may choose from a variety of educational programs. Most military installations have tuition assistance programs for people wishing to take courses during off-duty hours. The courses may be correspondence courses or courses in degree programs offered by local colleges or universities. Tuition assistance pays up to 100 percent of college costs up to a credit-hour and annual limit. Each branch of the service provides opportunities for full-time study to a limited number of exceptional applicants. Military personnel accepted into these highly competitive programs—in law or medicine, for example—receive full pay, allowances, tuition, and related fees. In return, they must agree to serve an additional amount of time in the service. Other highly selective programs enable enlisted personnel to qualify as commissioned officers through additional military training.

Warrant officers. Warrant officers are technical and tactical leaders who specialize in a specific technical area; for example, Army avia-

tors make up one group of warrant officers. The Army Warrant Officer Corps constitutes less than 5 percent of the total Army. Although the Corps is small in size, its level of responsibility is high. Its members receive extended career opportunities, worldwide leadership assignments, and increased pay and retirement benefits. Selection to attend the Warrant Officer Candidate School is highly competitive and restricted to those who meet rank and length-of-service requirements. The only exception is the Army aviator warrant officer, which has no prior military service requirements (table 1).

Officers. Officer training in the Armed Forces is provided through the federal service academies (Military, Naval, Air Force, and Coast Guard); the Reserve Officers Training Corps (ROTC) program offered at many colleges and universities; Officer Candidate School (OCS) or Officer Training School (OTS); the National Guard (State Officer Candidate School programs); the Uniformed Services University of Health Sciences; and other programs. All are highly selective and are good options for those wishing to make the military a career. Persons interested in obtaining training through the federal service academies must be single to enter and graduate, while those seeking training through OCS, OTS, or ROTC need not be single. Single parents with one or more minor dependents are not eligible to become commissioned officers.

Federal service academies provide a 4-year college program leading to a bachelor-of-science degree. Midshipmen or cadets are provided free room and board, tuition, medical and dental care, and a monthly allowance. Graduates receive regular or reserve commissions and have a 5-year active-duty obligation, or more if they are entering flight training. ·

To become a candidate for appointment as a cadet or midshipman in one of the service academies, applicants are required to obtain a nomination from an authorized source, usually a member of Congress. Candidates do not need to know a member of Congress personally to request a nomination. Nominees must have an academic record of the requisite quality, college aptitude test scores above an established minimum, and recommendations from teachers or school officials; they also must pass a medical examination. Appointments are made from the list of eligible nominees. Appointments to the Coast Guard Academy, however, are based strictly on merit and do not require a nomination.

ROTC programs train students in about 575 Army, 130 Navy and Marine Corps, and 300 Air Force units at participating colleges and universities. Trainees take 3 to 5 hours of military instruction a week in addition to regular college courses. After graduation, they may serve as officers on active duty for a stipulated period. Some may serve their obligation in the Reserves or National Guard. In the last 2 years of a ROTC program, students typically receive a monthly allowance while attending school, as well as additional pay for summer training. ROTC scholarships for 2, 3, and 4 years are available on a competitive basis. All scholarships pay for tuition and have allowances for textbooks, supplies, and other costs.

College graduates can earn a commission in the Armed Forces through OCS or OTS programs in the Army, Navy, Air Force, Marine Corps, Coast Guard, and National Guard. These officers generally must serve their obligation on active duty. Those with training in certain health professions may qualify for direct appointment as officers. In the case of persons studying for the health professions, financial assistance and internship opportunities are available from the military in return for specified periods of military service. Prospective medical students can apply to the Uniformed Services University of Health Sciences, which offers a salary and free tuition in a program leading to a doctor-of-medicine (M.D.) degree. In return, graduates must serve for 7 years in either the military or the U.S. Public Health Service. Direct appointments also are available for those qualified to serve in other specialty areas, such as the judge advocate general (legal) or chaplain corps. Flight training is available to commissioned officers in each branch of the Armed Forces. In addition, the Army has a direct enlistment option to become a warrant officer aviator.

Each service has different criteria for promoting personnel. Generally, the first few promotions for both enlisted and officer personnel come easily; subsequent promotions are much more competitive. Criteria for promotion may include time in service and in grade, job performance, a fitness report (supervisor's recommendation), and passing scores on written examinations. Table 1 shows the officer, warrant officer, and enlisted ranks by service.

Employment

In 2005, more than 2.6 million people served in the Armed Forces. More than 1.4 million were on active duty in the Armed Forces—about 487,000 in the Army, 350,000 in the Navy, 356,000 in the Air Force, and 185,000 in the Marine Corps. In addition, more than 1.2 million people served in their Reserve components, and the Air and Army National Guard. In addition, 33,000 individuals served in the Coast Guard, which is now part of the U.S. Department of Homeland Security. Table 2 shows the occupational composition of the 1.2 million active-duty enlisted personnel in February 2005; table 3 presents similar information for the 216,000 active-duty officers.

Military personnel are stationed throughout the United states and in many countries around the world. About half of all military jobs in the U.S. are located in California, Texas, North Carolina, Virginia, Florida, and Georgia. Approximately 169,000 service members were deployed to Operation Iraqi Freedom either in or around Iraq in June 2005. An additional 278,000 individuals were stationed outside the United States, including 21,000 assigned to ships at sea. About 106,000 were stationed in Europe, mainly in Germany, and another 81,000 were assigned to East Asia and the Pacific area, mostly in Japan and the Republic of Korea.

Table 1. Military rank and employment for active duty personnel, January 2005

Grade	Army	Navy	Air Force	Marine Corps	Employment Total
Commissioned officers:					
O-10	General	Admiral	General	General	34
O-9	Lieutenant General	Vice Admiral	Lieutenant General	Lieutenant General	125
O-8	Major General	Rear Admiral Upper	Major General	Major General	276
O-7	Brigadier General	Rear Admiral Lower	Brigadier General	Brigadier General	439
O-6	Colonel	Captain	Colonel	Colonel	11,483
O-5	Lieutenant Colonel	Commander	Lieutenant Colonel	Lieutenant Colonel	28,378
O-4	Major	Lieutenant Commander	Major	Major	43,846
O-3	Captain	Lieutenant	Captain	Captain	70,500
O-2	1st Lieutenant	Lieutenant (JG)	1st Lieutenant	1st Lieutenant	30,853
O-1	2nd Lieutenant	Ensign	2nd Lieutenant	2nd Lieutenant	24,948
Warrant officers:					
W-5	Chief Warrant Officer	Chief Warrant Officer	—	Chief Warrant Officer	540
W-4	Chief Warrant Officer	Chief Warrant Officer	—	Chief Warrant Officer	2,180
W-3	Chief Warrant Officer	Chief Warrant Officer	—	Chief Warrant Officer	4,618
W-2	Chief Warrant Officer	Chief Warrant Officer	—	Chief Warrant Officer	6,227
W-1	Warrant Officer	Warrant Officer	—	Warrant Officer	2,193
Enlisted personnel:					
E-9	Sergeant Major	Master Chief Petty Officer	Chief Master Sergeant	Sergeant Major/ Master Gunnery Sergeant	10,704
E-8	1st Sergeant/ Master Sergeant	Senior Chief Petty Officer	Senior Master Sergeant	1st Sergeant/ Master Sergeant	27,229
E-7	Sergeant First Class	Chief Petty Officer	Master Sergeant	Gunnery Sergeant	100,458
E-6	Staff Sergeant	Petty Officer 1st Class	Technical Sergeant	Staff Sergeant	174,467
E-5	Sergeant	Petty Officer 2nd Class	Staff Sergeant	Sergeant	249,816

Grade	Army	Navy	Air Force	Marine Corps	Employment Total
E-4	Corporal	Petty Officer 3rd Class	Senior Airman	Corporal	260,631
E-3	Private First Class	Seaman	Airman 1st Class	Lance Corporal	216,321
E-2	Private	Seaman Apprentice	Airman	Private 1st Class	82,008
E-1	Private	Seaman Recruit	Airman Basic	Private	48,818

SOURCE: U.S. Department of Defense

Table 2. Military enlisted personnel by broad occupational category and branch of military service, February 2005

Occupational Group - Enlisted	Army	Air Force	Coast Guard	Marine Corps	Navy	Total, all services
Administrative occupations	14,016	25,008	2,241	9,612	25,923	76,800
Combat specialty occupations	113,689	398	851	52,256	6,264	173,458
Construction occupations	15,544	6,407		5,147	5,085	32,183
Electronic and electrical repair occupations	39,601	40,083	3,045	15,586	58,992	157,307
Engineering, science, and technical occupations	35,482	50,732	986	23,656	41,951	152,807
Health care occupations	27,031	17,924	682		26,614	72,251
Human resource development occupations	15,908	12,468		6,803	4,822	40,001
Machine operator and precision work occupations	4,103	7,409	1,548	2,439	12,274	27,773
Media and public affairs occupations	4,867	6,453	121	2,258	5,047	18,746
Protective service occupations	23,270	31,716	2,695	5,733	12,215	75,629
Support services occupations	13,438	1,667	1,146	2,264	10,699	29,214
Transportation and material handling occupations	53,349	34,588	10,549	22,825	42,860	164,171
Vehicle machinery mechanic occupations	48,577	50,532	5,538	18,076	50,020	172,743
Total, by service	408,875	285,385	29,402	166,655	302,766	1,193,083

SOURCE: U.S. Department of Defense, Defense Manpower Data Center

Table 3. Military officer personnel by broad occupational category and branch of service, February 2005

Occupational Group - Officer	Army	Air Force	Coast Guard	Marine Corps	Navy	Total, all services
Combat specialty occupations	18,835	6,007		4,662	5,463	34,967
Engineering, science, and technical occupations	19,137	17,503	1,576	3,576	9,778	51,087
Executive, administrative, and managerial occupations	11,262	10,395	282	2,582	7,450	31,971
Health care occupations	9,792	9,413	43		6,983	26,231
Human resource development occupations	2,128	2,418	213	299	3,258	8,316
Media and public affairs occupations	224	500	20	44	282	1,070
Protective service occupations	2,237	1,410	104	309	890	4,950
Support services occupations	1,525	830		38	1,003	3,396
Transportation occupations	13,216	19,729	2,250	7,082	11,975	54,252
Total, by service	78,356	68,205	4,005	18,592	47,082	216,240

SOURCE: U.S. Department of Defense, Defense Manpower Data Center

Job Outlook

Opportunities should be good for qualified individuals in all branches of the Armed Forces through 2014. Many military personnel retire with a pension after 20 years of service, while they still are young enough to start a new career. About 170,000 personnel must be recruited each year to replace those who complete their commitment or retire. Since the end of the draft in 1973, the military has met its personnel requirements with volunteers. When the economy is good and civilian employment opportunities generally are more favorable, it is more difficult for all the services to meet their recruitment quotas. It is also more difficult to meet these goals during times of war, when recruitment goals typically rise.

America's strategic position is stronger than it has been in decades. Despite reductions in personnel due to the elimination of the threats of the Cold War, the number of active-duty personnel is expected to remain roughly constant through 2014. However, recent conflicts and the resulting strain on the Armed Forces may lead to an increasing number of active-duty personnel. The Armed Forces' current goal is to maintain a sufficient force to fight and win two major regional conflicts at the same time. Political events, however, could lead to a significant restructuring with or without an increase in size.

Educational requirements will continue to rise as military jobs become more technical and complex. High school graduates and applicants with a college background will be sought to fill the ranks of enlisted personnel, while virtually all officers will need at least a bachelor's degree and, in some cases, an advanced degree as well.

Earnings

The earnings structure for military personnel is shown in table 4. Most enlisted personnel started as recruits at Grade E-1 in 2004; however, those with special skills or above-average education started as high as Grade E-4. Most warrant officers had started at Grade W-1 or W-2, depending upon their occupational and academic qualifications and the branch of service of which they were a member, but warrant officer typically is not an entry-level occupation and, consequently, most of these individuals had previous military service. Most commissioned officers started at Grade O-1; some with advanced education started at Grade O-2, and some highly trained officers—for example, physicians and dentists—started as high as Grade O-3. Pay varies by total years of service as well as rank. Because it usually takes many years to reach the higher ranks, most personnel in higher ranks receive the higher pay rates awarded to those with many years of service.

In addition to receiving their basic pay, military personnel are provided with free room and board (or a tax-free housing and subsistence allowance), free medical and dental care, a military clothing allowance, military supermarket and department store shopping privileges, 30 days of paid vacation a year (referred to as leave), and travel opportunities. In many duty stations, military personnel may receive a housing allowance that can be used for off-base housing. This allowance can be substantial, but varies greatly by rank and

duty station. For example, in fiscal year 2005, the average housing allowance for an E-4 with dependents was $958 per month; for a comparable individual without dependents, it was $752. The allowance for an O-4 with dependents was $1,645 per month; for a comparable individual without dependents, it was $1,428. Other allowances are paid for foreign duty, hazardous duty, submarine and flight duty, and employment as a medical officer. Athletic and other facilities—such as gymnasiums, tennis courts, golf courses, bowling centers, libraries, and movie theaters—are available on many military installations. Military personnel are eligible for retirement benefits after 20 years of service.

The Veterans Administration (VA) provides numerous benefits to those who have served at least 24 months of continuous active duty in the Armed Forces. Veterans are eligible for free care in VA hospitals for all service-related disabilities, regardless of time served; those with other medical problems are eligible for free VA care if they are unable to pay the cost of hospitalization elsewhere. Admission to a VA medical center depends on the availability of beds, however. Veterans also are eligible for certain loans, including loans to purchase a home. Veterans, regardless of health, can convert a military life insurance policy to an individual policy with any participating company upon separation from the military. In addition, job counseling, testing, and placement services are available.

Veterans who participate in the Montgomery GI Bill Program receive education benefits. Under this program, Armed Forces personnel may elect to deduct up to $100 a month from their pay during the first 12 months of active duty, putting the money toward their future education. In fiscal year 2005, veterans who served on active duty for 3 or more years or who spent 2 years in active duty plus 4 years in the Selected Reserve received $1,004 a month in basic benefits for 36 months of full-time institutional training. Those who enlisted and serve less than 3 years received $816 a month for 36 months for the same. In addition, each service provides its own contributions to the enlistee's future education. The sum of the amounts from all these sources becomes the service member's educational fund. Upon separation from active duty, the fund can be used to finance educational costs at any VA-approved institution. Among those institutions which are approved by the VA are many vocational, correspondence, certification, business, technical, and flight-training schools; community and junior colleges; and colleges and universities.

Table 4. Military basic monthly pay by grade for active duty personnel, January, 2005

Grade	Years of service					
	Less than 2	Over 4	Over 8	Over 12	Over 16	Over 20
O-10	—	—	—	—	—	$12,963.00
O-9	—	—	—	—	—	11,337.90
O-8	$8,022.30	$8,508.30	$9,089.40	$9,519.00	$9,915.30	10,742.40
O-7	6,666.00	6,233.00	7,642.50	8,113.50	9,089.40	9,714.60
O-6	4,940.70	5,784.00	6,054.90	6,087.90	7,045.50	7,763.40
O-5	4,118.70	5,021.40	5,341.80	5,799.00	6,431.10	6,793.20
O-4	3,553.80	4,449.60	4,977.60	5,582.70	5,872.20	5,933.70

| | | Years of service | | | |
Grade	Less than 2	Over 4	Over 8	Over 12	Over 16	Over 20
O-3	$3,124.50	$4,168.20	$4,586.70	$4,962.00	$5,083.20	$5,083.20
O-2	2,699.40	3,660.90	3,736.20	3,736.20	3,736.20	3,736.20
O-1	2,343.60	2,948.10	2,948.10	2,948.10	2,948.10	2,948.10
W-5	—	—	—	—	—	5,548.20
W-4	3,228.60	3,671.40	4,007.10	4,341.00	4,779.00	5,117.40
W-3	2,948.40	3,238.80	3,522.30	3,918.90	4,285.50	4,509.30
W-2	2,593.50	2,965.50	3,268.20	3,564.00	3,771.30	3,977.40
W-1	2,290.20	2,684.40	3,030.90	3,275.40	3,438.30	3,659.70
E-9	—	—	—	3,989.70	4,232.40	4,575.90
E-8	—	—	3,193.50	3,442.10	3,640.50	3,949.20
E-7	2,220.00	2,638.80	2,899.50	3,084.60	3,332.40	3,458.70
E-6	1,920.30	2,296.50	2,604.30	2,779.20	2,888.70	2,908.20
E-5	1,759.50	2,060.70	2,329.80	2,450.70	2,450.70	2,450.70
E-4	1,612.80	1,877.70	1,957.80	1,957.80	1,957.80	1,957.80
E-3	1,456.20	1,641.00	1,641.00	1,641.00	1,641.00	1,641.00
E-2	1,384.50	1,384.50	1,384.50	1,384.50	1,384.50	1,384.50
E-1 4mos+	1,235.10	1,235.10	1,235.10	1,235.10	1,235.10	1,235.10
E-1 <4mos	1,142.70	—	—	—	—	—

SOURCE: U.S. Department of Defense, Defense Finance and Accounting Service

Sources of Additional Information

Each of the military services publishes handbooks, fact sheets, and pamphlets describing entrance requirements, training and advancement opportunities, and other aspects of military careers. These publications are widely available at all recruiting stations, at most state employment service offices, and in high schools, colleges, and public libraries. Information on educational and other veterans' benefits is available from VA offices located throughout the country.

In addition, the Defense Manpower Data Center, an agency of the U.S. Department of Defense, publishes *Military Career Guide Online*, a compendium of military occupational, training, and career information designed for use by students and jobseekers. This information is available on the Internet: http://www.todaysmilitary.com

Atmospheric Scientists

(O*NET 19-2021.00)

Significant Points

- 4 in 10 atmospheric scientists work for the federal government, the largest employer of these workers.

- A bachelor's degree in meteorology, or in a closely related field with courses in meteorology, is the minimum educational requirement; a master's degree is necessary for some positions, and a doctoral degree (Ph.D.) is required for most basic research positions.

- Job opportunities are expected to be better in private industry than in the federal government; opportunities in broadcasting, however, are rare and highly competitive.

Nature of the Work

Atmospheric science is the study of the atmosphere—the blanket of air covering the Earth. *Atmospheric scientists*, commonly called *meteorologists*, study the atmosphere's physical characteristics, motions, and processes and the way in which these factors affect the rest of our environment. The best-known application of this knowledge is forecasting the weather. In addition to predicting the weather, atmospheric scientists attempt to identify and interpret climate trends, understand past weather, and analyze today's weather. Weather information and meteorological research are also applied in air-pollution control; agriculture; forestry; air and sea transportation; defense; and the study of possible trends in the Earth's climate, such as global warming, droughts, and ozone depletion.

Atmospheric scientists who forecast the weather, known professionally as *operational meteorologists*, are the largest group of specialists. They study information on air pressure, temperature, humidity, and wind velocity and they apply physical and mathematical relationships to make short-range and long-range weather forecasts. Their data come from weather satellites, radars, sensors, and stations in many parts of the world. Meteorologists use sophisticated computer models of the world's atmosphere to make long-term, short-term, and local-area forecasts. More accurate instruments for measuring and observing weather conditions, as well as high-speed computers to process and analyze weather data, have revolutionized weather forecasting. Using satellite data, climate theory, and sophisticated computer models of the world's atmosphere, meteorologists can more effectively interpret the results of these models to make local-area weather predictions. These forecasts inform not only the general public, but also those who need accurate weather information for both economic and safety reasons, such as the shipping, air transportation, agriculture, fishing, forestry, and utilities industries.

The use of weather balloons, launched a few times a day to measure wind, temperature, and humidity in the upper atmosphere, is currently supplemented by sophisticated atmospheric monitoring equipment that transmits data as frequently as every few minutes. Doppler radar, for example, can detect airflow patterns in violent storm systems—allowing forecasters to better predict thunderstorms, flash floods, tornadoes, and other hazardous winds and to monitor the direction and intensity of storms.

Some atmospheric scientists work in research. *Physical meteorologists*, for example, study the atmosphere's chemical and physical properties; the transmission of light, sound, and radio waves; and the transfer of energy in the atmosphere. They also study factors affecting the formation of clouds, rain, and snow; the dispersal of air pollutants over urban areas; and other weather phenomena, such as the mechanics of severe storms. *Synoptic meteorologists* develop new tools for weather forecasting, using computers and sophisticated mathematical models of atmospheric activity. *Climatologists* study climactic variations spanning hundreds or even millions of years. They also may collect, analyze, and interpret past records of wind, rainfall, sunshine, and temperature in specific areas or regions. Their studies are used to design buildings, plan heating and cooling systems, and aid in effective land use and agricultural production. Environmental problems, such as pollution and shortages of fresh water, have widened the scope of the meteorological profession. *Environmental meteorologists* study these problems and may evaluate and report on air quality for environmental impact statements. Other research meteorologists examine the most effective ways to control or diminish air pollution.

Working Conditions

Most weather stations operate around the clock, 7 days a week. Jobs in such facilities usually involve night, weekend, and holiday work, often with rotating shifts. During weather emergencies, such as hurricanes, operational meteorologists may work overtime. Operational meteorologists also are often under pressure to meet forecast deadlines. Weather stations are found everywhere—at airports, in or near cities, and in isolated and remote areas. Some atmospheric scientists also spend time observing weather conditions and collecting data from aircraft. Weather forecasters who work for radio or television stations broadcast their reports from station studios and may work evenings and weekends. Meteorologists in smaller weather offices often work alone; in larger ones, they work as part of a team. Meteorologists who are not involved in forecasting tasks work regular hours, usually in offices. Those who work for private consulting firms or for companies analyzing and monitoring emissions to improve air quality usually work with other scientists or engineers; fieldwork and travel may be common for these workers.

Training, Other Qualifications, and Advancement

A bachelor's degree in meteorology or atmospheric science, or in a closely related field with courses in meteorology, usually is the min-

imum educational requirement for an entry-level position as an atmospheric scientist.

The preferred educational requirement for entry-level meteorologists in the federal government is a bachelor's degree—not necessarily in meteorology—with at least 24 semester hours of meteorology courses, including 6 hours in the analysis and prediction of weather systems, 6 hours of atmospheric dynamics and thermodynamics, 3 hours of physical meteorology, and 2 hours of remote sensing of the atmosphere or instrumentation. Other required courses include 3 semester hours of ordinary differential equations, 6 hours of college physics, and at least 9 hours of courses appropriate for a physical science major—such as statistics, chemistry, physical oceanography, physical climatology, physical hydrology, radiative transfer, aeronomy, advanced thermodynamics, advanced electricity and magnetism, light and optics, and computer science. Sometimes, a combination of education and appropriate experience may be substituted for a degree.

Although positions in operational meteorology are available for those with only a bachelor's degree, obtaining a second bachelor's degree or a master's degree enhances employment opportunities, pay, and advancement potential. A master's degree usually is necessary for conducting applied research and development, and a Ph.D. is required for most basic research positions. Students planning on a career in research and development do not necessarily need to major in atmospheric science or meteorology as an undergraduate. In fact, a bachelor's degree in mathematics, physics, or engineering provides excellent preparation for graduate study in atmospheric science.

Because atmospheric science is a small field, relatively few colleges and universities offer degrees in meteorology or atmospheric science, although many departments of physics, earth science, geography, and geophysics offer atmospheric science and related courses. In 2005, the American Meteorological Society (AMS) approved approximately 100 undergraduate and graduate atmospheric science programs. Many of these programs combine the study of meteorology with another field, such as agriculture, hydrology, oceanography, engineering, or physics. For example, hydrometeorology is the blending of hydrology (the science of Earth's water) and meteorology and is the field concerned with the effect of precipitation on the hydrologic cycle and the environment.

Prospective students should make certain that courses required by the National Weather Service and other employers are offered at the college they are considering. Computer science courses, additional meteorology courses, a strong background in mathematics and physics, and good communication skills are important to prospective employers.

Students should also take courses in subjects that are most relevant to their desired area of specialization. For example, those who wish to become broadcast meteorologists for radio or television stations should develop excellent communication skills through courses in speech, journalism, and related fields. Students interested in air quality work should take courses in chemistry and supplement their technical training with coursework in policy or government affairs. Prospective meteorologists seeking opportunities at weather consulting firms should possess knowledge of business, statistics, and economics, as an increasing emphasis is being placed on long-range seasonal forecasting to assist businesses.

Beginning atmospheric scientists often do routine data collection, computation, or analysis and some basic forecasting. Entry-level operational meteorologists in the federal government usually are placed in intern positions for training and experience. During this period, they learn about the Weather Service's forecasting equipment and procedures and rotate to different offices to learn about various weather systems. After completing the training period, they are assigned to a permanent duty station. Experienced meteorologists may advance to supervisory or administrative jobs or may handle more complex forecasting jobs. After several years of experience, some meteorologists establish their own weather consulting services.

AMS offers professional certification of consulting meteorologists administered by a Board of Certified Consulting Meteorologists. Applicants must meet formal education requirements (but not necessarily have a college degree), pass an examination to demonstrate thorough meteorological knowledge, have a minimum of 5 years of experience or a combination of experience plus an advanced degree, and provide character references from fellow professionals. In addition, AMS also offers professional certification for broadcast meteorologists.

Employment

Atmospheric scientists held about 7,400 jobs in 2004. The federal government was the largest single employer of civilian meteorologists, accounting for about 2,900. The National Oceanic and Atmospheric Administration (NOAA) employed most federal meteorologists in National Weather Service stations throughout the nation; the remainder of NOAA's meteorologists worked mainly in research and development or management. The U.S. Department of Defense employed several hundred civilian meteorologists. Others worked for professional, scientific, and technical services firms, including private weather consulting services, radio and television broadcasting, air carriers, and state government.

Although several hundred people teach atmospheric science and related courses in college and university departments of meteorology or atmospheric science, physics, earth science, or geophysics, these individuals are classified as college or university faculty rather than atmospheric scientists. (See the description of teachers—postsecondary elsewhere in this book.)

In addition to civilian meteorologists, hundreds of Armed Forces members are involved in forecasting and other meteorological work. (See the description job opportunities in the Armed Forces elsewhere in this book.)

Job Outlook

Employment of atmospheric scientists is projected to increase about as fast as average for all occupations through 2014. The National Weather Service has completed an extensive modernization of its weather forecasting equipment and finished all hiring of meteorologists needed to staff the upgraded stations, however. The Service has no plans to increase the number of weather stations or the number of meteorologists in existing stations. Employment of meteorologists in other federal agencies is expected to remain stable.

In private industry, on the other hand, job opportunities for atmospheric scientists are expected to be better than in the federal government over the 2004–2014 period. As research leads to continuing improvements in weather forecasting, demand should grow for private weather consulting firms to provide more detailed information than has formerly been available, especially to climate-sensitive industries. Farmers; commodity investors; radio and television stations; and utilities, transportation, and construction firms can greatly benefit from additional weather information more closely targeted to their needs than the general information provided by the National Weather Service. Additionally, research on seasonal and other long-range forecasting is yielding positive results, which should spur demand for more atmospheric scientists to interpret these forecasts and advise climate-sensitive industries. However, because many customers for private weather services are in industries sensitive to fluctuations in the economy, the sales and growth of private weather services depend on the health of the economy.

There will continue to be demand for atmospheric scientists to analyze and monitor the dispersion of pollutants into the air to ensure compliance with federal environmental regulations, but related employment increases are expected to be small. Efforts toward making and improving global weather observations also could have a positive impact on employment. Opportunities in broadcasting are rare and highly competitive, however, making for very few job openings in this industry. Prospects for academic positions may improve. While a competitive job market will continue to exist for independent research positions in universities and for college and university faculty, opportunities are expected to be better than in the past as an increasing number of faculty are expected to retire through the projection period.

Earnings

Median annual earnings of atmospheric scientists in May 2004 were $70,100. The middle 50 percent earned between $48,880 and $86,610. The lowest 10 percent earned less than $34,590, and the highest 10 percent earned more than $106,020.

The average salary for meteorologists in nonsupervisory, supervisory, and managerial positions employed by the federal government was about $80,499 in 2005. Meteorologists in the federal government with a bachelor's degree and no experience received a starting salary of $27,955 or $34,544, depending on their college grades. Those with a master's degree could start at $42,090 or $54,393, and those with a Ph.D. could begin at $70,280. Beginning salaries for all degree levels are slightly higher in areas of the country where the prevailing local pay level is higher.

Related Occupations

Workers in other occupations concerned with the physical environment include environmental scientists and geoscientists; physicists and astronomers; mathematicians; and civil, chemical, and environmental engineers.

Sources of Additional Information

Information about careers in meteorology and a listing of colleges and universities offering meteorology programs is provided by the American Meteorological Society on the Internet at http://www.ametsoc.org/AMS.

Information on obtaining a position as a meteorologists with the federal government is available from the Office of Personnel Management through USAJOBS, the federal government's official employment information system. This resource for locating and applying for job opportunities can be accessed through the Internet at http://www.usajobs.opm.gov or through an interactive voice response telephone system at (703) 724-1850 or TDD (978) 461-8404. These numbers are not toll free, and charges may result.

Audiologists

(O*NET 29-1121.00)

Significant Points

■ Employment growth will be spurred by the expanding population in older age groups that are prone to medical conditions that result in hearing problems.

■ More than half work in health care facilities; many others are employed by educational services.

■ A master's degree in audiology has been the standard credential; however, a clinical doctoral degree is becoming more common for new entrants and is expected to become the new standard for the profession.

Nature of the Work

Audiologists work with people who have hearing, balance, and related ear problems. They examine individuals of all ages and identify those with the symptoms of hearing loss and other auditory, balance, and related sensory and neural problems. They then assess the nature and extent of the problems and help the individuals manage them. Using audiometers, computers, and other testing devices, they measure the loudness at which a person begins to hear sounds, the ability to distinguish between sounds, and the impact of hearing loss on an individual's daily life. In addition, audiologists use computer equipment to evaluate and diagnose balance disorders. Audiologists interpret these results and may coordinate them with medical, educational, and psychological information to make a diagnosis and determine a course of treatment.

Hearing disorders can result from a variety of causes, including trauma at birth, viral infections, genetic disorders, exposure to loud noise, certain medications, or aging. Treatment may include examining and cleaning the ear canal, fitting and dispensing hearing aids, and fitting and programming cochlear implants. Audiologic treatment also includes counseling on adjusting to hearing loss, training on the use of hearing instruments, and teaching communication strategies for use in a variety of environments. For example, they may provide instruction in listening strategies. Audiologists also

may recommend, fit, and dispense personal or large-area amplification systems and alerting devices.

In audiology (hearing) clinics, audiologists may independently develop and carry out treatment programs. They keep records on the initial evaluation, progress, and discharge of patients. In other settings, audiologists may work with other health and education providers as part of a team in planning and implementing services for children and adults, from birth to old age. Audiologists who diagnose and treat balance disorders often work in collaboration with physicians and physical and occupational therapists.

Some audiologists specialize in work with the elderly, children, or hearing-impaired individuals who need special treatment programs. Others develop and implement ways to protect workers' hearing from on-the-job injuries. They measure noise levels in workplaces and conduct hearing protection programs in factories, as well as in schools and communities.

Audiologists who work in private practice also manage the business aspects of running an office, such as developing a patient base, hiring employees, keeping records, and ordering equipment and supplies.

A few audiologists conduct research on types of—and treatment for—hearing, balance, and related disorders. Others design and develop equipment or techniques for diagnosing and treating these disorders.

Working Conditions

Audiologists usually work at a desk or table in clean, comfortable surroundings. The job is not physically demanding but does require attention to detail and intense concentration. The emotional needs of patients and their families may be demanding. Most full-time audiologists work about 40 hours per week, which may include weekends and evenings to meet the needs of patients. Some work part time. Those who work on a contract basis may spend a substantial amount of time traveling between facilities.

Training, Other Qualifications, and Advancement

Audiologists are regulated in 49 states; all require that individuals have at least a master's degree in audiology. However, a clinical doctoral degree is expected to become the new standard, and several states are currently in the process of changing their regulations to require the Doctor of Audiology (Au.D.) degree or equivalent. A passing score on the national examination on audiology offered through the Praxis Series of the Educational Testing Service also is needed. Other requirements typically are 300 to 375 hours of supervised clinical experience and 9 months of postgraduate professional clinical experience. Forty-one states have continuing education requirements for licensure renewal. An additional examination and license is required in order to dispense hearing aids in some states. Medicaid, Medicare, and private health insurers generally require practitioners to be licensed to qualify for reimbursement.

In 2005, there were 24 master's degree programs and 62 clinical doctoral programs offered at accredited colleges and universities. Graduation from an accredited program may be required to obtain a license. Requirements for admission to programs in audiology include courses in English, mathematics, physics, chemistry, biology, psychology, and communication. Graduate course work in audiology includes anatomy; physiology; physics; genetics; normal and abnormal communication development; auditory, balance, and neural systems assessment and treatment; diagnosis and treatment; pharmacology; and ethics.

Audiologists can acquire the Certificate of Clinical Competence in Audiology (CCC-A) offered by the American Speech-Language-Hearing Association. To earn a CCC, a person must have a graduate degree and 375 hours of supervised clinical experience, complete a 36-week postgraduate clinical fellowship, and pass the Praxis Series examination in audiology, administered by the Educational Testing Service. According to the American Speech-Language-Hearing Association, as of 2007, audiologists will need to have a bachelor's degree and complete 75 hours of credit toward a doctoral degree in order to seek certification. As of 2012, audiologists will have to earn a doctoral degree in order to be certified.

Audiologists may also be certified through the American Board of Audiology. Applicants must earn a master's or doctoral degree in audiology from a regionally accredited college or university, achieve a passing score on a national examination in audiology, and demonstrate that they have completed a minimum of 2,000 hours of mentored professional practice in a two-year period with a qualified audiologist. Certificants must apply for renewal every three years. They must demonstrate that they have earned 45 hours of approved continuing education within the three-year period. Beginning in 2007, all applicants must earn a doctoral degree in audiology.

Audiologists should be able to effectively communicate diagnostic test results, diagnoses, and proposed treatments in a manner easily understood by their patients. They must be able to approach problems objectively and provide support to patients and their families. Because a patient's progress may be slow, patience, compassion, and good listening skills are necessary.

Employment

Audiologists held about 10,000 jobs in 2004. More than half of all jobs were in offices of physicians or other health practitioners, including audiologists; in hospitals; and in outpatient care centers. About 1 in 7 jobs was in educational services, including elementary and secondary schools. Other jobs for audiologists were in health and personal care stores, including hearing aid stores; scientific research and development services; and state and local governments.

A small number of audiologists were self-employed in private practice. They provided hearing health care services in their own offices or worked under contract for schools, health care facilities, or other establishments.

Job Outlook

Employment of audiologists is expected to grow about as fast as the average for all occupations through the year 2014. Because hearing loss is strongly associated with aging, rapid growth in older population groups will cause the number of persons with hearing and balance impairments to increase markedly. Medical advances are also improving the survival rate of premature infants and trauma victims, who then need assessment and possible treatment. Greater awareness of the importance of early identification and diagnosis of hearing disorders in infants also will increase employment. Most states now require that all newborns be screened for hearing loss and receive appropriate early intervention services.

Employment in educational services will increase along with growth in elementary and secondary school enrollments, including enrollment of special education students. The number of audiologists in private practice will rise due to the increasing demand for direct services to individuals as well as increasing use of contract services by hospitals, schools, and nursing care facilities.

Growth in employment of audiologists will be moderated by limitations on insurance reimbursements for the services they provide. Additionally, increased educational requirements may limit the pool of workers entering the profession and any resulting higher salaries may cause doctors to hire more lower-paid ear technicians to perform the functions that audiologists held in doctor's offices. Only a few job openings for audiologists will arise from the need to replace those who leave the occupation, because the occupation is small.

Earnings

Median annual earnings of audiologists were $51,470 in May 2004. The middle 50 percent earned between $42,160 and $62,210. The lowest 10 percent earned less than $34,990, and the highest 10 percent earned more than $75,990.

According to a 2004 survey by the American Speech-Language-Hearing Association, the median annual salary for full-time certified audiologists who worked on a calendar-year basis, generally 11 or 12 months annually, was $56,000. For those who worked on an academic-year basis, usually 9 or 10 months annually, the median annual salary was $53,000. The median starting salary for certified audiologists with one to three years of experience was $45,000 on a calendar-year basis.

Related Occupations

Audiologists specialize in the prevention, diagnosis, and treatment of hearing problems. Workers in related occupations include occupational therapists, optometrists, physical therapists, psychologists, recreational therapists, rehabilitation counselors, and speech-language pathologists.

Sources of Additional Information

State licensing boards can provide information on licensure requirements. State departments of education can supply information on certification requirements for those who wish to work in public schools.

General information on careers in audiology is available from

▸ American Academy of Audiology, 11730 Plaza America Dr., Suite 300, Reston, VA 20190. Internet: http://www.audiology.org

Career information, a description of the CCC-A credential, and a listing of accredited graduate programs is available from

▸ American Speech-Language-Hearing Association, 10801 Rockville Pike, Rockville, MD 20852. Internet: http://www.asha.org

Information on American Board of Audiology certification is available from

▶ American Board of Audiology, 11730 Plaza America Dr., Suite 300, Reston, VA 20190. Internet: http://www.americanboardofaudiology.org

Automotive Body and Related Repairers

(O*NET 49-3021.00 and 49-3022.00)

Significant Points

■ To become a fully skilled automotive body repairer, formal training followed by on-the-job instruction is recommended because repair of newer automobiles requires more advanced skills to fix their new technologies and new body materials.

■ Repairers need good reading ability and basic mathematics and computer skills in order to follow instructions and diagrams in print and computer-based technical manuals.

Nature of the Work

While running errands or driving to and from work, we sometimes observe traffic accidents. Most of the vehicle damage resulting from these collisions can be repaired and the vehicle refinished to once again look and drive like new. Automotive body repairers, also often called collision repair technicians, straighten bent bodies, remove dents, and replace crumpled parts that cannot be fixed. They repair all types of vehicles, and although some work on large trucks, buses, or tractor-trailers, most work on cars and small trucks.

Automotive body repairers use special equipment to restore damaged metal frames and body sections. Repairers chain or clamp frames and sections to alignment machines that use hydraulic pressure to align damaged components. "Unibody" vehicles—designs built without frames—must be restored to precise factory specifications for the vehicle to operate correctly. To do so, repairers use benchmark systems to make accurate measurements of how much each section is out of alignment and hydraulic machinery to return the vehicle to its original shape.

Body repairers remove badly damaged sections of body panels with a pneumatic metal-cutting gun or by other means and then weld in replacement sections. Repairers pull out less-serious dents with a hydraulic jack or hand-prying bar or knock them out with hand tools or pneumatic hammers. They smooth out small dents and creases in the metal by holding a small anvil against one side of the damaged area while hammering the opposite side. Repairers also remove very small pits and dimples with pick hammers and punches in a process called metal finishing. Body repairers use plastic or solder to fill small dents that cannot be worked out of plastic or metal panels. On metal panels, they file or grind the hardened filler to the original shape and clean the surface with a media blaster before repainting the damaged portion of the vehicle.

Body repairers also repair or replace the plastic body parts that are increasingly being used on new-model vehicles. They remove damaged panels and identify the type and properties of the plastic used on the vehicle. With most types of plastic, repairers can apply heat from a hot-air welding gun or by immersion in hot water and press the softened panel back into its original shape by hand. They replace plastic parts that are badly damaged or very difficult to repair. A few body repairers specialize in repairing fiberglass car bodies.

The advent of assembly-line repairs in large shops enables the establishment to move away from the one-vehicle, one-repairer method to a team approach that allows body repairers to specialize in one type of repair, such as straightening frames, repairing doors and fenders, or painting and refinishing. In most shops, automotive painters do the painting. However, in small shops, workers often do both body repairing and painting. Some body repairers specialize in installing and repairing glass in automobiles and other vehicles. *Automotive glass installers and repairers* remove broken, cracked, or pitted windshields and window glass. Glass installers apply a moisture-proofing compound along the edges of the glass, place the glass in the vehicle, and install rubber strips around the sides of the windshield or window to make it secure and weatherproof.

Body repair work has variety and challenges: Each damaged vehicle presents a different problem. Using their broad knowledge of automotive construction and repair techniques, repairers must develop appropriate methods for each job. They usually work alone, with only general directions from supervisors. In some shops, helpers or apprentices assist experienced repairers.

Working Conditions

Most automotive body repairers work a standard 40-hour week, although some, including the self-employed, work more than 40 hours a week. Repairers work indoors in body shops that are noisy with the clatters of hammers against metal and the whine of power tools. Most shops are well ventilated in order to disperse dust and paint fumes. Body repairers often work in awkward or cramped positions, and much of their work is strenuous and dirty. Hazards include cuts from sharp metal edges, burns from torches and heated metal, injuries from power tools, and fumes from paint. However, serious accidents usually are avoided when the shop is kept clean and orderly and safety practices are observed.

Training, Other Qualifications, and Advancement

Automotive technology is rapidly increasing in sophistication, and most training authorities strongly recommend that persons seeking automotive body repair and related jobs complete a formal training program in automotive body repair or refinishing. Programs are offered in high school or in postsecondary vocational schools and community colleges, but these programs provide only a portion of the training needed to become fully skilled. Most new repairers receive primarily on-the-job training, supplemented with short-term training sessions given by vehicle, parts, and equipment manufacturers, when available. Training is necessary because advances in technology have greatly changed the structure, components, and materials used in automobiles. As a result, proficiency in new repair techniques is necessary. For example, the bodies of automobiles are usually a combination of materials—traditional steel, aluminum, and a growing variety of metal alloys and plastics. Each of these materials or composites requires the use of somewhat different techniques to reshape parts and smooth out dents and small pits.

Fully skilled automotive body repairers must have good reading ability and basic mathematics and computer skills. Restoring unibody automobiles to their original form requires body repairers to follow instructions and diagrams in technical manuals in order to make precise three-dimensional measurements of the position of one body section relative to another.

New repairers begin by assisting experienced body repairers in tasks such as removing damaged parts, sanding body panels, and installing repaired parts. Novices learn to remove small dents and to make other minor repairs. They then progress to more difficult tasks, such as straightening body parts and returning them to their correct alignment. Generally, to become skilled in all aspects of body repair requires 3 to 4 years of on-the-job training.

Certification by the National Institute for Automotive Service Excellence (ASE), although voluntary, is the recognized industry credential for automotive body repairers. Repairers may take from one to four ASE Master Collision Repair and Refinish Exams. Repairers who pass at least one exam and have 2 years of hands-on work experience earn ASE certification. The completion of a postsecondary program in automotive body repair may be substituted for 1 year of work experience. Those who pass all four exams become ASE Master Collision Repair and Refinish Technicians. Automotive body repairers must retake the examination at least every 5 years to retain their certification. While the ASE designations are the most widely recognized, many vehicle manufacturers and paint manufacturers also have product certification programs available for body repairers.

Continuing education is required throughout a career in automotive body repair. Automotive parts, body materials, and electronics continue to change and to become more complex and technologically advanced. To keep up with the technological advances, repairers must continue to gain new skills, read technical manuals, and attend seminars and classes. Many companies within the automotive body repair industry provide ongoing training for workers.

As beginners increase their skills, learn new techniques, and complete work more rapidly, their pay increases. An experienced automotive body repairer with managerial ability may advance to shop supervisor. Some workers even open their own body repair shops. Others become automobile damage appraisers for insurance companies.

Employment

Automotive body and related repairers held about 223,000 jobs in 2004; about 1 in 10 specialized in automotive glass installation and repair. Most repairers worked for automotive repair and maintenance shops or automobile dealers. Others worked for organizations that maintain their own motor vehicles, such as trucking companies. A small number worked for wholesalers of motor vehicles, parts, and supplies. More than 1 automotive body repairer in 5 was self-employed, more than double the proportion for all installation, maintenance, and repair occupations.

Job Outlook

Employment of automotive body repairers is expected to grow as fast as the average for all occupations through the year 2014. The need to replace experienced repairers who transfer to other occupations or who retire or stop working for other reasons will account for the majority of job openings. Opportunities will be best for persons with formal training in automotive body repair and refinishing. Those without formal training in automotive body refinishing or collision repair will face competition for these jobs.

Demand for qualified body repairers will increase as the number of motor vehicles in operation continues to grow in line with the nation's population. With each rise in the number of motor vehicles in use, the number of vehicles damaged in accidents also will grow. New automobile designs increasingly have body parts made of steel alloys, aluminum, and plastics—materials that are more difficult to work with than traditional steel body parts. In addition, new automotive designs of lighter weight are prone to greater collision damage than are older, heavier designs, so more time is consumed in repair.

However, increasing demand due to growth in the number of vehicles in operation will be somewhat tempered by improvements in the quality of vehicles and technological innovations that enhance safety and reduce the likelihood of accidents. Also, more body parts are simply being replaced rather than repaired. Larger shops also are instituting productivity enhancements, such as employing a team approach to repairs to decrease repair time and expand their volume of work. In addition, demand for automotive body repair services will be constrained as more vehicles are declared a total loss after accidents. In many such cases, the vehicles are not repaired because of the high cost of replacing the increasingly complex parts and electronic components and fixing the extensive damage that results when airbags deploy. Employment growth will continue to be concentrated in automotive body, paint, interior, and glass repair shops. Automobile dealers will employ a smaller portion of this occupation as the equipment needed for collision repair becomes more specialized and expensive to operate and maintain.

Experienced body repairers are rarely laid off during a general slowdown in the economy. Automotive repair business is not very sensitive to changes in economic conditions because major body damage must be repaired if a vehicle is to be restored to safe operating condition. However, repair of minor dents and crumpled fenders often can be deferred when drivers' budgets become tight.

Earnings

Median hourly earnings of automotive body and related repairers, including incentive pay, were $16.68 in May 2004. The middle 50 percent earned between $12.55 and $22.04 an hour. The lowest 10 percent earned less than $9.42, and the highest 10 percent earned more than $28.45 an hour. In May 2004, median hourly earnings of automotive body and related repairers were $17.73 in automobile dealers and $16.44 in automotive repair and maintenance.

Median hourly earnings of automotive glass installers and repairers, including incentive pay, were $13.45 in May 2004. The middle 50 percent earned between $10.36 and $17.04 an hour. The lowest 10 percent earned less than $8.53, and the highest 10 percent earned more than $20.63 an hour. Median hourly earnings in automotive repair and maintenance shops, the industry employing most automotive glass installers and repairers, were $13.43.

The majority of body repairers employed by independent repair shops and automotive dealers are paid on an incentive basis. Under this method, body repairers are paid a predetermined amount for various tasks, and earnings depend on the amount of work assigned to the repairer and how fast it is completed. Employers frequently guarantee workers a minimum weekly salary. Body repairers who work for trucking companies, bus lines, and other organizations that maintain their own vehicles usually receive an hourly wage.

Helpers and trainees typically earn from 30 percent to 60 percent of the earnings of skilled workers. Helpers and trainees usually receive an hourly rate until they are skilled enough to be paid on an incentive basis.

Related Occupations

Repairing damaged motor vehicles often involves working on mechanical components as well as vehicle bodies. Automotive body repairers often work closely with individuals in several related occupations, including automotive service technicians and mechanics; diesel service technicians and mechanics; auto damage insurance appraisers; and painting and coating workers, except construction and maintenance.

Sources of Additional Information

Additional details about work opportunities may be obtained from automotive body repair shops, automobile dealers, or local offices of your state employment service. State employment service offices also are a source of information about training programs.

For general information about automotive body repairer careers, contact any of the following sources:

▸ Automotive Service Association, P.O. Box 929, Bedford, TX 76095-0929. Internet: http://www.asashop.org

▸ National Automobile Dealers Association, 8400 Westpark Dr., McLean, VA 22102. Internet: http://www.nada.org

▸ Inter-Industry Conference On Auto Collision Repair Education Foundation (I-CAR), 5125 Trillium Blvd., Hoffman Estates, IL 60192. Telephone (toll free): 800-422-7872.

▸ Automotive Jobs Today, 8400 Westpark Drive, MS #2, McLean, VA 22102. Internet: http://www.autojobstoday.org

For general information about careers in automotive glass installation and repair, contact

▸ National Glass Association. 8200 Greensboro Drive, Suite 302, McLean, VA 22102-3881. Internet: http://www.glass.org

For information on how to become a certified automotive body repairer, write to

▸ National Institute for Automotive Service Excellence (ASE), 101 Blue Seal Dr. SE, Suite 101, Leesburg, VA 20175. Internet: http://www.asecert.org

For a directory of certified automotive body repairer programs, contact

▸ National Automotive Technician Education Foundation, 101 Blue Seal Dr. SE, Suite 101, Leesburg, VA 20175. Internet: http://www.natef.org

For a directory of accredited private trade and technical schools that offer training programs in automotive body repair, contact

▸ Accrediting Commission of Career Schools and Colleges of Technology, 2101 Wilson Blvd., Suite 302, Arlington, VA 22201. Internet: http://www.accsct.org

Automotive Service Technicians and Mechanics

(O*NET 49-3023.01 and 49-3023.02)

Significant Points

■ Formal automotive technician training is the best preparation for these challenging technology-based jobs.

■ Opportunities should be very good for automotive service technicians and mechanics with diagnostic and problem-solving skills, knowledge of electronics and mathematics, and mechanical aptitude.

■ Automotive service technicians and mechanics must continually adapt to changing technology and repair techniques as vehicle components and systems become increasingly sophisticated.

Nature of the Work

Anyone whose car or light truck has broken down knows the importance of the jobs of automotive service technicians and mechanics. The ability to diagnose the source of a problem quickly and accurately requires good reasoning ability and a thorough knowledge of automobiles. Many technicians consider diagnosing hard-to-find troubles one of their most challenging and satisfying duties.

The work of automotive service technicians and mechanics has evolved from mechanical repair to a high-technology job. As a result, these workers are now usually called "technicians" in automotive services and the term "mechanic" is falling into disuse. Today, integrated electronic systems and complex computers run vehicles and measure their performance while on the road. Technicians must have an increasingly broad base of knowledge about how vehicles' complex components work and interact, as well as the ability to work with electronic diagnostic equipment and computer-based technical reference materials.

Automotive service technicians use their high-tech skills to inspect, maintain, and repair automobiles and light trucks that run on gasoline; ethanol; and other alternative fuels, such as electricity. The increasing sophistication of automotive technology now requires workers who can use computerized shop equipment and work with electronic components while maintaining their skills with traditional hand tools. (Service technicians who work on diesel-powered trucks, buses, and equipment are discussed in the description of diesel service technicians and mechanics. Motorcycle technicians—who repair and service motorcycles, motor scooters, mopeds, and, occasionally, small all-terrain vehicles—are discussed in the description of small engine mechanics.)

When mechanical or electrical troubles occur, technicians first get a description of the symptoms from the owner or, if they work in a large shop, from the repair service estimator or service advisor who wrote the repair order. To locate the problem, technicians use a diagnostic approach. First, they test to see whether components and systems are proper and secure. Then, they isolate the components or systems that could not logically be the cause of the problem. For example, if an air-conditioner malfunctions, the technician's diagnostic approach can pinpoint a problem as simple as a low coolant level or as complex as a bad drive-train connection that has shorted out the air conditioner. Technicians may have to test-drive the vehicle or use a variety of testing equipment, such as onboard and hand-held diagnostic computers or compression gauges, to identify the source of the problem. These tests may indicate whether a component is salvageable or whether a new one is required to get the vehicle back in working order.

During routine service inspections, technicians test and lubricate engines and other major components. In some cases, the technician may repair or replace worn parts before they cause breakdowns that could damage critical components of the vehicle. Technicians usually follow a checklist to ensure that they examine every critical part. Belts, hoses, plugs, brake and fuel systems, and other potentially troublesome items are among those closely watched.

Service technicians use a variety of tools in their work—power tools, such as pneumatic wrenches to remove bolts quickly; machine tools like lathes and grinding machines to rebuild brakes; welding and flame-cutting equipment to remove and repair exhaust systems; and jacks and hoists to lift cars and engines. They also use common hand tools, such as screwdrivers, pliers, and wrenches, to work on small parts and in hard-to-reach places.

Computers also have become commonplace in modern repair shops. Service technicians compare the readouts from computerized diagnostic testing devices with the benchmarked standards given by the manufacturer of the components being tested. Deviations outside of acceptable levels are an indication to the technician that further attention to an area is necessary. A shop's computerized system provides automatic updates to technical manuals and unlimited access to manufacturers' service information, technical service bulletins, and other databases that allow technicians to keep current on problem spots and to learn new procedures.

Automotive service technicians in large shops have increasingly become specialized. For example, *transmission technicians and rebuilders* work on gear trains, couplings, hydraulic pumps, and other parts of transmissions. Extensive knowledge of computer controls, the ability to diagnose electrical and hydraulic problems, and other specialized skills are needed to work on these complex components, which employ some of the most sophisticated technology used in vehicles. *Tuneup technicians* adjust the ignition timing and valves and adjust or replace spark plugs and other parts to ensure efficient engine performance. They often use electronic testing equipment to isolate and adjust malfunctions in fuel, ignition, and emissions control systems.

Automotive air-conditioning repairers install and repair air conditioners and service their components, such as compressors, condensers, and controls. These workers require special training in federal and state regulations governing the handling and disposal of refrigerants. *Front-end mechanics* align and balance wheels and repair steering mechanisms and suspension systems. They frequently use special alignment equipment and wheel-balancing

machines. *Brake repairers* adjust brakes, replace brake linings and pads, and make other repairs on brake systems. Some technicians specialize in both brake and front-end work. Even though electronics and electronic systems in automobiles were a specialty in the past, electronics are now so common that it is essential for all types of service technicians to be familiar with at least the basic principles of electronics.

Working Conditions

Nearly half of automotive service technicians work more than 40 hours a week. Some may also work evenings and weekends to satisfy customer service needs. Generally, service technicians work indoors in well-ventilated and -lighted repair shops. However, some shops are drafty and noisy. Although some problems can be fixed with simple computerized adjustments, technicians frequently work with dirty and greasy parts and in awkward positions. They often lift heavy parts and tools. Minor cuts, burns, and bruises are common, but technicians can usually avoid serious accidents if the shop is kept clean and orderly and safety practices are observed.

Training, Other Qualifications, and Advancement

Automotive technology is rapidly increasing in sophistication, and most training authorities strongly recommend that persons seeking automotive service technician and mechanic jobs complete a formal training program in high school or in a postsecondary vocational school or community college. However, some service technicians still learn the trade solely by assisting and learning from experienced workers. Courses in automotive repair, electronics, physics, chemistry, English, computers, and mathematics provide a good educational background for a career as a service technician.

High school programs, while an asset, vary greatly in scope. Some aim to equip graduates with enough skills to get a job as a technician's helper or trainee technician. Other programs offer only an introduction to automotive technology and service for the future consumer or hobbyist. Some of the more extensive programs participate in Automotive Youth Education Service (AYES), which has about 500 participating schools and more than 4000 participating dealers. Students who complete these programs receive an AYES certification and upon high school graduation are better prepared to enter entry-level technician positions or to advance their technical education.

Postsecondary automotive technician training programs vary greatly in format, but normally provide intensive career preparation through a combination of classroom instruction and hands-on practice. Some trade and technical school programs provide concentrated training for 6 months to a year, depending on how many hours the student attends each week, and award a certificate. Community college programs normally award an associate degree or certificate and usually spread the training over 2 years by supplementing the automotive training with instruction in English, basic mathematics, computers, and other subjects. Some students earn repair certificates in one particular skill and opt to leave the program to begin their career before graduation. Recently, some programs have added to their curriculums training on employability skills such as customer service and stress management. Employers find that these skills help technicians handle the additional responsibilities of dealing with the customers and parts vendors.

The various automobile manufacturers and their participating dealers sponsor 2-year associate degree programs at postsecondary schools across the nation. The Accrediting Commission of Career Schools and Colleges of Technology (ACCSCT) currently certifies a number of automotive and diesel technology schools. Schools update their curriculums frequently to reflect changing technology and equipment. Students in these programs typically spend alternate 6- to 12-week periods attending classes full time and working full time in the service departments of sponsoring dealers. At these dealerships, students get practical experience while assigned to an experienced worker who provides hands-on instruction and timesaving tips.

The ASE certification is a nationally recognized standard for programs offered by high schools, postsecondary trade schools, technical institutes, and community colleges that train automobile service technicians. Some automotive manufacturers provide ASE-certified instruction programs with service equipment and current-model cars on which students practice new skills and learn the latest automotive technology. While ASE certification is voluntary, it does signify that the program meets uniform standards for instructional facilities, equipment, staff credentials, and curriculum. To ensure that programs keep up with ever-changing technology, repair techniques, and ASE standards, the certified programs are subjected to periodic compliance reviews and mandatory recertification, as are the ASE standards themselves. In 2004, about 2000 high school and postsecondary automotive service technician training programs had been certified by ASE.

For trainee automotive service technician jobs, employers look for people with strong communication and analytical skills. Technicians need good reading, mathematics, and computer skills to study technical manuals and to keep abreast of new technology and learn new service and repair procedures and specifications. Trainees also must possess mechanical aptitude and knowledge of how automobiles work. Most employers regard the successful completion of a vocational training program in automotive service technology as the best preparation for trainee positions. Experience working on motor vehicles in the Armed Forces or as a hobby also is valuable. Because of the complexity of new vehicles, a growing number of employers require completion of high school and additional postsecondary training.

Many new cars have several onboard computers that operate everything from the engine to the radio. Engine controls and dashboard instruments were among the first components to use electronics, but today most automotive systems, such as braking, transmission, and steering systems, are controlled primarily by computers and electronic components. Some of the more advanced vehicles have global positioning systems, Internet access, and other high-tech features integrated into the functions of the vehicle. The training in electronics is vital because electrical components, or a series of related components, account for nearly all malfunctions in modern vehicles.

In addition to electronics and computers, automotive service technicians will have to learn and understand the science behind the alternate-fuel vehicles that have begun to enter the market. The fuel for these vehicles will come from the dehydrogenization of water, elec-

tric fuel cells, natural gas, solar power, and other non-petroleum-based sources. Hybrid vehicles, for example, use the energy from braking to recharge batteries that power an electric motor, which supplements a gasoline engine. As vehicles with these new technologies become more common, technicians will need additional training to learn the science and engineering that makes them possible. Currently, the manufacturers of these alternate-fuel vehicles are providing the necessary training. However, as the warrantees begin to expire, technicians in all industries will need to be trained to service these vehicles. As the number of these automobiles on the road increases, some technicians will likely specialize in the service and repair of these vehicles.

Those new to automotive service usually start as trainee technicians, technicians' helpers, or lubrication workers and gradually acquire and practice their skills by working with experienced mechanics and technicians. With a few months' experience, beginners perform many routine service tasks and make simple repairs. While some graduates of postsecondary automotive training programs are often able to earn promotion to the journey level after only a few months on the job, it typically takes 2 to 5 years of experience to become a journey-level service technician, who is expected to quickly perform the more difficult types of routine service and repairs. An additional 1 to 2 years of experience familiarizes technicians with all types of repairs. Complex specialties, such as transmission repair, require another year or two of training and experience. In contrast, brake specialists may learn their jobs in considerably less time because they do not need a complete knowledge of automotive repair.

At work, the most important possessions of technicians are their hand tools. Technicians usually provide their own tools, and many experienced workers have thousands of dollars invested in them. Employers typically furnish expensive power tools, engine analyzers, and other diagnostic equipment, but technicians accumulate hand tools with experience. Some formal training programs have alliances with tool manufacturers that help entry-level technicians accumulate tools during their training period.

Employers increasingly send experienced automotive service technicians to manufacturer training centers to learn to repair new models or to receive special training in the repair of components such as electronic fuel injection or air conditioners. Motor vehicle dealers and other automotive service providers also may send promising beginners to manufacturer-sponsored technician training programs; most employers periodically send experienced technicians to manufacturer-sponsored technician training programs for additional training to maintain or upgrade employees' skills and thus increase the employees' value to the employer. Factory representatives also visit many shops to conduct short training sessions.

Voluntary certification by the National Institute for Automotive Service Excellence (ASE) has become a standard credential for automotive service technicians. Certification is available in 1 or more of 8 different areas of automotive service, such as electrical systems, engine repair, brake systems, suspension and steering, and heating and air conditioning. For certification in each area, technicians must have at least 2 years of experience and pass the examination. Completion of an automotive training program in high school, vocational or trade school, or community or junior college may be substituted for 1 year of experience. For ASE certification as a master automobile technician, technicians must be certified in all eight areas. Technicians must retake each examination once every 5 years to maintain their certifications.

Experienced technicians who have leadership ability sometimes advance to shop supervisor or service manager. Those who work well with customers may become automotive repair service estimators. Some with sufficient funds open independent repair shops.

Employment

Automotive service technicians and mechanics held about 803,000 jobs in 2004. The majority worked for automotive repair and maintenance shops; automobile dealers; and retailers and wholesalers of automotive parts, accessories, and supplies. Others found employment in gasoline stations; home and auto supply stores; automotive equipment rental and leasing companies; federal, state, and local governments; and other organizations. More than 16 percent of service technicians were self-employed, more than twice the proportion for all installation, maintenance, and repair occupations.

Job Outlook

Job opportunities in this occupation are expected to be very good for persons who complete automotive training programs in high school, vocational and technical schools, or community colleges, as employers report difficulty in finding workers with the right skills. Persons with good diagnostic and problem-solving abilities, and whose training includes basic electronics and computer courses, should have the best opportunities. For well-prepared people with a technical background, automotive service technician careers offer an excellent opportunity for good pay and the satisfaction of highly skilled work with vehicles incorporating the latest in advanced technology. However, persons without formal automotive training are likely to face competition for entry-level jobs.

Employment of automotive service technicians and mechanics is expected to increase as fast as the average through the year 2014. Over the 2004–2014 period, demand for technicians will grow as the number of vehicles in operation increases, reflecting continued growth in the number of multi-car families. Growth in demand will be offset somewhat by slowing population growth and the continuing increase in the quality and durability of automobiles, which will require less frequent service. Additional job openings will be due to the need to replace a growing number of retiring technicians, who tend to be the most experienced workers.

Most persons who enter the occupation can expect steady work, even through downturns in the economy. While car owners may postpone maintenance and repair on their vehicles when their budgets become strained, and employers of automotive technicians may cutback hiring new workers, changes in economic conditions generally have minor effects on the automotive service and repair business.

Employment growth will continue to be concentrated in automobile dealerships and independent automotive repair shops. Many new jobs also will be created in small retail operations that offer after-warranty repairs, such as oil changes, brake repair, air-conditioner service, and other minor repairs generally taking less than 4 hours to complete. Employment of automotive service technicians and

mechanics in gasoline service stations will continue to decline as fewer stations offer repair services.

Earnings

Median hourly earnings of automotive service technicians and mechanics, including commission, were $15.60 in May 2004. The middle 50 percent earned between $11.31 and $20.75 per hour. The lowest 10 percent earned less than $8.70, and the highest 10 percent earned more than $26.22 per hour. Median annual earnings in the industries employing the largest numbers of service technicians in May 2004 were as follows:

Local government	$38,160
Automobile dealers	38,060
Automotive repair and maintenance	28,810
Gasoline stations	28,030
Automotive parts, accessories, and tire stores	27,180

Many experienced technicians employed by automobile dealers and independent repair shops receive a commission related to the labor cost charged to the customer. Under this method, weekly earnings depend on the amount of work completed. Employers frequently guarantee commissioned technicians a minimum weekly salary.

Some automotive service technicians are members of labor unions such as the International Association of Machinists and Aerospace Workers; the International Union, United Automobile, Aerospace, and Agricultural Implement Workers of America; the Sheet Metal Workers' International Association; and the International Brotherhood of Teamsters.

Related Occupations

Other workers who repair and service motor vehicles include automotive body and related repairers, diesel service technicians and mechanics, and small engine mechanics.

Sources of Additional Information

For more details about work opportunities, contact local automobile dealers and repair shops or local offices of the state employment service. The state employment service also may have information about training programs.

A list of certified automotive service technician training programs can be obtained from

▸ National Automotive Technicians Education Foundation, 101 Blue Seal Dr. SE, Suite 101, Leesburg, VA 20175. Internet: http://www.natef.org

For a directory of accredited private trade and technical schools that offer programs in automotive service technician training, contact

▸ Accrediting Commission of Career Schools and Colleges of Technology, 2101 Wilson Blvd., Suite 302, Arlington, VA 22201. Internet: http://www.accsct.org

Information on automobile manufacturer-sponsored programs in automotive service technology can be obtained from

▸ Automotive Youth Educational Systems (AYES), 100 W. Big Beaver, Suite 300, Troy, MI 48084. Internet: http://www.ayes.org

Information on how to become a certified automotive service technician is available from

▸ National Institute for Automotive Service Excellence (ASE), 101 Blue Seal Dr. SE, Suite 101, Leesburg, VA 20175. Internet: http://www.asecert.org

For general information about a career as an automotive service technician, contact

▸ National Automobile Dealers Association, 8400 Westpark Dr., McLean, VA 22102. Internet: http://www.nada.org

▸ Automotive Retailing Today, 8400 Westpark Dr., MS #2, McLean, VA 22102. Internet: http://www.autoretailing.org

▸ Automotive Jobs Today, 8400 Westpark Dr., MS #2, McLean, VA 22102. Internet: http://www.autojobstoday.org

▸ Career Voyages, U.S. Department of Labor, 200 Constitution Ave. NW, Washington, DC 20210. Internet: http://www.careervoyages.gov/automotive-main.cfm

Biological Scientists

(O*NET 19-1020.01, 19-1021.01, 19-1021.02, 19-1022.00, 19-1023.00, and 19-1029.99)

Significant Points

■ A Ph.D. degree usually is required for independent research, but a master's degree is sufficient for some jobs in applied research or product development; a bachelor's degree is adequate for some nonresearch jobs.

■ Doctoral degree holders face competition for basic research positions; holders of bachelor's or master's degrees in biological science can expect better opportunities in nonresearch positions.

■ Biotechnological research and development will continue to drive employment growth.

Nature of the Work

Biological scientists study living organisms and their relationship to their environment. They research problems dealing with life processes and living organisms. Most specialize in some area of biology, such as zoology (the study of animals) or microbiology (the study of microscopic organisms). (Medical scientists, whose work is closely related to that of biological scientists, are discussed elsewhere in this book.)

Many biological scientists work in research and development. Some conduct basic research to advance knowledge of living organisms, including viruses, bacteria, and other infectious agents. Basic biological research continues to provide the building blocks necessary to develop solutions to human health problems and to preserve and repair the natural environment. Biological scientists mostly work independently in private industry, university, or government laboratories, often exploring new areas of research or expanding on specialized research started in graduate school. Those who are not wage and salary workers in private industry typically submit grant proposals to obtain funding for their projects. Colleges and universities, private industry, and federal government agencies such as the National Institutes of Health and the National Science Foundation contribute to the support of scientists whose research proposals are determined to be financially feasible and to have the potential to advance new ideas or processes.

Biological scientists who work in applied research or product development use knowledge provided by basic research to develop new drugs, treatments, and medical diagnostic tests; increase crop yields; and protect and clean up the environment by developing new biofuels. They usually have less autonomy than basic researchers to choose the emphasis of their research, relying instead on market-driven directions based on their firms' products and goals. Because biological scientists doing applied research and product development in private industry may be required to describe their research plans or results to nonscientists who are in a position to veto or approve their ideas, they must understand the potential cost of their work and its impact on business. Scientists often work in teams, interacting with engineers, scientists of other disciplines, business managers, and technicians. Some biological scientists also work with customers or suppliers and manage budgets.

Those who conduct research usually work in laboratories and use electron microscopes, computers, thermal cyclers, and a wide variety of other equipment. Some conduct experiments using laboratory animals or greenhouse plants. This is particularly true of botanists, physiologists, and zoologists. For some biological scientists, research also is performed outside of laboratories. For example, a botanist might do research in tropical rain forests to see what plants grow there, or an ecologist might study how a forest area recovers after a fire. Some marine biologists also work outdoors, often on research vessels from which they study various marine organisms such as marine plankton or fish.

Some biological scientists work in managerial or administrative positions, usually after spending some time doing research and learning about a particular firm, agency, or project. They may plan and administer programs for testing foods and drugs, for example, or direct activities at zoos or botanical gardens. Some work as consultants to businesses or to government agencies.

Recent advances in biotechnology and information technology are transforming the industries in which biological scientists work. In the 1980s, swift advances in basic biological knowledge related to genetics and molecules spurred growth in the field of biotechnology. Biological scientists using this technology manipulate the genetic material of animals or plants, attempting to make organisms more productive or resistant to disease. Research using biotechnology techniques, such as recombining DNA, has led to the production of important substances, including human insulin and growth hormone. Many other substances not previously available in large quantities are starting to be produced by biotechnological means; some may be useful in treating cancer and other diseases. Today, many biological scientists are involved in biotechnology. Those who work on the Human Genome Project isolate genes and determine their function. This work continues to lead to the discovery of the genes associated with specific diseases and inherited traits, such as certain types of cancer or obesity. These advances in biotechnology have created research opportunities in almost all areas of biology, with commercial applications in the food industry, agriculture, and environmental remediation and in other emerging areas such as DNA fingerprinting.

Most biological scientists are further classified by the type of organism they study or by the specific activity they perform, although recent advances in the understanding of basic life processes at the molecular and cellular levels have blurred some traditional classifications.

Aquatic biologists study micro-organisms, plants, and animals living in water. *Marine biologists* study saltwater organisms, and *limnologists* study freshwater organisms. Much of the work of marine biology centers on molecular biology, the study of the biochemical processes that take place inside living cells. Marine biologists sometimes are mistakenly called oceanographers, but oceanography is the study of the physical characteristics of oceans and the ocean floor. (See this book's descriptions of environmental scientists and hydrologists and of geoscientists.)

Biochemists study the chemical composition of living things. They analyze the complex chemical combinations and reactions involved in metabolism, reproduction, growth, and heredity. Biochemists and molecular biologists do most of their work in biotechnology, which involves understanding the complex chemistry of life.

Botanists study plants and their environment. Some study all aspects of plant life, including algae, fungi, lichens, mosses, ferns, conifers, and flowering plants; others specialize in areas such as identification and classification of plants, the structure and function of plant parts, the biochemistry of plant processes, the causes and cures of plant diseases, the interaction of plants with other organisms and the environment, and the geological record of plants.

Microbiologists investigate the growth and characteristics of microscopic organisms such as bacteria, algae, or fungi. Most microbiologists specialize in environmental, food, agricultural, or industrial microbiology; virology (the study of viruses); immunology (the study of mechanisms that fight infections); or bioinformatics (the process of integrating molecular biology and information science). Many microbiologists use biotechnology to advance knowledge of cell reproduction and human disease.

Physiologists study life functions of plants and animals, both in the whole organism and at the cellular or molecular level, under normal and abnormal conditions. Physiologists often specialize in functions such as growth, reproduction, photosynthesis, respiration, or movement or in the physiology of a certain area or system of the organism.

Biophysicists study the application of principles of physics, such as electrical and mechanical energy and related phenomena, to living cells and organisms.

Zoologists and wildlife biologists study animals and wildlife—their origin, behavior, diseases, and life processes. Some experiment with live animals in controlled or natural surroundings, while others dissect dead animals to study their structure. Zoologists and wildlife biologists also may collect and analyze biological data to determine the environmental effects of current and potential use of land and water areas. Zoologists usually are identified by the animal group studied—ornithologists (birds), mammalogists (mammals), herpetologists (reptiles), and ichthyologists (fish).

Ecologists study the relationships among organisms and between organisms and their environments, examining the effects of population size, pollutants, rainfall, temperature, and altitude. Using knowledge of various scientific disciplines, ecologists may collect, study, and report data on the quality of air, food, soil, and water.

Agricultural and food scientists, sometimes referred to as biological scientists, are discussed elsewhere in this book.

Working Conditions

Biological scientists usually work regular hours in offices or laboratories and usually are not exposed to unsafe or unhealthy conditions. Those who work with dangerous organisms or toxic substances in the laboratory must follow strict safety procedures to avoid contamination. Many biological scientists such as botanists, ecologists, and zoologists take field trips that involve strenuous physical activity and primitive living conditions. Biological scientists in the field may work in warm or cold climates in all kinds of weather. In their research, they may dig, chip with a hammer, scoop with a net, and carry equipment in a backpack. They also may climb, stand, kneel, or dive.

Marine biologists encounter a variety of working conditions. Some marine biologists work in laboratories; others work on research ships. Marine biologists who work underwater must practice safe diving while working around sharp coral reefs and hazardous marine life. Although some marine biologists obtain their specimens from the sea, many still spend a good deal of their time in laboratories and offices, conducting tests, running experiments, recording results, and compiling data.

Some biological scientists depend on grant money to support their research. They may be under pressure to meet deadlines and to conform to rigid grant-writing specifications when preparing proposals to seek new or extended funding.

Training, Other Qualifications, and Advancement

A Ph.D. degree usually is necessary for independent research, industrial research, and college teaching, as well as for advancement to administrative positions. A master's degree is sufficient for some jobs in basic research, applied research or product development, management, or inspection; it also may qualify one to work as a research technician or as a teacher in an aquarium. The bachelor's degree is adequate for some nonresearch jobs. For example, some graduates with a bachelor's degree start as biological scientists in testing and inspection or get jobs related to biological science, such as technical sales or service representatives. In some cases, graduates with a bachelor's degree are able to work in a laboratory environment on their own projects, but this is unusual. Some may work as research assistants, whereas others become biological laboratory technicians or, with courses in education, high school biology teachers. (Elsewhere in this book, see the descriptions of clinical laboratory technologists and technicians and of science technicians.) Many with a bachelor's degree in biology enter medical, dental, veterinary, or other health profession schools.

In addition to required courses in chemistry and biology, undergraduate biological science majors usually study allied disciplines such as mathematics, physics, engineering, and computer science. Computer courses are essential because employers prefer job applicants who are able to apply computer skills to modeling and simulation tasks and to operate computerized laboratory equipment, particularly in emerging fields such as bioinformatics. Those interested in studying the environment also should take courses in environmental studies and become familiar with current legislation and regulations. Prospective biological scientists who hope to work as marine biologists should have at least a bachelor's degree in a biological or marine science. However, students should not overspecialize in undergraduate study, as knowledge of marine biology often is acquired in graduate study. Most colleges and universities offer bachelor's degrees in biological science, and many offer advanced degrees. Curriculums for advanced degrees often emphasize a subfield such as microbiology or botany, but not all universities offer all curriculums. Larger universities frequently have separate departments specializing in different areas of biological science. For example, a program in botany might cover agronomy, horticulture, or plant pathology. Advanced degree programs include classroom and fieldwork, laboratory research, and a thesis or dissertation.

Biological scientists with a Ph.D. often take temporary postdoctoral research positions that provide specialized research experience. Postdoctoral positions may offer the opportunity to publish research findings. A solid record of published research is essential in obtaining a permanent position involving basic research, especially for those seeking a permanent college or university faculty position. In private industry, some may become managers or administrators within the field of biology; others leave biology for nontechnical managerial, administrative, or sales jobs.

Biological scientists should be able to work independently or as part of a team and be able to communicate clearly and concisely, both orally and in writing. Those in private industry, especially those who aspire to management or administrative positions, should possess strong business and communication skills and be familiar with regulatory issues and marketing and management techniques. Those doing field research in remote areas must have physical stamina. Biological scientists also must have patience and self-discipline to conduct long and detailed research projects.

Employment

Biological scientists held about 77,000 jobs in 2004. Slightly more than half of all biological scientists were employed by federal, state, and local governments. Federal biological scientists worked mainly for the U.S. Departments of Agriculture, Interior, and Defense and for the National Institutes of Health. Most of the rest worked in scientific research and testing laboratories, the pharmaceutical and medicine manufacturing industry, or hospitals.

In addition, many biological scientists held biology faculty positions in colleges and universities. (See the description of teachers—postsecondary elsewhere in this book.)

Job Outlook

Employment of biological scientists is projected to grow about as fast as average for all occupations over the 2004–2014 period, as biotechnological research and development continues to drive job growth. However, doctoral degree holders face competition for basic research positions. The federal government funds much basic research and development, including many areas of medical research that relate to biological science. Recent budget increases at the National Institutes of Health have led to large increases in federal basic research and development expenditures, with research grants growing both in number and in dollar amount. Nevertheless, the increase in expenditures is expected to slow significantly over the 2004–2014 projection period, resulting in a highly competitive environment for winning and renewing research grants. Furthermore, should the number of advanced degrees awarded continue to grow, applicants for research grants are likely to face even more competition. Currently, about 1 in 3 grant proposals are approved for long-term research projects. In addition, applied research positions in private industry may become more difficult to obtain if increasing numbers of scientists seek jobs in private industry because of the competitive job market for independent research positions in universities and for college and university faculty.

Opportunities for those with a bachelor's or master's degree in biological science are expected to be better. The number of science-related jobs in sales, marketing, and research management for which non-Ph.D.s usually qualify is expected to exceed the number of independent research positions. Non-Ph.D.s also may fill positions as science or engineering technicians or as medical health technologists and technicians. Some may become high school biology teachers.

Biological scientists enjoyed very rapid gains in employment between the mid-1980s and mid-1990s—reflecting, in part, increased staffing requirements in new biotechnology companies. Employment growth should slow somewhat, along with a slowdown in the number of new biotechnology firms; some existing firms will merge or be absorbed by larger biotechnology or pharmaceutical firms. However, much of the basic biological research done in recent years has resulted in new knowledge, including the isolation and identification of genes. Biological scientists will be needed to take this knowledge to the next stage, which is understanding how certain genes function within an entire organism, so that gene therapies can be developed to treat diseases. Even pharmaceutical and other firms not solely engaged in biotechnology use biotechnology techniques extensively, spurring employment increases for biological scientists. For example, biological scientists are continuing to help farmers increase crop yields by pinpointing genes that can help crops such as wheat grow worldwide in areas that currently are hostile to the crop. Expected expansion of research related to health issues such as AIDS, cancer, and Alzheimer's disease also should create more jobs for these scientists. In addition, efforts to discover new and improved ways to clean up and preserve the environment will continue to add to job growth. More biological scientists will be needed to determine the environmental impact of industry and government actions and to prevent or correct environmental problems such as the negative effects of pesticide use. Some biological scientists will find opportunities in environmental regulatory agencies; others will use their expertise to advise lawmakers on legislation to save environmentally sensitive areas. There will continue to be demand for biological scientists specializing in botany, zoology, and marine biology, but opportunities will be limited because of the small size of these fields. New industrial applications of biotechnology, such as changing how companies make ethanol for transportation fuel, also will spur demand for biological scientists.

Marine biology, despite its attractiveness as a career, is a very small specialty within biological science. Prospective marine biology students should be aware that those who would like to enter this specialty far outnumber the very few openings that occur each year for the type of glamorous research jobs that many would like to obtain. Almost all marine biologists who do basic research have a Ph.D.

Biological scientists are less likely to lose their jobs during recessions than are those in many other occupations because many are employed on long-term research projects. However, an economic downturn could influence the amount of money allocated to new research and development efforts, particularly in areas of risky or innovative research. An economic downturn also could limit the possibility of extension or renewal of existing projects.

Earnings

Median annual earnings of biochemists and biophysicists were $68,950 in May 2004. The middle 50 percent earned between $49,430 and $88,540. The lowest 10 percent earned less than $38,710, and the highest 10 percent earned more than $110,660. Median annual earnings of microbiologists were $54,840 in May 2004. The middle 50 percent earned between $41,000 and $74,260. The lowest 10 percent earned less than $32,630, and the highest 10 percent earned more than $101,720. Median annual earnings of zoologists and wildlife biologists were $50,330 in May 2004. The middle 50 percent earned between $39,150 and $63,800. The lowest 10 percent earned less than $31,450, and the highest 10 percent earned more than $81,200. Median annual earnings of biochemists and biophysicists employed in scientific research and development services were $73,900 in May 2004.

According to the National Association of Colleges and Employers, beginning salary offers in July 2005 averaged $31,258 a year for bachelor's degree recipients in biological and life sciences.

In the federal government in 2005, general biological scientists in nonsupervisory, supervisory, and managerial positions earned an average salary of $69,908; microbiologists, $80,798; ecologists, $72,021; physiologists, $93,208; geneticists, $85,170; zoologists, $101,601; and botanists, $62,207.

Related Occupations

Many other occupations deal with living organisms and require a level of training similar to that of biological scientists. These include medical scientists, agricultural and food scientists, and conservation scientists and foresters as well as health occupations such as physicians and surgeons, dentists, and veterinarians.

Sources of Additional Information

For information on careers in the biological sciences, contact

▸ American Institute of Biological Sciences, 1444 I St. NW, Suite 200, Washington, DC 20005. Internet: http://www.aibs.org

For information on careers in biochemistry or biological sciences, contact

▸ Federation of American Societies for Experimental Biology, 9650 Rockville Pike, Bethesda, MD 20814. Internet: http://www.faseb.org

For a brochure titled *Careers in Botany*, contact

▸ The Botanical Society of America, 4475 Castleman Ave., P.O. Box 299, St. Louis, MO 63166. Internet: http://www.botany.org

For information on careers in microbiology, contact

▸ American Society for Microbiology, Career Information–Education Department, 1752 N St. NW, Washington, DC 20036. Internet: http://www.asm.org

Information on obtaining a biological scientist position with the federal government is available from the Office of Personnel Management through USAJOBS, the federal government's official employment information system. This resource for locating and applying for job opportunities can be accessed through the Internet at http://www.usajobs.opm.gov or through an interactive voice response telephone system at (703) 724-1850 or TDD (978) 461-8404. These numbers are not toll free, and charges may result.

Broadcast and Sound Engineering Technicians and Radio Operators

(O*NET 27-4011.00, 27-4012.00, 27-4013.00, and 27-4014.00)

Significant Points

■ Job applicants will face keen competition for jobs in major metropolitan areas, where pay generally is higher; prospects are expected to be better in small cities and towns.

■ Technical school, community college, or college training in broadcast technology, electronics, or computer networking provides the best preparation.

■ About 30 percent work in broadcasting, mainly for radio and television stations, and 17 percent work in the motion picture, video, and sound recording industries.

■ Evening, weekend, and holiday work is common.

Nature of the Work

Broadcast and sound engineering technicians and radio operators set up, operate, and maintain a wide variety of electrical and electronic equipment involved in almost any radio or television broadcast, concert, play, musical recording, television show, or movie. With such a range of work, there are many specialized occupations within the field.

Audio and video equipment technicians set up and operate audio and video equipment, including microphones, sound speakers, video screens, projectors, video monitors, recording equipment, connecting wires and cables, sound and mixing boards, and related electronic equipment for concerts, sports events, meetings and conventions, presentations, and news conferences. They also may set up and operate associated spotlights and other custom lighting systems.

Broadcast technicians set up, operate, and maintain equipment that regulates the signal strength, clarity, and range of sounds and colors of radio or television broadcasts. These technicians also operate control panels to select the source of the material. Technicians may switch from one camera or studio to another, from film to live programming, or from network to local programming.

Sound engineering technicians operate machines and equipment to record, synchronize, mix, or reproduce music, voices, or sound effects in recording studios, sporting arenas, theater productions, or movie and video productions.

Radio operators mainly receive and transmit communications using a variety of tools. These workers also repair equipment, using such devices as electronic testing equipment, hand tools, and power tools. One of their major duties is to help to maintain communication systems in good condition.

The transition to digital recording, editing, and broadcasting has greatly changed the work of broadcast and sound engineering technicians and radio operators. Software on desktop computers has replaced specialized electronic equipment in many recording and editing functions. Most radio and television stations have replaced videotapes and audiotapes with computer hard drives and other computer data storage systems. Computer networks linked to specialized equipment dominate modern broadcasting. This transition has forced technicians to learn computer networking and software skills. (See the description of computer support specialists and systems administrators elsewhere in this book.)

Broadcast and sound engineering technicians and radio operators perform a variety of duties in small stations. In large stations and at the networks, technicians are more specialized, although job assignments may change from day to day. The terms "operator," "engineer," and "technician" often are used interchangeably to describe these jobs. Workers in these positions may monitor and log outgoing signals and operate transmitters; set up, adjust, service, and repair electronic broadcasting equipment; and regulate fidelity, brightness, contrast, volume, and sound quality of television broadcasts.

Technicians also work in program production. *Recording engineers* operate and maintain video and sound recording equipment. They may operate equipment designed to produce special effects, such as the illusions of a bolt of lightning or a police siren. *Sound mixers* or *re-recording mixers* produce soundtracks for movies or television programs. After filming or recording is complete, these workers may use a process called "dubbing" to insert sounds. *Field technicians* set up and operate portable transmission equipment outside the studio. Because television news coverage requires so much electronic equipment and the technology is changing so rapidly, many stations assign technicians exclusively to news.

Chief engineers, transmission engineers, and *broadcast field supervisors* oversee other technicians and maintain broadcasting equipment.

Working Conditions

Broadcast and sound engineering technicians and radio operators generally work indoors in pleasant surroundings. However, those who broadcast news and other programs from locations outside the studio may work outdoors in all types of weather. Technicians doing maintenance may climb poles or antenna towers, while those setting up equipment do heavy lifting.

Technicians at large stations and the networks usually work a 40-hour week under great pressure to meet broadcast deadlines and may occasionally work overtime. Technicians at small stations routinely work more than 40 hours a week. Evening, weekend, and holiday work is usual because most stations are on the air 18 to 24 hours a day, 7 days a week. Even though a technician may not be on duty when the station is broadcasting, some technicians may be on call during nonwork hours; these workers must handle any problems that occur when they are on call.

Technicians who work on motion pictures may be on a tight schedule and may work long hours to meet contractual deadlines.

Training, Other Qualifications, and Advancement

The best way to prepare for a broadcast and sound engineering technician job is to obtain technical school, community college, or college training in broadcast technology, electronics, or computer networking. In the motion picture industry, people are hired as apprentice editorial assistants and work their way up to more skilled jobs. Employers in the motion picture industry usually hire experienced freelance technicians on a picture-by-picture basis. Reputation and determination are important in getting jobs.

When starting out, broadcast and sound engineering technicians learn skills on the job from experienced technicians and supervisors. These beginners often start their careers in small stations and, once experienced, move on to larger ones. Large stations usually hire only technicians with experience. Experienced technicians can become supervisory technicians or chief engineers. A college degree in engineering is needed in order to become chief engineer at a large television station. Many employers pay tuition and expenses for courses or seminars to help technicians keep abreast of developments in the field.

Audio and video equipment technicians generally need a high school diploma. Many recent entrants have a community college degree or other forms of postsecondary degrees, although they are not always required. These technicians may substitute on-the-job training for formal education requirements. Working in a studio as an assistant is a great way of gaining experience and knowledge.

Radio operators usually are not required to complete any formal training. This is an entry-level position that generally requires on-the-job training.

Licensing is not required for broadcast technicians. However, certification by the Society of Broadcast Engineers is a mark of competence and experience. The certificate is issued to experienced technicians who pass an examination.

Prospective technicians should take high school courses in math, physics, and electronics. Building electronic equipment from hobby kits and operating a "ham," or amateur, radio are good experience, as is working in college radio and television stations.

Broadcast and sound engineering technicians and radio operators must have manual dexterity and an aptitude for working with electrical, electronic, and mechanical systems and equipment.

Employment

Broadcast and sound engineering technicians and radio operators held about 95,000 jobs in 2004. Their employment was distributed among the following detailed occupations:

Audio and video equipment technicians 46,000

Broadcast technicians 34,000

Sound engineering technicians 13,000

Radio operators 2,000

About 30 percent worked in broadcasting (except Internet) and 17 percent worked in the motion picture, video, and sound recording industries. About 7 percent were self-employed. Television stations employ, on average, many more technicians than radio stations. Some technicians are employed in other industries, producing employee communications, sales, and training programs. Technician jobs in television and radio are located in virtually all cities; jobs in radio also are found in many small towns. The highest-paying and most specialized jobs are concentrated in New York City, Los Angeles, Chicago, and Washington, DC—the originating centers for most network or news programs. Motion picture production jobs are concentrated in Los Angeles and New York City.

Job Outlook

People seeking entry-level jobs as technicians in broadcasting are expected to face keen competition in major metropolitan areas, where pay generally is higher and the number of qualified jobseekers typically exceeds the number of openings. Prospects for entry-level positions are expected to be better in small cities and towns for beginners with appropriate training.

Overall employment of broadcast and sound engineering technicians and radio operators is expected to grow about as fast as average for all occupations through the year 2014. Job growth in radio and television broadcasting will be limited by consolidation of ownership of radio and television stations and by labor-saving technical advances, such as computer-controlled programming and remotely controlled transmitters. The Federal Communications Commission (FCC) is required to examine its media ownership rules quadrennially. Thus, the rules can change periodically. In 2005, FCC regulations stated that a single owner could own up to eight radio stations in a single large market and that a single owner could not own television stations that would reach more than 39 percent of households. Revisions to these rules have been passed by the FCC, but have not been implemented because of legal challenges. When broader common ownership is allowed, stations often are consolidated and operated from a single location, reducing employment because one or a few technicians can provide support to multiple stations. Technicians who know how to install transmitters will be in demand as television stations install digital transmitters. Although most television stations are broadcasting in both analog and digital formats and plan to switch entirely to digital, radio stations are only beginning to broadcast digital signals.

Employment of broadcast and sound engineering technicians in the cable and pay television portion of the broadcasting industry is expected to grow as the range of products and services expands, including cable Internet access and video-on-demand. Employment of these workers in the motion picture industry is expected to grow rapidly. However, job prospects are expected to remain competitive because of the large number of people who are attracted by the glamour of working in motion pictures.

Projected job growth varies among detailed occupations in this field. Employment of audio and video equipment technicians and sound engineering technicians is expected to grow faster than the average for all occupations. Not only will these workers have to set up audio and video equipment, but they will have to maintain and repair it as well. Employment of broadcast technicians is expected to grow about as fast as the average for all occupations through 2014 as advancements in technology enhance the capabilities of technicians to produce higher-quality radio and television programming. Employment of radio operators, on the other hand, is projected to decline as more stations control programming and operate transmitters remotely.

In addition to employment growth, job openings also will result from the need to replace experienced technicians who leave this field. Some of these workers leave for other jobs that require knowledge of electronics, such as computer repairer or industrial machinery repairer.

Earnings

Television stations usually pay higher salaries than radio stations, commercial broadcasting usually pays more than public broadcasting, and stations in large markets pay more than those in small markets.

Median annual earnings of audio and video equipment technicians in May 2004 were $32,570. The middle 50 percent earned between $24,180 and $44,290. The lowest 10 percent earned less than $19,110, and the highest 10 percent earned more than $58,620. Median annual earnings in motion picture and video industries, which employed the largest number of audio and video equipment technicians, were $33,670.

Median annual earnings of broadcast technicians in May 2004 were $28,010. The middle 50 percent earned between $19,240 and $42,760. The lowest 10 percent earned less than $14,960, and the highest 10 percent earned more than $62,850. Median annual earnings in radio and television broadcasting, which employed the largest number of broadcast technicians, were $25,220.

Median annual earnings of sound engineering technicians in May 2004 were $38,110. The middle 50 percent earned between $25,470 and $56,320. The lowest 10 percent earned less than $19,180, and the highest 10 percent earned more than $80,450.

Median annual earnings of radio operators in May 2004 were $32,720. The middle 50 percent earned between $23,960 and $43,850. The lowest 10 percent earned less than $17,960, and the highest 10 percent earned more than $57,420.

Related Occupations

Broadcast and sound engineering technicians and radio operators need the electronics training necessary to operate technical equipment, and they generally complete specialized postsecondary programs. Occupations with similar characteristics include engineering technicians, science technicians, and electrical and electronics installers and repairers. Broadcast and sound engineering technicians also may operate computer networks, as do computer support specialists and systems administrators. Broadcast technicians on some live radio and television programs screen incoming calls; these workers have responsibilities similar to those of communications equipment operators.

Sources of Additional Information

For career information and links to employment resources, contact

▸ National Association of Broadcasters, 1771 N St. NW, Washington, DC 20036. Internet: http://www.nab.org

For information on certification, contact

▸ Society of Broadcast Engineers, 9247 North Meridian St., Suite 305, Indianapolis, IN 46260. Internet: http://www.sbe.org

Cardiovascular Technologists and Technicians

(O*NET 29-2031.00)

Significant Points

■ About 3 out of 4 jobs are in hospitals.

■ The vast majority of cardiovascular technologists and technicians complete a 2-year junior or community college program.

■ Employment will grow much faster than the average, but the number of job openings created will be low because the occupation is small.

■ Employment of most specialties will grow, but fewer EKG technicians will be needed.

Nature of the Work

Cardiovascular technologists and technicians assist physicians in diagnosing and treating cardiac (heart) and peripheral vascular (blood vessel) ailments. Cardiovascular technologists may specialize in any of three areas of practice: invasive cardiology, echocardiography, and vascular technology. Cardiovascular technicians who specialize in electrocardiograms (EKGs), stress testing, and Holter monitors are known as *cardiographic technicians* or *EKG technicians*.

Cardiovascular technologists specializing in invasive procedures are called *cardiology technologists*. They assist physicians with cardiac catheterization procedures in which a small tube, or catheter, is threaded through a patient's artery from a spot on the patient's groin to the heart. The procedure can determine whether a blockage exists in the blood vessels that supply the heart muscle. The procedure also can help to diagnose other problems. Part of the procedure may involve balloon angioplasty, which can be used to treat blockages of blood vessels or heart valves without the need for heart surgery. Cardiology technologists assist physicians as they insert a catheter with a balloon on the end to the point of the obstruction.

Technologists prepare patients for cardiac catheterization and balloon angioplasty by first positioning them on an examining table and then shaving, cleaning, and administering anesthesia to the top of their leg near the groin. During the procedures, they monitor patients' blood pressure and heart rate with EKG equipment and notify the physician if something appears to be wrong. Technologists also may prepare and monitor patients during open-heart surgery and during the insertion of pacemakers and stents that open up blockages in arteries to the heart and major blood vessels.

Cardiovascular technologists who specialize in echocardiography or vascular technology often run noninvasive tests using ultrasound instrumentation, such as Doppler ultrasound. Tests are called "noninvasive" if they do not require the insertion of probes or other instruments into the patient's body. The ultrasound instrumentation transmits high-frequency sound waves into areas of the patient's body and then processes reflected echoes of the sound waves to form an image. Technologists view the ultrasound image on a screen and may record the image on videotape or photograph it for interpretation and diagnosis by a physician. As the instrument scans the image, technologists check the image on the screen for subtle differences between healthy and diseased areas, decide which images to include in the report to the physician, and judge whether the images are satisfactory for diagnostic purposes. They also explain the procedure to patients, record any additional medical history the patient relates, select appropriate equipment settings, and change the patient's position as necessary.

Those who assist physicians in the diagnosis of disorders affecting the circulation are known as *vascular technologists* or *vascular sonographers*. They perform a medical history, evaluate pulses, and assess blood flow in arteries and veins by listening to the vascular flow sounds for abnormalities. Then they perform a noninvasive procedure using ultrasound instrumentation to record vascular information such as vascular blood flow, blood pressure, changes in limb volume, oxygen saturation, cerebral circulation, peripheral circulation, and abdominal circulation. Many of these tests are performed during or immediately after surgery.

Technologists who use ultrasound to examine the heart chambers, valves, and vessels are referred to as *cardiac sonographers* or *echocardiographers*. They use ultrasound instrumentation to create images called echocardiograms. An echocardiogram may be performed while the patient is either resting or physically active. Technologists may administer medication to physically active patients to assess their heart function. Cardiac sonographers also may assist physicians who perform transesophageal echocardiography, which involves placing a tube in the patient's esophagus to obtain ultrasound images.

Cardiovascular technicians who obtain EKGs are known as *electrocardiograph* (or *EKG*) *technicians*. To take a basic EKG, which traces electrical impulses transmitted by the heart, technicians attach electrodes to the patient's chest, arms, and legs and then manipulate switches on an EKG machine to obtain a reading. An EKG is printed out for interpretation by the physician. This test is done before most kinds of surgery or as part of a routine physical examination, especially on persons who have reached middle age or who have a history of cardiovascular problems.

EKG technicians with advanced training perform Holter monitor and stress testing. For Holter monitoring, technicians place electrodes on the patient's chest and attach a portable EKG monitor to the patient's belt. Following 24 or more hours of normal activity by the patient, the technician removes a tape from the monitor and places it in a scanner. After checking the quality of the recorded impulses on an electronic screen, the technician usually prints the information from the tape for analysis by a physician. Physicians use the output from the scanner to diagnose heart ailments, such as heart rhythm abnormalities or problems with pacemakers.

For a treadmill stress test, EKG technicians document the patient's medical history, explain the procedure, connect the patient to an EKG monitor, and obtain a baseline reading and resting blood pressure. Next, they monitor the heart's performance while the patient is walking on a treadmill, gradually increasing the treadmill's speed to observe the effect of increased exertion. Like vascular technologists and cardiac sonographers, cardiographic technicians who perform EKG, Holter monitor, and stress tests are known as "noninvasive" technicians.

Some cardiovascular technologists and technicians schedule appointments, type doctors' interpretations, maintain patient files, and care for equipment.

Working Conditions

Technologists and technicians generally work a 5-day, 40-hour week that may include weekends. Those in catheterization laboratories tend to work longer hours and may work evenings. They also may be on call during the night and on weekends.

Cardiovascular technologists and technicians spend a lot of time walking and standing. Heavy lifting may be involved to move equipment or transfer patients. These workers wear heavy protective aprons while conducting some procedures. Those who work in catheterization laboratories may face stressful working conditions because they are in close contact with patients with serious heart ailments. For example, some patients may encounter complications that have life-or-death implications.

Training, Other Qualifications, and Advancement

Although a few cardiovascular technologists, vascular technologists, and cardiac sonographers are currently trained on the job, most receive training in 2- to 4-year programs. The majority of technologists complete a 2-year junior or community college program, but 4-year programs are increasingly available. The first year is dedicated to core courses and is followed by a year of specialized instruction in either invasive, noninvasive cardiovascular, or noninvasive vascular technology. Those who are qualified in an allied health profession need to complete only the year of specialized instruction.

Graduates of the 33 programs accredited by the Joint Review Committee on Education in Cardiovascular Technology are eligible to obtain professional certification in cardiac catheterization, echocardiography, vascular ultrasound, and cardiographic techniques from Cardiovascular Credentialing International. Cardiac sonographers and vascular technologists also may obtain certification from the American Registry of Diagnostic Medical Sonographers.

Most EKG technicians are trained on the job by an EKG supervisor or a cardiologist. On-the-job training usually lasts about 8 to 16 weeks. Most employers prefer to train people already in the health care field—nursing aides, for example. Some EKG technicians are students enrolled in 2-year programs to become technologists, working part time to gain experience and make contact with employers.

One-year certification programs exist for basic EKGs, Holter monitoring, and stress testing.

Cardiovascular technologists and technicians must be reliable, have mechanical aptitude, and be able to follow detailed instructions. A pleasant, relaxed manner for putting patients at ease is an asset.

Employment

Cardiovascular technologists and technicians held about 45,000 jobs in 2004. About 3 out 4 jobs were in hospitals (private and government), primarily in cardiology departments. The remaining jobs were mostly in offices of physicians, including cardiologists, or in medical and diagnostic laboratories, including diagnostic imaging centers.

Job Outlook

Employment of cardiovascular technologists and technicians is expected to grow much faster than the average for all occupations through the year 2014. Growth will occur as the population ages because older people have a higher incidence of heart problems and use more diagnostic imaging. Employment of vascular technologists and echocardiographers will grow as advances in vascular technology and sonography reduce the need for more costly and invasive procedures. However, fewer EKG technicians will be needed as hospitals train nursing aides and others to perform basic EKG procedures. Individuals trained in Holter monitoring and stress testing are expected to have more favorable job prospects than are those who can perform only a basic EKG.

Some job openings for cardiovascular technologists and technicians will arise from replacement needs as individuals transfer to other jobs or leave the labor force. However, job growth and replacement needs will produce relatively few job openings because the occupation is small.

Earnings

Median annual earnings of cardiovascular technologists and technicians were $38,690 in May 2004. The middle 50 percent earned between $27,890 and $50,130. The lowest 10 percent earned less than $21,790, and the highest 10 percent earned more than $59,000. Median annual earnings of cardiovascular technologists and technicians in May 2004 were $36,890 in offices of physicians and $38,150 in general medical and surgical hospitals.

Related Occupations

Cardiovascular technologists and technicians operate sophisticated equipment that helps physicians and other health practitioners to diagnose and treat patients. So do diagnostic medical sonographers, nuclear medicine technologists, radiation therapists, radiologic technologists and technicians, and respiratory therapists.

Sources of Additional Information

For general information about a career in cardiovascular technology, contact

▸ Alliance of Cardiovascular Professionals, Thalia Landing Offices, Bldg. 2, 4356 Bonney Rd., Suite 103, Virginia Beach, VA 23452-1200. Internet: http://www.acp-online.org

For a list of accredited programs in cardiovascular technology, contact

▸ Committee on Accreditation for Allied Health Education Programs, 39 East Wacker Dr., Chicago, IL 60601. Internet: http://www.caahep.org

▸ Joint Review Committee on Education in Cardiovascular Technology, 1248 Harwood Rd., Bedford, TX 76021.

For information on vascular technology, contact

▸ Society for Vascular Ultrasound, 4601 Presidents Dr., Suite 260, Lanham, MD 20706-4381. Internet: http://www.svunet.org

For information on echocardiography, contact

▸ American Society of Echocardiography, 1500 Sunday Dr., Suite 102, Raleigh, NC 27607. Internet: http://www.asecho.org

For information regarding registration and certification, contact

▸ Cardiovascular Credentialing International, 1500 Sunday Dr., Suite 102, Raleigh, NC 27607. Internet: http://www.cci-online.org

▸ American Registry of Diagnostic Medical Sonographers, 51 Monroe St., Plaza East One, Rockville, MD 20850-2400. Internet: http://www.ardms.org

Chemists and Materials Scientists

(O*NET 19-2031.00 and 19-2032.00)

Significant Points

■ A bachelor's degree in chemistry or a related discipline is the minimum educational requirement; however, many research jobs require a master's degree or, more often, a Ph.D.

■ Slower-than-average growth in employment is projected.

■ Job growth will be concentrated in pharmaceutical and medicine manufacturing companies and in professional, scientific, and technical services firms.

■ Graduates with a bachelor's degree will have opportunities at smaller research organizations; those with a master's degree, and particularly those with a Ph.D., will enjoy better opportunities at larger pharmaceutical and biotechnology firms.

Nature of the Work

Everything in the environment, whether naturally occurring or of human design, is composed of chemicals. Chemists and materials scientists search for and use new knowledge about chemicals. Chemical research has led to the discovery and development of new and improved synthetic fibers, paints, adhesives, drugs, cosmetics, electronic components, lubricants, and thousands of other products. Chemists and materials scientists also develop processes such as improved oil refining and petrochemical processing that save energy and reduce pollution. Research on the chemistry of living things spurs advances in medicine, agriculture, food processing, and other fields.

Materials scientists study the structures and chemical properties of various materials to develop new products or enhance existing ones. They also determine ways to strengthen or combine materials or develop new materials for use in a variety of products. Materials science encompasses the natural and synthetic materials used in a wide range of products and structures, from airplanes, cars, and bridges to clothing and household goods. Companies whose products are made of metals, ceramics, and rubber employ most materials scientists. Other applications of materials science include studies of superconducting materials, graphite materials, integrated-circuit chips, and fuel cells. Materials scientists, applying chemistry and physics, study all aspects of these materials. Chemistry plays an increasingly dominant role in materials science because it provides information about the structure and composition of materials. Materials scientists often specialize in specific areas such as ceramics or metals.

Many chemists and materials scientists work in research and development (R&D). In basic research, they investigate properties, composition, and structure of matter and the laws that govern the combination of elements and reactions of substances. In applied R&D, they create new products and processes or improve existing ones, often using knowledge gained from basic research. For example, synthetic rubber and plastics resulted from research on small molecules uniting to form large ones, a process called polymerization. R&D chemists and materials scientists use computers and a wide variety of sophisticated laboratory instrumentation for modeling and simulation in their work.

The use of computers to analyze complex data has allowed chemists and materials scientists to practice combinatorial chemistry. This technique makes and tests large quantities of chemical compounds simultaneously to find those with certain desired properties. Combinatorial chemistry has allowed chemists to produce thousands of compounds more quickly and inexpensively than was formerly possible and assisted in the completion of the sequencing of human genes. Today, specialty chemists, such as medicinal and organic chemists, are working with life scientists to translate this knowledge into new drugs.

Chemists also work in production and quality control in chemical manufacturing plants. They prepare instructions for plant workers that specify ingredients, mixing times, and temperatures for each stage in the process. They also monitor automated processes to ensure proper product yield and test samples of raw materials or finished products to ensure that they meet industry and government standards, including regulations governing pollution. Chemists report and document test results and analyze those results in hopes of improving existing theories or developing new test methods.

Chemists often specialize. *Analytical chemists* determine the structure, composition, and nature of substances by examining and identifying their various elements or compounds. These chemists are absolutely crucial to the pharmaceutical industry because pharmaceutical companies need to know the identity of compounds that they hope to turn into drugs. Furthermore, analytical chemists study the relations and interactions of the parts of compounds and develop analytical techniques. They also identify the presence and concentration of chemical pollutants in air, water, and soil. *Organic chemists* study the chemistry of the vast number of carbon compounds that make up all living things. Organic chemists who synthesize elements or simple compounds to create new compounds or substances that have different properties and applications have developed many commercial products, such as drugs, plastics, and elastomers (elastic substances similar to rubber). *Inorganic chemists* study compounds consisting mainly of elements other than carbon, such as those in electronic components. *Physical* and *theoretical chemists* study the physical characteristics of atoms and molecules and the theoretical properties of matter and investigate how chemical reactions work. Their research may result in new and better energy sources. *Macromolecular chemists* study the behavior of atoms and molecules. *Medicinal chemists* study the structural properties of compounds intended for applications to human medicine. *Materials chemists* study and develop new materials to improve existing products or make new ones. In fact, virtually all chemists are involved in this quest in one way or another. Developments in the field of chemistry that involve life sciences will expand, resulting in more interaction among biologists, engineers, computer specialists, and chemists. (*Biochemists*, whose work encompasses both biology and chemistry, are discussed in this book's description of biological scientists.)

Working Conditions

Chemists and materials scientists usually work regular hours in offices and laboratories. R&D chemists and materials scientists spend much time in laboratories but also work in offices when they do theoretical research or plan, record, and report on their lab research. Although some laboratories are small, others are large enough to incorporate prototype chemical manufacturing facilities as well as advanced equipment for chemists. In addition to working in a laboratory, materials scientists also work with engineers and processing specialists in industrial manufacturing facilities. After a material is sold, materials scientists often help customers tailor the material to suit their needs. Chemists do some of their work in a chemical plant or outdoors—while gathering water samples to test for pollutants, for example. Some chemists are exposed to health or safety hazards when handling certain chemicals, but there is little risk if proper procedures are followed.

Training, Other Qualifications, and Advancement

A bachelor's degree in chemistry or a related discipline usually is the minimum educational requirement for entry-level chemist jobs. However, many research jobs require a master's degree, or more often a Ph.D. While some materials scientists hold a degree in materials science, a bachelor's degree in chemistry, physics, or electrical engineering also is accepted. Many R&D jobs require a Ph.D. in materials science or a related science.

Many colleges and universities offer degree programs in chemistry. In 2005, the American Chemical Society (ACS) approved 631 bachelor's, 308 master's, and 192 doctoral degree programs. In addition to these schools, several hundred colleges and universities also offer

advanced degree programs in chemistry. The number of colleges that offer a degree program in materials science is small but gradually increasing.

Students planning careers as chemists and materials scientists should take courses in science and mathematics, should like working with their hands building scientific apparatus and performing laboratory experiments, and should like computer modeling. Perseverance, curiosity, and the ability to concentrate on detail and to work independently are essential. Interaction among specialists in this field is increasing, especially for specialty chemists in drug development. One type of chemist often relies on the findings of another type of chemist. For example, an organic chemist must understand findings on the identity of compounds prepared by an analytical chemist.

In addition to required courses in analytical, inorganic, organic, and physical chemistry, undergraduate chemistry majors usually study biological sciences; mathematics; physics; and increasingly, computer science. Computer courses are essential because employers prefer job applicants who are able to apply computer skills to modeling and simulation tasks and operate computerized laboratory equipment. This is increasingly important as combinatorial chemistry and high-throughput screening (HTS)—the ability to enhance processing capacity—techniques are more widely applied. Those interested in the environmental field also should take courses in environmental studies and become familiar with current legislation and regulations. Specific courses should include atmospheric chemistry, water chemistry, soil chemistry, and energy. Courses in statistics are useful because both chemists and materials scientists need the ability to apply basic statistical techniques.

Because R&D chemists and materials scientists are increasingly expected to work on interdisciplinary teams, some understanding of other disciplines, including business and marketing or economics, is desirable, along with leadership ability and good oral and written communication skills. Experience, either in academic laboratories or through internships, fellowships, or work-study programs in industry, also is useful. Some employers of research chemists, particularly in the pharmaceutical industry, prefer to hire individuals with several years of postdoctoral experience.

Graduate students typically specialize in a subfield of chemistry, such as analytical chemistry or polymer chemistry, depending on their interests and the kind of work they wish to do. For example, those interested in doing drug research in the pharmaceutical industry usually develop a strong background in medicinal or synthetic organic chemistry. However, students normally need not specialize at the undergraduate level. In fact, undergraduates who are broadly trained have more flexibility when job hunting or changing jobs than if they have narrowly defined their interests. Most employers provide new graduates additional training or education.

In government or industry, beginning chemists with a bachelor's degree work in quality control, perform analytical testing, or assist senior chemists in R&D laboratories. Many employers prefer chemists and materials scientists with a Ph.D., or at least a master's degree, to lead basic and applied research. Chemists who hold a Ph.D. and have previous industrial experience may be particularly attractive to employers because such people are more likely to understand the complex regulations that apply to the pharmaceutical industry. Within materials science, a broad background in various sciences is preferred. This broad base may be obtained through degrees in physics, engineering, or chemistry. While many companies prefer hiring Ph.D.s, some may employ materials scientists with bachelor's and master's degrees.

Employment

Chemists and materials scientists held about 90,000 jobs in 2004. About 43 percent of all chemists and material scientists are employed in manufacturing firms—mostly in the chemical manufacturing industry, which includes firms that produce plastics and synthetic materials, drugs, soaps and cleaners, pesticides and fertilizers, paint, industrial organic chemicals, and other chemical products. About 15 percent of chemists and material scientists work in scientific research and development services; 12 percent work in architectural, engineering, and related services. In addition, thousands of people with a background in chemistry and materials science hold teaching positions in high schools and in colleges and universities. (See the descriptions of teachers—postsecondary elsewhere in this book.)

Chemists and materials scientists are employed in all parts of the country, but they are mainly concentrated in large industrial areas.

Job Outlook

Employment of chemists is expected to grow more slowly than the average rate for all occupations through 2014. Job growth will be concentrated in pharmaceutical and medicine manufacturing and in professional, scientific, and technical services firms. Employment in the nonpharmaceutical segments of the chemical industry, a major employer of chemists, is expected to decline over the projection period. Consequently, new chemists at all levels may experience competition for jobs in these segments, including basic chemical manufacturing and synthetic materials. Graduates with a bachelor's degree may find science-related jobs in sales, marketing, and middle management. Some become chemical technicians or technologists or high school chemistry teachers. In addition, bachelor's degree holders are increasingly finding assistant research positions at smaller research organizations. Graduates with a master's degree, and particularly those with a Ph.D., will enjoy better opportunities at larger pharmaceutical and biotechnology firms. Furthermore, those with an advanced degree will continue to fill most senior research and upper management positions, although applicants are likely to experience competition for these jobs.

Within the chemical industry, job opportunities are expected to be most plentiful in pharmaceutical and biotechnology firms. Biotechnological research, including studies of human genes, continues to offer possibilities for the development of new drugs and products to combat illnesses and diseases that have previously been unresponsive to treatments derived by traditional chemical processes. Stronger competition among drug companies and an aging population are contributing to the need for new drugs.

Employment in the remaining segments of the chemical industry is expected to decline as companies downsize. To control costs, most chemical companies, including many large pharmaceutical and biotechnology companies, will increasingly turn to scientific R&D services firms to perform specialized research and other work formerly done by in-house chemists. As a result, these firms will experience healthy growth. Despite downsizing, some job openings will result from the need to replace chemists who retire or otherwise leave the labor force, although not all positions will be filled. Quality control will continue to be an important issue in chemical manufacturing and other industries that use chemicals in their manufacturing processes.

Chemists also will be needed to develop and improve the technologies and processes used to produce chemicals for all purposes and to monitor and measure air and water pollutants to ensure compliance with local, state, and federal environmental regulations. Environmental research will offer many new opportunities for chemists and materials scientists. To satisfy public concerns and to comply with government regulations, the chemical industry will continue to invest billions of dollars each year in technology that reduces pollution and cleans up existing waste sites. Chemists also are needed to find ways to use less energy and to discover alternative sources of energy.

During periods of economic recession, layoffs of chemists may occur—especially in the industrial chemicals industry. Layoffs are less likely in the pharmaceutical industry, where long development cycles generally overshadow short-term economic effects. The traditional chemical industry, however, provides many raw materials to the auto manufacturing and construction industries, both of which are vulnerable to temporary slowdowns during recessions.

Earnings

Median annual earnings of chemists in May 2004 were $56,060. The middle 50 percent earned between $41,900 and $76,080. The lowest 10 percent earned less than $33,170, and the highest 10 percent earned more than $98,010. Median annual earnings of materials scientists in May 2004 were $72,390. The middle 50 percent earned between $53,350 and $92,340. The lowest 10 percent earned less than $40,030, and the highest 10 percent earned more than $113,460. Median annual earnings in the industries employing the largest numbers of chemists in May 2004 are shown here:

Federal government $80,550

Scientific research and development services 62,460

Pharmaceutical and medicine manufacturing 57,050

Architectural, engineering, and related services 42,370

The ACS reports that in 2004 the median salary of all of its members with a bachelor's degree was $62,000; for those with a master's degree, it was $72,300; and for those with a Ph.D., it was $91,600. The median salary was highest for those working in private industry and lowest for those in academia. According to an ACS survey of recent graduates, inexperienced chemistry graduates with a bachelor's degree earned a median starting salary of $32,500 in October 2004; those with a master's degree earned a median salary of $43,600; and those with a Ph.D. had median earnings of $65,000. Among bachelor's degree graduates, those who had completed internships or had other work experience while in school commanded the highest starting salaries.

In 2005, chemists in nonsupervisory, supervisory, and managerial positions in the federal government averaged $83,777 a year.

Related Occupations

The research and analysis conducted by chemists and materials scientists is closely related to work done by agricultural and food scientists, biological scientists, medical scientists, chemical engineers, materials engineers, physicists, and science technicians.

Sources of Additional Information

General information on career opportunities and earnings for chemists is available from

▸ American Chemical Society, Education Division, 1155 16th St. NW, Washington, DC 20036. Internet: http://www.acs.org

Information on obtaining a position as a chemist with the federal government is available from the Office of Personnel Management through USAJOBS, the federal government's official employment information system. This resource for locating and applying for job opportunities can be accessed through the Internet at http://www.usajobs.opm.gov or through an interactive voice response telephone system at (703) 724-1850 or TDD (978) 461-8404. These numbers are not toll free, and charges may result.

Chiropractors

(O*NET 29-1011.00)

Significant Points

■ Job prospects should be good; employment is expected to increase faster than average as consumer demand for alternative health care grows.

■ Chiropractors must be licensed, requiring 2 to 4 years of undergraduate education, the completion of a 4-year chiropractic college course, and passing scores on national and state examinations.

■ About 58 percent of chiropractors are self-employed.

■ Earnings are relatively low in the beginning, but increase as the practice grows.

Nature of the Work

Chiropractors, also known as *doctors of chiropractic* or *chiropractic physicians*, diagnose and treat patients whose health problems are associated with the body's muscular, nervous, and skeletal systems, especially the spine. Chiropractors believe that interference with these systems impairs the body's normal functions and lowers its resistance to disease. They also hold that spinal or vertebral dysfunction alters many important body functions by affecting the nervous system and that skeletal imbalance through joint or articular dysfunction, especially in the spine, can cause pain.

The chiropractic approach to health care is holistic, stressing the patient's overall health and wellness. It recognizes that many factors affect health, including exercise, diet, rest, environment, and heredity. Chiropractors provide natural, drugless, nonsurgical health treat-

ments and rely on the body's inherent recuperative abilities. They also recommend changes in lifestyle—in eating, exercise, and sleeping habits, for example—to their patients. When appropriate, chiropractors consult with and refer patients to other health practitioners.

Like other health practitioners, chiropractors follow a standard routine to secure the information they need for diagnosis and treatment. They take the patient's medical history; conduct physical, neurological, and orthopedic examinations; and may order laboratory tests. X rays and other diagnostic images are important tools because of the chiropractor's emphasis on the spine and its proper function. Chiropractors also employ a postural and spinal analysis common to chiropractic diagnosis.

In cases in which difficulties can be traced to the involvement of musculoskeletal structures, chiropractors manually adjust the spinal column. Some chiropractors use water, light, massage, ultrasound, electric, acupuncture, and heat therapy. They also may apply supports such as straps, tapes, and braces. Chiropractors counsel patients about wellness concepts such as nutrition, exercise, changes in lifestyle, and stress management, but do not prescribe drugs or perform surgery.

Some chiropractors specialize in sports injuries, neurology, orthopedics, pediatrics, nutrition, internal disorders, or diagnostic imaging.

Many chiropractors are solo or group practitioners who also have the administrative responsibilities of running a practice. In larger offices, chiropractors delegate these tasks to office managers and chiropractic assistants. Chiropractors in private practice are responsible for developing a patient base, hiring employees, and keeping records.

Working Conditions

Chiropractors work in clean, comfortable offices. Their average workweek is about 40 hours, although longer hours are not uncommon. Solo practitioners set their own hours, but may work evenings or weekends to accommodate patients.

Like other health practitioners, chiropractors are sometimes on their feet for long periods. Chiropractors who take X rays must employ appropriate precautions against the dangers of repeated exposure to radiation.

Training, Other Qualifications, and Advancement

All states and the District of Columbia regulate the practice of chiropractic and grant licenses to chiropractors who meet the educational and examination requirements established by the state. Chiropractors can practice only in states where they are licensed. Some states have agreements permitting chiropractors licensed in one state to obtain a license in another without further examination, provided that their educational, examination, and practice credentials meet state specifications.

Most state boards require at least 2 years of undergraduate education; an increasing number are requiring a 4-year bachelor's degree. All boards require the completion of a 4-year program at an accredited chiropractic college leading to the Doctor of Chiropractic degree.

For licensure, most state boards recognize either all or part of the four-part test administered by the National Board of Chiropractic Examiners. State examinations may supplement the National Board tests, depending on state requirements. All states except New Jersey require the completion of a specified number of hours of continuing education each year in order to maintain licensure. Chiropractic associations and accredited chiropractic programs and institutions offer continuing education programs.

In 2005, 15 chiropractic programs and 2 chiropractic institutions in the United States were accredited by the Council on Chiropractic Education. Applicants are required to have at least 90 semester hours of undergraduate study leading toward a bachelor's degree, including courses in English, the social sciences or humanities, organic and inorganic chemistry, biology, physics, and psychology. Many applicants have a bachelor's degree, which may eventually become the minimum entry requirement. Several chiropractic colleges offer prechiropractic study as well as a bachelor's degree program. Recognition of prechiropractic education offered by chiropractic colleges varies among the state boards.

Chiropractic programs require a minimum of 4,200 hours of combined classroom, laboratory, and clinical experience. During the first 2 years, most chiropractic programs emphasize classroom and laboratory work in basic science subjects such as anatomy, physiology, public health, microbiology, pathology, and biochemistry. The last 2 years stress courses in manipulation and spinal adjustment and provide clinical experience in physical and laboratory diagnosis, neurology, orthopedics, geriatrics, physiotherapy, and nutrition. Chiropractic programs and institutions grant the degree of Doctor of Chiropractic.

Chiropractic colleges also offer postdoctoral training in orthopedics, neurology, sports injuries, nutrition, rehabilitation, radiology, industrial consulting, family practice, pediatrics, and applied chiropractic sciences. Once such training is complete, chiropractors may take specialty exams leading to "diplomate" status in a given specialty. Exams are administered by specialty chiropractic associations.

Chiropractic requires keen observation to detect physical abnormalities. It also takes considerable manual dexterity, but not unusual strength or endurance, to perform adjustments. Chiropractors should be able to work independently and handle responsibility. As in other health-related occupations, empathy, understanding, and the desire to help others are good qualities for dealing effectively with patients.

Newly licensed chiropractors can set up a new practice, purchase an established one, or enter into partnership with an established practitioner. They also may take a salaried position with an established chiropractor, a group practice, or a health care facility.

Employment

Chiropractors held about 53,000 jobs in 2004. Approximately 58 percent of chiropractors are self-employed. Most chiropractors are in solo practice, although some are in group practice or work for other chiropractors. A small number teach, conduct research at chiropractic institutions, or work in hospitals and clinics.

Many chiropractors are located in small communities. However, there still often are geographic imbalances in the distribution of chi-

ropractors, in part because many establish practices close to one of the few chiropractic institutions.

Job Outlook

Job prospects are expected to be good for persons who enter the practice of chiropractic. Employment of chiropractors is expected to grow faster than the average for all occupations through the year 2014 as consumer demand for alternative health care grows. Because chiropractors emphasize the importance of healthy lifestyles and do not prescribe drugs or perform surgery, chiropractic care is appealing to many health-conscious Americans. Chiropractic treatment of the back, neck, extremities, and joints has become more accepted as a result of research and changing attitudes about alternative, noninvasive health care practices. The rapidly expanding older population, with its increased likelihood of mechanical and structural problems, also will increase demand for chiropractors.

Demand for chiropractic treatment, however, is related as well to the ability of patients to pay, either directly or through health insurance. Although more insurance plans now cover chiropractic services, the extent of such coverage varies among plans. Increasingly, chiropractors must educate communities about the benefits of chiropractic care in order to establish a successful practice.

In this occupation, replacement needs arise almost entirely from retirements. Chiropractors usually remain in the occupation until they retire; few transfer to other occupations. Establishing a new practice will be easiest in areas with a low concentration of chiropractors.

Earnings

Median annual earnings of salaried chiropractors were $69,910 in May 2004. The middle 50 percent earned between $46,710 and $118,280 a year.

In 2005, the mean salary for chiropractors was $104,363, according to a survey conducted by *Chiropractic Economics* magazine.

In chiropractic, as in other types of independent practice, earnings are relatively low in the beginning and increase as the practice grows. Geographic location and the characteristics and qualifications of the practitioner also may influence earnings. Self-employed chiropractors must provide their own health insurance and retirement.

Related Occupations

Chiropractors treat patients and work to prevent bodily disorders and injuries. So do athletic trainers, massage therapists, occupational therapists, physical therapists, physicians and surgeons, podiatrists, and veterinarians.

Sources of Additional Information

General information on a career as a chiropractor is available from the following organizations:

▸ American Chiropractic Association, 1701 Clarendon Blvd., Arlington, VA 22209. Internet: http://www.amerchiro.org

▸ International Chiropractors Association, 1110 North Glebe Rd., Suite 1000, Arlington, VA 22201. Internet: http://www.chiropractic.org

For a list of chiropractic programs and institutions, as well as general information on chiropractic education, contact

▸ Council on Chiropractic Education, 8049 North 85th Way, Scottsdale, AZ 85258-4321. Internet: http://www.cce-usa.org

For information on state education and licensure requirements, contact

▸ Federation of Chiropractic Licensing Boards, 5401 W. 10th St., Suite 101, Greeley, CO 80634-4400. Internet: http://www.fclb.org

For more information on the national chiropractic licensing exam, contact

▸ National Board of Chiropractic Examiners, 901 54th Ave., Suite 101, Greeley, CO 80634-4400. Internet: http://www.nbce.org

For information on admission requirements to a specific chiropractic college, as well as scholarship and loan information, contact the college's admissions office.

Clinical Laboratory Technologists and Technicians

(O*NET 29-2011.00 and 29-2012.00)

Significant Points

■ Faster-than-average employment growth is expected as the volume of laboratory tests continues to increase with both population growth and the development of new types of tests.

■ Clinical laboratory technologists usually have a bachelor's degree with a major in medical technology or in one of the life sciences; clinical laboratory technicians generally need either an associate degree or a certificate.

■ Job opportunities are expected to be excellent.

Nature of the Work

Clinical laboratory testing plays a crucial role in the detection, diagnosis, and treatment of disease. Clinical laboratory technologists, also referred to as clinical laboratory scientists or medical technologists and clinical laboratory technicians, also known as medical technicians or medical laboratory technicians, perform most of these tests.

Clinical laboratory personnel examine and analyze body fluids and cells. They look for bacteria, parasites, and other microorganisms; analyze the chemical content of fluids; match blood for transfusions; and test for drug levels in the blood to show how a patient is responding to treatment. Technologists also prepare specimens for examination, count cells, and look for abnormal cells in blood and body fluids. They use automated equipment and computerized instruments capable of performing a number of tests simultaneously, as well as microscopes, cell counters, and other sophisticated laboratory equipment. Then they analyze the results and relay them to physicians. With increasing automation and the use of computer

technology, the work of technologists and technicians has become less hands-on and more analytical.

The complexity of tests performed, the level of judgment needed, and the amount of responsibility workers assume depend largely on the amount of education and experience they have.

Clinical laboratory technologists perform complex chemical, biological, hematological, immunologic, microscopic, and bacteriological tests. Technologists microscopically examine blood and other body fluids. They make cultures of body fluid and tissue samples to determine the presence of bacteria, fungi, parasites, or other microorganisms. Clinical laboratory technologists analyze samples for chemical content or a chemical reaction and determine concentrations of compounds such as blood glucose and cholesterol levels. They also type and cross-match blood samples for transfusions.

Clinical laboratory technologists evaluate test results, develop and modify procedures, and establish and monitor programs to ensure the accuracy of tests. Some technologists supervise clinical laboratory technicians.

Technologists in small laboratories perform many types of tests, whereas those in large laboratories generally specialize. Technologists who prepare specimens and analyze the chemical and hormonal contents of body fluids are called clinical chemistry technologists. Those who examine and identify bacteria and other microorganisms are microbiology technologists. Blood bank technologists, or immunohematology technologists, collect, type, and prepare blood and its components for transfusions. Immunology technologists examine elements of the human immune system and its response to foreign bodies. Cytotechnologists prepare slides of body cells and examine these cells microscopically for abnormalities that may signal the beginning of a cancerous growth. Molecular biology technologists perform complex protein and nucleic acid testing on cell samples.

Clinical laboratory technicians perform less-complex tests and laboratory procedures than technologists perform. Technicians may prepare specimens and operate automated analyzers, for example, or they may perform manual tests in accordance with detailed instructions. Like technologists, they may work in several areas of the clinical laboratory or specialize in just one. Histotechnicians cut and stain tissue specimens for microscopic examination by pathologists, and phlebotomists collect blood samples. They usually work under the supervision of medical and clinical laboratory technologists or laboratory managers.

Working Conditions

Hours and other working conditions of clinical laboratory technologists and technicians vary with the size and type of employment setting. In large hospitals or in independent laboratories that operate continuously, personnel usually work the day, evening, or night shift and may work weekends and holidays. Laboratory personnel in small facilities may work on rotating shifts rather than on a regular shift. In some facilities, laboratory personnel are on call several nights a week or on weekends in case of an emergency.

Clinical laboratory personnel are trained to work with infectious specimens. When proper methods of infection control and sterilization are followed, few hazards exist. Protective masks, gloves, and goggles are often necessary to ensure the safety of laboratory personnel.

Laboratories usually are well lighted and clean; however, specimens, solutions, and reagents used in the laboratory sometimes produce fumes. Laboratory workers may spend a great deal of time on their feet.

Training, Other Qualifications, and Advancement

The usual requirement for an entry-level position as a clinical laboratory technologist is a bachelor's degree with a major in medical technology or in one of the life sciences, although it is possible to qualify through a combination of education, on-the-job, and specialized training. Universities and hospitals offer medical technology programs.

Bachelor's degree programs in medical technology include courses in chemistry, biological sciences, microbiology, mathematics, and statistics, as well as specialized courses devoted to knowledge and skills used in the clinical laboratory. Many programs also offer or require courses in management, business, and computer applications. The Clinical Laboratory Improvement Act requires technologists who perform highly complex tests to have at least an associate degree.

Medical and clinical laboratory technicians generally have either an associate degree from a community or junior college or a certificate from a hospital, a vocational or technical school, or one of the U.S. Armed Forces. A few technicians learn their skills on the job.

The National Accrediting Agency for Clinical Laboratory Sciences (NAACLS) fully accredits 469 programs for medical and clinical laboratory technologists, medical and clinical laboratory technicians, histotechnologists and histotechnicians, cytogenetic technologists, and diagnostic molecular scientists. NAACLS also approves 57 programs in phlebotomy and clinical assisting. Other nationally recognized accrediting agencies that accredit specific areas for clinical laboratory workers include the Commission on Accreditation of Allied Health Education Programs and the Accrediting Bureau of Health Education Schools.

Some states require laboratory personnel to be licensed or registered. Information on licensure is available from state departments of health or boards of occupational licensing. Certification is a voluntary process by which a nongovernmental organization, such as a professional society or certifying agency, grants recognition to an individual whose professional competence meets prescribed standards. Widely accepted by employers in the health care industry, certification is a prerequisite for most jobs and often is necessary for advancement. Agencies certifying medical and clinical laboratory technologists and technicians include the Board of Registry of the American Society for Clinical Pathology, the American Medical Technologists, the National Credentialing Agency for Laboratory Personnel, and the Board of Registry of the American Association of Bioanalysts. These agencies have different requirements for certification and different organizational sponsors.

Clinical laboratory personnel need good analytical judgment and the ability to work under pressure. Close attention to detail is essential because small differences or changes in test substances or numerical readouts can be crucial for patient care. Manual dexterity and normal color vision are highly desirable. With the widespread use of automated laboratory equipment, computer skills are important. In addition, technologists in particular are expected to be good at problem solving.

Technologists may advance to supervisory positions in laboratory work or may become chief medical or clinical laboratory technologists or laboratory managers in hospitals. Manufacturers of home diagnostic testing kits and laboratory equipment and supplies seek experienced technologists to work in product development, marketing, and sales. A graduate degree in medical technology, one of the biological sciences, chemistry, management, or education usually speeds advancement. A doctorate is needed to become a laboratory director; however, federal regulation allows directors of moderately complex laboratories to have either a master's degree or a bachelor's degree, combined with the appropriate amount of training and experience. Technicians can become technologists through additional education and experience.

Employment

Clinical laboratory technologists and technicians held about 302,000 jobs in 2004. More than half of jobs were in hospitals. Most of the remaining jobs were in offices of physicians and in medical and diagnostic laboratories. A small proportion was in educational services and in all other ambulatory health care services.

Job Outlook

Job opportunities are expected to be excellent because the number of job openings is expected to continue to exceed the number of job seekers. Employment of clinical laboratory workers is expected to grow faster than the average for all occupations through the year 2014 as the volume of laboratory tests continues to increase with both population growth and the development of new types of tests.

Technological advances will continue to have two opposing effects on employment. On the one hand, new, increasingly powerful diagnostic tests will encourage additional testing and spur employment. On the other hand, research and development efforts targeted at simplifying routine testing procedures may enhance the ability of non-laboratory personnel—physicians and patients in particular—to perform tests now conducted in laboratories. Although hospitals are expected to continue to be the major employer of clinical laboratory workers, employment is expected to grow faster in medical and diagnostic laboratories, offices of physicians, and all other ambulatory health care services.

Although significant, job growth will not be the only source of opportunities. As in most occupations, many openings will result from the need to replace workers who transfer to other occupations, retire, or stop working for some other reason.

Earnings

Median annual earnings of medical and clinical laboratory technologists were $45,730 in May 2004. The middle 50 percent earned between $38,740 and $54,310. The lowest 10 percent earned less than $32,240, and the highest 10 percent earned more than $63,120.

Median annual earnings in the industries employing the largest numbers of medical and clinical laboratory technologists in May 2004 were as follows:

General medical and surgical hospitals	$46,020
Medical and diagnostic laboratories	45,840
Offices of physicians	41,070

Median annual earnings of medical and clinical laboratory technicians were $30,840 in May 2004. The middle 50 percent earned between $24,890 and $37,770. The lowest 10 percent earned less than $20,410, and the highest 10 percent earned more than $45,680. Median annual earnings in the industries employing the largest numbers of medical and clinical laboratory technicians in May 2004 were as follows:

Colleges, universities, and professional schools	$32,410
General medical and surgical hospitals	31,830
Offices of physicians	29,620
Medical and diagnostic laboratories	29,220
Other ambulatory health care services	28,130

According to the American Society for Clinical Pathology, median hourly wages of staff clinical laboratory technologists and technicians in 2003 varied by specialty and laboratory type as follows:

	Hospital	Private clinic	Physician office laboratory
Cytotechnologist	$24.70	$24.07	$25.66
Histotechnologist	19.88	19.22	20.50
Medical technologist	20.40	19.00	18.00
Histotechnician	16.97	16.13	20.00
Medical laboratory technician	16.12	15.00	14.75
Phlebotomist	11.13	10.57	10.50

Related Occupations

Clinical laboratory technologists and technicians analyze body fluids, tissue, and other substances, using a variety of tests. Similar or related procedures are performed by chemists and materials scientists, science technicians, and veterinary technologists and technicians.

Sources of Additional Information

For a list of accredited and approved educational programs for clinical laboratory personnel, contact

▸ National Accrediting Agency for Clinical Laboratory Sciences, 8410 W. Bryn Mawr Ave., Suite 670, Chicago, IL 60631. Internet: http://www.naacls.org

Information on certification is available from

▸ American Association of Bioanalysts, Board of Registry, 906 Olive St., Suite 1200, St. Louis, MO 63101-1434. Internet: http://www.aab.org

▸ American Medical Technologists, 710 Higgins Rd., Park Ridge, IL 60068.

▸ American Society for Clinical Pathology, 2100 West Harrison St., Chicago, IL 60612. Internet: http://www.ascp.org

▸ National Credentialing Agency for Laboratory Personnel, P.O. Box 15945, Lenexa, KS 66285. Internet: http://www.nca-info.org

Additional career information is available from

▸ American Association of Blood Banks, 8101 Glenbrook Rd., Bethesda, MD 20814-2749. Internet: http://www.aabb.org

▸ American Society for Clinical Laboratory Science, 6701 Democracy Blvd., Suite 300, Bethesda, MD 20817. Internet: http://www.ascls.org

▸ American Society for Cytopathology, 400 West 9th St., Suite 201, Wilmington, DE 19801. Internet: http://www.cytopathology.org

▸ Clinical Laboratory Management Association, 989 Old Eagle School Rd., Suite 815, Wayne, PA 19087. Internet: http://www.clma.org

Computer Control Programmers and Operators

(O*NET 51-4011.01 and 51-4012.00)

Significant Points

■ Manufacturing industries employ almost all of these workers.

■ Workers learn in apprenticeship programs; informally on the job; and in secondary, vocational, or postsecondary schools; many entrants have previously worked as machinists or machine setters, operators, and tenders.

■ Despite the projected decline in employment, job opportunities should be good, as employers are expected to continue to have difficulty finding qualified workers.

Nature of the Work

Computer control programmers and operators use computer numerically controlled (CNC) machines to cut and shape precision products, such as automobile parts, machine parts, and compressors. CNC machines include machining tools such as lathes, multiaxis spindles, milling machines, laser cutting, water jet cutting, and wire electrical discharge machines (EDM), but the functions formerly performed by human operators are performed by a computer-control module. CNC machines cut away material from a solid block of metal, plastic, or glass—known as a workpiece—to form a finished part. Computer control programmers and operators normally produce large quantities of one part, although they may produce small batches or one-of-a-kind items. They use their knowledge of the working properties of metals and their skill with CNC programming to design and carry out the operations needed to make machined products that meet precise specifications.

Before CNC programmers—also referred to as numerical tool and process control programmers—machine a part, they must carefully plan and prepare the operation. First, these workers review three-dimensional computer-aided/automated design (CAD) blueprints of the part. Next, they calculate where to cut or bore into the workpiece, how fast to feed the metal into the machine, and how much metal to remove. They then select tools and materials for the job and plan the sequence of cutting and finishing operations.

Next, CNC programmers turn the planned machining operations into a set of instructions. These instructions are translated into a computer-aided/automated manufacturing (CAM) program containing a set of commands for the machine to follow. These commands normally are a series of numbers (hence, numerical control) that describes where cuts should occur, what type of cut should be used, and the speed of the cut. CNC programmers and operators check new programs to ensure that the machinery will function properly and that the output will meet specifications. Because a problem with the program could damage costly machinery and cutting tools or simply waste valuable time and materials, computer simulations may be used to check the program instead of a trial run. If errors are found, the program must be changed and retested until the problem is resolved. In addition, growing connectivity between CAD/CAM software and CNC machine tools is raising productivity by automatically translating designs into instructions for the computer controller on the machine tool. These new CAM technologies enable programs to be easily modified for use on other jobs with similar specifications.

After the programming work is completed, CNC operators—also referred to as computer-controlled machine tool operators, metal and plastic—perform the necessary machining operations. The CNC operators transfer the commands from the server to the CNC control module using a computer network link or floppy disk. Many advanced control modules are conversational, meaning that they ask the operator a series of questions about the nature of the task. CNC operators position the metal stock on the CNC machine tool—spindle, lathe, milling machine, or other—set the controls, and let the computer make the cuts. Heavier objects may be loaded with the assistance of other workers, autoloaders, a crane, or a forklift. During the machining process, computer-control operators constantly check to see if any problems exist. Machine tools have unique characteristics, which can be problematic. During a machining operation, the operator modifies the cutting program to account for any problems encountered. Operators who make these adjustments need a basic knowledge of CNC programming. Unique, modified CNC programs are saved for every different machine that performs a task.

In order to boost productivity, manufacturers increasingly prefer workers who can quickly adapt to new technology and perform a wide range of tasks. As a result, CNC operators often are required to perform many of the basic skills of a machinist and a CNC programmer. However, some manufacturers simply need CNC operators to be "button-pushers." They primarily start and stop machines, load cutting programs, and load and unload parts and tools.

Regardless of skill level, all CNC operators detect some problems by listening for specific sounds—for example, a dull cutting tool that needs changing or excessive vibration. Machine tools rotate at high speeds, which can create problems with harmonic vibrations in the workpiece. Vibrations cause the machine tools to make minor cutting errors, hurting the quality of the product. Operators listen for vibrations and then adjust the cutting speed to compensate. In older, slower machine tools, the cutting speed would be reduced to eliminate the vibrations, but the amount of time needed to finish the product would increase as a result. In newer, high-speed CNC machines, increasing the cutting speed normally eliminates the vibrations and reduces production time. CNC operators also ensure that the work-piece is being properly lubricated and cooled, because the machining of metal products generates a significant amount of heat.

Since CNC machines can operate with limited input from the operator, a single operator may monitor several machines simultaneously. Typically, an operator might monitor two machines cutting relatively simple parts from softer materials, while devoting most of his or her attention to a third machine cutting a much more difficult part from a hard metal, such as stainless steel. Operators are often expected to carefully schedule their work so that all of the machines are always operating.

Working Conditions

Most machine shops are clean, well lit, and ventilated. Most modern CNC machines are partially or totally enclosed, minimizing the exposure of workers to noise, debris, and the lubricants used to cool workpieces during machining. Nevertheless, working around machine tools presents certain dangers, and workers must follow safety precautions. Computer-controlled machine tool operators, metal and plastic, wear protective equipment, such as safety glasses to shield against bits of flying metal and earplugs to dampen machinery noise. They also must exercise caution when handling hazardous coolants and lubricants. The job requires stamina because operators stand most of the day and, at times, may need to lift moderately heavy workpieces.

Numerical tool and process control programmers work on desktop computers in offices that typically are near, but separate from, the shop floor. These work areas usually are clean, well lit, and free of machine noise. Numerical tool and process control programmers occasionally need to enter the shop floor to monitor CNC machining operations. On the shop floor, CNC programmers encounter the same hazards and exercise the same safety precautions as do CNC operators.

Most computer control programmers and operators work a 40-hour week. CNC operators increasingly work evening and weekend shifts as companies justify investments in more expensive machinery by extending hours of operation. Overtime is common during peak production periods.

Training, Other Qualifications, and Advancement

Computer control programmers and operators train in various ways—in apprenticeship programs; informally on the job; and in secondary, vocational, or postsecondary schools. In general, the more skills needed for the job, the more education and training that is needed to qualify. For example, a growing number of computer control programmers and the more skilled operators are receiving their formal training from community or technical colleges. For some specialized types of programming, such as that needed to produce complex parts for the aerospace or shipbuilding industries, employers may prefer individuals with a degree in engineering.

Less-skilled CNC operators (button-pushers) may need only a couple of weeks of on-the-job training.

Employers prefer to hire workers who have a basic knowledge of computers and electronics and experience with machine tools. In fact, many entrants to these occupations have previously worked as machinists or machine setters, operators, and tenders. Due to a shortage of applicants with the appropriate training, many employers are providing introductory courses in operating metalworking machines, safety, and blueprint reading. Persons interested in becoming computer control programmers or operators should be mechanically inclined and able to work independently and do highly accurate work.

High school or vocational school courses in mathematics (trigonometry and algebra), blueprint reading, computer programming, metalworking, and drafting are recommended. Apprenticeship programs consist of shop training and related classroom instruction. In shop training, apprentices learn filing, handtapping, and dowel fitting, as well as the operation of various machine tools. Classroom instruction includes math, physics, programming, blueprint reading, CAD software, safety, and shop practices. Skilled computer control programmers and operators need an understanding of the machining process, including the complex physics that occur at the cutting point. Thus, most training programs teach CNC operators and programmers to perform operations on manual machines prior to operating CNC machines.

To boost the skill level of all metalworkers and to create a more uniform standard of competency, a number of training facilities and colleges have recently begun implementing curriculums incorporating national skills standards developed by the National Institute of Metalworking Skills (NIMS). After completing such a curriculum and passing a performance requirement and written exam, trainees are granted a NIMS credential that provides formal recognition of competency in a metalworking field. Completion of a formal certification program provides expanded career opportunities.

Classroom training includes an introduction to computer numerical control; the basics of programming; and more complex topics, such as computer-aided manufacturing. Trainees start writing simple programs under the direction of an experienced programmer. Although machinery manufacturers are trying to standardize programming languages, there are numerous languages in use. Because of this, computer control programmers and operators should be able to learn new programming languages.

As new automation is introduced, computer control programmers and operators normally receive additional training to update their skills. This training usually is provided by a representative of the equipment manufacturer or a local technical school. Many employers offer tuition reimbursement for job-related courses.

Computer control programmers and operators can advance in several ways. Experienced CNC operators may become CNC programmers, and some are promoted to supervisory or administrative positions in their firms. A few open their own shops.

Employment

Computer control programmers and operators held about 143,000 jobs in 2004, mostly working in machine shops, plastics products manufacturing, machinery manufacturing, or transportation equipment manufacturing making mostly aerospace and automobile parts. Although computer control programmers and operators work in all parts of the country, jobs are most plentiful in the areas where manufacturing is concentrated.

Job Outlook

Computer control programmers and operators should have good job opportunities despite the projected decline in employment. Due to the limited number of people entering training programs, employers are expected to continue to have difficulty finding workers with the necessary skills and knowledge.

Employment of both computer-controlled machine tool operators and numerical tool and process control programmers is expected to decline through 2014. While CNC machine tools will be increasingly used, advances in CNC machine tools and manufacturing technology will further automate the production process, boosting CNC operator productivity and limiting employment. The demand for computer control programmers also will be negatively affected by the increasing use of software (CAD/CAM) that automatically translates part and product designs into CNC machine tool instructions.

Employment levels of computer control programmers and operators are influenced by economic cycles—as the demand for machined goods falls, programmers and operators involved in production may be laid off or forced to work fewer hours.

Earnings

Median hourly earnings of computer-controlled machine tool operators, metal and plastic, were $14.75 in May 2004. The middle 50 percent earned between $11.65 and $18.21. The lowest 10 percent earned less than $9.47, whereas the top 10 percent earned more than $21.67. Median hourly earnings in the manufacturing industries employing the largest numbers of computer-controlled machine tool operators, metal and plastic, in May 2004 were

Metalworking machinery manufacturing $16.34
Other fabricated metal product manufacturing 15.62
Machine shops; turned product; and screw,
    nut, and bolt manufacturing...............................14.73
Motor vehicle parts manufacturing.........................13.55
Plastics product manufacturing 11.78

Median hourly earnings of numerical tool and process control programmers were $19.31 in May 2004. The middle 50 percent earned between $15.67 and $24.00. The lowest 10 percent earned less than $12.89, while the top 10 percent earned more than $28.89.

Related Occupations

Occupations most closely related to computer control programmers and operators are other metal and plastic working occupations, which include machinists; tool and die makers; machine setters, operators, and tenders—metal and plastic; and welding, soldering, and brazing workers. Numerical tool and process control programmers apply their knowledge of machining operations, metals, blueprints, and machine programming to write programs that run machine tools. Computer programmers also write detailed programs to meet precise specifications.

Sources of Additional Information

For general information about computer control programmers and operators, contact

▸ Precision Machine Products Association, 6700 West Snowville Rd., Brecksville, OH 44141-3292. Internet: http://www.pmpa.org

For a list of training centers and apprenticeship programs, contact

▸ National Tooling and Metalworking Association, 9300 Livingston Rd., Fort Washington, MD 20744. Internet: http://www.ntma.org

For general occupational information, including a list of training programs, contact

▸ Precision Metalforming Association Educational Foundation, 6363 Oak Tree Blvd., Independence, OH 44131-2500. Internet: http://www.pmaef.org

Computer Programmers

(O*NET 15-1021.00)

Significant Points

■ Sixty-seven percent of computer programmers held a college or higher degree in 2004; nearly half held a bachelor's degree, and about 1 in 5 held a graduate degree.

■ Employment is expected to grow much more slowly than that for other computer specialists.

■ Prospects likely will be best for college graduates with knowledge of a variety of programming languages and tools; those with less formal education or its equivalent in work experience are apt to face strong competition for programming jobs.

Nature of the Work

Computer programmers write, test, and maintain the detailed instructions, called programs, that computers must follow to perform their functions. Programmers also conceive, design, and test logical structures for solving problems by computer. Many technical innovations in programming—advanced computing technologies and sophisticated new languages and programming tools—have redefined the role of a programmer and elevated much of the programming work done today. Job titles and descriptions may vary, depending on the organization. In this occupational description, *computer programmers* are individuals whose main job function is programming; this group has a wide range of responsibilities and educational backgrounds.

Computer programs tell the computer what to do—which information to identify and access, how to process it, and what equipment to use. Programs vary widely depending on the type of information to be accessed or generated. For example, the instructions involved in updating financial records are very different from those required to duplicate conditions on an aircraft for pilots training in a flight simulator. Although simple programs can be written in a few hours, programs that use complex mathematical formulas whose solutions can only be approximated or that draw data from many existing systems may require more than a year of work. In most cases, several programmers work together as a team under a senior programmer's supervision.

Programmers write programs according to the specifications determined primarily by computer software engineers and systems analysts. (Separate descriptions of computer software engineers and of computer systems analysts appear elsewhere in this book.) After the design process is complete, it is the job of the programmer to convert that design into a logical series of instructions that the computer can follow. The programmer codes these instructions in a conventional programming language such as COBOL; an artificial intelligence language such as Prolog; or one of the most advanced object-oriented languages, such as Java, C++, or ACTOR. Different programming languages are used depending on the purpose of the program. COBOL, for example, is commonly used for business applications, whereas Fortran (short for "formula translation") is used in science and engineering. C++ is widely used for both scientific and business applications. Extensible Markup Language (XML) has become a popular programming tool for Web programmers, along with J2EE (Java 2 Platform). Programmers generally know more than one programming language and, because many languages are similar, they often can learn new languages relatively easily. In practice, programmers often are referred to by the language they know, such as Java programmers, or by the type of function they perform or environment in which they work—for example, database programmers, mainframe programmers, or Web programmers.

Many programmers update, repair, modify, and expand existing programs. When making changes to a section of code, called a routine, programmers need to make other users aware of the task that the routine is to perform. They do this by inserting comments in the coded instructions so that others can understand the program. Many programmers use computer-assisted software engineering (CASE) tools to automate much of the coding process. These tools enable a programmer to concentrate on writing the unique parts of the program because the tools automate various pieces of the program being built. CASE tools generate whole sections of code automatically rather than line by line. Programmers also use libraries of basic code that can be modified or customized for a specific application. This approach yields more reliable and consistent programs and increases programmers' productivity by eliminating some routine steps.

Programmers test a program by running it to ensure that the instructions are correct and that the program produces the desired outcome. If errors do occur, the programmer must make the appropriate change and recheck the program until it produces the correct results. This process is called testing and debugging. Programmers may continue to fix these problems throughout the life of a program. Programmers working in a mainframe environment, which involves a large centralized computer, may prepare instructions for a computer operator who will run the program. Programmers also may contribute to a manual for persons who will be using the program.

Computer programmers often are grouped into two broad types—applications programmers and systems programmers. *Applications programmers* write programs to handle a specific job, such as a program to track inventory within an organization. They also may revise existing packaged software or customize generic applications that are frequently purchased from vendors. *Systems programmers*, in contrast, write programs to maintain and control computer systems software, such as operating systems, networked systems, and database systems. These workers make changes in the instructions that determine how the network, workstations, and central processing unit of the system handle the various jobs they have been given and how they communicate with peripheral equipment such as terminals, printers, and disk drives. Because of their knowledge of the entire computer system, systems programmers often help applications programmers determine the source of problems that may occur with their programs.

Programmers in software development companies may work directly with experts from various fields to create software—either programs designed for specific clients or packaged software for general use—ranging from games and educational software to programs for desktop publishing and financial planning. Programming of packaged software constitutes one of the most rapidly growing segments of the computer services industry.

In some organizations, particularly small ones, workers commonly known as *programmer-analysts* are responsible for both the systems analysis and the actual programming work. (A more detailed description of the work of programmer-analysts is presented in the description of computer systems analysts elsewhere in this book.) Advanced programming languages and new object-oriented programming capabilities are increasing the efficiency and productivity of both programmers and users. The transition from a mainframe environment to one that is based primarily on personal computers (PCs) has blurred the once-rigid distinction between the programmer and the user. Increasingly, adept end users are taking over many of the tasks previously performed by programmers. For example, the growing use of packaged software, such as spreadsheet and database management software packages, allows users to write simple programs to access data and perform calculations.

Working Conditions

Programmers generally work in offices in comfortable surroundings. Many programmers may work long hours or weekends to meet deadlines or fix critical problems that occur during off hours. Telecommuting is becoming common for a wide range of computer professionals, including computer programmers. As computer networks expand, more programmers are able to make corrections or fix problems remotely by using modems, e-mail, and the Internet to connect to a customer's computer.

Like other workers who spend long periods in front of a computer terminal typing at a keyboard, programmers are susceptible to eyestrain, back discomfort, and hand and wrist problems such as carpal tunnel syndrome.

Training, Other Qualifications, and Advancement

Although there are many training paths available for programmers, mainly because employers' needs are so varied, the level of education and experience employers seek has been rising due to the growing number of qualified applicants and the specialization involved with most programming tasks. Bachelor's degrees are commonly required, although some programmers may qualify for certain jobs with 2-year degrees or certificates. The associate degree is a widely used entry-level credential for prospective computer programmers. Most community colleges and many independent technical institutes and proprietary schools offer an associate degree in computer science or a related information technology field.

Employers primarily are interested in programming knowledge, and computer programmers can become certified in a programming language such as C++ or Java. College graduates who are interested in changing careers or developing an area of expertise also may return to a 2-year community college or technical school for additional training. In the absence of a degree, substantial specialized experience or expertise may be needed. Even when hiring programmers with a degree, employers appear to place more emphasis on previous experience.

Some computer programmers hold a college degree in computer science, mathematics, or information systems, whereas others have taken special courses in computer programming to supplement their degree in a field such as accounting, inventory control, or another area of business. As the level of education and training required by employers continues to rise, the proportion of programmers with a college degree should increase in the future. As indicated by the following tabulation, more than two-thirds of computer programmers had a bachelor's or higher degree in 2004.

High school graduate or less	8.3%
Some college, no degree	14.1
Associate degree	10.2
Bachelor's degree	49.1
Graduate degree	18.3

Required skills vary from job to job, but the demand for various skills generally is driven by changes in technology. Employers using computers for scientific or engineering applications usually prefer college graduates who have degrees in computer or information science, mathematics, engineering, or the physical sciences. Graduate degrees in related fields are required for some jobs. Employers who use computers for business applications prefer to hire people who have had college courses in management information systems and business and who possess strong programming skills. Although knowledge of traditional languages still is important, employers are placing increasing emphasis on newer, object-oriented programming languages and tools such as C++ and Java. Additionally, employers are seeking persons familiar with fourth-generation and fifth-generation languages that involve graphic user interface and systems programming. Employers also prefer applicants who have general business skills and experience related to the operations of the firm. Students can improve their employment prospects by participating in a college work-study program or by undertaking an internship.

Most systems programmers hold a 4-year degree in computer science. Extensive knowledge of a variety of operating systems is essential for such workers. This includes being able to configure an operating system to work with different types of hardware and having the skills needed to adapt the operating system to best meet the needs of a particular organization. Systems programmers also must be able to work with database systems, such as DB2, Oracle, or Sybase.

When hiring programmers, employers look for people with the necessary programming skills who can think logically and pay close attention to detail. The job calls for patience, persistence, and the ability to work on exacting analytical work, especially under pressure. Ingenuity and creativity are particularly important when programmers design solutions and test their work for potential failures. The ability to work with abstract concepts and to do technical analysis is especially important for systems programmers because they work with the software that controls the computer's operation. Because programmers are expected to work in teams and interact directly with users, employers want programmers who are able to communicate with nontechnical personnel.

Entry-level or junior programmers may work alone on simple assignments after some initial instruction, or they may be assigned to work on a team with more experienced programmers. Either way, beginning programmers generally must work under close supervision. Because technology changes so rapidly, programmers must continuously update their knowledge and skills by taking courses sponsored by their employer or by software vendors or offered through local community colleges and universities.

For skilled workers who keep up to date with the latest technology, the prospects for advancement are good. In large organizations, programmers may be promoted to lead programmer and be given supervisory responsibilities. Some applications programmers may move into systems programming after they gain experience and take courses in systems software. With general business experience, programmers may become programmer-analysts or systems analysts or be promoted to managerial positions. Other programmers, with specialized knowledge and experience with a language or operating system, may work in research and development for multimedia or Internet technology and may even become computer software engineers. As employers increasingly contract with outside firms to do programming jobs, more opportunities should arise for experienced programmers with expertise in a specific area to work as consultants.

Certification is a way to demonstrate a level of competence and may provide a jobseeker with a competitive advantage. In addition to language-specific certificates that a programmer can obtain, product vendors or software firms also offer certification and may require professionals who work with their products to be certified. Voluntary certification also is available through various other organizations.

Employment

Computer programmers held about 455,000 jobs in 2004. Programmers are employed in almost every industry, but the largest concentration is in computer systems design and related services. Large numbers of programmers also work for telecommunications companies, software publishers, financial institutions, insurance carriers, educational institutions, and government agencies.

Many computer programmers are employed on a temporary or contract basis or work as independent consultants, providing companies expertise with new programming languages or specialized areas of application. Rather than hiring programmers as permanent employees and then laying them off after a job is completed, employers can contract with temporary help agencies, with consulting firms, or with programmers themselves. A marketing firm, for example, may require programming services only to write and debug the software necessary to get a new customer database running. Bringing in an independent contractor or consultant with experience in a new or advanced programming language enables the firm to complete the

job without having to retrain existing workers. Such jobs may last anywhere from several weeks to a year or longer. There were 25,000 self-employed computer programmers in 2004.

Job Outlook

As programming tasks become increasingly sophisticated and additional levels of skill and experience are demanded by employers, graduates of 2-year programs and people with less than a 2-year degree or its equivalent in work experience will face strong competition for programming jobs. Competition for entry-level positions, however, also can affect applicants with a bachelor's degree. Prospects should be best for college graduates with knowledge of, and experience working with, a variety of programming languages and tools—including C++ and other object-oriented languages such as Java as well as newer, domain-specific languages that apply to computer networking, database management, and Internet application development. Obtaining vendor-specific or language-specific certification also can provide a competitive edge. Because demand fluctuates with employers' needs, jobseekers should keep up to date with the latest skills and technologies. Individuals who want to become programmers can enhance their prospects by combining the appropriate formal training with practical work experience.

Employment of programmers is expected to grow more slowly than the average for all occupations through the year 2014. Sophisticated computer software now has the capability to write basic code, eliminating the need for many programmers to do this routine work. The consolidation and centralization of systems and applications; developments in packaged software; advances in programming languages and tools; and the growing ability of users to design, write, and implement more of their own programs mean that more of the programming functions can be transferred from programmers to other types of information workers, such as computer software engineers.

Another factor limiting growth in employment is the outsourcing of these jobs to other countries. Computer programmers can perform their job function from anywhere in the world and can digitally transmit their programs to any location via e-mail. Programmers are at a much higher risk of having their jobs outsourced abroad than are workers involved in more complex and sophisticated information technology functions, such as software engineering, because computer programming has become an international language requiring little localized or specialized knowledge. Additionally, the work of computer programmers can be routinized once knowledge of a particular programming language is mastered.

Nevertheless, employers will continue to need programmers who have strong technical skills and who understand an employer's business and its programming requirements. This means that programmers will have to keep abreast of changing programming languages and techniques. Given the importance of networking and the expansion of client/server, Web-based, and wireless environments, organizations will look for programmers who can support data communications and help implement electronic commerce and intranet strategies. Demand for programmers with strong object-oriented programming capabilities and technical specialization in areas such as client/server programming, wireless applications, multimedia technology, and graphic user interface likely will stem from the expansion of intranets, extranets, and Internet applications. Programmers also will be needed to create and maintain expert systems and embed these technologies in more products. Finally, a growing emphasis on cybersecurity will lead to increased demand for programmers who are familiar with digital security issues and skilled in using appropriate security technology.

Jobs for both systems and applications programmers should be most plentiful in data-processing service firms, software houses, and computer consulting businesses. These types of establishments are part of computer systems design and related services and software publishers, which are projected to be among the fastest-growing industries in the economy over the 2004–2014 period. As organizations attempt to control costs and keep up with changing technology, they will need programmers to assist in conversions to new computer languages and systems. In addition, numerous job openings will result from the need to replace programmers who leave the labor force or transfer to other occupations such as manager or systems analyst.

Earnings

Median annual earnings of computer programmers were $62,890 in May 2004. The middle 50 percent earned between $47,580 and $81,280 a year. The lowest 10 percent earned less than $36,470; the highest 10 percent earned more than $99,610. Median annual earnings in the industries employing the largest numbers of computer programmers in May 2004 are shown here:

Software publishers $73,060

Computer systems design and related services 67,600

Data-processing, hosting, and related services........64,540

Insurance carriers 62,990

Management of companies and enterprises 62,160

According to the National Association of Colleges and Employers, starting salary offers for graduates with a bachelor's degree in computer science averaged $50,820 a year in 2005.

According to Robert Half International, a firm providing specialized staffing services, average annual starting salaries in 2005 ranged from $52,500 to $83,250 for applications development programmers/analysts and from $55,000 to $88,250 for software developers. Average starting salaries for mainframe systems programmers ranged from $50,250 to $67,500 in 2005.

Related Occupations

Other professional workers who deal extensively with data include computer software engineers, computer scientists and database administrators, computer systems analysts, statisticians, mathematicians, engineers, and operations research analysts.

Sources of Additional Information

State employment service offices can provide information about job openings for computer programmers. Municipal chambers of commerce are an additional source of information on an area's largest employers.

Further information about computer careers is available from

▸ Association for Computing Machinery, 1515 Broadway, New York, NY 10036. Internet: http://www.acm.org

▸ Institute of Electrical and Electronics Engineers Computer Society, Headquarters Office, 1730 Massachusetts Ave. NW, Washington, DC 20036-1992. Internet: http://www.computer.org

▸ National Workforce Center for Emerging Technologies, 3000 Landerholm Circle SE, Bellevue, WA 98007. Internet: http://www.nwcet.org

Computer Scientists and Database Administrators

(O*NET 15-1011.00, 15-1061.00, and 15-1099.99)

Significant Points

■ Education requirements range from an associate degree to a doctoral degree.

■ Employment is expected to increase much faster than the average as organizations continue to adopt increasingly sophisticated technologies.

■ Job prospects are favorable.

Nature of the Work

The rapid spread of computers and information technology has generated a need for highly trained workers proficient in various job functions. These workers—computer scientists, database administrators, and network systems and data communication analysts—include a wide range of computer specialists. Job tasks and occupational titles used to describe these workers evolve rapidly, reflecting new areas of specialization or changes in technology as well as the preferences and practices of employers.

Computer scientists work as theorists, researchers, or inventors. Their jobs are distinguished by the higher level of theoretical expertise and innovation they apply to complex problems and the creation or application of new technology. Those employed by academic institutions work in areas ranging from complexity theory to hardware to programming-language design. Some work on multidisciplinary projects, such as developing and advancing uses of virtual reality, extending human–computer interaction, or designing robots. Their counterparts in private industry work in areas such as applying theory; developing specialized languages or information technologies; or designing programming tools, knowledge-based systems, or even computer games.

With the Internet and electronic business generating large volumes of data, there is a growing need to be able to store, manage, and extract data effectively. *Database administrators* work with database management systems software and determine ways to organize and store data. They identify user requirements, set up computer databases, and test and coordinate modifications to the computer database systems. An organization's database administrator ensures the performance of the system, understands the platform on which the database runs, and adds new users to the system. Because they also may design and implement system security, database administrators often plan and coordinate security measures. With the volume of sensitive data generated every second growing rapidly, data integrity, backup systems, and database security have become increasingly important aspects of the job of database administrators.

Because networks are configured in many ways, *network systems and data communications analysts* are needed to design, test, and evaluate systems such as local area networks (LANs), wide area networks (WANs), the Internet, intranets, and other data communications systems. Systems can range from a connection between two offices in the same building to globally distributed networks, voice mail, and e-mail systems of a multinational organization. Network systems and data communications analysts perform network modeling, analysis, and planning; they also may research related products and make necessary hardware and software recommendations. *Telecommunications specialists* focus on the interaction between computer and communications equipment. These workers design voice and data communication systems, supervise the installation of the systems, and provide maintenance and other services to clients after the systems are installed.

The growth of the Internet and the expansion of the World Wide Web (the graphical portion of the Internet) have generated a variety of occupations related to the design, development, and maintenance of Web sites and their servers. For example, *Webmasters* are responsible for all technical aspects of a Web site, including performance issues such as speed of access, and for approving the content of the site. *Internet developers* or *Web developers*, also called *Web designers*, are responsible for day-to-day site creation and design.

Working Conditions

Computer scientists and database administrators normally work in offices or laboratories in comfortable surroundings. They usually work about 40 hours a week—the same as many other professional or office workers do. However, evening or weekend work may be necessary to meet deadlines or solve specific problems. With the technology available today, telecommuting is common for computer professionals. As networks expand, more work can be done from remote locations through modems, laptops, electronic mail, and the Internet.

Like other workers who spend long periods in front of a computer terminal typing on a keyboard, computer scientists and database administrators are susceptible to eyestrain, back discomfort, and hand and wrist problems such as carpal tunnel syndrome or cumulative trauma disorder.

Training, Other Qualifications, and Advancement

Rapidly changing technology requires an increasing level of skill and education on the part of employees. Companies look for professionals with an ever-broader background and range of skills including not only technical knowledge, but also communication and other interpersonal skills. While there is no universally accepted way to prepare for a job as a network systems analyst, computer scientist, or database administrator, most employers place a premium on some

formal college education. A bachelor's degree is a prerequisite for many jobs; however, some jobs may require only a 2-year degree. Relevant work experience also is very important. For more technically complex jobs, persons with graduate degrees are preferred.

For database administrator positions, many employers seek applicants who have a bachelor's degree in computer science, information science, or management information systems (MIS). MIS programs usually are part of the business school or college and differ considerably from computer science programs, emphasizing business and management-oriented coursework and business computing courses. Employers increasingly seek individuals with a master's degree in business administration (MBA), with a concentration in information systems, as more firms move their business to the Internet. For some network systems and data communication analysts, such as Webmasters, an associate degree or certificate is sufficient, although more advanced positions might require a computer-related bachelor's degree. For computer and information scientists, a doctoral degree generally is required because of the highly technical nature of their work.

Despite employers' preference for those with technical degrees, persons with degrees in a variety of majors find employment in these occupations. The level of education and the type of training that employers require depend on their needs. One factor affecting these needs is changes in technology. Employers often scramble to find workers capable of implementing new technologies. Workers with formal education or experience in information security, for example, are in demand because of the growing need for their skills and services. Employers also look for workers skilled in wireless technologies as wireless networks and applications have spread into many firms and organizations.

Most community colleges and many independent technical institutes and proprietary schools offer an associate's degree in computer science or a related information technology field. Many of these programs may be geared more toward meeting the needs of local businesses and are more occupation-specific than are 4-year degree programs. Some jobs may be better suited to the level of training that such programs offer. Employers usually look for people who have broad knowledge and experience related to computer systems and technologies, strong problem-solving and analytical skills, and good interpersonal skills. Courses in computer science or systems design offer good preparation for a job in these computer occupations. For jobs in a business environment, employers usually want systems analysts to have business management or closely related skills, while a background in the physical sciences, applied mathematics, or engineering is preferred for work in scientifically oriented organizations. Art or graphic design skills may be desirable for Webmasters or Web developers.

Jobseekers can enhance their employment opportunities by participating in internship or co-op programs offered through their schools. Because many people develop advanced computer skills in a non-computer occupation and then transfer those skills to a computer occupation, a background in the industry in which the person's job is located, such as financial services, banking, or accounting, can be important. Others have taken computer science courses to supplement their study in fields such as accounting, inventory control, or other business areas.

Computer scientists and database administrators must be able to think logically and have good communication skills. Because they often deal with a number of tasks simultaneously, the ability to concentrate and pay close attention to detail is important. Although these computer specialists sometimes work independently, they frequently work in teams on large projects. They must be able to communicate effectively with computer personnel, such as programmers and managers, as well as with users or other staff who may have no technical computer background.

Computer scientists employed in private industry may advance into managerial or project leadership positions. Those employed in academic institutions can become heads of research departments or published authorities in their field. Database administrators may advance into managerial positions, such as chief technology officer, on the basis of their experience managing data and enforcing security. Computer specialists with work experience and considerable expertise in a particular subject or a certain application may find lucrative opportunities as independent consultants or may choose to start their own computer consulting firms.

Technological advances come so rapidly in the computer field that continuous study is necessary to keep one's skills up to date. Employers, hardware and software vendors, colleges and universities, and private training institutions offer continuing education. Additional training may come from professional development seminars offered by professional computing societies.

Certification is a way to demonstrate a level of competence in a particular field. Some product vendors or software firms offer certification and require professionals who work with their products to be certified. Many employers regard these certifications as the industry standard. For example, one method of acquiring enough knowledge to get a job as a database administrator is to become certified in a specific type of database management. Voluntary certification also is available through various organizations associated with computer specialists. Professional certification may afford a jobseeker a competitive advantage.

Employment

Computer scientists and database administrators held about 507,000 jobs in 2004, including about 66,000 who were self-employed. Employment was distributed among the detailed occupations as follows:

Network systems and data communication analysts	231,000
Database administrators	104,000
Computer and information scientists, research	22,000
Computer specialists, all other	149,000

Although they are increasingly employed in every sector of the economy, the greatest concentration of these workers is in the computer systems design and related services industry. Firms in this industry provide services related to the commercial use of computers on a contract basis, including custom computer programming services; computer systems integration design services; computer facilities management services, including computer systems or data-processing facilities support services for clients; and other computer-related services, such as disaster recovery services and

software installation. Many computer scientists and database administrators are employed by Internet service providers; Web search portals; and data-processing, hosting, and related services firms. Others work for government, manufacturers of computer and electronic products, insurance companies, financial institutions, and universities.

A growing number of computer specialists, such as network and data communications analysts, are employed on a temporary or contract basis; many of these individuals are self-employed, working independently as contractors or consultants. For example, a company installing a new computer system may need the services of several network systems and data communication analysts just to get the system running. Because not all of the analysts would be needed once the system is functioning, the company might contract for such employees with a temporary help agency or a consulting firm or with the network systems analysts themselves. Such jobs may last from several months to 2 years or more. This growing practice enables companies to bring in people with the exact skills they need to complete a particular project instead of having to spend time or money training or retraining existing workers. Often, experienced consultants then train a company's in-house staff as a project develops.

Job Outlook

Computer scientists and database administrators should continue to enjoy favorable job prospects. As technology becomes more sophisticated and complex, however, employers demand a higher level of skill and expertise from their employees. Individuals with an advanced degree in computer science or computer engineering or with an MBA with a concentration in information systems should enjoy favorable employment prospects. College graduates with a bachelor's degree in computer science, computer engineering, information science, or MIS also should enjoy favorable prospects, particularly if they have supplemented their formal education with practical experience. Because employers continue to seek computer specialists who can combine strong technical skills with good interpersonal and business skills, graduates with degrees in fields other than computer science who have had courses in computer programming, systems analysis, and other information technology areas also should continue to find jobs in these computer fields. In fact, individuals with the right experience and training can work in these computer occupations regardless of their college major or level of formal education.

Computer scientists and database administrators are expected to be among the fastest-growing occupations through 2014. Employment of these computer specialists is expected to grow much faster than the average for all occupations as organizations continue to adopt and integrate increasingly sophisticated technologies. Job increases will be driven by very rapid growth in computer systems design and related services, which is projected to be one of the fastest-growing industries in the U.S. economy. Job growth will not be as rapid as during the previous decade, however, as the information technology sector begins to mature and as routine work is increasingly outsourced overseas. In addition to growth, many job openings will arise annually from the need to replace workers who move into managerial positions or other occupations or who leave the labor force.

The demand for networking to facilitate the sharing of information, the expansion of client–server environments, and the need for computer specialists to use their knowledge and skills in a problem-solving capacity will be major factors in the rising demand for computer scientists and database administrators. Moreover, falling prices of computer hardware and software should continue to induce more businesses to expand their computerized operations and integrate new technologies into them. To maintain a competitive edge and operate more efficiently, firms will keep demanding computer specialists who are knowledgeable about the latest technologies and are able to apply them to meet the needs of businesses.

Increasingly, more sophisticated and complex technology is being implemented across all organizations, fueling demand for computer scientists and database administrators. There is growing demand for network systems and data communication analysts to help firms maximize their efficiency with available technology. Expansion of electronic commerce—doing business on the Internet—and the continuing need to build and maintain databases that store critical information on customers, inventory, and projects are fueling demand for database administrators familiar with the latest technology. Also, the increasing importance placed on cybersecurity—the protection of electronic information—will result in a need for workers skilled in information security.

The development of new technologies usually leads to demand for various kinds of workers. The expanding integration of Internet technologies into businesses, for example, has resulted in a growing need for specialists who can develop and support Internet and intranet applications. The growth of electronic commerce means that more establishments use the Internet to conduct their business online. The introduction of the wireless Internet, known as WiFi, creates new systems to be analyzed and new data to be administered. The spread of such new technologies translates into a need for information technology professionals who can help organizations use technology to communicate with employees, clients, and consumers. Explosive growth in these areas also is expected to fuel demand for specialists who are knowledgeable about network, data, and communications security.

Earnings

Median annual earnings of computer and information scientists, research, were $85,190 in May 2004. The middle 50 percent earned between $64,860 and $108,440. The lowest 10 percent earned less than $48,930, and the highest 10 percent earned more than $132,700. Median annual earnings of computer and information scientists employed in computer systems design and related services in May 2004 were $85,530.

Median annual earnings of database administrators were $60,650 in May 2004. The middle 50 percent earned between $44,490 and $81,140. The lowest 10 percent earned less than $33,380, and the highest 10 percent earned more than $97,450. In May 2004, median annual earnings of database administrators employed in computer systems design and related services were $70,530, and for those in management of companies and enterprises, earnings were $65,990.

Median annual earnings of network systems and data communication analysts were $60,600 in May 2004. The middle 50 percent

earned between $46,480 and $78,060. The lowest 10 percent earned less than $36,260, and the highest 10 percent earned more than $95,040. Median annual earnings in the industries employing the largest numbers of network systems and data communications analysts in May 2004 are shown here:

Wired telecommunications carriers	$65,130
Insurance carriers	64,660
Management of companies and enterprises	64,170
Computer systems design and related services	63,910
Local government	52,300

Median annual earnings of all other computer specialists were $59,480 in May 2004. Median annual earnings of all other computer specialists employed in computer systems design and related services were $57,430, and, for those in management of companies and enterprises, earnings were $68,590 in May 2004.

According to the National Association of Colleges and Employers, starting offers for graduates with a doctoral degree in computer science averaged $93,050 in 2005. Starting offers averaged $50,820 for graduates with a bachelor's degree in computer science; $46,189 for those with a degree in computer systems analysis; $44,417 for those with a degree in management information systems; and $44,775 for those with a degree in information sciences and systems.

According to Robert Half International, a firm providing specialized staffing services, starting salaries in 2005 ranged from $67,750 to $95,500 for database administrators. Salaries for networking and Internet-related occupations ranged from $47,000 to $68,500 for LAN administrators and from $51,750 to $74,520 for Web developers. Starting salaries for information security professionals ranged from $63,750 to $93,000 in 2005.

Related Occupations

Others who work with large amounts of data are computer programmers, computer software engineers, computer and information systems managers, engineers, mathematicians, and statisticians.

Sources of Additional Information

Further information about computer careers is available from:

▸ Association for Computing Machinery (ACM), 1515 Broadway, New York, NY 10036. Internet: http://www.acm.org

▸ Institute of Electrical and Electronics Engineers Computer Society, Headquarters Office, 1730 Massachusetts Ave. NW, Washington, DC 20036-1992. Internet: http://www.computer.org

▸ National Workforce Center for Emerging Technologies, 3000 Landerholm Circle SE, Bellevue, WA 98007. Internet: http://www.nwcet.org

Computer Software Engineers

(O*NET 15-1031.00 and 15-1032.00)

Significant Points

■ Computer software engineers are projected to be one of the fastest-growing occupations over the 2004–2014 period.

- Very good opportunities are expected for college graduates with at least a bachelor's degree in computer engineering or computer science and with practical work experience.

- Computer software engineers must continually strive to acquire new skills in conjunction with the rapid changes that are occurring in computer technology.

Nature of the Work

The explosive impact of computers and information technology on our everyday lives has generated a need to design and develop new computer software systems and to incorporate new technologies into a rapidly growing range of applications. The tasks performed by workers known as computer software engineers evolve quickly, reflecting new areas of specialization or changes in technology as well as the preferences and practices of employers. Computer software engineers apply the principles and techniques of computer science, engineering, and mathematical analysis to the design, development, testing, and evaluation of the software and systems that enable computers to perform their many applications. (A separate description of engineers appears elsewhere in this book.)

Software engineers working in applications or systems development analyze users' needs and design, construct, test, and maintain computer applications software or systems. Software engineers can be involved in the design and development of many types of software, including software for operating systems and network distribution and compilers, which convert programs for execution on a computer. In programming, or coding, software engineers instruct a computer, line by line, how to perform a function. They also solve technical problems that arise. Software engineers must possess strong programming skills but are more concerned with developing algorithms and analyzing and solving programming problems than with actually writing code. (A separate description of computer programmers appears elsewhere in this book.)

Computer applications software engineers analyze users' needs and design, construct, and maintain general computer applications software or specialized utility programs. These workers use different programming languages, depending on the purpose of the program. The programming languages most often used are C, C++, and Java, with Fortran and COBOL used less commonly. Some software engineers develop both packaged systems and systems software or create customized applications.

Computer systems software engineers coordinate the construction and maintenance of a company's computer systems and plan their future growth. Working with the company, they coordinate each department's computer needs—ordering, inventory, billing, and payroll recordkeeping, for example—and make suggestions about its technical direction. They also might set up the company's intranets—networks that link computers within the organization and ease communication among the various departments.

Systems software engineers work for companies that configure, implement, and install complete computer systems. These workers may be members of the marketing or sales staff, serving as the primary technical resource for sales workers and customers. They also may be involved in product sales and in providing their customers with continuing technical support. Since the selling of complex computer systems often requires substantial customization for the purchaser's organization, software engineers help to explain the requirements necessary for installing and operating the new system in the purchaser's computing environment. In addition, systems software engineers are responsible for ensuring security across the systems they are configuring.

Computer software engineers often work as part of a team that designs new hardware, software, and systems. A core team may comprise engineering, marketing, manufacturing, and design people, who work together until the product is released.

Working Conditions

Computer software engineers normally work in well-lighted and comfortable offices or laboratories in which computer equipment is located. Most software engineers work at least 40 hours a week; however, due to the project-oriented nature of the work, they also may have to work evenings or weekends to meet deadlines or solve unexpected technical problems. Like other workers who sit for hours at a computer, typing on a keyboard, software engineers are susceptible to eyestrain, back discomfort, and hand and wrist problems such as carpal tunnel syndrome.

As they strive to improve software for users, many computer software engineers interact with customers and co-workers. Computer software engineers who are employed by software vendors and consulting firms, for example, spend much of their time away from their offices, frequently traveling overnight to meet with customers. They call on customers in businesses ranging from manufacturing plants to financial institutions.

As networks expand, software engineers may be able to use modems, laptops, e-mail, and the Internet to provide more technical support and other services from their main office, connecting to a customer's computer remotely to identify and correct developing problems.

Training, Other Qualifications, and Advancement

Most employers prefer to hire persons who have at least a bachelor's degree and broad knowledge of, and experience with, a variety of computer systems and technologies. The usual degree concentration for applications software engineers is computer science or software engineering; for systems software engineers, it is computer science or computer information systems. Graduate degrees are preferred for some of the more complex jobs.

Academic programs in software engineering emphasize software and may be offered as a degree option or in conjunction with computer science degrees. Increasing emphasis on computer security suggests that software engineers with advanced degrees that include mathematics and systems design will be sought after by software developers, government agencies, and consulting firms specializing in information assurance and security. Students seeking software engineering jobs enhance their employment opportunities by participating in internship or co-op programs offered through their schools. These experiences provide the students with broad knowledge and experience, making them more attractive candidates to employers. Inexperienced college graduates may be hired by large computer and consulting firms that train new employees in intensive company-based programs. In many firms, new hires are mentored, and their mentors have an input into the performance evaluations of these new employees.

For systems software engineering jobs that require workers to have a college degree, a bachelor's degree in computer science or computer information systems is typical. For systems engineering jobs that place less emphasis on workers having a computer-related degree, computer training programs leading to certification are offered by systems software vendors. Nonetheless, most training authorities feel that program certification alone is not sufficient for the majority of software engineering jobs.

Persons interested in jobs as computer software engineers must have strong problem-solving and analytical skills. They also must be able to communicate effectively with team members, other staff, and the customers they meet. Because they often deal with a number of tasks simultaneously, they must be able to concentrate and pay close attention to detail.

As is the case with most occupations, advancement opportunities for computer software engineers increase with experience. Entry-level computer software engineers are likely to test and verify ongoing designs. As they become more experienced, they may become involved in designing and developing software. Eventually, they may advance to become a project manager, manager of information systems, or chief information officer. Some computer software engineers with several years of experience or expertise find lucrative opportunities working as systems designers or independent consultants or starting their own computer consulting firms.

As technological advances in the computer field continue, employers demand new skills. Computer software engineers must continually strive to acquire such skills if they wish to remain in this extremely dynamic field. For example, computer software engineers interested in working for a bank should have some expertise in finance as they integrate new technologies into the computer system of the bank. To help them keep up with the changing technology, continuing education and professional development seminars are offered by employers, software vendors, colleges and universities, private training institutions, and professional computing societies.

Employment

Computer software engineers held about 800,000 jobs in 2004. Approximately 460,000 were computer applications software engineers, and around 340,000 were computer systems software engineers. Although they are employed in most industries, the largest concentration of computer software engineers—almost 30 percent—are in computer systems design and related services. Many computer software engineers also work for establishments in other industries, such as software publishers, government agencies, manufacturers of computers and related electronic equipment, and management of companies and enterprises.

Employers of computer software engineers range from startup companies to established industry leaders. The proliferation of Internet, e-mail, and other communications systems is expanding electronics to engineering firms that are traditionally associated with unrelated disciplines. Engineering firms specializing in building bridges and

power plants, for example, hire computer software engineers to design and develop new geographic data systems and automated drafting systems. Communications firms need computer software engineers to tap into growth in the personal communications market. Major communications companies have many job openings for both computer software applications engineers and computer systems engineers.

An increasing number of computer software engineers are employed on a temporary or contract basis, with many being self-employed, working independently as consultants. Some consultants work for firms that specialize in developing and maintaining client companies' Web sites and intranets. About 23,000 computer software engineers were self-employed in 2004.

Job Outlook

Computer software engineers are projected to be one of the fastest-growing occupations from 2004 to 2014. Rapid employment growth in the computer systems design and related services industry, which employs the greatest number of computer software engineers, should result in very good opportunities for those college graduates with at least a bachelor's degree in computer engineering or computer science and practical experience working with computers. Employers will continue to seek computer professionals with strong programming, systems analysis, interpersonal, and business skills. With the software industry beginning to mature, however, and with routine software engineering work being increasingly outsourced overseas, job growth will not be as rapid as during the previous decade.

Employment of computer software engineers is expected to increase much faster than the average for all occupations as businesses and other organizations adopt and integrate new technologies and seek to maximize the efficiency of their computer systems. Competition among businesses will continue to create an incentive for increasingly sophisticated technological innovations, and organizations will need more computer software engineers to implement these changes. In addition to jobs created through employment growth, many job openings will result annually from the need to replace workers who move into managerial positions, transfer to other occupations, or leave the labor force.

Demand for computer software engineers will increase as computer networking continues to grow. For example, the expanding integration of Internet technologies and the explosive growth in electronic commerce—doing business on the Internet—have resulted in rising demand for computer software engineers who can develop Internet, intranet, and World Wide Web applications. Likewise, expanding electronic data-processing systems in business, telecommunications, government, and other settings continue to become more sophisticated and complex. Growing numbers of systems software engineers will be needed to implement, safeguard, and update systems and resolve problems. Consulting opportunities for computer software engineers also should continue to grow as businesses seek help to manage, upgrade, and customize their increasingly complicated computer systems.

New growth areas will continue to arise from rapidly evolving technologies. The increasing uses of the Internet, the proliferation of Web sites, and mobile technology such as the wireless Internet have created a demand for a wide variety of new products. As individuals and businesses rely more on hand-held computers and wireless networks, it will be necessary to integrate current computer systems with this new, more mobile technology. Also, information security concerns have given rise to new software needs. Concerns over "cyber security" should result in businesses and government continuing to invest heavily in software that protects their networks and vital electronic infrastructure from attack. The expansion of this technology in the next 10 years will lead to an increased need for computer engineers to design and develop the software and systems to run these new applications and integrate them into older systems.

As with other information technology jobs, employment growth of computer software engineers may be tempered somewhat as more software development is contracted out abroad. Firms may look to cut costs by shifting operations to lower-wage foreign countries with highly educated workers who have strong technical skills. At the same time, jobs in software engineering are less prone to being sent abroad compared with jobs in other computer specialties because the occupation requires innovation and intense research and development.

Earnings

Median annual earnings of computer applications software engineers who worked full time in May 2004 were about $74,980. The middle 50 percent earned between $59,130 and $92,130. The lowest 10 percent earned less than $46,520, and the highest 10 percent earned more than $113,830. Median annual earnings in the industries employing the largest numbers of computer applications software engineers in May 2004 were as follows:

Software publishers	$79,930
Management, scientific, and technical consulting services	78,460
Computer systems design and related services	76,910
Management of companies and enterprises	70,520
Insurance carriers	68,440

Median annual earnings of computer systems software engineers who worked full time in May 2004 were about $79,740. The middle 50 percent earned between $63,150 and $98,220. The lowest 10 percent earned less than $50,420, and the highest 10 percent earned more than $118,350. Median annual earnings in the industries employing the largest numbers of computer systems software engineers in May 2004 are as follows:

Scientific research and development services	$91,390
Computer and peripheral equipment manufacturing	87,800
Software publishers	83,670
Computer systems design and related services	79,950
Wired telecommunications carriers	74,370

According to the National Association of Colleges and Employers, starting salary offers for graduates with a bachelor's degree in computer engineering averaged $52,464 in 2005; offers for those with a master's degree averaged $60,354. Starting salary offers for graduates with a bachelor's degree in computer science averaged $50,820.

According to Robert Half International, starting salaries for software engineers in software development ranged from $63,250 to $92,750 in 2005. For network engineers, starting salaries in 2005 ranged from $61,250 to $88,250.

Related Occupations

Other workers who use mathematics and logic extensively include computer systems analysts, computer scientists and database administrators, computer programmers, computer hardware engineers, computer support specialists and systems administrators, engineers, statisticians, mathematicians, and actuaries.

Sources of Additional Information

Additional information on a career in computer software engineering is available from the following organizations:

▸ Association for Computing Machinery (ACM), 1515 Broadway, New York, NY 10036. Internet: http://www.acm.org

▸ Institute of Electronics and Electrical Engineers Computer Society, Headquarters Office, 1730 Massachusetts Ave. NW, Washington, DC 20036-1992. Internet: http://www.computer.org

▸ National Workforce Center for Emerging Technologies, 3000 Landerholm Circle SE, Bellevue, WA 98007. Internet: http://www.nwcet.org

Computer Support Specialists and Systems Administrators

(O*NET 15-1041.00, 15-1071.00, and 15-1071.01)

Significant Points

■ Rapid job growth is projected over the 2004–2014 period.

■ There are many paths of entry to these occupations.

■ Job prospects should be best for college graduates who are up to date with the latest skills and technologies; certifications and practical experience are essential for persons without degrees.

Nature of the Work

In the last decade, computers have become an integral part of everyday life, used for a variety of reasons at home, in the workplace, and at schools. Of course, almost every computer user encounters a problem occasionally, whether it is the disaster of a crashing hard drive or the annoyance of a forgotten password. The explosive use of computers has created a high demand for specialists to provide advice to users as well as for day-to-day administration, maintenance, and support of computer systems and networks.

Computer support specialists provide technical assistance, support, and advice to customers and other users. This occupational group includes *technical support specialists* and *help-desk technicians*. These troubleshooters interpret problems and provide technical support for hardware, software, and systems. They answer telephone calls, analyze problems by using automated diagnostic programs, and resolve recurring difficulties. Support specialists may work either within a company that uses computer systems or directly for a computer hardware or software vendor. Increasingly, these specialists work for help-desk or support services firms, for which they provide computer support to clients on a contract basis.

Technical support specialists answer telephone calls from their organizations' computer users and may run automatic diagnostics programs to resolve problems. Working on monitors, keyboards, printers, and mice, they install, modify, clean, and repair computer hardware and software. They also may write training manuals and train computer users in how to use new computer hardware and software. In addition, technical support specialists oversee the daily performance of their company's computer systems and evaluate software programs with regard to their usefulness.

Help-desk technicians assist computer users with the inevitable hardware and software questions that are not addressed in a product's instruction manual. Help-desk technicians field telephone calls and e-mail messages from customers who are seeking guidance on technical problems. In responding to these requests for guidance, help-desk technicians must listen carefully to the customer, ask questions to diagnose the nature of the problem, and then patiently walk the customer through the problem-solving steps.

Help-desk technicians deal directly with customer issues, and companies value them as a source of feedback on their products. These technicians are consulted for information about what gives customers the most trouble as well as other customer concerns. Most computer support specialists start out at the help desk.

Network administrators and *computer systems administrators* design, install, and support an organization's local area network (LAN), wide area network (WAN), network segment, Internet, or intranet system. They provide day-to-day onsite administrative support for software users in a variety of work environments, including professional offices, small businesses, government, and large corporations. They maintain network hardware and software, analyze problems, and monitor the network to ensure its availability to system users. These workers gather data to identify customer needs and then use the information to identify, interpret, and evaluate system and network requirements. Administrators also may plan, coordinate, and implement network security measures.

Systems administrators are the information technology employees responsible for the efficient use of networks by organizations. They ensure that the design of an organization's computer site allows all of the components, including computers, the network, and software, to fit together and work properly. Furthermore, they monitor and adjust the performance of existing networks and continually survey the current computer site to determine future network needs. Administrators also troubleshoot problems reported by users and by automated network monitoring systems and make recommendations for enhancements in the implementation of future servers and networks.

In some organizations, *computer security specialists* may plan, coordinate, and implement the organization's information security. These workers may be called upon to educate users about computer security, install security software, monitor the network for security breaches, respond to cyber attacks, and, in some cases, gather data and evidence to be used in prosecuting cyber crime. The responsibilities of computer security specialists have increased in recent years, as there has been a large increase in the number of cyber attacks on data and networks. This and other growing specialty occupations reflect an increasing emphasis on client-server applications, the expansion of Internet and intranet applications, and the demand for more end-user support.

Working Conditions

Computer support specialists and systems administrators normally work in well-lighted, comfortable offices or computer laboratories. They usually work about 40 hours a week, but that may include being "on call" via pager or telephone for rotating evening or weekend work if the employer requires computer support over extended hours. Overtime may be necessary when unexpected technical problems arise. Like other workers who type on a keyboard for long periods, computer support specialists and systems administrators are susceptible to eyestrain, back discomfort, and hand and wrist problems such as carpal tunnel syndrome.

Due to the heavy emphasis on helping all types of computer users, computer support specialists and systems administrators constantly interact with customers and fellow employees as they answer questions and give valuable advice. Those who work as consultants are away from their offices much of the time, sometimes spending months working in a client's office.

As computer networks expand, more computer support specialists and systems administrators may be able to connect to a customer's computer remotely, using modems, laptops, e-mail, and the Internet, to provide technical support to computer users. This capability would reduce or eliminate travel to the customer's workplace. Systems administrators also can administer and configure networks and servers remotely, although this practice is not as common as it is among computer support specialists.

Training, Other Qualifications, and Advancement

Due to the wide range of skills required, there are many paths of entry to a job as a computer support specialist or systems administrator. While there is no universally accepted way to prepare for a job as a computer support specialist, many employers prefer to hire persons with some formal college education. A bachelor's degree in computer science or information systems is a prerequisite for some jobs; however, other jobs may require only a computer-related associate's degree. For systems administrators, many employers seek applicants with bachelor's degrees, although not necessarily in a computer-related field.

A number of companies are becoming more flexible about requiring a college degree for support positions. However, certification and practical experience demonstrating these skills will be essential for applicants without a degree. The completion of a certification training program, offered by a variety of vendors and product makers, may help some people to qualify for entry-level positions. Relevant computer experience may substitute for formal education.

Beginning computer support specialists usually work for organizations that deal directly with customers or in-house users. Then they may advance into more responsible positions in which they use what they have learned from customers to improve the design and efficiency of future products. Job promotions usually depend more on performance than on formal education. Eventually, some computer support specialists become applications developers, designing products rather than assisting users. Computer support specialists at hardware and software companies often enjoy great upward mobility; advancement sometimes comes within months of one's initial employment.

Entry-level network and computer systems administrators are involved in routine maintenance and monitoring of computer systems, typically working behind the scenes in an organization. After gaining experience and expertise, they often are able to advance into more senior-level positions in which they take on more responsibilities. For example, senior network and computer systems administrators may present recommendations to management on matters related to a company's network. They also may translate the needs of an organization into a set of technical requirements based on the available technology. As with support specialists, administrators may become software engineers, actually involved in the designing of the system or network and not just its day-to-day administration.

Persons interested in becoming a computer support specialist or systems administrator must have strong problem-solving, analytical, and communication skills because troubleshooting and helping others are vital parts of the job. The constant interaction with other computer personnel, customers, and employees requires computer support specialists and systems administrators to communicate effectively on paper, via e-mail, or in person. Strong writing skills are useful in preparing manuals for employees and customers.

As technology continues to improve, computer support specialists and systems administrators must keep their skills current and acquire new ones. Many continuing education programs are provided by employers, hardware and software vendors, colleges and universities, and private training institutions. Professional development seminars offered by computing services firms also can enhance one's skills and advancement opportunities.

Employment

Computer support specialists and systems administrators held about 797,000 jobs in 2004. Of these, approximately 518,000 were computer support specialists and around 278,000 were network and computer systems administrators. Although they worked in a wide range of industries, about 23 percent of all computer support specialists and systems administrators were employed in professional, scientific, and technical services industries, principally computer systems design and related services. Other organizations that employed substantial numbers of these workers include administrative and support services companies; banks; government agencies; insurance companies; educational institutions; and wholesale and retail vendors of computers, office equipment, appliances, and home electronic equipment. Many computer support specialists worked for manufacturers of computers, semiconductors, and other electronic components.

Employers of computer support specialists and systems administrators range from startup companies to established industry leaders. With the continued development of the Internet, telecommunications, and e-mail, industries not typically associated with computers—such as construction—increasingly need computer workers.

Small and large firms across all industries are expanding or developing computer systems, creating an immediate need for computer support specialists and systems administrators.

Job Outlook

Job prospects should be best for college graduates who are up to date with the latest skills and technologies, particularly if they have supplemented their formal education with some relevant work experience. Employers will continue to seek computer specialists who possess a strong background in fundamental computer skills combined with good interpersonal and communication skills. Due to the demand for computer support specialists and systems administrators over the next decade, those who have strong computer skills but do not have a bachelor's degree should continue to qualify for some entry-level positions. However, certifications and practical experience are essential for persons without degrees.

Employment of computer support specialists is expected to increase faster than the average for all occupations through 2014 as organizations continue to adopt increasingly sophisticated technology and integrate it into their systems. Job growth will continue to be driven by the ongoing expansion of the computer system design and related services industry, which is projected to remain one of the fastest-growing industries in the U.S. economy. Growth will not be as explosive as during the previous decade, however, as the information technology industry matures and some of these jobs are increasingly outsourced overseas.

Job growth among computer support specialists reflects the rapid pace of improved technology. As computers and software become more complex, support specialists will be needed to provide technical assistance to customers and other users. New mobile technologies, such as wireless Internet access, will continue to create a demand for these workers to familiarize and educate computer users. Consulting opportunities for computer support specialists also should continue to grow as businesses increasingly need help managing, upgrading, and customizing ever more complex computer systems. However, growth in employment of support specialists may be tempered somewhat as firms continue to cut costs by shifting more routine work abroad to countries where workers are highly skilled and labor costs are lower. Physical location is not as important for computer support specialists as it is for others because these workers can provide assistance remotely and support services can be provided around the clock.

Employment of systems administrators is expected to increase much faster than the average for all occupations as firms continue to invest heavily in securing computer networks. Companies are looking for workers who are knowledgeable about the function and administration of networks. Such employees have become increasingly hard to find as systems administration has moved from being a separate function within corporations to one that forms a crucial element of business in an increasingly high-technology economy. Also, demand for computer security specialists will grow as businesses and government continue to invest heavily in "cyber security," protecting vital computer networks and electronic infrastructures from attack. The information security field is expected to generate many opportunities over the next decade as firms across all industries place a high priority on safeguarding their data and systems.

The growth of electronic commerce means that more establishments use the Internet to conduct their business online. This growth translates into a need for information technology specialists who can help organizations use technology to communicate with employees, clients, and consumers. Growth in these areas also is expected to fuel demand for specialists who are knowledgeable about network, data, and communications security.

Earnings

Median annual earnings of computer support specialists were $40,430 in May 2004. The middle 50 percent earned between $30,980 and $53,010. The lowest 10 percent earned less than $24,190, and the highest 10 percent earned more than $69,110. Median annual earnings in the industries employing the largest numbers of computer support specialists in May 2004 were as follows:

Software publishers $44,890

Management of companies and enterprises 42,780

Computer systems design and related services 42,750

Colleges, universities, and professional schools 37,940

Elementary and secondary schools 35,500

Median annual earnings of network and computer systems administrators were $58,190 in May 2004. The middle 50 percent earned between $46,260 and $73,620. The lowest 10 percent earned less than $37,100, and the highest 10 percent earned more than $91,300. Median annual earnings in the industries employing the largest numbers of network and computer systems administrators in May 2004 were as follows:

Wired telecommunications carriers $65,120

Computer systems design and related services 63,710

Management of companies and enterprises 61,600

Elementary and secondary schools 51,420

Colleges, universities, and professional schools 51,170

According to Robert Half International, starting salaries in 2005 ranged from $26,250 to $53,750 for help-desk and technical support staff and from $44,500 to $63,250 for more senior technical support specialists. For systems administrators, starting salaries in 2005 ranged from $47,250 to $70,500.

Related Occupations

Other computer specialists include computer programmers, computer software engineers, computer systems analysts, and computer scientists and database administrators.

Sources of Additional Information

For additional information about a career as a computer support specialist, contact the following organizations:

▸ Association of Computer Support Specialists, 333 Mamaroneck Ave., #129, White Plains, NY 10605. Internet: http://www.acss.org

▸ Association of Support Professionals, 122 Barnard Ave., Watertown, MA 02472.

For additional information about a career as a systems administrator, contact

▸ System Administrators Guild, 2560 9th St., Suite 215, Berkeley, CA 94710. Internet: http://www.sage.org

Further information about computer careers is available from

▸ National Workforce Center for Emerging Technologies, 3000 Landerholm Circle SE, Bellevue, WA 98007. Internet: http://www.nwcet.org

Computer Systems Analysts

(O*NET 15-1051.00)

Significant Points

■ Employers generally prefer applicants who have at least a bachelor's degree in computer science, information science, or management information systems (MIS).

■ Employment is expected to increase much faster than the average as organizations continue to adopt increasingly sophisticated technologies.

■ Job prospects are favorable.

Nature of the Work

All organizations rely on computer and information technology to conduct business and operate more efficiently. The rapid spread of technology across all industries has generated a need for highly trained workers to help organizations incorporate new technologies. The tasks performed by workers known as computer systems analysts evolve rapidly, reflecting new areas of specialization or changes in technology as well as the preferences and practices of employers.

Computer systems analysts solve computer problems and apply computer technology to meet the individual needs of an organization. They help an organization to realize the maximum benefit from its investment in equipment, personnel, and business processes. Systems analysts may plan and develop new computer systems or devise ways to apply existing systems' resources to additional operations. They may design new systems, including both hardware and software, or add a new software application to harness more of the computer's power. Most systems analysts work with specific types of systems—for example, business, accounting, or financial systems or scientific and engineering systems—that vary with the kind of organization. Some systems analysts also are known as *systems developers* or *systems architects*.

Systems analysts begin an assignment by discussing the systems problem with managers and users to determine its exact nature. Defining the goals of the system and dividing the solutions into individual steps and separate procedures, systems analysts use techniques such as structured analysis, data modeling, information engineering, mathematical model building, sampling, and cost accounting to plan the system. They specify the inputs to be accessed by the system, design the processing steps, and format the output to meet users' needs. They also may prepare cost-benefit and return-on-investment analyses to help management decide whether implementing the proposed technology will be financially feasible.

When a system is accepted, systems analysts determine what computer hardware and software will be needed to set the system up. They coordinate tests and observe the initial use of the system to ensure that it performs as planned. They prepare specifications, flow charts, and process diagrams for computer programmers to follow; then, they work with programmers to "debug," or eliminate, errors from the system. Systems analysts who do more in-depth testing of products may be referred to as *software quality assurance analysts*. In addition to running tests, these individuals diagnose problems, recommend solutions, and determine whether program requirements have been met.

In some organizations, *programmer-analysts* design and update the software that runs a computer. Because they are responsible for both programming and systems analysis, these workers must be proficient in both areas. (A separate description of computer programmers appears elsewhere in this book.) As this dual proficiency becomes more commonplace, these analysts are increasingly working with databases and object-oriented programming languages as well as client-server applications development and multimedia and Internet technology.

One obstacle associated with expanding computer use is the need for different computer systems to communicate with each other. Because of the importance of maintaining up-to-date information— accounting records, sales figures, or budget projections, for example—systems analysts work on making the computer systems within an organization, or among organizations, compatible so that information can be shared among them. Many systems analysts are involved with "networking," connecting all the computers internally—in an individual office, department, or establishment—or externally because many organizations rely on e-mail or the Internet. A primary goal of networking is to allow users to retrieve data from a mainframe computer or a server and use it on their desktop computer. Systems analysts must design the hardware and software to allow the free exchange of data, custom applications, and the computer power to process it all. For example, analysts are called upon to ensure the compatibility of computing systems between and among businesses to facilitate electronic commerce.

Working Conditions

Computer systems analysts work in offices or laboratories in comfortable surroundings. They usually work about 40 hours a week— the same as many other professional or office workers do. However, evening or weekend work may be necessary to meet deadlines or solve specific problems. Given the technology available today, telecommuting is common for computer professionals. As networks expand, more work can be done from remote locations through modems, laptops, electronic mail, and the Internet.

Like other workers who spend long periods in front of a computer terminal typing on a keyboard, computer systems analysts are susceptible to eyestrain, back discomfort, and hand and wrist problems such as carpal tunnel syndrome or cumulative trauma disorder.

Training, Other Qualifications, and Advancement

Rapidly changing technology requires an increasing level of skill and education on the part of employees. Companies increasingly look for professionals with a broad background and range of skills, including not only technical knowledge but also communication and other interpersonal skills. This shift from requiring workers to possess solely sound technical knowledge emphasizes workers who can handle various responsibilities. While there is no universally accepted way to prepare for a job as a systems analyst, most employers place a premium on some formal college education. Relevant work experience also is very important. For more technically complex jobs, persons with graduate degrees are preferred.

Many employers seek applicants who have at least a bachelor's degree in computer science, information science, or management information systems (MIS). MIS programs usually are part of the business school or college and differ considerably from computer science programs, emphasizing business and management-oriented coursework and business computing courses. Employers are increasingly seeking individuals with a master's degree in business administration (MBA), with a concentration in information systems, as more firms move their business to the Internet.

Despite employers' preference for those with technical degrees, persons with degrees in a variety of majors find employment as system analysts. The level of education and type of training that employers require depend on their needs. One factor affecting these needs is changes in technology. Employers often scramble to find workers capable of implementing "hot" new technologies such as wireless Internet. Those workers with formal education or experience in information security, for example, are in demand because of the growing need for their skills and services. Another factor driving employers' needs is the timeframe during which a project must be completed.

Employers usually look for people who have broad knowledge and experience related to computer systems and technologies, strong problem-solving and analytical skills, and good interpersonal skills. Courses in computer science or systems design offer good preparation for a job in these computer occupations. For jobs in a business environment, employers usually want systems analysts to have business management or closely related skills, while a background in the physical sciences, applied mathematics, or engineering is preferred for work in scientifically oriented organizations.

Job seekers can enhance their employment opportunities by participating in internship or co-op programs offered through their schools. Because many people develop advanced computer skills in a non-computer-related occupation and then transfer those skills to a computer occupation, a background in the industry in which the person's job is located, such as financial services, banking, or accounting, can be important. Others have taken computer science courses to supplement their study in fields such as accounting, inventory control, or other business areas.

Computer systems analysts must be able to think logically and have good communication skills. Because they often deal with a number of tasks simultaneously, the ability to concentrate and pay close attention to detail is important. Although these workers sometimes work independently, they frequently work in teams on large projects. They must be able to communicate effectively with computer personnel, such as programmers and managers, as well as with users or other staff who may have no technical computer background.

Systems analysts may be promoted to senior or lead systems analyst. Those who show leadership ability also can become project managers or advance into management positions such as manager of information systems or chief information officer. Workers with work experience and considerable expertise in a particular subject or a certain application may find lucrative opportunities as independent consultants or may choose to start their own computer consulting firms.

Technological advances come so rapidly in the computer field that continuous study is necessary to keep one's skills up to date. Employers, hardware and software vendors, colleges and universities, and private training institutions offer continuing education. Additional training may come from professional development seminars offered by professional computing societies.

Employment

Computer systems analysts held about 487,000 jobs in 2004; about 28,000 were self-employed.

Although they are increasingly employed in every sector of the economy, the greatest concentration of these workers is in the computer systems design and related services industry. Firms in this industry provide services related to the commercial use of computers on a contract basis, including custom computer programming services; computer systems integration design services; computer facilities management services, including computer systems or data-processing facilities; support services for clients; and other computer services, such as disaster recovery services and software installation. Computer systems analysts are also employed by governments, insurance companies, financial institutions, Internet service providers, data-processing services firms, and universities.

A growing number of systems analysts are employed on a temporary or contract basis; many of these individuals are self-employed, working independently as contractors or consultants. For example, a company installing a new computer system may need the services of several systems analysts just to get the system running. Because not all of the analysts would be needed once the system is functioning, the company might contract for such employees with a temporary help agency or a consulting firm or with the systems analysts themselves. Such jobs may last from several months up to 2 years or more. This growing practice enables companies to bring in people with the exact skills the firm needs to complete a particular project instead of having to spend time or money training or retraining existing workers. Often, experienced consultants then train a company's in-house staff as a project develops.

Job Outlook

Employment of computer systems analysts is expected to grow much faster than the average for all occupations through the year 2014 as organizations continue to adopt and integrate increasingly sophisticated technologies. Job increases will be driven by very rapid growth in computer system design and related services, which is projected to be among the fastest-growing industries in the U.S. economy. In addition, many job openings will arise annually from the need to replace workers who move into managerial positions or other occupations or who leave the labor force. Job growth will not be as rapid as during the previous decade, however, as the information technology sector begins to mature and as routine work is increasingly outsourced to lower-wage foreign countries.

Workers in the occupation should enjoy favorable job prospects. The demand for networking to facilitate the sharing of information, the expansion of client-server environments, and the need for computer specialists to use their knowledge and skills in a problem-solving capacity will be major factors in the rising demand for computer systems analysts. Moreover, falling prices of computer hardware and software should continue to induce more businesses to expand their computerized operations and integrate new technologies into them. In order to maintain a competitive edge and operate more efficiently, firms will keep demanding system analysts who are knowledgeable about the latest technologies and are able to apply them to meet the needs of businesses.

Increasingly, more sophisticated and complex technology is being implemented across all organizations, which should fuel the demand for these computer occupations. There is a growing demand for system analysts to help firms maximize their efficiency with available technology. Expansion of electronic commerce—doing business on the Internet—and the continuing need to build and maintain databases that store critical information on customers, inventory, and projects are fueling demand for database administrators familiar with the latest technology. Also, the increasing importance being placed on "cybersecurity"—the protection of electronic information—will result in a need for workers skilled in information security.

The development of new technologies usually leads to demand for various kinds of workers. The expanding integration of Internet technologies into businesses, for example, has resulted in a growing need for specialists who can develop and support Internet and intranet applications. The growth of electronic commerce means that more establishments use the Internet to conduct their business online. The introduction of wireless Internet, known as WiFi, creates new systems to be analyzed. The spread of such new technologies translates into a need for information technology professionals who can help organizations use technology to communicate with employees, clients, and consumers. Explosive growth in these areas also is expected to fuel demand for analysts who are knowledgeable about network, data, and communications security.

As technology becomes more sophisticated and complex, employers demand a higher level of skill and expertise from their employees. Individuals with an advanced degree in computer science or computer engineering, or with an MBA with a concentration in information systems, should enjoy favorable employment prospects. College graduates with a bachelor's degree in computer science, computer engineering, information science, or MIS also should enjoy favorable prospects for employment, particularly if they have supplemented their formal education with practical experience.

Because employers continue to seek computer specialists who can combine strong technical skills with good interpersonal and business skills, graduates with non-computer-science degrees who have had courses in computer programming, systems analysis, and other information technology subjects also should continue to find jobs in computer fields. In fact, individuals with the right experience and training can work in computer occupations regardless of their college major or level of formal education.

Earnings

Median annual earnings of computer systems analysts were $66,460 in May 2004. The middle 50 percent earned between $52,400 and $82,980 a year. The lowest 10 percent earned less than $41,730, and the highest 10 percent earned more than $99,180. Median annual earnings in the industries employing the largest numbers of computer systems analysts in May 2004 were

Federal government $71,770

Computer systems design and related services 69,560

Management of companies and enterprises 67,230

Insurance carriers 66,840

State government 57,040

According to the National Association of Colleges and Employers, starting offers for graduates with a master's degree in computer science averaged $62,727 in 2005. Starting offers averaged $50,820 for graduates with a bachelor's degree in computer science, $46,189 for those with a degree in computer systems analysis, $44,417 for those with a degree in management information systems, and $44,775 for those with a degree in information sciences and systems.

According to Robert Half International, starting salaries for systems analysts ranged from $61,500 to $82,500 in 2005.

Related Occupations

Other workers who use computers extensively and who use logic and creativity to solve business and technical problems include computer programmers, computer software engineers, computer and information systems managers, engineers, mathematicians, statisticians, operations research analysts, management analysts, and actuaries.

Sources of Additional Information

Further information about computer careers is available from

▸ Association for Computing Machinery (ACM), 1515 Broadway, New York, NY 10036. Internet: http://www.acm.org

▸ Institute of Electrical and Electronics Engineers Computer Society, Headquarters Office, 1730 Massachusetts Ave. NW, Washington, DC 20036-1992. Internet: http://www.computer.org

▸ National Workforce Center for Emerging Technologies, 3000 Landerholm Circle SE, Bellevue, WA 98007. Internet: http://www.nwcet.org

Computer, Automated Teller, and Office Machine Repairers

(O*NET 49-2011.01, 49-2011.02, and 49-2011.03)

Significant Points

■ Workers qualify for these jobs by receiving training in electronics from associate degree programs, the military, vocational schools, equipment manufacturers, or employers.

■ Job growth reflects the increasing dependence of businesses and individuals on computers and other sophisticated office machines.

■ Job prospects will be best for applicants with knowledge of electronics as well as repair experience.

Nature of the Work

Computer repairers, also known as *computer service technicians or data-processing equipment repairers,* service mainframe, server, and personal computers; printers; and disc drives. These workers perform primarily hands-on repair, maintenance, and installation of computers and related equipment. Workers who provide technical assistance, in person or by telephone, to computer system users are known as computer support specialists or computer support technicians. (See the description of computer support specialists and systems administrators elsewhere in this book.)

Automated teller machines (ATMs) allow customers to carry out bank transactions without the assistance of a teller. ATMs now also provide a growing variety of other services, including stamp, phone card, and ticket sales. *Automated teller machine servicers* repair and service these machines.

Office machine and cash register servicers work on photocopiers, cash registers, mail-processing equipment, and fax machines. Newer models of office machinery include computerized components that allow them to function more effectively than earlier models.

To install large equipment, such as mainframe computers and ATMs, repairers connect the equipment to power sources and communication lines that allow the transmission of information over computer networks. For example, when an ATM dispenses cash, it transmits the withdrawal information to the customer's bank. Workers also may install operating software and peripheral equipment, checking that all components are configured to function together correctly. The installation of personal computers and other small office machines is less complex and may be handled by the purchaser.

When equipment breaks down, many repairers travel to customers' workplaces or other locations to make the necessary repairs. These workers, known as *field technicians*, often have assigned areas in which they perform preventive maintenance on a regular basis. *Bench technicians* work in repair shops located in stores, factories, or service centers. In small companies, repairers may work both in repair shops and at customer locations.

Computer repairers usually replace subsystems instead of repairing them. Replacement is common because subsystems are inexpensive and businesses are reluctant to shut down their computers for time-consuming repairs. Subsystems commonly replaced by computer repairers include video cards, which transmit signals from the computer to the monitor; hard drives, which store data; and network cards, which allow communication over the network. Defective modules may be given to bench technicians, who use software programs to diagnose the problem and who may repair the modules, if possible.

When ATMs malfunction, computer networks recognize the problem and alert repairers. Common problems include worn magnetic heads on card readers, which prevent the equipment from recognizing customers' bank cards, and "pick failures," which prevent the equipment from dispensing the correct amount of cash. Field technicians travel to the locations of ATMs and usually repair equipment by removing and replacing defective components. Broken components are taken to a repair shop, where bench technicians make the necessary repairs. Field technicians perform routine maintenance on a regular basis, replacing worn parts and running diagnostic tests to ensure that the equipment functions properly.

Office machine repairers usually work on machinery at the customer's workplace; alternatively, if the machines are small enough, customers may bring them to a repair shop for maintenance. Common malfunctions include paper misfeeds caused by worn or dirty parts and poor-quality copy resulting from problems with lamps, lenses, or mirrors. These malfunctions usually can be resolved simply by cleaning the relevant components. Breakdowns also may result from the failure of commonly used parts. For example, heavy use of a photocopier may wear down the print head, which applies ink to the final copy. In such cases, the repairer usually replaces the part instead of repairing it.

Workers use a variety of tools for diagnostic tests and repair. To diagnose malfunctions, they use multimeters to measure voltage, current, resistance, and other electrical properties; signal generators to provide test signals; and oscilloscopes to monitor equipment signals. To diagnose computerized equipment, repairers use software programs. To repair or adjust equipment, workers use hand tools, such as pliers, screwdrivers, soldering irons, and wrenches.

Working Conditions

Repairers usually work in clean, well-lighted surroundings. Because computers and office machines are sensitive to extreme temperatures and to humidity, repair shops usually are air-conditioned and well ventilated. Field repairers must travel frequently to various locations to install, maintain, or repair customers' equipment. ATM repairers may have to perform their jobs in small, confined spaces that house the equipment.

Because computers and ATMs are critical for many organizations to function efficiently, data processing equipment repairers and ATM field technicians often work around the clock. Their schedules may include evening, weekend, and holiday shifts, sometimes assigned on the basis of seniority. Office machine and cash register servicers usually work regular business hours because the equipment they repair is not as critical.

Although their job is not strenuous, repairers must lift equipment and work in a variety of postures. Repairers of computer monitors need to discharge voltage from the equipment to avoid electrocution. Workers may have to wear protective goggles.

Training, Other Qualifications, and Advancement

Knowledge of electronics is necessary for employment as a computer, automated teller, or office machine repairer. Employers prefer workers who are certified as repairers or who have training in electronics from associate degree programs, the military, vocational schools, or equipment manufacturers. Employers generally provide some training to new repairers on specific equipment; however, workers are expected to arrive on the job with a basic understanding of equipment repair. Employers may send experienced workers to training sessions to keep up with changes in technology and service procedures.

Most office machine and ATM repairer positions require an associate degree in electronics. A basic understanding of mechanical equipment also is important, because many of the parts that fail in office machines and ATMs, such as paper loaders, are mechanical. Entry-level employees at large companies normally receive on-the-job training lasting several months. Such training may include a week of classroom instruction, followed by a period of 2 weeks to several months assisting an experienced repairer.

Field technicians work closely with customers and must have good communications skills and a neat appearance. Employers normally require that field technicians have a driver's license.

Various organizations offer certification. To receive certification, repairers must pass qualifying examinations corresponding to their level of training and experience.

Newly hired computer repairers may work on personal computers or peripheral equipment. With experience, they can advance to positions maintaining more sophisticated systems, such as networking equipment and servers. Field repairers of ATMs may advance to bench technician positions responsible for more complex repairs. Experienced workers may become specialists who help other repairers diagnose difficult problems or who work with engineers in designing equipment and developing maintenance procedures. Experienced workers also may move into management positions responsible for supervising other repairers.

Because of their familiarity with equipment, experienced repairers may move into customer service or sales positions. Some experienced workers open their own repair shops or become wholesalers or retailers of electronic equipment.

Employment

Computer, automated teller, and office machine repairers held about 168,000 jobs in 2004. Wholesale trade establishments employed about 35 percent of the workers in this occupation; most of these establishments were wholesalers of professional and commercial equipment and supplies. Many workers also were employed in electronics, appliance, and office supply stores. Others worked in electronic and precision equipment repair shops and computer systems design firms. A small number found employment with computer and peripheral equipment manufacturers, government agencies, and Internet service providers. About 15 percent of computer, automated teller, and office machine repairers were self-employed, which is more than twice the proportion for all installation, maintenance, and repair occupations.

Job Outlook

Employment of computer, automated teller, and office machine repairers is expected to grow more slowly than the average for all occupations through 2014. Limited job growth will be driven by the increasing dependence of business and individuals on computers and other sophisticated office machines. The need to maintain this equipment will create new jobs for repairers. In addition, openings will result from the need to replace repairers who retire or transfer to new occupations.

Job prospects will be best for applicants with knowledge of electronics as well as repair experience. Although computer equipment continues to become less expensive and more reliable, malfunctions still occur and can cause severe problems for users, most of whom lack the knowledge to make repairs. Computers are critical to most businesses today and will become even more so to companies that do business on the Internet and to individuals that bank, pay bills, or make purchases online.

People also are becoming increasingly reliant on ATMs. Besides offering bank and retail transactions, ATMs provide an increasing number of other services, such as employee information processing and distribution of government payments. Improvements in ATM design have increased reliability and simplified repair tasks, reducing the number and extent of repairs. However, opportunities for ATM repairers should still be available; they will arise primarily from the need to replace workers who leave the specialty, rather than from employment growth.

Conventional office machines, such as calculators, are inexpensive and often are replaced instead of repaired. However, digital copiers and other, newer office machines are more costly and complex. This equipment often is computerized, designed to work on a network, and capable of performing multiple functions. The growing need for repairers to service such sophisticated equipment should result in job opportunities for office machine repairers.

Earnings

Median hourly earnings of computer, automated teller, and office machine repairers were $16.90 in May 2004. The middle 50 percent earned between $13.11 and $21.36. The lowest 10 percent earned less than $10.31, and the highest 10 percent earned more than $26.28. Median hourly earnings in the industries employing the largest numbers of computer, automated teller, and office machine repairers in May 2004 are shown here:

Professional and commercial equipment and
   supplies merchant wholesalers $18.51
Computer systems design and related services 18.08
Office supplies, stationery, and gift stores 15.69
Electronic and precision equipment repair
   and maintenance 14.95
Electronics and appliance stores 14.04

Related Occupations

Workers in other occupations who repair and maintain electronic equipment include broadcast and sound engineering technicians and radio operators; electronic home entertainment equipment installers and repairers; electrical and electronics installers and repairers; industrial machinery mechanics and maintenance workers; and radio and telecommunications equipment installers and repairers.

Sources of Additional Information

For information on careers and certification, contact

▸ ACES International, 5241 Princess Anne Rd., Suite 110, Virginia Beach, VA 23462. Internet: http://www.acesinternational.org

▸ Electronics Technicians Association International, 5 Depot St., Greencastle, IN 46135.

▸ International Society of Certified Electronics Technicians, 3608 Pershing Ave., Fort Worth, TX 76107-4527. Internet: http://www.iscet.org

Conservation Scientists and Foresters

(O*NET 19-1031.01, 19-1031.02, 19-1031.03, and 19-1032.00)

Significant Points

■ About two-thirds of salaried conservation scientists and foresters work for federal, state, or local governments.

■ A bachelor's degree in forestry, range management, or a related discipline is the minimum educational requirement.

■ Slower-than-average job growth is projected; most new jobs will be in state and local governments and in private-sector forestry and conservation consulting.

Nature of the Work

Forests and rangelands supply wood products, livestock forage, minerals, and water; serve as sites for recreational activities; and provide habitats for wildlife.

Conservation scientists and foresters manage their use and development and help to protect these and other natural resources, and for this reason, they are becoming known as natural resource managers.

Foresters manage forested lands for a variety of purposes. Those working in private industry may manage company-owned forest land or procure timber from private landowners. Company forests usually are managed to produce a sustainable supply of wood for company mills. *Procurement foresters* contact local forest owners and gain permission to take inventory of the type, amount, and location of all standing timber on the property, a process known as timber cruising. These foresters then appraise the timber's worth, negotiate its purchase, and draw up a contract for procurement. Next, they subcontract with loggers or pulpwood cutters for tree removal and aid in laying out roads to access the timber. Throughout the process, foresters maintain close contact with the subcontractor's workers and the landowner to ensure that the work meets the landowner's requirements, as well as federal, state, and local environmental specifications. Forestry consultants often act as agents for forest owners, monitoring the growth of the timber on the owners' property and negotiating timber sales with industrial procurement foresters.

Foresters, referred to as *land management foresters,* work for both government and private industry and manage and protect the forests and supervise harvests. These foresters supervise the planting and growing of new trees, called regeneration. They choose and direct the preparation of the site, using controlled burning, bulldozers, or herbicides to clear weeds, brush, and logging debris. They advise on the type, number, and placement of trees to be planted. Foresters then monitor the seedlings to ensure healthy growth and to determine the best time for harvesting. If they detect signs of disease or harmful insects, they consult with specialists in forest pest management to decide on the best course of treatment. They may also design campgrounds and recreation areas on public lands.

Throughout the forest management and procurement processes, foresters consider the economics as well as the environmental impact on natural resources. To do this, they determine how to conserve wildlife habitats, creek beds, water quality, and soil stability and how best to comply with environmental regulations. Foresters must balance the desire to conserve forested ecosystems for future generations with the need to use forest resources for recreational or economic purposes.

Foresters use a number of tools to perform their jobs. Clinometers measure the height of trees, diameter tapes measure the diameter, and increment borers and bark gauges measure the growth of trees so that timber volumes can be computed and growth rates estimated. Remote sensing (aerial photographs and other imagery taken from airplanes and satellites) and Geographic Information Systems (GIS) data often are used for mapping large forest areas and for detecting widespread trends of forest and land use. Once the map is generated, the data are digitized to create a computerized inventory of information required to manage the forest land and its resources. Moreover, hand-held computers, Global Positioning Systems (GPS), and World Wide Web–based applications are used extensively.

Conservation scientists manage, improve, and protect the country's natural resources. They work with the landowners and federal, state, and local governments to devise ways to use and improve the land without damaging the environment. Although conservation scientists mainly advise farmers, farm managers, and ranchers on ways they can improve their land for agricultural purposes and to control erosion, a growing number are advising landowners and governments on recreational uses for the land.

Two of the more common conservation scientists are range managers and soil conservationists. *Range managers,* also called *range conservationists*, *range ecologists*, or *range scientists*, study, manage, improve, and protect rangelands to maximize their use without damaging the environment. Rangelands cover hundreds of millions of acres of the United States, mostly in western states and Alaska. They contain many natural resources, including grass and shrubs for animal grazing, wildlife habitats, water from vast watersheds, recreation facilities, and valuable mineral and energy resources. Range managers may inventory soils, plants, and animals; develop resource management plans; help to restore degraded ecosystems; or assist in managing a ranch. For example, they may help ranchers attain optimum livestock production by determining the number and kind of animals to graze, the grazing system to use, and the best season for grazing. At the same time, however, range managers maintain soil stability and vegetation for other uses such as wildlife habitats and outdoor recreation. They also plan and implement revegetation of disturbed sites.

Soil and water conservationists provide technical assistance to farmers, ranchers, forest managers, state and local agencies, and others concerned with the conservation of soil, water, and related natural resources. They develop programs for private landowners designed to make the most productive use of land without damaging it. Soil conservationists also assist landowners by visiting areas with erosion problems, finding the source of the problem, and helping landowners and managers develop management practices to combat it. Water conservationists also assist private landowners and federal, state, and local governments by advising on a broad range of natural resource topics—specifically, issues of water quality, preserving water supplies, groundwater contamination, and management and conservation of water resources.

Conservation scientists and foresters often specialize in one area, such as wildlife management, urban forestry, pest management, native species, or forest economics.

Working Conditions

Working conditions vary considerably. Although some of the work is solitary, foresters and conservation scientists also deal regularly with landowners, loggers, forestry technicians and aides, farmers, ranchers, government officials, special interest groups, and the public in general. Some foresters and conservation scientists work regular hours in offices or labs. Others may split their time between fieldwork and office work, while independent consultants and especially new, less experienced workers spend the majority of their time outdoors overseeing or participating in hands-on work.

The work can be physically demanding. Some conservation scientists and foresters work outdoors in all types of weather, sometimes in isolated areas, and consequently may need to walk long distances through densely wooded land to carry out their work. Foresters also may work long hours fighting fires. Conservation scientists often are called to prevent erosion after a forest fire, and they provide emergency help after floods, mudslides, and tropical storms.

Training, Other Qualifications, and Advancement

A bachelor's degree in forestry, biology, natural resource management, environmental sciences, or a related discipline is the minimum educational requirement for careers in forestry or conservation science. In the federal government, a combination of experience and appropriate education occasionally may substitute for a 4-year forestry degree, but job competition makes this difficult. Foresters who wish to perform specialized research or teach should have an advanced degree, preferably a Ph.D.

Seventeen states have mandatory licensing and/or voluntary registration requirements that a forester must meet in order to acquire the title "professional forester" and practice forestry in the state. Of those 17 states, 9 have mandatory licensing; 8 have mandatory registration. Both licensing and registration requirements usually entail completing a 4-year degree in forestry and several years of forestry work experience. Candidates pursuing licensing also may be required to pass a comprehensive written exam.

Most land-grant colleges and universities offer a bachelor's or higher degree in forestry. The Society of American Foresters accredits about 48 such programs throughout the country. Curriculums stress four components: forest ecology and biology, measurement of forest resources, management of forest resources, and public policy. Students should balance general science courses such as ecology, biology, tree physiology, taxonomy, and soil formation with technical forestry courses, such as forest inventory or wildlife habitat assessment, remote sensing, land surveying, GPS technology, integrated forest resource management, silviculture, and forest protection. In addition, mathematics, statistics, and computer science courses also are recommended. Many forestry curriculums include advanced computer applications such as GIS and resource assessment programs. Courses in resource policy and administration, specifically forest economics and business administration, supplement the student's scientific and technical knowledge. Forestry curriculums increasingly include courses on best management practices, wetlands analysis, and sustainability and regulatory issues in response to the growing focus on protecting forested lands during timber harvesting operations. Prospective foresters should have a strong grasp of federal, state, and local policy issues and of increasingly numerous and complex environmental regulations that affect many forestry-related activities. Many colleges require students to complete a field session either in a camp operated by the college or in a cooperative work-study program with a federal or state agency or with private industry. All schools encourage students to take summer jobs that provide experience in forestry or conservation work.

Conservation scientists generally hold a minimum of a bachelor's degree in fields such as ecology, natural resource management, agriculture, biology, environmental science, or a related field. A master's or Ph.D. degree is usually required for teaching and research positions.

Range managers usually have a degree in range management or range science. Nine colleges and universities offer degrees in range management that are accredited by the Society of Range Management. More than forty other schools offer course work in range science or in a closely related discipline offering a range management or range science option. Specialized range management courses combine plant, animal, and soil sciences with principles of ecology and resource management. Desirable electives include economics, statistics, forestry, hydrology, agronomy, wildlife, animal husbandry, computer science, and recreation. Selection of a minor in range management, such as wildlife ecology, watershed management, animal science, or agricultural economics, can often enhance qualifications for certain types of employment.

The Society for Range Management offers two types of certification: one as a certified professional in rangeland management (CPRM) and another as a certified range management consultant. Candidates seeking certification must have at least a bachelor's degree in range science or a closely related field, have a minimum of 6 years of full-time work experience, and pass a comprehensive written exam.

The Society of American Foresters has a Certified Forester Program. To become certified through this program, a candidate must graduate with at least a bachelor's degree from a forestry program accredited by the Society or from a forestry program that, though not accredited by the Society, is substantially equivalent. In addition, the candidate must have five years of qualifying professional experience and pass an examination.

Additionally, a graduate with the proper coursework in college can seek certification as a wetland scientist through the Society of Wetland Scientists and certification as a professional wildlife biologist through the Wildlife Society.

Very few colleges and universities offer degrees in soil conservation. Most soil conservationists have degrees in environmental studies, agronomy, general agriculture, hydrology, or crop or soil science; a few have degrees in related fields such as wildlife biology, forestry, and range management. Programs of study usually include 30 semester hours in natural resources or agriculture, including at least 3 hours in soil science.

In addition to meeting the demands of forestry and conservation research and analysis, foresters and conservation scientists generally must enjoy working outdoors, be able to tolerate extensive walking and other types of physical exertion, and be willing to move to where the jobs are. They also must work well with people and have good communication skills.

Recent forestry and conservation scientist graduates usually work under the supervision of experienced foresters or scientists. After gaining experience, they may advance to more responsible positions. In the federal government, most entry-level foresters work in forest resource management. An experienced federal forester may supervise a ranger district and may advance to forest supervisor, to regional forester, or to a top administrative position in the national headquarters. In private industry, foresters start by learning the practical and administrative aspects of the business and acquiring comprehensive technical training. They are then introduced to contract writing, timber harvesting, and decisionmaking. Some foresters work their way up to top managerial positions within their companies. Foresters in management usually leave the fieldwork behind, spending more of their time in an office, working with teams to develop management plans and supervising others. After gaining several years of experience, some foresters may become consulting foresters, working alone or with one or several partners. They contract with state or local governments, private landowners, private industry, or other forestry consulting groups.

Soil conservationists usually begin working within one county or conservation district and, with experience, may advance to the area, state, regional, or national level. Also, soil conservationists can transfer to related occupations, such as farm or ranch management advisor or land appraiser.

Employment

Conservation scientists and foresters held about 32,000 jobs in 2004. More than 1 in 3 workers were employed by the federal government, mostly in the U.S. Departments of Agriculture (USDA) and Interior. Foresters were concentrated in the USDA's Forest Service; soil conservationists were employed primarily in the USDA's Natural Resource Conservation Service. Most range managers worked in the U.S. Department of the Interior's Bureau of Land Management, the Natural Resource Conservation Service, or the Forest Service. Another 21 percent of conservation scientists and foresters worked for state governments, and about 11 percent worked for local governments. The remainder worked in private industry, mainly in support activities for agriculture and forestry or in wood product manufacturing. Some were self-employed as consultants for private landowners, federal and state governments, and forestry-related businesses.

Although conservation scientists and foresters work in every state, employment of foresters is concentrated in the western and southeastern states, where many national and private forests and parks, and most of the lumber and pulpwood-producing forests, are located. Range managers work almost entirely in the western states, where most of the rangeland is located. Soil conservationists, on the other hand, are employed in almost every county in the country. Besides the jobs described here, some foresters and conservation scientists held faculty positions in colleges and universities. (See the description of teachers—postsecondary elsewhere in this book.)

Job Outlook

Employment of conservation scientists and foresters is expected to increase more slowly than the average for all occupations through 2014. Growth should be strongest in private-sector consulting firms. Demand will be spurred by a continuing emphasis on environmental protection, responsible land management, and water-related issues. Growing interest in developing private lands and forests for recreational purposes will generate additional jobs for foresters and conservation scientists. Fire prevention is another area of growth for these two occupations.

Job opportunities for conservation scientists will arise because government regulations, such as those regarding the management of storm water and coastlines, have created demand for persons knowledgeable about runoff and erosion on farms and in cities and suburbs. Soil and water quality experts will be needed as states design initiatives to improve water resources by preventing pollution by agricultural producers and industrial plants.

Overall employment of conservation scientists and foresters is expected to decline slightly in the federal government, mostly because of budgetary constraints and the trend among all levels of government toward contracting these functions out to private consulting firms. Also, federal land management agencies, such as the USDA Forest Service, have de-emphasized their timber programs and increasingly focused on wildlife, recreation, and sustaining ecosystems, thereby spurring demand for other life and

social scientists rather than for foresters. However, departures of foresters who retire or leave the government for other reasons will result in many job openings. Additionally, state governments are expected to increase their hiring of conservation scientists and foresters as their budgetary situations improve. A small number of new jobs will result from the need for range and soil conservationists to provide technical assistance to owners of grazing land through the Natural Resource Conservation Service.

Foresters involved with timber harvesting will find good opportunities in the Southeast, where much forested land is privately owned. However, the recent opening of public lands, especially in the West, to commercial activity will also help the outlook for foresters. Salaried foresters working for private industry—such as paper companies, sawmills, and pulpwood mills—and consulting foresters will be needed to provide technical assistance and management plans to landowners.

Scientific research and development services have increased their hiring of conservation scientists and foresters in recent years in response to demand for professionals to prepare environmental impact statements and erosion and sediment control plans; monitor water quality near logging sites; and advise on tree harvesting practices required by federal, state, or local regulations. Hiring in these firms should continue during the 2004–2014 period.

Earnings

Median annual earnings of conservation scientists in May 2004 were $52,480. The middle 50 percent earned between $39,660 and $65,550. The lowest 10 percent earned less than $30,740, and the highest 10 percent earned more than $78,470.

Median annual earnings of foresters in 2004 were $48,230. The middle 50 percent earned between $37,260 and $60,500. The lowest 10 percent earned less than $29,770, and the highest 10 percent earned more than $72,050.

In 2005, most bachelor's degree graduates entering the federal government as foresters, range managers, or soil conservationists started at $24,677 or $30,567, depending on academic achievement. Those with a master's degree could start at $37,390 or $45,239. Holders of doctorates could start at $54,221. Beginning salaries were slightly higher in selected areas where the prevailing local pay level was higher. In 2005, the average federal salary for foresters in nonsupervisory, supervisory, and managerial positions was $63,492; for soil conservationists, $60,671; and for rangeland managers, $58,162.

According to the National Association of Colleges and Employers, graduates with a bachelor's degree in conservation and renewable natural resources received an average starting salary offer of $27,950 in 2005.

In private industry, starting salaries for students with a bachelor's degree were comparable with starting salaries in the federal government, but starting salaries in state and local governments were usually lower.

Conservation scientists and foresters who work for federal, state, and local governments and large private firms generally receive more generous benefits than do those working for smaller firms.

Related Occupations

Conservation scientists and foresters manage, develop, and protect natural resources. Other workers with similar responsibilities include environmental engineers; agricultural and food scientists; biological scientists; environmental scientists and geoscientists; and farmers, ranchers, and agricultural managers.

Sources of Additional Information

For information about the forestry profession and lists of schools offering education in forestry, send a self-addressed, stamped business envelope to

▶ Society of American Foresters, 5400 Grosvenor Lane, Bethesda, MD 20814-2198. Internet: http://www.safnet.org

Information about a career as a range manager, as well as a list of schools offering training, is available from

▶ Society for Range Management, 445 Union Blvd., Suite 230, Lakewood, CO 80228-1259. Internet: http://www.rangelands.org

For information on certification as a professional wildlife biologist, contact

▶ The Wildlife Society, 5410 Grosvenor Lane, Suite 200, Bethesda, MD 20814-2197. Internet: http://www.wildlife.org/certification/index.cfm

Information on obtaining a position as a conservation scientist or forester with the federal government is available from the Office of Personnel Management (OPM) through USAJOBS, the federal government's official employment information system. This resource for locating and applying for job opportunities can be accessed through the Internet at http://www.usajobs.opm.gov or through an interactive voice response telephone system at (703) 724-1850 or TDD (978)461-8404. These numbers are not toll free, and charges may result.

Dental Assistants

(O*NET 31-9091.00)

Significant Points

■ Job prospects should be excellent.

■ Dentists are expected to hire more assistants to perform routine tasks so that they may devote their own time to more complex procedures.

■ Most assistants learn their skills on the job, although an increasing number are trained in dental-assisting programs; most programs take 1 year or less to complete.

Nature of the Work

Dental assistants perform a variety of patient care, office, and laboratory duties. They work chairside as dentists examine and treat patients. They make patients as comfortable as possible in the dental chair, prepare them for treatment, and obtain their dental records. Assistants hand instruments and materials to dentists and keep patients' mouths dry and clear by using suction or other devices. Assistants also sterilize and disinfect instruments and equipment, prepare trays of instruments for dental procedures, and instruct patients on postoperative and general oral health care.

Some dental assistants prepare materials for impressions and restorations, take dental X rays, and process X-ray film as directed by a dentist. They also may remove sutures, apply topical anesthetics to gums or cavity-preventive agents to teeth, remove excess cement used in the filling process, and place rubber dams on the teeth to isolate them for individual treatment.

Those with laboratory duties make casts of the teeth and mouth from impressions, clean and polish removable appliances, and make temporary crowns. Dental assistants with office duties schedule and confirm appointments, receive patients, keep treatment records, send bills, receive payments, and order dental supplies and materials.

Dental assistants should not be confused with dental hygienists, who are licensed to perform different clinical tasks. (See the description of dental hygienists elsewhere in this book.)

Working Conditions

Dental assistants work in a well-lighted, clean environment. Their work area usually is near the dental chair so that they can arrange instruments, materials, and medication and hand them to the dentist when needed. Dental assistants must wear gloves, masks, eyewear, and protective clothing to protect themselves and their patients from infectious diseases. Assistants also follow safety procedures to minimize the risks associated with the use of X-ray machines.

About half of dental assistants have a 35- to 40-hour workweek, which may include work on Saturdays or evenings.

Training, Other Qualifications, and Advancement

Most assistants learn their skills on the job, although an increasing number are trained in dental-assisting programs offered by community and junior colleges, trade schools, technical institutes, or the Armed Forces. Assistants must be a second pair of hands for a dentist; therefore, dentists look for people who are reliable, work well with others, and have good manual dexterity. High school students interested in a career as a dental assistant should take courses in biology, chemistry, health, and office practices.

The Commission on Dental Accreditation within the American Dental Association (ADA) approved 265 dental-assisting training programs in 2005. Programs include classroom, laboratory, and preclinical instruction in dental-assisting skills and related theory. In addition, students gain practical experience in dental schools, clinics, or dental offices. Most programs take 1 year or less to complete and lead to a certificate or diploma. Two-year programs offered in community and junior colleges lead to an associate degree. All programs require a high school diploma or its equivalent, and some require science or computer-related courses for admission. A number of private vocational schools offer 4-month to 6-month courses in dental assisting, but the Commission on Dental Accreditation does not accredit these programs.

Most states regulate the duties that dental assistants are allowed to perform through licensure or registration. Licensure or registration may require passing a written or practical examination. States offering licensure or registration have a variety of schools offering courses—approximately 10 to 12 months in length—that meet their state's requirements. Other states require dental assistants to complete state-approved education courses of 4 to 12 hours in length. Some states offer registration of other dental assisting credentials with little or no education required. Some states require continuing education to maintain licensure or registration. A few states allow dental assistants to perform any function delegated to them by the dentist.

Individual states have adopted different standards for dental assistants who perform certain advanced duties, such as radiological procedures. Completion of the Radiation Health and Safety examination offered by the Dental Assisting National Board (DANB) meets those standards in more than 30 states. Some states require completion of a state-approved course in radiology as well.

Certification is available through DANB and is recognized or required in more than 30 states. Other organizations offer registration, most often at the state level. Certification is an acknowledgment of an assistant's qualifications and professional competence and may be an asset when one is seeking employment. Candidates may qualify to take the DANB certification examination by graduating from an ADA-accredited dental assisting education program or by having 2 years of full-time, or 4 years of part-time, experience as a dental assistant. In addition, applicants must have current certification in cardiopulmonary resuscitation. For annual recertification, individuals must earn continuing education credits.

Without further education, advancement opportunities are limited. Some dental assistants become office managers, dental-assisting instructors, or dental product sales representatives. Others go back to school to become dental hygienists. For many, this entry-level occupation provides basic training and experience and serves as a stepping-stone to more highly skilled and higher-paying jobs.

Employment

Dental assistants held about 267,000 jobs in 2004. Almost all jobs for dental assistants were in offices of dentists. A small number of jobs were in the federal, state, and local governments or in offices of physicians. About 2 out of 5 dental assistants worked part time, sometimes in more than one dental office.

Job Outlook

Job prospects for dental assistants should be excellent. Employment is expected to grow much faster than average for all occupations through the year 2014. In fact, dental assistants is expected to be one of the fastest-growing occupations over the 2004–2014 projection period.

In addition to job openings due to employment growth, numerous job openings will arise out of the need to replace assistants who transfer to other occupations, retire, or leave for other reasons. Many opportunities are for entry-level positions offering on-the-job training.

Population growth and greater retention of natural teeth by middle-aged and older people will fuel demand for dental services. Older dentists, who have been less likely to employ assistants, are leaving the occupation and will be replaced by recent graduates, who are more likely to use one or even two assistants. In addition, as dentists' workloads increase, they are expected to hire more assistants to perform routine tasks so that they may devote their own time to more complex procedures.

Earnings

Median hourly earnings of dental assistants were $13.62 in May 2004. The middle 50 percent earned between $11.06 and $16.65 an hour. The lowest 10 percent earned less than $9.11, and the highest 10 percent earned more than $19.97 an hour.

Benefits vary substantially by practice setting and may be contingent upon full-time employment. According to the American Dental Association (ADA), almost all full-time dental assistants employed by private practitioners received paid vacation time. The ADA also found that 9 out of 10 full-time and part-time dental assistants received dental coverage.

Related Occupations

Other workers supporting health practitioners include medical assistants, occupational therapist assistants and aides, pharmacy aides, pharmacy technicians, and physical therapist assistants and aides.

Sources of Additional Information

Information about career opportunities and accredited dental assistant programs is available from

▸ Commission on Dental Accreditation, American Dental Association, 211 East Chicago Ave., Suite 1814, Chicago, IL 60611. Internet: http://www.ada.org

For information on becoming a Certified Dental Assistant and a list of state boards of dentistry, contact

▸ Dental Assisting National Board, Inc., 676 North Saint Clair St., Suite 1880, Chicago, IL 60611. Internet: http://www.danb.org

For more information on a career as a dental assistant and general information about continuing education, contact

▸ American Dental Assistants Association, 35 East Wacker Dr., Suite 1730, Chicago, IL 60601. Internet: http://www.dentalassistant.org

For more information about continuing education courses, contact

▸ National Association of Dental Assistants, 900 South Washington St., Suite G-13, Falls Church, VA 22046.

Dental Hygienists

(O*NET 29-2021.00)

Significant Points

■ Most dental hygiene programs grant an associate degree; others offer a certificate, a bachelor's degree, or a master's degree.

■ Dental hygienists rank among the fastest-growing occupations.

■ Job prospects are expected to remain excellent.

■ More than half work part time, and flexible scheduling is a distinctive feature of this job.

Nature of the Work

Dental hygienists remove soft and hard deposits from teeth, teach patients how to practice good oral hygiene, and provide other preventive dental care. Hygienists examine patients' teeth and gums, recording the presence of diseases or abnormalities. They remove calculus, stains, and plaque from teeth; perform root planing as a periodontal therapy; take and develop dental X rays; and apply cavity-preventive agents such as fluorides and pit and fissure sealants. In some states, hygienists administer anesthetics; place and carve filling materials, temporary fillings, and periodontal dressings; remove sutures; and smooth and polish metal restorations. Although hygienists may not diagnose diseases, they can prepare clinical and laboratory diagnostic tests for the dentist to interpret. Hygienists sometimes work chairside with the dentist during treatment.

Dental hygienists also help patients develop and maintain good oral health. For example, they may explain the relationship between diet and oral health or inform patients how to select toothbrushes and show them how to brush and floss their teeth.

Dental hygienists use hand and rotary instruments and ultrasonics to clean and polish teeth, X-ray machines to take dental pictures, syringes with needles to administer local anesthetics, and models of teeth to explain oral hygiene.

Working Conditions

Flexible scheduling is a distinctive feature of this job. Full-time, part-time, evening, and weekend schedules are widely available. Dentists frequently hire hygienists to work only 2 or 3 days a week, so hygienists may hold jobs in more than one dental office.

Dental hygienists work in clean, well-lighted offices. Important health safeguards include strict adherence to proper radiological procedures and the use of appropriate protective devices when administering anesthetic gas. Dental hygienists also wear safety glasses, surgical masks, and gloves to protect themselves and patients from infectious diseases.

Training, Other Qualifications, and Advancement

Dental hygienists must be licensed by the state in which they practice. To qualify for licensure in nearly all states, a candidate must graduate from an accredited dental hygiene school and pass both a written and clinical examination. The American Dental Association's Joint Commission on National Dental Examinations administers the written examination, which is accepted by all states and the District of Columbia. State or regional testing agencies administer the clinical examination. In addition, most states require an examination on the legal aspects of dental hygiene practice. Alabama allows candidates to take its examinations if they have been trained through a state-regulated on-the-job program in a dentist's office.

In 2004, the Commission on Dental Accreditation accredited 266 programs in dental hygiene. Most dental hygiene programs grant an associate degree, although some also offer a certificate, a bachelor's degree, or a master's degree. A minimum of an associate degree or certificate in dental hygiene is generally required for practice in a private dental office. A bachelor's or master's degree usually is required for research, teaching, or clinical practice in public or school health programs.

A high school diploma and college entrance test scores are usually required for admission to a dental hygiene program. Also, some dental hygiene programs prefer applicants who have completed at least 1 year of college. Requirements vary from one school to another. Schools offer laboratory, clinical, and classroom instruction in subjects such as anatomy, physiology, chemistry, microbiology, pharmacology, nutrition, radiography, histology (the study of tissue structure), periodontology (the study of gum diseases), pathology, dental materials, clinical dental hygiene, and social and behavioral sciences.

Dental hygienists should work well with others and must have good manual dexterity, because they use dental instruments within a patient's mouth with little room for error. High school students interested in becoming a dental hygienist should take courses in biology, chemistry, and mathematics.

Employment

Dental hygienists held about 158,000 jobs in 2004. Because multiple jobholding is common in this field, the number of jobs exceeds the number of hygienists. More than half of all dental hygienists worked part time—less than 35 hours a week.

Almost all jobs for dental hygienists were in offices of dentists. A very small number worked for employment services or in offices of physicians.

Job Outlook

Employment of dental hygienists is expected to grow much faster than the average for all occupations through 2014, ranking among the fastest-growing occupations, in response to increasing demand for dental care and the greater utilization of hygienists to perform services previously performed by dentists. Job prospects are expected to remain excellent.

Population growth and greater retention of natural teeth will stimulate demand for dental hygienists. Older dentists, who have been less likely to employ dental hygienists, are leaving the occupation and will be replaced by recent graduates, who are more likely to employ one or even two hygienists. In addition, as dentists' workloads increase, they are expected to hire more hygienists to perform preventive dental care, such as cleaning, so that they may devote their own time to more profitable procedures.

Earnings

Median hourly earnings of dental hygienists were $28.05 in May 2004. The middle 50 percent earned between $22.72 and $33.82 an hour. The lowest 10 percent earned less than $18.05, and the highest 10 percent earned more than $40.70 an hour.

Earnings vary by geographic location, employment setting, and years of experience. Dental hygienists may be paid on an hourly, daily, salary, or commission basis.

Benefits vary substantially by practice setting and may be contingent upon full-time employment. According to the American Dental Association (ADA), almost all full-time dental hygienists employed by private practitioners received paid vacation. The ADA also found that 9 out of 10 full-time and part-time dental hygienists received dental coverage. Dental hygienists who work for school systems, public health agencies, the federal government, or state agencies usually have substantial benefits.

Related Occupations

Other workers supporting health practitioners in an office setting include dental assistants, medical assistants, occupational therapist assistants and aides, physical therapist assistants and aides, physician assistants, and registered nurses.

Sources of Additional Information

For information on a career in dental hygiene, including educational requirements, contact

▸ Division of Education, American Dental Hygienists Association, 444 N. Michigan Ave., Suite 3400, Chicago, IL 60611. Internet: http://www.adha.org

For information about accredited programs and educational requirements, contact

▸ Commission on Dental Accreditation, American Dental Association, 211 E. Chicago Ave., Suite 1814, Chicago, IL 60611. Internet: http://www.ada.org

The State Board of Dental Examiners in each state can supply information on licensing requirements.

Dentists

(O*NET 29-1021.00, 29-1022.00, 29-1023.00, 29-1024.00, and 29-1029.99)

Significant Points

■ Most dentists are solo practitioners.

■ Dentists usually complete at least 8 years of education beyond high school.

■ Employment is projected to grow about as fast as average, and most job openings will result from the need to replace the large number of dentists expected to retire.

■ Job prospects should be good.

Nature of the Work

Dentists diagnose, prevent, and treat problems with teeth or mouth tissue. They remove decay, fill cavities, examine X rays, place protective plastic sealants on children's teeth, straighten teeth, and repair fractured teeth. They also perform corrective surgery on gums and supporting bones to treat gum diseases. Dentists

extract teeth and make models and measurements for dentures to replace missing teeth. They provide instruction on diet, brushing, flossing, the use of fluorides, and other aspects of dental care. They also administer anesthetics and write prescriptions for antibiotics and other medications.

Dentists use a variety of equipment, including X-ray machines; drills; and instruments such as mouth mirrors, probes, forceps, brushes, and scalpels. They wear masks, gloves, and safety glasses to protect themselves and their patients from infectious diseases.

Dentists in private practice oversee a variety of administrative tasks, including bookkeeping and buying equipment and supplies. They may employ and supervise dental hygienists and dental assistants. (These occupations are described elsewhere in this book.)

Most dentists are general practitioners, handling a variety of dental needs. Other dentists practice in any of nine specialty areas. *Orthodontists*, the largest group of specialists, straighten teeth by applying pressure to the teeth with braces or retainers. The next largest group, *oral and maxillofacial surgeons*, operates on the mouth and jaws. The remainder may specialize as *pediatric dentists* (focusing on dentistry for children); *periodontists* (treating gums and bone supporting the teeth); *prosthodontists* (replacing missing teeth with permanent fixtures, such as crowns and bridges, or with removable fixtures such as dentures); *endodontists* (performing root canal therapy); *public health dentists* (promoting good dental health and preventing dental diseases within the community); *oral pathologists* (studying oral diseases); or *oral and maxillofacial radiologists* (diagnosing diseases in the head and neck through the use of imaging technologies).

Working Conditions

Most dentists work 4 or 5 days a week. Some work evenings and weekends to meet their patients' needs. Most full-time dentists work between 35 and 40 hours a week, but others work more. Initially, dentists may work more hours as they establish their practice. Experienced dentists often work fewer hours. Many continue in part-time practice well beyond the usual retirement age.

Most dentists are solo practitioners, meaning that they own their own businesses and work alone or with a small staff. Some dentists have partners, and a few work for other dentists as associate dentists.

Training, Other Qualifications, and Advancement

All 50 states and the District of Columbia require dentists to be licensed. To qualify for a license in most states, candidates must graduate from 1 of the 56 dental schools accredited by the American Dental Association's (ADA's) Commission on Dental Accreditation in 2004 and then must pass written and practical examinations. Candidates may fulfill the written part of the state licensing requirements by passing the National Board Dental Examinations. Individual states or regional testing agencies administer the written or practical examinations.

Dental schools require a minimum of 2 years of college-level predental education, regardless of the major chosen. However, most dental students have at least a bachelor's degree. Predental education emphasizes coursework in science, and many applicants to dental school major in a science such as biology or chemistry, while other applicants major in another subject and take many science courses as well. A few applicants are accepted to dental school after 2 or 3 years of college and complete their bachelor's degree while attending dental school.

All dental schools require applicants to take the Dental Admissions Test (DAT). When selecting students, schools consider scores earned on the DAT, applicants' grade point averages, and information gathered through recommendations and interviews. Competition for admission to dental school is keen.

Dental school usually lasts 4 academic years. Studies begin with classroom instruction and laboratory work in basic sciences, including anatomy, microbiology, biochemistry, and physiology. Beginning courses in clinical sciences, including laboratory techniques, also are provided at this time. During the last 2 years, students treat patients, usually in dental clinics, under the supervision of licensed dentists. Most dental schools award the degree of Doctor of Dental Surgery (DDS). The rest award an equivalent degree, Doctor of Dental Medicine (DMD).

Some dental school graduates work for established dentists as associates for 1 to 2 years to gain experience and save money to equip an office of their own. Most dental school graduates, however, purchase an established practice or open a new one immediately after graduation.

In 2004, 17 states licensed or certified dentists who intended to practice in a specialty area. Requirements include 2 to 4 years of postgraduate education and, in some cases, the completion of a special state examination. Most state licenses permit dentists to engage in both general and specialized practice. Dentists who want to teach or conduct research usually spend an additional 2 to 5 years in advanced dental training in programs operated by dental schools or hospitals. According to the ADA, each year about 12 percent of new graduates enroll in postgraduate training programs to prepare for a dental specialty.

Dentistry requires diagnostic ability and manual skills. Dentists should have good visual memory, excellent judgment regarding space and shape, a high degree of manual dexterity, and scientific ability. Good business sense, self-discipline, and good communication skills are helpful for success in private practice. High school and college students who want to become dentists should take courses in biology, chemistry, physics, health, and mathematics.

Employment

Dentists held about 150,000 jobs in 2004. Employment was distributed among general practitioners and specialists as follows:

Dentists, general	128,000
Orthodontists	10,000
Oral and maxillofacial surgeons	6,000
Prosthodontists	1,000
Dentists, all other specialists	5,000

About one third of dentists were self-employed and not incorporated. Almost all dentists work in private practice. According to ADA, 78 percent of dentists in private practice are sole proprietors,

and 14 percent belong to a partnership. A few salaried dentists work in hospitals and offices of physicians.

Job Outlook

Employment of dentists is projected to grow about as fast as average for all occupations through 2014. Although employment growth will provide some job opportunities, most jobs will result from the need to replace the large number of dentists expected to retire. Job prospects should be good as new dentists take over established practices or start their own.

Demand for dental care should grow substantially through 2014. As members of the baby-boom generation advance into middle age, a large number will need complicated dental work, such as bridges. In addition, elderly people are more likely to retain their teeth than were their predecessors, so they will require much more care than in the past. The younger generation will continue to need preventive checkups despite treatments such as fluoridation of the water supply, which decreases the incidence of tooth decay. However, employment of dentists is not expected to grow as rapidly as the demand for dental services. As their practices expand, dentists are likely to hire more dental hygienists and dental assistants to handle routine services.

Dentists will increasingly provide care and instruction aimed at preventing the loss of teeth rather than simply providing treatments such as fillings. Improvements in dental technology also will allow dentists to offer more effective and less painful treatment to their patients.

Earnings

Median annual earnings of salaried dentists were $129,920 in May 2004. Earnings vary according to number of years in practice, location, hours worked, and specialty.

Self-employed dentists in private practice tend to earn more than do salaried dentists, and a relatively large proportion of dentists is self-employed. Like other business owners, these dentists must provide their own health insurance, life insurance, and retirement benefits.

Related Occupations

Dentists examine, diagnose, prevent, and treat diseases and abnormalities. Chiropractors, optometrists, physicians and surgeons, podiatrists, psychologists, and veterinarians do related work.

Sources of Additional Information

For information on dentistry as a career, a list of accredited dental schools, and a list of state boards of dental examiners, contact

▶ American Dental Association, Commission on Dental Accreditation, 211 E. Chicago Ave., Chicago, IL 60611. Internet: http://www.ada.org

For information on admission to dental schools, contact

▶ American Dental Education Association, 1400 K St. NW, Suite 1100, Washington, DC 20005. Internet: http://www.adea.org

Persons interested in practicing dentistry should obtain the requirements for licensure from the board of dental examiners of the state in which they plan to work.

To obtain information on scholarships, grants, and loans, including federal financial aid, prospective dental students should contact the office of student financial aid at the schools to which they apply.

Desktop Publishers

(0*NET 43-9031.00)

Significant Points

- About 4 out of 10 work for newspaper, periodical, book, and directory publishers, while 1 out of 4 works in printing and related support activities.

- Employment is expected to grow faster than the average for all occupations.

- Most employers prefer to hire experienced desktop publishers; among persons without experience, opportunities should be best for those with certificates or degrees in desktop publishing or graphic design.

Nature of the Work

Using computer software, desktop publishers format and combine text, numerical data, photographs, charts, and other visual graphic elements to produce publication-ready material. Depending on the nature of a particular project, desktop publishers may write and edit text, create graphics to accompany text, convert photographs and drawings into digital images and then manipulate those images, design page layouts, create proposals, develop presentations and advertising campaigns, typeset and do color separation, and translate electronic information onto film or other traditional forms. Materials produced by desktop publishers include books, business cards, calendars, magazines, newsletters and newspapers, packaging, slides, and tickets. As companies have brought the production of marketing, promotional, and other kinds of materials in-house, they increasingly have employed people who can produce such materials.

Desktop publishers use a keyboard to enter and select formatting properties, such as the size and style of type, column width, and spacing, and store them in the computer, which then displays and arranges columns of type on a video display terminal or computer monitor. An entire newspaper, catalog, or book page, complete with artwork and graphics, can be created on the screen exactly as it will appear in print. Operators transmit the pages for production either into film and then into printing plates or directly into plates.

Desktop publishing is a rapidly changing field that encompasses a number of different kinds of jobs. Personal computers enable desktop publishers to perform publishing tasks that would otherwise require complicated equipment and extensive human effort. Advances in computer software and printing technology continue to change and enhance desktop publishing work. Instead of receiving simple typed text from customers, desktop publishers get the material over the Internet or on a computer disk. Other innovations in the occupation include digital color page makeup systems, electronic page layout systems, and off-press color proofing systems. In addition, because most materials today often are published on the Internet, desktop publishers may need to know electronic publishing technologies such as Hypertext Markup Language (HTML) and may be responsible for converting text and graphics to an Internet-ready format.

Typesetting and page layout have been affected by the technological changes shaping desktop publishing. Increasingly, desktop publishers are using computers to do much of the typesetting and page-layout work formerly done by prepress workers, posing new challenges for the printing industry. The old "hot type" method of text composition—which used molten lead to create individual letters, paragraphs, and full pages of text—is nearly extinct. Today, composition work is done primarily with computers. Improvements in desktop-publishing software also allow customers to do much more of their own typesetting.

Desktop publishers use scanners to capture photographs, images, or art as digital data that can be either incorporated directly into electronic page layouts or further manipulated with the use of computer software. The desktop publisher then can correct mistakes or compensate for deficiencies in the original color print or transparency. Digital files are used to produce printing plates. Like photographers and multimedia artists and animators, desktop publishers also can create special effects or other visual images using film, video, computers, or other electronic media. (A separate description of photographers appears elsewhere in this book.)

Desktop publishers often perform writing and editing tasks as well as page layout and design. For example, in addition to laying out articles for a newsletter, desktop publishers may be responsible for editing content they receive or for writing original content themselves. A desktop publisher's writing and editing responsibilities vary widely from employer to employer. Small firms typically need desktop publishers to perform a wide range of tasks, while desktop publishers at large firms specialize in a certain part of the publishing process.

Depending on the establishment employing these workers, desktop publishers also may be referred to as publications specialists, electronic publishers, DTP operators, desktop publishing editors, electronic prepress technicians, electronic publishing specialists, image designers, typographers, compositors, layout artists, and Web publications designers.

Working Conditions

Desktop publishers usually work in clean, air-conditioned office areas with little noise. They generally work an 8-hour day, 5 days a week. Some workers work night shifts, weekends, and holidays.

Desktop publishers often are subject to stress and the pressures of short deadlines and tight work schedules. Like other workers who spend long hours working in front of a computer monitor, they may be susceptible to eyestrain, back discomfort, and hand and wrist problems.

Training, Other Qualifications, and Advancement

Most workers qualify for jobs as desktop publishers by taking classes or completing certificate programs at vocational schools, universities, and colleges or through the Internet. Programs range in length, but the average certificate program takes approximately 1 year. However, some desktop publishers train on the job to develop the necessary skills. The length of on-the-job training varies by company. An internship or part-time desktop-publishing assignment is another way to gain experience as a desktop publisher.

Students interested in pursuing a career in desktop publishing may obtain an associate degree in applied science or a bachelor's degree in graphic arts, graphic communications, or graphic design. Graphic arts programs are a good way to learn about desktop publishing software used to format pages, assign type characteristics, and import text and graphics into electronic page layouts to produce printed materials such as advertisements, brochures, newsletters, and forms. Applying this knowledge of graphic arts techniques and computerized typesetting usually is intended for students who may eventually move into management positions, while 2-year associate degree programs are designed to train skilled workers. Students also develop finely tuned skills in typography, print media, packaging, branding and identity, Web site design, and motion graphics. The programs teach print and graphic design fundamentals and provide an extensive background in imaging, prepress operations, print reproduction, and emerging media. Courses in other aspects of printing also are available at vocational-technical institutes, industry-sponsored update and retraining programs, and private trade and technical schools.

Although formal training is not always required, those with certificates or degrees will have the best job opportunities. Most employers prefer to hire people who have at least a high school diploma and who possess good communication skills, basic computer skills, and a strong work ethic. Desktop publishers should be able to deal courteously with people because, in small shops, they may have to take customers' orders. They also may have to add, subtract, multiply, divide, and compute ratios to estimate job costs. Persons interested in working for firms using advanced printing technology need to know the basics of electronics and computers.

Desktop publishers need good manual dexterity, and they must be able to pay attention to detail and work independently. Good eyesight, including visual acuity, depth perception, a wide field of view, color vision, and the ability to focus quickly also are assets. Artistic ability often is a plus. Employers also seek persons who are even-tempered and adaptable—important qualities for workers who often must meet deadlines and learn how to operate new equipment.

Workers with limited training and experience may start as helpers. They begin with instruction from an experienced desktop publisher and advance on the basis of their demonstrated mastery of skills at each level. All workers should expect to be retrained from time to time to handle new, improved software and equipment. As workers gain experience, they advance to positions with greater responsibility. Some move into supervisory or management positions. Other desktop publishers may start their own company or work as independent consultants, while those with more artistic talent and further education may find opportunities in graphic design or commercial art.

Employment

Desktop publishers held about 34,000 jobs in 2004. About 4 out of 10 worked for newspaper, periodical, book, and directory publishers, while 1 out of 4 worked in printing and related support activities; the rest worked in a wide variety of industries.

Firms in the publishing industry publish newspapers, periodicals, books, directory and mailing lists, and greeting cards. Printing and related support activities firms print a wide range of products—newspapers, books, labels, business cards, stationery, inserts, catalogs, pamphlets, and advertisements—while business form establishments print material such as sales receipts and business forms and perform support activities such as data imaging and bookbinding. Establishments in printing and related support activities typically perform custom composition, platemaking, and related prepress services. (A separate description of prepress technicians and workers appears elsewhere in this book.). Other desktop publishers print or publish materials in-house or in-plant for business services firms, government agencies, hospitals, or universities, typically in a reproduction or publications department that operates within the organization.

The printing and publishing industries are two of the most geographically dispersed industries in the United States, and desktop publishing jobs are found throughout the country. However, most jobs are in large metropolitan cities.

Job Outlook

Employment of desktop publishers is expected to grow faster than the average for all occupations through 2014 as more page layout and design work is performed in-house using computers and sophisticated publishing software. Desktop publishing is replacing much of the prepress work done by compositors and typesetters, enabling organizations to reduce costs while increasing production speeds. Many new jobs for desktop publishers are expected to emerge in commercial printing and publishing establishments. However, more companies also are turning to in-house desktop publishers, as computers with elaborate text and graphics capabilities have become common and desktop publishing software has become cheaper and easier to use. In addition to employment growth, many job openings for desktop publishers also will result from the need to replace workers who move into managerial positions, transfer to other occupations, or leave the labor force.

Printing and publishing costs represent a significant portion of a corporation's expenses, and firms are finding it more profitable to print their own newsletters and other reports than to send them out to trade shops. Desktop publishing reduces the time needed to complete a printing job and allows commercial printers to make inroads into new markets that require fast turnaround.

Most employers prefer to hire experienced desktop publishers. As more people gain desktop-publishing experience, however, competition for jobs may increase. Among persons without experience, opportunities should be best for those with computer backgrounds who are certified or who have completed postsecondary programs in desktop publishing or graphic design. Many employers prefer graduates of these programs because the comprehensive training they receive helps them learn the page layout process and adapt more rapidly to new software and techniques.

Earnings

Earnings for desktop publishers vary according to level of experience, training, location, and size of firm. Median annual earnings of desktop publishers were $32,340 in May 2004. The middle 50 percent earned between $24,660 and $42,070. The lowest 10 percent earned less than $19,460, and the highest 10 percent earned more than $52,460 a year. Median annual earnings of desktop publishers in May 2004 were $36,040 in printing and related support services and $29,040 in newspaper, periodical, book, and directory publishers.

Related Occupations

Desktop publishers use artistic and editorial skills in their work. These skills also are essential for artists and related workers; commercial and industrial designers; news analysts, reporters, and correspondents; prepress technicians and workers; public relations specialists; and writers and editors.

Sources of Additional Information

Details about training programs may be obtained from local employers such as newspapers and printing shops or from local offices of the state employment service.

For information on careers and training in printing, desktop publishing, and graphic arts, write to

▸ Graphic Communications Council, 1899 Preston White Dr., Reston, VA 20191-4367. Internet: http://www.makeyourmark.org

▸ Graphic Arts Information Network, 200 Deer Run Rd., Sewickley, PA 15143. Internet: http://www.gain.org

Diagnostic Medical Sonographers

(O*NET 29-2032.00)

Significant Points

■ Job opportunities should be favorable as sonography becomes an increasingly attractive alternative to radiologic procedures.

■ About 6 out of 10 sonographers are employed by hospitals, and most of the rest work in offices of physicians or in medical and diagnostic laboratories, including diagnostic imaging centers.

■ Sonographers may train in hospitals, vocational-technical institutions, colleges and universities, and the Armed Forces.

Nature of the Work

Diagnostic imaging embraces several procedures that aid in diagnosing ailments. Besides the familiar X ray, another common diagnostic imaging method is magnetic resonance imaging, which uses giant magnets that create radio waves, rather than radiation, to form an image. Not all imaging technologies use ionizing radiation or radio waves, however. Sonography, or ultrasonography, is the use of sound waves to generate an image for the assessment and diagnosis of various medical conditions. Sonography usually is associated with obstetrics and the use of ultrasound imaging during pregnancy, but this technology has many other applications in the diagnosis and treatment of medical conditions.

Diagnostic medical sonographers, also known as *ultrasonographers*, use special equipment to direct nonionizing, high-frequency sound waves into areas of the patient's body. Sonographers operate the equipment, which collects reflected echoes and forms an image that may be videotaped, transmitted, or photographed for interpretation and diagnosis by a physician.

Sonographers begin by explaining the procedure to the patient and recording any medical history that may be relevant to the condition being viewed. They then select appropriate equipment settings and direct the patient to move into positions that will provide the best view. To perform the exam, sonographers use a transducer, which transmits sound waves in a cone- or rectangle-shaped beam. Although techniques vary with the area being examined, sonographers usually spread a special gel on the skin to aid the transmission of sound waves.

Viewing the screen during the scan, sonographers look for subtle visual cues that contrast healthy areas with unhealthy ones. They decide whether the images are satisfactory for diagnostic purposes and select which ones to show to the physician. Sonographers take measurements, calculate values, and analyze the results in preliminary reports for the physicians.

Diagnostic medical sonographers may specialize in obstetric and gynecologic sonography (the female reproductive system), abdominal sonography (the liver, kidneys, gallbladder, spleen, and pancreas), neurosonography (the brain), or breast sonography. In addition, sonographers may specialize in vascular technology or echocardiography. (Vascular technologists and echocardiographers are covered in this book's description of cardiovascular technologists and technicians.)

Obstetric and gynecologic sonographers specialize in the study of the female reproductive system. Included in the discipline is one of the more well-known uses of sonography: examining the fetus of a pregnant woman to track the baby's growth and health.

Abdominal sonographers inspect a patient's abdominal cavity to help diagnose and treat conditions primarily involving the gallbladder, bile ducts, kidneys, liver, pancreas, and spleen. Abdominal sonographers also are able to scan parts of the chest, although studies of the heart using sonography usually are done by echocardiographers.

Neurosonographers focus on the nervous system, including the brain. In neonatal care, neurosonographers study and diagnose neurological and nervous system disorders in premature infants. They also may scan blood vessels to check for abnormalities indicating a stroke in infants diagnosed with sickle-cell anemia. Like other sonographers, neurosonographers operate transducers to perform the sonogram, but use frequencies and beam shapes different from those used by obstetric and abdominal sonographers.

Breast sonographers use sonography to study the disease in breasts. Sonography aids mammography in the detection of breast cancer. Breast sonography can also track tumors and blood supply conditions and assist in the accurate biopsy of breast tissue. Breast sonographers use high-frequency transducers made exclusively to study breast tissue.

In addition to working directly with patients, diagnostic medical sonographers keep patient records and adjust and maintain equipment. They also may prepare work schedules, evaluate equipment purchases, or manage a sonography or diagnostic imaging department.

Working Conditions

Most full-time sonographers work about 40 hours a week. Hospital-based sonographers may have evening and weekend hours and times when they are on call and must be ready to report to work on short notice.

Sonographers typically work in health care facilities that are clean and well lighted. Some travel to patients in large vans equipped with sophisticated diagnostic equipment. A growing number of sonographers work as contract employees and may perform tests at a number of different hospitals. Sonographers are on their feet for long periods and may have to lift or turn disabled patients. They work at diagnostic imaging machines, but also may perform some procedures at patients' bedsides.

Training, Other Qualifications, and Advancement

There are several avenues for entry into the field of diagnostic medical sonography. Sonographers may train in hospitals, vocational-technical institutions, colleges and universities, and the Armed Forces. Some training programs prefer applicants with a background in science or experience in other health care professions, but also will consider high school graduates with courses in mathematics and science, as well as applicants with liberal arts backgrounds.

Colleges and universities offer formal training in both 2- and 4-year programs, culminating in an associate or a bachelor's degree. Two-year programs are most prevalent. Course work includes classes in anatomy, physiology, instrumentation, basic physics, patient care, and medical ethics. The Commission on Accreditation for Allied Health Education Programs accredits most formal training programs—132 programs in 2005.

Some health care workers, such as obstetric nurses and radiologic technologists, increase their marketability by seeking training in fields such as sonography. This usually requires completion of an additional 1-year program that may result in a certificate. In addition, sonographers specializing in one particular discipline often seek competency in others; for example, obstetric sonographers might seek training in abdominal sonography to broaden their opportunities.

Although no state requires licensure in diagnostic medical sonography, organizations such as the American Registry for Diagnostic Medical Sonography (ARDMS) certify the competency of sonographers through registration. Because registration provides an independent, objective measure of an individual's professional standing, many employers prefer to hire registered sonographers. Registration with ARDMS requires passing a general physical principles and instrumentation examination in addition to passing an exam in a spe-

cialty such as obstetric and gynecologic sonography, abdominal sonography, or neurosonography. To keep their registration current, sonographers must complete continuing education to stay abreast of technological advances related to the occupation.

Sonographers need good communication and interpersonal skills because they must be able to explain technical procedures and results to their patients, some of whom may be nervous about the exam or the problems it may reveal. Sonographers also should have a background in mathematics and science.

Employment

Diagnostic medical sonographers held about 42,000 jobs in 2004. About 6 out of 10 sonographer jobs were in hospitals—public and private. Most of the rest were in offices of physicians or in medical and diagnostic laboratories, including diagnostic imaging centers.

Job Outlook

Employment of diagnostic medical sonographers is expected to grow much faster than the average for all occupations through 2014 as the population grows and ages, increasing the demand for diagnostic imaging and therapeutic technology. In addition to job openings from growth, some job openings will arise from the need to replace sonographers who leave the occupation permanently.

Opportunities should be favorable because sonography is becoming an increasingly attractive alternative to radiologic procedures as patients seek safer treatment methods. Unlike most diagnostic imaging methods, sonography does not involve radiation, so harmful side effects and complications from repeated use are rarer for both the patient and the sonographer. Sonographic technology is expected to evolve rapidly and to spawn many new sonography procedures, such as 3D- and 4D-sonography for use in obstetric and ophthalmologic diagnosis. However, high costs may limit the rate at which some promising new technologies are adopted.

Hospitals will remain the principal employer of diagnostic medical sonographers. However, employment is expected to grow more rapidly in offices of physicians and in medical and diagnostic laboratories, including diagnostic imaging centers. Health care facilities such as these are expected to grow very rapidly through 2014 because of the strong shift toward outpatient care encouraged by third-party payers and made possible by technological advances that permit more procedures to be performed outside the hospital.

Earnings

Median annual earnings of diagnostic medical sonographers were $52,490 in May 2004. The middle 50 percent earned between $44,720 and $61,360 a year. The lowest 10 percent earned less than $37,800, and the highest 10 percent earned more than $72,230. Median annual earnings of diagnostic medical sonographers in May 2004 were $53,790 in offices of physicians and $51,860 in general medical and surgical hospitals.

Related Occupations

Diagnostic medical sonographers operate sophisticated equipment to help physicians and other health practitioners diagnose and treat patients. Workers in related occupations include cardiovascular technologists and technicians, clinical laboratory technologists and technicians, nuclear medicine technologists, radiologic technologists and technicians, and respiratory therapists.

Sources of Additional Information

For information on a career as a diagnostic medical sonographer, contact

▸ Society of Diagnostic Medical Sonography, 2745 Dallas Pkwy., Suite 350, Plano, TX 75093-8730. Internet: http://www.sdms.org

For information on becoming a registered diagnostic medical sonographer, contact

▸ American Registry for Diagnostic Medical Sonography, 51 Monroe St., Plaza East 1, Rockville, MD 20850-2400. Internet: http://www.ardms.org

For a current list of accredited education programs in diagnostic medical sonography, contact

▸ Joint Review Committee on Education in Diagnostic Medical Sonography, 2025 Woodlane Dr., St. Paul, MN 55125-2998. Internet: http://www.jrcdms.org

▸ Commission on Accreditation for Allied Health Education Programs, 35 East Wacker Dr., Suite 1970, Chicago, IL 60601. Internet: http://www.caahep.org

Diesel Service Technicians and Mechanics

(O*NET 49-3031.00)

Significant Points

■ A career as a diesel service technician or mechanic can offer relatively high wages and the challenge of skilled repair work.

■ Opportunities are expected to be very good for persons who complete formal training programs.

■ National certification is the recognized standard of achievement for diesel service technicians and mechanics.

Nature of the Work

The diesel engine is the workhorse powering the nation's trucks and buses because it delivers more power, is more efficient, and is more durable than its gasoline-burning counterpart. Diesel-powered engines also are becoming more prevalent in light vehicles, including passenger vehicles, pickups, and other work trucks.

Diesel service technicians and mechanics, which includes *bus and truck mechanics* and *diesel engine specialists*, repair and maintain the diesel engines that power transportation equipment such as heavy trucks, buses, and locomotives. Some diesel technicians and mechanics also work on heavy vehicles and mobile equipment, including bulldozers, cranes, road graders, farm tractors, and combines. Other technicians repair diesel-powered passenger automobiles, light trucks, or boats. (For information on technicians and

mechanics working primarily on gasoline-powered automobiles, heavy vehicles, mobile equipment, or boats, see this book's descriptions of automotive service technicians and mechanics; heavy vehicle and mobile equipment service technicians and mechanics; and small engine mechanics.)

Technicians who work for organizations that maintain their own vehicles spend most of their time doing preventive maintenance to ensure that equipment will operate safely. These workers also eliminate unnecessary wear on, and damage to, parts that could result in costly breakdowns. During a routine maintenance check on a vehicle, technicians follow a checklist that includes inspecting brake systems, steering mechanisms, wheel bearings, and other important parts. Following inspection, technicians repair or adjust parts that do not work properly or remove and replace parts that cannot be fixed.

Increasingly, technicians must be versatile in order to adapt to customers' needs and new technologies. It is common for technicians to handle all kinds of repairs, from working on a vehicle's electrical system one day to doing major engine repairs the next. Diesel maintenance is becoming increasingly complex as more electronic components are used to control the operation of an engine. For example, microprocessors now regulate and manage fuel timing, increasing the engine's efficiency. Also, new emissions standards are requiring mechanics to retrofit engines to comply with pollution regulations. In modern shops, diesel service technicians use hand-held or laptop computers to diagnose problems and adjust engine functions. Because of continual advances in automotive technology, technicians must regularly learn new techniques to repair vehicles.

Diesel service technicians use a variety of tools in their work, including power tools, such as pneumatic wrenches, to remove bolts quickly; machine tools, such as lathes and grinding machines, to rebuild brakes; welding and flame-cutting equipment to remove and repair exhaust systems; and jacks and hoists to lift and move large parts. Common hand tools—screwdrivers, pliers, and wrenches—are used to work on small parts and get at hard-to-reach places. Diesel service technicians and mechanics also use a variety of computerized testing equipment to pinpoint and analyze malfunctions in electrical systems and engines.

In large shops, technicians generally receive their assignments from shop supervisors or service managers. Most supervisors and managers are experienced technicians who also assist in diagnosing problems and maintaining quality standards. Technicians may work as a team or be assisted by an apprentice or helper when doing heavy work, such as removing engines and transmissions.

Working Conditions

Diesel technicians usually work indoors, although they occasionally make repairs to vehicles on the road. Diesel technicians may lift heavy parts and tools, handle greasy and dirty parts, and stand or lie in awkward positions to repair vehicles and equipment. Minor cuts, burns, and bruises are common, although serious accidents can usually be avoided if the shop is kept clean and orderly and if safety procedures are followed. Technicians normally work in well-lighted, heated, and ventilated areas; however, some shops are drafty and noisy. Many employers provide lockers and shower facilities.

Training, Other Qualifications, and Advancement

Although many persons qualify for diesel service technician and mechanic jobs through years of on-the-job training, authorities on diesel engines recommend the completion of a formal diesel engine training program. Employers prefer to hire graduates of formal training programs because those workers often have a head start in training and are able to advance quickly to the journey level of diesel service.

Many community colleges and trade and vocational schools offer programs in diesel repair. These programs, lasting 6 months to 2 years, lead to a certificate of completion or an associate degree. Programs vary in the degree of hands-on training they provide on equipment. Some offer about 30 hours per week on equipment, whereas others offer more lab or classroom instruction. Training provides a foundation in the latest diesel technology and instruction in the service and repair of the vehicles and equipment that technicians will encounter on the job. Training programs also improve the skills needed to interpret technical manuals and to communicate with co-workers and customers. In addition to the hands-on aspects of the training, many institutions teach communication skills, customer service, basic understanding of physics, and logical thought. Increasingly, employers work closely with representatives of training programs, providing instructors with the latest equipment, techniques, and tools and offering jobs to graduates.

Whereas most employers prefer to hire persons who have completed formal training programs, some technicians and mechanics continue to learn their skills on the job. Unskilled beginners generally are assigned tasks such as cleaning parts, fueling and lubricating vehicles, and driving vehicles into and out of the shop. Beginners usually are promoted to trainee positions as they gain experience and as vacancies become available. In some shops, beginners with experience in automobile service start as trainee technicians.

After a few months' experience, most trainees can perform routine service tasks and make minor repairs. These workers advance to increasingly difficult jobs as they prove their ability and competence. After technicians master the repair and service of diesel engines, they learn to work on related components, such as brakes, transmissions, and electrical systems. Generally, technicians with at least 3 to 4 years of on-the-job experience will qualify as journey-level diesel technicians. The completion of a formal training program speeds advancement to the journey level.

For unskilled entry-level jobs, employers usually look for applicants who have mechanical aptitude and strong problem-solving skills and who are at least 18 years of age and in good physical condition. Nearly all employers require the completion of high school. Courses in automotive repair, electronics, English, mathematics, and physics provide a strong educational background for a career as a diesel service technician or mechanic. Technicians need a state commercial driver's license to test-drive trucks or buses on public roads. Many companies also require applicants to pass a drug test. Practical experience in automobile repair at an automotive service station, in the Armed Forces, or as a hobby is valuable as well.

Employers often send experienced technicians and mechanics to special training classes conducted by manufacturers and vendors in which workers learn the latest technology and repair techniques. Technicians constantly receive updated technical manuals and instructions outlining changes in techniques and standards for repair. It is essential for technicians to read, interpret, and comprehend service manuals in order to keep abreast of engineering changes.

Voluntary certification by the National Institute for Automotive Service Excellence (ASE) is the recognized industry credential for diesel service technicians and mechanics. Diesel service technicians may be certified as master medium/heavy truck technicians, master school bus technicians, or master truck equipment technicians. They may also be ASE-certified in specific areas of truck repair, such as gasoline engines, drivetrains, brakes, suspension and steering, electrical and electronic systems, or preventive maintenance and inspection.

For certification in each area, a technician must pass one or more of the ASE-administered exams and present proof of 2 years of relevant hands-on work experience. Two years of relevant formal training from a high school, vocational or trade school, or community or junior college program may be substituted for up to 1 year of the work experience requirement. To remain certified, technicians must be retested every 5 years. Retesting ensures that service technicians and mechanics keep up with changing technology.

The most important work possessions of technicians and mechanics are their hand tools. Technicians usually provide their own tools, and many experienced workers have thousands of dollars invested in them. Employers typically furnish expensive power tools, computerized engine analyzers, and other diagnostic equipment, but individual workers ordinarily accumulate their own hand tools with experience.

Experienced diesel service technicians and mechanics with leadership ability may advance to shop supervisor or service manager. Technicians and mechanics with sales ability sometimes become sales representatives. Some open their own repair shops.

Employment

Diesel service technicians and mechanics held about 270,000 jobs in 2004. They were employed by almost every industry; in particular, those that use trucks, buses, and equipment to haul, deliver, and transport materials, goods, and people. The largest employer, the truck transportation industry, employed nearly one out of six diesel service technicians and mechanics. Slightly fewer were employed by local governments, mainly to repair school buses, waste removal trucks, and road equipment. About 1 out of 10 was employed by automotive and commercial equipment repair and maintenance facilities. The rest were employed throughout the economy, including construction, manufacturing, retail and wholesale trade, and automotive leasing. A relatively small number were self-employed. Nearly every section of the country employs diesel service technicians and mechanics, although most work in towns and cities where trucking companies, bus lines, and other fleet owners have large operations.

Job Outlook

Employment of diesel service technicians and mechanics is expected to increase about as fast as the average for all occupations through the year 2014. Besides openings resulting from employment growth, opportunities will be created by the need to replace workers who retire or transfer to other occupations.

Employment of diesel service technicians and mechanics is expected to grow as freight transportation by truck increases. Additional trucks will be needed to keep pace with the increasing volume of freight shipped nationwide. Trucks also serve as intermediaries for other forms of transportation, such as rail and air. Due to the greater durability and economy of the diesel engine relative to the gasoline engine, the number of buses, trucks, and passenger vehicles that are powered by diesel engines is expected to increase.

While diesel engines are a more efficient and powerful option, diesel engines tend to produce more pollutants than gasoline-powered engines. As governments have applied emissions-lowering standards to diesel engines, many older diesel engines must be retrofitted to comply. These new emissions control systems, such as emissions filters and catalysts, may create additional jobs for diesel service technicians and mechanics.

Careers as diesel service technicians attract many because they offer relatively high wages and the challenge of skilled repair work. Opportunities should be very good for persons who complete formal training in diesel mechanics at community and junior colleges or vocational and technical schools. Applicants without formal training may face stiffer competition for entry-level jobs.

Most persons entering this occupation can expect relatively steady work because changes in economic conditions have less of an effect on the diesel repair business than on other sectors of the economy. During a downturn in the economy, however, some employers may lay off workers or be reluctant to hire new workers.

Earnings

Median hourly earnings of bus and truck mechanics and diesel engine specialists, including incentive pay, were $17.20 in May 2004. The middle 50 percent earned between $13.73 and $21.13 an hour. The lowest 10 percent earned less than $11.19, and the highest 10 percent earned more than $25.67 an hour. Median hourly earnings in the industries employing the largest numbers of bus and truck mechanics and diesel engine specialists in May 2004 were as follows:

Local government, excluding schools	$20.18
Motor vehicle and motor vehicle parts and supplies merchant wholesalers	17.97
Automotive repair and maintenance	16.65
General freight trucking	16.33
Elementary and secondary schools	15.73

Because many experienced technicians employed by truck fleet dealers and independent repair shops receive a commission related to the labor cost charged to the customer, weekly earnings depend on the amount of work completed. Beginners usually earn from 50 to 75 percent of the rate of skilled workers and receive increases as they become more skilled.

The majority of service technicians work a standard 40-hour week, although some work longer hours, particularly if they are self-employed. A growing number of shops have expanded their hours, either to perform repairs and routine service in a more timely fashion or as a convenience to customers. Those technicians employed by truck and bus firms providing service around the clock may work evenings, nights, and weekends, usually at a higher rate of pay than those working traditional hours.

Many diesel service technicians and mechanics are members of labor unions, including the International Association of Machinists and Aerospace Workers; the Amalgamated Transit Union; the International Union, United Automobile, Aerospace, and Agricultural Implement Workers of America; the Transport Workers Union of America; the Sheet Metal Workers' International Association; and the International Brotherhood of Teamsters.

Related Occupations

Diesel service technicians and mechanics repair trucks, buses, and other diesel-powered equipment. Related technician and mechanic occupations include aircraft and avionics equipment mechanics and service technicians, automotive service technicians and mechanics, heavy vehicle and mobile equipment service technicians and mechanics, and small engine mechanics.

Sources of Additional Information

More details about work opportunities for diesel service technicians and mechanics may be obtained from local employers such as trucking companies, truck dealers, or bus lines; locals of the unions previously mentioned; and local offices of your state employment service. Local state employment service offices also may have information about training programs. State boards of postsecondary career schools have information on licensed schools with training programs for diesel service technicians and mechanics.

For general information about a career as a diesel service technician or mechanic, write

▸ Association of Diesel Specialists, 10 Laboratory Dr., PO Box 13966, Research Triangle Park, NC 27709. Internet: http://www.diesel.org

Information on how to become a certified diesel technician of medium to heavy-duty vehicles or a certified bus technician is available from

▸ National Institute for Automotive Service Excellence (ASE), 101 Blue Seal Dr. SE, Suite 101, Leesburg, VA 20175. Internet: http://www.asecert.org

For a directory of accredited private trade and technical schools with training programs for diesel service technicians and mechanics, contact

▸ Accrediting Commission of Career Schools and Colleges of Technology, 2101 Wilson Blvd., Suite 302, Arlington, VA 22201. Internet: http://www.accsct.org

▸ National Automotive Technicians Education Foundation, 101 Blue Seal Dr. SE, Suite 101, Leesburg, VA 20175. Internet: http://www.natef.org

Dietitians and Nutritionists

(O*NET 29-1031.00)

Significant Points

■ Most jobs are in hospitals, nursing care facilities, and offices of physicians or other health practitioners.

■ Dietitians and nutritionists need at least a bachelor's degree in dietetics, foods and nutrition, food service systems management, or a related area.

■ Faster-than-average employment growth is expected; however, growth may be constrained if employers substitute other workers for dietitians and if limitations are placed on insurance reimbursement for dietetic services.

■ Those who have specialized training in renal or diabetic diets or have a master's degree should experience good employment opportunities.

Nature of the Work

Dietitians and nutritionists plan food and nutrition programs and supervise the preparation and serving of meals. They help to prevent and treat illnesses by promoting healthy eating habits and recommending dietary modifications, such as the use of less salt for those with high blood pressure or the reduction of fat and sugar intake for those who are overweight.

Dietitians manage food service systems for institutions such as hospitals and schools, promote sound eating habits through education, and conduct research. Major areas of practice include clinical, community, management, and consultant dietetics.

Clinical dietitians provide nutritional services for patients in institutions such as hospitals and nursing care facilities. They assess patients' nutritional needs, develop and implement nutrition programs, and evaluate and report the results. They also confer with doctors and other health care professionals to coordinate medical and nutritional needs. Some clinical dietitians specialize in the management of overweight patients or in the care of critically ill or renal (kidney) and diabetic patients. In addition, clinical dietitians in nursing care facilities, small hospitals, or correctional facilities may manage the food service department.

Community dietitians counsel individuals and groups on nutritional practices designed to prevent disease and promote health. Working in places such as public health clinics, home health agencies, and health maintenance organizations, community dietitians evaluate individual needs, develop nutritional care plans, and instruct individuals and their families. Dietitians working in home health agencies provide instruction on grocery shopping and food preparation to the elderly, individuals with special needs, and children.

Increased public interest in nutrition has led to job opportunities in food manufacturing, advertising, and marketing. In these areas, dietitians analyze foods; prepare literature for distribution; or report on issues such as the nutritional content of recipes, dietary fiber, or vitamin supplements.

Management dietitians oversee large-scale meal planning and preparation in health care facilities, company cafeterias, prisons, and schools. They hire, train, and direct other dietitians and food service workers; budget for and purchase food, equipment, and supplies; enforce sanitary and safety regulations; and prepare records and reports.

Consultant dietitians work under contract with health care facilities or in their own private practice. They perform nutrition screenings for their clients and offer advice on diet-related concerns such as weight loss and cholesterol reduction. Some work for wellness programs, sports teams, supermarkets, and other nutrition-related businesses. They may consult with food service managers, providing expertise in sanitation, safety procedures, menu development, budgeting, and planning.

Working Conditions

Most full-time dietitians and nutritionists work a regular 40-hour week, although some work weekends. About 1 in 4 worked part time in 2004.

Dietitians and nutritionists usually work in clean, well-lighted, and well-ventilated areas. However, some dietitians work in warm, congested kitchens. Many dietitians and nutritionists are on their feet for much of the workday.

Training, Other Qualifications, and Advancement

High school students interested in becoming a dietitian or nutritionist should take courses in biology, chemistry, mathematics, health, and communications. Dietitians and nutritionists need at least a bachelor's degree in dietetics, foods and nutrition, food service systems management, or a related area. College students in these majors take courses in foods, nutrition, institution management, chemistry, biochemistry, biology, microbiology, and physiology. Other suggested courses include business, mathematics, statistics, computer science, psychology, sociology, and economics.

Of the 46 states and jurisdictions with laws governing dietetics, 31 require licensure, 14 require certification, and 1 requires registration. Requirements vary by state. As a result, interested candidates should determine the requirements of the state in which they want to work before sitting for any exam. Although not required, the Commission on Dietetic Registration of the American Dietetic Association (ADA) awards the Registered Dietitian credential to those who pass an exam after completing their academic coursework and supervised experience.

As of 2004, there were about 227 bachelor's and master's degree programs approved by the ADA's Commission on Accreditation for Dietetics Education (CADE).

Supervised practice experience can be acquired in two ways. The first requires the completion of a CADE-accredited program. As of 2004, there were more than 50 accredited programs, which combined academic and supervised practice experience and generally lasted 4 to 5 years. The second option requires the completion of 900 hours of supervised practice experience in any of the 265 CADE-accredited internships. These internships may be full-time programs lasting 6 to 12 months or part-time programs lasting 2 years. To maintain a registered dietitian status, at least 75 credit hours in approved continuing education classes are required every 5 years.

Students interested in research, advanced clinical positions, or public health may need an advanced degree.

Experienced dietitians may advance to management positions, such as assistant director, associate director, or director of a dietetic department, or may become self-employed. Some dietitians specialize in areas such as renal, diabetic, cardiovascular, or pediatric dietetics. Others may leave the occupation to become sales representatives for equipment, pharmaceutical, or food manufacturers.

Employment

Dietitians and nutritionists held about 50,000 jobs in 2004. More than half of all jobs were in hospitals, nursing care facilities, outpatient care centers, or offices of physicians and other health practitioners. State and local government agencies provided about 1 job in 5—mostly in correctional facilities, health departments, and other public-health-related areas. Some dietitians and nutritionists were employed in special food services, an industry made up of firms providing food services on contract to facilities such as colleges and universities, airlines, correctional facilities, and company cafeterias. Other jobs were in public and private educational services, community care facilities for the elderly (which includes assisted-living facilities), individual and family services, home health care services, and the federal government—mostly in the U.S. Department of Veterans Affairs.

Some dietitians were self-employed, working as consultants to facilities such as hospitals and nursing care facilities or providing dietary counseling to individuals.

Job Outlook

Employment of dietitians is expected to grow faster than the average for all occupations through 2014 as a result of increasing emphasis on disease prevention through improved dietary habits. A growing and aging population will boost the demand for meals and nutritional counseling in hospitals, residential care facilities, schools, prisons, community health programs, and home health care agencies. Public interest in nutrition and increased emphasis on health education and prudent lifestyles also will spur demand, especially in management. In addition to employment growth, job openings will result from the need to replace experienced workers who leave the occupation.

The number of dietitian positions in nursing care facilities and in state government hospitals is expected to decline as these establishments continue to contract with outside agencies for food services. However, employment is expected to grow rapidly in contract providers of food services, in outpatient care centers, and in offices of physicians and other health practitioners. With increased public awareness of obesity and diabetes, Medicare coverage may be expanded to include medical nutrition therapy for renal and diabetic patients. As a result, dietitians that have specialized training in renal or diabetic diets or have a master's degree should experience good employment opportunities.

Employment growth for dietitians and nutritionists may be constrained if some employers substitute other workers, such as health educators, food service managers, and dietetic technicians. Growth also may be curbed by limitations on insurance reimbursement for dietetic services.

Earnings

Median annual earnings of dietitians and nutritionists were $43,630 in May 2004. The middle 50 percent earned between $35,940 and $53,370. The lowest 10 percent earned less than $27,500, and the highest 10 percent earned more than $63,760. In May 2004, median annual earnings in general medical and surgical hospitals, the industry employing the largest number of dietitians and nutritionists, were $44,050.

According to the American Dietetic Association, median annualized wages for registered dietitians in 2005 varied by practice area as follows: $53,800 in consultation and business; $60,000 in food and nutrition management; $60,200 in education and research; $48,800 in clinical nutrition/ambulatory care; $50,000 in clinical nutrition/long-term care; $44,800 in community nutrition; and $45,000 in clinical nutrition/acute care. Salaries also vary by years in practice, education level, geographic region, and size of the community.

Related Occupations

Workers in other occupations who may apply the principles of dietetics include food service managers, health educators, dietetic technicians, and registered nurses.

Sources of Additional Information

For a list of academic programs, scholarships, and other information about dietetics, contact

▸ The American Dietetic Association, 120 South Riverside Plaza, Suite 2000, Chicago, IL 60606-6995. Internet: http://www.eatright.org

Drafters

(O*NET 17-3011.01, 17-3011.02, 17-3012.01, 17-3012.02, and 17-3013.00)

Significant Points

■ The type and quality of postsecondary drafting programs vary considerably; prospective students should be careful in selecting a program.

■ Employment is projected to grow more slowly than average.

■ Opportunities should be best for individuals with at least 2 years of postsecondary training in drafting and considerable skill and experience using computer-aided design and drafting (CADD) systems.

■ Demand for drafters varies by specialty and depends on the needs of local industry, particularly architectural and engineering services and manufacturing.

Nature of the Work

Drafters prepare technical drawings and plans used by production and construction workers to build everything from manufactured products such as toys, toasters, industrial machinery, and spacecraft to structures such as houses, office buildings, and oil and gas pipelines. Drafters' drawings provide visual guidelines; show the technical details of the products and structures; and specify dimensions, materials, and procedures. Drafters fill in technical details using drawings, rough sketches, specifications, codes, and calculations previously made by engineers, surveyors, architects, or scientists. For example, drafters use their knowledge of standardized building techniques to draw in the details of a structure. Some use their knowledge of engineering and manufacturing theory and standards to draw the parts of a machine to determine design elements, such as the numbers and kinds of fasteners needed to assemble the machine. Drafters use technical handbooks, tables, calculators, and computers to complete their work.

Traditionally, drafters sat at drawing boards and used pencils, pens, compasses, protractors, triangles, and other drafting devices to prepare a drawing manually. Most drafters now use CADD systems to prepare drawings. Consequently, some drafters may be referred to as *CADD operators*. CADD systems employ computers to create and store drawings electronically that can then be viewed, printed, or programmed directly into automated manufacturing systems. These systems also permit drafters to quickly prepare variations of a design. Although drafters use CADD extensively, it is only a tool. Persons who produce technical drawings with CADD still function as drafters and need the knowledge of traditional drafters in addition to CADD skills. Despite the nearly universal use of CADD systems, manual drafting and sketching still are used in certain applications.

Drafting work has many specialties, and titles may denote a particular discipline of design or drafting.

Aeronautical drafters prepare engineering drawings detailing plans and specifications used in the manufacture of aircraft, missiles, and related parts.

Architectural drafters draw architectural and structural features of buildings and other structures. These workers may specialize in a type of structure, such as residential or commercial, or in a kind of material used, such as reinforced concrete, masonry, steel, or timber.

Civil drafters prepare drawings and topographical and relief maps used in major construction or civil engineering projects, such as highways, bridges, pipelines, flood control projects, and water and sewage systems.

Electrical drafters prepare wiring and layout diagrams used by workers who erect, install, and repair electrical equipment and wiring in communication centers, power plants, electrical distribution systems, and buildings.

Electronics drafters draw wiring diagrams, circuit board assembly diagrams, schematics, and layout drawings used in the manufacture, installation, and repair of electronic devices and components.

Mechanical drafters prepare drawings showing the detail and assembly of a wide variety of machinery and mechanical devices, indicating dimensions, fastening methods, and other requirements.

Process piping or *pipeline drafters* prepare drawings used in the layout, construction, and operation of oil and gas fields, refineries, chemical plants, and process piping systems.

Working Conditions

Most drafters work a standard 40-hour week; only a small number work part time. Drafters usually work in comfortable offices furnished to accommodate their tasks. They may sit at adjustable drawing boards or drafting tables when doing manual drawings, although most drafters work at computer terminals much of the time. Because they spend long periods in front of computer terminals doing detailed work, drafters may be susceptible to eyestrain, back discomfort, and hand and wrist problems.

Training, Other Qualifications, and Advancement

Employers prefer applicants who have completed postsecondary school training in drafting, training that is offered by technical institutes, community colleges, and some 4-year colleges and universities. Employers are most interested in applicants with well-developed drafting and mechanical drawing skills; knowledge of drafting standards, mathematics, science, and engineering technology; and a solid background in CADD techniques. In addition, communication and problem-solving skills are important.

Training and coursework differ somewhat within the drafting specialties. The initial training for each specialty is similar. All incorporate math and communication skills, for example, but coursework relating to the specialty varies. In an electronics drafting program, for example, students learn how to depict electronic components and circuits in drawings.

Many types of publicly and privately operated schools provide some form of training in drafting. Because the kind and quality of programs vary considerably, prospective students should be careful in selecting a program. They should contact prospective employers regarding their preferences and ask schools to provide information about the kinds of jobs that are obtained by the school's graduates, the types and conditions of the instructional facilities and equipment, and the faculty's qualifications.

Technical institutes offer intensive technical training but less general education than do junior and community colleges. Certificates or diplomas based on the completion of a certain number of course hours may be awarded. Many technical institutes offer 2-year associate degree programs, which are similar to, or part of, the programs offered by community colleges or state university systems. Their programs vary considerably in both length and type of courses offered. Some area vocational-technical schools are postsecondary public institutions that serve local students and emphasize the type of training preferred by local employers. Many offer introductory drafting instruction. Most require a high school diploma or its equivalent for admission. Other technical institutes are run by private, often for-profit, organizations sometimes called proprietary schools.

Community colleges offer curricula similar to those in technical institutes but include more courses on theory and liberal arts. Often, there is little or no difference between technical institute and community college programs. However, courses taken at community colleges are more likely than those given at technical institutes to be accepted for credit at 4-year colleges. After completing a 2-year associate degree program, graduates may obtain jobs as drafters or continue their education in a related field at 4-year colleges. Most 4-year colleges usually do not offer training in drafting, but college courses in engineering, architecture, and mathematics are useful for obtaining a job as a drafter.

Technical training obtained in the Armed Forces also can be applied in civilian drafting jobs. Some additional training may be necessary, depending on the technical area or military specialty.

The American Design Drafting Association (ADDA) has established a certification program for drafters. Although employers usually do not require drafters to be certified, certification demonstrates an understanding of nationally recognized practices and standards of knowledge. Individuals who wish to become certified must pass the Drafter Certification Test, which is administered periodically at ADDA-authorized sites. Applicants are tested on their knowledge and understanding of basic drafting concepts, such as geometric construction, working drawings, and architectural terms and standards.

Individuals planning careers in drafting should take courses in mathematics, science, computer technology, design, and computer graphics, as well as any high school drafting courses available. Mechanical ability and visual aptitude are important. Prospective drafters should be able to draw well and perform detailed work accurately and neatly. Artistic ability is helpful in some specialized fields, as is knowledge of manufacturing and construction methods. In addition, prospective drafters should have good interpersonal skills because they work closely with engineers, surveyors, architects, and other professionals and, sometimes, with customers.

Entry-level or junior drafters usually do routine work under close supervision. After gaining experience, they may become intermediate drafters and progress to more difficult work with less supervision. At the intermediate level, they may need to exercise more judgment and perform calculations when preparing and modifying drawings. Drafters may eventually advance to senior drafter, designer, or supervisor. Many employers pay for continuing education, and, with appropriate college degrees, drafters may go on to become engineering technicians, engineers, or architects.

Employment

Drafters held about 254,000 jobs in 2004. Architectural and civil drafters held 43 percent of all jobs for drafters, mechanical drafters held about 32 percent of all jobs, and about 15 percent of jobs were held by electrical and electronics drafters.

About 44 percent of all jobs for drafters were in architectural, engineering, and related services firms that design construction projects or do other engineering work on a contract basis for other industries. Another 27 percent of jobs were in manufacturing industries such as machinery manufacturing, including metalworking and other general machinery; fabricated metal products manufacturing, including architectural and structural metals; computer and electronic products manufacturing, including navigational, measuring, electromedical, and control instruments; and transportation equipment manufacturing, including aerospace products and parts manufacturing, as well as ship and boat building. Most of the rest were employed in construction, government, wholesale trade, utilities, and employment services. Approximately 6 percent were self-employed in 2004.

Job Outlook

Employment of drafters is expected to grow more slowly than the average for all occupations through 2014. Industrial growth and increasingly complex design problems associated with new products and manufacturing processes will increase the demand for drafting services. Further, drafters are beginning to break out of the traditional drafting role and do work traditionally performed by engineers and architects, thus also increasing demand for drafters. However, drafters tend to be concentrated in slowly growing or declining manufacturing industries. CADD systems that are more powerful and easier to use also should limit demand for lesser-skilled drafters as simple tasks are increasingly done quickly and easily by other drafters or other technical professionals, resulting in slower-than-average overall employment growth. Because some drafting work can be done in other locations by using the Internet to send CADD files internationally, the offshoring of some drafting jobs also should dampen growth. Most job openings are expected to arise from the need to replace drafters who transfer to other occupations, leave the labor force, or retire.

Opportunities should be best for individuals with at least 2 years of postsecondary training in a drafting program that provides strong technical skills as well as considerable experience with CADD systems. CADD has increased the complexity of drafting applications while enhancing the productivity of drafters. It also has enhanced the nature of drafting by creating more possibilities for design and drafting. As technology continues to advance, employers will look for drafters with a strong background in fundamental drafting principles, a high level of technical sophistication, and the ability to apply their knowledge to a broader range of responsibilities.

While growth is expected to be greatest for mechanical, architectural, and civil drafters, demand for particular drafting specialties varies throughout the country because employment usually is contingent on the needs of local industry. Employment of drafters remains highly concentrated in industries that are sensitive to cyclical changes in the economy, primarily manufacturing industries. During recessions, drafters may be laid off. However, a growing number of drafters should continue to find employment on a temporary or contract basis as more companies turn to the employment services industry to meet their changing needs.

Earnings

Drafters' earnings vary by specialty, location, and level of responsibility. Median annual earnings of architectural and civil drafters were $39,190 in May 2004. The middle 50 percent earned between $31,460 and $47,800. The lowest 10 percent earned less than $25,670, and the highest 10 percent earned more than $57,670. Median annual earnings for architectural and civil drafters in architectural, engineering, and related services were $38,760.

Median annual earnings of mechanical drafters were $43,000 in May 2004. The middle 50 percent earned between $34,090 and $54,240. The lowest 10 percent earned less than $27,490, and the highest 10 percent earned more than $67,650. Median annual earnings for mechanical drafters in architectural, engineering, and related services were $44,560.

Median annual earnings of electrical and electronics drafters were $43,180 in May 2004. The middle 50 percent earned between $33,920 and $56,110. The lowest 10 percent earned less than $27,600, and the highest 10 percent earned more than $72,050. In architectural, engineering, and related services, median annual earnings for electrical and electronics drafters were $42,200.

Related Occupations

Other workers who prepare or analyze detailed drawings and make precise calculations and measurements include architects, except landscape and naval; landscape architects; commercial and industrial designers; engineers; engineering technicians; science technicians; and surveyors, cartographers, photogrammetrists, and surveying technicians.

Sources of Additional Information

Information on schools offering programs in drafting and related fields is available from

▸ Accrediting Commission of Career Schools and Colleges of Technology, 2101 Wilson Blvd., Suite 302, Arlington, VA 22201. Internet: http://www.accsct.org

Information about certification is available from

▸ American Design Drafting Association, 105 E. Main St., Newbern, TN 38059. Internet: http://www.adda.org

Economists

(O*NET 19-3011.00)

Significant Points

■ Slower-than-average job growth is expected as firms increasingly employ workers to perform more-specialized tasks with titles that reflect the specific duties of the job rather than the general title of economist.

■ Job seekers with a background in economics should have good opportunities, although some of these opportunities will be in related occupations.

■ Candidates who hold a master's or Ph.D. degree in economics will have the best employment prospects and advancement opportunities.

■ Quantitative skills are important in all economics specialties.

Nature of the Work

Economists study how society distributes scarce resources, such as land, labor, raw materials, and machinery, to produce goods and services. They conduct research, collect and analyze data, monitor economic trends, and develop forecasts. They research issues such as energy costs, inflation, interest rates, exchange rates, business cycles, taxes, or employment levels.

Economists devise methods and procedures for obtaining the data they need. For example, sampling techniques may be used to conduct a survey, and various mathematical modeling techniques may be used to develop forecasts. Preparing reports, including tables and charts, on research results is an important part of an economist's job. Presenting economic and statistical concepts in a clear and meaningful way is particularly important for economists whose research is directed toward making policies for an organization. Some economists also might perform economic analysis for the media.

Many economists specialize in a particular area of economics, although general knowledge of basic economic principles is useful in each area. *Microeconomists* study the supply and demand decisions of individuals and firms, such as how profits can be maximized and how much of a good or service consumers will demand at a certain price. *Industrial economists* or *organizational economists* study the market structure of particular industries in terms of the number of competitors within those industries and examine the market decisions of competitive firms and monopolies. These economists also may be concerned with antitrust policy and its impact on market structure. *Macroeconomists* study historical trends in the whole economy and forecast future trends in areas such as unemployment, inflation, economic growth, productivity, and investment. Closely related to macroeconomists are *monetary economists* or *financial economists*, who study the money and banking system and the effects of changing interest rates. *International economists* study international financial markets, exchange rates, and the effects of various trade policies such as tariffs. *Labor economists* or *demographic economists* study the supply and demand for labor and the determination of wages. These economists also try to explain the reasons for unemployment and the effects of changing demographic trends, such as an aging population and increasing immigration, on labor markets. *Public finance economists* are involved primarily in studying the role of the government in the economy and the effects of tax cuts, budget deficits, and welfare policies. *Econometricians* investigate all areas of economics and use mathematical techniques such as calculus, game theory, and regression analysis to formulate economic models that help to explain economic relationships and that are used to develop forecasts related to the nature and length of business cycles, the effects of a specific rate of inflation on the economy, the effects of tax legislation on unemployment levels, and other economic phenomena. Many economists have applied these fundamental areas of economics to specific applications such as health, education, agriculture, urban and regional economics, law, history, energy, and the environment.

Most economists are concerned with practical applications of economic policy and work for a variety of organizations. Economists working for corporations are involved primarily in microeconomic issues, such as forecasting consumer demand and sales of the firm's products. Some analyze their competitors' growth and market share and advise their company on how to handle the competition. Others monitor legislation passed by Congress, such as environmental and worker safety regulations, and assess its impact on their business. Corporations with many international branches or subsidiaries might employ economists to monitor the economic situations in countries where they do business or to provide a risk assessment of a country into which the company might expand.

Economists working in economic consulting or research firms may perform the same tasks as economists working for corporations. Economists in consulting firms also perform much of the macroeconomic analysis and forecasting that is conducted in the United States. These economists collect data on various indicators; maintain databases; analyze historical trends; and develop models to forecast growth, inflation, unemployment, or interest rates. Their analyses and forecasts are frequently published in newspapers and journal articles.

Another large employer of economists is the government. Economists in the federal government administer most of the surveys and collect the majority of the economic data characterizing the United States. For example, economists in the U.S. Department of Commerce collect and analyze data on the production, distribution, and consumption of commodities produced in the United States and overseas, while economists employed by the U.S. Department of Labor collect and analyze data on the domestic economy, including data on prices, wages, employment, productivity, and safety and health. Economists who work for government agencies also assess economic conditions in the United States or abroad in order to estimate the economic effects of specific changes in legislation or public policy. Government economists advise policy makers in areas such as telecommunications deregulation, Social Security revamping, the effects of tax cuts on the budget deficit, and the effectiveness of imposing tariffs on imported steel. An economist working in state or local government might analyze data on the growth of school-age or prison populations and on employment and unemployment rates in order to project future spending needs.

Working Conditions

Economists have structured work schedules. They often work alone, writing reports, preparing statistical charts, and using computers, but they also may be an integral part of a research team. Most work under pressure of deadlines and tight schedules, which may require overtime. Their routine may be interrupted by special requests for data and by the need to attend meetings or conferences. Frequent travel may be necessary.

Training, Other Qualifications, and Advancement

A master's or Ph.D. degree in economics is required for many private-sector economist jobs and for advancement to more responsible positions. Economics includes numerous specialties at the graduate level, such as advanced economic theory, econometrics, international economics, and labor economics. Students should select graduate schools that are strong in specialties in which they are interested. Undergraduate economics majors can choose from a variety of courses ranging from microeconomics, macroeconomics, and econometrics to more philosophical courses, such as the history of economic thought. Because of the importance of quantitative skills to economists, courses in mathematics, statistics, economet-

rics, sampling theory and survey design, and computer science are extremely helpful. Some schools help graduate students find internships or part-time employment in government agencies, economic consulting or research firms, or financial institutions prior to graduation.

In the federal government, candidates for entry-level economist positions must have a bachelor's degree with a minimum of 21 semester hours of economics and 3 hours of statistics, accounting, or calculus.

Whether working in government, industry, research organizations, or consulting firms, economists with a bachelor's degree usually qualify for most entry-level positions as a research assistant, for administrative or management trainee positions, or for various sales jobs. A master's degree usually is required to qualify for more responsible research and administrative positions. Many businesses, research and consulting firms, and government agencies seek individuals who have strong computer and quantitative skills and can perform complex research. A Ph.D. is necessary for top economist positions in many organizations. Many corporation and government executives have a strong background in economics.

A master's degree usually is the minimum requirement for a job as an instructor in a junior or community college. In most colleges and universities, however, a Ph.D. is necessary for appointment as an instructor. A Ph.D. and extensive publications in academic journals are required for a professorship, tenure, and promotion.

Aspiring economists should gain experience gathering and analyzing data, conducting interviews or surveys, and writing reports on their findings while in college. This experience can prove invaluable later in obtaining a full-time position in the field because much of the economist's work, especially in the beginning, may center on these duties. With experience, economists eventually are assigned their own research projects. Related job experience, such as work as a stock or bond trader, might be advantageous.

Those considering careers as economists should be able to pay attention to details because much time is spent on precise data analysis. Patience and persistence are necessary qualities, given that economists must spend long hours on independent study and problem solving. Good communication skills also are useful, as economists must be able to present their findings, both orally and in writing, in a clear, concise manner.

Employment

Economists held about 13,000 jobs in 2004. The government employed 58 percent of economists in a wide range of government agencies, with 34 percent in federal government and 24 percent in state and local government. The U.S. Departments of Labor, Agriculture, and State are the largest federal employers of economists. The remaining jobs were spread throughout private industry, particularly in scientific research and development services and management, scientific, and technical consulting services. A number of economists combine a full-time job in government, academia, or business with part-time or consulting work in another setting.

Employment of economists is concentrated in large cities. Some work abroad for companies with major international operations; for

U.S. government agencies; and for international organizations, such as the World Bank, International Monetary Fund, and United Nations.

In addition to the previously mentioned jobs, economists hold faculty positions in colleges and universities. Economics faculties have flexible work schedules and may divide their time among teaching, research, consulting, and administration. (See the description of teachers—postsecondary elsewhere in this book.)

Job Outlook

Employment of economists is expected to grow more slowly than average for all occupations through 2014. Employment growth should be the fastest in private industry, especially in management, scientific, and technical consulting services. Rising demand for economic analysis in virtually every industry should stem from the growing complexity of the global economy; the effects of competition on businesses; and increased reliance on quantitative methods for analyzing and forecasting business, sales, and other economic trends. Some corporations choose to hire economic consultants to fill these needs rather than keeping an economist on staff. This practice should result in more economists being employed in consulting services. However, job growth will be limited as firms increasingly employ workers to perform more-specialized tasks with titles that reflect the specific duties of the job instead of the general title of economist. In addition, few new jobs are expected in government, but the need to replace experienced workers who transfer to other occupations or who retire or leave the labor force for other reasons will lead to job openings for economists across all industries in which they are employed.

Individuals with a background in economics should have job opportunities, although some of these opportunities will be in related occupations. As firms increasingly employ workers to perform more-specialized tasks, the best opportunities for individuals with backgrounds in economics are expected to be in positions that have titles other than economist. Some examples of job titles often held by those with an economics background are financial analyst, market analyst, public policy consultant, researcher or research assistant, and econometrician.

A master's or Ph.D. degree, coupled with a strong background in economic theory, mathematics, statistics, and econometrics, provides the basis for acquiring any specialty within the economics field. Economists who are skilled in quantitative techniques and their application to economic modeling and forecasting, and who also have good communications skills, should have the best job opportunities. Like those in many other disciplines, however, Ph.D. holders are likely to face keen competition for tenured teaching positions in colleges and universities.

Bachelor's degree holders may face competition for the limited number of economist positions for which they qualify. However, they will qualify for a number of other positions in which they can take advantage of their economic knowledge by conducting research, developing surveys, or analyzing data. Many graduates with bachelor's degrees will find jobs in industry and business as management or sales trainees or as administrative assistants. Bachelor's degree holders with good quantitative skills and a strong background in mathematics, statistics, survey design, and computer science also may be hired by private firms as researchers. Some will find jobs in government.

Candidates who meet state certification requirements may become high school economics teachers. The demand for secondary school economics teachers is expected to grow as economics becomes an increasingly important and popular course.

Earnings

Median annual wage and salary earnings of economists were $72,780 in May 2004. The middle 50 percent earned between $53,650 and $96,240. The lowest 10 percent earned less than $41,040, and the highest 10 percent earned more than $129,170.

The federal government recognizes education and experience in certifying applicants for entry-level positions. The starting salary for economists having a bachelor's degree was about $24,667 a year in 2005; however, those with superior academic records could begin at $30,567. Those having a master's degree could qualify for positions at an annual salary of $37,390. Those with a Ph.D. could begin at $45,239, while some individuals with experience and an advanced degree could start at $54,221. Starting salaries were slightly higher in selected geographical areas where the prevailing local pay was higher. The average annual salary for economists employed by the federal government was $89,441 a year in 2005.

Related Occupations

Economists are concerned with understanding and interpreting financial matters, among other subjects. Other occupations in this area include accountants and auditors; actuaries; budget analysts; financial analysts and personal financial advisors; financial managers; insurance underwriters; loan officers; and purchasing managers, buyers, and purchasing agents. Other occupations involved in market research and data collection are management analysts and market and survey researchers.

Sources of Additional Information

For information on careers in business economics, contact

▸ National Association for Business Economics, 1233 20th St. NW, Suite 505, Washington, DC 20036.

Information on obtaining positions as economists with the federal government is available from the Office of Personnel Management through USAJOBS, the federal government's official employment information system. This resource for locating and applying for job opportunities can be accessed through the Internet at http://www.usajobs.opm.gov or through an interactive voice response telephone system at (703) 724-1850 or TDD (978) 461-8404. These numbers are not toll free, and charges may result.

Electrical and Electronics Installers and Repairers

(O*NET 49-2092.01, 49-2092.02, 49-2092.03, 49-2092.04, 49-2092.05, 49-2092.06, 49-2093.00, 49-2094.00, 49-2095.00, and 49-2096.00)

Significant Points

- Knowledge of electrical equipment and electronics is necessary for employment; many applicants complete 1 to 2 years at vocational schools and community colleges, although some less-skilled repairers may have only a high school diploma.

- Employment is projected to grow more slowly than average, but prospects vary by occupational specialty.

- Job opportunities will be best for applicants with a thorough knowledge of electrical and electronic equipment as well as repair experience.

Nature of the Work

Businesses and other organizations depend on complex electronic equipment for a variety of functions. Industrial controls automatically monitor and direct production processes on the factory floor. Transmitters and antennae provide communication links for many organizations. Electric power companies use electronic equipment to operate and control generating plants, substations, and monitoring equipment. The federal government uses radar and missile control systems to provide for the national defense and to direct commercial air traffic. These complex pieces of electronic equipment are installed, maintained, and repaired by electrical and electronics installers and repairers.

Electrical equipment and electronic equipment are two distinct types of industrial equipment, although much equipment contains both electrical and electronic components. In general, electrical portions provide the power for the equipment, while electronic components control the device, although many types of equipment still are controlled with electrical devices. Electronic sensors monitor the equipment and the manufacturing process, providing feedback to the programmable logic control (PLC), which controls the equipment. The PLC processes the information provided by the sensors and makes adjustments to optimize output. To adjust the output, the PLC sends signals to the electrical, hydraulic, and pneumatic devices that power the machine—changing feed rates, pressures, and other variables in the manufacturing process. Many installers and repairers, known as *field technicians*, travel to factories or other locations to repair equipment. These workers often have assigned areas in which they perform preventive maintenance on a regular basis. When equipment breaks down, field technicians go to a customer's site to repair the equipment. *Bench technicians* work in repair shops located in factories and service centers, fixing components that cannot be repaired on the factory floor.

Some industrial electronic equipment is self-monitoring and alerts repairers to malfunctions. When equipment breaks down, repairers first check for common causes of trouble, such as loose connections or obviously defective components. If routine checks do not locate the trouble, repairers may refer to schematics and manufacturers' specifications that show connections and provide instructions on how to locate problems. Automated electronic control systems are increasing in complexity, making diagnosis more challenging. With these systems, repairers use software programs and testing equipment to diagnose malfunctions. Among their diagnostic tools are multimeters, which measure voltage, current, and resistance, and advanced multimeters, which measure capacitance, inductance, and current gain of transistors. Repairers also use signal generators, which provide test signals, and oscilloscopes, which display signals graphically. Finally, repairers use hand tools such as pliers, screwdrivers, soldering irons, and wrenches to replace faulty parts and adjust equipment.

Because repairing components is a complex activity and factories cannot allow production equipment to stand idle, repairers on the factory floor usually remove and replace defective units, such as circuit boards, instead of fixing them. Defective units are discarded or returned to the manufacturer or a specialized shop for repair. Bench technicians at these locations have the training, tools, and parts needed to thoroughly diagnose and repair circuit boards or other complex components. These workers also locate and repair circuit defects, such as poorly soldered joints, blown fuses, or malfunctioning transistors.

Electrical and electronics installers often fit older manufacturing equipment with new automated control devices. Older manufacturing machines are frequently in good working order but are limited by inefficient control systems for which replacement parts are no longer available. Installers replace old electronic control units with new PLCs. Setting up and installing a new PLC involves connecting it to different sensors and electrically powered devices (electric motors, switches, and pumps) and writing a computer program to operate the PLC. Electronics installers coordinate their efforts with those of other workers who are installing and maintaining equipment. (See the description of industrial machinery mechanics and maintenance workers elsewhere in this book.)

Electrical and electronics installers and repairers, transportation equipment install, adjust, or maintain mobile electronic communication equipment, including sound, sonar, security, navigation, and surveillance systems on trains, watercraft, or other vehicles. *Electrical and electronics repairers, powerhouse, substation, and relay* inspect, test, maintain, or repair electrical equipment used in generating stations, substations, and in-service relays. These workers may be known as powerhouse electricians, relay technicians, or power transformer repairers. *Electric motor, power tool, and related repairers*—such as armature winders, generator mechanics, and electric golf cart repairers—specialize in installing, maintaining, and repairing electric motors, wiring, or switches.

Electronic equipment installers and repairers, motor vehicles have a significantly different job. They install, diagnose, and repair communication, sound, security, and navigation equipment in motor vehicles. Most installation work involves either new alarm or sound systems. New sound systems vary significantly in cost and complexity of installation. Replacing a head unit (radio) with a new CD player is simple, requiring the removal of a few screws and the connection of a few wires. Installing a new sound system with a subwoofer, amplifier, and fuses is far more complicated. The installer builds a fiberglass or wood box designed to hold the subwoofer and to fit inside the unique dimensions of the automobile. Installing sound-deadening material, which often is necessary with more powerful speakers, requires an installer to remove many parts of a car (for example, seats, carpeting, or interiors of doors), add sound-absorbing material in empty spaces, and reinstall the interior parts. The installer also runs new speaker and electrical cables. The new system may require additional fuses, a new electrical line to be run from the battery through a newly drilled hole in the firewall into the interior of the vehicle, or an additional or more powerful alternator or battery. Motor vehicle installers and repairers work with an increasingly complex range of electronic equipment, including DVD players, satellite navigation equipment, passive security systems, and active security systems.

Working Conditions

Many electrical and electronics installers and repairers work on factory floors, where they are subject to noise, dirt, vibration, and heat. Bench technicians work primarily in repair shops, where the surroundings are relatively quiet, comfortable, and well lighted.

Installers and repairers may have to do heavy lifting and work in a variety of positions. They must follow safety guidelines and often wear protective goggles and hardhats. When working on ladders or on elevated equipment, repairers must wear harnesses to avoid falls. Before repairing a piece of machinery, these workers must follow procedures to ensure that others cannot start the equipment during the repair process. They also must take precautions against electric shock by locking off power to the unit under repair.

Motor vehicle electronic equipment installers and repairers normally work indoors in well-ventilated and well-lighted repair shops. Minor cuts and bruises are common, but serious accidents usually are avoided when safety practices are observed.

Training, Other Qualifications, and Advancement

Knowledge of electrical equipment and electronics is necessary for employment. Many applicants gain this knowledge through programs lasting 1 to 2 years at vocational schools or community colleges, although some less-skilled repairers may have only a high school diploma. Entry-level repairers may work closely with more experienced technicians who provide technical guidance.

Installers and repairers should have good eyesight and color perception to work with the intricate components used in electronic equipment. Field technicians work closely with customers and should have good communication skills and a neat appearance. Employers also may require that field technicians have a driver's license.

Various organizations offer certification. Repairers may specialize—in industrial electronics, for example. To receive certification, repairers must pass qualifying exams corresponding to their level of training and experience.

Experienced repairers with advanced training may become specialists or troubleshooters who help other repairers diagnose difficult problems. Workers with leadership ability may become supervisors of other repairers. Some experienced workers open their own repair shops.

Employment

Electrical and electronics installers and repairers held about 158,000 jobs in 2004. The following tabulation breaks down their employment by occupational specialty:

Electrical and electronics repairers, commercial and industrial equipment	72,000
Electric motor, power tool, and related repairers	28,000
Electrical and electronics repairers, powerhouse, substation, and relay	21,000
Electronic equipment installers and repairers, motor vehicles	19,000
Electrical and electronics installers and repairers, transportation equipment	18,000

Many repairers worked for utilities; building equipment contractors; machinery and equipment repair shops; wholesalers; the federal government; retailers of automotive parts and accessories; rail transportation companies; and manufacturers of electrical, electronic, and transportation equipment.

Job Outlook

Job opportunities should be best for applicants with a thorough knowledge of electrical equipment and electronics as well as with repair experience. Overall employment of electrical and electronics installers and repairers is expected to grow more slowly than the average for all occupations during the 2004–2014 period, but prospects vary by occupational specialty. In addition to employment growth, the need to replace workers who transfer to other occupations or leave the labor force will result in many job openings.

Average employment growth is projected for electrical and electronics installers and repairers of commercial and industrial equipment. This equipment will become more sophisticated and will be used more frequently as businesses strive to lower costs by increasing and improving automation. Companies will install electronic controls, robots, sensors, and other equipment to automate processes such as assembly and testing. As prices decline, applications will be found across a number of industries, including services, utilities, and construction, as well as manufacturing. Improved reliability of equipment should not constrain employment growth, however: Companies increasingly will rely on repairers because malfunctions that idle commercial and industrial equipment will continue to be costly.

Employment of motor vehicle electronic equipment installers and repairers also is expected to grow about as fast as the average. However, as motor vehicle manufacturers install more and better sound, security, entertainment, and navigation systems in new vehicles, and as newer electronic systems require progressively less maintenance, employment growth for aftermarket electronic equipment installers will be limited.

Employment of electric motor, power tool, and related repairers is expected to grow more slowly than average. Improvements in electrical and electronic equipment design should limit job growth by simplifying repair tasks. The design of more parts that are easily disposable will further reduce employment growth.

Employment of electrical and electronic installers and repairers of transportation equipment is also expected to grow more slowly than the average because of declining industry employment in railroad rolling stock manufacturing and shipbuilding and boatbuilding.

Employment of electrical and electronics installers and repairers, powerhouse, substation, and relay is expected to decline slightly. Consolidation and privatization in utilities industries should improve productivity, reducing employment. Newer equipment will be more reliable and easier to repair, further limiting employment.

Earnings

Median hourly earnings of electrical and electronics repairers, commercial and industrial equipment were $20.48 in May 2004. The middle 50 percent earned between $16.04 and $25.07. The lowest 10 percent earned less than $12.55, and the highest 10 percent earned more than $28.68. In May 2004, median hourly earnings were $23.79 in the federal government and $17.82 in building equipment contractors, the industries employing the largest numbers of electrical and electronics repairers, commercial and industrial equipment.

Median hourly earnings of electric motor, power tool, and related repairers were $15.54 in May 2004. The middle 50 percent earned between $12.12 and $19.71. The lowest 10 percent earned less than $9.48, and the highest 10 percent earned more than $23.90. In May 2004, median hourly earnings were $15.02 in commercial and industrial machinery and equipment (except automotive and electronic) repair and maintenance, the industry employing the largest number of electronic motor, power tool, and related repairers.

Median hourly earnings of electrical and electronics repairers, powerhouse, substation, and relay were $25.86 in May 2004. The middle 50 percent earned between $22.47 and $29.73. The lowest 10 percent earned less than $18.01, and the highest 10 percent earned more than $33.82. In May 2004, median hourly earnings were $26.37 in electric power generation, transmission, and distribution—the industry employing the largest number of these repairers.

Median hourly earnings of electronics installers and repairers, motor vehicles were $12.79 in May 2004. The middle 50 percent earned between $10.27 and $16.55. The lowest 10 percent earned less than $8.85, and the highest 10 percent earned more than $22.02.

Median hourly earnings of electrical and electronics repairers, transportation equipment were $19.25 in May 2004. The middle 50 percent earned between $15.06 and $23.57. The lowest 10 percent earned less than $11.86, and the highest 10 percent earned more than $27.70.

Related Occupations

Workers in other occupations who install and repair electronic equipment include broadcast and sound technicians and radio operators; computer, automated teller, and office machine repairers; electronic home entertainment equipment installers and repairers; and radio and telecommunications equipment installers and repairers. Industrial machinery mechanics and maintenance workers also install, maintain, and repair industrial machinery.

Sources of Additional Information

For information on careers and certification, contact any of the following organizations:

▶ ACES International, 5241 Princess Anne Rd., Suite 110, Virginia Beach, VA 23462. Internet: http://www.acesinternational.org

▶ Electronics Technicians Association International, 5 Depot St., Greencastle, IN 46135.

▶ International Society of Certified Electronics Technicians, 3608 Pershing Ave., Fort Worth, TX 76107-4527. Internet: http://www.iscet.org

Electronic Home Entertainment Equipment Installers and Repairers

(O*NET 49-2097.00)

Significant Points

■ Employers prefer applicants who have basic knowledge and skills in electronics; many applicants gain these skills at vocational training programs and community colleges.

■ Employment is expected to grow more slowly than the average for all occupations because it often is cheaper to replace equipment than to repair it.

■ Job opportunities will be best for applicants with knowledge of electronics and with related hands-on experience.

Nature of the Work

Electronic home entertainment equipment installers and repairers, also called *service technicians*, repair a variety of equipment, including televisions and radios, stereo components, video and audio disc players, video cameras, and video recorders. They also install and repair home security systems, intercom equipment, satellite television dishes, and home theater systems, which consist of large-screen televisions and sophisticated surround-sound audio components.

Customers usually bring small, portable equipment to repair shops for servicing. Repairers at these locations, known as *bench technicians*, are equipped with a full array of electronic tools and parts. When larger, less mobile equipment breaks down, customers may pay repairers to come to their homes. These repairers, known as *field technicians*, travel with a limited set of tools and parts and attempt to complete the repair at the customer's location. If the job is complex, technicians may bring defective components back to the shop for thorough diagnosis and repair.

When equipment breaks down, repairers check for common causes of trouble, such as dirty or defective components. Many repairs consist simply of cleaning and lubricating equipment. If routine checks do not locate the trouble, repairers may refer to schematics and manufacturers' specifications that provide instructions on how to locate problems. Repairers use a variety of test equipment to diagnose and identify malfunctions. Multimeters detect short circuits, failed capacitors, and blown fuses by measuring voltage, current, and resistance. Color-bar and dot generators provide on-screen test patterns, signal generators test signals, and oscilloscopes and digital storage scopes measure complex waveforms produced by electronic equipment. Repairs may involve removing and replacing a failed capacitor, transistor, or fuse. Repairers use hand tools, such as pliers, screwdrivers, soldering irons, and wrenches, to replace faulty parts. They also make adjustments to equipment, such as focusing and converging the picture of a television set or balancing the audio on a surround-sound system.

Improvements in technology have miniaturized and digitized many audio and video recording devices. Miniaturization has made repair work significantly more difficult because both the components and the acceptable tolerances are smaller. For example, an analog video camera operates at 1,800 revolutions per minute (rpm), while a digital video camera may operate at 9,000 rpm. Also, components now are mounted on the surface of circuit boards, rather than plugged into slots, requiring more precise soldering when a new part is installed. Improved technologies have lowered the price of electronic home entertainment equipment to the point where customers often replace broken equipment instead of repairing it.

Working Conditions

Most repairers work in well-lighted electrical repair shops. Field technicians, however, spend much time traveling in service vehicles and working in customers' residences.

Repairers may have to work in a variety of positions and carry heavy equipment. Although the work of repairers is comparatively safe, they must take precautions against minor burns and electric shock. Because television monitors carry high voltage even when they are turned off, repairers need to discharge the voltage before servicing such equipment.

Training, Other Qualifications, and Advancement

Employers prefer applicants who have basic knowledge and skills in electronics. Applicants should be familiar with schematics and have some hands-on experience repairing electronic equipment. Many applicants gain these skills at vocational training programs and community colleges. Training programs should include both hands-on experience and theoretical education in digital consumer electronics. Entry-level repairers may work closely with more experienced technicians, who provide technical guidance.

Field technicians work closely with customers and must have good communication skills and a neat appearance. Employers also may require that field technicians have a driver's license.

Various organizations offer certification for electronic home entertainment equipment installers and repairers. Repairers may specialize in a variety of skill areas, including consumer electronics. To receive certification, repairers must pass qualifying exams corresponding to their level of training and experience.

Experienced repairers with advanced training may become specialists or troubleshooters, helping other repairers to diagnose difficult problems. Workers with leadership ability may become supervisors of other repairers. Some experienced workers open their own repair shops.

Employment

Electronic home entertainment equipment installers and repairers held about 47,000 jobs in 2004. Most repairers worked in electronics and appliance stores that sell and service electronic home entertainment products or in electronic and precision equipment repair and maintenance shops. About 1 electronic home entertainment equipment installer and repairer in 3 were self-employed, more than 4 times the proportion for all installation, maintenance, and repair occupations.

Job Outlook

Employment of electronic home entertainment equipment installers and repairers is expected to grow more slowly than average through 2014, due to decreased demand for repair work. Nevertheless, job openings will come about because of employment growth; some openings will also result from the need to replace workers who retire or who transfer to higher-paying jobs in other occupations requiring electronics experience. Opportunities will be best for applicants with knowledge of electronics and with related hands-on experience.

The need for repairers is expected to grow slowly because home entertainment equipment is less expensive than in the past. As technological developments have lowered the price and improved the reliability of equipment, the demand for repair services has decreased. When malfunctions do occur, it often is cheaper for consumers to replace equipment rather than to pay for repairs.

Employment growth will be spurred somewhat by the introduction of sophisticated digital equipment, such as DVDs, high-definition digital televisions, and digital camcorders. So long as the price of such equipment remains high, purchasers will be willing to hire repairers when malfunctions occur. There also will be demand to install sophisticated home entertainment systems, such as home theaters.

Earnings

Median hourly earnings of electronic home entertainment equipment installers and repairers were $13.44 in May 2004. The middle 50 percent earned between $10.39 and $17.10. The lowest 10 percent earned less than $8.17, and the highest 10 percent earned more than $21.36. In May 2004, median hourly earnings of electronic home entertainment equipment installers and repairers were $12.86 in electronics and appliance stores and $12.28 in electronic and precision equipment repair and maintenance.

Related Occupations

Other workers who repair and maintain electronic equipment include broadcast and sound engineering technicians and radio operators; computer, automated teller, and office machine repairers; electrical and electronics installers and repairers; and radio and telecommunications equipment installers and repairers.

Sources of Additional Information

For information on careers and certification, contact

▸ ACES International, 5241 Princess Anne Rd., Suite 110, Virginia Beach, VA 23462. Internet: http://www.acesinternational.org

▸ Electronics Technicians Association International, 5 Depot St., Greencastle, IN 46135.

▸ International Society of Certified Electronics Technicians, 3608 Pershing Ave., Fort Worth, TX 76107-4527. Internet: http://www.iscet.org

Elevator Installers and Repairers

(O*NET 47-4021.00)

Significant Points

■ Most workers belong to a union and enter the occupation through a 4-year apprenticeship program.

■ High pay and good benefits, together with expected slow job growth and few separations, should result in keen competition for the few job opportunities that arise in this small occupation; prospects should be best for those with postsecondary education in electronics.

■ Elevator installers and repairers are less affected by downturns in the economy and inclement weather than other construction trades workers.

Nature of the Work

Elevator installers and repairers—also called *elevator constructors* or *elevator mechanics*—assemble, install, and replace elevators, escalators, dumbwaiters, moving walkways, and similar equipment in new and old buildings. Once the equipment is in service, they maintain and repair it as well. They also are responsible for modernizing older equipment.

To install, repair, and maintain modern elevators, which are almost all electronically controlled, elevator installers and repairers must have a thorough knowledge of electronics, electricity, and hydraulics. Many elevators are controlled with microprocessors, which are programmed to analyze traffic conditions in order to dispatch elevators in the most efficient manner. With these computer controls, it is possible to get the greatest amount of service with the least number of cars.

When installing a new elevator, installers and repairers begin by studying blueprints to determine the equipment needed to install rails, machinery, car enclosures, motors, pumps, cylinders, and plunger foundations. Once this has been done, they begin equipment installation. Working on scaffolding or platforms, installers bolt or weld steel rails to the walls of the shaft to guide the elevator.

Elevator installers put in electrical wires and controls by running tubing, called conduit, along a shaft's walls from floor to floor. Once the conduit is in place, mechanics pull plastic-covered electrical wires through it. They then install electrical components and related devices required at each floor and at the main control panel in the machine room.

Installers bolt or weld together the steel frame of an elevator car at the bottom of the shaft; install the car's platform, walls, and doors; and attach guide shoes and rollers to minimize the lateral motion of the car as it travels through the shaft. They also install the outer doors and door frames at the elevator entrances on each floor.

For cabled elevators, these workers install geared or gearless machines with a traction drive wheel that guides and moves heavy steel cables connected to the elevator car and counterweight. (The counterweight moves in the opposite direction from the car and balances most of the weight of the car to reduce the weight that the elevator's motor must lift.) Elevator installers also install elevators in which a car sits on a hydraulic plunger that is driven by a pump. The plunger pushes the elevator car up from underneath, similar to a lift in an auto service station.

Installers and repairers also install escalators. They put in place the steel framework, the electrically powered stairs, and the tracks and install associated motors and electrical wiring. In addition to elevators and escalators, installers and repairers also may install devices such as dumbwaiters and material lifts—which are similar to elevators in design—as well as moving walkways, stair lifts, and wheelchair lifts.

The most highly skilled elevator installers and repairers, called *adjusters,* specialize in fine-tuning all the equipment after installation. Adjusters make sure that an elevator is working according to specifications and is stopping correctly at each floor within a specified time. Once an elevator is operating properly, it must be maintained and serviced regularly to keep it in safe working condition. Elevator installers and repairers generally do preventive maintenance—such as oiling and greasing moving parts, replacing worn parts, testing equipment with meters and gauges, and adjusting equipment for optimal performance. They also troubleshoot and may be called to do emergency repairs.

A service crew usually handles major repairs—for example, replacing cables, elevator doors, or machine bearings. This may require the use of cutting torches or rigging equipment—tools that an elevator repairer normally would not carry. Service crews also do major modernization and alteration work, such as moving and replacing electrical motors, hydraulic pumps, and control panels.

Elevator installers and repairers usually specialize in installation, maintenance, or repair work. Maintenance and repair workers generally need greater knowledge of electricity and electronics than do installers, because a large part of maintenance and repair work is troubleshooting. Similarly, adjusters need a thorough knowledge of electricity, electronics, and computers to ensure that newly installed elevators operate properly.

Working Conditions

Most elevator installers and repairers work a 40-hour week. However, overtime is required when essential elevator equipment must be repaired, and some workers are on 24-hour call. Unlike most elevator installers, workers who specialize in elevator maintenance are on their own most of the day and typically service the same elevators periodically.

Elevator installers lift and carry heavy equipment and parts and may work in cramped spaces or awkward positions. Potential hazards include falls, electrical shock, muscle strains, and other injuries related to handling heavy equipment. Because most of their work is performed indoors in buildings under construction or in existing buildings, elevator installers and repairers lose less work time due to inclement weather than do other construction trades workers.

Training, Other Qualifications, and Advancement

Most elevator installers and repairers apply for their jobs through a local of the International Union of Elevator Constructors. Applicants for apprenticeship positions must be at least 18 years old, have a high school diploma or equivalent, and pass an aptitude test. Good physical condition and mechanical aptitude also are important.

Elevator installers and repairers learn their trade in a program administered by local joint educational committees representing the employers and the union. These programs, through which the apprentice learns everything from installation to repair, combine on-the-job training with classroom instruction in blueprint reading, electrical and electronic theory, mathematics, applications of physics, and safety. In nonunion shops, workers may complete training programs sponsored by independent contractors.

Apprentices generally must complete a 6-month probationary period. After successful completion, they work toward becoming fully qualified within 4 years. To be classified as a fully qualified elevator installer or repairer, union trainees must pass a standard examination administered by the National Elevator Industry Educational Program. Most states and cities also require elevator installers and repairers to pass a licensing examination. Both union and nonunion technicians may take the Certified Elevator Technician (CET) or the Certified Accessibility and Private Residence Lift Technician (CAT) program courses offered by the National Association of Elevator Contractors.

Most apprentices assist experienced elevator installers and repairers. Beginners carry materials and tools, bolt rails to walls, and assemble elevator cars. Eventually, apprentices learn more difficult tasks such as wiring, which requires knowledge of local and national electrical codes.

High school courses in electricity, mathematics, and physics provide a useful background. As elevators become increasingly sophisticated, workers may find it necessary to acquire more advanced formal education—for example, in a postsecondary technical school or junior college—with an emphasis on electronics. Workers with more formal education, such as an associate degree, usually advance more quickly than do their counterparts without a degree.

Many elevator installers and repairers also receive training from their employers or through manufacturers to become familiar with a particular company's equipment. Retraining is very important if a worker is to keep abreast of technological developments in elevator repair. In fact, union elevator installers and repairers typically receive continual training throughout their careers, through correspondence courses, seminars, or formal classes. Although voluntary, this training greatly improves one's chances for promotion and retention.

Some installers may receive further training in specialized areas and advance to the position of mechanic-in-charge, adjuster, supervisor, or elevator inspector. Adjusters, for example, may be picked for their position because they possess particular skills or are electronically inclined. Other workers may move into management, sales, or product design jobs.

Employment

Elevator installers and repairers held about 22,000 jobs in 2004. Most were employed by specialty trades contractors, particularly elevator maintenance and repair contractors. Others were employed by field offices of elevator manufacturers, machinery wholesalers, government agencies, or businesses that do their own elevator maintenance and repair.

Job Outlook

Workers should expect keen competition when seeking to enter this occupation. Elevator installer and repairer jobs have relatively high earnings and good benefits and involve a significant investment in training, and a large proportion are unionized. As a result, workers tend to stay in this occupation for a long time and few leave and need to be replaced, thus reducing job opportunities. Job prospects should be best for those with postsecondary education in electronics.

Employment of elevator installers and repairers is expected to increase as fast as the average for all occupations through the year 2014. Most of the demand for workers will be due to replacements. Demand for additional elevator installers depends greatly on growth in nonresidential construction, such as commercial office buildings and stores that have elevators and escalators. This sector of the construction industry is expected to grow during the decade in response to expansion of the economy. In addition, the need to continually update and repair old equipment, expand access to the disabled, and install increasingly sophisticated equipment and computerized controls also should add to the demand for elevator installers and repairers. Adding to the demand for elevator installers and repairers is a growing residential market where an increasing number of the elderly require easier access to their homes through stair lifts and residential elevators.

Elevators, escalators, lifts, moving walkways, and related equipment need to be kept in good working condition year round, so employment of elevator repairers is less affected by economic downturns and seasonality than other construction trades.

Earnings

Earnings of elevator installers and repairers are among the highest of all construction trades. Median hourly earnings of elevator installers and repairers were $28.23 in May 2004. The middle 50 percent earned between $22.96 and $33.68. The lowest 10 percent earned less than $17.36, and the top 10 percent earned more than $39.65. In May 2004, median hourly earnings in the miscellaneous special trade contractors industry were $28.68.

Three out of four elevator installers and repairers were members of unions or covered by a union contract, one of the highest proportions of all occupations. The largest numbers were members of the International Union of Elevator Constructors. In addition to free continuing education, elevator installers and repairers receive basic benefits enjoyed by most other workers.

Related Occupations

Elevator installers and repairers combine electrical and mechanical skills with construction skills, such as welding, rigging, measuring, and blueprint reading. Other occupations that require many of these skills are boilermakers; electricians; electrical and electronics installers and repairers; industrial machinery installation, repair, and maintenance workers; sheet metal workers; and structural and reinforcing iron and metal workers.

Sources of Additional Information

For further information on opportunities as an elevator installer and repairer, contact

▸ International Union of Elevator Constructors, 7154 Columbia Gateway Dr., Columbia, MD 21046. Internet: http://www.iuec.org

For additional information about the Certified Elevator Technician (CET) program, contact

▸ National Association of Elevator Contractors, 1298 Wellbrook Circle, Suite A, Conyers, GA 30012. Internet: http://www.naec.org

Engineering and Natural Sciences Managers

(O*NET 11-9041.00 and 11-9121.00)

Significant Points

■ Most engineering and natural sciences managers have previous experience as engineers, scientists, or mathematicians.

■ Projected employment growth for engineering and natural sciences managers should be closely related to growth in employment of the engineers and scientists they supervise and of the industries in which they are found.

■ Opportunities will be best for workers with strong communication and business management skills.

Nature of the Work

Engineering and natural sciences managers plan, coordinate, and direct research, design, and production activities. They may supervise engineers, scientists, and technicians, along with support personnel. These managers use their knowledge of engineering and natural sciences to oversee a variety of activities. They determine scientific and technical goals within broad outlines provided by top executives. These goals may include improving manufacturing processes, advancing scientific research, or developing new products. Managers make detailed plans to accomplish these goals. For example, they may develop the overall concepts of a new product or identify technical problems preventing the completion of a project.

To perform effectively, they also must acquire knowledge of administrative procedures, such as budgeting, hiring, and supervision. These managers propose budgets for projects and programs and determine staff, training, and equipment needs. They hire and assign scientists, engineers, and support personnel to carry out specific parts of each project. They also supervise the work of these employees, review their output, and establish administrative procedures and policies—including environmental standards, for example.

In addition, these managers use communication skills extensively. They spend a great deal of time coordinating the activities of their unit with those of other units or organizations. They confer with higher levels of management; with financial, production, marketing, and other managers; and with contractors and equipment and materials suppliers.

Engineering managers may supervise people who design and develop machinery, products, systems, and processes, or they may direct and coordinate production, operations, quality assurance, testing, or maintenance in industrial plants. Many are plant engineers, who direct and coordinate the design, installation, operation, and maintenance of equipment and machinery in industrial plants. Others manage research and development teams that produce new products and processes or improve existing ones.

Natural sciences managers oversee the work of life and physical scientists (including agricultural scientists, chemists, biologists, geoscientists, medical scientists, and physicists). These managers direct research and development projects and coordinate activities such as testing, quality control, and production. They may work on basic research projects or on commercial activities. Science managers sometimes conduct their own research in addition to managing the work of others.

Working Conditions

Engineering and natural sciences managers spend most of their time in an office. Some managers, however, also may work in laboratories, where they may be exposed to the same conditions as research scientists, or in industrial plants, where they may be exposed to the same conditions as production workers. Most managers work at least 40 hours a week and may work much longer on occasion to meet project deadlines. Some may experience considerable pressure to meet technical or scientific goals on a short deadline or within a tight budget.

Training, Other Qualifications, and Advancement

Strong technical knowledge is essential for engineering and natural sciences managers, who must understand and guide the work of their subordinates and explain the work in nontechnical terms to senior management and potential customers. Therefore, these management positions usually require work experience and formal education as an engineer, scientist, or mathematician.

Most engineering managers begin their careers as engineers after completing a bachelor's degree in the field. To advance to higher-level positions, engineers generally must assume management responsibility. To fill management positions, employers seek engineers who possess administrative and communication skills in addition to technical knowledge in their specialty. Many engineers gain these skills by obtaining a master's degree in engineering management or a master's degree in business administration (MBA). Employers often pay for such training. In large firms, some courses required in these degree programs may be offered onsite. Typically, engineers who prefer to manage in technical areas pursue a master's degree in engineering management, while those interested in non-technical management earn an MBA.

Many science managers begin their careers as scientists, such as chemists, biologists, geologists, or mathematicians. Most scientists or mathematicians engaged in basic research have a Ph.D.; some in applied research and other activities may have a bachelor's or master's degree. Science managers must be specialists in the work they supervise. In addition, employers prefer managers with good communication and administrative skills. Graduate programs allow scientists to augment their undergraduate training with instruction in other fields, such as management or computer technology. Given the rapid pace of scientific developments, science managers must continuously upgrade their knowledge.

Engineering and natural sciences managers may advance to progressively higher leadership positions within their discipline. Some may become managers in nontechnical areas such as marketing, human resources, or sales. In high technology firms, managers in nontechnical areas often must possess the same specialized knowledge as do managers in technical areas. For example, employers in an engineering firm may prefer to hire experienced engineers as sales workers because the complex services offered by the firm can be marketed only by someone with specialized engineering knowledge. Such sales workers could eventually advance to jobs as sales managers.

Employment

Engineering and natural sciences managers held about 233,000 jobs in 2004. About 27 percent worked in professional, scientific, and technical services industries, primarily for firms providing architectural, engineering, and related services; computer systems design and related services; and scientific research and development services. Manufacturing industries employed 37 percent of engineering and natural sciences managers. Manufacturing industries with the largest employment include those producing computer and electronic equipment; transportation equipment, including aerospace products and parts; chemicals, including pharmaceuticals; and machinery manufacturing. Other large employers include government agencies and telecommunications and utilities companies.

Job Outlook

Employment of engineering and natural sciences managers is expected to grow about as fast as the average for all occupations through the year 2014—in line with projected employment growth in engineering and most sciences. However, many additional jobs will result from the need to replace managers who retire or move into other occupations. Opportunities for obtaining a management position will be best for workers with advanced technical knowledge and strong communication skills. Because engineering and natural sciences managers are involved in their firms' financial, production, and marketing activities, business management skills are also important.

Projected employment growth for engineering and natural sciences managers should be closely related to the growth of the occupations they supervise and of the industries in which they are found. For example, opportunities for managers should be better in rapidly growing areas of engineering—such as environmental and biomedical engineering—than in more slowly growing areas, such as nuclear and aerospace engineering. (See the description of engineers elsewhere in this book.) In addition, many employers are finding it more efficient to contract engineering and science management services to outside companies and consultants, creating good opportunities for managers in management services and management, scientific, and technical consulting firms.

Earnings

Earnings for engineering and natural sciences managers vary by specialty and by level of responsibility. Median annual earnings of engineering managers were $97,630 in May 2004. The middle 50 percent earned between $78,820 and $121,090. Median annual earnings in the industries employing the largest numbers of engineering managers in May 2004 are shown here:

Semiconductor and other electronic component
   manufacturing $116,400
Navigational, measuring, electromedical, and
   control instruments manufacturing....................107,160
Aerospace product and parts manufacturing..........103,570
Federal government 97,000
Architectural, engineering, and related services......96,020

Median annual earnings of natural sciences managers were $88,660 in May 2004. The middle 50 percent earned between $64,550 and $118,210. Median annual earnings in the industries employing the largest numbers of natural sciences managers in May 2004 are shown here:

Scientific research and development services $106,530
Federal government 81,460

A survey of manufacturing firms, conducted by Abbot, Langer, and Associates, found that engineering department managers and superintendents earned a median annual income of $89,232 in 2004, while research and development managers earned $90,377.

In addition, engineering and natural sciences managers, especially those at higher levels, often receive more benefits—such as expense accounts, stock option plans, and bonuses—than do nonmanagerial workers in their organizations.

Related Occupations

The work of engineering and natural sciences managers is closely related to that of engineers; mathematicians; and physical and life scientists, including agricultural and food scientists, atmospheric scientists, biological scientists, conservation scientists and foresters, chemists and materials scientists, environmental scientists and hydrologists, geoscientists, medical scientists, and physicists and astronomers. It also is related to the work of other managers, especially top executives.

Sources of Additional Information

For information about a career as an engineering and natural sciences manager, contact the sources of additional information for engineers that are listed at the end of the engineers job description elsewhere in this book.

Engineering Technicians

(O*NET 17-3021.00, 17-3022.00, 17-3023.01, 17-3023.02, 17-3023.03, 17-3024.00, 17-3025.00, 17-3026.00, 17-3027.00, and 17-3029.99)

Significant Points

- Because the type and quality of training programs vary considerably, prospective students should carefully investigate training programs before enrolling.

- Electrical and electronic engineering technicians make up 34 percent of all engineering technicians.

- Employment of engineering technicians often is influenced by the same local and national economic conditions that affect engineers; as a result, job outlook varies with industry and specialization.

- Opportunities will be best for individuals with an associate degree or extensive job training in engineering technology.

Nature of the Work

Engineering technicians use the principles and theories of science, engineering, and mathematics to solve technical problems in research and development, manufacturing, sales, construction, inspection, and maintenance. Their work is more limited in scope and application-oriented than that of scientists and engineers. Many engineering technicians assist engineers and scientists, especially in research and development. Others work in quality control, inspecting products and processes, conducting tests, or collecting data. In manufacturing, they may assist in product design, development, or production.

Engineering technicians who work in research and development build or set up equipment; prepare and conduct experiments; collect data; calculate or record results; and help engineers or scientists in other ways, such as making prototype versions of newly designed equipment. They also assist in design work, often using computer-aided design and drafting (CADD) equipment.

Most engineering technicians specialize, learning skills and working in the same disciplines as engineers. Occupational titles, therefore, tend to reflect engineering specialties. Some branches of engineering technology for which there are accredited programs of study are not covered in detail in this book, such as chemical engineering technology (the development of new chemical products and processes) and bioengineering technology (the development and implementation of biomedical equipment).

Aerospace engineering and operations technicians construct, test, and maintain aircraft and space vehicles. They may calibrate test equipment and determine causes of equipment malfunctions.

Using computer and communications systems, aerospace engineering and operations technicians often record and interpret test data.

Civil engineering technicians help civil engineers plan and build highways, buildings, bridges, dams, wastewater treatment systems, and other structures, as well as do related research. Some estimate construction costs and specify materials to be used, and some may even prepare drawings or perform land-surveying duties. Others may set up and monitor instruments used to study traffic conditions. (Drafters, as well as surveyors, cartographers, photogrammetrists, and surveying technicians, are covered elsewhere in this book.)

Electrical and electronics engineering technicians help design, develop, test, and manufacture electrical and electronic equipment such as communication equipment; radar, industrial, and medical monitoring or control devices; navigational equipment; and computers. They may work in product evaluation and testing, using measuring and diagnostic devices to adjust, test, and repair equipment. (Workers whose jobs are limited to repairing electrical and electronic equipment, who often are referred to as electronics technicians, are included with electrical and electronics installers and repairers elsewhere in this book.)

Electromechanical engineering technicians combine fundamental principles of mechanical engineering technology with knowledge of electrical and electronic circuits to design, develop, test, and manufacture electrical and computer-controlled mechanical systems. Their work often overlaps that of both electrical and electronics engineering technicians and mechanical engineering technicians.

Environmental engineering technicians work closely with environmental engineers and scientists in developing methods and devices used in the prevention, control, or correction of environmental hazards. They inspect and maintain equipment related to air pollution and recycling. Some inspect water and wastewater treatment systems to ensure that pollution control requirements are met.

Industrial engineering technicians study the efficient use of personnel, materials, and machines in factories, stores, repair shops, and offices. They prepare layouts of machinery and equipment, plan the flow of work, make statistical studies, and analyze production costs.

Mechanical engineering technicians help engineers design, develop, test, and manufacture industrial machinery, consumer products, and other equipment. They may assist in product tests—for example, by setting up instrumentation for auto crash tests. They may make sketches and rough layouts, record and analyze data, make calculations and estimates, and report on their findings. When planning production, mechanical engineering technicians prepare layouts and drawings of the assembly process and of parts to be manufactured. They estimate labor costs, equipment life, and plant space. Some test and inspect machines and equipment or work with engineers to eliminate production problems.

Working Conditions

Most engineering technicians work at least 40 hours a week in laboratories, offices, or manufacturing or industrial plants or on construction sites. Some may be exposed to hazards from equipment, chemicals, or toxic materials.

Training, Other Qualifications, and Advancement

Although it may be possible to qualify for certain engineering technician jobs without formal training, most employers prefer to hire someone with at least a 2-year associate degree in engineering technology. Training is available at technical institutes, community colleges, extension divisions of colleges and universities, and public and private vocational-technical schools and in the Armed Forces. Persons with college courses in science, engineering, and mathematics may qualify for some positions but may need additional specialized training and experience. Although employers usually do not require engineering technicians to be certified, such certification may provide jobseekers a competitive advantage.

Prospective engineering technicians should take as many high school science and math courses as possible to prepare for postsecondary programs in engineering technology. Most 2-year associate degree programs accredited by the Technology Accreditation Commission of the Accreditation Board for Engineering and Technology (ABET) require, at a minimum, college algebra and trigonometry and one or two basic science courses. Depending on the specialty, more math or science may be required. About 230 colleges offer ABET-accredited programs in engineering technology.

The type of technical courses required also depends on the specialty. For example, prospective mechanical engineering technicians may take courses in fluid mechanics, thermodynamics, and mechanical design; electrical engineering technicians may need classes in electrical circuits, microprocessors, and digital electronics; and those preparing to work in environmental engineering technology need courses in environmental regulations and safe handling of hazardous materials.

Because many engineering technicians assist in design work, creativity is desirable. Because these workers often are part of a team of engineers and other technicians, good communication skills and the ability to work well with others also are important.

Engineering technicians usually begin by performing routine duties under the close supervision of an experienced technician, technologist, engineer, or scientist. As they gain experience, they are given more difficult assignments with only general supervision. Some engineering technicians eventually become supervisors.

Many publicly and privately operated schools provide technical training, but the type and quality of training vary considerably. Therefore, prospective students should be careful in selecting a program. They should ascertain prospective employers' preferences and ask schools to provide information about the kinds of jobs obtained by program graduates, about instructional facilities and equipment, and about faculty qualifications. Graduates of ABET-accredited programs usually are recognized as having achieved an acceptable level of competence in the mathematics, science, and technical courses required for this occupation.

Technical institutes offer intensive technical training through application and practice, but they provide less theory and general education than do community colleges. Many technical institutes offer 2-year associate degree programs and are similar to or part of a community college or state university system. Other technical institutes are run by private, often for-profit organizations, sometimes called proprietary schools. Their programs vary considerably in length and types of courses offered, although some are 2-year associate degree programs.

Community colleges offer curriculums that are similar to those in technical institutes but include more theory and liberal arts. There may be little or no difference between programs at technical institutes and community colleges, as both offer associate degrees. After completing the 2-year program, some graduates get jobs as engineering technicians, whereas others continue their education at 4-year colleges. However, there is a difference between an associate degree in pre-engineering and one in engineering technology. Students who enroll in a 2-year pre-engineering program may find it very difficult to find work as an engineering technician if they decide not to enter a 4-year engineering program because pre-engineering programs usually focus less on hands-on applications and more on academic preparatory work. Conversely, graduates of 2-year engineering technology programs may not receive credit for some of the courses they have taken if they choose to transfer to a 4-year engineering program. Colleges with these 4-year programs usually do not offer engineering technician training, but college courses in science, engineering, and mathematics are useful for obtaining a job as an engineering technician. Many 4-year colleges offer bachelor's degrees in engineering technology, but graduates of these programs often are hired to work as technologists or applied engineers, not technicians.

Area vocational-technical schools, another source of technical training, include postsecondary public institutions that serve local students and emphasize training needed by local employers. Most require a high school diploma or its equivalent for admission.

Other training in technical areas may be obtained in the Armed Forces. Many military technical training programs are highly regarded by employers. However, skills acquired in military programs are often narrowly focused and may be of limited applicability in civilian industry, which often requires broader training. Therefore, some additional training may be needed, depending on the acquired skills and the kind of job.

The National Institute for Certification in Engineering Technologies has established a voluntary certification program for engineering technicians. Certification is available at various levels, each level combining a written examination in 1 of about 30 specialties with a certain amount of job-related experience, a supervisory evaluation, and a recommendation.

Employment

Engineering technicians held 532,000 jobs in 2004. About a third were electrical and electronics engineering technicians, as indicated by the following tabulation.

Electrical and electronic engineering technicians	182,000
Civil engineering technicians	94,000
Industrial engineering technicians	69,000
Mechanical engineering technicians	48,000
Environmental engineering technicians	20,000

Electro-mechanical technicians 19,000

Aerospace engineering and operations
   technicians 9,500

Engineering technicians, except drafters,
   all other 91,000

About 36 percent of all engineering technicians worked in manufacturing, mainly in the computer and electronic equipment, transportation equipment, and machinery manufacturing industries. Another 22 percent worked in professional, scientific, and technical service industries, mostly in engineering or business services companies that do engineering work on contract for government, manufacturing firms, or other organizations.

In 2004, the federal government employed 37,000 engineering technicians. State governments employed 39,000, and local governments employed 27,000.

Job Outlook

Opportunities will be best for individuals with an associate degree or extensive job training in engineering technology. As technology becomes more sophisticated, employers will continue to look for technicians who are skilled in new technology and require a minimum of additional job training. An increase in the number of jobs related to public health and safety should create job opportunities for engineering technicians with the appropriate training and certification.

Overall employment of engineering technicians is expected to increase about as fast as the average for all occupations through 2014. Competitive pressures will force companies to improve and update manufacturing facilities and product designs, resulting in more jobs for engineering technicians. In addition to growth, many job openings will stem from the need to replace technicians who retire or leave the labor force.

Growth of engineering technician employment in some design functions may be dampened by increasing globalization of the development process. To reduce costs and speed project completion, some companies may relocate part of their development operations to facilities overseas, impacting both engineers and the engineering technicians that support them—particularly in electronics and computer-related areas. However, much of the work of engineering technicians requires on-site presence, so demand for engineering technicians within the United States should continue to grow.

Because engineering technicians work closely with engineers, employment of engineering technicians is often influenced by the same local and national economic conditions that affect engineers. As a result, the employment outlook varies with industry and specialization. Growth in the largest specialty—electrical and electronics engineering technicians—is expected to be about as fast as the average, while employment of environmental engineering technicians is expected to grow faster than average to meet the environmental demands of an ever-growing population.

Earnings

Median annual earnings in May 2004 of engineering technicians by specialty are shown in the following tabulation.

Aerospace engineering and operations
   technicians...$52,500

Electrical and electronic engineering
   technicians 46,310

Industrial engineering technicians 43,590

Mechanical engineering technicians 43,400

Electro-mechanical technicians 41,440

Environmental engineering technicians 38,550

Civil engineering technicians..............................38,480

Median annual earnings of electrical and electronics engineering technicians were $46,310 in May 2004. The middle 50 percent earned between $36,290 and $55,750. The lowest 10 percent earned less than $29,000, and the highest 10 percent earned more than $67,900. Median annual earnings in the industries employing the largest numbers of electrical and electronics engineering technicians in May 2004 are shown here.

Federal government $64,160

Wired telecommunications carriers 51,250

Architectural, engineering, and related services 44,800

Navigational, measuring, electromedical, and
   control instruments manufacturing 42,780

Semiconductor and other electronic component
   manufacturing 41,300

Median annual earnings of civil engineering technicians were $38,480 in May 2004. The middle 50 percent earned between $29,880 and $48,590. The lowest 10 percent earned less than $24,180, and the highest 10 percent earned more than $57,550. Median annual earnings in the industries employing the largest numbers of civil engineering technicians in May 2004 are shown here.

Local government $43,700

Architectural, engineering, and related services 37,470

State government 35,970

In May 2004, the average annual salary for aerospace engineering and operations technicians in the aerospace products and parts manufacturing industry was $52,250, and the average annual salary for environmental engineering technicians in the architectural, engineering, and related services industry was $36,530. The average annual salary for industrial engineering technicians in the semiconductor and other electronic component manufacturing industry was $40,020. In the architectural, engineering, and related services industry, the average annual salary for mechanical engineering technicians was $43,190.

Related Occupations

Engineering technicians apply scientific and engineering principles usually acquired in postsecondary programs below the baccalaureate level. Similar occupations include science technicians; drafters; surveyors, cartographers, photogrammetrists, and surveying technicians; and broadcast and sound engineering technicians and radio operators.

Sources of Additional Information

For information about careers in engineering technology, contact

▸ JETS (Junior Engineering Technical Society)—Guidance, 1420 King St., Suite 405, Alexandria, VA 22314-2794. Internet: http://www.jets.org

Information on ABET-accredited engineering technology programs is available from

▸ Accreditation Board for Engineering and Technology, Inc., 111 Market Plc., Suite 1050, Baltimore, MD 21202-4012. Internet: http://www.abet.org

Information on certification of engineering technicians, as well as job and career information, is available from

▸ National Institute for Certification in Engineering Technologies, 1420 King St., Alexandria, VA 22314-2794. Internet: http://www.nicet.org

Engineers

(O*NET 17-2011.00, 17-2021.00, 17-2031.00, 17-2041.00, 17-2051.00, 17-2061.00, 17-2071.00, 17-2072.00, 17-2081.00, 17-2111.01, 17-2111.02, 17-2111.03, 17-2112.00, 17-2121.01, 17-2121.02, 17-2131.00, 17-2141.00, 17-2151.00, 17-2161.00, 17-2171.00, and 17-2199.99)

Significant Points

■ Overall job opportunities in engineering are expected to be good, but will vary by specialty.

■ A bachelor's degree is required for most entry-level jobs.

■ Starting salaries are significantly higher than those of college graduates in other fields.

■ Continuing education is critical for engineers wishing to enhance their value to employers as technology evolves.

Nature of the Work

Engineers apply the principles of science and mathematics to develop economical solutions to technical problems. Their work is the link between perceived social needs and commercial applications.

Engineers consider many factors when developing a new product. For example, in developing an industrial robot, engineers precisely specify the functional requirements; design and test the robot's components; integrate the components to produce the final design; and evaluate the design's overall effectiveness, cost, reliability, and safety. This process applies to the development of many different products, such as chemicals, computers, gas turbines, helicopters, and toys.

In addition to design and development, many engineers work in testing, production, or maintenance. These engineers supervise production in factories, determine the causes of component failure, and test manufactured products to maintain quality. They also estimate the time and cost to complete projects. Some move into engineering management or into sales. In sales, an engineering background enables them to discuss technical aspects and assist in product planning, installation, and use. Supervisory engineers are responsible for major components or entire projects. (See the descriptions of sales engineers and engineering and natural sciences managers elsewhere in this book.)

Engineers use computers extensively to produce and analyze designs; to simulate and test how a machine, structure, or system operates; and to generate specifications for parts. Many engineers also use computers to monitor product quality and control process efficiency. The field of nanotechnology, which involves the creation of high-performance materials and components by integrating atoms and molecules, also is introducing entirely new principles to the design process.

Most engineers specialize. This section provides details on the 17 engineering specialties covered in the federal government's Standard Occupational Classification system and on engineering in general. Numerous specialties are recognized by professional societies, and the major branches of engineering have numerous subdivisions. Some examples include structural and transportation engineering, which are subdivisions of civil engineering, and ceramic, metallurgical, and polymer engineering, which are subdivisions of materials engineering. Engineers also may specialize in one industry, such as motor vehicles, or in one type of technology, such as turbines or semiconductor materials.

■ **Aerospace engineers** design, develop, and test aircraft, spacecraft, and missiles and supervise the manufacture of these products. Those who work with aircraft are called *aeronautical engineers*, and those working specifically with spacecraft are *astronautical engineers*. Aerospace engineers develop new technologies for use in aviation, defense systems, and space exploration, often specializing in areas such as structural design, guidance, navigation and control, instrumentation and communication, or production methods. They also may specialize in a particular type of aerospace product, such as commercial aircraft, military fighter jets, helicopters, spacecraft, or missiles and rockets, and may become experts in aerodynamics, thermodynamics, celestial mechanics, propulsion, acoustics, or guidance and control systems.

■ **Agricultural engineers** apply knowledge of engineering technology and science to agriculture and the efficient use of biological resources. (See biological scientists and agricultural and food scientists elsewhere in this book.) They design agricultural machinery and equipment and agricultural structures. Some specialize in areas such as power systems and machinery design, structures and environment engineering, and food and bioprocess engineering. They develop ways to conserve soil and water and to improve the processing of agricultural products. Agricultural engineers often work in research and development, production, sales, or management.

■ **Biomedical engineers** develop devices and procedures that solve medical and health-related problems by combining their knowledge of biology and medicine with engineering principles and practices. Many do research, along with life scientists, chemists, and medical scientists, to develop and evaluate systems and products such as artificial organs, prostheses (artificial devices that replace missing body parts), instrumentation, medical information systems, and health management and care delivery systems. (See biological scientists, medical scientists, and chemists and materials scientists elsewhere in this book.)

Biomedical engineers may also design devices used in various medical procedures, imaging systems such as magnetic resonance imaging (MRI), and devices for automating insulin injections or controlling body functions. Most engineers in this specialty need a sound background in another engineering specialty, such as mechanical or electronics engineering, in addition to specialized biomedical training. Some specialties within biomedical engineering include biomaterials, biomechanics, medical imaging, rehabilitation engineering, and orthopedic engineering.

- **Chemical engineers** apply the principles of chemistry to solve problems involving the production or use of chemicals and biochemicals. They design equipment and processes for large-scale chemical manufacturing, plan and test methods of manufacturing products and treating byproducts, and supervise production. Chemical engineers also work in a variety of manufacturing industries other than chemical manufacturing, such as those producing energy, electronics, food, clothing, and paper. They also work in health care, biotechnology, and business services. Chemical engineers apply principles of chemistry, physics, mathematics, and mechanical and electrical engineering. (See chemists and materials scientists, physicists and astronomers, and mathematicians elsewhere in this book.) Some may specialize in a particular chemical process, such as oxidation or polymerization. Others specialize in a particular field, such as materials science, or in the development of specific products. They must be aware of all aspects of chemicals manufacturing and how the manufacturing process affects the environment and the safety of workers and consumers.

- **Civil engineers** design and supervise the construction of roads, buildings, airports, tunnels, dams, bridges, and water supply and sewage systems. They must consider many factors in the design process, from the construction costs and expected lifetime of a project to government regulations and potential environmental hazards such as earthquakes. Civil engineering, considered one of the oldest engineering disciplines, encompasses many specialties. The major specialties are structural, water resources, construction, environmental, transportation, and geotechnical engineering. Many civil engineers hold supervisory or administrative positions, from supervisor of a construction site to city engineer. Others may work in design, construction, research, and teaching.

- **Computer hardware engineers** research, design, develop, test, and oversee the installation of computer hardware and supervise its manufacture and installation. Hardware refers to computer chips; circuit boards; computer systems; and related equipment such as keyboards, modems, and printers. (Computer software engineers—often simply called computer engineers—design and develop the software systems that control computers. These workers are covered elsewhere in this book.) The work of computer hardware engineers is very similar to that of electronics engineers, but, unlike electronics engineers, computer hardware engineers work exclusively with computers and computer-related equipment. The rapid advances in computer technology are largely a result of the research, development, and design efforts of computer hardware engineers.

- **Electrical engineers** design, develop, test, and supervise the manufacture of electrical equipment. Some of this equipment includes electric motors; machinery controls, lighting, and wiring in buildings; automobiles; aircraft; radar and navigation systems; and power-generating, -controlling, and -transmission devices used by electric utilities. Although the terms "electrical" and "electronics" engineering often are used interchangeably in academia and industry, electrical engineers have traditionally focused on the generation and supply of power, whereas electronics engineers have worked on applications of electricity to control systems or signal processing. Electrical engineers specialize in areas such as power systems engineering or electrical equipment manufacturing.

- **Electronics engineers, except computer,** are responsible for a wide range of technologies, from portable music players to the global positioning system (GPS), which can continuously provide the location of a vehicle. Electronics engineers design, develop, test, and supervise the manufacture of electronic equipment such as broadcast and communications systems. Many electronics engineers also work in areas closely related to computers. However, engineers whose work is related exclusively to computer hardware are considered computer hardware engineers. Electronics engineers specialize in areas such as communications, signal processing, and control systems or have a specialty within one of these areas—industrial robot control systems or aviation electronics, for example.

- **Environmental engineers** develop solutions to environmental problems using the principles of biology and chemistry. They are involved in water and air pollution control, recycling, waste disposal, and public health issues. Environmental engineers conduct hazardous-waste management studies in which they evaluate the significance of the hazard, advise on treatment and containment, and develop regulations to prevent mishaps. They design municipal water supply and industrial wastewater treatment systems. They conduct research on the environmental impact of proposed construction projects, analyze scientific data, and perform quality-control checks. Environmental engineers are concerned with local and worldwide environmental issues. They study and attempt to minimize the effects of acid rain, global warming, automobile emissions, and ozone depletion. They may also be involved in the protection of wildlife. Many environmental engineers work as consultants, helping their clients to comply with regulations and to clean up hazardous sites.

- **Health and safety engineers, except mining safety engineers and inspectors,** promote worksite or product safety by applying knowledge of industrial processes and mechanical, chemical, and human performance principles. Using this specialized knowledge, they identify and measure potential hazards to people or property, such as the risk of fires or the dangers involved in the handling of toxic chemicals. Health and safety engineers develop procedures and designs to reduce the risk of injury or damage. Some work in manufacturing industries to ensure that the designs of new products do not create unnecessary hazards. They must be able to anticipate, recognize, and evaluate hazardous conditions, as well as develop hazard control methods.

- **Industrial engineers** determine the most effective ways to use the basic factors of production—people, machines, materials, information, and energy—to make a product or to provide a service. They are mostly concerned with increasing productivity through the management of people, methods of business organization, and technology. To solve organizational, production, and related problems efficiently, industrial engineers carefully study the product requirements, use mathematical methods to meet those requirements, and design manufacturing and information systems. They develop management control systems to aid in financial planning and cost analysis and design production planning and control systems to coordinate activities and ensure product quality. They also design or improve systems for the physical distribution of goods and services as well as determine the most efficient plant locations. Industrial engineers develop wage and salary administration systems and job evaluation programs. Many industrial engineers move into management positions because the work is closely related to the work of managers.

- **Marine engineers and naval architects** are involved in the design, construction, and maintenance of ships, boats, and related equipment. They design and supervise the construction of everything from aircraft carriers to submarines and from sailboats to tankers. Naval architects work on the basic design of ships, including hull form and stability. Marine engineers work on the propulsion, steering, and other systems of ships. Marine engineers and naval architects apply knowledge from a range of fields to the entire design and production process of all water vehicles. Workers who operate or supervise the operation of marine machinery on ships and other vessels also may be called marine engineers or, more frequently, ship engineers.

- **Materials engineers** are involved in the development, processing, and testing of the materials used to create a range of products, from computer chips and television screens to golf clubs and snow skis. They work with metals, ceramics, plastics, semiconductors, and composites to create new materials that meet certain mechanical, electrical, and chemical requirements. They also are involved in selecting materials for new applications. Materials engineers have developed the ability to create and then study materials at an atomic level, using advanced processes to replicate the characteristics of materials and their components with computers. Most materials engineers specialize in a particular material. For example, metallurgical engineers specialize in metals such as steel, and ceramic engineers develop ceramic materials and the processes for making ceramic materials into useful products such as glassware or fiber-optic communication lines.

- **Mechanical engineers** research, develop, design, manufacture, and test tools, engines, machines, and other mechanical devices. They work on power-producing machines such as electric generators, internal combustion engines, and steam and gas turbines, as well as power-using machines such as refrigeration and air-conditioning equipment, machine tools, material handling systems, elevators and escalators, industrial production equipment, and robots used in manufacturing. Mechanical engineers also design tools that other engineers need for their work. Mechanical engineering is one of the broadest engineering disciplines. Mechanical engineers may work in production operations in manufacturing or agriculture, maintenance, or technical sales; many are administrators or managers.

- **Mining and geological engineers, including mining safety engineers,** find, extract, and prepare coal, metals, and minerals for use by manufacturing industries and utilities. They design open-pit and underground mines, supervise the construction of mine shafts and tunnels in underground operations, and devise methods for transporting minerals to processing plants. Mining engineers are responsible for the safe, economical, and environmentally sound operation of mines. Some mining engineers work with geologists and metallurgical engineers to locate and appraise new ore deposits. Others develop new mining equipment or direct mineral-processing operations that separate minerals from the dirt, rock, and other materials with which they are mixed. Mining engineers frequently specialize in the mining of one mineral or metal, such as coal or gold. With increased emphasis on protecting the environment, many mining engineers work to solve problems related to land reclamation and water and air pollution. Mining safety engineers use their knowledge of mine design and practices to ensure the safety of workers and to comply with state and federal safety regulations. They inspect walls and roof surfaces, monitor air quality, and examine mining equipment for compliance with safety practices.

- **Nuclear engineers** research and develop the processes, instruments, and systems used to derive benefits from nuclear energy and radiation. They design, develop, monitor, and operate nuclear plants to generate power. They may work on the nuclear fuel cycle—the production, handling, and use of nuclear fuel and the safe disposal of waste produced by the generation of nuclear energy—or on the development of fusion energy. Some specialize in the development of nuclear power sources for spacecraft; others find industrial and medical uses for radioactive materials, as in equipment used to diagnose and treat medical problems.

- **Petroleum engineers** search the world for reservoirs containing oil or natural gas. Once these resources are discovered, petroleum engineers work with geologists and other specialists to understand the geologic formation and properties of the rock containing the reservoir, determine the drilling methods to be used, and monitor drilling and production operations. They design equipment and processes to achieve the maximum profitable recovery of oil and gas. Because only a small proportion of oil and gas in a reservoir flows out under natural forces, petroleum engineers develop and use various enhanced recovery methods. These include injecting water, chemicals, gases, or steam into an oil reservoir to force out more of the oil and doing computer-controlled drilling or fracturing to connect a larger area of a reservoir to a single well. Because even the best techniques in use today recover only a portion of the oil and gas in a reservoir, petroleum engineers research and develop technology and methods to increase recovery and lower the cost of drilling and production operations.

Working Conditions

Most engineers work in office buildings, laboratories, or industrial plants. Others may spend time outdoors at construction sites and oil and gas exploration and production sites, where they monitor or direct operations or solve onsite problems. Some engineers travel extensively to plants or worksites.

Many engineers work a standard 40-hour week. At times, deadlines or design standards may bring extra pressure to a job, requiring engineers to work longer hours.

Training, Other Qualifications, and Advancement

A bachelor's degree in engineering is required for almost all entry-level engineering jobs. College graduates with a degree in a physical science or mathematics occasionally may qualify for some engineering jobs, especially in specialties in high demand. Most engineering degrees are granted in electrical, electronics, mechanical, or civil engineering. However, engineers trained in one branch may work in related branches. For example, many aerospace engineers have training in mechanical engineering. This flexibility allows employers to meet staffing needs in new technologies and specialties in which engineers may be in short supply. It also allows engineers to shift to fields with better employment prospects or to those that more closely match their interests.

Most engineering programs involve a concentration of study in an engineering specialty along with courses in both mathematics and the physical and life sciences. General courses not directly related to engineering, such as those in the social sciences or humanities, are often a required component of programs. Many programs also include courses in general engineering. A design course, sometimes accompanied by a computer or laboratory class or both, is part of the curriculum of most programs.

In addition to the standard engineering degree, many colleges offer 2- or 4-year degree programs in engineering technology. These programs, which usually include various hands-on laboratory classes that focus on current issues in the application of engineering principles, prepare students for practical design and production work rather than for jobs that require more theoretical and scientific knowledge. Graduates of 4-year technology programs may get jobs similar to those obtained by graduates with a bachelor's degree in engineering. Engineering technology graduates, however, are not qualified to register as professional engineers under the same terms as graduates with degrees in engineering. Some employers regard technology program graduates as having skills between those of a technician and an engineer.

Graduate training is essential for engineering faculty positions and many research and development programs, but is not required for the majority of entry-level engineering jobs. Many engineers obtain graduate degrees in engineering or business administration to learn new technology and broaden their education. Many high-level executives in government and industry began their careers as engineers.

About 360 colleges and universities offer bachelor's degree programs in engineering that are accredited by the Accreditation Board for Engineering and Technology, Inc. (ABET), and about 230 colleges offer accredited programs in engineering technology. ABET accreditation is based on an examination of an engineering program's student achievement, program improvement, faculty, curriculum, facilities, and institutional commitment to certain principles of quality and ethics. Although most institutions offer programs in the major branches of engineering, only a few offer programs in the smaller specialties. Also, programs of the same title may vary in content. For example, some programs emphasize industrial practices, preparing students for a job in industry, whereas others are more theoretical and are designed to prepare students for graduate work. Therefore, students should investigate curriculums and check accreditations carefully before selecting a college.

Admissions requirements for undergraduate engineering schools include a solid background in mathematics (algebra, geometry, trigonometry, and calculus) and science (biology, chemistry, and physics), with courses in English, social studies, and humanities. Bachelor's degree programs in engineering typically are designed to last 4 years, but many students find that it takes between 4 and 5 years to complete their studies. In a typical 4-year college curriculum, the first 2 years are spent studying mathematics, basic sciences, introductory engineering, humanities, and social sciences. In the last 2 years, most courses are in engineering, usually with a concentration in one specialty. Some programs offer a general engineering curriculum; students then specialize on the job or in graduate school.

Some engineering schools and 2-year colleges have agreements whereby the 2-year college provides the initial engineering education and the engineering school automatically admits students for their last 2 years. In addition, a few engineering schools have arrangements that allow students who spend 3 years in a liberal arts college studying pre-engineering subjects and 2 years in an engineering school studying core subjects to receive a bachelor's degree from each school. Some colleges and universities offer 5-year master's degree programs. Some 5-year or even 6-year cooperative plans combine classroom study and practical work, permitting students to gain valuable experience and to finance part of their education.

All 50 states and the District of Columbia require licensure for engineers who offer their services directly to the public. Engineers who are licensed are called professional engineers (PE). This licensure generally requires a degree from an ABET-accredited engineering program, 4 years of relevant work experience, and successful completion of a state examination. Recent graduates can start the licensing process by taking the examination in two stages. The initial Fundamentals of Engineering (FE) examination can be taken upon graduation. Engineers who pass this examination commonly are called engineers in training (EIT) or engineer interns (EI). After acquiring suitable work experience, EITs can take the second examination, the Principles and Practice of Engineering exam. Several states have imposed mandatory continuing education requirements for relicensure. Most states recognize licensure from other states, provided that the manner in which the initial license was obtained meets or exceeds their own licensure requirements. Many civil, electrical, mechanical, and chemical engineers are licensed PEs. Independent of licensure, various certification programs are offered by professional organizations to demonstrate competency in specific fields of engineering.

Engineers should be creative, inquisitive, analytical, and detail oriented. They should be able to work as part of a team and to communicate well, both orally and in writing. Communication abilities are important because engineers often interact with specialists in a wide range of fields outside engineering.

Beginning engineering graduates usually work under the supervision of experienced engineers and, in large companies, also may receive formal classroom or seminar-type training. As new engineers gain knowledge and experience, they are assigned more difficult projects with greater independence to develop designs, solve problems, and make decisions. Engineers may advance to become technical specialists or to supervise a staff or team of engineers and technicians. Some may eventually become engineering managers or enter other managerial or sales jobs.

Employment

In 2004, engineers held 1.4 million jobs. The distribution of employment by engineering specialty is as follows:

Total, all engineers	1,449,000	100%
Civil	237,000	16.4
Mechanical	226,000	15.6
Industrial	177,000	12.2
Electrical	156,000	10.8
Electronics, except computer	143,000	9.9
Computer hardware	77,000	5.3
Aerospace	76,000	5.2
Environmental	49,000	3.4
Chemical	31,000	2.1
Health and safety, except mining safety	27,000	1.8
Materials	21,000	1.5
Nuclear	17,000	1.2
Petroleum	16,000	1.1
Biomedical	9,700	0.7
Marine engineers and naval architects	6,800	0.5
Mining and geological, including mining safety	5,200	0.4
Agricultural	3,400	0.2
All other engineers	172,000	11.8

About 555,000 engineering jobs were found in manufacturing industries, and another 378,000 wage and salary jobs were in the professional, scientific, and technical services sector, primarily in architectural, engineering, and related services and in scientific research and development services. Many engineers also worked in the construction and transportation, telecommunications, and utilities industries.

Federal, state, and local governments employed about 194,000 engineers in 2004. About 91,000 of these were in the federal government, mainly in the U.S. Departments of Defense, Transportation, Agriculture, Interior, and Energy and in the National Aeronautics and Space Administration. Most engineers in state and local government agencies worked in highway and public works departments. In 2004, about 41,000 engineers were self-employed, many as consultants.

Engineers are employed in every state, in small and large cities and in rural areas. Some branches of engineering are concentrated in particular industries and geographic areas—for example, petroleum engineering jobs tend to be located in areas with sizable petroleum deposits, such as Texas, Louisiana, Oklahoma, Alaska, and California. Others, such as civil engineering, are widely dispersed, and engineers in these fields often move from place to place to work on different projects.

Engineers are employed in every major industry. The industries employing the most engineers in each specialty are given in the table below, along with the percent of occupational employment in the industry.

Table 1. Percent concentration of engineering specialty employment in key industries, 2004

Specialty/Industry	Percent
Aerospace	
Aerospace product and parts manufacturing	59.6
Agricultural	
State and local government	22.6
Biomedical	
Scientific research and development services	18.7
Pharmaceutical and medicine manufacturing	15.6
Chemical	
Chemical manufacturing	27.8
Architectural, engineering, and related services	16.3
Civil	
Architectural, engineering, and related services	46.0
Computer hardware	
Computer and electronic product manufacturing	43.2
Computer systems design and related services	15.0
Electrical	
Architectural, engineering, and related services	19.6
Navigational, measuring, electromedical, and control instruments manufacturing	10.8
Electronics, except computer	
Telecommunications	17.5
Federal government	14.4
Environmental	
Architectural, engineering, and related services	28.9
State and local government	19.6
Health and safety, except mining safety	
State and local government	12.4
Industrial	
Machinery manufacturing	7.8
Motor vehicle parts manufacturing	7.1
Marine engineers and naval architects	
Architectural, engineering, and related services	34.5
Materials	
Computer and electronic product manufacturing	14.3
Mechanical	
Architectural, engineering, and related services	18.1
Machinery manufacturing	13.4

(continued)

(continued)

Specialty/Industry	Percent
Mining and geological, including mining safety	
Mining	49.9
Nuclear	
Electric power generation, transmission and distribution	36.1
Petroleum	
Oil and gas extraction	47.4

Job Outlook

Overall engineering employment is expected to grow about as fast as the average for all occupations over the 2004–2014 period. Engineers have traditionally been concentrated in slow-growing manufacturing industries, in which they will continue to be needed to design, build, test, and improve manufactured products. However, increasing employment of engineers in faster-growing service industries should generate most of the employment growth. Overall job opportunities in engineering are expected to be favorable because the number of engineering graduates should be in rough balance with the number of job openings over this period. However, job outlook varies by specialty, as discussed later in this section.

Competitive pressures and advancing technology will force companies to improve and update product designs and optimize their manufacturing processes. Employers will rely on engineers to further increase productivity as investments in plant and equipment increase to expand output of goods and services. New technologies continue to improve the design process, enabling engineers to produce and analyze various product designs much more rapidly than in the past. Unlike in other fields, however, technological advances are not expected to limit employment opportunities substantially, because they will permit the development of new products and processes.

There are many well-trained, often English-speaking engineers available around the world willing to work at much lower salaries than are U.S. engineers. The rise of the Internet has made it relatively easy for much of the engineering work previously done by engineers in this country to be done by engineers in other countries, a factor that will tend to hold down employment growth. Even so, the need for onsite engineers to interact with other employees and with clients will remain.

Compared with most other workers, a smaller proportion of engineers leave their jobs each year. Nevertheless, many job openings will arise from replacement needs, reflecting the large size of this profession. Numerous job openings will be created by engineers who transfer to management, sales, or other professional occupations; additional openings will arise as engineers retire or leave the labor force for other reasons.

Many engineers work on long-term research and development projects or in other activities that continue even during economic slowdowns. In industries such as electronics and aerospace, however, large cutbacks in defense expenditures and in government funding for research and development have resulted in significant layoffs of engineers in the past. The trend toward contracting for engineering work with engineering services firms, both domestic and foreign, has had the same result.

It is important for engineers, as it is for those working in other technical and scientific occupations, to continue their education throughout their careers because much of their value to their employer depends on their knowledge of the latest technology. Engineers in high-technology areas, such as advanced electronics or information technology, may find that technical knowledge can become outdated rapidly. By keeping current in their field, engineers are able to deliver the best solutions and greatest value to their employers. Engineers who have not kept current in their field may find themselves passed over for promotions or vulnerable to layoffs.

The following list discusses job outlook by engineering specialty.

- **Aerospace engineers** are expected to have slower-than-average growth in employment over the projection period. Although increases in the number and scope of military aerospace projects likely will generate new jobs, increased efficiency will limit the number of new jobs in the design and production of commercial aircraft. Even with slow growth, the employment outlook for aerospace engineers through 2014 appears favorable: The number of degrees granted in aerospace engineering declined for many years because of a perceived lack of opportunities in this field, and, although this trend is reversing, new graduates continue to be needed to replace aerospace engineers who retire or leave the occupation for other reasons.

- **Agricultural engineers** are expected to have employment growth about as fast as the average for all occupations through 2014. The growing interest in worldwide standardization of agricultural equipment should result in increased employment of agricultural engineers. Job opportunities also should result from the need to feed a growing population, develop more efficient agricultural production, and conserve resources.

- **Biomedical engineers** are expected to have employment growth that is much faster than the average for all occupations through 2014. The aging of the population and the focus on health issues will drive demand for better medical devices and equipment designed by biomedical engineers. Along with the demand for more sophisticated medical equipment and procedures, an increased concern for cost-effectiveness will boost demand for biomedical engineers, particularly in pharmaceutical manufacturing and related industries. However, because of the growing interest in this field, the number of degrees granted in biomedical engineering has increased greatly. Biomedical engineers, particularly those with only a bachelor's degree, may face competition for jobs. Unlike the case for many other engineering specialties, a graduate degree is recommended or required for many entry-level jobs.

- **Chemical engineers** are expected to have employment growth about as fast as the average for all occupations though 2014. Although overall employment in the chemical manufacturing industry is expected to decline, chemical companies will continue to research and develop new chemicals and more efficient processes to increase output of existing chemicals. Among manufacturing industries, pharmaceuticals may provide the best opportunities for jobseekers. However, most employment growth for chemical engineers will be in service industries such as scientific research and development services, particularly in energy and the developing fields of biotechnology and nanotechnology.

■ **Civil engineers** are expected to see average employment growth through 2014. Spurred by general population growth and an increased emphasis on infrastructure security, more civil engineers will be needed to design and construct safe and higher-capacity transportation, water supply, and pollution control systems, as well as large buildings and building complexes. They also will be needed to repair or replace existing roads, bridges, and other public structures. Because construction and related industries—including those providing design services—employ many civil engineers, employment opportunities will vary by geographic area and may decrease during economic slowdowns, when construction often is curtailed.

■ **Computer hardware engineers** are expected to have average employment growth through 2014. Although the use of information technology continues to expand rapidly, the manufacture of computer hardware is expected to be adversely affected by intense foreign competition. As computer and semiconductor manufacturing contract out more of their engineering needs, much of the growth in employment should occur in the computer systems design and related services industry. However, use of foreign computer hardware engineering services also will serve to limit job growth. Computer engineers should still have favorable employment opportunities, as the number of new entrants is expected to be in balance with demand.

■ **Electrical engineers** should have favorable employment opportunities. The number of job openings resulting from employment growth and from the need to replace electrical engineers who transfer to other occupations or leave the labor force is expected to be in rough balance with the supply of graduates. Employment of electrical engineers is expected to increase about as fast as the average for all occupations through 2014. Although international competition and the use of engineering services performed in other countries may limit employment growth, strong demand for electrical devices such as giant electric power generators or wireless phone transmitters should boost growth. Prospects should be particularly good for electrical engineers working in engineering services firms providing technical expertise to other companies on specific projects.

■ **Electronics engineers, except computer,** should have good job opportunities, and employment is expected to increase about as fast as the average for all occupations through 2014. Although rising demand for electronic goods—including advanced communications equipment, defense-related electronic equipment, medical electronics, and consumer products—should continue to increase employment, foreign competition in electronic products development and the use of engineering services performed in other countries will act to limit employment growth. Job growth is expected to be fastest in service-providing industries—particularly consulting firms that provide expertise in electronics engineering.

■ **Environmental engineers** should have favorable job opportunities. Employment of environmental engineers is expected to increase much faster than the average for all occupations through 2014. More environmental engineers will be needed to comply with environmental regulations and to develop methods of cleaning up existing hazards. A shift in emphasis toward preventing problems rather than controlling those that already exist, as well as increasing public health concerns, also will spur demand for environmental engineers. Even though employment of environmental engineers should be less affected by economic conditions than that of most other types of engineers, a significant economic downturn could reduce the emphasis on environmental protection, reducing environmental engineers' job opportunities.

■ **Health and safety engineers, except mining safety engineers and inspectors,** are projected to experience average employment growth through 2014. Because the main function of health and safety engineers is to make products and production processes as safe as possible, their services should be in demand as concern for health and safety within work environments increases. As new technologies for production or processing are developed, health and safety engineers will be needed to ensure their safety.

■ **Industrial engineers** are expected to have employment growth about as fast as the average for all occupations through 2014. As firms seek to reduce costs and increase productivity, they increasingly will turn to industrial engineers to develop more efficient processes to reduce costs, delays, and waste. Because their work is similar to that done in management occupations, many industrial engineers leave the occupation to become managers. Many openings will be created by the need to replace industrial engineers who transfer to other occupations or leave the labor force.

■ **Marine engineers and naval architects** likely will experience employment growth that is slower than the average for all occupations. Strong demand for naval vessels and for yachts and other small craft should more than offset the long-term decline in the domestic design and construction of large oceangoing vessels. There should be good prospects for marine engineers and naval architects because of growth in employment, the need to replace workers who retire or take other jobs, and the limited number of students pursuing careers in this occupation.

■ **Materials engineers, including mining safety engineers,** are expected to have employment growth about as fast as the average for all occupations through 2014. Although many of the manufacturing industries in which materials engineers are concentrated are expected to experience declining employment, materials engineers still will be needed to develop new materials for electronics, biotechnology, and plastics products. Growth should be particularly strong for materials engineers working on nanomaterials and biomaterials. As manufacturing firms contract for their materials engineering needs, employment growth is expected in professional, scientific, and technical services industries.

■ **Mechanical engineers** are projected to have an average rate of employment growth through 2014. Although total employment in manufacturing industries—in which employment of mechanical engineers is concentrated—is expected to decline, employment of mechanical engineers in manufacturing should increase as the demand for improved machinery and machine tools grows and as industrial machinery and processes become increasingly complex. Also, emerging technologies in biotechnology, materials science, and nanotechnology will create new job opportunities for mechanical engineers. Additional opportunities for mechanical engineers will arise because the skills acquired through earning a degree in mechanical engineering often can be applied in other engineering specialties.

■ **Mining and geological engineers, including mining safety engineers**, are expected to have good employment opportunities, despite a projected decline in employment. Many mining engineers currently employed are approaching retirement age, a factor that should create some job openings over the 2004–2014 period. In addition, relatively few schools offer mining engineering programs, and the small number of yearly graduates is not expected to increase substantially. Favorable job opportunities also may be available worldwide as mining operations around the world recruit graduates of U.S. mining engineering programs. As a result, some graduates may travel frequently or even live abroad. Employment of mining and geological engineers, including mining safety engineers, is projected to decline through 2014, primarily because most of the industries in which mining engineers are concentrated—such as coal, metal, and copper mining—are expected to experience declines in employment.

■ **Nuclear engineers** are expected to have good opportunities because the small number of nuclear engineering graduates is likely to be in rough balance with the number of job openings. Employment of nuclear engineers is expected to grow more slowly than the average for all occupations through 2014. Most openings will result from the need to replace nuclear engineers who transfer to other occupations or leave the labor force. Although no commercial nuclear power plants have been built in the United States for many years, nuclear engineers will be needed to operate existing plants. In addition, nuclear engineers may be needed to research and develop future nuclear power sources. They also will be needed to work in defense-related areas, to develop nuclear medical technology, and to improve and enforce waste management and safety standards.

■ **Petroleum engineers** are expected to have a decline in employment through 2014 because most of the potential petroleum-producing areas in the United States already have been explored. Even so, favorable opportunities are expected for petroleum engineers because the number of job openings is likely to exceed the relatively small number of graduates. All job openings should result from the need to replace petroleum engineers who transfer to other occupations or leave the labor force. Petroleum engineers work around the world and, in fact, the best employment opportunities may be in other countries. Many foreign employers seek U.S.-trained petroleum engineers, and many U.S. employers maintain overseas branches.

Earnings

Earnings for engineers vary significantly by specialty, industry, and education. Even so, as a group, engineers earn some of the highest

average starting salaries among those holding bachelor's degrees. The following tabulation shows average starting salary offers for engineers, according to a 2005 survey by the National Association of Colleges and Employers.

Curriculum	Bachelor's	Master's	Ph.D.
Aerospace/aeronautical/ astronautical	$50,993	$62,930	$72,529
Agricultural	46,172	53,022	
Bioengineering & biomedical		48,503	59,667
Chemical	53,813	57,260	79,591
Civil	43,679	48,050	59,625
Computer	52,464	60,354	69,625
Electrical/electronics & communications	51,888	64,416	80,206
Environmental/ environmental health	47,384		
Industrial/manufacturing	49,567	56,561	85,000
Materials	50,982		
Mechanical	50,236	59,880	68,299
Mining & mineral	48,643		
Nuclear	51,182	58,814	
Petroleum	61,516	58,000	

Variation in median earnings and in the earnings distributions for engineers in the various branches of engineering also is significant. For engineers in specialties covered in this job description, earnings distributions by percentile in May 2004 are shown in the following tabulation.

Specialty	10%	25%	50%	75%	90%
Aerospace	$52,820	$64,380	$79,100	$94,900	$113,520
Agricultural	37,680	43,270	56,520	77,740	90,410
Biomedical	41,260	51,620	67,690	86,400	107,530
Chemical	49,030	60,920	76,770	94,740	115,180
Civil	42,610	51,430	64,230	79,920	94,660
Computer hardware	50,490	63,730	81,150	102,100	123,560
Electrical	47,310	57,540	71,610	88,400	108,070
Electronics, except computer	49,120	60,280	75,770	92,870	112,200
Environmental	40,620	50,740	66,480	83,690	100,050
Health and safety, except mining safety	39,930	49,900	63,730	79,500	92,870
Industrial	42,450	52,210	65,020	79,830	93,950
Marine engineers and naval architects	43,790	54,530	72,040	89,900	109,190
Materials	44,130	53,510	67,110	83,830	101,120
Mechanical	43,900	53,070	66,320	82,380	97,850

Specialty	10%	25%	50%	75%	90%
Mining and geological, including mining safety	39,700	50,500	64,690	83,050	103,790
Nuclear	61,790	73,340	84,880	100,220	118,870
Petroleum	48,260	65,350	88,500	113,180	140,800

In the federal government, mean annual salaries for engineers ranged from $100,059 in ceramic engineering to $70,086 in agricultural engineering in 2005.

Related Occupations

Engineers apply the principles of physical science and mathematics in their work. Other workers who use scientific and mathematical principles include architects, except landscape and naval; engineering and natural sciences managers; computer and information systems managers; computer programmers; computer software engineers; mathematicians; drafters; engineering technicians; sales engineers; science technicians; and physical and life scientists, including agricultural and food scientists, biological scientists, conservation scientists and foresters, atmospheric scientists, chemists and materials scientists, environmental scientists and hydrologists, geoscientists, and physicists and astronomers.

Sources of Additional Information

Information about careers in engineering is available from

▸ JETS, 1420 King St., Suite 405, Alexandria, VA 22314-2794. Internet: http://www.jets.org

Information on ABET-accredited engineering programs is available from

▸ Accreditation Board for Engineering and Technology, Inc., 111 Market Place, Suite 1050, Baltimore, MD 21202-4012. Internet: http://www.abet.org

Those interested in information on the Professional Engineer licensure should contact

▸ National Society of Professional Engineers, 1420 King St., Alexandria, VA 22314-2794. Internet: http://www.nspe.org

▸ National Council of Examiners for Engineering and Surveying, P.O. Box 1686, Clemson, SC 29633-1686. Internet: http://www.ncees.org

Information on general engineering education and career resources is available from

▸ American Society for Engineering Education, 1818 N St. NW, Suite 600, Washington, DC 20036-2479. Internet: http://www.asee.org

Information on obtaining positions as engineers with the federal government is available from the Office of Personnel Management through USAJOBS, the federal government's official employment information system. This resource for locating and applying for job opportunities can be accessed through the Internet at http://www.usajobs.opm.gov or through an interactive voice response telephone system at (703) 724-1850 or TDD (978) 461-8404. These numbers are not toll free, and charges may result.

For more detailed information on an engineering specialty, contact societies representing the individual branches of engineering. Each can provide information about careers in the particular branch.

Aerospace engineers

▸ Aerospace Industries Association, 1000 Wilson Blvd., Suite 1700, Arlington, VA 22209-3901. Internet: http://www.aia-aerospace.org

▸ American Institute of Aeronautics and Astronautics, Inc., 1801 Alexander Bell Dr., Suite 500, Reston, VA 20191-4344. Internet: http://www.aiaa.org

Agricultural engineers

▸ American Society of Agricultural and Biological Engineers, 2950 Niles Rd., St. Joseph, MI 49085-9659. Internet: http://www.asabe.org

Biomedical engineers

▸ Biomedical Engineering Society, 8401 Corporate Dr., Suite 225, Landover, MD 20785-2224. Internet: http://www.bmes.org

Chemical engineers

▸ American Institute of Chemical Engineers, 3 Park Ave., New York, NY 10016-5991. Internet: http://www.aiche.org

▸ American Chemical Society, Department of Career Services, 1155 16th St. NW, Washington, DC 20036. Internet: http://www.chemistry.org/portal/Chemistry

Civil engineers

▸ American Society of Civil Engineers, 1801 Alexander Bell Dr., Reston, VA 20191-4400. Internet: http://www.asce.org

Computer hardware engineers

▸ IEEE Computer Society, 1730 Massachusetts Ave. NW, Washington, DC 20036-1992. Internet: http://www.computer.org

Electrical and electronics engineers

▸ Institute of Electrical and Electronics Engineers—USA, 1828 L St. NW, Suite 1202, Washington, DC 20036. Internet: http://www.ieeeusa.org

Environmental engineers

▸ American Academy of Environmental Engineers, 130 Holiday Court, Suite 100, Annapolis, MD 21401. Internet: http://www.aaee.net

Health and safety engineers

▸ American Society of Safety Engineers, 1800 E Oakton St., Des Plaines, IL 60018. Internet: http://www.asse.org

▸ Board of Certified Safety Professionals, 208 Burwash Ave., Savoy, IL 61874. Internet: http://www.bcsp.org

Industrial engineers

▸ Institute of Industrial Engineers, 3577 Parkway Lane, Suite 200, Norcross, GA 30092. Internet: http://www.iienet.org

Materials engineers

▸ The Minerals, Metals, & Materials Society, 184 Thorn Hill Rd., Warrendale, PA 15086-7514. Internet: http://www.tms.org

▸ ASM International, 9639 Kinsman Rd., Materials Park, OH 44073-0002. Internet: http://www.asminternational.org

Mechanical engineers

▸ The American Society of Mechanical Engineers, 3 Park Ave., New York, NY 10016-5990. Internet: http://www.asme.org

▸ American Society of Heating, Refrigerating, and Air-Conditioning Engineers, Inc., 1791 Tullie Circle NE, Atlanta, GA 30329. Internet: http://www.ashrae.org

▸ Society of Automotive Engineers, 400 Commonwealth Dr., Warrendale, PA 15096-0001. Internet: http://www.sae.org

Marine engineers and naval architects

▸ Society of Naval Architects and Marine Engineers, 601 Pavonia Ave., Jersey City, NJ 07306. Internet: http://www.sname.org

Mining and geological engineers, including mining safety engineers

▸ The Society for Mining, Metallurgy, and Exploration, Inc., 8307 Shaffer Parkway, Littleton, CO 80127-4102. Internet: http://www.smenet.org

Nuclear engineers

▸ American Nuclear Society, 555 North Kensington Ave., LaGrange Park, IL 60526. Internet: http://www.ans.org

Petroleum engineers

▸ Society of Petroleum Engineers, P.O. Box 833836, Richardson, TX 75083-3836. Internet: http://www.spe.org

Environmental Scientists and Hydrologists

(O*NET 19-2041.00 and 19-2043.00)

Significant Points

■ Environmental scientists and hydrologists often split their work between offices, laboratories, and field sites.

■ Federal, state, and local governments employ over half of all environmental scientists and hydrologists.

■ Although a bachelor's degree in an earth science is adequate for a few entry-level jobs, employers increasingly prefer a master's degree; a Ph.D. degree is required for most high-level research or college teaching positions.

■ The strongest job growth should be in private-sector consulting firms.

Nature of the Work

Environmental scientists and hydrologists use their knowledge of the physical makeup and history of the Earth to protect the environment, study the properties of underground and surface waters, locate water and energy resources, predict water-related geologic hazards, and offer environmental site assessments and advice on indoor air quality and hazardous-waste-site remediation.

Environmental scientists conduct research to identify and abate or eliminate sources of pollutants or hazards that affect people, wildlife, and their environments. These workers analyze and report measurements or observations of air, food, water, soil, and other sources and make recommendations on how best to clean and preserve the environment. Understanding the issues involved in protecting the environment—degradation, conservation, recycling, and replenishment—is central to the work of environmental scientists, who often use their skills and knowledge to design and monitor waste disposal sites, preserve water supplies, and reclaim contaminated land and water to comply with federal environmental regulations.

Many environmental scientists do work and have training that is similar to other physical or life scientists, but is applied to environmental areas. Many specialize in some specific area, such as environmental ecology and conservation, environmental chemistry, environmental biology, or fisheries science. Most environmental scientists are further classified by the specific activity they perform, although recent advances in the understanding of basic life processes within the ecosystem have blurred some traditional classifications. For example, environmental ecologists study the relationships between organisms and their environments and the effects of influences such as population size, pollutants, rainfall, temperature, and altitude. Utilizing their knowledge of various scientific disciplines, they may collect, study, and report data on air, food, soil, and water. Ecological modelers study ecosystems, the control of environmental pollution, and the management of resources. These environmental scientists may use mathematical modeling, systems analysis, thermodynamics, and computer techniques. Environmental chemists may study the toxicity of various chemicals—how those chemicals affect plants, animals, and people.

Hydrologists study the quantity, distribution, circulation, and physical properties of underground and surface waters. Often, they specialize in either underground water or surface water. They examine the form and intensity of precipitation, its rate of infiltration into the soil, its movement through the earth, and its return to the ocean and atmosphere. Hydrologists use sophisticated techniques and instruments. For example, they may use remote sensing technology, data assimilation, and numerical modeling to monitor the change in regional and global water cycles. Some surface-water hydrologists use sensitive stream-measuring devices to assess flow rates and the quality of water. The work hydrologists do is particularly important in flood control and environmental preservation, including groundwater decontamination.

Many environmental scientists and hydrologists work at consulting firms, advising and helping businesses and government agencies comply with environmental policy, particularly with regard to groundwater decontamination and flood control. Environmental scientists and hydrologists at consulting firms are generally hired to solve problems. Most firms fall into two categories: large multidisciplinary engineering companies, the largest of which may employ more than 15,000 workers, and small niche firms that may employ fewer than 50 workers. When entering the field, prospects should consider the type of firm and the scope of the projects it undertakes. In larger firms, environmental scientists are more likely to engage in large, long-term projects in which their role will mesh with those of workers in other scientific disciplines. In smaller specialty firms, however, they may be responsible for many skills beyond traditional environmental disciplines, such as working with environmental laws and regulations; making environmental risk assessments; writing technical proposals; giving presentations to managers and regulators; and working with other specialists on a variety of issues, including engineering remediation.

Environmental scientists who determine policy may help identify how human behavior can be modified in the future to avoid such problems as groundwater contamination and depletion of the ozone layer. Some environmental scientists work in managerial positions, usually after spending some time performing research or learning about environmental laws and regulations. (Information on geoscientists, whose work is closely related to that of environmental scientists and hydrologists, is located elsewhere in this book.)

Working Conditions

Most entry-level environmental scientists and hydrologists spend the majority of their time in the field, while more experienced workers generally devote more of their time to office or laboratory work. Many beginning hydrologists and some environmental scientists, such as environmental ecologists and environmental chemists, often take field trips that involve physical activity. Environmental scientists and hydrologists in the field may work in warm or cold climates in all kinds of weather. In their research, they may dig or chip with a hammer, scoop with a net, come in contact with water, and carry equipment in a backpack. Travel often is required to meet with prospective clients or investors. Those in laboratories may conduct tests, run experiments, record results, and compile data.

Environmental scientists and hydrologists in research positions with the federal government or in colleges and universities frequently are required to design programs and write grant proposals in order to continue their data collection and research. Environmental scientists and hydrologists in consulting jobs face similar pressures to market their skills and write proposals so that they will have steady work. Occasionally, those who write technical reports to business clients and regulators may be under pressure to meet deadlines.

Training, Other Qualifications, and Advancement

A bachelor's degree is adequate for a few entry-level positions, but environmental scientists are increasingly needing a master's degree in a natural science. A master's degree also is the minimum educational requirement for most entry-level applied research positions in private industry, in state and federal agencies, and at state geological surveys. A doctoral degree is necessary for college teaching and most high-level research positions.

Many environmental scientists earn degrees in life science, chemistry, geology, geophysics, atmospheric science, or physics and then, either through further education or through their research interests and work experience, apply their education to environmental areas. Others earn a degree in environmental science. A bachelor's degree in environmental science offers an interdisciplinary approach to the natural sciences with an emphasis on biology, chemistry, and geology. In addition, undergraduate environmental science majors should focus on data analysis and physical geography, particularly if they are interested in studying pollution abatement; water resources; or ecosystem protection, restoration, or management. Understanding the geochemistry of inorganic compounds is becoming increasingly important in developing remediation goals. Those students interested in working in the environmental or regulatory fields, either in environmental consulting firms or for federal or state governments, should take courses in hydrology, hazardous-waste management, environmental legislation, chemistry, fluid mechanics, and geologic logging. An understanding of environmental regulations and government permit issues also is valuable for those planning to work in mining and oil and gas extraction.

Students interested in the field of hydrology should take courses in the physical sciences, geophysics, chemistry, engineering science, soil science, mathematics, aquatic biology, atmospheric science, geology, oceanography, hydrogeology, and the management or conservation of water resources. In some cases, graduates with a bachelor's degree in a hydrologic science are qualified for positions in environmental consulting and planning regarding water quality or wastewater treatment. Curricula for advanced degrees often emphasize the natural sciences, but not all universities offer all curricula.

The American Institute of Hydrology offers certification programs in professional hydrology. Certification is recommended for those seeking advancement and for those seeking to upgrade their knowledge.

For environmental scientists and hydrologists who enter the field of consulting, courses in business, finance, marketing, or economics may be useful. In addition, combining environmental science training with other disciplines such as engineering, or a technical degree coupled with a master's degree in business administration, qualifies these scientists for the widest range of jobs. Environmental scientists and hydrologists also should have some knowledge of the potential liabilities associated with some environmental work.

Computer skills are essential for prospective environmental scientists and hydrologists. Students who have some experience with computer modeling, data analysis and integration, digital mapping, remote sensing, and geographic information systems will be the most prepared to enter the job market. A knowledge of the Geographic Information System (GIS) and Global Positioning System (GPS)—a locator system that uses satellites—is vital.

Environmental scientists and hydrologists must have excellent interpersonal skills because they usually work as part of a team with other scientists, engineers, and technicians. Strong oral and written communication skills also are essential because writing technical reports and research proposals and communicating technical and research results to company managers, regulators, and the public are important aspects of the work. Those involved in fieldwork must have physical stamina.

Environmental scientists and hydrologists often begin their careers in field exploration or, occasionally, as research assistants or technicians in laboratories or offices. They are given more difficult assignments as they gain experience. Eventually, they may be promoted to project leader, program manager, or some other management and research position.

Because international work is becoming increasingly pervasive, knowledge of a second language can be a valuable skill to employers.

Employment

Environmental scientists and hydrologists held about 81,000 jobs in 2004. Jobs for hydrologists accounted for only 10 percent of the total. Many more individuals held environmental science faculty positions in colleges and universities, but they are classified as college and university faculty. (See the description of teachers—postsecondary elsewhere in this book.)

About 44 percent of environmental scientists were employed in state and local governments; 15 percent in management, scientific, and technical consulting services; 14 percent in architectural, engineering and related services; and 8 percent in the federal government. About 5 percent were self-employed.

Among hydrologists, 22 percent were employed in architectural, engineering, and related services, and 18 percent worked for management, scientific, and technical consulting services. In 2004, the federal government employed about 2,500 hydrologists, mostly within the U.S. Department of the Interior for the U.S. Geological Survey (USGS) and within the U.S. Department of Defense. Another 15 percent worked for state agencies, such as state geological surveys and state departments of conservation. About 5 percent of hydrologists were self-employed, most as consultants to industry or government.

Job Outlook

Employment of environmental scientists is expected to grow about as fast as the average for all occupations through 2014, while employment of hydrologists should grow much faster than average. Job growth for environmental scientists and hydrologists should be strongest at private-sector consulting firms. Demand for environmental scientists and hydrologists will be spurred largely by public policy, which will oblige companies and organizations to comply with complex environmental laws and regulations, particularly those regarding groundwater decontamination, clean air, and flood control.

Job opportunities also will be spurred by a continued general awareness regarding the need to monitor the quality of the environment, to interpret the impact of human actions on terrestrial and aquatic ecosystems, and to develop strategies for restoring ecosystems.

Many environmental scientists and hydrologists work in consulting. Consulting firms have hired these scientists to advise and help businesses and government comply with new regulations on issues related to underground tanks, land disposal areas, and other hazardous-waste-management facilities. Currently, environmental consulting is maturing and evolving from investigations to remediation and engineering solutions. At the same time, the regulatory climate is evolving from a rigid structure to a more flexible risk-based approach. These factors, coupled with new federal and state initiatives that integrate environmental activities into the business process itself, will result in a greater focus on waste minimization, resource recovery, pollution prevention, and the consideration of environmental effects during product development. This shift in focus from reactive solutions to preventive management will provide many new opportunities for environmental scientists and hydrologists in consulting roles.

Some opportunities are expected for environmental scientists at state geological surveys, stemming from the need to conduct environmental site assessments for local governments to help improve the flow of railroad and automobile traffic in urban areas. In addition, environmental scientists will be needed to help planners and communities develop and construct buildings, transportation corridors, and utilities that protect water resources and reflect efficient and beneficial land use.

Opportunities will be better for hydrologists as the population increases and moves to more environmentally sensitive locations. For example, as people increasingly migrate toward coastal regions,

hydrologists will be needed to assess building sites for potential geologic hazards and to mitigate the effects of natural hazards such as floods and landslides. Hydrologists also will be needed to conduct research on hazardous-waste sites in order to determine the impact of hazardous pollutants on soil and groundwater so that engineers can design remediation systems. Demand is growing for hydrologists who understand both the scientific and engineering aspects of waste remediation. As states design initiatives to improve water resources by preventing pollution, there should be opportunities for hydrologists in state government. Increased government regulations, such as those regarding the management of storm water, and issues related to water conservation, deteriorating coastal environments, and rising sea levels also will stimulate employment growth for these workers.

Federal and state geological surveys depend to a large extent on the public climate and the current budget. Thus, job security for environmental scientists and hydrologists within a state survey may be cyclical. During periods of economic recession, layoffs of environmental scientists and hydrologists may occur in consulting firms; layoffs are much less likely in government.

Earnings

Median annual earnings of environmental scientists were $51,080 in May 2004. The middle 50 percent earned between $39,100 and $67,360. The lowest 10 percent earned less than $31,610, and the highest 10 percent earned more than $85,940.

Median annual earnings of hydrologists were $61,510 in May 2004, with the middle 50 percent earning between $47,080 and $77,910, the lowest 10 percent earning less than $38,580, and the highest 10 percent earning more than $94,460.

Median annual earnings in the industries employing the largest number of environmental scientists in May 2004 were as follows:

Federal government $73,530
Management, scientific, and technical
    consulting services 51,190
Architectural, engineering, and related services 49,160
Local government 48,870
State government 46,850

According to the National Association of Colleges and Employers, beginning salary offers in July 2005 for graduates with bachelor's degrees in a environmental science averaged $31,366 a year.

In 2005, the federal government's average salary for hydrologists in managerial, supervisory, and nonsupervisory positions was $77,182.

Related Occupations

Environmental scientists and hydrologists perform investigations for the purpose of abating or eliminating sources of pollutants or hazards that affect the environment or some population—plant, animal, or human. Many other occupations deal with preserving or researching the natural environment, including conservation scientists and foresters, atmospheric scientists, and some biological scientists and science and engineering technicians.

Environmental scientists and hydrologists have extensive training in physical sciences, and many apply their knowledge of chemistry, physics, biology, and mathematics to explain certain phenomena closely related to the work of geoscientists.

Using their qualitative and quantitative problem-solving skills, physicists; chemists; engineers; mathematicians; surveyors, cartographers, photogrammetrists, and surveying technicians; computer systems analysts; and computer scientists and database administrators may perform similar work in environment-related activities.

Sources of Additional Information

Information on training and career opportunities for environmental scientists is available from

▸ American Geological Institute, 4220 King St., Alexandria, VA 22302-1502. Internet: http://www.agiweb.org

For information on careers in hydrology, contact

▸ American Institute of Hydrology, 300 Village Green Circle, Suite #201, Smyrna, GA 30080. Internet: http://www.aihydro.org

For career information and a list of education and training programs in oceanography and related fields, contact

▸ Marine Technology Society, 5565 Sterrett Place, Suite 108, Columbia, MD 21004. Internet: http://www.mtsociety.org

Information on obtaining a position as a hydrologist or an environmental protection specialist with the federal government is available from the Office of Personnel Management through USAJOBS, the federal government's official employment information system. This resource for locating and applying for job opportunities can be accessed through the Internet at http://www.usajobs.opm.gov or through an interactive voice response telephone system at (703) 724-1850 or TDD (978) 461-8404. These numbers are not toll free, and charges may result.

Geoscientists

(O*NET 19-2041.00, 19-2042.01, and 19-2043.00)

Significant Points

■ Work at remote field sites is common.

■ Federal, state, and local governments employ 24 percent of all geoscientists.

■ A master's degree is usually the minimum educational requirement; a Ph.D. degree is required for most high-level research and college teaching positions.

■ Although employment of geoscientists is expected to grow more slowly than average, good job opportunities are expected in most areas of geoscience.

Nature of the Work

Geoscientists study the composition, structure, and other physical aspects of the Earth. With the use of sophisticated instruments and by analyzing the composition of the earth and water, geoscientists study the Earth's geologic past and present. Many geoscientists are involved in searching for adequate supplies of natural resources such as groundwater, metals, and petroleum, while others work closely with environmental and other scientists in preserving and cleaning up the environment.

Geoscientists usually study, and are subsequently classified into, one of several closely related fields of geoscience. *Geologists* study the composition, processes, and history of the Earth. They try to find out how rocks were formed and what has happened to them since their formation. They also study the evolution of life by analyzing plant and animal fossils. *Geophysicists* use the principles of physics, mathematics, and chemistry to study not only the Earth's surface, but also its internal composition; ground and surface waters; atmosphere; oceans; and magnetic, electrical, and gravitational forces.

Oceanographers use their knowledge of geology and geophysics, in addition to biology and chemistry, to study the world's oceans and coastal waters. They study the motion and circulation of the ocean waters; the physical and chemical properties of the oceans; and how these properties affect coastal areas, climate, and weather. Oceanographers are further broken down according to their areas of expertise. For example, *physical oceanographers* study the tides, waves, currents, temperatures, density, and salinity of the ocean. They examine the interaction of various forms of energy, such as light, radar, sound, heat, and wind, with the sea, in addition to investigating the relationship between the sea, weather, and climate. *Chemical oceanographers* study the distribution of chemical compounds and chemical interactions that occur in the ocean and on the sea floor. They may investigate how pollution affects the chemistry of the ocean. *Geological and geophysical oceanographers* study the topographic features and the physical makeup of the ocean floor. Their knowledge can help companies find oil and gas off coastal waters. (*Biological oceanographers*, often called marine biologists, study the distribution and migration patterns of the many diverse forms of sea life in the ocean, but because they are considered biological scientists, they are not covered in this description of geoscientists. See the description of biological scientists elsewhere in this book.)

Geoscientists can spend a large part of their time in the field identifying and examining rocks, studying information collected by remote sensing instruments in satellites, conducting geological surveys, constructing field maps, and using instruments to measure the Earth's gravity and magnetic field. For example, they often perform seismic studies, which involve bouncing energy waves off buried layers of rock, to search for oil and gas or to understand the structure of the subsurface layers. Seismic signals generated by an earthquake are used to determine the earthquake's location and intensity. In laboratories, geologists and geophysicists examine the chemical and physical properties of specimens. They study fossil remains of animal and plant life or experiment with the flow of water and oil through rocks.

Numerous specialties that further differentiate the type of work geoscientists do fall under the two major disciplines of geology and geophysics. For example, *petroleum geologists* map the subsurface of the ocean or land as they explore the terrain for oil and gas deposits. They use sophisticated geophysical instrumentation and computers to interpret geological information. *Engineering geologists* apply geologic principles to the fields of civil and environmental engineering, offering advice on major construction projects and assisting in environmental remediation and natural hazard-reduction projects. *Mineralogists* analyze and classify minerals and precious stones according to their composition and structure. They study the environment surrounding rocks in order to find new mineral resources. *Sedimentologists* study the nature, origin, distribution, and alteration of sediments, such as sand, silt, and mud. These sediments may contain oil, gas, coal, and many other mineral deposits. *Paleontologists* study fossils found in geological formations to trace the evolution of plant and animal life and the geologic history of the Earth. *Stratigraphers* examine the formation and layering of rocks to understand the environment in which they were formed. *Volcanologists* investigate volcanoes and volcanic phenomena to try to predict the potential for future eruptions and hazards to human health and welfare. *Glacial geologists* study the physical properties and movement of glaciers and ice sheets. *Geochemists* study the nature and distribution of chemical elements in groundwater and earth materials.

Geophysicists specialize in areas such as geodesy, seismology, and magnetic geophysics. *Geodesists* study the Earth's size, shape, gravitational field, tides, polar motion, and rotation. *Seismologists* interpret data from seismographs and other geophysical instruments to detect earthquakes and locate earthquake-related faults. *Geomagnetists* measure the Earth's magnetic field and use measurements taken over the past few centuries to devise theoretical models that explain the Earth's origin. *Paleomagnetists* interpret fossil magnetization in rocks and sediments from the continents and oceans to record the spreading of the sea floor, the wandering of the continents, and the many reversals of polarity that the Earth's magnetic field has undergone through time. Other geophysicists study atmospheric sciences and space physics. (See the descriptions of atmospheric scientists and of physicists and astronomers elsewhere in this book.)

Working Conditions

Some geoscientists spend the majority of their time in an office, but many others divide their time between fieldwork and office or laboratory work. Work at remote field sites is common. Many geoscientists, such as volcanologists, often take field trips that involve physical activity. Geoscientists in the field may work in warm or cold climates and in all kinds of weather. In their research, they may dig or chip with a hammer, scoop with a net, and carry equipment in a backpack. Oceanographers may spend considerable time at sea on academic research ships. Fieldwork often requires working long hours. Geologists frequently travel to remote field sites by helicopter or four-wheel-drive vehicle and cover large areas on foot. An increasing number of exploration geologists and geophysicists work in foreign countries, sometimes in remote areas and under difficult conditions. Travel often is required to meet with prospective clients or investors.

Geoscientists in research positions with the federal government or in colleges and universities frequently are required to design programs and write grant proposals in order to continue their data collection and research. Geoscientists in consulting jobs face similar pressures to market their skills and write proposals so that they will have steady work.

Training, Other Qualifications, and Advancement

A bachelor's degree is adequate for a few entry-level positions, but most geoscientists need at least a master's degree in general geology or earth science. A master's degree also is the minimum educational requirement for most entry-level research positions in private industry, federal agencies, and state geological surveys. A Ph.D. degree is necessary for most high-level research and college teaching positions.

Many colleges and universities offer a bachelor's or higher degree in a geoscience. In 2005, more than 100 universities offered accredited bachelor's degree programs in geoscience, about 80 universities had master's degree programs, and about 60 offered doctoral degree programs.

Traditional geoscience courses emphasizing classical geologic methods and topics (such as mineralogy, petrology, paleontology, stratigraphy, and structural geology) are important for all geoscientists. Persons studying physics, chemistry, biology, mathematics, engineering, or computer science may also qualify for some geoscience positions if their course work includes study in geology or natural sciences.

Computer skills are essential for prospective geoscientists; students who have experience with computer modeling, data analysis and integration, digital mapping, remote sensing, and geographic information systems will be the most prepared entering the job market. A knowledge of the Global Information System (GIS) and Global Positioning System (GPS)—a locator system that uses satellites—has also become essential. Some employers seek applicants with field experience, so a summer internship may be beneficial to prospective geoscientists.

Geoscientists must have excellent interpersonal skills because they usually work as part of a team with other geoscientists and with environmental scientists, engineers, and technicians. Strong oral and written communication skills also are important because writing technical reports and research proposals, as well as communicating research results to others, are important aspects of the work. Because many jobs require foreign travel, knowledge of a second language is becoming an important attribute to employers. Geoscientists must be inquisitive; be able to think logically; and be capable of complex analytical thinking, including spatial visualization and the ability to develop comprehensive conclusions, often from sparse data. Those involved in fieldwork must have physical stamina.

Geoscientists often begin their careers in field exploration or as research assistants or technicians in laboratories or offices. They are given more difficult assignments as they gain experience. Eventually, they may be promoted to project leader, program manager, or some other management or research position.

Employment

Geoscientists held about 28,000 jobs in 2004. Many more individuals held geoscience faculty positions in colleges and universities, but they are classified as college and university faculty. (See the description of teachers—postsecondary elsewhere in this book.)

About 25 percent of geoscientists were employed in architectural, engineering, and related services, and 20 percent worked for oil and gas extraction companies. In 2004, state agencies such as state geological surveys and state departments of conservation employed about 3,600 geoscientists. Another 2,900 worked for the federal government, including geologists, geophysicists, and oceanographers, mostly within the U.S. Department of the Interior for the U.S. Geological Survey (USGS) and within the U.S. Department of Defense. About 5 percent of geoscientists were self-employed, most as consultants to industry or government.

Job Outlook

Although employment growth will vary by occupational specialty, overall employment of geoscientists is expected to grow more slowly than the average for all occupations through 2014. However, due to the relatively low number of qualified geoscience graduates and the large number of expected retirements, opportunities are expected to be good in most areas of geoscience.

Graduates with a master's degree may have the best opportunities. Those with a Ph.D. who wish to become college and university faculty or to do advanced research may face competition. There are few openings for graduates with only a bachelor's degree in geoscience, but these graduates may find excellent opportunities as high school science teachers. They also can become science technicians or enter a wide variety of related occupations.

Few opportunities for geoscientists are expected in federal and state government, mostly because of budgetary constraints at key agencies, such as the USGS, and the trend among governments toward contracting out to consulting firms. However, departures of geoscientists who retire or leave the government for other reasons will result in some job openings over the next decade. A small number of new jobs will result from the need for oceanographers to conduct research for the military or for federal agencies such as the National Oceanic and Atmospheric Administration (NOAA) on issues related to maintaining healthy and productive oceans.

Many geoscientists work in the exploration and production of oil and gas. Historically, employment of petroleum geologists, geophysicists, and some other geoscientists has been cyclical and affected considerably by the price of oil and gas. When prices were low, oil and gas producers curtailed exploration activities and laid off geologists. When prices were higher, companies had the funds and incentive to renew exploration efforts and hire geoscientists in larger numbers. In recent years, a growing worldwide demand for oil and gas and for new exploration and recovery techniques—particularly in deep water and previously inaccessible sites in Alaska and the Gulf of Mexico—has returned some stability to the petroleum industry. Growth in this area, though, will be limited due to increasing efficiencies in finding oil and gas. Geoscientists who speak a foreign language and who are willing to work abroad should enjoy the best opportunities as the need for energy, construction materials, and a broad range of geoscience expertise grows in developing nations.

Job growth is expected within management, scientific, and technical consulting services. Demand will be spurred by a continuing emphasis on the need for energy, environmental protection, responsible land management, and water-related issues. Management, scientific,

and technical consulting services have increased their hiring of many geoscientists in recent years due to increased government contracting and also in response to demand for professionals to provide technical assistance and management plans to corporations. Moreover, many of these workers will be needed to monitor the quality of the environment, including aquatic ecosystems, issues related to water conservation, deteriorating coastal environments, and rising sea levels—all of which will stimulate employment growth of geoscientists.

An expected increase in highway building and other infrastructure projects will be a source of jobs for engineering geologists.

During periods of economic recession, geoscientists may be laid off. Especially vulnerable to layoffs are those in consulting and, to a lesser extent, workers in government. Employment for those working in the production of oil and gas, however, will largely be dictated by the cyclical nature of the energy sector and changes in government policy.

Earnings

Median annual earnings of geoscientists were $68,730 in May 2004. The middle 50 percent earned between $49,260 and $98,380; the lowest 10 percent earned less than $37,700, the highest 10 percent more than $130,750.

According to the National Association of Colleges and Employers, beginning salary offers in July 2005 for graduates with bachelor's degrees in geology and related sciences averaged $39,365 a year.

In 2005, the federal government's average salary for geologists in managerial, supervisory, and nonsupervisory positions was $83,178 for geologists, $94,836 for geophysicists, and $87,007 for oceanographers.

The petroleum, mineral, and mining industries are vulnerable to recessions and to changes in oil and gas prices, among other factors, and usually release workers when exploration and drilling slow down. Consequently, they offer higher salaries, but less job security, than other industries.

Related Occupations

Many geoscientists work in the petroleum and natural-gas industry, an industry that also employs numerous other workers whose jobs deal with the scientific and technical aspects of the exploration and extraction of petroleum and natural gas. Among these other workers are engineering technicians, science technicians, petroleum engineers, surveyors, cartographers, photogrammetrists, and surveying technicians. Also, some physicists, chemists, atmospheric scientists, biological scientists, and environmental scientists and hydrologists—as well as mathematicians, computer systems analysts, computer scientists and database administrators—perform related work both in the exploration and extraction of petroleum and natural gas and in activities having to do with the environment.

Sources of Additional Information

Information on training and career opportunities for geologists is available from either of the following organizations:

▶ American Geological Institute, 4220 King St., Alexandria, VA 22302-1502. Internet: http://www.agiweb.org

▶ American Association of Petroleum Geologists, P.O. Box 979, Tulsa, OK 74101. Internet: http://www.aapg.org

Information on oceanography and related fields is available from

▶ Marine Technology Society, 5565 Sterrett Place, Suite 108, Columbia, MD 21004. Internet: http://www.mtsociety.org

Information on obtaining a position as a geologist, geophysicist, or oceanographer with the federal government is available from the Office of Personnel Management through USAJOBS, the federal government's official employment information system. This resource for locating and applying for job opportunities can be accessed through the Internet at http://www.usajobs.opm.gov or through an interactive voice response telephone system at (703) 724-1850 or TDD (978) 461-8404. These numbers are not toll free, and charges may result.

Heating, Air-Conditioning, and Refrigeration Mechanics and Installers

(O*NET 49-9021.01 and 49-9021.02)

Significant Points

■ Employment is projected to grow faster than average.

■ Job prospects are expected to be excellent, particularly for those with training from an accredited technical school or with formal apprenticeship training.

■ Obtaining certification through one of several organizations is increasingly recommended by employers and may increase advancement opportunities.

Nature of the Work

Heating and air-conditioning systems control the temperature, humidity, and the total air quality in residential, commercial, industrial, and other buildings. Refrigeration systems make it possible to store and transport food, medicine, and other perishable items. Heating, air-conditioning, and refrigeration mechanics and installers—also called technicians—install, maintain, and repair such systems. Because heating, ventilation, air-conditioning, and refrigeration systems often are referred to as HVACR systems, these workers also may be called HVACR technicians.

Heating, air-conditioning, and refrigeration systems consist of many mechanical, electrical, and electronic components, such as motors, compressors, pumps, fans, ducts, pipes, thermostats, and switches. In central forced-air heating systems, for example, a furnace heats air that is distributed throughout the building via a system of metal or fiberglass ducts. Technicians must be able to maintain, diagnose, and correct problems throughout the entire system. To do this, they adjust system controls to recommended settings and test the performance of the entire system, using special tools and test equipment.

Technicians often specialize in either installation or maintenance and repair, although they are trained to do both. They also may specialize in doing heating work or air-conditioning or refrigeration work. Some specialize in one type of equipment—for example, hydronics (water-based heating systems), solar panels, or commercial refrigeration. Technicians also try to sell service contracts to their clients. Service contracts provide for regular maintenance of the heating and cooling systems and they help to reduce the seasonal fluctuations of this type of work.

Technicians follow blueprints or other specifications to install oil, gas, electric, solid-fuel, and multiple-fuel heating systems and air-conditioning systems. After putting the equipment in place, they install fuel and water supply lines, air ducts and vents, pumps, and other components. They may connect electrical wiring and controls and check the unit for proper operation. To ensure the proper functioning of the system, furnace installers often use combustion test equipment, such as carbon dioxide testers, carbon monoxide testers, combustion analyzers, and oxygen testers.

After a furnace or air-conditioning unit has been installed, technicians often perform routine maintenance and repair work to keep the systems operating efficiently. They may adjust burners and blowers and check for leaks. If the system is not operating properly, they check the thermostat, burner nozzles, controls, or other parts to diagnose and then correct the problem.

During the summer, when the heating system is not being used, heating equipment technicians do maintenance work, such as replacing filters, ducts, and other parts of the system that may accumulate dust and impurities during the operating season. During the winter, air-conditioning mechanics inspect the systems and do required maintenance, such as overhauling compressors.

Refrigeration mechanics install, service, and repair industrial and commercial refrigerating systems and a variety of refrigeration equipment. They follow blueprints, design specifications, and manufacturers' instructions to install motors, compressors, condensing units, evaporators, piping, and other components. They connect this equipment to the ductwork, refrigerant lines, and electrical power source. After making the connections, they charge the system with refrigerant, check it for proper operation, and program control systems.

When air-conditioning and refrigeration technicians service equipment, they must use care to conserve, recover, and recycle chlorofluorocarbon (CFC), hydrochlorofluorocarbon (HCFC), hydrofluorocarbon (HFC), and other refrigerants used in air-conditioning and refrigeration systems. The release of these refrigerants can be harmful to the environment. Technicians conserve the refrigerant by making sure that there are no leaks in the system; they recover it by venting the refrigerant into proper cylinders; they recycle it for reuse with special filter-dryers; or they insure that the refrigerant is properly disposed.

Heating, air-conditioning, and refrigeration mechanics and installers are adept at using a variety of tools, including hammers, wrenches, metal snips, electric drills, pipe cutters and benders, measurement gauges, and acetylene torches, to work with refrigerant lines and air ducts. They use voltmeters, thermometers, pressure gauges, manometers, and other testing devices to check airflow, refrigerant pressure, electrical circuits, burners, and other components.

Other craftworkers sometimes install or repair cooling and heating systems. For example, on a large air-conditioning installation job, especially where workers are covered by union contracts, ductwork might be done by sheet metal workers and duct installers; electrical work by electricians; and installation of piping, condensers, and other components by pipelayers, plumbers, pipefitters, and steamfitters. Home appliance repairers usually service room air conditioners and household refrigerators.

Working Conditions

Heating, air-conditioning, and refrigeration mechanics and installers work in homes, retail establishments, hospitals, office buildings, and factories—anywhere there is climate-control equipment. They may be assigned to specific job sites at the beginning of each day or may be dispatched to a variety of locations if they are making service calls.

Technicians may work outside in cold or hot weather or in buildings that are uncomfortable because the air-conditioning or heating equipment is broken. In addition, technicians might have to work in awkward or cramped positions and sometimes are required to work in high places. Hazards include electrical shock, burns, muscle strains, and other injuries from handling heavy equipment. Appropriate safety equipment is necessary when handling refrigerants because contact can cause skin damage, frostbite, or blindness. Inhalation of refrigerants when working in confined spaces also is a possible hazard.

The majority of mechanics and installers work at least a 40-hour week. During peak seasons, they often work overtime or irregular hours. Maintenance workers, including those who provide maintenance services under contract, often work evening or weekend shifts and are on call. Most employers try to provide a full workweek year-round by scheduling both installation and maintenance work, and many manufacturers and contractors now provide or even require service contracts. In most shops that service both heating and air-conditioning equipment, employment is stable throughout the year.

Training, Other Qualifications, and Advancement

Because of the increasing sophistication of heating, air-conditioning, and refrigeration systems, employers prefer to hire those with technical school training or those who have completed an apprenticeship. Some mechanics and installers, however, still learn the trade informally on the job.

Many secondary and postsecondary technical and trade schools, junior and community colleges, and the U.S. Armed Forces offer 6-month to 2-year programs in heating, air-conditioning, and refrigeration. Students study theory, design, and equipment construction, as well as electronics. They also learn the basics of installation, maintenance, and repair. There are three accrediting agencies that have set academic standards for HVACR programs. These accrediting bodies are HVAC Excellence, the National Center for Construction Education and Research (NCCER), and the Partnership for Air Conditioning, Heating, and Refrigeration Accreditation (PHARA). After completing these programs, new technicians generally need between an additional 6 months and 2 years of field experience before they can be considered proficient.

Apprenticeship programs frequently are run by joint committees representing local chapters of the Air-Conditioning Contractors of America, the Mechanical Contractors Association of America, Plumbing-Heating-Cooling Contractors—National Association, and locals of the sheet metal workers' International Association or the United Association of Journeymen and Apprentices of the Plumbing and Pipefitting Industry of the United States and Canada. Other apprenticeship programs are sponsored by local chapters of the Associated Builders and Contractors and the National Association of Home Builders. Formal apprenticeship programs normally last 3 to 5 years and combine on-the-job training with classroom instruction. Classes include subjects such as the use and care of tools; safety practices; blueprint reading; and the theory and design of heating, ventilation, air-conditioning, and refrigeration systems. Applicants for these programs must have a high school diploma or equivalent. Math and reading skills are essential. After completing an apprenticeship program, technicians are considered skilled trades workers and capable of working alone. These programs are also a pathway to certification and, in some cases, college credits.

Those who acquire their skills on the job usually begin by assisting experienced technicians. They may begin by performing simple tasks such as carrying materials, insulating refrigerant lines, or cleaning furnaces. In time, they move on to more difficult tasks, such as cutting and soldering pipes and sheet metal and checking electrical and electronic circuits.

Courses in shop math, mechanical drawing, applied physics and chemistry, electronics, blueprint reading, and computer applications provide a good background for those interested in entering this occupation. Some knowledge of plumbing or electrical work also is helpful. A basic understanding of electronics is becoming more important because of the increasing use of this technology in equipment controls. Because technicians frequently deal directly with the public, they should be courteous and tactful, especially when dealing with an aggravated customer. They also should be in good physical condition because they sometimes have to lift and move heavy equipment.

All technicians who purchase or work with refrigerants must be certified in their proper handling. To become certified to purchase and handle refrigerants, technicians must pass a written examination specific to the type of work in which they specialize. The three possible areas of certification are Type I—servicing small appliances, Type II—high-pressure refrigerants, and Type III—low-pressure refrigerants. Exams are administered by organizations approved by the U.S. Environmental Protection Agency, such as trade schools, unions, contractor associations, or building groups.

Several organizations have begun to offer basic self-study, classroom, and Internet courses for individuals with limited experience. In addition to understanding how systems work, technicians also must learn about refrigerant products and the legislation and regulations that govern their use.

Throughout the learning process, job candidates may have to take a number of tests that measure their skills in the field. For those with less than 1 year of experience and taking classes, the industry has developed a series of exams to test basic competency in residential heating and cooling, light commercial heating and cooling, and commercial refrigeration. These are referred to as "entry-level" certification exams and are commonly conducted at both secondary and postsecondary technical and trade schools. For HVACR technicians who have at least one year of experience performing installations and 2 years of experience performing maintenance and repair, they can take a number of different tests to certify their competency in working with more specific types of equipment, such as oil-burning furnaces. The tests are offered through Refrigeration Service Engineers Society (RSES), HVAC Excellence, The Carbon Monoxide Safety Association (COSA), Air Conditioning and Refrigeration Safety Coalition, and North American Technician Excellence, Inc. (NATE), among others. Passing these tests and obtaining certification is increasingly recommended by employers and may increase advancement opportunities.

Advancement usually takes the form of higher wages. Some technicians, however, may advance to positions as supervisor or service manager. Others may move into areas such as sales and marketing. Still others may become building superintendents, cost estimators, or, with the necessary certification, teachers. Those with sufficient money and managerial skill can open their own contracting business.

Employment

Heating, air-conditioning, and refrigeration mechanics and installers held about 270,000 jobs in 2004; almost half worked for plumbing, heating, and air-conditioning contractors. The remainder was employed in a variety of industries throughout the country, reflecting a widespread dependence on climate-control systems. Some worked for fuel oil dealers, refrigeration and air-conditioning service and repair shops, schools, and stores that sell heating and air-conditioning systems. Local governments, the federal government, hospitals, office buildings, and other organizations that operate large air-conditioning, refrigeration, or heating systems employed others. About 15 percent of mechanics and installers were self-employed.

Job Outlook

Job prospects for heating, air-conditioning, and refrigeration mechanics and installers are expected to be excellent, particularly for those with training from an accredited technical school or with formal apprenticeship training and especially in the fastest-growing areas of the country. A growing number of retirements of highly skilled technicians is expected to generate many job openings. In addition, employment of heating, air-conditioning, and refrigeration mechanics and installers is projected to increase faster than the average for all occupations through the year 2014. As the population and stock of buildings grows, so does the demand for residential, commercial, and industrial climate-control systems. The increased complexity of HVACR systems, increasing the possibility that equipment may malfunction, also will create opportunities for service technicians. Technicians who specialize in installation work may experience periods of unemployment when the level of new construction activity declines, but maintenance and repair work usually remains relatively stable. People and businesses depend on their cli-

mate-control systems and must keep them in good working order, regardless of economic conditions.

Concern for the environment has prompted the development of new energy-saving heating and air-conditioning systems. An emphasis on better energy management should lead to the replacement of older systems and the installation of newer, more efficient systems in existing homes and buildings. Also, demand for maintenance and service work should increase as businesses and homeowners strive to keep increasingly complex systems operating at peak efficiency. Regulations prohibiting the discharge and production of CFC and HCFC refrigerants should continue to result in the need to replace many existing air-conditioning systems or modify them to use new environmentally safe refrigerants. The pace of replacement in the commercial and industrial sectors will quicken if Congress or individual states cut the time needed to fully depreciate the cost of new HVACR systems, which is being considered.

A growing focus on improving indoor air quality, as well as the increasing use of refrigerated equipment by a growing number of stores and gasoline stations that sell food, also should contribute to the creation of more jobs for heating, air-conditioning, and refrigeration technicians.

Earnings

Median hourly earnings of heating, air-conditioning, and refrigeration mechanics and installers were $17.43 in May 2004. The middle 50 percent earned between $13.51 and $22.21 an hour. The lowest 10 percent earned less than $10.88, and the top 10 percent earned more than $27.11. Median hourly earnings in the industries employing the largest numbers of heating, air-conditioning, and refrigeration mechanics and installers in May 2004 were

Hardware and plumbing and heating equipment and supplies merchant wholesalers	$19.51
Direct selling establishments	17.81
Elementary and secondary schools	17.56
Commercial and industrial machinery and equipment (except automotive and electronic) repair and maintenance	17.52
Building equipment contractors	16.80

Apprentices usually begin at about 50 percent of the wage rate paid to experienced workers. As they gain experience and improve their skills, they receive periodic increases until they reach the wage rate of experienced workers.

Heating, air-conditioning, and refrigeration mechanics and installers enjoy a variety of employer-sponsored benefits. In addition to typical benefits such as health insurance and pension plans, some employers pay for work-related training and provide uniforms, company vans, and tools.

About 16 percent of heating, air-conditioning, and refrigeration mechanics and installers are members of a union. The unions to which the greatest numbers of mechanics and installers belong are the sheet metal workers International Association and the United Association of Journeymen and Apprentices of the Plumbing and Pipefitting Industry of the United States and Canada.

Related Occupations

Heating, air-conditioning, and refrigeration mechanics and installers work with sheet metal and piping and repair machinery such as electrical motors, compressors, and burners. Other workers who have similar skills include boilermakers; home appliance repairers; electricians; sheet metal workers; and pipelayers, plumbers, pipefitters, and steamfitters.

Sources of Additional Information

For more information about opportunities for training, certification, and employment in this trade, contact local vocational and technical schools; local heating, air-conditioning, and refrigeration contractors; a local of the unions or organizations previously mentioned; a local joint union-management apprenticeship committee; or the nearest office of the state employment service or apprenticeship agency.

For information on career opportunities, training, and technician certification, contact

▶ Air-Conditioning Contractors of America (ACCA), 2800 Shirlington Rd., Suite 300, Arlington, VA 22206. Internet: http://www.acca.org

▶ Refrigeration Service Engineers Society (RSES), 1666 Rand Rd., Des Plaines, IL 60016-3552. Internet: http://www.rses.org

▶ Plumbing-Heating-Cooling Contractors (PHCC), 180 S. Washington St., P.O. Box 6808, Falls Church, VA 22046. Internet: http://www.phccweb.org

▶ Sheet Metal and Air-Conditioning Contractors National Association, 4201 Lafayette Center Dr., Chantilly, VA 20151-1209. Internet: http://www.smacna.org

▶ HVAC Excellence, P.O. Box 491, Mt. Prospect, IL 60056. Internet: http://www.hvacexcellence.org

▶ North American Technician Excellence (NATE), 4100 North Fairfax Dr., Suite 210, Arlington, VA 22203. Internet: http://www.natex.org

▶ Air-Conditioning and Refrigeration Institute, 4100 North Fairfax Dr., Suite 200, Arlington, VA 22203. Internet: http://www.coolcareers.org or http://www.ari.org

▶ Carbon Monoxide Safety Association, P.O. Box 669, Eastlake, CO 80614. Internet: http://www.cosafety.org

▶ National Occupational Competency Testing Institute. Internet: http://www.nocti.org

▶ Associated Builders and Contractors, Workforce Development Department, 4250 North Fairfax Dr., 9th Floor, Arlington, VA 22203. Internet: http://www.trytools.org

▶ Home Builders Institute, National Association of Home Builders, 1201 15th St. NW, 6th Floor, Washington, DC 20005-2800. Internet: http://www.hbi.org

▶ Mechanical Contractors Association of America, 1385 Piccard Dr., Rockville, MD 20850-4329. Internet: http://www.mcaa.org

▶ National Center for Construction Education and Research, P.O. Box 141104, Gainesville FL, 32601. Internet: http://www.nccer.org

Heavy Vehicle and Mobile Equipment Service Technicians and Mechanics

(O*NET 49-3041.00, 49-3042.00, and 49-3043.00)

Significant Points

■ Opportunities should be good for persons with formal postsecondary training in diesel or heavy equipment mechanics, especially if they also have training in basic electronics and hydraulics.

■ This occupation offers relatively high wages and the challenge of skilled repair work.

■ Skill in using computerized diagnostic equipment is important in this occupation.

Nature of the Work

Heavy vehicles and mobile equipment are indispensable to many industrial activities, from construction to railroads. Various types of equipment move materials, till land, lift beams, and dig earth to pave the way for development and production. *Heavy vehicle and mobile equipment service technicians and mechanics* repair and maintain engines and hydraulic, transmission, and electrical systems powering farm machinery, cranes, bulldozers, and railcars, for example. (For more detailed information on service technicians specializing in diesel engines, see the description of diesel service technicians and mechanics elsewhere in this book.)

Service technicians perform routine maintenance checks on diesel engines and on fuel, brake, and transmission systems to ensure peak performance, safety, and longevity of the equipment. Maintenance checks and comments from equipment operators usually alert technicians to problems. With many types of modern heavy and mobile equipment, technicians can plug diagnostic computers into onboard computers to diagnose a component needing adjustment or repair. After locating the problem, these technicians rely on their training and experience to use the best possible technique to solve the problem. If necessary, they may partially dismantle the component to examine parts for damage or excessive wear. Then, using hand-held tools, they repair, replace, clean, and lubricate parts as necessary. In some cases, technicians calibrate systems by typing codes into the onboard computer. After reassembling the component and testing it for safety, they put it back into the equipment and return the equipment to the field.

Many types of heavy and mobile equipment use hydraulics to raise and lower movable parts. When hydraulic components malfunction, technicians examine them for fluid leaks, ruptured hoses, or worn gaskets on fluid reservoirs. Occasionally, the equipment requires extensive repairs, as when a defective hydraulic pump needs replacing.

In addition to conducting routine maintenance checks, service technicians perform a variety of other repairs. They diagnose electrical problems and adjust or replace defective components. They also disassemble and repair undercarriages and track assemblies. Occasionally, technicians weld broken equipment frames and structural parts, using electric or gas welders.

It is common for technicians in large shops to specialize in one or two types of repair. For example, a shop may have individual specialists in major engine repair, transmission work, electrical systems, and suspension or brake systems. Technicians in smaller shops, on the other hand, generally perform multiple functions.

The technology used in heavy equipment is becoming more sophisticated with the increased use of electronic and computer-controlled components that run much of the equipment's functions. These onboard computers are accessed using other computers and electronic devices that are manipulated by the technician. As a result, technicians need training in electronics and the use of hand-held diagnostic computers to make engine adjustments and diagnose problems.

Service technicians use a variety of tools in their work: power tools, such as pneumatic wrenches, to remove bolts quickly; machine tools, like lathes and grinding machines, to rebuild brakes; welding and flame-cutting equipment to remove and repair exhaust systems; and jacks and hoists to lift and move large parts. Service technicians also use common hand tools—screwdrivers, pliers, and wrenches—to work on small parts and to get at hard-to-reach places. They may use a variety of computerized testing equipment to pinpoint and analyze malfunctions in electrical systems and other essential systems. Tachometers and dynamometers, for example, serve to locate engine malfunctions. Service technicians also use ohmmeters, ammeters, and voltmeters when working on electrical systems.

Mobile heavy equipment mechanics and service technicians keep construction and surface mining equipment, such as bulldozers, cranes, crawlers, draglines, graders, excavators, and other equipment, in working order. Typically, these workers are employed by equipment wholesale distribution and leasing firms, large construction and mining companies, local and federal governments, and other organizations operating and maintaining heavy machinery and equipment fleets. Service technicians employed by the federal government may work on tanks and other armored equipment.

Farm equipment mechanics service, maintain, and repair farm equipment, as well as smaller lawn and garden tractors sold to suburban homeowners. What typically was a general repairer's job around the farm has evolved into a specialized technical career. Farmers have increasingly turned to farm equipment dealers to service and repair their equipment because the machinery has grown in complexity. Modern equipment uses more computers, electronics, and hydraulics, making it difficult to perform repairs without some specialized training.

Railcar repairers specialize in servicing railroad locomotives and other rolling stock, streetcars and subway cars, or mine cars. Most work for railroads, public and private transit companies, and railcar manufacturers.

Working Conditions

Heavy vehicle and mobile equipment service technicians usually work indoors, although if repairs are needed urgently or the machinery cannot be moved to a shop, many technicians make repairs at the worksite. To repair vehicles and equipment, technicians often lift heavy parts and tools, handle greasy and dirty parts, and stand or lie in awkward positions. Minor cuts, burns, and bruises are common; serious accidents normally are avoided when the shop is kept clean and orderly and when safety practices are observed. Technicians usually work in well-lighted, heated, and ventilated areas. However, some shops are drafty and noisy. Many employers provide uniforms, locker rooms, and shower facilities.

When heavy or mobile equipment breaks down at a construction site, it may be too difficult or expensive to bring into a repair shop, so the shop will send a field service technician to the site to make repairs. Field service technicians work outdoors and spend much of their time away from the shop. Generally, the more experienced service technicians specialize in field service. They usually drive trucks specially equipped with replacement parts and tools. On occasion, they must travel many miles to reach disabled machinery. Field technicians normally earn a higher wage than their counterparts because they are required to make on-the-spot decisions that are necessary to serve their customers.

The hours of work for farm equipment mechanics vary according to the season of the year. During the busy planting and harvesting seasons, mechanics often work 6 or 7 days a week, 10 to 12 hours daily. In slow winter months, however, mechanics may work fewer than 40 hours a week.

Training, Other Qualifications, and Advancement

Many persons qualify for service technician jobs through years of on-the-job training, but most employers prefer that applicants complete a formal diesel or heavy equipment mechanic training program after graduating from high school. They seek persons with mechanical aptitude who are knowledgeable about the fundamentals of diesel engines, transmissions, electrical systems, computers, and hydraulics. In addition, the constant change in equipment technology makes it necessary for technicians to be flexible and have the capacity to learn new skills quickly.

Many community colleges and vocational schools offer programs in diesel technology. Some tailor programs to heavy equipment mechanics. These programs educate the student in the basics of analytical and diagnostic techniques, electronics, and hydraulics. The increased use of electronics and computers makes training in the fundamentals of electronics essential for new heavy and mobile equipment mechanics. Some 1- to 2-year programs lead to a certificate of completion, whereas others lead to an associate degree in diesel or heavy equipment mechanics. These programs not only provide a foundation in the components of diesel and heavy equipment technology, but also enable trainee technicians to advance to the journey, or experienced worker, level sooner than would otherwise be possible.

A combination of formal and on-the-job training prepares trainee technicians with the knowledge to service and repair equipment typically seen by a shop. After a few months' experience, most beginners perform routine service tasks and make minor repairs. As they prove their ability and competence, they advance to harder jobs. After trainees master the repair and service of diesel engines, they learn to work on related components, such as brakes, transmissions, and electrical systems. Generally, a service technician with at least 3 to 4 years of on-the-job experience is accepted as fully qualified.

Many employers send trainee technicians to training sessions conducted by heavy equipment manufacturers. The sessions, which typically last up to 1 week, provide intensive instruction in the repair of the manufacturer's equipment. Some sessions focus on particular components found in the equipment, such as diesel engines, transmissions, axles, and electrical systems. Other sessions focus on particular types of equipment, such as crawler-loaders and crawler-dozers. As they progress, trainees may periodically attend additional training sessions. When appropriate, experienced technicians attend training sessions to gain familiarity with new technology or equipment.

High school courses in automobile repair, physics, chemistry, and mathematics provide a strong foundation for a career as a service technician or mechanic. It is also essential for technicians to be able to read and interpret service manuals in order to keep abreast of engineering changes. Experience working on diesel engines and heavy equipment acquired in the Armed Forces is valuable as well.

Voluntary certification by the National Institute for Automotive Service Excellence is the recognized industry credential for heavy vehicle and mobile equipment service technicians, who may be certified as a master medium/heavy truck technician or in a specific area of heavy-duty equipment repair, such as brakes, gasoline engines, diesel engines, drivetrains, electrical systems, or suspension and steering. For certification in each area, technicians must pass a written examination and have at least 2 years' experience. High school, vocational or trade school, or community or junior college training in gasoline or diesel engine repair may substitute for up to 1 year's experience. To remain certified, technicians must be retested every 5 years. Retesting ensures that service technicians keep up with changing technology. However, ASE currently offers no certification programs for more advanced heavy vehicle and mobile equipment repair specialties.

The most important work possessions of technicians are their hand tools. Service technicians typically buy their own hand tools, and many experienced technicians have thousands of dollars invested in them. Employers typically furnish expensive power tools, computerized engine analyzers, and other diagnostic equipment, but hand tools are normally accumulated with experience.

Experienced technicians may advance to field service jobs, wherein they have a greater opportunity to tackle problems independently and earn additional pay. Field positions may require a commercial driver's license and a clean driving record. Technicians with leadership ability may become shop supervisors or service managers. Some technicians open their own repair shops or invest in a franchise.

Employment

Heavy vehicle and mobile equipment service technicians and mechanics held about 178,000 jobs in 2004. Approximately 125,000 were mobile heavy equipment mechanics, 33,000 were farm equipment mechanics, and 20,000 were railcar repairers. About 30 percent were employed by machinery, equipment, and supplies merchant wholesalers. More than 13 percent worked in construction, primarily for specialty trade contractors and highway, street, and bridge construction companies; another 12 percent were employed by federal, state, and local governments. Other service technicians worked in agriculture; mining; rail transportation and support activities; and commercial and industrial machinery and equipment rental, leasing, and repair. A small number repaired equipment for machinery and railroad rolling stock manufacturers or lawn and garden equipment and supplies stores. Less than 4 percent of service technicians were self-employed.

Nearly every section of the country employs heavy and mobile equipment service technicians and mechanics, although most work in towns and cities where equipment dealers, equipment rental and leasing companies, and construction companies have repair facilities.

Job Outlook

Opportunities for heavy vehicle and mobile equipment service technicians and mechanics should be good for those who have completed formal training programs in diesel or heavy equipment mechanics. Persons without formal training are expected to encounter growing difficulty entering these jobs.

Employment of heavy vehicle and mobile equipment service technicians and mechanics is expected to grow slower than the average for all occupations through the year 2014. Most job openings will arise from the need to replace experienced repairers who retire. Employers report difficulty finding candidates with formal postsecondary training to fill available service technician positions because many young people with mechanic training and experience opt to take jobs as automotive service technicians, diesel service technicians, or industrial machinery repairers—jobs that offer more openings and a wider variety of locations in which to work.

Faster employment growth is expected for mobile heavy equipment mechanics than for farm equipment mechanics or railcar repairers. Increasing numbers of heavy duty and mobile equipment service technicians will be required to support growth in the construction industry, equipment dealers, and rental and leasing companies. Because of the nature of construction activity, demand for service technicians follows the nation's economic cycle. As the economy expands, construction activity increases, resulting in the use of more mobile heavy equipment to grade construction sites, excavate basements, and lay water and sewer lines. The increased use of such equipment increases the need for periodic service and repair. In addition, the construction and repair of highways and bridges requires more technicians to service equipment. As equipment becomes more complicated, repairs increasingly must be made by specially trained technicians. Job openings for farm equipment mechanics and railcar repairers are expected to arise mostly because of replacement needs.

Construction and mining are particularly sensitive to changes in the level of economic activity; therefore, heavy and mobile equipment may be idled during downturns. In addition, winter is traditionally the slow season for construction and farming activity, particularly in cold regions. During periods when equipment is used less, few technicians may be needed, and employers may be reluctant to hire inexperienced workers. However, employers usually try to retain experienced workers during these slow periods.

Earnings

Median hourly earnings of mobile heavy equipment mechanics were $18.34 in May 2004. The middle 50 percent earned between $14.96 and $21.75. The lowest 10 percent earned less than $12.11, and the highest 10 percent earned more than $26.27. Median hourly earnings in the industries employing the largest numbers of mobile heavy equipment mechanics in May 2004 were as follows:

Federal government	$20.41
Local government	19.22
Machinery, equipment, and supplies merchant wholesalers	18.49
Other specialty trade contractors	17.81
Highway, street, and bridge construction	17.79

Median hourly earnings of farm equipment mechanics were $13.40 in May 2004. The middle 50 percent earned between $10.77 and $16.34. The lowest 10 percent earned less than $9.08, and the highest 10 percent earned more than $19.40. In May 2004, median hourly earnings were $13.66 in machinery, equipment, and supplies merchant wholesalers, the industry employing the largest number of farm equipment mechanics.

Median hourly earnings of railcar repairers were $19.48 in May 2004. The middle 50 percent earned between $16.12 and $21.76. The lowest 10 percent earned less than $12.07, and the highest 10 percent earned more than $25.52. In May 2004, median hourly earnings were $20.38 in rail transportation, the industry employing the largest number of railcar repairers.

Many heavy vehicle and mobile equipment service technicians and mechanics are members of unions, including the International Association of Machinists and Aerospace Workers, the International Union of Operating Engineers, and the International Brotherhood of Teamsters.

Related Occupations

Workers in related repair occupations include aircraft and avionics equipment mechanics and service technicians; automotive service technicians and mechanics; diesel service technicians and mechanics; industrial machinery mechanics and maintenance workers; and small engine mechanics.

Sources of Additional Information

More details about job openings for heavy vehicle and mobile equipment service technicians and mechanics may be obtained from local heavy and mobile equipment dealers and distributors, construction contractors, and government agencies. Local offices of the state employment service also may have information on job openings and training programs.

For general information about a career as a heavy vehicle and mobile equipment service technician or mechanic, contact

▸ The AED Foundation (Associated Equipment Dealers affiliate), 615 W. 22nd St., Oak Brook, IL 60523. Internet: http://www.aednet.org/aed_foundation

A list of certified diesel service technician training programs can be obtained from

▸ National Automotive Technician Education Foundation (NATEF), 101 Blue Seal Dr., Suite 101, Leesburg, VA 20175. Internet: http://www.natef.org

Information on certification as a heavy-duty diesel service technician is available from

▸ National Institute for Automotive Service Excellence (ASE), 101 Blue Seal Dr. SE, Suite 101, Leesburg, VA 20175. Internet: http://www.asecert.org

Industrial Machinery Mechanics and Maintenance Workers

(O*NET 49-9041.00 and 49-9043.00)

Significant Points

■ Highly skilled mechanics usually learn their trade through a 4-year apprenticeship program, while lower-skilled maintenance workers receive short-term on-the-job training.

■ Employment is projected to grow more slowly than average, but applicants with broad skills in machine repair and maintenance should have favorable job prospects.

■ Unlike some manufacturing occupations, these workers usually are not affected by changes in production.

Nature of the Work

A wide range of employees is required to keep sophisticated industrial machinery running smoothly—from highly skilled industrial machinery mechanics to lower-skilled machinery maintenance workers who perform routine tasks. Their work is vital to the success of industrial facilities, not only because an idle machine will delay production, but also because a machine that is not properly repaired and maintained may damage the machine or the final product or injure an operator.

The most basic tasks in this process are performed by *machinery maintenance workers*. These employees are responsible for cleaning and lubricating machinery, performing basic diagnostic tests, checking performance, and testing damaged machine parts to determine whether major repairs are necessary. In carrying out these tasks, maintenance workers must follow machine specifications and adhere to maintenance schedules. Maintenance workers may perform minor repairs, but major repairs are generally left to machinery mechanics.

Industrial machinery mechanics, also called industrial machinery repairers or maintenance machinists, are highly skilled workers who maintain and repair machinery in a plant or factory. To do this effectively, they must be able to detect minor problems and correct them before they become major problems. Machinery mechanics use their understanding of the equipment, technical manuals, and careful observation to discover the cause. For example, after hearing a vibration from a machine, the mechanic must decide whether it is due to worn belts, weak motor bearings, or some other problem. Computerized diagnostic systems and vibration analysis techniques are aiding in determining the problem, but mechanics still need years of training and experience.

After diagnosing the problem, the industrial machinery mechanic disassembles the equipment to repair or replace the necessary parts. When repairing electronically controlled machinery, mechanics may work closely with electronic repairers or electricians who maintain the machine's electronic parts. (A description of electrical and electronic installers and repairers appears elsewhere in this book.) Increasingly, mechanics need electronic and computer skills in order to repair sophisticated equipment on their own. Once a repair is made, mechanics perform tests to ensure that the machine is running smoothly.

Primary responsibilities of industrial machinery mechanics include repair, preventive maintenance, and installation of new machinery. For example, they adjust and calibrate automated manufacturing equipment, such as industrial robots. As plants retool and invest in new equipment, they increasingly rely on mechanics to properly situate and install the machinery. In many plants, this has traditionally been the job of millwrights, but mechanics are increasingly called upon to carry out this task. (See the description of millwrights elsewhere in this book.)

Industrial machinery mechanics and machinery maintenance workers use a variety of tools to perform repairs and preventive maintenance. They may use a screwdriver and wrench to adjust a motor or use a hoist to lift a printing press off the ground. When replacements for broken or defective parts are not readily available, or when a machine must be quickly returned to production, mechanics may sketch a part to be fabricated by the plant's machine shop. Mechanics use catalogs to order replacement parts and often follow blueprints, technical manuals, and engineering specifications to maintain and fix equipment. By keeping complete and up-to-date records, mechanics try to anticipate trouble and service equipment before factory production is interrupted.

Working Conditions

In production facilities, these workers are subject to common shop injuries such as cuts, bruises, and strains. They also may work in awkward positions, including on top of ladders or in cramped conditions under large machinery, which exposes them to additional hazards. They often use protective equipment such as hardhats, safety glasses, steel-tipped shoes, hearing protectors, and belts.

Because factories and other facilities cannot afford to have industrial machinery out of service for long periods, mechanics may be called to the plant at night or on weekends for emergency repairs. Overtime is common among industrial machinery mechanics; about 30 percent work over 40 hours a week.

Training, Other Qualifications, and Advancement

Machinery maintenance workers typically receive short-term on-the-job training in order to perform routine tasks, such as setting up, cleaning, lubricating, and starting machinery. This training may be offered by experienced workers, professional trainers, or product representatives.

Industrial machinery mechanics, on the other hand, often learn their trade through 4-year apprenticeship programs that combine classroom instruction with on-the-job-training. These programs usually are sponsored by a local trade union. Other mechanics start as helpers and learn the skills of the trade informally or by taking courses offered by machinery manufacturers and community colleges.

Mechanics learn from experienced repairers how to operate, disassemble, repair, and assemble machinery. Classroom instruction focuses on subjects such as shop mathematics, blueprint reading, welding, electronics, and computer training.

Employers prefer to hire those who have completed high school or technical school and have taken courses in mechanical drawing, mathematics, blueprint reading, computers, and electronics. Mechanical aptitude and manual dexterity are important characteristics for workers in this trade. Good reading comprehension is also necessary to understand the technical manuals of a wide range of machines. And, in general, good physical conditioning and agility are necessary because repairers sometimes have to lift heavy objects or climb to reach equipment.

Opportunities for advancement vary by specialty. Machinery maintenance workers may gain additional skills to make more complex repairs to machinery or work as supervisors. Industrial machinery mechanics also may advance either by working with more complicated equipment or by becoming supervisors. The most highly skilled repairers can be promoted to master mechanic or can become millwrights.

Employment

Industrial machinery mechanics and maintenance workers held about 306,000 jobs in 2004. Of these, 220,000 were held by the more highly skilled industrial machinery mechanics, while machinery maintenance workers accounted for 86,000 jobs. Two out of three workers were employed in the manufacturing sector, in industries such as food processing, textile mills, chemicals, fabricated metal products, motor vehicles, and primary metals. Others worked for government agencies, public utilities, mining companies, and other establishments in which industrial machinery is used.

Job Outlook

Employment of industrial machinery mechanics and maintenance workers is projected to grow more slowly than the average for all occupations through 2014. Nevertheless, applicants with broad skills in machine repair and maintenance should have favorable job prospects. Many mechanics are expected to retire in coming years, and employers have reported difficulty in recruiting young workers with the necessary skills to be industrial machinery mechanics. Most job openings will stem from the need to replace workers who transfer to other occupations or who retire or leave the labor force for other reasons.

As more firms introduce automated production equipment, these workers will be needed to ensure that these machines are properly maintained and consistently in operation. However, many new machines are capable of self-diagnosis, increasing their reliability and somewhat reducing the need for repairers.

Industrial machinery mechanics and maintenance workers are not usually affected by changes in production. During slack periods, when some plant workers are laid off, mechanics often are retained to do major overhaul jobs and to keep expensive machinery in working order. Although these workers may face layoffs or a reduced workweek when economic conditions are particularly severe, they usually are less affected than other workers because machines have to be maintained regardless of production level.

Earnings

Median hourly earnings of industrial machinery mechanics were $18.78 in May 2004. The middle 50 percent earned between $15.09 and $22.95. The lowest 10 percent earned less than $12.14, and the highest 10 percent earned more than $27.59.

Machinery maintenance workers earned less than the higher-skilled industrial machinery mechanics. Median hourly earnings of machinery maintenance workers were $15.79 in May 2004. The middle 50 percent earned between $12.21 and $20.18. The lowest 10 percent earned less than $9.60, and the highest 10 percent earned more than $24.59.

Earnings vary by industry and geographic region. Median hourly earnings in the industries employing the largest numbers of industrial machinery mechanics in May 2004 were

Electric power generation, transmission, and
distribution $25.78

Motor vehicle parts manufacturing..........................21.79

Plastics product manufacturing 18.04

Machinery, equipment, and supplies merchant
wholesalers 17.74

Commercial and industrial machinery and equipment
(except automotive and electronic) repair and
maintenance 16.93

About 25 percent of industrial machinery mechanics and maintenance workers are union members. Labor unions that represent these workers include the United Steelworkers of America; the United Auto Workers; the International Association of Machinists and Aerospace Workers; the United Brotherhood of Carpenters and Joiners of America; and the International Union of Electronic, Electrical, Salaried, Machine, and Furniture Workers-Communications Workers of America.

Related Occupations

Other occupations that involve repairing and maintaining machinery include aircraft and avionics equipment mechanics and service technicians; automotive service technicians and mechanics; diesel service technicians and mechanics; elevator installers and repairers;

heating, air-conditioning, and refrigeration mechanics and installers; heavy vehicle and mobile equipment service technicians and mechanics; machinists; maintenance and repair workers, general; millwrights; and small engine mechanics.

Sources of Additional Information

Information about employment and apprenticeship opportunities may be obtained from local employers, from local offices of the state employment service, or from

▶ United Brotherhood of Carpenters and Joiners of America, 6801 Placid St., Las Vegas, NV 89119. Internet: http://www.carpenters.org

▶ National Tooling and Machining Association, 9300 Livingston Rd., Fort Washington, MD 20744. Internet: http://www.ntma.org

Licensed Practical and Licensed Vocational Nurses

(O*NET 29-2061.00)

Significant Points

■ Training lasting about 1 year is available in about 1,200 state-approved programs, mostly in vocational or technical schools.

■ Applicants for jobs in hospitals may face competition as the number of hospital jobs for licensed practical nurses declines; however, rapid employment growth is projected in other health care industries, with the best job opportunities occurring in nursing care facilities and in home health care services.

■ Replacement needs will be a major source of job openings, as many workers leave the occupation permanently.

Nature of the Work

Licensed practical nurses (LPNs) or licensed vocational nurses (LVNs) care for the sick, injured, convalescent, and disabled under the direction of physicians and registered nurses. (The work of physicians and surgeons and of registered nurses is described elsewhere in this book.)

Most LPNs provide basic bedside care, taking vital signs such as temperature, blood pressure, pulse, and respiration. They also prepare and give injections and enemas, monitor catheters, apply dressings, treat bedsores, and give alcohol rubs and massages. LPNs monitor their patients and report adverse reactions to medications or treatments. They collect samples for testing, perform routine laboratory tests, feed patients, and record food and fluid intake and output. To help keep patients comfortable, LPNs assist with bathing, dressing, and personal hygiene. In states where the law allows, they may administer prescribed medicines or start intravenous fluids. Some LPNs help to deliver, care for, and feed infants. Experienced LPNs may supervise nursing assistants and aides.

In addition to providing routine bedside care, LPNs in nursing care facilities help to evaluate residents' needs, develop care plans, and supervise the care provided by nursing aides. In doctors' offices and clinics, they also may make appointments, keep records, and perform other clerical duties. LPNs who work in private homes may prepare meals and teach family members simple nursing tasks.

Working Conditions

Most licensed practical nurses in hospitals and nursing care facilities work a 40-hour week, but because patients need round-the-clock care, some work nights, weekends, and holidays. They often stand for long periods and help patients move in bed, stand, or walk.

LPNs may face hazards from caustic chemicals, radiation, and infectious diseases such as hepatitis. They are subject to back injuries when moving patients and shock from electrical equipment. They often must deal with the stress of heavy workloads. In addition, the patients they care for may be confused, irrational, agitated, or uncooperative.

Training, Other Qualifications, and Advancement

All states and the District of Columbia require LPNs to pass a licensing examination, known as the NCLEX-PN, after completing a state-approved practical nursing program. A high school diploma or its equivalent usually is required for entry, although some programs accept candidates without a diploma and some are designed as part of a high school curriculum.

In 2004, approximately 1,200 state-approved programs provided training in practical nursing. Most training programs are available from technical and vocational schools or from community and junior colleges. Other programs are available through high schools, hospitals, and colleges and universities.

Most practical nursing programs last about 1 year and include both classroom study and supervised clinical practice (patient care). Classroom study covers basic nursing concepts and patient care–related subjects, including anatomy, physiology, medical-surgical nursing, pediatrics, obstetrics, psychiatric nursing, the administration of drugs, nutrition, and first aid. Clinical practice usually is in a hospital, but sometimes includes other settings.

In some employment settings, such as nursing homes, LPNs can advance to become charge nurses who oversee the work of other LPNs and of nursing aides. Some LPNs also choose to become registered nurses through numerous LPN-to-RN training programs.

LPNs should have a caring, sympathetic nature. They should be emotionally stable because working with the sick and injured can be stressful. They also should have keen observational, decision-making, and communication skills. As part of a health care team, they must be able to follow orders and work under close supervision.

Employment

Licensed practical nurses held about 726,000 jobs in 2004. About 27 percent of LPNs worked in hospitals, 25 percent in nursing care facilities, and another 12 percent in offices of physicians. Others worked for home health care services; employment services; community care facilities for the elderly; public and private educational services; outpatient care centers; and federal, state, and local government agencies. About 1 in 5 worked part time.

Job Outlook

Employment of LPNs is expected to grow about as fast as average for all occupations through 2014 in response to the long-term care needs of an increasing elderly population and the general growth of health care services. Replacement needs will be a major source of job openings, as many workers leave the occupation permanently. Applicants for jobs in hospitals may face competition as the number of hospital jobs for LPNs declines; however, rapid employment growth is projected in other health care industries, with the best job opportunities occurring in nursing care facilities and in home health care services.

Employment of LPNs in hospitals is expected to continue to decline. Sophisticated procedures once performed only in hospitals are being performed in physicians' offices and in outpatient care centers such as ambulatory surgical and emergency medical centers, largely because of advances in technology. Consequently, employment of LPNs in most health care industries outside the traditional hospital setting is projected to grow faster than average.

Employment of LPNs is expected to grow much faster than average in home health care services. Home health care agencies also will offer the most new jobs for LPNs because of an increasing number of older persons with functional disabilities, consumer preference for care in the home, and technological advances that make it possible to bring increasingly complex treatments into the home.

Employment of LPNs in nursing care facilities is expected to grow about as fast as average because of the growing number of aged and disabled persons in need of long-term care. In addition, LPNs in nursing care facilities will be needed to care for the increasing number of patients who have been discharged from the hospital but who have not recovered enough to return home. However, changes in consumer preferences towards less restrictive and more cost-effective care from assisted living facilities and home health care agencies will limit employment growth.

Earnings

Median annual earnings of licensed practical nurses were $33,970 in May 2004. The middle 50 percent earned between $28,830 and $40,670. The lowest 10 percent earned less than $24,480, and the highest 10 percent earned more than $46,270. Median annual earnings in the industries employing the largest numbers of licensed practical nurses in May 2004 were

Employment services	$41,550
Nursing care facilities	35,460
Home health care services	35,180
General medical and surgical hospitals	32,570
Offices of physicians	30,400

Related Occupations

LPNs work closely with people while helping them. So do emergency medical technicians and paramedics; medical assistants; nursing, psychiatric, and home health aides; registered nurses; social and human service assistants; and surgical technologists.

Sources of Additional Information

For information about practical nursing, contact any of the following organizations:

▶ National Association for Practical Nurse Education and Service, Inc., P.O. Box 25647, Alexandria, VA 22313. Internet: http://www.napnes.org

▶ National League for Nursing, 61 Broadway, New York, NY 10006. Internet: http://www.nln.org

▶ National Federation of Licensed Practical Nurses, Inc., 605 Poole Dr., Garner, NC 27529. Internet: http://www.nflpn.org

Information on the NCLEX-PN licensing exam is available from

▶ National Council of State Boards of Nursing, 111 East Wacker Dr., Suite 2900, Chicago, IL 60611. Internet: http://www.ncsbn.org

A list of state-approved LPN programs is available from individual state boards of nursing.

Machinists

(O*NET 51-4041.00)

Significant Points

■ Machinists learn in apprenticeship programs, informally on the job, and in vocational schools or community or technical colleges.

■ Many entrants previously have worked as machine setters, operators, or tenders.

■ Job opportunities are expected to be good.

Nature of the Work

Machinists use machine tools, such as lathes, milling machines, and machining centers, to produce precision metal parts. Although they may produce large quantities of one part, precision machinists often produce small batches or one-of-a-kind items. They use their knowledge of the working properties of metals and their skill with machine tools to plan and carry out the operations needed to make machined products that meet precise specifications.

Before they machine a part, machinists must carefully plan and prepare the operation. These workers first review electronic or written blueprints or specifications for a job. Next, they calculate where to cut or bore into the workpiece (the piece of steel, aluminum, titanium, plastic, silicon, or any other material that is being shaped), how fast to feed the workpiece into the machine, and how much material to remove. They then select tools and materials for the job, plan the sequence of cutting and finishing operations, and mark the workpiece to show where cuts should be made.

After this layout work is completed, machinists perform the necessary machining operations. They position the workpiece on the machine tool—drill press, lathe, milling machine, or other type of machine—set the controls, and make the cuts. During the machining process, they must constantly monitor the feed rate and speed of the machine. Machinists also ensure that the workpiece is being properly lubricated and cooled, because the machining of metal products generates a significant amount of heat. The temperature of the workpiece is a key concern because most metals expand when heated;

machinists must adjust the size of their cuts relative to the temperature. Some rare but increasingly popular metals, such as titanium, are machined at extremely high temperatures.

Machinists detect some problems by listening for specific sounds—for example, a dull cutting tool or excessive vibration. Dull cutting tools are removed and replaced. Cutting speeds are adjusted to compensate for harmonic vibrations, which can decrease the accuracy of cuts, particularly on newer high-speed spindles and lathes. After the work is completed, machinists use both simple and highly sophisticated measuring tools to check the accuracy of their work against blueprints.

Some machinists, often called *production machinists*, may produce large quantities of one part, especially parts requiring the use of complex operations and great precision. Many modern machine tools are computer numerically controlled (CNC). CNC machines, following a computer program, control the cutting tool speed, change dull tools, and perform all of the necessary cuts to create a part. Frequently, machinists work with computer control programmers to determine how the automated equipment will cut a part. (See the description of computer control programmers and operators elsewhere in this book.) The programmer may determine the path of the cut, while the machinist determines the type of cutting tool, the speed of the cutting tool, and the feed rate. Because most machinists train in CNC programming, they may write basic programs themselves and often set offsets (modify programs) in response to problems encountered during test runs. After the production process is designed, relatively simple and repetitive operations normally are performed by machine setters, operators, and tenders.

Some manufacturing techniques employ automated parts loaders, automatic tool changers, and computer controls, allowing machine tools to operate without anyone present. One production machinist, working 8 hours a day, might monitor equipment, replace worn cutting tools, check the accuracy of parts being produced, adjust offsets, and perform other tasks on several CNC machines that operate 24 hours a day (lights-out manufacturing). During lights-out manufacturing, a factory may need only a few machinists to monitor the entire factory.

Other machinists do maintenance work—repairing or making new parts for existing machinery. To repair a broken part, maintenance machinists may refer to blueprints and perform the same machining operations that were needed to create the original part.

Because the technology of machining is changing rapidly, machinists must learn to operate a wide range of machines. Along with operating machines that use metal cutting tools to shape workpieces, machinists operate machines that cut with lasers, water jets, or electrified wires. While some of the computer controls may be similar, machinists must understand the unique cutting properties of these different machines. As engineers create new types of machine tools and new materials to machine, machinists must constantly learn new machining properties and techniques.

Working Conditions

Today, most machine shops are relatively clean, well lit, and ventilated. Many computer-controlled machines are partially or totally enclosed, minimizing the exposure of workers to noise, debris, and the lubricants used to cool workpieces during machining. Nevertheless, working around machine tools presents certain dangers, and workers must follow safety precautions. Machinists wear protective equipment, such as safety glasses to shield against bits of flying metal and earplugs to dampen machinery noise. They also must exercise caution when handling hazardous coolants and lubricants, although many common water-based lubricants present little hazard. The job requires stamina, because machinists stand most of the day and, at times, may need to lift moderately heavy workpieces. Modern factories extensively employ autoloaders and overhead cranes, reducing heavy lifting.

Many machinists work a 40-hour week. Evening and weekend shifts are becoming more common as companies justify investments in more expensive machinery by extending hours of operation. However, this trend is somewhat offset by the increasing use of lights-out manufacturing and the use of machine operators for less desirable shifts. Overtime is common during peak production periods.

Training, Other Qualifications, and Advancement

Machinists train in apprenticeship programs, informally on the job, and in vocational schools or community or technical colleges. Experience with machine tools is helpful. In fact, many entrants previously have worked as machine setters, operators, or tenders. Persons interested in becoming machinists should be mechanically inclined, have good problem-solving abilities, be able to work independently, and be able to do highly accurate work (tolerances may reach 1/10,000th of an inch) that requires concentration and physical effort.

High school or vocational school courses in mathematics (especially trigonometry), blueprint reading, metalworking, and drafting are highly recommended. Apprenticeship programs consist of shop training and related classroom instruction lasting up to 4 years. In shop training, apprentices work almost full time and are supervised by an experienced machinist while learning to operate various machine tools. Classroom instruction includes math, physics, materials science, blueprint reading, mechanical drawing, and quality and safety practices. In addition, as machine shops have increased their use of computer-controlled equipment, training in the operation and programming of CNC machine tools has become essential. Apprenticeship classes are often taught in cooperation with local community or vocational colleges. A growing number of machinists learn the trade through 2-year associate degree programs at community or technical colleges. Graduates of these programs still need significant on-the-job experience before they are fully qualified.

To boost the skill level of machinists and to create a more uniform standard of competency, a number of training facilities and colleges are implementing curriculums that incorporate national skills standards developed by the National Institute of Metalworking Skills (NIMS). After completing such a curriculum and passing a performance requirement and written exam, trainees are granted a NIMS credential, which provides formal recognition of competency in a metalworking field. Completing a recognized certification program provides a machinist with better career opportunities.

As new automation is introduced, machinists normally receive additional training to update their skills. This training usually is provided by a representative of the equipment manufacturer or a local technical school. Some employers offer tuition reimbursement for job-related courses.

Machinists can advance in several ways. Experienced machinists may become CNC programmers, tool and die makers, or mold makers or be promoted to supervisory or administrative positions in their firms. A few open their own shops.

Employment

Machinists held about 370,000 jobs in 2004. Most machinists work in small machining shops or in manufacturing industries, such as machinery manufacturing and transportation equipment manufacturing (motor vehicle parts and aerospace products and parts). Maintenance machinists work in most industries that use production machinery.

Job Outlook

Despite relatively slow employment growth, job opportunities for machinists should continue to be good. Many young people with the necessary educational and personal qualifications needed to obtain machining skills often prefer to attend college or may not wish to enter production occupations. Therefore, the number of workers obtaining the skills and knowledge necessary to fill machinist jobs is expected to be less than the number of job openings arising each year from the need to replace experienced machinists who transfer to other occupations or retire and from job growth.

Employment of machinists is projected to grow more slowly than the average for all occupations over the 2004–2014 period because of rising productivity among these workers and strong foreign competition. Machinists will become more efficient as a result of the expanded use of and improvements in technologies such as CNC machine tools, autoloaders, and high-speed machining. This allows fewer machinists to accomplish the same amount of work previously performed by more workers. Technology is not expected to affect the employment of machinists as significantly as that of most other production occupations, however, because machinists monitor and maintain many automated systems. Due to modern production techniques, employers prefer workers, such as machinists, who have a wide range of skills and are capable of performing almost any task in a machine shop.

Employment levels in this occupation are influenced by economic cycles—as the demand for machined goods falls, machinists involved in production may be laid off or forced to work fewer hours. Employment of machinists involved in plant maintenance, however, often is more stable because proper maintenance and repair of costly equipment remain critical to manufacturing operations, even when production levels fall.

Earnings

Median hourly earnings of machinists were $16.33 in May 2004. The middle 50 percent earned between $12.84 and $20.33. The lowest 10 percent earned less than $10.08, while the top 10 percent earned more than $24.34. Median hourly earnings in the manufacturing industries employing the largest number of machinists in May 2004 were

Aerospace product and parts manufacturing $17.78

Motor vehicle parts manufacturing.........................17.46

Metalworking machinery manufacturing 17.06

Machine shops; turned product; and screw, nut,
and bolt manufacturing 15.87

Employment services 11.09

Apprentices earn much less than machinists, but earnings increase quickly as they improve their skills. Also, most employers pay for apprentices' training classes.

Related Occupations

Occupations most closely related to that of machinist are other machining occupations, which include tool and die makers; machine setters, operators, and tenders—metal and plastic; and computer control programmers and operators. Another occupation that requires precision and skill in working with metal is welding, soldering, and brazing workers.

Sources of Additional Information

For general information about machinists, contact

▸ Precision Machine Products Association, 6700 West Snowville Rd., Brecksville, OH 44141-3292. Internet: http://www.pmpa.org

For a list of training centers and apprenticeship programs, contact

▸ National Tooling and Machining Association, 9300 Livingston Rd., Fort Washington, MD 20744. Internet: http://www.ntma.org

For general occupational information and a list of training programs, contact

▸ Precision Metalforming Association Educational Foundation, 6363 Oak Tree Blvd., Independence, OH 44131-2500. Internet: http://www.pmaef.org

Mathematicians

(O*NET 15-2021.00)

Significant Points

■ A Ph.D. degree in mathematics usually is the minimum educational requirement, except in the federal government.

■ The number of jobs with the title "mathematician" is declining as the workforce becomes increasingly specialized; competition will be keen for the limited number of available jobs.

■ Master's and Ph.D. degree holders with a strong background in mathematics and a related field, such as computer science or engineering, should have better employment opportunities in related occupations.

Nature of the Work

Mathematics is one of the oldest and most fundamental sciences. Mathematicians use mathematical theory, computational techniques, algorithms, and the latest computer technology to solve economic, scientific, engineering, physics, and business problems. The work of mathematicians falls into two broad classes—theoretical (pure) mathematics and applied mathematics. These classes, however, are not sharply defined and often overlap.

Theoretical mathematicians advance mathematical knowledge by developing new principles and recognizing previously unknown relationships between existing principles of mathematics. Although these workers seek to increase basic knowledge without necessarily considering its practical use, such pure and abstract knowledge has been instrumental in producing or furthering many scientific and engineering achievements. Many theoretical mathematicians are employed as university faculty, dividing their time between teaching and conducting research. (See the description of teachers—postsecondary elsewhere in this book.)

Applied mathematicians, on the other hand, use theories and techniques, such as mathematical modeling and computational methods, to formulate and solve practical problems in business, government, and engineering and in the physical, life, and social sciences. For example, they may analyze the most efficient way to schedule airline routes between cities, the effects and safety of new drugs, the aerodynamic characteristics of an experimental automobile, or the cost-effectiveness of alternative manufacturing processes. Applied mathematicians working in industrial research and development may develop or enhance mathematical methods when solving a difficult problem. Some mathematicians, called cryptanalysts, analyze and decipher encryption systems designed to transmit military, political, financial, or law enforcement-related information in code.

Applied mathematicians start with a practical problem, envision the separate elements of the process under consideration, and then reduce the elements to mathematical variables. They often use computers to analyze relationships among the variables and solve complex problems by developing models with alternative solutions.

Much of the work in applied mathematics is done by individuals with titles other than mathematician. In fact, because mathematics is the foundation on which so many other academic disciplines are built, the number of workers using mathematical techniques is much greater than the number formally designated as mathematicians. For example, engineers, computer scientists, physicists, and economists are among those who use mathematics extensively. Some professionals, including statisticians, actuaries, and operations research analysts, actually are specialists in a particular branch of mathematics. Frequently, applied mathematicians are required to collaborate with other workers in their organizations to achieve common solutions to problems. (For more information, see the descriptions of actuaries, operations research analysts, and statisticians elsewhere in this book.)

Working Conditions

Mathematicians usually work in comfortable offices. They often are part of interdisciplinary teams that may include economists, engineers, computer scientists, physicists, technicians, and others. Deadlines, overtime work, special requests for information or analysis, and prolonged travel to attend seminars or conferences may be part of their jobs. Mathematicians who work in academia usually have a mix of teaching and research responsibilities. These mathematicians may conduct research alone or in close collaboration with other mathematicians. Collaborators may work together at the same institution or from different locations, using technology such as e-mail to communicate. Mathematicians in academia also may be aided by graduate students.

Training, Other Qualifications, and Advancement

A Ph.D. degree in mathematics usually is the minimum educational requirement for prospective mathematicians, except in the federal government. In the federal government, entry-level job candidates usually must have a 4-year degree with a major in mathematics or a 4-year degree with the equivalent of a mathematics major—24 semester hours of mathematics courses.

In private industry, candidates for mathematician jobs typically need a Ph.D., although there may be opportunities for those with a master's degree. Most of the positions designated for mathematicians are in research and development laboratories as part of technical teams. In such settings, mathematicians engage either in basic research on pure mathematical principles or in applied research on developing or improving specific products or processes. The majority of those with a bachelor's or master's degree in mathematics who work in private industry do so not as mathematicians but in related fields such as computer science, where they have titles such as computer programmer, systems analyst, or systems engineer.

A bachelor's degree in mathematics is offered by most colleges and universities. Mathematics courses usually required for this degree include calculus, differential equations, and linear and abstract algebra. Additional courses might include probability theory and statistics, mathematical analysis, numerical analysis, topology, discrete mathematics, and mathematical logic. Many colleges and universities urge or require students majoring in mathematics to take courses in a field that is closely related to mathematics, such as computer science, engineering, life science, physical science, or economics. A double major in mathematics and another related discipline is particularly desirable to many employers. High school students who are prospective college mathematics majors should take as many mathematics courses as possible while in high school.

In 2004, about 200 colleges and universities offered a master's degree as the highest degree in either pure or applied mathematics; about 200 offered a Ph.D. degree in pure or applied mathematics. In graduate school, students conduct research and take advanced courses, usually specializing in a subfield of mathematics.

For jobs in applied mathematics, training in the field in which the mathematics will be used is very important. Mathematics is used extensively in physics, actuarial science, statistics, engineering, and operations research. Computer science, business and industrial management, economics, finance, chemistry, geology, life sciences, and behavioral sciences are likewise dependent on applied mathematics. Mathematicians also should have substantial knowledge of computer programming because most complex mathematical computation and much mathematical modeling are done on a computer.

Mathematicians need good reasoning ability and persistence to identify, analyze, and apply basic principles to technical problems. Communication skills also are important, as mathematicians must be able to interact and discuss proposed solutions with people who may not have extensive knowledge of mathematics.

Employment

Mathematicians held about 2,500 jobs in 2004. Many people with mathematical backgrounds also worked in other occupations. For example, about 53,000 persons held positions as postsecondary mathematical science teachers in 2004.

Many mathematicians work for federal or state governments. The U.S. Department of Defense is the primary federal employer, accounting for about three-fourths of the mathematicians employed by the federal government. Many of the other mathematicians employed by the federal government work for the National Aeronautics and Space Administration (NASA). In the private sector, major employers include scientific research and development services and management, scientific, and technical consulting services. Some mathematicians also work for software publishers, for insurance companies, and in aerospace or pharmaceutical manufacturing.

Job Outlook

Employment of mathematicians is expected to decline through 2014, reflecting the reduction in the number of jobs with the title "mathematician." As a result, competition is expected to be keen for the limited number of jobs as mathematicians. Master's and Ph.D. degree holders with a strong background in mathematics and a related discipline, such as engineering or computer science, should have the best opportunities. Many of these workers have job titles that reflect their occupation, such as systems analyst, rather than the title mathematician, reflecting their primary educational background.

Advancements in technology usually lead to expanding applications of mathematics, and more workers with knowledge of mathematics will be required in the future. However, jobs in industry and government often require advanced knowledge of related scientific disciplines in addition to mathematics. The most common fields in which mathematicians study and find work are computer science and software development, physics, engineering, and operations research. More mathematicians also are becoming involved in financial analysis. Mathematicians must compete for jobs, however, with people who have degrees in these other disciplines. The most successful jobseekers will be able to apply mathematical theory to real-world problems and will possess good communication, teamwork, and computer skills.

Private industry jobs require at least a master's degree in mathematics or in a related field. Bachelor's degree holders in mathematics usually are not qualified for most jobs, and many seek advanced degrees in mathematics or a related discipline. However, bachelor's degree holders who meet state certification requirements may become primary or secondary school mathematics teachers.

Holders of a master's degree in mathematics will face very strong competition for jobs in theoretical research. Because the number of Ph.D. degrees awarded in mathematics continues to exceed the number of university positions available, many of these graduates will need to find employment in industry and government.

Earnings

Median annual earnings of mathematicians were $81,240 in May 2004. The middle 50 percent earned between $60,050 and $101,360.

The lowest 10 percent had earnings of less than $43,160, while the highest 10 percent earned over $120,900.

In early 2005, the average annual salary for mathematicians employed by the federal government in supervisory, nonsupervisory, and managerial positions was $88,194; that for mathematical statisticians was $91,446; and for cryptanalysts the average was $70,774.

Related Occupations

Other occupations that require extensive knowledge of mathematics or, in some cases, a degree in mathematics include actuaries, statisticians, computer programmers, computer systems analysts, computer scientists and database administrators, computer software engineers, and operations research analysts. A strong background in mathematics also facilitates employment as teachers—postsecondary; teachers—preschool, kindergarten, elementary, middle, and secondary; engineers; economists; market and survey researchers; financial analysts and personal financial advisors; and physicists and astronomers.

Sources of Additional Information

For more information about careers and training in mathematics, especially for doctoral-level employment, contact

▸ American Mathematical Society, 201 Charles St., Providence, RI 02904-2294. Internet: http://www.ams.org

For specific information on careers in applied mathematics, contact

▸ Society for Industrial and Applied Mathematics, 3600 University City Science Center, Philadelphia, PA 19104-2688. Internet: http://www.siam.org

Information on obtaining positions as mathematicians with the federal government is available from the Office of Personnel Management through USAJOBS, the federal government's official employment information system. This resource for locating and applying for job opportunities can be accessed through the Internet at http://www.usajobs.opm.gov or through an interactive voice response telephone system at (703) 724-1850 or TDD (978) 461-8404. These numbers are not toll free, and charges may result.

Medical Records and Health Information Technicians

(O*NET 29-2071.00)

Significant Points

- Employment is expected to grow much faster than average.
- Job prospects should be very good; technicians with a strong background in medical coding will be in particularly high demand.
- Entrants usually have an associate degree; courses include anatomy, physiology, medical terminology, statistics, and computer science.
- This is one of the few health occupations in which there is little or no direct contact with patients.

Nature of the Work

Every time a patient receives health care, a record is maintained of the observations, medical or surgical interventions, and treatment outcomes. This record includes information that the patient provides concerning his or her symptoms and medical history, the results of examinations, reports of X rays and laboratory tests, diagnoses, and treatment plans. Medical records and health information technicians organize and evaluate these records for completeness and accuracy.

Technicians assemble patients' health information. They make sure that patients' initial medical charts are complete, that all forms are completed and properly identified and signed, and that all necessary information is in the computer. They regularly communicate with physicians and other health care professionals to clarify diagnoses or to obtain additional information.

Some medical records and health information technicians specialize in coding patients' medical information for insurance purposes. Technicians who specialize in coding are called *health information coders*, *medical record coders*, *coder/abstractors*, or *coding specialists*. These technicians assign a code to each diagnosis and procedure. They consult classification manuals and also rely on their knowledge of disease processes. Technicians then use computer software to assign the patient to one of several hundred "diagnosis-related groups," or DRGs. The DRG determines the amount for which the hospital will be reimbursed if the patient is covered by Medicare or other insurance programs using the DRG system. In addition to the DRG system, coders use other coding systems, such as those geared toward ambulatory settings or long-term care.

Some technicians also use computer programs to tabulate and analyze data to improve patient care, control costs, provide documentation for use in legal actions, respond to surveys, or use in research studies. For example, *cancer* (or tumor) *registrars* maintain facility, regional, and national databases of cancer patients. Registrars review patient records and pathology reports and assign codes for the diagnosis and treatment of different cancers and selected benign tumors. Registrars conduct annual followups on all patients in the registry to track their treatment, survival, and recovery. Physicians and public health organizations then use this information to calculate survivor rates and success rates of various types of treatment, locate geographic areas with high incidences of certain cancers, and identify potential participants for clinical drug trials. Cancer registry data also is used by public health officials to target areas for the allocation of resources to provide intervention and screening.

Medical records and health information technicians' duties vary with the size of the facility where they work. In large to medium-sized facilities, technicians might specialize in one aspect of health information or might supervise health information clerks and transcriptionists while a medical records and health information administrator manages the department. In small facilities, a credentialed medical records and health information technician sometimes manages the department.

Working Conditions

Medical records and health information technicians usually work a 40-hour week. Some overtime may be required. In hospitals—where health information departments often are open 24 hours a day, 7 days a week—technicians may work day, evening, and night shifts.

Medical records and health information technicians work in pleasant and comfortable offices. This is one of the few health occupations in which there is little or no direct contact with patients. Because accuracy is essential in their jobs, technicians must pay close attention to detail. Technicians who work at computer monitors for prolonged periods must guard against eyestrain and muscle pain.

Training, Other Qualifications, and Advancement

Medical records and health information technicians entering the field usually have an associate degree from a community or junior college. In addition to general education, coursework includes medical terminology, anatomy and physiology, legal aspects of health information, coding and abstraction of data, statistics, database management, quality improvement methods, and computer science. Applicants can improve their chances of admission into a program by taking biology, chemistry, health, and computer science courses in high school.

Hospitals sometimes advance promising health information clerks to jobs as medical records and health information technicians, although this practice may be less common in the future. Advancement usually requires 2 to 4 years of job experience and completion of a hospital's in-house training program.

Most employers prefer to hire Registered Health Information Technicians (RHIT), who must pass a written examination offered by the American Health Information Management Association (AHIMA). To take the examination, a person must graduate from a 2-year associate degree program accredited by the Commission on Accreditation for Health Informatics and Information Management Education (CAHIIM). Technicians trained in non–CAHIIM-accredited programs or trained on the job are not eligible to take the examination. In 2005, CAHIIM accredited 184 programs for health information technicians.

Experienced medical records and health information technicians usually advance in one of two ways—by specializing or managing. Many senior technicians specialize in coding, particularly Medicare coding, or in cancer registry. Most coding and registry skills are learned on the job. Some schools offer certificates in coding as part of the associate degree program for health information technicians, although there are no formal degree programs in coding. For cancer registry, there were 11 formal 2-year certificate programs in 2005 approved by the National Cancer Registrars Association (NCRA). Some schools and employers offer intensive 1- to 2-week training programs in either coding or cancer registry. Once coders and registrars gain some on-the-job experience, many choose to become certified. Certifications in coding are available either from AHIMA or from the American Academy of Professional Coders. Certification in cancer registry is available from the NCRA.

In large medical records and health information departments, experienced technicians may advance to section supervisor, overseeing the work of the coding, correspondence, or discharge sections, for example. Senior technicians with RHIT credentials may become director or assistant director of a medical records and health infor-

mation department in a small facility. However, in larger institutions, the director usually is an administrator with a bachelor's degree in medical records and health information administration.

Employment

Medical records and health information technicians held about 159,000 jobs in 2004. About 2 out of 5 jobs were in hospitals. The rest were mostly in offices of physicians, nursing care facilities, outpatient care centers, and home health care services. Insurance firms that deal in health matters employ a small number of health information technicians to tabulate and analyze health information. Public health departments also hire technicians to supervise data collection from health care institutions and to assist in research.

Job Outlook

Job prospects should be very good. Employment of medical records and health information technicians is expected to grow much faster than the average for all occupations through 2014 because of rapid growth in the number of medical tests, treatments, and procedures that will be increasingly scrutinized by health insurance companies, regulators, courts, and consumers. Also, technicians will be needed to enter patient information into computer databases to comply with federal legislation mandating the use of electronic patient records.

Although employment growth in hospitals will not keep pace with growth in other health care industries, many new jobs will, nevertheless, be created. The majority of new jobs is expected in offices of physicians as a result of increasing demand for detailed records, especially in large group practices. Rapid growth also is expected in home health care services, outpatient care centers, and nursing and residential care facilities. Additional job openings will result from the need to replace technicians who retire or leave the occupation permanently.

Technicians with a strong background in medical coding will be in particularly high demand. Changing government regulations and the growth of managed care have increased the amount of paperwork involved in filing insurance claims. Additionally, health care facilities are having difficulty attracting qualified workers, primarily because of the lack of both formal training programs and sufficient resources to provide on-the-job training for coders. Job opportunities may be especially good for coders employed through temporary help agencies or by professional services firms.

Some cancer registrars may have difficulty finding open positions in their geographic area because of a limited number of registrars employed by health care facilities and low job turnover. However, when a position does become vacant, qualified cancer registrars have excellent prospects because of the limited number of trained registrars available for employment.

Earnings

Median annual earnings of medical records and health information technicians were $25,590 in 2004. The middle 50 percent earned between $20,650 and $32,990. The lowest 10 percent earned less than $17,720, and the highest 10 percent earned more than $41,760. Median annual earnings in the industries employing the largest numbers of medical records and health information technicians in 2004 were as follows:

General medical and surgical hospitals	$26,640
Nursing care facilities	26,330
Outpatient care centers	23,870
Offices of physicians	22,130

Related Occupations

Medical records and health information technicians need a strong clinical background to analyze the contents of medical records. Other workers who need knowledge of medical terminology, anatomy, and physiology but have little or no direct contact with patients include medical secretaries and medical transcriptionists.

Sources of Additional Information

Information on careers in medical records and health information technology, including a list of programs accredited by CAHIIM, is available from

▶ American Health Information Management Association, 233 N. Michigan Ave., Suite 2150, Chicago, IL 60601-5800. Internet: http://www.ahima.org

Information on training and certification for medical coders is available from

▶ American Academy of Professional Coders, P.O. Box 45855, Salt Lake City, UT 84145-0855.

Information on a career as a cancer registrar is available from

▶ National Cancer Registrars Association, 1340 Braddock Pl. #203, Alexandria, VA 22314. Internet: http://www.ncra-usa.org

Medical Scientists

(O*NET 19-1041.00 and 19-1042.00)

Significant Points

■ Most medical scientists work in research and development.

■ Most medical scientists need a Ph.D. degree in a biological science; however, epidemiologists typically require a master's degree in public health or, in some cases, a Ph.D. or medical degree.

■ Despite projected rapid job growth, competition is expected for most positions.

Nature of the Work

Medical scientists research human diseases in order to improve human health. Most medical scientists conduct biomedical research and development to advance knowledge of life processes and living organisms, including viruses, bacteria, and other infectious agents. Past research has resulted in advances in diagnosis, treatment, and prevention of many diseases. Basic medical research continues to provide the building blocks necessary to develop solutions to human health problems, such as vaccines and medicines. Medical scientists

also engage in clinical investigation, technical writing, drug application review, patent examination, and related activities.

Medical scientists study biological systems to understand the causes of disease and other health problems and to develop treatments and research tools and techniques, many of which have medical applications. These scientists try to identify changes in a cell or in chromosomes that signal the development of medical problems, such as different types of cancer. For example, medical scientists involved in cancer research may formulate a combination of drugs that will lessen the effects of the disease. Medical scientists who are also physicians can administer these drugs to patients in clinical trials, monitor their reactions, and observe the results. Those who are not physicians normally collaborate with a physician who deals directly with patients. Medical scientists examine the results of clinical trials and, if necessary, adjust the dosage levels to reduce negative side effects or to try to induce even better results. In addition to developing treatments for health problems, medical scientists attempt to discover ways to prevent health problems—for example, by affirming the link between smoking and lung cancer or between alcoholism and liver disease.

Many medical scientists work independently in private industry, university, or government laboratories, often exploring new areas of research or expanding on specialized research that they began in graduate school. Medical scientists working in colleges and universities, hospitals, and nonprofit medical research organizations typically submit grant proposals to obtain funding for their projects. Colleges and universities; private industry; and federal government agencies, such as the National Institutes of Health and the National Science Foundation, contribute greatly to the support of scientists whose research proposals are determined to be financially feasible and to have the potential to advance new ideas or processes.

Medical scientists who work in applied research or product development use knowledge discovered through basic research to develop new drugs and medical treatments. They usually have less autonomy than basic medical researchers to choose the emphasis of their research, relying instead on market-driven forces arising from their firm's products and goals. Medical scientists doing applied research and product development in private industry may be required to express their research plans or results to nonscientists who are in a position to reject or approve their ideas; thus, they must understand the impact of their work on business. Scientists increasingly work as part of teams, interacting with engineers, scientists of other disciplines, business managers, and technicians.

Medical scientists who conduct research usually work in laboratories and use electron microscopes, computers, thermal cyclers, or a wide variety of other equipment. Some may work directly with individual patients or larger groups as they administer drugs and monitor and observe the patients during clinical trials. Medical scientists who are also physicians may administer gene therapy to human patients, draw blood, excise tissue, or perform other invasive procedures.

Some medical scientists work in managerial, consulting, or administrative positions, usually after spending some time doing research and learning about the firm, agency, or project. In the 1980s, swift advances in basic medical knowledge related to genetics and molecules spurred growth in the field of biotechnology. Medical scientists using this technology manipulate the genetic material of animals, attempting to make organisms more productive or resistant to disease. Research using biotechnology techniques, such as recombining DNA, has led to the discovery of important drugs, including human insulin and growth hormone. Many other substances not previously available in large quantities are now produced by biotechnological means; some may one day be useful in treating diseases such as Parkinson's or Alzheimer's. Today, many medical scientists are involved in the science of genetic engineering—isolating, identifying, and sequencing human genes and then determining their function. This work continues to lead to the discovery of the genes associated with specific diseases and inherited traits, such as certain types of cancer or obesity. These advances in biotechnology have opened up research opportunities in almost all areas of medical science.

Some medical scientists specialize in epidemiology. This branch of medical science investigates and describes the determinants of disease, disability, and other health outcomes and develops the means for prevention and control. Epidemiologists may study many different diseases, such as tuberculosis, influenza, or cholera, often focusing on epidemics.

Epidemiologists can be separated into two groups—research and clinical. *Research epidemiologists* conduct research in an effort to eradicate or control infectious diseases that affect the entire body, such as AIDS or typhus. Others may focus only on localized infections of the brain, lungs, or digestive tract, for example. Research epidemiologists work at colleges and universities, schools of public health, medical schools, and research and development services firms. For example, federal government agencies, such as the U.S. Department of Defense, may contract with a research firm's epidemiologists to evaluate the incidence of malaria in certain parts of the world. While some perform consulting services, other research epidemiologists may work as college and university faculty.

Clinical epidemiologists work primarily in consulting roles at hospitals, informing the medical staff of infectious outbreaks and providing containment solutions. These epidemiologists sometimes are referred to as infection control professionals, and some of them are also physicians. Epidemiologists who are not physicians often collaborate with physicians to find ways to contain diseases and outbreaks. In addition to traditional duties of studying and controlling diseases, clinical epidemiologists also may be required to develop standards and guidelines for the treatment and control of communicable diseases. Some clinical epidemiologists may work in outpatient settings.

Working Conditions

Medical scientists typically work regular hours in offices or laboratories and usually are not exposed to unsafe or unhealthy conditions. However, those scientists who work with dangerous organisms or toxic substances in the laboratory must follow strict safety procedures to avoid contamination. Medical scientists also spend time working in clinics and hospitals administering drugs and treatments to patients in clinical trials. On occasion, epidemiologists may be required to work evenings and weekends to attend meetings and hearings for medical investigations.

Some medical scientists depend on grant money to support their research. They may be under pressure to meet deadlines and to con-

form to rigid grant-writing specifications when preparing proposals to seek new or extended funding.

Training, Other Qualifications, and Advancement

A Ph.D. degree in a biological science is the minimum education required for most prospective medical scientists, except epidemiologists, because the work of medical scientists is almost entirely research oriented. A Ph.D. degree qualifies one to do research on basic life processes or on particular medical problems or diseases and to analyze and interpret the results of experiments on patients. Some medical scientists obtain a medical degree instead of a Ph.D., but may not be licensed physicians because they have not taken the state licensing examination or completed a residency program, typically because they prefer research to clinical practice. Medical scientists who administer drug or gene therapy to human patients, or who otherwise interact medically with patients—drawing blood, excising tissue, or performing other invasive procedures—must be licensed physicians. To be licensed, physicians must graduate from an accredited medical school, pass a licensing examination, and complete 1 to 7 years of graduate medical education. (See physicians and surgeons elsewhere in this book.) It is particularly helpful for medical scientists to earn both Ph.D. and medical degrees.

Students planning careers as medical scientists should have a bachelor's degree in a biological science. In addition to required courses in chemistry and biology, undergraduates should study allied disciplines, such as mathematics, engineering, physics, and computer science, or courses in their field of interest. Once they have completed undergraduate studies, they can then select a specialty area for their advanced degree, such as cytology, bioinformatics, genomics, or pathology. In addition to formal education, medical scientists usually spend several years in a postdoctoral position before they apply for permanent jobs. Postdoctoral work provides valuable laboratory experience, including experience in specific processes and techniques such as gene splicing, which is transferable to other research projects. In some institutions, the postdoctoral position can lead to a permanent job.

Medical scientists should be able to work independently or as part of a team and be able to communicate clearly and concisely, both orally and in writing. Those in private industry, especially those who aspire to consulting and administrative positions, should possess strong communication skills so that they can provide instruction and advice to physicians and other health care professionals.

The minimum educational requirement for epidemiology is a master's degree from a school of public health. Some jobs require a Ph.D. or medical degree, depending on the work performed. Epidemiologists who work in hospitals and health care centers often must have a medical degree with specific training in infectious diseases. Currently, about 140 infectious disease training programs exist in 42 states. Some employees in research epidemiology positions are required to be licensed physicians because they must administer drugs in clinical trials.

Epidemiologists who perform laboratory tests often require the knowledge and expertise of a licensed physician in order to administer drugs to patients in clinical trials. Epidemiologists who are not physicians frequently work closely with one.

Few students select epidemiology for undergraduate study. Undergraduates, nonetheless, should study biological sciences and should have a solid background in chemistry, mathematics, and computer science. Once a student is prepared for graduate studies, he or she can choose a specialty within epidemiology. For example, those interested in studying environmental epidemiology should focus on environmental coursework, such as water pollution, air pollution, or pesticide use. The core work of environmental studies includes toxicology and molecular biology, and students may continue with advanced coursework in environmental or occupational epidemiology. Other specialty areas that students can pursue include infectious process, infection control precautions, surveillance methodology, and outbreak investigation. Some epidemiologists begin their careers in other health care occupations, such as registered nurse and medical technologist.

The Association for Professionals in Infection Control and Epidemiology (APIC) offers continuing-education courses and certification programs in infection prevention and control and applied epidemiology. To become certified as an infection control professional, applicants are required by a certified board to pass an examination for a one-time fee. Certification is recommended for those seeking advancement and for those seeking to continually upgrade their knowledge in a rapidly evolving field.

Employment

Medical scientists held about 77,000 jobs in 2004. Epidemiologists accounted for only 4,800 of that total. In addition, many medical scientists held faculty positions in colleges and universities, but they are classified as college or university faculty. (See teachers—postsecondary elsewhere in this book.)

About 24 percent of medical scientists were employed in government; 24 percent were employed in scientific research and development services firms; 14 percent were employed in pharmaceutical and medicine manufacturing; 9 percent were employed in private hospitals; and most of the remainder were employed in private educational services and ambulatory health care services.

Among epidemiologists, 50 percent were employed in government; 23 percent were employed in management, scientific, and technical consulting services; 12 percent were employed in scientific research and development services; and 8 percent were employed in private hospitals.

Job Outlook

Employment of medical scientists is expected to grow much faster than average for all occupations through 2014. Despite projected rapid job growth, doctoral degree holders can expect to face considerable competition for basic research positions. The federal government funds much basic research and development, including many areas of medical research. Recent budget increases at the National Institutes of Health have led to large increases in federal basic research and development expenditures, with the number of grants awarded to researchers growing in number and dollar amount. However, the increase in expenditures is expected to slow significantly over the 2004–2014 projection period, resulting in a highly competitive environment for winning and renewing research grants. In addition, if the number of advanced degrees awarded continues to grow, applicants are likely to face even more competition.

Medical scientists enjoyed rapid gains in employment between the mid-1980s and mid-1990s—reflecting, in part, increased staffing requirements in new biotechnology companies. Job growth should be dampened somewhat as increases in the number of new biotechnology firms slow down and as existing firms merge or are absorbed by larger, more established biotechnology or pharmaceutical firms. However, much of the basic medical research done in recent years has resulted in new knowledge, including the isolation and identification of new genes. Medical scientists will be needed to take this knowledge to the next stage—understanding how certain genes function within an entire organism—so that gene therapies can be developed to treat diseases. Even pharmaceutical and other firms not solely engaged in biotechnology are expected to increasingly use biotechnology techniques, thus creating employment for medical scientists.

Expected expansion in research related to health issues such as AIDS, cancer, and Alzheimer's disease, along with treating growing threats such as the increase in antibiotic resistance, also should result in employment growth. Moreover, environmental conditions such as overcrowding and the increasing frequency of international travel will tend to spread existing diseases and give rise to new ones. Medical scientists will continue to be needed because they greatly contribute to the development of many treatments and medicines that improve human health.

Opportunities in epidemiology also should be highly competitive, as the number of available positions remains limited. However, an increasing focus on monitoring patients at hospitals and health care centers to ensure positive patient outcomes will contribute to job growth. In addition, a heightened awareness of bioterrorism and rare, but infectious, diseases such as West Nile Virus or severe acute respiratory syndrome (SARS) should spur demand for these workers. As hospitals enhance their infection control programs, many will seek to boost the quality and quantity of their staff. Besides job openings due to employment growth, additional openings will result as workers leave the labor force or transfer to other occupations.

Medical scientists and some epidemiologists are less likely to lose their jobs during recessions than are those in many other occupations because they are employed on long-term research projects. However, a recession could influence the amount of money allocated to new research and development, particularly in areas of risky or innovative medical research. A recession also could limit extensions or renewals of existing projects.

Earnings

Median annual earnings of medical scientists, except epidemiologists, were $61,320 in May 2004. The middle 50 percent of these workers earned between $44,120 and $86,830. The lowest 10 percent earned less than $33,030, and the highest 10 percent earned more than $114,360. Median annual earnings in the industries employing the largest numbers of medical scientists in May 2004 were

Pharmaceutical and medicine manufacturing $76,800

Scientific research and development services 65,110

General medical and surgical hospitals 55,410

Colleges, universities, and professional schools 45,600

Median annual earnings of epidemiologists were $54,800 in May 2004. The middle 50 percent earned between $45,320 and $67,160. The lowest 10 percent earned less than $36,130, and the highest 10 percent earned more than $82,310.

Related Occupations

Many other occupations deal with living organisms and require a level of training similar to that of medical scientists. These occupations include biological scientists; agricultural and food scientists; and health occupations such as physicians and surgeons, dentists, and veterinarians.

Sources of Additional Information

For a brochure entitled *Is a Career in the Pharmaceutical Sciences Right for Me*, contact

▸ American Association of Pharmaceutical Scientists (AAPS), 2107 Wilson Blvd., Suite 700, Arlington, VA 22201.

For a career brochure entitled *A Million and One*, contact

▸ American Society for Microbiology, Career Information—Education Department, 1752 N St. NW, Washington, DC 20036-2804. Internet: http://www.asm.org

For information on infectious diseases training programs, contact

▸ Infectious Diseases Society of America, Guide to Training Programs, 66 Canal Center Plaza, Suite 600, Alexandria, VA 22314. Internet: http://www.idsociety.org

Information on obtaining a medical scientist position with the federal government is available from the Office of Personnel Management through USAJOBS, the federal government's official employment information system. This resource for locating and applying for job opportunities can be accessed through the Internet at http://www.usajobs.opm.gov or through an interactive voice response telephone system at (703) 724-1850 or TDD (978) 461-8404. These numbers are not toll free, and charges may result.

Medical Transcriptionists

(O*NET 31-9094.00)

Significant Points

■ Job opportunities will be good.

■ Employers prefer medical transcriptionists who have completed a postsecondary training program at a vocational school or community college.

■ Many medical transcriptionists telecommute from home-based offices as employees or subcontractors for hospitals and transcription services or as self-employed independent contractors.

■ About 4 out of 10 work in hospitals and another 3 out of 10 work in offices of physicians.

Nature of the Work

Medical transcriptionists listen to dictated recordings made by physicians and other health care professionals and transcribe them into medical reports, correspondence, and other administrative material. They generally listen to recordings on a headset, using a foot pedal to pause the recording when necessary, and key the text into a personal computer or word processor, editing as necessary for grammar and clarity. The documents they produce include discharge summaries, history and physical examination reports, operative reports, consultation reports, autopsy reports, diagnostic imaging studies, progress notes, and referral letters. Medical transcriptionists return transcribed documents to the physicians or other health care professionals who dictated them for review and signature or correction. These documents eventually become part of patients' permanent files.

To understand and accurately transcribe dictated reports into a format that is clear and comprehensible for the reader, medical transcriptionists must understand medical terminology, anatomy and physiology, diagnostic procedures, pharmacology, and treatment assessments. They also must be able to translate medical jargon and abbreviations into their expanded forms. To help identify terms appropriately, transcriptionists refer to standard medical reference materials—both printed and electronic; some of these are available over the Internet. Medical transcriptionists must comply with specific standards that apply to the style of medical records in addition to the legal and ethical requirements involved with keeping patient information confidential.

Experienced transcriptionists spot mistakes or inconsistencies in a medical report and check to correct the information. Their ability to understand and correctly transcribe patient assessments and treatments reduces the chance of patients receiving ineffective or even harmful treatments and ensures high-quality patient care.

Currently, most health care providers transmit dictation to medical transcriptionists using either digital or analog dictating equipment. The Internet has grown to be a popular mode for transmitting documentation. Many transcriptionists receive dictation over the Internet and are able to quickly return transcribed documents to clients for approval. Another increasingly popular method utilizes speech recognition technology, which electronically translates sound into text and creates drafts of reports. Reports are then formatted; edited for mistakes in translation, punctuation, or grammar; and checked for consistency and any possible medical errors. Transcriptionists working in areas with standardized terminology, such as radiology or pathology, are more likely to encounter speech recognition technology. However, use of speech recognition technology will become more widespread as the technology becomes more sophisticated.

Medical transcriptionists who work in physicians' offices may have other office duties, such as receiving patients, scheduling appointments, answering the telephone, and handling incoming and outgoing mail. Medical secretaries also may transcribe as part of their jobs. Court reporters have similar duties, but with a different focus. They take verbatim reports of speeches, conversations, legal proceedings, meetings, and other events when written accounts of spoken words are necessary for correspondence, records, or legal proof.

Working Conditions

The majority of these workers are employed in comfortable settings, such as hospitals, physicians' offices, transcription service offices, clinics, laboratories, medical libraries, government medical facilities, or their own homes. Many medical transcriptionists telecommute from home-based offices as employees or subcontractors for hospitals and transcription services or as self-employed independent contractors.

Work in this occupation presents hazards from sitting in the same position for long periods. Workers can suffer wrist, back, neck, or eye problems due to strain and risk repetitive motion injuries such as carpal tunnel syndrome. The constant pressure to be accurate and productive also can be stressful.

Many medical transcriptionists work a standard 40-hour week. Self-employed medical transcriptionists are more likely to work irregular hours—including part time, evenings, weekends, or on call at any time.

Training, Other Qualifications, and Advancement

Employers prefer to hire transcriptionists who have completed post-secondary training in medical transcription, which is offered by many vocational schools, community colleges, and distance-learning programs. Completion of a 2-year associate degree or 1-year certificate program—including coursework in anatomy, medical terminology, legal issues relating to health care documentation, and English grammar and punctuation—is highly recommended, but not always required. Many of these programs include supervised on-the-job experience. Some transcriptionists, especially those already familiar with medical terminology from previous experience as a nurse or medical secretary, become proficient through refresher courses and training.

The American Association for Medical Transcription (AAMT) awards the voluntary designation Certified Medical Transcriptionist (CMT) to those who earn a passing score on a certification examination. As in many other fields, certification is recognized as a sign of competence. Because medicine is constantly evolving, medical transcriptionists are encouraged to update their skills regularly. Every 3 years, CMTs must earn continuing education credits to be recertified.

In addition to understanding medical terminology, transcriptionists must have good English grammar and punctuation skills, as well as proficiency with personal computers and word processing software. Normal hearing acuity and good listening skills also are necessary. Employers require applicants to take pre-employment tests and usually prefer individuals with experience.

With experience, medical transcriptionists can advance to supervisory positions, home-based work, editing, consulting, or teaching. With additional education or training, some become medical records and health information technicians, medical coders, or medical records and health information administrators.

Employment

Medical transcriptionists held about 105,000 jobs in 2004. About 4 out of 10 worked in hospitals and another 3 out of 10 worked in offices of physicians. Others worked for business support services; medical and diagnostic laboratories; outpatient care centers; and offices of physical, occupational and speech therapists and audiologists.

Job Outlook

Job opportunities will be good. Employment of medical transcriptionists is projected to grow faster than the average for all occupations through 2014. Demand for medical transcription services will be spurred by a growing and aging population. Older age groups receive proportionately greater numbers of medical tests, treatments, and procedures that require documentation. A high level of demand for transcription services also will be sustained by the continued need for electronic documentation that can easily be shared among providers, third-party payers, regulators, consumers, and health information systems. Growing numbers of medical transcriptionists will be needed to amend patients' records, edit documents from speech recognition systems, and identify discrepancies in medical reports.

Contracting out transcription work overseas and advancements in speech recognition technology are not expected to significantly reduce the need for well-trained medical transcriptionists. Outsourcing transcription work abroad—to countries such as India, Pakistan, Philippines, and the Caribbean—has grown more popular as transmitting confidential health information over the Internet has become more secure; however, the demand for overseas transcription services is expected only to supplement the demand for well-trained domestic medical transcriptionists. In addition, reports transcribed by overseas medical transcription services usually require editing for accuracy by domestic medical transcriptionists before they meet domestic quality standards. Speech-recognition technology allows physicians and other health professionals to dictate medical reports to a computer that immediately creates an electronic document. In spite of the advances in this technology, the software has been slow to grasp and analyze the human voice, the English language, and the medical vernacular with all its diversity. As a result, there will continue to be a need for skilled medical transcriptionists to identify and appropriately edit the inevitable errors created by speech recognition systems and to create a final document.

Hospitals will continue to employ a large percentage of medical transcriptionists, but job growth there will not be as fast as in other industries. An increasing demand for standardized records should result in rapid employment growth in physicians' offices, especially in large group practices.

Earnings

Medical transcriptionists had median hourly earnings of $13.64 in May 2004. The middle 50 percent earned between $11.50 and $16.32. The lowest 10 percent earned less than $9.67, and the highest 10 percent earned more than $19.11. Median hourly earnings in the industries employing the largest numbers of medical transcriptionists in May 2004 were

General medical and surgical hospitals $13.83

Offices of physicians 13.40

Business support services 13.40

Compensation methods for medical transcriptionists vary. Some are paid based on the number of hours they work or on the number of lines they transcribe. Others receive a base pay per hour with incentives for extra production. Employees of transcription services and independent contractors almost always receive production-based pay. Independent contractors earn more than do transcriptionists who work for others, but independent contractors have higher expenses than their corporate counterparts, receive no benefits, and may face higher risk of termination than do employed transcriptionists.

Related Occupations

A number of other workers type, record information, and process paperwork. Among these are court reporters; human resources assistants, except payroll and timekeeping; receptionists and information clerks; and secretaries and administrative assistants. Other workers who provide medical support include medical assistants and medical records and health information technicians.

Sources of Additional Information

For information on a career as a medical transcriptionist, send a self-addressed, stamped envelope to

▸ American Association for Medical Transcription, 100 Sycamore Ave., Modesto, CA 95354-0550. Internet: http://www.aamt.org

State employment service offices can provide information about job openings for medical transcriptionists.

Medical, Dental, and Ophthalmic Laboratory Technicians

(O*NET 51-9081.00, 51-9082.00, 51-9083.01, and 51-9083.02)

Significant Points

■ Around 3 out of 5 salaried jobs are in medical equipment and supply manufacturing laboratories, which usually are small, privately owned businesses with fewer than 5 employees.

■ Most medical, dental, and ophthalmic laboratory technicians learn their craft on the job; however, many employers prefer to hire those with formal training in a related field.

■ Slower-than-average employment growth is expected for dental and ophthalmic laboratory technicians, while average employment growth is expected for medical appliance technicians.

■ Job opportunities should be favorable as employers have difficulty filling trainee positions.

Nature of the Work

When patients require a special appliance to see clearly, chew and speak well, or walk, their health care providers send requests to medical, dental, and ophthalmic laboratory technicians. These technicians produce a wide variety of appliances to help patients.

Medical appliance technicians construct, fit, maintain, and repair braces, artificial limbs, joints, arch supports, and other surgical and medical appliances. They read prescriptions or detailed information from orthotists, podiatrists, or prosthetists. Orthotists treat patients who need braces, supports, or corrective shoes. Podiatrists are doctors who treat foot problems and request the same appliances as orthotists. Prosthetists work with patients who need a replacement limb, such as an arm, leg, hand, or foot, due to a birth defect or an accident. The appliances are called orthoses and prostheses. Medical appliance technicians are also referred to as orthotic and prosthetic technicians.

For orthoses such as arch supports, technicians first make a wax or plastic impression of the patient's foot. Then they bend and form a material so that it conforms to prescribed contours required to fabricate structural components. If a support is mainly required to correct the balance of a patient with legs of different lengths, a rigid material is used. If the support is primarily intended to protect those with arthritic or diabetic feet, a soft material is used. Supports and braces are polished with grinding and buffing wheels. Technicians may cover arch supports with felt to make them more comfortable.

For prostheses, technicians construct or receive a plaster cast of the patient's limb to use as a pattern. Then, they lay out parts and use precision measuring instruments to measure them. Technicians may use wood, plastic, metal, or other material for the parts of the artificial limb. Next, they carve, cut, or grind the material, using hand or power tools. Then, they drill holes for rivets and glue, rivet, or weld the parts together. They are able to do very precise work using common tools. Next, technicians use grinding and buffing wheels to smooth and polish artificial limbs. Lastly, they may cover or pad the limbs with rubber, leather, felt, plastic, or another material. Also, technicians may mix pigments according to formulas to match the patient's skin color and apply the mixture to the artificial limb.

After fabrication, medical appliance technicians test devices for proper alignment, movement, and biomechanical stability using meters and alignment fixtures. They also may fit the appliance on the patient and adjust them as necessary. Over time the appliance will wear down, so technicians must repair and maintain the device. They also may service and repair the machinery used for the fabrication of orthotic and prosthetic devices.

Dental laboratory technicians fill prescriptions from dentists for crowns, bridges, dentures, and other dental prosthetics. First, dentists send a specification of the item to be manufactured, along with an impression (mold) of the patient's mouth or teeth. Then, dental laboratory technicians, also called dental technicians, create a model of the patient's mouth by pouring plaster into the impression and allowing it to set. Next, they place the model on an apparatus that mimics the bite and movement of the patient's jaw. The model serves as the basis of the prosthetic device. Technicians examine the model, noting the size and shape of the adjacent teeth, as well as gaps within the gumline. Based upon these observations and the dentist's specifications, technicians build and shape a wax tooth or teeth model, using small hand instruments called wax spatulas and wax carvers. They use this wax model to cast the metal framework for the prosthetic device.

After the wax tooth has been formed, dental technicians pour the cast and form the metal and, using small hand-held tools, prepare the surface to allow the metal and porcelain to bond. They then apply porcelain in layers to arrive at the precise shape and color of a tooth. Technicians place the tooth in a porcelain furnace to bake the porcelain onto the metal framework and then adjust the shape and color, with subsequent grinding and addition of porcelain to achieve a sealed finish. The final product is a nearly exact replica of the lost tooth or teeth.

In some laboratories, technicians perform all stages of the work, whereas in other labs, each technician does only a few. Dental laboratory technicians can specialize in 1 of 5 areas: orthodontic appliances, crowns and bridges, complete dentures, partial dentures, or ceramics. Job titles can reflect specialization in these areas. For example, technicians who make porcelain and acrylic restorations are called *dental ceramists.*

Ophthalmic laboratory technicians—also known as *manufacturing opticians, optical mechanics,* or *optical goods workers*—make prescription eyeglass or contact lenses. Prescription lenses are curved in such a way that light is correctly focused onto the retina of the patient's eye, improving his or her vision. Some ophthalmic laboratory technicians manufacture lenses for other optical instruments, such as telescopes and binoculars. Ophthalmic laboratory technicians cut, grind, edge, and finish lenses according to specifications provided by dispensing opticians, optometrists, or ophthalmologists and may insert lenses into frames to produce finished glasses. Although some lenses still are produced by hand, technicians are increasingly using automated equipment to make lenses.

Ophthalmic laboratory technicians should not be confused with workers in other vision care occupations. Ophthalmologists and optometrists are "eye doctors" who examine eyes, diagnose and treat vision problems, and prescribe corrective lenses. Ophthalmologists are physicians who perform eye surgery. Dispensing opticians, who also may do the work of ophthalmic laboratory technicians, help patients select frames and lenses and adjust finished eyeglasses. (See the description of physicians and surgeons, which includes ophthalmologists, as well as the descriptions of optometrists and opticians, dispensing, elsewhere in this book.)

Ophthalmic laboratory technicians read prescription specifications, select standard glass or plastic lens blanks, and then mark them to indicate where the curves specified on the prescription should be ground. They place the lens in the lens grinder, set the dials for the prescribed curvature, and start the machine. After a minute or so, the lens is ready to be "finished" by a machine that rotates it against a fine abrasive to grind it and smooth out rough edges. The lens is then placed in a polishing machine with an even finer abrasive to polish it to a smooth, bright finish.

Next, the technician examines the lens through a lensometer, an instrument similar in shape to a microscope, to make sure that the degree and placement of the curve are correct. The technician then cuts the lenses and bevels the edges to fit the frame, dips each lens into dye if the prescription calls for tinted or coated lenses, polishes the edges, and assembles the lenses and frame parts into a finished pair of glasses.

In small laboratories, technicians usually handle every phase of the operation. In large ones, in which virtually every phase of the operation is automated, technicians may be responsible for operating computerized equipment. Technicians also inspect the final product for quality and accuracy.

Working Conditions

Medical, dental, and ophthalmic laboratory technicians generally work in clean, well-lighted, and well-ventilated laboratories. They have limited contact with the public. Salaried laboratory technicians usually work 40 hours a week, but some work part time. At times, technicians wear goggles to protect their eyes, gloves to handle hot objects, or masks to avoid inhaling dust. They may spend a great deal of time standing.

Dental technicians usually have their own workbenches, which can be equipped with Bunsen burners; grinding and polishing equipment; and hand instruments, such as wax spatulas and wax carvers. Some dental technicians have computer-aided milling equipment to assist them with creating artificial teeth.

Training, Other Qualifications, and Advancement

Most medical, dental, and ophthalmic laboratory technicians learn their craft on the job; however, many employers prefer to hire those with formal training in a related field.

Medical appliance technicians begin as a helper and gradually learn new skills as they gain experience. Formal training is also available. There are currently 4 programs actively accredited by the National Commission on Orthotic and Prosthetic Education (NCOPE). These programs offer either an associate degree for orthotics and prosthetic technicians or one-year certificate for orthotic technicians or prosthetic technicians. The programs instruct students on human anatomy and physiology, orthotic and prosthetic equipment and materials, and applied biomechanical principles to customize orthoses or prostheses. The programs also include clinical rotations to provide hands-on experience.

Voluntary certification is available through the American Board for Certification in Orthotics and Prosthetics (ABC). Applicants are eligible for an exam after completing a program accredited by NCOPE or obtaining two years of experience as a technician under the direct supervision of an ABC-certified practitioner. After successfully passing the appropriate exam, technicians receive the Registered Orthotic Technician, Registered Prosthetic Technician, or Registered Prosthetic-Orthotic Technician credential.

High school students interested in becoming medical appliance technicians should take mathematics, metal and wood shop, and drafting. With additional formal education, medical appliance technicians can advance to become orthotists or prosthetists.

Dental laboratory technicians begin with simple tasks, such as pouring plaster into an impression, and progress to more complex procedures, such as making porcelain crowns and bridges. Becoming a fully trained technician requires an average of 3 to 4 years, depending upon the individual's aptitude and ambition, but it may take a few years more to become an accomplished technician.

Training in dental laboratory technology also is available through community and junior colleges, vocational-technical institutes, and the U.S. Armed Forces. Formal training programs vary greatly both in length and in the level of skill they impart.

In 2004, 25 programs in dental laboratory technology were approved (accredited) by the Commission on Dental Accreditation in conjunction with the American Dental Association (ADA). These programs provide classroom instruction in dental materials science, oral anatomy, fabrication procedures, ethics, and related subjects. In addition, each student is given supervised practical experience in a school or an associated dental laboratory. Accredited programs normally take 2 years to complete and lead to an associate degree. A few programs take about 4 years to complete and offer a bachelor's degree in dental technology.

Graduates of 2-year training programs need additional hands-on experience to become fully qualified. Each dental laboratory owner operates in a different way, and classroom instruction does not necessarily expose students to techniques and procedures favored by individual laboratory owners. Students who have taken enough courses to learn the basics of the craft usually are considered good candidates for training regardless of whether they have completed a formal program. Many employers will train someone without any classroom experience.

The National Board for Certification, an independent board established by the National Association of Dental Laboratories, offers certification in dental laboratory technology. Certification, which is voluntary, can be obtained in five specialty areas: crowns and bridges, ceramics, partial dentures, complete dentures, and orthodontic appliances.

In large dental laboratories, technicians may become supervisors or managers. Experienced technicians may teach or may take jobs with dental suppliers in such areas as product development, marketing, and sales. Still, for most technicians, opening one's own laboratory is the way toward advancement and higher earnings.

A high degree of manual dexterity, good vision, and the ability to recognize very fine color shadings and variations in shape are necessary. An artistic aptitude for detailed and precise work also is important. High school students interested in becoming dental laboratory technicians should take courses in art, metal and wood shop, drafting, and sciences. Courses in management and business may help those wishing to operate their own laboratories.

Ophthalmic laboratory technicians start on simple tasks if they are trained to produce lenses by hand. They may begin with marking or blocking lenses for grinding; then, they progress to grinding, cutting, edging, and beveling lenses; finally, they are trained in assembling the eyeglasses. Depending on individual aptitude, it may take up to 6 months to become proficient in all phases of the work.

Employers filling trainee jobs prefer applicants who are high school graduates. Courses in science, mathematics, and computers are valuable; manual dexterity and the ability to do precision work are essential. Technicians using automated systems will find computer skills valuable.

A very small number of ophthalmic laboratory technicians learn their trade in the Armed Forces or in the few programs in optical technology offered by vocational-technical institutes or trade schools. These programs have classes in optical theory, surfacing and lens finishing, and the reading and applying of prescriptions. Programs vary in length from 6 months to 1 year and award certificates or diplomas.

Ophthalmic laboratory technicians can become supervisors and managers. Some become dispensing opticians, although further education or training generally is required in that occupation.

Employment

Medical, dental, and ophthalmic laboratory technicians held about 87,000 jobs in 2004. Around 3 out of 5 salaried jobs were in medical equipment and supply manufacturing laboratories, which usually are small, privately owned businesses with fewer than five employees. However, some laboratories are large; a few employ more than 1,000 workers.

Employment by detailed occupation is presented in the following tabulation:

Dental laboratory technicians 50,000
Ophthalmic laboratory technicians 25,000
Medical appliance technicians 11,000

Some medical appliance technicians worked in health and personal care stores, while others worked in public and private hospitals, professional and commercial equipment and supplies merchant wholesalers, offices of physicians, or consumer goods rental centers. Some were self-employed.

Some dental laboratory technicians work in offices of dentists. Others work for hospitals providing dental services, including U.S. Department of Veterans Affairs hospitals. Some dental laboratory technicians open their own offices or work in dental laboratories in their homes.

Around 30 percent of ophthalmic laboratory technicians were in health and personal care stores, such as optical goods stores that manufacture and sell prescription glasses and contact lenses. Some were in offices of optometrists or ophthalmologists. Others worked at professional and commercial equipment and supplies merchant wholesalers. A few worked in commercial and service industry machine manufacturing firms that produce lenses for other optical instruments, such as telescopes and binoculars.

Job Outlook

Job opportunities for medical, dental, and ophthalmic laboratory technicians should be favorable, despite expected slower-than-average growth in overall employment through the year 2014. Employers have difficulty filling trainee positions, probably because entry-level salaries are relatively low and because the public is not familiar with these occupations. Most job openings will arise from the need to replace technicians who transfer to other occupations or who leave the labor force.

Medical appliance technicians will grow faster than dental and ophthalmic laboratory technicians, with employment projected to increase about as fast as the average for all occupations due to the increasing prevalence of the two leading causes of limb loss—diabetes and cardiovascular disease. Advances in technology may spur demand for prostheses that allow for greater movement.

During the last few years, demand has arisen from an aging public that is growing increasingly interested in cosmetic prostheses. For example, many dental laboratories are filling orders for composite fillings that are the same shade of white as natural teeth to replace older, less attractive fillings. However, job growth for dental laboratory technicians will be limited. The overall dental health of the population has improved because of fluoridation of drinking water, which has reduced the incidence of dental cavities, and greater emphasis on preventive dental care since the early 1960s. As a result, full dentures will be less common, as most people will need only a bridge or crown.

Demographic trends also make it likely that many more Americans will need vision care in the years ahead. Not only will the population grow, but also, the proportion of middle-aged and older adults is projected to increase rapidly. Middle age is a time when many people use corrective lenses for the first time, and elderly persons usually require more vision care than others. However, the increasing use of automated machinery will limit job growth for ophthalmic laboratory technicians.

Earnings

Median hourly earnings of medical appliance technicians were $13.38 in May 2004. The middle 50 percent earned between $10.46 and $18.22 an hour. The lowest 10 percent earned less than $8.21, and the highest 10 percent earned more than $23.66 an hour. Median hourly earnings of medical appliance technicians in May 2004 were $13.00 in medical equipment and supplies manufacturing.

Median hourly earnings of dental laboratory technicians were $14.93 in May 2004. The middle 50 percent earned between $11.18 and $19.71 an hour. The lowest 10 percent earned less than $8.86, and the highest 10 percent earned more than $25.48 an hour. Median hourly earnings of dental laboratory technicians in May 2004 were $15.95 in offices of dentists and $14.40 in medical equipment and supplies manufacturing.

Dental technicians in large laboratories tend to specialize in a few procedures and, therefore, tend to be paid a lower wage than those employed in small laboratories who perform a variety of tasks.

Median hourly earnings of ophthalmic laboratory technicians were $11.40 in May 2004. The middle 50 percent earned between $9.33 and $14.67 an hour. The lowest 10 percent earned less than $7.89, and the highest 10 percent earned more than $17.61 an hour. Median hourly earnings of ophthalmic laboratory technicians in May 2004 were $10.88 in health and personal care stores and $10.79 in medical equipment and supplies manufacturing.

Related Occupations

Medical, dental, and ophthalmic laboratory technicians manufacture a variety of health implements, such as artificial limbs, corrective lenses, and artificial teeth, following specifications and instructions provided by health care practitioners. Other workers who make and repair medical devices or other items include dispensing opticians, orthotists and prosthetists, and precision instrument and equipment repairers.

Sources of Additional Information

For information on careers in orthotics and prosthetics, contact

▸ American Academy of Orthotists and Prosthetists, 526 King St., Suite 201, Alexandria, VA 22314. Internet: http://www.opcareers.org

For a list of accredited programs for orthotic and prosthetic technicians, contact

▸ National Commission on Orthotic and Prosthetic Education, 330 John Carlyle St., Suite 200, Alexandria, VA 22314. Internet: http://www.ncope.org

For a list of accredited programs in dental laboratory technology, contact

▸ Commission on Dental Accreditation, American Dental Association, 211 E. Chicago Ave., Chicago, IL 60611. Internet: http://www.ada.org

For information on requirements for certification of dental laboratory technicians, contact

▸ National Board for Certification in Dental Technology, 325 John Knox Rd., L103, Tallahassee, FL 32303. Internet: http://www.nbccert.org

For information on career opportunities in commercial dental laboratories, contact

▸ National Association of Dental Laboratories, 325 John Knox Rd., L103, Tallahassee, FL 32303. Internet: http://www.nadl.org

For information on an accredited program in ophthalmic laboratory technology, contact

▸ Commission on Opticianry Accreditation, 8665 Sudley Rd., #341, Manassas VA 20110.

General information on grants and scholarships is available from individual schools. State employment service offices can provide information about job openings for medical, dental, and ophthalmic laboratory technicians.

Millwrights

(O*NET 49-9044.00)

Significant Points

■ Training through apprenticeship programs, or through community colleges coupled with on-the-job training, generally lasts 4 years.

■ Despite projected slower-than-average employment growth, skilled applicants should have good job opportunities.

■ About 54 percent of millwrights belong to labor unions, one of the highest rates of membership in the economy.

Nature of the Work

Millwrights install, repair, replace, and dismantle the machinery and heavy equipment used in many industries. About half of all millwrights work in a variety of manufacturing industries; another third work for construction builders and contractors. The wide range of facilities and the development of new technologies require millwrights to continually update their skills—from blueprint reading and pouring concrete for machinery to set on to diagnosing and solving mechanical problems.

The millwright's responsibilities begin when machinery arrives at the jobsite. New equipment must be unloaded, inspected, and moved into position. To lift and move light machinery, millwrights use rigging and hoisting devices, such as pulleys and cables. With heavier equipment, they may require the assistance of hydraulic lift-truck or crane operators to position the machinery. Because millwrights often decide which device to use for moving machinery, they must know the load-bearing properties of rope, cables, hoists, and cranes.

Millwrights consult with production managers and others to determine the optimal placement of machines in a plant. When this placement requires building a new foundation, millwrights either prepare the foundation themselves or supervise its construction. As a result, they must know how to read blueprints and work with a variety of building materials.

To assemble machinery, millwrights fit bearings, align gears and wheels, attach motors, and connect belts, according to the manufacturer's blueprints and drawings. Precision leveling and alignment are important in the assembly process, so millwrights measure angles, material thickness, and small distances with tools such as squares, calipers, and micrometers. When a high level of precision is required, devices such as lasers and ultrasonic measuring and alignment tools may be used. Millwrights also work with hand and power tools, such as cutting torches, welding machines, hydraulic torque wrenches, hydraulic stud tensioners, and soldering guns, and with metalworking equipment, including lathes and grinding machines.

In addition to installing and dismantling machinery, many millwrights work with mechanics and maintenance workers to repair and maintain equipment. This includes preventive maintenance, such as lubrication and fixing or replacing worn parts.

Increasingly sophisticated automation means more complicated machines for millwrights to install and maintain, requiring millwrights to specialize in certain machines or brand names. For example, millwrights install and maintain turbines in power plants that can weigh hundreds of tons and contain thousands of parts. This machinery requires special care and knowledge, so millwrights receive additional training and are required to be certified by the manufacturer of the turbine.

Working Conditions

Working conditions vary by industry. Millwrights employed in manufacturing often work in a typical shop setting and use protective equipment to avoid common hazards. For example, protective devices, such as safety belts, protective glasses, and hardhats may be worn to prevent injuries from falling objects or machinery. Those employed in construction may work outdoors in difficult weather conditions.

Advances in some equipment, such as hydraulic wrenches and hydraulic stud tensioners, have made the work safer and eliminated the need for millwrights to use a sledgehammer to pound bolts into position. Other equipment has reduced the amount of heavy lifting and other strenuous tasks that would often cause injuries in the past.

Millwrights work independently or as part of a team. Their tasks must be performed quickly and precisely, because disabled machinery costs a company time and money. Many millwrights work overtime; about 4 in 10 millwrights report working more than 40 hours during a typical week. During power outages or other emergencies, millwrights are often assigned overtime and shift work.

Millwrights that work at construction sites may have to travel long distances to reach different worksites. For example, millwrights who specialize in turbine installation travel to wherever new power plants are being built.

Training, Other Qualifications, and Advancement

Millwrights normally receive training through 4- to 5-year apprenticeship programs that combine on-the-job training with classroom instruction or through community college programs coupled with informal on-the-job training. These programs include training in dismantling, moving, erecting, and repairing machinery. Trainees also may work with concrete and receive instruction in related skills, such as carpentry, welding, and sheet-metal work. Millwright apprentices attend about one week of classes every three months. Classroom instruction covers mathematics, blueprint reading, hydraulics, electricity, computers, electronics, and instruction in specific machinery.

Employers prefer applicants with a high school diploma or equivalency and some vocational training or experience. Courses in science, mathematics, mechanical drawing, computers, and machine shop practice are useful. Millwrights are expected to keep their skills up to date and may need additional training on technological advances, such as laser shaft alignment and vibration analysis.

Because millwrights assemble and disassemble complicated machinery, mechanical aptitude is very important. Strength and agility also are necessary for lifting and climbing. Millwrights need good interpersonal and communication skills to work as part of a team and to effectively give detailed instructions to others.

Advancement for millwrights usually takes the form of higher wages. Some advance to the position of supervisor or superintendent, while others may become self-employed contractors.

Employment

Millwrights held about 59,000 jobs in 2004. Most work in manufacturing, primarily in durable goods industries, such as motor vehicle and parts manufacturing and iron and steel mills. About 1 in 3 millwrights are employed in construction, where most work for contracting firms. Although millwrights work in every state, employment is concentrated in heavily industrialized areas.

Job Outlook

Employment of millwrights is projected to grow more slowly than the average for all occupations through the year 2014. Because millwrights will always be needed to maintain and repair existing machinery, dismantle old machinery, and install new equipment, skilled applicants should have good job opportunities. Prospects will be best for millwrights with training in installing newer production technologies. In addition to employment growth, many job openings for these workers will stem from the need to replace experienced millwrights who transfer to other occupations or retire.

Employment of millwrights has historically been cyclical, rising and falling in line with investments in automation in the nation's factories and production facilities. To remain competitive in coming years, firms will continue to require the services of millwrights to dismantle old equipment and install new high-technology machinery. Additionally, as the services sector of the economy grows, there is an increasing number of companies in this sector employing new technology to make them more efficient, which will likely offset the loss of manufacturing work. Warehouse and distribution companies, for example, are deploying highly automated conveyor systems that are being maintained by millwrights. Employment growth from new automation will be dampened somewhat by foreign competition and the introduction of new technologies, such as hydraulic torque wrenches, ultrasonic measuring tools, and laser shaft alignment, which allow fewer millwrights to perform more work. In addition, the demand for millwrights may be adversely affected as lower-paid workers, such as electronics technicians and industrial machinery mechanics and maintenance workers, assume some installation and maintenance duties.

Earnings

Median hourly earnings of millwrights were $21.02 in May 2004. The middle 50 percent earned between $16.53 and $27.07. The lowest 10 percent earned less than $13.02, and the highest 10 percent earned more than $32.17. Earnings vary by industry and geographic location. Median hourly earnings in the industries employing the largest numbers of millwrights in May 2004 were as follows:

Motor vehicle parts manufacturing $28.76
Building equipment contractors.............................19.88

About 54 percent of millwrights belong to labor unions, one of the highest rates of membership in the economy.

Related Occupations

To set up machinery for use in a plant, millwrights must know how to use hoisting devices and how to assemble, disassemble, and sometimes repair machinery. Other workers with similar job duties include industrial machinery installation, repair, and maintenance workers, except millwrights; tool and die makers; aircraft and avionics equipment mechanics and service technicians; structural and reinforcing iron and metal workers; assemblers and fabricators; and heavy vehicle and mobile equipment service technicians and mechanics. Millwrights also machine parts and operate computer-controlled machine tools like machinists and computer control machine tool programmers and operators. Millwrights often use welding and soldering to assemble and repair machines like welding, soldering and brazing workers.

Sources of Additional Information

For further information on apprenticeship programs, write to the Apprenticeship Council of your state's labor department, local offices of your state employment service, or local firms that employ millwrights. In addition, you may contact

▸ United Brotherhood of Carpenters and Joiners of America, 6801 Placid St., Las Vegas, NV 89119. Internet: http://www.carpenters.org

▸ Associated General Contractors of America, 333 John Carlyle St., Suite 200, Alexandria, VA 22314. Internet: http://www.agc.org

▸ Associated Builders and Contractors, Workforce Development Dept., 2300 Wilson Blvd., Suite 400, Arlington, VA 22201. Internet: http://www.trytools.org

▸ National Tooling and Machining Association, 9300 Livingston Rd., Fort Washington, MD 20744. Internet: http://www.ntma.org

Nuclear Medicine Technologists

(O*NET 29-2033.00)

Significant Points

■ About 7 out of 10 work in hospitals.

■ Nuclear medicine technology programs range in length from 1 to 4 years and lead to a certificate, an associate degree, or a bachelor's degree.

■ Faster-than-average growth will arise from an increase in the number of middle-aged and elderly persons, who are the primary users of diagnostic procedures.

■ The number of job openings each year will be relatively low because the occupation is small; technologists who also are trained in other diagnostic methods, such as radiologic technology or diagnostic medical sonography, will have the best prospects.

Nature of the Work

Diagnostic imaging embraces several procedures that aid in diagnosing ailments, the most familiar being the X ray. Another increasingly common diagnostic imaging method, called magnetic resonance imaging (MRI), uses giant magnets and radio waves, rather than radiation, to create an image. In nuclear medicine, radionuclides—unstable atoms that emit radiation spontaneously—are used to diagnose and treat disease. Radionuclides are purified and compounded to form radiopharmaceuticals. Nuclear medicine technologists administer radiopharmaceuticals to patients and then monitor the characteristics and functions of tissues or organs in which the drugs localize. Abnormal areas show higher-than-expected or lower-than-expected concentrations of radioactivity. Nuclear medicine differs from other diagnostic imaging technologies because it determines the presence of disease on the basis of biological changes rather than changes in organ structure.

Nuclear medicine technologists operate cameras that detect and map the radioactive drug in a patient's body to create diagnostic images. After explaining test procedures to patients, technologists prepare a dosage of the radiopharmaceutical and administer it by mouth, injection, inhalation, or other means. They position patients and start a gamma scintillation camera, or "scanner," which creates images of the distribution of a radiopharmaceutical as it localizes in, and emits signals from, the patient's body. The images are produced on a computer screen or on film for a physician to interpret.

When preparing radiopharmaceuticals, technologists adhere to safety standards that keep the radiation dose to workers and patients as low as possible. Technologists keep patient records and record the amount and type of radionuclides that they receive, use, and discard.

Radiologic technologists and technicians and cardiovascular technologists and technicians also operate diagnostic imaging equipment, but their equipment creates images by means of a different technology. (See the descriptions of these occupations elsewhere in this book.)

Nuclear medicine technologists also perform radioimmunoassay studies that assess the behavior of a radioactive substance inside the body. For example, technologists may add radioactive substances to blood or serum to determine levels of hormones or of therapeutic drugs in the body. Most nuclear medicine studies, such as cardiac function studies, are processed with the aid of a computer.

Working Conditions

Nuclear medicine technologists generally work a 40-hour week, perhaps including evening or weekend hours, in departments that operate on an extended schedule. Opportunities for part-time and shift work also are available. In addition, technologists in hospitals may have on-call duty on a rotational basis.

Physical stamina is important because technologists are on their feet much of the day and may lift or turn disabled patients.

Although the potential for radiation exposure exists in this field, it is kept to a minimum by the use of shielded syringes, gloves, and other protective devices and by adherence to strict radiation safety guidelines. The amount of radiation in a nuclear medicine procedure is comparable to that received during a diagnostic X-ray procedure. Technologists also wear badges that measure radiation levels. Because of safety programs, badge measurements rarely exceed established safety levels.

Training, Other Qualifications, and Advancement

Many employers and an increasing number of states require certification or licensure. Aspiring nuclear medicine technologists should check the requirements of the state in which they plan to work. Certification is available from the American Registry of Radiologic Technologists and from the Nuclear Medicine Technology Certification Board. Some workers receive certification from both agencies. Nuclear medicine technologists must meet the minimum federal standards on the administration of radioactive drugs and the operation of radiation detection equipment.

Nuclear medicine technology programs range in length from 1 to 4 years and lead to a certificate, an associate degree, or a bachelor's degree. Generally, certificate programs are offered in hospitals, associate degree programs in community colleges, and bachelor's degree programs in 4-year colleges and universities. Courses cover the physical sciences, biological effects of radiation exposure, radi-

ation protection and procedures, the use of radiopharmaceuticals, imaging techniques, and computer applications.

One-year certificate programs are for health professionals who already possess an associate degree—especially radiologic technologists and diagnostic medical sonographers—but who wish to specialize in nuclear medicine. The programs also attract medical technologists, registered nurses, and others who wish to change fields or specialize. Others interested in nuclear medicine technology have three options: a 2-year certificate program, a 2-year associate degree program, or a 4-year bachelor's degree program.

The Joint Review Committee on Education Programs in Nuclear Medicine Technology accredits most formal training programs in nuclear medicine technology. In 2005, there were 100 accredited programs in the continental United States and Puerto Rico.

Nuclear medicine technologists should be sensitive to patients' physical and psychological needs. They must pay attention to detail, follow instructions, and work as part of a team. In addition, operating complicated equipment requires mechanical ability and manual dexterity.

Technologists may advance to supervisor, then to chief technologist, and, finally, to department administrator or director. Some technologists specialize in a clinical area such as nuclear cardiology or computer analysis or leave patient care to take positions in research laboratories. Some become instructors in, or directors of, nuclear medicine technology programs, a step that usually requires a bachelor's or master's degree in the subject. Others leave the occupation to work as sales or training representatives for medical equipment and radiopharmaceutical manufacturing firms or as radiation safety officers in regulatory agencies or hospitals.

Employment

Nuclear medicine technologists held about 18,000 jobs in 2004. About 7 out of 10 were in hospitals—private and government. Most of the rest were in offices of physicians or in medical and diagnostic laboratories, including diagnostic imaging centers.

Job Outlook

Employment of nuclear medicine technologists is expected to grow faster than the average for all occupations through the year 2014. Growth will arise from technological advancement; the development of new nuclear medicine treatments; and an increase in the number of middle-aged and older persons, who are the primary users of diagnostic procedures, including nuclear medicine tests. However, the number of openings each year will be relatively low because the occupation is small. Technologists who also are trained in other diagnostic methods, such as radiologic technology or diagnostic medical sonography, will have the best prospects.

Technological innovations may increase the diagnostic uses of nuclear medicine. One example is the use of radiopharmaceuticals in combination with monoclonal antibodies to detect cancer at far earlier stages than is customary today and without resorting to surgery. Another is the use of radionuclides to examine the heart's ability to pump blood. New nuclear medical imaging technologies, including positron emission tomography (PET) and single photon emission computed tomography (SPECT), are expected to be used increasingly and to contribute further to employment growth. The wider use of nuclear medical imaging to observe metabolic and biochemical changes during neurology, cardiology, and oncology procedures also will spur demand for nuclear medicine technologists.

Nonetheless, cost considerations will affect the speed with which new applications of nuclear medicine grow. Some promising nuclear medicine procedures, such as positron emission tomography, are extremely costly, and hospitals contemplating these procedures will have to consider equipment costs, reimbursement policies, and the number of potential users.

Earnings

Median annual earnings of nuclear medicine technologists were $56,450 in May 2004. The middle 50 percent earned between $48,720 and $67,460. The lowest 10 percent earned less than $41,800, and the highest 10 percent earned more than $80,300. Median annual earnings of nuclear medicine technologists in May 2004 were $54,920 in general medical and surgical hospitals.

Related Occupations

Nuclear medical technologists operate sophisticated equipment to help physicians and other health practitioners diagnose and treat patients. Cardiovascular technologists and technicians, clinical laboratory technologists and technicians, diagnostic medical sonographers, radiation therapists, radiologic technologists and technicians, and respiratory therapists perform similar functions.

Sources of Additional Information

Additional information on a career as a nuclear medicine technologist is available from

▶ Society of Nuclear Medicine Technologists, 1850 Samuel Morse Dr., Reston, VA 20190-5316. Internet: http://www.snm.org

For career information, send a stamped, self-addressed, business-size envelope with your request to

▶ American Society of Radiologic Technologists, 15000 Central Ave. SE, Albuquerque, NM 87123-3917. Internet: http://www.asrt.org

For a list of accredited programs in nuclear medicine technology, write to

▶ Joint Review Committee on Educational Programs in Nuclear Medicine Technology, 1716 Black Point Rd., P.O. Box 1149, Polson, MT 59860-1149. Internet: http://www.jrcnmt.org

Information on certification is available from

▶ American Registry of Radiologic Technologists, 1255 Northland Dr., St. Paul, MN 55120-1155. Internet: http://www.arrt.org

▶ Nuclear Medicine Technology Certification Board, 2970 Clairmont Rd., Suite 935, Atlanta, GA 30329-4421. Internet: http://www.nmtcb.org

Nursing, Psychiatric, and Home Health Aides

(O*NET 31-1011.00, 31-1012.00, and 31-1013.00)

Significant Points

■ Home health aides is projected to be the fastest-growing occupation through 2014.

■ Numerous job openings and excellent job opportunities are expected.

■ Most jobs are in nursing and residential care facilities, hospitals, and home health care services.

■ Modest entry requirements, low pay, high physical and emotional demands, and lack of advancement opportunities characterize this occupation.

Nature of the Work

Nursing and psychiatric aides help care for physically or mentally ill, injured, disabled, or infirm individuals confined to hospitals, nursing care facilities, and mental health settings. Home health aides have duties that are similar, but they work in patients' homes or residential care facilities.

Nursing aides—also known as *nursing assistants, certified nursing assistants, geriatric aides, unlicensed assistive personnel, orderlies,* or *hospital attendants*—perform routine tasks under the supervision of nursing and medical staff. They answer patients' call lights; deliver messages; serve meals; make beds; and help patients to eat, dress, and bathe. Aides also may provide skin care to patients; take their temperature, pulse rate, respiration rate, and blood pressure; and help them to get into and out of bed and walk. They also may escort patients to operating and examining rooms, keep patients' rooms neat, set up equipment, store and move supplies, and assist with some procedures. Aides observe patients' physical, mental, and emotional conditions and report any change to the nursing or medical staff.

Nursing aides employed in nursing care facilities often are the principal caregivers, having far more contact with residents than do other members of the staff. Because some residents may stay in a nursing care facility for months or even years, aides develop ongoing relationships with them and interact with them in a positive, caring way.

Home health aides help elderly, convalescent, or disabled persons live in their own homes instead of in a health care facility. Under the direction of nursing or medical staff, they provide health-related services, such as administering oral medications. Like nursing aides, home health aides may check patients' pulse rate, temperature, and respiration rate; help with simple prescribed exercises; keep patients' rooms neat; and help patients to move from bed, bathe, dress, and groom. Occasionally, they change nonsterile dressings, give massages and alcohol rubs, or assist with braces and artificial limbs. Experienced home health aides also may assist with medical equipment such as ventilators, which help patients breathe.

Most home health aides work with elderly or disabled persons who need more extensive care than family or friends can provide. Some help discharged hospital patients who have relatively short-term needs.

In home health agencies, a registered nurse, physical therapist, or social worker usually assigns specific duties to and supervises home health aides, who keep records of the services they perform and record each patient's condition and progress. The aides report changes in a patient's condition to the supervisor or case manager.

Psychiatric aides, also known as mental health assistants or psychiatric nursing assistants, care for mentally impaired or emotionally disturbed individuals. They work under a team that may include psychiatrists, psychologists, psychiatric nurses, social workers, and therapists. In addition to helping patients to dress, bathe, groom themselves, and eat, psychiatric aides socialize with them and lead them in educational and recreational activities. Psychiatric aides may play games such as cards with the patients; watch television with them; or participate in group activities, such as sports or field trips. They observe patients and report any physical or behavioral signs that might be important for the professional staff to know. They accompany patients to and from examinations and treatment. Because they have such close contact with patients, psychiatric aides can have a great deal of influence on their patients' outlook and treatment.

Working Conditions

Most full-time aides work about 40 hours a week, but, because patients need care 24 hours a day, some aides work evenings, nights, weekends, and holidays. Many work part time. In 2004, 25 percent of aides worked part time compared with 16 percent of all workers. Aides spend many hours standing and walking, and they often face heavy workloads. Aides must guard against back injury because they may have to move patients into and out of bed or help them to stand or walk. Aides also may face hazards from minor infections and major diseases, such as hepatitis, but can avoid infections by following proper procedures.

Aides often have unpleasant duties, such as emptying bedpans and changing soiled bed linens. The patients they care for may be disoriented, irritable, or uncooperative. Psychiatric aides must be prepared to care for patients whose illness may cause violent behavior. While their work can be emotionally demanding, many aides gain satisfaction from assisting those in need.

Home health aides may go to the same patient's home for months or even years. However, most aides work with a number of different patients, each job lasting a few hours, days, or weeks. Home health aides often visit multiple patients on the same day.

Home health aides generally work alone, with periodic visits from their supervisor. They receive detailed instructions explaining when to visit patients and what services to perform. Aides are individually responsible for getting to patients' homes, and they may spend a good portion of the working day traveling from one patient to another. Because mechanical lifting devices available in institutional settings are seldom available in patients' homes, home health aides are particularly susceptible to injuries resulting from overexertion when they assist patients.

Training, Other Qualifications, and Advancement

In many cases, a high school diploma or equivalent is necessary for a job as a nursing or psychiatric aide. However, a high school diploma generally is not required for jobs as home health aides. Hospitals may require previous experience as a nursing aide or home health aide. Nursing care facilities often hire inexperienced workers, who must complete a minimum of 75 hours of mandatory training and pass a competency evaluation as part of a state-approved training program within 4 months of their employment. Aides who complete the program are known as certified nurse assistants (CNAs) and are placed on the state registry of nursing aides. Some states also require psychiatric aides to complete a formal training program. However, most psychiatric aides learn their skills on the job from experienced workers.

Nursing and psychiatric aide training is offered in high schools, vocational-technical centers, some nursing care facilities, and some community colleges. Courses cover body mechanics, nutrition, anatomy and physiology, infection control, communication skills, and resident rights. Personal care skills, such as how to help patients to bathe, eat, and groom themselves, also are taught.

Some employers provide classroom instruction for newly hired aides, while others rely exclusively on informal on-the-job instruction by a licensed nurse or an experienced aide. Such training may last from several days to a few months. Aides also may attend lectures, workshops, and in-service training.

The federal government has guidelines for home health aides whose employers receive reimbursement from Medicare. Federal law requires home health aides to pass a competency test covering a wide range of areas: communication; documentation of patient status and care provided; reading and recording of vital signs; basic infection-control procedures; basic bodily functions; maintenance of a healthy environment; emergency procedures; physical, emotional, and developmental characteristics of patients; personal hygiene and grooming; safe transfer techniques; normal range of motion and positioning; and basic nutrition.

A home health aide may receive training before taking the competency test. Federal law suggests at least 75 hours of classroom and practical training supervised by a registered nurse. Training and testing programs may be offered by the employing agency but must meet the standards of the Center for Medicare and Medicaid Services. State regulations for training programs vary.

The National Association for Home Care offers national certification for home health aides. The certification is a voluntary demonstration that the individual has met industry standards. Some states also require aides to be licensed.

Aides must be in good health. A physical examination, including state-regulated tests such as those for tuberculosis, may be required. A criminal background check also is usually required for employment.

Applicants should be tactful, patient, understanding, emotionally stable, and dependable and should have a desire to help people. They also should be able to work as part of a team; have good communication skills; and be willing to perform repetitive, routine tasks. Home health aides should be honest and discreet because they work in private homes. They also will need access to their own car or public transportation to reach patients' homes.

For some individuals, these occupations serve as entry-level jobs, as in the case of high school and college students who may work while also attending school. In addition, experience as an aide can help individuals decide whether to pursue a career in health care. Opportunities for advancement within these occupations are limited. Aides generally need additional formal training or education in order to enter other health occupations. The most common health care occupations for former aides are licensed practical nurse, registered nurse, and medical assistant.

Employment

Nursing, psychiatric, and home health aides held about 2.1 million jobs in 2004. Nursing aides held the most jobs—approximately 1.5 million. Home health aides held roughly 624,000 jobs, and psychiatric aides held about 59,000 jobs. Around 42 percent of nursing aides worked in nursing care facilities, and another 27 percent worked in hospitals. Most home health aides—about 34 percent—were employed by home health care services. Others were employed in nursing and residential care facilities and social assistance agencies. Around 54 percent of all psychiatric aides worked in hospitals, primarily in psychiatric and substance abuse hospitals, although some also worked in the psychiatric units of general medical and surgical hospitals. Others were employed in state government agencies; residential mental retardation, mental health, and substance abuse facilities; outpatient care centers; and nursing care facilities.

Job Outlook

Numerous job openings for nursing, psychiatric, and home health aides will arise from a combination of fast employment growth and high replacement needs. High replacement needs in this large occupation reflect modest entry requirements, low pay, high physical and emotional demands, and lack of opportunities for advancement. For these same reasons, many people are unwilling to perform the kind of work required by the occupation, limiting the number of entrants. Many aides also leave the occupation to attend training programs for other health care occupations. Therefore, persons who are interested in, and suited for, this work should have excellent job opportunities.

Overall employment of nursing, psychiatric, and home health aides is projected to grow much faster than the average for all occupations through the year 2014, although individual occupational growth rates will vary. Home health aides is expected to be the fastest-growing occupation as a result of both growing demand for home services from an aging population and efforts to contain costs by moving patients out of hospitals and nursing care facilities as quickly as possible. Consumer preference for care in the home and improvements in medical technologies for in-home treatment also will contribute to much-faster-than-average employment growth for home health aides.

Nursing aide employment will not grow as fast as home health aide employment, largely because nursing aides are concentrated in slower-growing nursing care facilities and hospitals. Employment of nursing aides is expected to grow faster than the average for all occupations through 2014 in response to the long-term care needs of

an increasing elderly population. Financial pressures on hospitals to discharge patients as soon as possible should boost admissions to nursing care facilities. As a result, job opportunities will be more numerous in nursing and residential care facilities than in hospitals. Modern medical technology also will drive demand for nursing aides because, as the technology saves and extends more lives, it increases the need for long-term care provided by aides.

Employment of psychiatric aides—the smallest of the three occupations—is expected to grow more slowly than the average for all occupations. Most psychiatric aides currently work in hospitals, but most job growth will be in residential mental health facilities and in home health care agencies. There is a long-term trend toward treating mental health patients outside of hospitals because it is more cost effective and allows patients to live more normal lives. Demand for psychiatric aides in residential facilities will rise in response to growth in the number of older persons—many of whom will require mental health services—but also as an increasing number of mentally disabled adults, who were formerly cared for by their elderly parents, seek care. Job growth also could be affected by changes in government funding of programs for the mentally ill.

Earnings

Median hourly earnings of nursing aides, orderlies, and attendants were $10.09 in May 2004. The middle 50 percent earned between $8.59 and $12.09 an hour. The lowest 10 percent earned less than $7.31, and the highest 10 percent earned more than $14.02 an hour. Median hourly earnings in the industries employing the largest numbers of nursing aides, orderlies, and attendants in May 2004 were as follows:

Employment services	$11.29
Local government	11.10
General medical and surgical hospitals	10.44
Nursing care facilities	9.86
Community care facilities for the elderly	9.56

Nursing and psychiatric aides in hospitals generally receive at least 1 week of paid vacation after 1 year of service. Paid holidays and sick leave, hospital and medical benefits, extra pay for late-shift work, and pension plans also are available to many hospital employees and to some nursing care facility employees.

Median hourly earnings of home health aides were $8.81 in May 2004. The middle 50 percent earned between $7.52 and $10.38 an hour. The lowest 10 percent earned less than $6.52, and the highest 10 percent earned more than $12.32 an hour. Median hourly earnings in the industries employing the largest numbers of home health aides in May 2004 were as follows:

Nursing care facilities	$9.11
Residential mental retardation, mental health, and substance abuse facilities	8.97
Home health care services	8.57
Community care facilities for the elderly	8.57
Individual and family services	8.47

Home health aides receive slight pay increases with experience and added responsibility. Usually, they are paid only for the time worked in the home, not for travel time between jobs. Most employers hire only on-call hourly workers and provide no benefits.

Median hourly earnings of psychiatric aides were $11.19 in May 2004. The middle 50 percent earned between $9.09 and $14.09 an hour. The lowest 10 percent earned less than $7.63, and the highest 10 percent earned more than $16.74 an hour. Median hourly earnings in the industries employing the largest numbers of psychiatric aides in May 2004 were as follows:

General medical and surgical hospitals	$11.31
Psychiatric and substance abuse hospitals	11.06
Residential mental retardation, mental health, and substance abuse facilities	9.37

Related Occupations

Nursing, psychiatric, and home health aides help people who need routine care or treatment. So do childcare workers, licensed practical and licensed vocational nurses, medical assistants, occupational therapist assistants and aides, personal and home care aides, physical therapist assistants and aides, and registered nurses.

Sources of Additional Information

Information about employment opportunities may be obtained from local hospitals, nursing care facilities, home health care agencies, psychiatric facilities, state boards of nursing, and local offices of the state employment service.

Information on licensing requirements for nursing and home health aides and lists of state-approved nursing aide programs are available from state departments of public health, departments of occupational licensing, boards of nursing, and home care associations.

Occupational Health and Safety Specialists and Technicians

(O*NET 29-9011.00 and 29-9012.00)

Significant Points

■ About 2 out of 5 specialists work in federal, state, and local government agencies that enforce rules on safety, health, and the environment.

■ Many employers, including the federal government, require a bachelor's degree in occupational health, safety, or a related field for some specialist positions.

■ Projected average employment growth reflects a balance of continuing public demand for a safe and healthy work environment against the desire for smaller government and fewer regulations.

Nature of the Work

Occupational health and safety specialists and technicians, also known as *safety and health practitioners* or *occupational health and*

safety inspectors, help prevent harm to workers, property, the environment, and the general public. They promote occupational health and safety within organizations in many ways, such as by advising management on how to increase worker productivity through raising morale and reducing absenteeism, turnover, and equipment downtime while securing savings on insurance premiums, workers' compensation benefits, and litigation expenses. (Industrial engineers, including health and safety, have similar goals. See the description of engineers elsewhere in this book.)

Occupational health and safety specialists analyze work environments and design programs to control, eliminate, and prevent disease or injury caused by chemical, physical, radiological, and biological agents or ergonomic factors that involve the impact of equipment design on a worker's comfort or fatigue. They may conduct inspections and inform the management of a business which areas may not be in compliance with state and federal laws or employer policies in order to gain their support for addressing these areas. They advise management on the cost and effectiveness of safety and health programs.

Occupational health and safety technicians collect data on work environments for analysis by occupational health and safety specialists. Usually working under the supervision of specialists, they help implement and evaluate programs designed to limit risks to workers.

The specific responsibilities of occupational health and safety specialists and technicians vary by industry, workplace, and types of hazards affecting employees. In most settings, they initially focus on identifying hazardous conditions and practices. Sometimes they develop methods to predict hazards from experience, historical data, workplace analysis, and other information sources. Then they identify potential hazards in systems, equipment, products, facilities, or processes planned for use in the future. For example, they might uncover patterns in injury data that implicate a specific cause such as system failure, human error, incomplete or faulty decision making, or a weakness in existing policies or practices. After reviewing the causes or effects of hazards, they evaluate the probability and severity of accidents or exposures to hazardous materials that may result. Then they identify where controls need to be implemented to reduce or eliminate hazards and advise if a new program or practice is required. As necessary, they conduct training sessions for management, supervisors, and workers on health and safety practices and regulations to promote an understanding of a new or existing process. After implementation, they may monitor and evaluate the program's progress, making additional suggestions when needed.

To ensure the machinery and equipment meet appropriate safety regulations, occupational health and safety specialists and technicians may examine and test machinery and equipment, such as lifting devices, machine guards, or scaffolding. They may check that personal protective equipment, such as masks, respirators, protective eyewear, or hardhats, is being used in workplaces according to regulations. They also check that hazardous materials are stored correctly. They test and identify work areas for potential accident and health hazards, such as toxic vapors, mold, mildew, and explosive gas-air mixtures, and help implement appropriate control measures, such as adjustments to ventilation systems. Their survey of the workplace might involve talking with workers and observing their work as well as inspecting elements in their work environment such as lighting, tools, and equipment.

To measure and control hazardous substances, such as the noise or radiation levels, occupational health and safety specialists and technicians prepare and calibrate scientific equipment. They must properly collect and handle samples of dust, gases, vapors, and other potentially toxic materials to ensure personal safety and accurate test results.

If an injury or illness occurs, occupational health and safety specialists and technicians help investigate unsafe working conditions, study possible causes, and recommend remedial action. Some occupational health and safety specialists and technicians assist with the rehabilitation of workers after accidents and injuries and make sure they return to work successfully.

Frequent communication with management may be necessary to report on the status of occupational health and safety programs. Consultation with engineers or physicians also may be required.

Occupational health and safety specialists and technicians prepare reports, including accident reports, Occupational Safety and Health Administration record-keeping forms, observations, analysis of contaminants, and recommendations for control and correction of hazards. They may prepare documents to be used in legal proceedings and give testimony in court proceedings. Those who develop expertise in certain areas may develop occupational health and safety systems, including policies, procedures, and manuals.

Specialists and technicians that concentrate in particular areas include environmental protection officers, ergonomists, health physicists, industrial hygienists, and mine examiners. *Environmental protection officers* evaluate and coordinate programs that impact the environment, such as the storage and handling of hazardous waste or monitoring the cleanup of contaminated soil or water. *Ergonomists* help ensure that the work environment allows employees to maximize their comfort, safety, and productivity. *Health physicists* help protect people and the environment from hazardous radiation exposure by monitoring the manufacture, handling, and disposal of radioactive material. *Industrial hygienists* examine the workplace for health hazards, such as worker exposure to lead, asbestos, pesticides, or communicable diseases. *Mine examiners* are technicians who inspect mines for proper air flow and health hazards such as the buildup of methane or other noxious gases.

Working Conditions

Occupational health and safety specialists and technicians work with many different people in a variety of environments. Their jobs often involve considerable fieldwork, and some travel frequently. Many occupational health and safety specialists and technicians work long and often irregular hours.

Occupational health and safety specialists and technicians may be exposed to many of the same physically strenuous conditions and hazards as industrial employees, and the work may be performed in unpleasant, stressful, and dangerous working conditions. They may find themselves in an adversarial role if the management of an organization disagrees with the recommendations for ensuring a safe working environment.

Training, Other Qualifications, and Advancement

All occupational health and safety specialists and technicians are trained in the applicable laws or inspection procedures through some combination of classroom and on-the-job training. Awards and degrees in programs related to occupational safety and health include 1-year certificates, associate degrees, bachelor's degrees, and graduate degrees. The Accreditation Board for Engineering and Technology (ABET) accredits health physics, industrial hygiene, and safety programs in addition to engineering programs. Many employers, including the federal government, require a bachelor's degree in occupational health; safety; or a related field, such as engineering, biology, or chemistry, for some specialist positions. Many industrial hygiene programs result in a master's degree. Experience as an occupational health and safety professional is also a prerequisite for many positions. Advancement to senior specialist positions is likely to require an advanced degree and substantial experience in several areas of practice.

In general, people who want to enter this occupation should be responsible and like detailed work. Occupational health and safety specialists and technicians should be able to communicate well. Recommended high school courses include English, mathematics, chemistry, biology, and physics.

Certification is available through the Board of Certified Safety Professionals (BCSP) and the American Board of Industrial Hygiene (ABIH). The BCSP offers the Certified Safety Professional (CSP) credential, while the ABIH offers the Certified Industrial Hygienist (CIH) and Certified Associate Industrial Hygienist (CAIH) credentials. Also, the Council on Certification of Health, Environmental, and Safety Technologists, a joint effort between the BCSP and ABIH, awards the Occupational Health and Safety Technologist (OHST) and Construction Health and Safety Technician (CHST) credentials. Requirements for the OHST and CHST credentials are less stringent than those for the CSP, CIH, or CAIH credentials. Once education and experience requirements have been met, certification may be obtained through an examination. Continuing education is required for recertification. Although voluntary, many employers encourage certification.

Federal government occupational health and safety specialists and technicians whose job performance is satisfactory advance through their career ladder to a specified full-performance level. For positions above this level, usually supervisory positions, advancement is competitive and based on agency needs and individual merit. Advancement opportunities in state and local governments and the private sector are often similar to those in the federal government.

Research or related teaching positions at the college level require advanced education.

Employment

Occupational health and safety specialists held about 40,000 jobs in 2004. While the majority of jobs were spread throughout the private sector, about 2 out of 5 specialists worked for government agencies. Local governments employed 19 percent, state governments employed 18 percent, and the federal government employed 4 percent. Other occupational health and safety specialists were employed in manufacturing firms; private general medical and surgical hospitals; management, scientific, and technical consulting services; management of companies and enterprises; support activities for mining; research and development in the physical, engineering, and life sciences; private colleges, universities, and professional schools; and electric power generation, transmission, and distribution. Some were self-employed.

Occupational health and safety technicians held about 12,000 jobs in 2004. Nearly 3 out of 10 technicians worked in government agencies. Local governments employed 13 percent, state governments employed 7 percent, and the federal government employed 9 percent. Other occupational health and safety technicians were employed in manufacturing firms; private general medical and surgical hospitals; private colleges, universities, and professional schools; employment services; management, scientific, and technical consulting services; testing laboratories for architectural, engineering, and related services; research and development in the physical, engineering, and life sciences; and electric power generation, transmission, and distribution.

Within the federal government, most jobs are as Occupational Safety and Health Administration (OSHA) inspectors, who enforce U.S. Department of Labor regulations that ensure adequate safety principles, practices, and techniques are applied in workplaces. Employers may be fined for violation of OSHA standards. Within the U.S. Department of Health and Human Services, occupational health and safety specialists working for the National Institute of Occupational Safety and Health (NIOSH) provide private companies with an avenue to evaluate the health and safety of their employees without the risk of being fined. Most large government agencies also employ occupational health and safety specialists and technicians who work to protect agency employees.

Most private companies either employ their own occupational health and safety personnel or contract with occupational health and safety professionals to ensure the safety of their workers and compliance with federal, state, and local government agencies that enforce rules on safety, health, and the environment.

Job Outlook

Employment of occupational health and safety specialists and technicians is expected to grow about as fast as average for all occupations through 2014, reflecting a balance of continuing public demand for a safe and healthy work environment against the desire for smaller government and fewer regulations. Since the September 11, 2001 attacks, emergency preparedness has become a greater focus for the public and private sectors and for occupational health and safety specialists and technicians. Additional job openings will arise from the need to replace those who transfer to other occupations, retire, or leave for other reasons. In private industry, employment growth will reflect industry growth and the continuing self-enforcement of government and company regulations and policies.

Employment of occupational health and safety specialists and technicians in the private sector is somewhat affected by general economic fluctuations. Federal, state, and local governments, which

employ about 2 out of 5 of all specialists and technicians, provide considerable job security; workers are less likely to be affected by changes in the economy.

Earnings

Median annual earnings of occupational health and safety specialists were $51,570 in May 2004. The middle 50 percent earned between $39,580 and $65,370. The lowest 10 percent earned less than $30,590, and the highest 10 percent earned more than $79,530. Median annual earnings of occupational health and safety specialists in May 2004 were $48,710 in local government and $44,400 in state government.

Median annual earnings of occupational health and safety technicians were $42,130 in May 2004. The middle 50 percent earned between $29,900 and $56,640. The lowest 10 percent earned less than $22,860, and the highest 10 percent earned more than $70,460.

Most occupational health and safety specialists and technicians work in large private firms or for federal, state, and local governments, most of which generally offer more generous benefits than smaller firms.

Related Occupations

Occupational health and safety specialists and technicians help to ensure that laws and regulations are obeyed. Others who enforce laws and regulations include agricultural inspectors, construction and building inspectors, correctional officers, financial examiners, fire inspectors, police and detectives, and transportation inspectors.

Sources of Additional Information

Information about jobs in federal, state, and local governments and in private industry is available from state employment service offices.

For information on a career as an industrial hygienist, including a list of colleges and universities offering industrial hygiene and related degrees, contact

▸ American Industrial Hygiene Association, 2700 Prosperity Ave., Suite 250, Fairfax, VA 22031. Internet: http://www.aiha.org

For information on the Certified Industrial Hygienist or Certified Associate Industrial Hygienist credential, contact

▸ American Board of Industrial Hygiene, 6015 West St. Joseph Hwy., Suite 102, Lansing, MI 48917. Internet: http://www.abih.org

For more information on professions in safety, a comprehensive list of colleges and universities offering safety and related degrees, and applications for scholarships, contact

▸ American Society of Safety Engineers, 1800 E Oakton St., Des Plaines, IL 60018. Internet: http://www.asse.org

For more information on professions in safety, a list of programs in safety and related academic fields, and the Certified Safety Professional credential, contact

▸ Board of Certified Safety Professionals, 208 Burwash Ave., Savoy, IL 61874. Internet: http://www.bcsp.org

For information on the Occupational Health and Safety Technologist and Construction Health and Safety Technician credentials, contact

▸ Council on Certification of Health, Environmental, and Safety Technologists, 208 Burwash Ave., Savoy, IL 61874. Internet: http://www.cchest.org

For information on a career as a health physicist, contact

▸ Health Physics Society, 1313 Dolley Madison Blvd., Suite 402, McLean, VA 22101. Internet: http://www.hps.org

For additional career information, contact

▸ U.S. Department of Health and Human Services, Center for Disease Control and Prevention, National Institute of Occupational Safety and Health, Hubert H. Humphrey Bldg., 200 Independence Ave. SW, Room 715H, Washington, DC 20201. Internet: http://www.cdc.gov/niosh

▸ U.S. Department of Labor, Occupational Safety and Health Administration, Office of Communication, 200 Constitution Ave. NW, Washington, DC 20210. Internet: http://www.osha.gov

Information on obtaining positions as occupational health and safety specialists and technicians with the federal government is available from the Office of Personnel Management through USAJOBS, the federal government's official employment information system. This resource for locating and applying for job opportunities can be accessed through the Internet at http://www.usajobs.opm.gov or through an interactive voice response telephone system at (703) 724-1850 or TDD (978) 461-8404. These numbers are not toll free, and charges may result.

Occupational Therapist Assistants and Aides

(O*NET 31-2011.00 and 31-2012.00)

Significant Points

■ Employment is projected to increase much faster than the average, reflecting growth in the number of individuals with disabilities or limited function who require therapeutic services.

■ Occupational therapist assistants generally must complete an associate degree or a certificate program; in contrast, occupational therapist aides usually receive most of their training on the job.

■ In an effort to control rising health care costs, third-party payers are expected to encourage occupational therapists to delegate more hands-on therapy work to lower-paid occupational therapist assistants and aides.

Nature of the Work

Occupational therapist assistants and aides work under the direction of occupational therapists to provide rehabilitative services to persons with mental, physical, emotional, or developmental impairments. The ultimate goal is to improve clients' quality of life and ability to perform daily activities. For example, occupational therapist assistants help injured workers re-enter the labor force by teaching them how to compensate for lost motor skills or help individuals with learning disabilities increase their independence.

Occupational therapist assistants, commonly known as *occupational therapy assistants,* help clients with rehabilitative activities and exercises outlined in a treatment plan developed in collaboration with an occupational therapist. Activities range from teaching the proper method of moving from a bed into a wheelchair to the best way to stretch and limber the muscles of the hand. Assistants monitor an individual's activities to make sure that they are performed correctly and to provide encouragement. They also record their client's progress for the occupational therapist. If the treatment is not having the intended effect or the client is not improving as expected, the therapist may alter the treatment program in hopes of obtaining better results. In addition, occupational therapist assistants document the billing of the client's health insurance provider.

Occupational therapist aides typically prepare materials and assemble equipment used during treatment. They are responsible for a range of clerical tasks, including scheduling appointments, answering the telephone, restocking or ordering depleted supplies, and filling out insurance forms or other paperwork. Aides are not licensed, so the law does not allow them to perform as wide a range of tasks as occupational therapist assistants.

Working Conditions

The hours and days that occupational therapist assistants and aides work vary with the facility and with whether they are full- or part-time employees. Many outpatient therapy offices and clinics have evening and weekend hours to help coincide with patients' personal schedules.

Occupational therapist assistants and aides need to have a moderate degree of strength because of the physical exertion required in assisting patients with their treatment. For example, assistants and aides may need to lift patients. Constant kneeling, stooping, and standing for long periods also are part of the job.

Training, Other Qualifications, and Advancement

An associate degree or a certificate from an accredited community college or technical school is generally required to qualify for occupational therapist assistant jobs. In contrast, occupational therapist aides usually receive most of their training on the job.

There were 135 accredited occupational therapist assistant programs in 2005. The first year of study typically involves an introduction to health care, basic medical terminology, anatomy, and physiology. In the second year, courses are more rigorous and usually include occupational therapist courses in areas such as mental health, adult physical disabilities, gerontology, and pediatrics. Students also must complete 16 weeks of supervised fieldwork in a clinic or community setting. Applicants to occupational therapist assistant programs can improve their chances of admission by taking high school courses in biology and health and by performing volunteer work in nursing care facilities, occupational or physical therapists' offices, or other health care settings.

Occupational therapist assistants are regulated in most states and must pass a national certification examination after they graduate. Those who pass the test are awarded the title "Certified Occupational Therapy Assistant."

Occupational therapist aides usually receive most of their training on the job. Qualified applicants must have a high school diploma, strong interpersonal skills, and a desire to help people in need. Applicants may increase their chances of getting a job by volunteering their services, thus displaying initiative and aptitude to the employer.

Assistants and aides must be responsible, patient, and willing to take directions and work as part of a team. Furthermore, they should be caring and want to help people who are not able to help themselves.

Employment

Occupational therapist assistants and aides held about 27,000 jobs in 2004. Occupational therapist assistants held about 21,000 jobs, and occupational therapist aides held approximately 5,400. About 30 percent of jobs for assistants and aides were in hospitals, 23 percent were in offices of occupational therapists, and 18 percent were in nursing care facilities. The rest were primarily in community care facilities for the elderly, home health care services, individual and family services, and state government agencies.

Job Outlook

Employment of occupational therapist assistants and aides is expected to grow much faster than the average for all occupations through 2014. The impact of proposed federal legislation imposing limits on reimbursement for therapy services may adversely affect the job market for occupational therapist assistants and aides in the short run. Over the long run, however, demand for occupational therapist assistants and aides will continue to rise because of the increasing number of individuals with disabilities or limited function. Job growth will result from an aging population, including the baby-boom generation, which will need more occupational therapy services. The increased prevalence of sensory disorders in children will increase the demand for occupational therapy services. Increasing demand also will result from advances in medicine that allow more people with critical problems to survive and then need rehabilitative therapy. In an effort to control rising health care costs, third-party payers are expected to encourage occupational therapists to delegate more hands-on therapy work to lower-paid occupational therapist assistants and aides.

Earnings

Median annual earnings of occupational therapist assistants were $38,430 in May 2004. The middle 50 percent earned between $31,970 and $44,390. The lowest 10 percent earned less than $25,880, and the highest 10 percent earned more than $52,700. Median annual earnings of occupational therapist assistants were $40,130 in offices of other health practitioners, which includes offices of occupational therapists.

Median annual earnings of occupational therapist aides were $23,150 in May 2004. The middle 50 percent earned between $19,080 and $31,910. The lowest 10 percent earned less than $15,820, and the highest 10 percent earned more than $41,560.

Related Occupations

Occupational therapist assistants and aides work under the supervision and direction of occupational therapists. Other workers in the health care field who work under similar supervision include dental assistants, medical assistants, pharmacy aides, pharmacy technicians, and physical therapist assistants and aides.

Sources of Additional Information

For information on a career as an occupational therapist assistant or aide and a list of accredited programs, contact

‣ American Occupational Therapy Association, 4720 Montgomery Lane, Bethesda, MD 20824-1220. Internet: http://www.aota.org

Occupational Therapists

(O*NET 29-1122.00)

Significant Points

■ Employment is projected to increase much faster than the average as rapid growth in the number of middle-aged and elderly individuals increases the demand for therapeutic services.

■ Beginning in 2007, a master's degree or higher in occupational therapy will be the minimum educational requirement.

■ Occupational therapists are increasingly taking on supervisory roles, allowing assistants and aides to work more closely with clients under the guidance of a therapist, in an effort to reduce the cost of therapy.

■ More than a quarter of occupational therapists work part time.

Nature of the Work

Occupational therapists (OTs) help people improve their ability to perform tasks in their daily living and working environments. They work with individuals who have conditions that are mentally, physically, developmentally, or emotionally disabling. They also help them to develop, recover, or maintain daily living and work skills. Occupational therapists help clients not only to improve their basic motor functions and reasoning abilities, but also to compensate for permanent loss of function. Their goal is to help clients have independent, productive, and satisfying lives.

Occupational therapists assist clients in performing activities of all types, ranging from using a computer to caring for daily needs such as dressing, cooking, and eating. Physical exercises may be used to increase strength and dexterity, while other activities may be chosen to improve visual acuity and the ability to discern patterns. For example, a client with short-term memory loss might be encouraged to make lists to aid recall, and a person with coordination problems might be assigned exercises to improve hand-eye coordination. Occupational therapists also use computer programs to help clients improve decisionmaking, abstract-reasoning, problem-solving, and perceptual skills, as well as memory, sequencing, and coordination—all of which are important for independent living.

Therapists instruct those with permanent disabilities, such as spinal cord injuries, cerebral palsy, or muscular dystrophy, in the use of adaptive equipment, including wheelchairs, orthotics, and aids for eating and dressing. They also design or make special equipment needed at home or at work. Therapists develop computer-aided adaptive equipment and teach clients with severe limitations how to use that equipment in order to communicate better and control various aspects of their environment.

Some occupational therapists treat individuals whose ability to function in a work environment has been impaired. These practitioners arrange employment, evaluate the work environment, plan work activities, and assess the client's progress. Therapists also may collaborate with the client and the employer to modify the work environment so that the work can be successfully completed.

Occupational therapists may work exclusively with individuals in a particular age group or with particular disabilities. In schools, for example, they evaluate children's abilities, recommend and provide therapy, modify classroom equipment, and help children participate as fully as possible in school programs and activities. A therapist may work with children individually, lead small groups in the classroom, consult with a teacher, or serve on a curriculum or other administrative committee. Early intervention therapy services are provided to infants and toddlers who have, or are at risk of having, developmental delays. Specific therapies may include facilitating the use of the hands, promoting skills for listening and following directions, fostering social play skills, or teaching dressing and grooming skills.

Occupational therapy also is beneficial to the elderly population. Therapists help the elderly lead more productive, active, and independent lives through a variety of methods, including the use of adaptive equipment. Therapists with specialized training in driver rehabilitation assess an individual's ability to drive, using both clinical and on-the-road tests. The evaluations allow the therapist to make recommendations for adaptive equipment, training to prolong driving independence, and alternative transportation options. Occupational therapists also work with the client to asses the home for hazards and to identify environmental factors that contribute to falls.

Occupational therapists in mental health settings treat individuals who are mentally ill, mentally retarded, or emotionally disturbed. To treat these problems, therapists choose activities that help people learn to engage in and cope with daily life. Activities include time management skills, budgeting, shopping, homemaking, and the use of public transportation. Occupational therapists also may work with individuals who are dealing with alcoholism, drug abuse, depression, eating disorders, or stress-related disorders.

Assessing and recording a client's activities and progress is an important part of an occupational therapist's job. Accurate records are essential for evaluating clients, for billing, and for reporting to physicians and other health care providers.

Working Conditions

Occupational therapists in hospitals and other health care and community settings usually work a 40-hour week. Those in schools may participate in meetings and other activities during and after the school day. In 2004, more than a quarter of occupational therapists worked part time.

In large rehabilitation centers, therapists may work in spacious rooms equipped with machines, tools, and other devices generating noise. The work can be tiring because therapists are on their feet much of the time. Those providing home health care services may spend time driving from appointment to appointment. Therapists also face hazards such as back strain from lifting and moving clients and equipment.

Therapists increasingly are taking on supervisory roles. Because of rising health care costs, third-party payers are beginning to encourage occupational therapist assistants and aides to take more hands-on responsibility. By having assistants and aides work more closely with clients under the guidance of a therapist, the cost of therapy should decline.

Training, Other Qualifications, and Advancement

Currently, a bachelor's degree in occupational therapy is the minimum requirement for entry into the field. Beginning in 2007, however, a master's degree or higher will be the minimum educational requirement. As a result, students in bachelor's-level programs must complete their coursework and fieldwork before 2007. All states, Puerto Rico, Guam, and the District of Columbia regulate the practice of occupational therapy. To obtain a license, applicants must graduate from an accredited educational program and pass a national certification examination. Those who pass the exam are awarded the title "Occupational Therapist Registered (OTR)." Some states have additional requirements for therapists who work in schools or early intervention programs. These requirements may include education-related classes, an education practice certificate, or early intervention certification requirements.

In 2005, 122 master's degree programs offered entry-level education, 65 programs offered a combined bachelor's and master's degree, and 5 offered an entry-level doctoral degree. Most schools have full-time programs, although a growing number are offering weekend or part-time programs as well. Bachelor's degree programs in occupational therapy are no longer offered because of the requirement for a master's degree or higher beginning in 2007. In addition, post-baccalaureate certificate programs for students with a degree other than occupational therapy are no longer offered.

Occupational therapy coursework includes the physical, biological, and behavioral sciences and the application of occupational therapy theory and skills. The completion of 6 months of supervised fieldwork also is required.

Persons considering this profession should take high school courses in biology, chemistry, physics, health, art, and the social sciences. College admissions offices also look favorably at paid or volunteer experience in the health care field. Relevant undergraduate majors include biology, psychology, sociology, anthropology, liberal arts, and anatomy.

Occupational therapists need patience and strong interpersonal skills to inspire trust and respect in their clients. Patience is necessary because many clients may not show rapid improvement. Ingenuity and imagination in adapting activities to individual needs are assets. Those working in home health care services must be able to adapt to a variety of settings.

Employment

Occupational therapists held about 92,000 jobs in 2004. About 1 in 10 occupational therapists held more than one job. The largest number of jobs were in hospitals. Other major employers were offices of other health practitioners (including offices of occupational therapists), public and private educational services, and nursing care facilities. Some occupational therapists were employed by home health care services, outpatient care centers, offices of physicians, individual and family services, community care facilities for the elderly, and government agencies.

A small number of occupational therapists were self-employed in private practice. These practitioners saw clients referred by physicians or other health professionals or provided contract or consulting services to nursing care facilities, schools, adult day care programs, and home health care agencies.

Job Outlook

Employment of occupational therapists is expected to increase much faster than the average for all occupations through 2014. The impact of proposed federal legislation imposing limits on reimbursement for therapy services may adversely affect the job market for occupational therapists in the short run. However, over the long run, the demand for occupational therapists should continue to rise as a result of growth in the number of individuals with disabilities or limited function who require therapy services. The baby-boom generation's movement into middle age, a period when the incidence of heart attack and stroke increases, will spur demand for therapeutic services. Growth in the population 75 years and older—an age group that suffers from high incidences of disabling conditions—also will increase demand for therapeutic services. Driver rehabilitation and fall-prevention training for the elderly are emerging practice areas for occupational therapy. In addition, medical advances now enable more patients with critical problems to survive—patients who ultimately may need extensive therapy.

Hospitals will continue to employ a large number of occupational therapists to provide therapy services to acutely ill inpatients. Hospitals also will need occupational therapists to staff their outpatient rehabilitation programs.

Employment growth in schools will result from the expansion of the school-age population, the extension of services for disabled students, and an increasing prevalence of sensory disorders in children. Therapists will be needed to help children with disabilities prepare to enter special education programs.

Earnings

Median annual earnings of occupational therapists were $54,660 in May 2004. The middle 50 percent earned between $45,690 and $67,010. The lowest 10 percent earned less than $37,430, and the highest 10 percent earned more than $81,600. Median annual earnings in the industries employing the largest numbers of occupational therapists in May 2004 were

Home health care services	$58,720
Offices of other health practitioners	56,620
Nursing care facilities	56,570
General medical and surgical hospitals	55,710
Elementary and secondary schools	48,580

Related Occupations

Occupational therapists use specialized knowledge to help individuals perform daily living skills and achieve maximum independence. Other workers performing similar duties include audiologists, chiropractors, physical therapists, recreational therapists, rehabilitation counselors, respiratory therapists, and speech-language pathologists.

Sources of Additional Information

For more information on occupational therapy as a career, contact

▸ American Occupational Therapy Association, 4720 Montgomery Lane, Bethesda, MD 20824-1220. Internet: http://www.aota.org

For information regarding the requirements to practice as an occupational therapist in schools, contact the appropriate occupational therapy regulatory agency for your state.

Operations Research Analysts

(O*NET 15-2031.00)

Significant Points

■ Employers generally prefer applicants with at least a master's degree in operations research or management science or a closely related field such as computer science, engineering, business, mathematics, or information systems.

■ Employment growth is projected to be slower than average, reflecting slow growth in the number of jobs with the title "operations research analyst."

■ Individuals with a master's or Ph.D. degree in management science, operations research, or equivalent should have good job opportunities as operations research analysts or in closely related occupations such as systems analysts, computer scientists, or management analysts.

Nature of the Work

"Operations research" and "management science" are terms that are used interchangeably to describe the discipline of applying advanced analytical techniques to help make better decisions and to solve problems. The procedures of operations research have been used effectively during wartime in areas such as deploying radar, searching for enemy submarines, and getting supplies to where they were needed most. New analytical methods have been developed and numerous peacetime applications have emerged, leading to the use of operations research in many industries and occupations.

The prevalence of operations research in the nation's economy reflects the growing complexity of managing large organizations that require the effective use of money, materials, equipment, and people. Operations research analysts help determine better ways to coordinate these elements by applying analytical methods from mathematics, science, and engineering. Analysts often find multiple possible solutions for meeting the particular goals of a project. These potential solutions are then presented to managers, who choose the course of action that they perceive to be best for the organization.

Operations research analysts often have one area of specialization, such as working in the transportation or the financial services industry, but the issues and industries in which operations research can be used are many. In general, operations research analysts may be involved in top-level strategizing, planning, forecasting, allocating resources, measuring performance, scheduling, designing production facilities and systems, managing the supply chain, pricing, coordinating transportation and distribution, or analyzing large databases.

The duties of the operations research analyst vary according to the structure and management of the employer's or client's organization. Some firms centralize operations research in one department; others use operations research in each division. Operations research analysts also may work closely with senior managers to identify and solve a variety of problems. Some organizations contract with consulting firms to provide operations research services. Economists, computer systems analysts, mathematicians, and others may apply operations research techniques to address problems in their respective fields. (These occupations are discussed elsewhere in this book.)

Regardless of the type or structure of the client organization, operations research entails following a standard set of procedures and conducting analysis to help managers improve performance. Managers begin the process by describing the symptoms of a problem to the analyst, who then formally defines the problem. For example, an operations research analyst for an auto manufacturer may be asked to determine the best inventory level for each of the parts needed on a production line and to ascertain the optimal number of windshields to be kept in stock. Too many windshields would be wasteful and expensive, whereas too few could result in an unintended halt in production.

Operations research analysts study such problems, breaking them into their components. Analysts then gather information about each of the components from a variety of sources. To determine the optimal inventory, for example, operations research analysts might talk with engineers about production levels, discuss purchasing arrangements with buyers, and examine storage-cost data provided by the accounting department.

With the relevant information in hand, the analyst determines the most appropriate analytical technique. Techniques used may include Monte Carlo simulation, linear and nonlinear programming, dynamic programming, queuing and other stochastic-process models, Markov decision processes, econometric methods, data envelopment analysis, neural networks, expert systems, decision analysis, and the analytic hierarchy process. Nearly all of these techniques involve the construction of a mathematical model that attempts to describe the system being studied. The use of models enables the analyst to explicitly describe the different components and clarify the relationships among them. The descriptions can be altered to examine what may happen to the system under different circumstances. In most cases, a computer program is developed to numerically evaluate the model.

Usually the model chosen is modified and run repeatedly to obtain different solutions. A model for airline flight scheduling, for example, might stipulate such things as connecting cities, the amount of fuel required to fly the routes, projected levels of passenger demand, varying ticket and fuel prices, pilot scheduling, and maintenance costs. By assessing different possible schedules, the analyst is able to determine the best flight schedule consistent with particular assumptions.

Based on the results of the analysis, the operations research analyst presents recommendations to managers. The analyst may need to modify and rerun the computer program to consider different assumptions before presenting the final recommendation. Once managers reach a decision, the analyst usually works with others in the organization to ensure the plan's successful implementation.

Working Conditions

Operations research analysts generally work regular hours in an office environment. However, because they work on projects that are of immediate interest to top managers, operations research analysts often are under pressure to meet deadlines and may work more than a 40-hour week.

Training, Other Qualifications, and Advancement

Employers generally prefer applicants with at least a master's degree in operations research or a closely related field, such as computer science, engineering, business, mathematics, information systems, or management science, coupled with a bachelor's degree in computer science or a quantitative discipline such as economics, mathematics, or statistics. Dual graduate degrees in operations research and computer science are especially attractive to employers. Operations research analysts must be able to think logically, use computers proficiently, work well with people, and demonstrate good oral and written communication skills.

In addition to supporting formal education in one manner or another, employers often sponsor training for experienced workers, helping them keep up with new developments in operations research techniques and computer science. Some analysts attend advanced university classes on these subjects at their employer's expense.

Computers are the most important tools used by operations research analysts for performing in-depth analysis. As a result, training and experience in programming are required. Analysts typically need to be proficient in database collection and management, programming, and the development and use of sophisticated software packages.

Beginning analysts usually perform routine work under the supervision of more experienced analysts. As the novices gain knowledge and experience, they are assigned more complex tasks and are given greater autonomy to design models and solve problems. Operations research analysts can advance by assuming positions as technical specialists or supervisors. Analysts also gain valuable insights into the industry or field in which they specialize and may assume higher-level nontechnical managerial or administrative positions. Operations research analysts with significant experience may become consultants, and some may even open their own consulting practices.

Employment

Operations research analysts held about 58,000 jobs in 2004. Major employers include computer systems design firms; insurance carriers and other financial institutions; telecommunications companies; management, scientific, and technical consulting services firms; and federal, state, and local governments. More than 4 out of 5 operations research analysts in the federal government work for the Department of Defense, and many in private industry work directly or indirectly on national defense.

Job Outlook

Employment of operations research analysts is expected to grow more slowly than average for all occupations through 2014, reflecting slow growth in the number of jobs with the title "operations research analyst." Job opportunities in operations research should be good, however, because organizations throughout the economy will strive to improve their productivity, effectiveness, and competitiveness and because of the extensive availability of data, computers, and software. Many jobs in operations research have other titles, such as operations analyst, management analyst, systems analyst, and computer scientist. Individuals who hold a master's or Ph.D. degree in operations research, management science, or a closely related field should find good job opportunities because the number of openings generated by employment growth and the need to replace those leaving the occupation is expected to exceed the number of persons graduating with these credentials.

Organizations face pressure today from growing domestic and international competition and must work to make their operations as effective as possible. As a result, businesses increasingly will rely on operations research analysts to optimize profits by improving productivity and reducing costs. As new technology is introduced into the marketplace, operations research analysts will be needed to determine how to utilize the technology in the best way.

Opportunities for operations research analysts exist in almost every industry because of the diversity of applications for their work. As businesses and government agencies continue to contract out jobs to cut costs, opportunities for operations research analysts will be best in management, scientific, and technical consulting firms. Opportunities in the military will exist as well, but will depend on the size of future military budgets. Military leaders will rely on operations research analysts to test and evaluate the accuracy and effectiveness of new weapons systems and strategies. (See this book's description of job opportunities in the Armed Forces.)

Earnings

Median annual earnings of operations research analysts were $60,190 in May 2004. The middle 50 percent earned between $45,640 and $78,420. The lowest 10 percent had earnings of less than $36,180, while the highest 10 percent earned more than $95,990.

The average annual salary for operations research analysts in the federal government in nonsupervisory, supervisory, and managerial positions was $89,882 in 2005.

Related Occupations

Operations research analysts apply advanced analytical methods to large, complicated problems. Workers in other occupations that stress advanced analysis include computer systems analysts, computer scientists and database administrators, computer programmers, engineers, mathematicians, statisticians, economists, and market and survey researchers. Because its goal is improved organizational effectiveness, operations research also is closely allied to managerial occupations such as computer and information systems managers and management analysts.

Sources of Additional Information

Information on career opportunities for operations research analysts is available from

▸ Institute for Operations Research and the Management Sciences, 7240 Parkway Dr., Suite 310, Hanover, MD 21076. Internet: http://www.informs.org

For information on operations research careers in the Armed Forces and the U.S. Department of Defense, contact

▸ Military Operations Research Society, 1703 N. Beauregard St., Suite 450, Alexandria, VA 22311. Internet: http://www.mors.org

Information on obtaining positions as operations research analysts with the federal government is available from the Office of Personnel Management through USAJOBS, the federal government's official employment information system. This resource for locating and applying for job opportunities can be accessed through the Internet at http://www.usajobs.opm.gov or through an interactive voice response telephone system at (703) 724-1850 or TDD (978) 461-8404. These numbers are not toll free, and charges may result.

Opticians, Dispensing

(O*NET 29-2081.00)

Significant Points

■ Most dispensing opticians receive training on the job or through apprenticeships lasting 2 or more years; however, some employers seek graduates of postsecondary training programs in opticianry.

■ About 20 states require a license.

■ Projected average employment growth reflects the steady demand for corrective lenses and eyeglass frames that are in fashion.

Nature of the Work

Dispensing opticians fit eyeglasses and contact lenses, following prescriptions written by ophthalmologists or optometrists. (The work of optometrists is outlined in a description elsewhere in this book. See the description of physicians and surgeons for information about ophthalmologists.)

Dispensing opticians examine written prescriptions to determine the specifications of lenses. They recommend eyeglass frames, lenses, and lens coatings after considering the prescription and the customer's occupation, habits, and facial features. Dispensing opticians measure clients' eyes, including the distance between the centers of the pupils and the distance between the ocular surface and the lens. For customers without prescriptions, dispensing opticians may use a focimeter to record eyeglass measurements in order to duplicate the eyeglasses. They also may obtain a customer's previous record to re-make eyeglasses or contact lenses, or they may verify a prescription with the examining optometrist or ophthalmologist.

Dispensing opticians prepare work orders that give ophthalmic laboratory technicians information needed to grind and insert lenses into a frame. The work order includes prescriptions for lenses and information on their size, material, color, and style. Some dispensing opticians grind and insert lenses themselves. After the glasses are made, dispensing opticians verify that the lenses have been ground to specifications. Then they may reshape or bend the frame, by hand or using pliers, so that the eyeglasses fit the customer properly and comfortably. Some also fix, adjust, and refit broken frames. They instruct clients about adapting to, wearing, or caring for eyeglasses.

Some dispensing opticians, after additional education and training, specialize in fitting contacts, artificial eyes, or cosmetic shells to cover blemished eyes.

To fit contact lenses, dispensing opticians measure the shape and size of the eye, select the type of contact lens material, and prepare work orders specifying the prescription and lens size. Fitting contact lenses requires considerable skill, care, and patience. Dispensing opticians observe customers' eyes, corneas, lids, and contact lenses with specialized instruments and microscopes. During several follow-up visits, opticians teach proper insertion, removal, and care of contact lenses. Opticians do all this to ensure that the fit is correct.

Dispensing opticians keep records on customers' prescriptions, work orders, and payments; track inventory and sales; and perform other administrative duties.

Working Conditions

Dispensing opticians work indoors in attractive, well-lighted, and well-ventilated surroundings. They may work in medical offices or small stores where customers are served one at a time. Some work in large stores where several dispensing opticians serve a number of customers at once. Opticians spend a fair amount of time on their feet. If they prepare lenses, they need to take precautions against the hazards associated with glass cutting, chemicals, and machinery.

Most dispensing opticians work about 40 hours a week, although a few work longer hours. Those in retail stores may work evenings and weekends. Some work part time.

Training, Other Qualifications, and Advancement

Employers usually hire individuals with no background as an optician or as an ophthalmic laboratory technician. The employers then provide the required training. Most dispensing opticians receive training on the job or through apprenticeships lasting 2 or more years. Some employers, however, seek people with postsecondary training in the field.

Knowledge of physics, basic anatomy, algebra, and trigonometry as well as experience with computers are particularly valuable because training usually includes instruction in optical mathematics, optical physics, and the use of precision measuring instruments and other machinery and tools. Dispensing opticians deal directly with the public, so they should be tactful and pleasant and communicate well. Manual dexterity and the ability to do precision work are essential.

Large employers usually offer structured apprenticeship programs; small employers provide more informal, on-the-job training. About 20 states require dispensing opticians to be licensed. States may require individuals to pass one of more of the following for licensure: a state practical examination, a state written examination, and certification examinations offered by the American Board of Opticianry (ABO) and the National Contact Lens Examiners (NCLE). To qualify for the examinations, states often require applicants to complete postsecondary training or work from 2 to 4 years as apprentices. Continuing education is commonly required for licensure renewal. Information about specific licensing requirements is available from the state board of occupational licensing. Apprenticeships or formal training programs are offered in other states as well.

Apprentices receive technical training and learn office management and sales. Under the supervision of an experienced optician, optometrist, or ophthalmologist, apprentices work directly with patients, fitting eyeglasses and contact lenses.

Formal training in the field is offered in community colleges and a few colleges and universities. In 2004, the Commission on Opticianry Accreditation accredited 24 programs that awarded 2-year associate degrees. There also are shorter programs of 1 year or less. Some states that offer a license to dispensing opticians allow graduates to take the licensure exam immediately upon graduation; others require a few months to a year of experience.

Dispensing opticians may apply to the ABO and the NCLE for certification of their skills. All applicants age 18 or older with a high school diploma or equivalent are eligible for the exam; however, some state licensing boards have additional eligibility requirements. Certification must be renewed every 3 years through continuing education. Those licensed in states where licensure renewal requirements include continuing education credits may use proof of their renewed state license to meet the recertification requirements of the ABO. Likewise, the NCLE will accept proof of renewal from any state that has contact lens requirements.

Many experienced dispensing opticians open their own optical stores. Others become managers of optical stores or sales representatives for wholesalers or manufacturers of eyeglasses or lenses.

Employment

Dispensing opticians held about 66,000 jobs in 2004. Nearly one-third worked in health and personal care stores, including optical goods stores. Many of these stores offer one-stop shopping. Customers may have their eyes examined, choose frames, and have glasses made on the spot. About 30 percent of dispensing opticians worked in offices of other health practitioners, including offices of optometrists. Over 10 percent worked in offices of physicians, including ophthalmologists who sell glasses directly to patients. Some work in optical departments of department stores or other general merchandise stores, such as warehouse clubs and superstores. Nearly 6 percent are self-employed and run their own unincorporated businesses.

Job Outlook

Employment of dispensing opticians is expected to grow about as fast as the average for all occupations through 2014 as demand grows for corrective lenses. The number of middle-aged and elderly persons is projected to increase rapidly. Middle age is a time when many individuals use corrective lenses for the first time, and elderly persons generally require more vision care than others. Fashion also influences demand. Frames come in a growing variety of styles and colors, encouraging people to buy more than one pair.

Increasing awareness of laser surgery that corrects some vision problems will have an impact on demand for eyewear. Although the surgery remains relatively more expensive than eyewear, patients who successfully undergo this surgery may not require glasses or contact lenses for several years.

The need to replace those who leave the occupation will result in additional job openings. Nevertheless, the number of job openings will be limited because the occupation is small. Dispensing opticians are vulnerable to changes in the business cycle because eyewear purchases often can be deferred for a time.

Earnings

Median annual earnings of dispensing opticians were $27,950 in May 2004. The middle 50 percent earned between $21,360 and $35,940. The lowest 10 percent earned less than $17,390, and the highest 10 percent earned more than $45,340. Median annual earnings in the industries employing the largest numbers of dispensing opticians in May 2004 were

Health and personal care stores	$30,890
Offices of physicians	30,560
Offices of other health practitioners	26,970

Related Occupations

Other workers who deal with customers and perform delicate work include jewelers and precious stone and metal workers, locksmiths and safe repairers, orthotists and prosthetists, and precision instrument and equipment repairers.

Sources of Additional Information

For general information about opticians and a list of home-study programs, seminars, and review materials, contact

▸ National Academy of Opticianry, 8401 Corporate Dr., Suite 605, Landover, MD 20785. Telephone (toll free): 800-229-4828. Internet: http://www.nao.org

For a list of accredited programs in opticianry, contact

▸ Commission on Opticianry Accreditation, 8665 Sudley Rd., #341, Manassas, VA 20110.

To learn about voluntary certification for opticians who fit eyeglasses, as well as a list of state licensing boards for opticians, contact

▸ American Board of Opticianry, 6506 Loisdale Rd., Suite 209, Springfield, VA 22150. Internet: http://www.abo.org

For information on voluntary certification for dispensing opticians who fit contact lenses, contact

▸ National Contact Lens Examiners, 6506 Loisdale Rd., Suite 209, Springfield, VA 22150. Internet: http://www.abo-ncle.org/

Optometrists

(O*NET 29-1041.00)

Significant Points

■ Admission to optometry school is competitive.

■ To be licensed, optometrists must earn a Doctor of Optometry degree from an accredited optometry school and pass a written National Board exam and a clinical examination.

■ Employment is expected to grow faster than average in response to the vision care needs of a growing and aging population.

Nature of the Work

Optometrists, also known as *doctors of optometry,* or *ODs*, provide most primary vision care. They examine people's eyes to diagnose vision problems and eye diseases, and they test patients' visual acuity, depth and color perception, and ability to focus and coordinate the eyes. Optometrists prescribe eyeglasses and contact lenses and provide vision therapy and low-vision rehabilitation. Optometrists analyze test results and develop a treatment plan. They administer drugs to patients to aid in the diagnosis of vision problems and prescribe drugs to treat some eye diseases. Optometrists often provide preoperative and postoperative care to cataract patients as well as to patients who have had laser vision correction or other eye surgery. They also diagnose conditions caused by systemic diseases such as diabetes and high blood pressure, referring patients to other health practitioners as needed.

Optometrists should not be confused with *ophthalmologists* or *dispensing opticians*. *Ophthalmologists* are physicians who perform eye surgery, as well as diagnose and treat eye diseases and injuries. Like optometrists, they also examine eyes and prescribe eyeglasses and contact lenses. *Dispensing opticians* fit and adjust eyeglasses and, in some states, may fit contact lenses according to prescriptions written by ophthalmologists or optometrists. (See the sections on physicians and surgeons and opticians, dispensing, elsewhere in this book.)

Most optometrists are in general practice. Some specialize in work with the elderly, children, or partially sighted persons who need specialized visual devices. Others develop and implement ways to protect workers' eyes from on-the-job strain or injury. Some specialize in contact lenses, sports vision, or vision therapy. A few teach optometry, perform research, or consult.

Most optometrists are private practitioners who also handle the business aspects of running an office, such as developing a patient base, hiring employees, keeping paper and electronic records, and ordering equipment and supplies. Optometrists who operate franchise optical stores also may have some of these duties.

Working Conditions

Optometrists work in places—usually their own offices—that are clean, well lighted, and comfortable. Most full-time optometrists work about 40 hours a week. Many work weekends and evenings to suit the needs of patients. Emergency calls, once uncommon, have increased with the passage of therapeutic-drug laws expanding optometrists' ability to prescribe medications.

Training, Other Qualifications, and Advancement

All states and the District of Columbia require that optometrists be licensed. Applicants for a license must have a Doctor of Optometry degree from an accredited optometry school and must pass both a written National Board examination and a national, regional, or state clinical board examination. The written and clinical examinations of the National Board of Examiners in Optometry usually are taken during the student's academic career. Many states also require applicants to pass an examination on relevant state laws. Licenses are renewed every 1 to 3 years and, in all states, continuing education credits are needed for renewal.

The Doctor of Optometry degree requires the completion of a 4-year program at an accredited optometry school, preceded by at least 3 years of preoptometric study at an accredited college or university. Most optometry students hold a bachelor's or higher degree. In 2004, 17 U.S. schools and colleges of optometry offered programs accredited by the Accreditation Council on Optometric Education of the American Optometric Association.

Requirements for admission to schools of optometry include courses in English, mathematics, physics, chemistry, and biology. A few schools also require or recommend courses in psychology, history, sociology, speech, or business. Because a strong background in science is important, many applicants to optometry school major in a science such as biology or chemistry, while other applicants major in another subject and take many science courses offering laboratory experience. Applicants must take the Optometry Admissions Test, which measures academic ability and scientific comprehension. Admission to optometry school is competitive. As a result, most applicants take the test after their sophomore or junior year, allowing them an opportunity to take the test again and raise their score. A few applicants are accepted to optometry school after 3 years of

college and complete their bachelor's degree while attending optometry school.

Optometry programs include classroom and laboratory study of health and visual sciences, as well as clinical training in the diagnosis and treatment of eye disorders. Courses in pharmacology, optics, vision science, biochemistry, and systemic disease are included.

Business ability, self-discipline, and the ability to deal tactfully with patients are important for success. The work of optometrists requires attention to detail and manual dexterity.

Optometrists wishing to teach or conduct research may study for a master's or Ph.D. degree in visual science, physiological optics, neurophysiology, public health, health administration, health information and communication, or health education. One-year postgraduate clinical residency programs are available for optometrists who wish to obtain advanced clinical competence. Specialty areas for residency programs include family practice optometry, pediatric optometry, geriatric optometry, vision therapy and rehabilitation, low-vision rehabilitation, cornea and contact lenses, refractive and ocular surgery, primary eye care optometry, and ocular disease.

Employment

Optometrists held about 34,000 jobs in 2004. The number of jobs is greater than the number of practicing optometrists because some optometrists hold two or more jobs. For example, an optometrist may have a private practice but also work in another practice, in a clinic, or in a vision care center. According to the American Optometric Association, about three-fourths of practicing optometrists are in private practice. Although many practice alone, optometrists increasingly are in a partnership or group practice.

Salaried jobs for optometrists were primarily in offices of optometrists; offices of physicians, including ophthalmologists; and health and personal care stores, including optical goods stores. A few salaried jobs for optometrists were in hospitals, the federal government, or outpatient care centers, including health maintenance organizations. Almost one third of optometrists were self-employed and not incorporated.

Job Outlook

Employment of optometrists is expected to grow faster than the average for all occupations through 2014 in response to the vision care needs of a growing and aging population. As baby boomers age, they will be more likely to visit optometrists and ophthalmologists because of the onset of vision problems in middle age, including those resulting from the extensive use of computers. The demand for optometric services also will increase because of growth in the oldest age group, with its increased likelihood of cataracts, glaucoma, diabetes, and hypertension. Greater recognition of the importance of vision care, along with rising personal incomes and growth in employee vision care plans, also will spur job growth.

Employment of optometrists would grow more rapidly were it not for anticipated productivity gains that will allow each optometrist to see more patients. These expected gains stem from greater use of optometric assistants and other support personnel, who will reduce the amount of time optometrists need with each patient. Also, laser surgery that can correct some vision problems is available, and although optometrists still will be needed to provide preoperative and postoperative care for laser surgery patients, patients who successfully undergo this surgery may not require optometrists to prescribe glasses or contacts for several years.

In addition to growth, the need to replace optometrists who retire or leave the occupation for another reason will create employment opportunities.

Earnings

Median annual earnings of salaried optometrists were $88,410 in May 2004. The middle 50 percent earned between $63,840 and $118,320. Median annual earnings of salaried optometrists in May 2004 were $87,430 in offices of optometrists. Salaried optometrists tend to earn more initially than do optometrists who set up their own practices. In the long run, however, those in private practice usually earn more.

According to the American Optometric Association, median net annual income for all optometrists, including the self-employed, was $114,000 in 2004. The middle 50 percent earned between $84,000 and $166,000.

Related Occupations

Other workers who apply scientific knowledge to prevent, diagnose, and treat disorders and injuries are chiropractors, dentists, physicians and surgeons, psychologists, podiatrists, and veterinarians.

Sources of Additional Information

For information on optometry as a career and a list of accredited optometric institutions of education, contact

▶ Association of Schools and Colleges of Optometry, 6110 Executive Blvd., Suite 510, Rockville, MD 20852. Internet: http://www.opted.org

Additional career information is available from

▶ American Optometric Association, Educational Services, 243 North Lindbergh Blvd., St. Louis, MO 63141. Internet: http://www.aoanet.org

The board of optometry in each state can supply information on licensing requirements.

For information on specific admission requirements and sources of financial aid, contact the admissions officers of individual optometry schools.

Paralegals and Legal Assistants

(O*NET 23-2011.00)

Significant Points

■ About 7 out of 10 work for law firms; others work for corporate legal departments and government agencies.

■ Most entrants have an associate's degree in paralegal studies or a bachelor's degree coupled with a certificate in paralegal studies.

■ Employment is projected to grow much faster than average as employers try to reduce costs by hiring paralegals to perform tasks formerly carried out by lawyers.

■ Competition for jobs should continue; experienced, formally trained paralegals should have the best employment opportunities.

Nature of the Work

While lawyers assume ultimate responsibility for legal work, they often delegate many of their tasks to paralegals. In fact, paralegals— also called legal assistants—are continuing to assume a growing range of tasks in the nation's legal offices and perform many of the same tasks as lawyers. Nevertheless, they are still explicitly prohibited from carrying out duties that are considered to be the practice of law, such as setting legal fees, giving legal advice, and presenting cases in court.

One of a paralegal's most important tasks is helping lawyers prepare for closings, hearings, trials, and corporate meetings. Paralegals investigate the facts of cases and ensure that all relevant information is considered. They also identify appropriate laws, judicial decisions, legal articles, and other materials that are relevant to assigned cases. After they analyze and organize the information, paralegals may prepare written reports that attorneys use in determining how cases should be handled. Should attorneys decide to file lawsuits on behalf of clients, paralegals may help prepare the legal arguments, draft pleadings and motions to be filed with the court, obtain affidavits, and assist attorneys during trials. Paralegals also organize and track files of all important case documents and make them available and easily accessible to attorneys.

In addition to this preparatory work, paralegals perform a number of other vital functions. For example, they help draft contracts, mortgages, separation agreements, and instruments of trust. They also may assist in preparing tax returns and planning estates. Some paralegals coordinate the activities of other law office employees and maintain financial office records. Various additional tasks may differ, depending on the employer.

Paralegals are found in all types of organizations, but most are employed by law firms, corporate legal departments, and various government offices. In these organizations, they can work in many different areas of the law, including litigation, personal injury, corporate law, criminal law, employee benefits, intellectual property, labor law, bankruptcy, immigration, family law, and real estate. As the law has become more complex, paralegals have responded by becoming more specialized. Within specialties, functions often are broken down further so that paralegals may deal with a specific area. For example, paralegals specializing in labor law may concentrate exclusively on employee benefits.

The duties of paralegals also differ widely with the type of organization in which they are employed. Paralegals who work for corporations often assist attorneys with employee contracts, shareholder agreements, stock-option plans, and employee benefit plans. They also may help prepare and file annual financial reports, maintain corporate minutes,' record resolutions, and prepare forms to secure loans for the corporation. Paralegals often monitor and review government regulations to ensure that the corporation is aware of new requirements and is operating within the law. Increasingly, experienced paralegals are assuming additional supervisory responsibilities such as overseeing team projects and serving as a communications link between the team and the corporation.

The duties of paralegals who work in the public sector usually vary within each agency. In general, paralegals analyze legal material for internal use, maintain reference files, conduct research for attorneys, and collect and analyze evidence for agency hearings. They may prepare informative or explanatory material on laws, agency regulations, and agency policy for general use by the agency and the public. Paralegals employed in community legal-service projects help the poor, the aged, and others who are in need of legal assistance. They file forms, conduct research, prepare documents, and, when authorized by law, may represent clients at administrative hearings.

Paralegals in small and medium-size law firms usually perform a variety of duties that require a general knowledge of the law. For example, they may research judicial decisions on improper police arrests or help prepare a mortgage contract. Paralegals employed by large law firms, government agencies, and corporations, however, are more likely to specialize in one aspect of the law.

Familiarity with computer use and technical knowledge have become essential to paralegal work. Computer software packages and the Internet are used to search legal literature stored in computer databases and on CD-ROM. In litigation involving many supporting documents, paralegals usually use computer databases to retrieve, organize, and index various materials. Imaging software allows paralegals to scan documents directly into a database, while billing programs help them to track hours billed to clients. Computer software packages also are used to perform tax computations and explore the consequences of various tax strategies for clients.

Working Conditions

Paralegals employed by corporations and government usually work a standard 40-hour week. Although most paralegals work year round, some are temporarily employed during busy times of the year and then are released when the workload diminishes. Paralegals who work for law firms sometimes work very long hours when they are under pressure to meet deadlines. Some law firms reward such loyalty with bonuses and additional time off.

These workers handle many routine assignments, particularly when they are inexperienced. As they gain experience, paralegals usually assume more varied tasks with additional responsibility. Paralegals do most of their work at desks in offices and law libraries. Occasionally, they travel to gather information and perform other duties.

Training, Other Qualifications, and Advancement

There are several ways to become a paralegal. The most common is through a community college paralegal program that leads to an associate's degree. The other common method of entry, mainly for those who already have a college degree, is through a program that leads to a certification in paralegal studies. A small number of schools also offer bachelor's and master's degrees in paralegal studies. Some employers train paralegals on the job, hiring college graduates with no legal experience or promoting experienced legal

secretaries. Other entrants have experience in a technical field that is useful to law firms, such as a background in tax preparation for tax and estate practice or in criminal justice, nursing, or health administration for personal injury practice.

An estimated 1,000 colleges and universities, law schools, and proprietary schools offer formal paralegal training programs. Approximately 260 paralegal programs are approved by the American Bar Association (ABA). Although many programs do not require such approval, graduation from an ABA-approved program can enhance one's employment opportunities. The requirements for admission to these programs vary. Some require certain college courses or a bachelor's degree, others accept high school graduates or those with legal experience, and a few schools require standardized tests and personal interviews.

Paralegal programs include 2-year associate degree's programs, 4-year bachelor's degree programs, and certificate programs that can take only a few months to complete. Most certificate programs provide intensive and, in some cases, specialized paralegal training for individuals who already hold college degrees, while associate's and bachelor's degree programs usually combine paralegal training with courses in other academic subjects. The quality of paralegal training programs varies; the better programs usually include job placement services. Programs generally offer courses introducing students to the legal applications of computers, including how to perform legal research on the Internet. Many paralegal training programs also offer an internship in which students gain practical experience by working for several months in a private law firm, the office of a public defender or attorney general, a bank, a corporate legal department, a legal aid organization, or a government agency. Experience gained in internships is an asset when one is seeking a job after graduation. Prospective students should examine the experiences of recent graduates before enrolling in a paralegal program.

Although most employers do not require certification, earning a voluntary certificate from a professional society may offer advantages in the labor market. The National Association of Legal Assistants (NALA), for example, has established standards for certification requiring various combinations of education and experience. Paralegals who meet these standards are eligible to take a 2-day examination, given three times each year at several regional testing centers. Those who pass this examination may use the Certified Legal Assistant (CLA) designation. The NALA also offers an advanced paralegal certification for those who want to specialize in other areas of the law. In addition, the Paralegal Advanced Competency Exam, administered through the National Federation of Paralegal Associations, offers professional recognition to paralegals with a bachelor's degree and at least 2 years of experience. Those who pass this examination may use the Registered Paralegal (RP) designation.

Paralegals must be able to document and present their findings and opinions to their supervising attorney. They need to understand legal terminology and have good research and investigative skills. Familiarity with the operation and applications of computers in legal research and litigation support also is important. Paralegals should stay informed of new developments in the laws that affect their area of practice. Participation in continuing legal education seminars allows paralegals to maintain and expand their knowledge of the law.

Because paralegals frequently deal with the public, they should be courteous and uphold the ethical standards of the legal profession. The National Association of Legal Assistants, the National Federation of Paralegal Associations, and a few states have established ethical guidelines for paralegals to follow.

Paralegals usually are given more responsibilities and require less supervision as they gain work experience. Experienced paralegals who work in large law firms, corporate legal departments, or government agencies may supervise and delegate assignments to other paralegals and clerical staff. Advancement opportunities also include promotion to managerial and other law-related positions within the firm or corporate legal department. However, some paralegals find it easier to move to another law firm when seeking increased responsibility or advancement.

Employment

Paralegals and legal assistants held about 224,000 jobs in 2004. Private law firms employed 7 out of 10 paralegals and legal assistants; most of the remainder worked for corporate legal departments and various levels of government. Within the federal government, the U.S. Department of Justice is the largest employer, followed by the Social Security Administration and the U.S. Department of the Treasury. A small number of paralegals own their own businesses and work as freelance legal assistants, contracting their services to attorneys or corporate legal departments.

Job Outlook

Employment for paralegals and legal assistants is projected to grow much faster than average for all occupations through 2014. Employers are trying to reduce costs and increase the availability and efficiency of legal services by hiring paralegals to perform tasks formerly carried out by lawyers. Besides new jobs created by employment growth, additional job openings will arise as people leave the occupation. Despite projections of rapid employment growth, competition for jobs should continue as many people seek to go into this profession; however, experienced, formally trained paralegals should have the best employment opportunities.

Private law firms will continue to be the largest employers of paralegals, but a growing array of other organizations, such as corporate legal departments, insurance companies, real estate and title insurance firms, and banks hire paralegals. Corporations in particular are boosting their in-house legal departments to cut costs. Demand for paralegals also is expected to grow as an expanding population increasingly requires legal services, especially in areas such as intellectual property, health care, international law, elder issues, criminal law, and environmental law. Paralegals who specialize in areas such as real estate, bankruptcy, medical malpractice, and product liability should have ample employment opportunities. The growth of prepaid legal plans also should contribute to the demand for legal services. Paralegal employment is expected to increase as organizations presently employing paralegals assign them a growing range of tasks and as paralegals are increasingly employed in small and medium-size establishments. A growing number of experienced paralegals are expected to establish their own businesses.

Job opportunities for paralegals will expand in the public sector as well. Community legal-service programs, which provide assistance to the poor, elderly, minorities, and middle-income families, will employ additional paralegals to minimize expenses and serve the most people. Federal, state, and local government agencies; consumer organizations; and the courts also should continue to hire paralegals in increasing numbers.

To a limited extent, paralegal jobs are affected by the business cycle. During recessions, demand declines for some discretionary legal services, such as planning estates, drafting wills, and handling real estate transactions. Corporations are less inclined to initiate certain types of litigation when falling sales and profits lead to fiscal belt tightening. As a result, full-time paralegals employed in offices adversely affected by a recession may be laid off or have their work hours reduced. However, during recessions, corporations and individuals are more likely to face other problems that require legal assistance, such as bankruptcies, foreclosures, and divorces. Paralegals, who provide many of the same legal services as lawyers at a lower cost, tend to fare relatively better in difficult economic conditions.

Earnings

Earnings of paralegals and legal assistants vary greatly. Salaries depend on education, training, experience, the type and size of employer, and the geographic location of the job. In general, paralegals who work for large law firms or in large metropolitan areas earn more than those who work for smaller firms or in less populated regions. In addition to earning a salary, many paralegals receive bonuses. In May 2004, full-time wage and salary paralegals and legal assistants had median annual earnings, including bonuses, of $39,130. The middle 50 percent earned between $31,040 and $49,950. The top 10 percent earned more than $61,390, while the bottom 10 percent earned less than $25,360. Median annual earnings in the industries employing the largest numbers of paralegals in May 2004 were as follows:

Federal government	$59,370
Local government	38,260
Legal services	37,870
State government	34,910

Related Occupations

Among the other occupations that call for a specialized understanding of the law and the legal system, but do not require the extensive training of a lawyer, are law clerks; title examiners, abstractors, and searchers; claims adjusters, appraisers, examiners, and investigators; and occupational health and safety specialists and technicians.

Sources of Additional Information

General information on a career as a paralegal can be obtained from

▸ Standing Committee on Paralegals, American Bar Association, 321 North Clark St., Chicago, IL 60610. Internet: http://www.abanet.org/legalservices/paralegals

For information on the Certified Legal Assistant exam, schools that offer training programs in a specific state, and standards and guidelines for paralegals, contact

▸ National Association of Legal Assistants, Inc., 1516 South Boston St., Suite 200, Tulsa, OK 74119. Internet: http://www.nala.org

Information on a career as a paralegal, schools that offer training programs, job postings for paralegals, the Paralegal Advanced Competency Exam, and local paralegal associations can be obtained from

▸ National Federation of Paralegal Associations, 2517 Eastlake Ave. East, Suite 200, Seattle, WA 98102. Internet: http://www.paralegals.org

Information on paralegal training programs, including the pamphlet *How to Choose a Paralegal Education Program*, may be obtained from

▸ American Association for Paralegal Education, 19 Mantua Rd., Mt. Royal, NJ 08061. Internet: http://www.aafpe.org

Information on obtaining positions as occupational health and safety specialists and technicians with the federal government is available from the Office of Personnel Management through USAJOBS, the federal government's official employment information system. This resource for locating and applying for job opportunities can be accessed through the Internet at http://www.usajobs.opm.gov or through an interactive voice response telephone system at (703) 724-1850 or TDD (978) 461-8404. These numbers are not toll free, and charges may result.

Pharmacists

(O*NET 29-1051.00)

Significant Points

■ Very good employment opportunities are expected for pharmacists.

■ Earnings are high, but some pharmacists work long hours, nights, weekends, and holidays.

■ Pharmacists are becoming more involved in making decisions regarding drug therapy and in counseling patients.

■ A license is required; the prospective pharmacist must graduate from an accredited college of pharmacy and pass a state examination.

Nature of the Work

Pharmacists distribute drugs prescribed by physicians and other health practitioners and provide information to patients about medications and their use. They advise physicians and other health practitioners on the selection, dosages, interactions, and side effects of medications. Pharmacists also monitor the health and progress of patients in response to drug therapy to ensure the safe and effective use of medication. Pharmacists must understand the use, clinical effects, and composition of drugs, including their chemical, biological, and physical properties. Compounding—the actual mixing of ingredients to form powders, tablets, capsules, ointments, and solutions—is a small part of a pharma-

cist's practice because most medicines are produced by pharmaceutical companies in a standard dosage and drug delivery form. Most pharmacists work in a community setting, such as a retail drugstore, or in a health care facility, such as a hospital, nursing home, mental health institution, or neighborhood health clinic.

Pharmacists in community and retail pharmacies counsel patients and answer questions about prescription drugs, including questions regarding possible side effects or interactions among various drugs. They provide information about over-the-counter drugs and make recommendations after talking with the patient. They also may give advice about the patient's diet, exercise, or stress management or about durable medical equipment and home health care supplies. In addition, they also may complete third-party insurance forms and other paperwork. Those who own or manage community pharmacies may sell non-health-related merchandise, hire and supervise personnel, and oversee the general operation of the pharmacy. Some community pharmacists provide specialized services to help patients manage conditions such as diabetes, asthma, smoking cessation, or high blood pressure. Some community pharmacists also are trained to administer vaccinations.

Pharmacists in health care facilities dispense medications and advise the medical staff on the selection and effects of drugs. They may make sterile solutions to be administered intravenously. They also assess, plan, and monitor drug programs or regimens. Pharmacists counsel hospitalized patients on the use of drugs and on their use at home when the patients are discharged. Pharmacists also may evaluate drug-use patterns and outcomes for patients in hospitals or managed care organizations.

Pharmacists who work in home health care monitor drug therapy and prepare infusions—solutions that are injected into patients—and other medications for use in the home.

Some pharmacists specialize in specific drug therapy areas, such as intravenous nutrition support, oncology (cancer), nuclear pharmacy (used for chemotherapy), geriatric pharmacy, and psychopharmacotherapy (the treatment of mental disorders by means of drugs).

Most pharmacists keep confidential computerized records of patients' drug therapies to prevent harmful drug interactions. Pharmacists are responsible for the accuracy of every prescription that is filled, but they often rely upon pharmacy technicians and pharmacy aides to assist them in the dispensing process. Thus, the pharmacist may delegate prescription-filling and administrative tasks and supervise their completion. Pharmacists also frequently oversee pharmacy students serving as interns in preparation for graduation and licensure.

Increasingly, pharmacists are pursuing nontraditional pharmacy work. Some are involved in research for pharmaceutical manufacturers, developing new drugs and therapies and testing their effects on people. Others work in marketing or sales, providing expertise to clients on a drug's use, effectiveness, and possible side effects. Some pharmacists work for health insurance companies, developing pharmacy benefit packages and carrying out cost-benefit analyses on certain drugs. Other pharmacists work for the government, public health care services, the armed services, and pharmacy associations. Finally, some pharmacists are employed full time or part time as college faculty, teaching classes and performing research in a wide range of areas.

Working Conditions

Pharmacists work in clean, well-lighted, and well-ventilated areas. Many pharmacists spend most of their workday on their feet. When working with sterile or dangerous pharmaceutical products, pharmacists wear gloves and masks and work with other special protective equipment. Many community and hospital pharmacies are open for extended hours or around the clock, so pharmacists may work nights, weekends, and holidays. Consultant pharmacists may travel to nursing homes or other facilities to monitor patients' drug therapy.

About 21 percent of pharmacists worked part time in 2004. Most full-time salaried pharmacists worked approximately 40 hours a week. Some, including many self-employed pharmacists, worked more than 50 hours a week.

Training, Other Qualifications, and Advancement

A license to practice pharmacy is required in all states, the District of Columbia, and all U.S. territories. To obtain a license, the prospective pharmacist must graduate from a college of pharmacy that is accredited by the Accreditation Council for Pharmacy Education (ACPE) and pass an examination. All states require the North American Pharmacist Licensure Exam (NAPLEX), which tests pharmacy skills and knowledge, and 43 states and the District of Columbia require the Multistate Pharmacy Jurisprudence Exam (MPJE), which tests pharmacy law. Both exams are administered by the National Association of Boards of Pharmacy. Pharmacists in the eight states that do not require the MPJE must pass a state-specific exam that is similar to the MPJE. In addition to the NAPLEX and MPJE, some states require additional exams unique to their state. All states except California currently grant a license without extensive reexamination to qualified pharmacists who already are licensed by another state. In Florida, reexamination is not required if a pharmacist has passed the NAPLEX and MPJE within 12 years of his or her application for a license transfer. Many pharmacists are licensed to practice in more than one state. Most states require continuing education for license renewal. Persons interested in a career as a pharmacist should check with individual state boards of pharmacy for details on examination requirements, license renewal requirements, and license transfer procedures.

In 2004, 89 colleges of pharmacy were accredited to confer degrees by the Accreditation Council for Pharmacy Education. Pharmacy programs grant the degree of Doctor of Pharmacy (Pharm.D.), which requires at least 6 years of postsecondary study and the passing of a state board of pharmacy's licensure examination. Courses offered at colleges of pharmacy are designed to teach students about all aspects of drug therapy. In addition, schools teach students how to communicate with patients and other health care providers about drug information and patient care. Students also learn professional ethics, how to develop and manage medication distribution systems, and concepts of public health. In addition to receiving classroom instruction, students in Pharm.D. programs spend about one-fourth of their time learning in a variety of pharmacy practice settings under the supervision of licensed pharmacists. The Pharm.D. degree has replaced the Bachelor of Pharmacy (B.Pharm.) degree, which is no longer being awarded.

The Pharm.D. is a 4-year program that requires at least 2 years of college study prior to admittance, although most applicants have completed 3 years. Entry requirements usually include courses in mathematics and natural sciences, such as chemistry, biology, and physics, as well as courses in the humanities and social sciences. Approximately two-thirds of all colleges require applicants to take the Pharmacy College Admissions Test (PCAT).

In 2003, the American Association of Colleges of Pharmacy (AACP) launched the Pharmacy College Application Service, known as PharmCAS, for students who are interested in applying to schools and colleges of pharmacy. This centralized service allows applicants to use a single Web-based application and one set of transcripts to apply to multiple schools of pharmacy. A total of 43 schools participated in 2003.

In the 2003–2004 academic year, 67 colleges of pharmacy awarded the master of science degree or the Ph.D. degree. Both degrees are awarded after the completion of a Pharm.D. degree and are designed for those who want more laboratory and research experience. Many master's and Ph.D. degree holders do research for a drug company or teach at a university. Other options for pharmacy graduates who are interested in further training include 1-year or 2-year residency programs or fellowships. Pharmacy residencies are postgraduate training programs in pharmacy practice and usually require the completion of a research study. There currently are more than 700 residency training programs nationwide. Pharmacy fellowships are highly individualized programs that are designed to prepare participants to work in a specialized area of pharmacy, such as clinical practice or research laboratories. Some pharmacists who run their own pharmacy obtain a master's degree in business administration (MBA). Others may obtain a degree in public administration or public health.

Areas of graduate study include pharmaceutics and pharmaceutical chemistry (physical and chemical properties of drugs and dosage forms), pharmacology (effects of drugs on the body), toxicology, and pharmacy administration.

Prospective pharmacists should have scientific aptitude, good communication skills, and a desire to help others. They also must be conscientious and pay close attention to detail because the decisions they make affect human lives.

In community pharmacies, pharmacists usually begin at the staff level. In independent pharmacies, after they gain experience and secure the necessary capital, some become owners or part owners of pharmacies. Pharmacists in chain drugstores may be promoted to pharmacy supervisor or manager at the store level, then to manager at the district or regional level, and later to an executive position within the chain's headquarters.

Hospital pharmacists may advance to supervisory or administrative positions. Pharmacists in the pharmaceutical industry may advance in marketing, sales, research, quality control, production, packaging, or other areas.

Employment

Pharmacists held about 230,000 jobs in 2004. About 61 percent work in community pharmacies that are either independently owned or part of a drugstore chain, grocery store, department store, or mass merchandiser. Most community pharmacists are salaried employees, but some are self-employed owners. About 24 percent of salaried pharmacists work in hospitals. Others work in clinics, mail-order pharmacies, pharmaceutical wholesalers, home health care agencies, or the federal government.

Job Outlook

Very good employment opportunities are expected for pharmacists over the 2004–2014 period because the number of job openings created by employment growth and the need to replace pharmacists who leave the occupation or retire are expected to exceed the number of degrees granted in pharmacy. Enrollments in pharmacy programs are rising as more students are attracted by high salaries and good job prospects. Despite this increase in enrollments, job openings should still be more numerous than those seeking employment.

Employment of pharmacists is expected to grow faster than the average for all occupations through the year 2014 because of the increasing demand for pharmaceuticals, particularly from the growing elderly population. The increasing numbers of middle-aged and elderly people—who use more prescription drugs than younger people—will continue to spur demand for pharmacists in all employment settings. Other factors likely to increase the demand for pharmacists include scientific advances that will make more drug products available, new developments in genome research and medication distribution systems, increasingly sophisticated consumers seeking more information about drugs, and coverage of prescription drugs by a greater number of health insurance plans and Medicare.

Community pharmacies are taking steps to manage an increasing volume of prescriptions. Automation of drug dispensing and greater employment of pharmacy technicians and pharmacy aides will help these establishments to dispense more prescriptions.

With its emphasis on cost control, managed care encourages the use of lower-cost prescription drug distributors, such as mail-order firms and online pharmacies, for purchases of certain medications. Prescriptions ordered through the mail and via the Internet are filled in a central location and shipped to the patient at a lower cost. Mail-order and online pharmacies typically use automated technology to dispense medication and employ fewer pharmacists. If the utilization of mail-order pharmacies increases rapidly, job growth among pharmacists could be limited.

Employment of pharmacists will not grow as fast in hospitals as in other industries because hospitals are reducing inpatient stays, downsizing, and consolidating departments. The number of outpatient surgeries is increasing, so more patients are being discharged and purchasing their medications through retail, supermarket, or mail-order pharmacies rather than through hospitals. An aging population means that more pharmacy services will be required in nursing homes, assisted-living facilities, and home care settings. The most rapid job growth among pharmacists is expected in these 3 settings.

New opportunities are emerging for pharmacists in managed care organizations where they analyze trends and patterns in medication use and in pharmacoeconomics—the cost and benefit analysis of different drug therapies. Opportunities also are emerging for pharmacists trained in research and disease management—the development of new methods for curing and controlling diseases.

Pharmacists also are finding jobs in research and development and in sales and marketing for pharmaceutical manufacturing firms. New breakthroughs in biotechnology will increase the potential for drugs to treat diseases and expand the opportunities for pharmacists to conduct research and sell medications. In addition, pharmacists are finding employment opportunities in pharmacy informatics, which uses information technology to improve patient care.

Job opportunities for pharmacists in patient care will arise as cost-conscious insurers and health systems continue to emphasize the role of pharmacists in primary and preventive health care. Health insurance companies realize that the expense of using medication to treat diseases and various health conditions often is considerably less than the costs for patients whose conditions go untreated. Pharmacists also can reduce the expenses resulting from unexpected complications due to allergic reactions or interactions among medications.

Earnings

Median annual wage and salary earnings of pharmacists in May 2004 were $84,900. The middle 50 percent earned between $75,720 and $94,850 a year. The lowest 10 percent earned less than $61,200, and the highest 10 percent earned more than $109,850 a year. Median annual earnings in the industries employing the largest numbers of pharmacists in May 2004 were

Department stores	$86,720
Grocery stores	85,680
Health and personal care stores	85,380
General medical and surgical hospitals	84,560
Other general merchandise stores	84,170

Related Occupations

Pharmacy technicians and pharmacy aides also work in pharmacies. Persons in other professions who may work with pharmaceutical compounds include biological scientists, medical scientists, and chemists and materials scientists. Increasingly, pharmacists are involved in patient care and therapy, work that they have in common with physicians and surgeons.

Sources of Additional Information

For information on pharmacy as a career, preprofessional and professional requirements, programs offered by colleges of pharmacy, and student financial aid, contact

▸ American Association of Colleges of Pharmacy, 1426 Prince St., Alexandria, VA 22314. Internet: http://www.aacp.org

General information on careers in pharmacy is available from

▸ American Society of Health-System Pharmacists, 7272 Wisconsin Ave., Bethesda, MD 20814. Internet: http://www.ashp.org

▸ National Association of Chain Drug Stores, 413 N. Lee St., P.O. Box 1417-D49, Alexandria, VA 22313-1480. Internet: http://www.nacds.org

▸ Academy of Managed Care Pharmacy, 100 North Pitt St., Suite 400, Alexandria, VA 22314. Internet: http://www.amcp.org

▸ American Pharmacists Association, 2215 Constitution Ave. NW, Washington, DC 20037-2985. Internet: http://www.aphanet.org

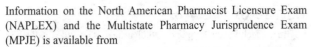

Information on the North American Pharmacist Licensure Exam (NAPLEX) and the Multistate Pharmacy Jurisprudence Exam (MPJE) is available from

▸ National Association of Boards of Pharmacy, 1600 Feehanville Dr., Mount Prospect, IL 60056. Internet: http://www.nabp.net

State licensure requirements are available from each state's board of pharmacy. Information on specific college entrance requirements, curriculums, and financial aid is available from any college of pharmacy.

Pharmacy Aides

(O*NET 31-9095.00)

Significant Points

■ Job opportunities are expected to be good for full-time and part-time work, especially for those with related work experience.

■ Many pharmacy aides work evenings, weekends, and holidays.

■ About 80 percent work in retail pharmacies, grocery stores, department stores, or mass retailers.

Nature of the Work

Pharmacy aides help licensed pharmacists with administrative duties in running a pharmacy. Aides often are clerks or cashiers who primarily answer telephones, handle money, stock shelves, and perform other clerical duties. They work closely with pharmacy technicians. *Pharmacy technicians* usually perform more complex tasks than do aides, although in some states the duties and titles of the jobs overlap. (See the description of pharmacy technicians elsewhere in this book.) Aides refer any questions regarding prescriptions, drug information, or health matters to a pharmacist. (See the description of pharmacists elsewhere in this book.)

Aides have several important duties that help the pharmacy to function smoothly. They may establish and maintain patient profiles, prepare insurance claim forms, and stock and take inventory of prescription and over-the-counter medications. Accurate recordkeeping is necessary to help avert dangerous drug interactions. In addition, because many people have medical insurance to help pay for prescriptions, it is essential that pharmacy aides correspond efficiently and correctly with the third-party insurance providers to obtain payment. Pharmacy aides also maintain inventory and inform the supervisor of stock needs so that the pharmacy does not run out of the vital medications that customers need. Some also clean pharmacy equipment, help with the maintenance of equipment and supplies, and manage the cash register.

Working Conditions

Pharmacy aides work in clean, organized, well-lighted, and well-ventilated areas. Most of their workday is spent on their feet. They may be required to lift heavy boxes or to use stepladders to retrieve supplies from high shelves.

Aides work the same hours that pharmacists work. These include evenings, nights, weekends, and some holidays, particularly in facilities such as hospitals and retail pharmacies that are open 24 hours a day. There are many opportunities for part-time work in both retail and hospital settings.

Training, Other Qualifications, and Advancement

Most pharmacy aides receive informal on-the-job training, but employers favor those with at least a high school diploma. Prospective pharmacy aides with experience working as cashiers may have an advantage when applying for jobs. Employers also prefer applicants with strong customer service and communication skills, experience managing inventories, and experience using computers. Aides entering the field need strong spelling, reading, and mathematics skills.

Successful pharmacy aides are organized, dedicated, friendly, and responsible. They should be willing and able to take directions. Candidates interested in becoming pharmacy aides cannot have prior records of drug or substance abuse. Strong interpersonal and communication skills are needed because pharmacy aides interact daily with patients, co-workers, and health care professionals. Teamwork is very important because aides are often required to work with technicians and pharmacists.

Pharmacy aides almost always are trained on the job. They may begin by observing a more experienced worker. After they become familiar with the store's equipment, policies, and procedures, they begin to work on their own. Once they become experienced, aides are not likely to receive additional training except when new equipment is introduced or when policies or procedures change.

To become a pharmacy aide, one should be able to perform repetitive work accurately. Aides need good basic mathematics skills and good manual dexterity. Pharmacy aides should be neat in appearance and able to deal pleasantly and tactfully with customers. Some employers may prefer people with experience typing; handling money; or operating specialized equipment, including computers.

Advancement usually is limited, although some aides may decide to become pharmacy technicians or to enroll in pharmacy school to become pharmacists.

Employment

Pharmacy aides held about 50,000 jobs in 2004. About 80 percent work in retail pharmacies, which are either independently owned or part of a drug store chain, grocery store, department store, or mass retailer; the vast majority of these are in drug stores. About 10 percent work in hospitals, and the rest work in mail-order pharmacies, clinics, and pharmaceutical wholesalers.

Job Outlook

Job opportunities for full-time and part-time work are expected to be good, especially for aides with related work experience in pharmacies or as cashiers or stock clerks in other retail settings. Job openings will be created by employment growth and by the need to replace workers who transfer to other occupations or leave the labor force.

Employment of pharmacy aides is expected to grow about as fast as the average for all occupations through 2014 because of the increasing use of medication in treating patients. In addition, a greater number of middle-aged and elderly people—who use more prescription drugs than younger people—will spur demand for aides in all practice settings.

Cost-conscious insurers, pharmacies, and health systems will continue to employ aides. As a result, pharmacy aides will assume some responsibility for routine tasks previously performed by pharmacists and pharmacy technicians, thereby giving pharmacists more time to interact with patients and technicians more time to prepare medications. Employment of pharmacy aides will not grow as fast as employment of pharmacists and pharmacy technicians, however, because of legal limitations regarding aides' duties. Many smaller pharmacies that can afford only a small staff will favor pharmacy technicians because of their more extensive training and job skills.

Earnings

Median hourly wage and salary earnings of pharmacy aides were $8.86 in May 2004. The middle 50 percent earned between $7.39 and $10.96, the lowest 10 percent earned less than $6.34, and the highest 10 percent earned more than $13.79. In May 2004, median hourly earnings of pharmacy aides were $8.29 in health and personal care stores and $9.80 in grocery stores.

Related Occupations

The work of pharmacy aides is closely related to that of pharmacy technicians, cashiers, and stock clerks and order fillers. Workers in other medical support occupations include dental assistants, licensed practical and licensed vocational nurses, medical transcriptionists, medical records and health information technicians, occupational therapist assistants and aides, physical therapist assistants and aides, and surgical technologists.

Sources of Additional Information

For information on employment opportunities, contact local employers or local offices of the state employment service.

Pharmacy Technicians

(O*NET 29-2052.00)

Significant Points

■ Job opportunities are expected to be good for full-time and part-time work, especially for those with certification or previous work experience.

■ Many technicians work evenings, weekends, and holidays.

■ About 7 out of 10 of jobs are in retail pharmacies, grocery stores, department stores, or mass retailers.

Nature of the Work

Pharmacy technicians help licensed pharmacists provide medication and other health care products to patients. Technicians usually perform routine tasks to help prepare prescribed medication for patients, such as counting tablets and labeling bottles. Technicians refer any questions regarding prescriptions, drug information, or health matters to a *pharmacist.* (See the description of pharmacists elsewhere in this book.)

Pharmacy aides work closely with pharmacy technicians. They often are clerks or cashiers who primarily answer telephones, handle money, stock shelves, and perform other clerical duties. (See the description of pharmacy aides elsewhere in this book.) Pharmacy technicians usually perform more complex tasks than do pharmacy aides, although in some states their duties and job titles may overlap.

Pharmacy technicians who work in retail or mail-order pharmacies have varying responsibilities, depending on state rules and regulations. Technicians receive written prescriptions or requests for prescription refills from patients. They also may receive prescriptions sent electronically from the doctor's office. They must verify that the information on the prescription is complete and accurate. To prepare the prescription, technicians must retrieve, count, pour, weigh, measure, and sometimes mix the medication. Then, they prepare the prescription labels, select the type of prescription container, and affix the prescription and auxiliary labels to the container. Once the prescription is filled, technicians price and file the prescription, which must be checked by a pharmacist before it is given to the patient. Technicians may establish and maintain patient profiles, prepare insurance claim forms, and stock and take inventory of prescription and over-the-counter medications.

In hospitals, nursing homes, and assisted-living facilities, technicians have added responsibilities, including reading patients' charts and preparing and delivering the medicine to patients. Still, the pharmacist must check the order before it is delivered to the patient. The technician then copies the information about the prescribed medication onto the patient's profile. Technicians also may assemble a 24-hour supply of medicine for every patient. They package and label each dose separately. The packages are then placed in the medicine cabinets of patients until the supervising pharmacist checks them for accuracy. The packages are then given to the patients.

Working Conditions

Pharmacy technicians work in clean, organized, well-lighted, and well-ventilated areas. Most of their workday is spent on their feet. They may be required to lift heavy boxes or to use stepladders to retrieve supplies from high shelves.

Technicians work the same hours that pharmacists work. These may include evenings, nights, weekends, and holidays, particularly in facilities, such as hospitals and retail pharmacies, that are open 24 hours a day. As their seniority increases, technicians often acquire increased control over the hours they work. There are many opportunities for part-time work in both retail and hospital settings.

Training, Other Qualifications, and Advancement

Although most pharmacy technicians receive informal on-the-job training, employers favor those who have completed formal training and certification. However, there are currently few state and no federal requirements for formal training or certification of pharmacy technicians. Employers who have insufficient resources to give on-the-job training often seek formally educated pharmacy technicians. Formal education programs and certification emphasize the technician's interest in and dedication to the work. In addition to the military, some hospitals, proprietary schools, vocational or technical colleges, and community colleges offer formal education programs.

Formal pharmacy technician education programs require classroom and laboratory work in a variety of areas, including medical and pharmaceutical terminology, pharmaceutical calculations, pharmacy recordkeeping, pharmaceutical techniques, and pharmacy law and ethics. Technicians also are required to learn medication names, actions, uses, and doses. Many training programs include internships, in which students gain hands-on experience in actual pharmacies. Students receive a diploma, a certificate, or an associate's degree, depending on the program.

Prospective pharmacy technicians with experience working as an aide in a community pharmacy or volunteering in a hospital may have an advantage. Employers also prefer applicants with strong customer service and communication skills, as well as those with experience managing inventories, counting tablets, measuring dosages, and using computers. Technicians entering the field need strong mathematics, spelling, and reading skills. A background in chemistry, English, and health education also may be beneficial. Some technicians are hired without formal training, but under the condition that they obtain certification within a specified period to retain their employment.

The Pharmacy Technician Certification Board administers the National Pharmacy Technician Certification Examination. This exam is voluntary in most states and displays the competency of the individual to act as a pharmacy technician. However, more states and employers are requiring certification as reliance on pharmacy technicians grows. Eligible candidates must have a high school diploma or GED and no felony convictions, and those who pass the exam earn the title of Certified Pharmacy Technician (CPhT). The exam is offered several times per year at various locations nationally. Employers—often pharmacists—know that individuals who pass the exam have a standardized body of knowledge and skills. Many employers also will reimburse the costs of the exam as an incentive for certification.

Certified technicians must be recertified every 2 years. Technicians must complete 20 contact hours of pharmacy-related topics within the 2-year certification period to become eligible for recertification. Contact hours are awarded for on-the-job training, attending lectures, and college coursework. At least 1 contact hour must be in pharmacy law. Contact hours can be earned from several different sources, including pharmacy associations, pharmacy colleges, and pharmacy technician training programs. Up to 10 contact hours can be earned when the technician is employed under the direct supervision and instruction of a pharmacist.

Successful pharmacy technicians are alert, observant, organized, dedicated, and responsible. They should be willing and able to take directions. They must be precise; details are sometimes a matter of life and death. Although a pharmacist must check and approve all their work, they should be able to work independently without constant instruction from the pharmacist. Candidates interested in becoming pharmacy technicians cannot have prior records of drug or substance abuse.

Strong interpersonal and communication skills are needed because pharmacy technicians interact daily with patients, co-workers, and health care professionals. Teamwork is very important because technicians often are required to work with pharmacists, aides, and other technicians.

Employment

Pharmacy technicians held about 258,000 jobs in 2004. About 7 out of 10 jobs were in retail pharmacies, either independently owned or part of a drugstore chain, grocery store, department store, or mass retailer. About 2 out of 10 jobs were in hospitals and a small proportion was in mail-order and Internet pharmacies, clinics, pharmaceutical wholesalers, and the federal government.

Job Outlook

Good job opportunities are expected for full-time and part-time work, especially for technicians with formal training or previous experience. Job openings for pharmacy technicians will result from the expansion of retail pharmacies and other employment settings and from the need to replace workers who transfer to other occupations or leave the labor force.

Employment of pharmacy technicians is expected to grow much faster than the average for all occupations through 2014 because as the population grows and ages, demand for pharmaceuticals will increase dramatically. The increased number of middle-aged and elderly people—who use more prescription drugs than younger people—will spur demand for technicians in all practice settings. With advances in science, more medications are becoming available to treat a greater number of conditions.

In addition, cost-conscious insurers, pharmacies, and health systems will continue to expand the role of technicians. As a result, pharmacy technicians will assume responsibility for some of the more routine tasks previously performed by pharmacists. Pharmacy technicians also will need to learn and master new pharmacy technology as it emerges. For example, robotic machines are being increasingly used to dispense medicine into containers; technicians must oversee the machines, stock the bins, and label the containers. Thus, while automation is increasingly incorporated into the job, it will not necessarily reduce the need for technicians.

Almost all states have legislated the maximum number of technicians who can safely work under a pharmacist at one time. In some states, technicians have assumed more medication-dispensing duties as pharmacists have become more involved in patient care, resulting in more technicians per pharmacist. Changes in these laws could directly affect employment.

Earnings

Median hourly earnings of wage and salary pharmacy technicians in May 2004 were $11.37. The middle 50 percent earned between $9.40 and $13.85. The lowest 10 percent earned less than $7.96, and the highest 10 percent earned more than $16.61. Median hourly earnings in the industries employing the largest numbers of pharmacy technicians in May 2004 were

General medical and surgical hospitals $12.93
Grocery stores...11.77
Other general merchandise stores 11.11
Department stores 10.56
Health and personal care stores 10.51

Certified technicians may earn more. Shift differentials for working evenings or weekends also can increase earnings. Some technicians belong to unions representing hospital or grocery store workers.

Related Occupations

This occupation is most closely related to pharmacists and pharmacy aides. Workers in other medical support occupations include dental assistants, licensed practical and licensed vocational nurses, medical transcriptionists, medical records and health information technicians, occupational therapist assistants and aides, physical therapist assistants and aides, and surgical technologists.

Sources of Additional Information

For information on the Certified Pharmacy Technician designation, contact

▸ Pharmacy Technician Certification Board, 2215 Constitution Ave. NW, Washington DC 20037-2985. Internet: http://www.ptcb.org

For a list of accredited pharmacy technician training programs, contact

▸ American Society of Health-System Pharmacists, 7272 Wisconsin Ave., Bethesda, MD 20814. Internet: http://www.ashp.org

For pharmacy technician career information, contact

▸ National Pharmacy Technician Association, P.O. Box 683148, Houston, TX 77268. Internet: http://www.pharmacytechnician.org

Photographers

(O*NET 27-4021.01 and 27-4021.02)

Significant Points

■ Competition for jobs is expected to be keen because the work is attractive to many people.

■ Technical expertise, a "good eye," imagination, and creativity are essential.

■ More than half of all photographers are self-employed; the most successful are adept at operating a business and able to take advantage of opportunities provided by rapidly changing technologies.

Nature of the Work

Photographers produce and preserve images that paint a picture, tell a story, or record an event. To create commercial-quality photographs, photographers need both technical expertise and creativity. Producing a successful picture requires choosing and presenting a subject to achieve a particular effect and selecting the appropriate equipment. For example, photographers may enhance the subject's appearance with natural or artificial light, shoot the subject from an interesting angle, draw attention to a particular aspect of the subject by blurring the background, or use various lenses to produce desired levels of detail at various distances from the subject.

Today, most photographers use digital cameras instead of traditional silver-halide film cameras, although some photographers use both types, depending on their own preference and the nature of the assignment. Regardless of the camera they use, photographers also employ an array of other equipment—from lenses, filters, and tripods to flash attachments and specially constructed lighting equipment—to improve the quality of their work.

Digital cameras capture images electronically, allowing them to be edited on a computer. Images can be stored on portable memory devices such as compact discs (CDs) or on smaller "minipocket" storage devices such as flash cards, which are small memory cards used in digital cameras. Once the raw image has been transferred to a computer, photographers can use processing software to crop or modify the image and enhance it through color correction and other specialized effects. As soon as a photographer has finished editing the image, it can be sent anywhere in the world over the Internet.

Photographers also can create electronic portfolios of their work and display them on their own Web page, allowing them to reach prospective customers directly. Digital technology also allows the production of larger, more colorful, and more accurate prints or images for use in advertising, photographic art, and scientific research. Photographers who process their own digital images need to have computers, high-quality printers, and editing software, as well as the technical knowledge to use these tools effectively.

Photographers who use cameras with silver-halide film often send their film to laboratories for processing. Color film requires expensive equipment and exacting conditions for correct processing and printing. (See the description of photographic process workers and processing machine operators elsewhere in this book.) Other photographers develop and print their own photographs using their own fully equipped darkroom, especially if they use black-and-white film or seek to achieve special effects. Photographers who do their own film developing must invest in additional developing and printing equipment and acquire the technical skills to operate it.

Some photographers specialize in areas such as portrait, commercial and industrial, scientific, news, or fine arts photography. *Portrait photographers* take pictures of individuals or groups of people and often work in their own studios. Some specialize in weddings, religious ceremonies, or school photographs and may work on location. Portrait photographers who own and operate their own business have many responsibilities in addition to taking pictures. They must arrange for advertising, schedule appointments, set and adjust equipment, purchase supplies, keep records, bill customers, pay bills, and—if they have employees—hire, train, and direct their workers.

Many also process their own images, design albums, and mount and frame the finished photographs.

Commercial and industrial photographers take pictures of various subjects, such as buildings, models, merchandise, artifacts, and landscapes. These photographs are used in a variety of media, including books, reports, advertisements, and catalogs. Industrial photographers often take pictures of equipment, machinery, products, workers, and company officials. The pictures are used for various purposes—for example, analysis of engineering projects; publicity; or records of equipment development or deployment, such as placement of an offshore oil rig. This photography frequently is done on location.

Scientific photographers take images of a variety of subjects to illustrate or record scientific or medical data or phenomena, using knowledge of scientific procedures. They typically possess additional knowledge in areas such as engineering, medicine, biology, or chemistry.

News photographers, also called *photojournalists*, photograph newsworthy people; places; and sporting, political, and community events for newspapers, journals, magazines, or television.

Fine arts photographers sell their photographs as fine artwork. In addition to technical proficiency, fine arts photographers need artistic talent and creativity.

Self-employed, or freelance, photographers usually specialize in one of the above fields. In addition to carrying out assignments under direct contract with clients, they may license the use of their photographs through stock-photo agencies or market their work directly to the public. Stock-photo agencies sell magazines and other customers the right to use photographs, and they pay the photographer a commission. These agencies require an application from the photographer and a sizable portfolio of pictures. Once accepted, photographers usually are required to submit a large number of new photographs each year.

Working Conditions

Working conditions for photographers vary considerably. Photographers employed in government and advertising studios usually work a 5-day, 40-hour week. On the other hand, news photographers often work long, irregular hours and must be available to work on short notice. Many photographers work part time or on variable schedules. Most photographers spend only a small portion of their work schedule actually taking photographs. Their most common activities are editing images on a computer—if they use a digital camera—and looking for new business—if they are self-employed.

Portrait photographers usually work in their own studios but also may travel to take photographs at the client's location, such as a school, a company office, or a private home. News and commercial photographers frequently travel locally, stay overnight on assignments, or travel to distant places for long periods.

Some photographers work in uncomfortable or even dangerous surroundings, especially news photographers covering accidents, natural disasters, civil unrest, or military conflicts. Many photographers must wait long hours in all kinds of weather for an event to take place and stand or walk for long periods while carrying heavy equipment. News photographers often work under strict deadlines.

Self-employment allows for greater autonomy, freedom of expression, and flexible scheduling. However, income can be uncertain and the continuous, time-consuming search for new clients can be stressful. Some self-employed photographers hire assistants who help seek out new business.

Training, Other Qualifications, and Advancement

Employers usually seek applicants with a "good eye," imagination, and creativity, as well as a good technical understanding of photography. Entry-level positions in photojournalism or in industrial or scientific photography generally require a college degree in photography or in a field related to the industry in which the photographer seeks employment. Freelance and portrait photographers need technical proficiency, gained through either a degree program, vocational training, or extensive photography experience.

Photography courses are offered by many universities, community and junior colleges, vocational-technical institutes, and private trade and technical schools. Basic courses in photography cover equipment, processes, and techniques. Bachelor's degree programs, especially those including business courses, provide a well-rounded education. Art schools offer useful training in design and composition.

Individuals interested in a career in photography should try to develop contacts in the field by subscribing to photographic newsletters and magazines; joining camera clubs; and seeking summer or part-time employment in camera stores, newspapers, or photo studios.

Photographers may start out as assistants to experienced photographers. Assistants acquire the technical knowledge needed to be a successful photographer and also learn other skills necessary to run a portrait or commercial photography business. Freelance photographers also should develop an individual style of photography to differentiate themselves from the competition. Some photographers enter the field by submitting an unsolicited portfolio of photographs to magazines and to art directors at advertising agencies; for freelance photographers, a good portfolio is critical.

Photographers need good eyesight, artistic ability, and good hand-eye coordination. They should be patient, accurate, and detail-oriented. Photographers should be able to work well with others, as they frequently deal with clients, graphic designers, and advertising and publishing specialists. Photographers need to know how to use computer software programs and applications that allow them to prepare and edit images, and those who market directly to clients should be familiar with using the Internet to display their work.

Portrait photographers need the ability to help people relax in front of the camera. Commercial and fine arts photographers must be imaginative and original. News photographers must not only be good with a camera, but also understand the story behind an event so that their pictures match the story. They must be decisive in recognizing a potentially good photograph and act quickly to capture it. Photographers who operate their own business, or freelance, need business skills as well as talent. These individuals must know how to prepare a business plan; submit bids; write contracts; keep financial records; market their work; hire models, if needed; get permission to shoot on locations that normally are not open to the public;

obtain releases to use photographs of people; license and price photographs; and secure copyright protection for their work. To protect their rights and their work, self-employed photographers require basic knowledge of licensing and copyright laws, as well as knowledge of contracts and negotiation procedures.

After several years of experience, magazine and news photographers may advance to photography or picture editor positions. Some photographers teach at technical schools, film schools, or universities.

Employment

Photographers held about 129,000 jobs in 2004. More than half were self-employed, a much higher proportion than for most occupations. Some self-employed photographers have contracts with advertising agencies, magazine publishers, or other businesses to do individual projects for a set fee, while others operate portrait studios or provide photographs to stock-photo agencies.

Most salaried photographers work in portrait or commercial photography studios; most of the others work for newspapers, magazines, and advertising agencies. Photographers work in all areas of the country, but most are employed in metropolitan areas.

Job Outlook

Photographers can expect keen competition for job openings because the work is attractive to many people. The number of individuals interested in positions as commercial and news photographers usually is much greater than the number of openings. Those who succeed in landing a salaried job or attracting enough work to earn a living by freelancing are likely to be adept at operating a business and to be among the most creative, able to find and exploit the new opportunities available from rapidly changing technologies. Related work experience, job-related training, or some unique skill or talent—such as a background in computers or electronics—also are beneficial to prospective photographers.

Employment of photographers is expected to increase about as fast as the average for all occupations through 2014. Demand for portrait photographers should increase as the population grows. Growth of Internet versions of magazines, journals, and newspapers will require increasing numbers of commercial photographers to provide digital images. The Internet also should make it easier for freelancers to market directly to their customers, increasing opportunities for self-employment.

Job growth, however, will be constrained somewhat by the widespread use of digital photography and the falling price of digital equipment. Improvements in digital technology reduce barriers of entry into this profession and allow more individual consumers and businesses to produce, store, and access photographic images on their own. Declines in the newspaper industry also will reduce demand for photographers to provide still images for print. Salaried jobs in particular may be difficult to find as more companies contract with freelancers rather than hire their own photographers.

Earnings

Median annual earnings of salaried photographers were $26,080 in May 2004. The middle 50 percent earned between $18,380 and

$37,370. The lowest 10 percent earned less than $15,000, and the highest 10 percent earned more than $54,180. Median annual earnings in the industries employing the largest numbers of salaried photographers were $32,800 for newspapers and periodicals and $23,100 for other professional, scientific, and technical services.

Salaried photographers—more of whom work full time—tend to earn more than those who are self-employed. Because most freelance and portrait photographers purchase their own equipment, they incur considerable expense acquiring and maintaining cameras and accessories. Unlike news and commercial photographers, few fine arts photographers are successful enough to support themselves solely through their art.

Related Occupations

Other occupations requiring artistic talent and creativity include architects, except landscape and naval; artists and related workers; commercial and industrial designers; fashion designers; graphic designers; and television, video, and motion picture camera operators and editors. Photojournalists are often required to cover news stories in much the same way as news analysts, reporters, and correspondents. The processing work that photographers do on computers is similar to the work of prepress technicians and workers and desktop publishers.

Sources of Additional Information

Career information on photography is available from

▸ Professional Photographers of America, Inc., 229 Peachtree St. NE, Suite 2200, Atlanta, GA 30303.

▸ National Press Photographers Association, Inc., 3200 Croasdaile Dr., Suite 306, Durham, NC 27705. Internet: http://www.nppa.org

▸ American Society of Media Photographers, Inc., 150 North Second St., Philadelphia, PA 19106. Internet: http://www.asmp.org

Photographic Process Workers and Processing Machine Operators

(O*NET 51-9131.01, 51-9131.02, 51-9131.03, 51-9131.04, and 51-9132.00)

Significant Points

- A decline in employment is expected as digital photography becomes commonplace.

- Most receive on-the-job training from their companies, manufacturers' representatives, and experienced workers.

- Job opportunities will be best for individuals with experience using computers and digital technology.

Nature of the Work

Both amateur and professional photographers rely heavily on photographic process workers and processing machine operators to develop film; make prints or slides; and do related tasks, such as enlarging or retouching photographs. *Photographic processing machine operators* operate various machines, such as mounting presses and motion picture film printing, photographic printing, and film-developing machines. *Photographic process workers* perform more delicate tasks, such as retouching photographic negatives, prints, and images to emphasize or correct specific features.

Photographic processing machine operators often have specialized jobs. *Film process technicians* operate machines that develop exposed photographic film or sensitized paper in a series of chemical and water baths to produce negative or positive images. First, technicians mix developing and fixing solutions, following a formula. They then load the film in the machine, which immerses the exposed film in a developer solution. This brings out the latent image. The next steps include immersing the negative in a stop-bath to halt the developer action, transferring it to a hyposolution to fix the image, and then immersing it in water to remove the chemicals. The technician then dries the film. In some cases, these steps are performed by hand.

Color printer operators control equipment that produces color prints from negatives. These workers read customer instructions to determine processing requirements. They load film into color printing equipment, examine negatives to determine equipment control settings, set controls, and produce a specified number of prints. Finally, they inspect the finished prints for defects, remove any that are found, and insert the processed negatives and prints into an envelope for return to the customer.

Processing machine operators who work with digital images first load the raw images onto a computer, either directly from the camera or, more commonly, from a storage device such as a flash card or CD. Most processing of the images is done automatically by software, but they may also be reviewed manually by the operator, who then selects which images the customer wants printed and the quantity. Some digital processors also upload images onto a Web site so that the customer can view them from a home computer and also share them with others through the Internet.

Photographic process workers, sometimes known as *digital imaging technicians*, use computer images of conventional negatives and specialized computer software to vary the contrast of images, remove unwanted background, or combine features from different photographs. Although computers and digital technology are replacing much manual work, some photographic process workers, especially those who work in portrait studios, still perform many specialized tasks by hand directly on the photo or negative. *Airbrush artists* restore damaged and faded photographs and may color or shade drawings to create photographic likenesses, using an airbrush. *Photographic retouchers* alter photographic negatives, prints, or images to accentuate the subject. *Colorists* apply oil colors to portrait photographs to create natural, lifelike appearances. *Photographic spotters* remove imperfections on photographic prints and images.

Working Conditions

Photographic process workers and processing machine operators generally spend their work hours in clean, appropriately lighted, well-ventilated, and air-conditioned offices, photofinishing laboratories, or 1-hour minilabs. In recent years, more commercial photo-

graphic processing has been done on computers than in darkrooms, and this trend is expected to continue.

Some photographic process workers and processing machine operators are exposed to the chemicals and fumes associated with developing and printing. These workers must wear rubber gloves and aprons and take precautions against these hazards. Those who use computers for extended periods may experience back pain, eyestrain, or fatigue.

Photographic processing machine operators must do repetitive work at a rapid pace without any loss of accuracy. Photographic process workers do detailed tasks, such as airbrushing and spotting, which can contribute to eye fatigue.

Many photo laboratory employees work a 40-hour week, including evenings and weekends, and may work overtime during peak seasons. About one in four work part time.

Training, Other Qualifications, and Advancement

Most photographic process workers and processing machine operators receive on-the-job training from their companies, manufacturers' representatives, and experienced workers. New employees gradually learn to use the machines and chemicals that develop and print film as well as the computer techniques to process and print digital images.

Employers prefer applicants who are high school graduates or those who have some experience in the field. Familiarity with computers is essential for photographic processing machine operators. The ability to perform simple mathematical calculations also is helpful. Photography courses that include instruction in film processing are valuable preparation. Such courses are available through high schools, vocational-technical institutes, private trade schools, and colleges and universities.

On-the-job training in photographic processing occupations can range from just a few hours for print machine operators to several months for photographic processing workers such as airbrush artists and colorists. Some workers attend periodic training seminars to maintain a high level of skill. Manual dexterity; good hand-eye coordination; and good vision, including normal color perception, are important qualifications for photographic process workers.

Photographic process machine workers can sometimes advance from jobs as machine operators to supervisory positions in laboratories or to management positions within retail stores.

Employment

Photographic process workers held about 32,000 jobs in 2004. About three in ten photographic process workers were employed in photofinishing laboratories and one-hour minilabs. More than one in six worked for portrait studios or commercial laboratories that specialize in processing the work of professional photographers for advertising and other industries. An additional one in nine was employed by general merchandise stores, and one in ten was in the printing, publishing, and motion picture industries.

Photographic processing machine operators held about 54,000 jobs in 2004. About half worked in retail establishments, primarily in general merchandise stores and drug stores. About one in three worked in photofinishing laboratories and one-hour minilabs. Small numbers were employed in the printing industry and in portrait studios and commercial laboratories that process the work of professional photographers.

Employment fluctuates somewhat over the course of the year. Typically, employment peaks during school graduation and summer vacation periods and again during the winter holiday season.

Job Outlook

A decline in employment is expected for photographic process workers and processing machine operators through the year 2014. Some openings will still result from replacement needs, which are higher for machine operators than for photographic process workers.

In recent years, digital cameras, which use electronic memory rather than film to record images, have become standard among professional photographers and are gaining in popularity among amateur photographers as the cost of these cameras continues to fall. This will reduce the demand for traditional photographic processing machine operators. However, while many digital camera owners will choose to print their own pictures with their own equipment, a growing number of casual photographers are choosing not to acquire the needed equipment and skills to print the photos themselves. For them, self-service machines will be able to meet some of the demand, but there will still be some demand for professionals to print digital photos, as well as to develop and print photos from those who continue to use film cameras.

Digital photography also will reduce demand for photographic process workers. Using digital cameras and technology, consumers who have a personal computer and the proper software will be able to download and view pictures on their computer, as well as manipulate, correct, and retouch their own photographs. No matter what improvements occur in camera technology, though, some photographic processing tasks will still require skillful manual treatment. Moreover, not all consumers will want to invest in the software. Job opportunities will be best for individuals with experience using computers and digital technology.

Earnings

Earnings of photographic process workers vary greatly depending on skill level, experience, and geographic location. Median hourly earnings for photographic process workers were $9.63 in May 2004. The middle 50 percent earned between $7.79 and $12.97. The lowest 10 percent earned less than $6.68, and the highest 10 percent earned more than $17.99. Median hourly earnings were $10.20 in photofinishing laboratories, the largest employer of photographic process workers.

Median hourly earnings for photographic processing machine operators were $9.33 in May 2004. The middle 50 percent earned between $7.78 and $11.88. The lowest 10 percent earned less than $6.84, and the highest 10 percent earned more than $15.21. Median hourly earnings in the two industries employing the largest numbers of photographic processing machine operators were $10.44 in photofinishing laboratories and $7.98 in health and personal care stores.

Related Occupations

Photographic process workers and processing machine operators need specialized knowledge of the photo developing process. Other workers who apply specialized technical knowledge include clinical laboratory technologists and technicians, computer operators, jewelers and precious stone and metal workers, prepress technicians and workers, printing machine operators, and science technicians.

Sources of Additional Information

For information about employment opportunities in photographic laboratories and schools that offer degrees in photographic technology, contact

▸ Photo Marketing Association International, 3000 Picture Place, Jackson, MI 49201. Internet: http://www.pmai.org

Physical Therapist Assistants and Aides

(O*NET 31-2021.00 and 31-2022.00)

Significant Points

■ Employment is projected to increase much faster than average; physical therapist aides may face keen competition from the large pool of qualified applicants.

■ Physical therapist assistants generally have an associate degree, but physical therapist aides usually learn skills on the job.

■ About 60 percent of jobs are in hospitals or offices of physical therapists.

Nature of the Work

Physical therapist assistants and aides perform components of physical therapy procedures and related tasks selected by a supervising physical therapist. These workers assist physical therapists in providing services that help improve mobility, relieve pain, and prevent or limit permanent physical disabilities of patients suffering from injuries or disease. Patients include accident victims and individuals with disabling conditions such as low-back pain, arthritis, heart disease, fractures, head injuries, and cerebral palsy.

Physical therapist assistants perform a variety of tasks. Components of treatment procedures performed by these workers, under the direction and supervision of physical therapists, involve exercises, massages, electrical stimulation, paraffin baths, hot and cold packs, traction, and ultrasound. Physical therapist assistants record the patient's responses to treatment and report the outcome of each treatment to the physical therapist.

Physical therapist aides help make therapy sessions productive under the direct supervision of a physical therapist or physical therapist assistant. They usually are responsible for keeping the treatment area clean and organized and for preparing for each patient's therapy. When patients need assistance moving to or from a treatment area, aides push them in a wheelchair or provide them with a shoulder to lean on. Because they are not licensed, aides do not perform the clinical tasks of a physical therapist assistant.

The duties of aides include some clerical tasks, such as ordering depleted supplies, answering the phone, and filling out insurance forms and other paperwork. The extent to which an aide or an assistant performs clerical tasks depends on the size and location of the facility.

Working Conditions

The hours and days that physical therapist assistants and aides work vary with the facility and with whether they are full- or part-time employees. Many outpatient physical therapy offices and clinics have evening and weekend hours to help coincide with patients' personal schedules. About 30 percent of all physical therapist assistants and aides work part time.

Physical therapist assistants and aides need a moderate degree of strength because of the physical exertion required in assisting patients with their treatment. In some cases, assistants and aides need to lift patients. Constant kneeling, stooping, and standing for long periods also are part of the job.

Training, Other Qualifications, and Advancement

Physical therapist aides are trained on the job, but physical therapist assistants typically earn an associate degree from an accredited physical therapist assistant program. Not all states require licensure or registration in order for the physical therapist assistant to practice. The states that require licensure stipulate specific educational and examination criteria. Complete information on practice acts and regulations can be obtained from the state licensing boards. Additional requirements may include certification in cardiopulmonary resuscitation (CPR) and other first aid and a minimum number of hours of clinical experience.

According to the American Physical Therapy Association, there were 238 accredited physical therapist assistant programs in the United States as of 2004. Accredited physical therapist assistant programs are designed to last 2 years, or 4 semesters, and culminate in an associate degree. Programs are divided into academic study and hands-on clinical experience. Academic coursework includes algebra, anatomy and physiology, biology, chemistry, and psychology. Many programs require that students complete a semester of anatomy and physiology and have certifications in CPR and other first aid even before they begin their clinical field experience. Both educators and prospective employers view clinical experience as integral to ensuring that students understand the responsibilities of a physical therapist assistant.

Employers typically require physical therapist aides to have a high school diploma, strong interpersonal skills, and a desire to assist people in need. Most employers provide clinical on-the-job training.

Employment

Physical therapist assistants and aides held about 101,000 jobs in 2004. Physical therapist assistants held about 59,000 jobs, physical

therapist aides approximately 43,000. Both work with physical therapists in a variety of settings. About 60 percent of jobs were in hospitals or in offices of physical therapists. Others worked primarily in nursing care facilities, offices of physicians, home health care services, and outpatient care centers.

Job Outlook

Employment of physical therapist assistants and aides is expected to grow much faster than the average for all occupations through the year 2014. The impact of proposed federal legislation imposing limits on reimbursement for therapy services may adversely affect the short-term job outlook for physical therapist assistants and aides. However, over the long run, demand for physical therapist assistants and aides will continue to rise in accordance with the increasing number of individuals with disabilities or limited function. The growing elderly population is particularly vulnerable to chronic and debilitating conditions that require therapeutic services. These patients often need additional assistance in their treatment, making the roles of assistants and aides vital. The large baby-boom generation is entering the prime age for heart attacks and strokes, further increasing the demand for cardiac and physical rehabilitation. In addition, future medical developments should permit an increased percentage of trauma victims to survive, creating added demand for therapy services.

Physical therapists are expected to increasingly utilize assistants to reduce the cost of physical therapy services. Once a patient is evaluated and a treatment plan is designed by the physical therapist, the physical therapist assistant can provide many aspects of treatment as prescribed by the therapist.

Physical therapist assistants and aides with prior experience working in a physical therapy office or other health care setting will have the best job opportunities. Physical therapist aides may face keen competition from the large pool of qualified individuals with a high school diploma.

Earnings

Median annual earnings of physical therapist assistants were $37,890 in May 2004. The middle 50 percent earned between $31,060 and $44,050. The lowest 10 percent earned less than $24,110, and the highest 10 percent earned more than $52,110. Median annual earnings in the industries employing the largest numbers of physical therapist assistants in May 2004 were

Nursing care facilities $40,360

General medical and surgical hospitals 37,790

Offices of other health practitioners......................37,120

Median annual earnings of physical therapist aides were $21,380 in May 2004. The middle 50 percent earned between $17,990 and $26,310. The lowest 10 percent earned less than $15,380, and the highest 10 percent earned more than $33,550. Median annual earnings of physical therapist aides in May 2004 were $21,120 in general medical and surgical hospitals and $20,360 in offices of physical therapists.

Related Occupations

Physical therapist assistants and aides work under the supervision of physical therapists. Other workers in the health care field who work under similar supervision include dental assistants, medical assistants, occupational therapist assistants and aides, pharmacy aides, pharmacy technicians, and social and human service assistants.

Sources of Additional Information

Career information on physical therapist assistants and a list of schools offering accredited programs can be obtained from

▸ The American Physical Therapy Association, 1111 North Fairfax St., Alexandria, VA 22314-1488. Internet: http://www.apta.org

Physical Therapists

(O*NET 29-1123.00)

Significant Points

■ Employment is expected to increase much faster than the average as growth in the number of individuals with disabilities or limited functioning spurs demand for therapy services.

■ Job opportunities should be particularly good in acute hospital, rehabilitation, and orthopedic settings.

■ After graduating from an accredited physical therapist educational program, therapists must pass a licensure exam before they can practice.

■ Nearly 6 out of 10 physical therapists work in hospitals or in offices of physical therapists.

Nature of the Work

Physical therapists provide services that help restore function, improve mobility, relieve pain, and prevent or limit permanent physical disabilities of patients suffering from injuries or disease. They restore, maintain, and promote overall fitness and health. Their patients include accident victims and individuals with disabling conditions such as low-back pain, arthritis, heart disease, fractures, head injuries, and cerebral palsy.

Therapists examine patients' medical histories and then test and measure the patients' strength, range of motion, balance and coordination, posture, muscle performance, respiration, and motor function. They also determine patients' ability to be independent and reintegrate into the community or workplace after injury or illness. Next, physical therapists develop plans describing a treatment strategy, its purpose, and its anticipated outcome. Physical therapist assistants, under the direction and supervision of a physical therapist, may be involved in implementing treatment plans with patients. Physical therapist aides perform routine support tasks, as directed by the therapist. (Physical therapist assistants and aides are discussed elsewhere in this book.)

Treatment often includes exercise for patients who have been immobilized and lack flexibility, strength, or endurance. Physical therapists encourage patients to use their own muscles to increase their flexibility and range of motion before finally advancing to other exercises that improve strength, balance, coordination, and endurance. The goal is to improve how an individual functions at work and at home.

Physical therapists also use electrical stimulation, hot packs or cold compresses, and ultrasound to relieve pain and reduce swelling. They may use traction or deep-tissue massage to relieve pain. Therapists also teach patients to use assistive and adaptive devices, such as crutches, prostheses, and wheelchairs. They also may show patients exercises to do at home to expedite their recovery.

As treatment continues, physical therapists document the patient's progress, conduct periodic examinations, and modify treatments when necessary. Besides tracking the patient's progress, such documentation identifies areas requiring more or less attention.

Physical therapists often consult and practice with a variety of other professionals, such as physicians, dentists, nurses, educators, social workers, occupational therapists, speech-language pathologists, and audiologists.

Some physical therapists treat a wide range of ailments; others specialize in areas such as pediatrics, geriatrics, orthopedics, sports medicine, neurology, and cardiopulmonary physical therapy.

Working Conditions

Physical therapists practice in hospitals, clinics, and private offices that have specially equipped facilities, or they treat patients in hospital rooms, homes, or schools.

In 2004, most full-time physical therapists worked a 40-hour week; some worked evenings and weekends to fit their patients' schedules. About 1 in 4 physical therapists worked part time. The job can be physically demanding because therapists often have to stoop, kneel, crouch, lift, and stand for long periods. In addition, physical therapists move heavy equipment and lift patients or help them turn, stand, or walk.

Training, Other Qualifications, and Advancement

All states require physical therapists to pass a licensure exam before they can practice and after graduating from an accredited physical therapist educational program.

According to the American Physical Therapy Association, there were 205 accredited physical therapist programs in 2004. Of the accredited programs, 94 offered master's degrees and 111 offered doctoral degrees. All physical therapist programs seeking accreditation are required to offer degrees at the master's degree level and above in accordance with the Commission on Accreditation in Physical Therapy Education.

Physical therapist programs start with basic science courses such as biology, chemistry, and physics and then introduce specialized courses, including biomechanics, neuroanatomy, human growth and development, manifestations of disease, examination techniques, and therapeutic procedures. Besides getting classroom and laboratory instruction, students receive supervised clinical experience. Among the courses that are useful when one applies to a physical therapist educational program are anatomy, biology, chemistry, social science, mathematics, and physics. Before granting admission, many professional education programs require experience as a volunteer in a physical therapy department of a hospital or clinic. For high school students, volunteering with the school athletic trainer is a good way to gain experience.

Physical therapists should have strong interpersonal skills in order to be able to educate patients about their physical therapy treatments. Physical therapists also should be compassionate and possess a desire to help patients. Similar traits are needed to interact with the patient's family.

Physical therapists are expected to continue their professional development by participating in continuing education courses and workshops. In fact, a number of states require continuing education as a condition of maintaining licensure.

Employment

Physical therapists held about 155,000 jobs in 2004. The number of jobs is greater than the number of practicing physical therapists because some physical therapists hold two or more jobs. For example, some may work in a private practice, but also work part time in another health care facility.

Nearly 6 out of 10 physical therapists worked in hospitals or in offices of physical therapists. Other jobs were in home health care services, nursing care facilities, outpatient care centers, and offices of physicians.

Some physical therapists were self-employed in private practices, seeing individual patients and contracting to provide services in hospitals, rehabilitation centers, nursing care facilities, home health care agencies, adult day care programs, and schools. Physical therapists also teach in academic institutions and conduct research.

Job Outlook

Employment of physical therapists is expected to grow much faster than the average for all occupations through 2014. The impact of proposed federal legislation imposing limits on reimbursement for therapy services may adversely affect the short-term job outlook for physical therapists. However, over the long run, the demand for physical therapists should continue to rise as growth in the number of individuals with disabilities or limited function spurs demand for therapy services. Job opportunities should be particularly good in acute hospital, rehabilitation, and orthopedic settings because the elderly receive the most treatment in these settings. The growing elderly population is particularly vulnerable to chronic and debilitating conditions that require therapeutic services. Also, the baby-boom generation is entering the prime age for heart attacks and strokes, increasing the demand for cardiac and physical rehabilitation. Further, young people will need physical therapy as technological advances save the lives of a larger proportion of newborns with severe birth defects.

Future medical developments also should permit a higher percentage of trauma victims to survive, creating additional demand for rehabilitative care. In addition, growth may result from advances in medical technology that could permit the treatment of more disabling conditions.

Widespread interest in health promotion also should increase demand for physical therapy services. A growing number of

employers are using physical therapists to evaluate worksites, develop exercise programs, and teach safe work habits to employees in the hope of reducing injuries in the workplace.

Earnings

Median annual earnings of physical therapists were $60,180 in May 2004. The middle 50 percent earned between $50,330 and $71,760. The lowest 10 percent earned less than $42,010, and the highest 10 percent earned more than $88,580. Median annual earnings in the industries employing the largest numbers of physical therapists in May 2004 were

Home health care services	$64,650
Nursing care facilities	61,720
Offices of physicians	61,270
General medical and surgical hospitals	60,350
Offices of other health practitioners	60,130

Related Occupations

Physical therapists rehabilitate persons with physical disabilities. Others who work in the rehabilitation field include audiologists, chiropractors, occupational therapists, recreational therapists, rehabilitation counselors, respiratory therapists, and speech-language pathologists.

Sources of Additional Information

Additional career information and a list of accredited educational programs in physical therapy are available from

▸ American Physical Therapy Association, 1111 North Fairfax St., Alexandria, VA 22314-1488. Internet: http://www.apta.org

Physician Assistants

(O*NET 29-1071.00)

Significant Points

■ Physician assistant programs usually last at least 2 years; admission requirements vary by program, but many require at least 2 years of college and some health care experience.

■ All states require physician assistants to complete an accredited education program and to pass a national exam in order to obtain a license.

■ Physician assistants rank among the fastest-growing occupations as physicians and health care institutions increasingly utilize physician assistants in order to contain costs.

■ Job opportunities should be good, particularly in rural and inner-city clinics.

Nature of the Work

Physician assistants (PAs) practice medicine under the supervision of physicians and surgeons. They should not be confused with medical assistants, who perform routine clinical and clerical tasks. PAs are formally trained to provide diagnostic, therapeutic, and preventive health care services, as delegated by a physician. Working as members of the health care team, they take medical histories, examine and treat patients, order and interpret laboratory tests and X rays, and make diagnoses. They also treat minor injuries by suturing, splinting, and casting. PAs record progress notes, instruct and counsel patients, and order or carry out therapy. In 48 states and the District of Columbia, physician assistants may prescribe medications. PAs also may have managerial duties. Some order medical supplies or equipment and supervise technicians and assistants.

Physician assistants work under the supervision of a physician. However, PAs may be the principal care providers in rural or inner-city clinics, where a physician is present for only 1 or 2 days each week. In such cases, the PA confers with the supervising physician and other medical professionals as needed and as required by law. PAs also may make house calls or go to hospitals and nursing care facilities to check on patients, after which they report back to the physician.

The duties of physician assistants are determined by the supervising physician and by state law. Aspiring PAs should investigate the laws and regulations in the states in which they wish to practice.

Many PAs work in primary care specialties, such as general internal medicine, pediatrics, and family medicine. Other specialty areas include general and thoracic surgery, emergency medicine, orthopedics, and geriatrics. PAs specializing in surgery provide preoperative and postoperative care and may work as first or second assistants during major surgery.

Working Conditions

Although PAs usually work in a comfortable, well-lighted environment, those in surgery often stand for long periods, and others do considerable walking. Schedules vary according to the practice setting and often depend on the hours of the supervising physician. The workweek of hospital-based PAs may include weekends, nights, or early morning hospital rounds to visit patients. These workers also may be on call. PAs in clinics usually work a 40-hour week.

Training, Other Qualifications, and Advancement

All states require that PAs complete an accredited, formal education program and pass a national exam to obtain a license. PA programs usually last at least 2 years and are full time. Most programs are in schools of allied health, academic health centers, medical schools, or 4-year colleges; a few are in community colleges, the military, or hospitals. Many accredited PA programs have clinical teaching affiliations with medical schools.

In 2005, more than 135 education programs for physician assistants were accredited or provisionally accredited by the American Academy of Physician Assistants. More than 90 of these programs offered the option of a master's degree, and the rest offered either a bachelor's degree or an associate degree. Most applicants to PA educational programs already have a bachelor's degree.

Admission requirements vary, but many programs require 2 years of college and some work experience in the health care field. Students should take courses in biology, English, chemistry, mathematics, psychology, and the social sciences. Many PAs have prior experience as registered nurses, while others come from varied backgrounds, including military corpsman/medics and allied health occupations such as respiratory therapists, physical therapists, and emergency medical technicians and paramedics.

PA education includes classroom instruction in biochemistry, pathology, human anatomy, physiology, microbiology, clinical pharmacology, clinical medicine, geriatric and home health care, disease prevention, and medical ethics. Students obtain supervised clinical training in several areas, including family medicine, internal medicine, surgery, prenatal care and gynecology, geriatrics, emergency medicine, psychiatry, and pediatrics. Sometimes, PA students serve one or more of these "rotations" under the supervision of a physician who is seeking to hire a PA. The rotations often lead to permanent employment.

All states and the District of Columbia have legislation governing the qualifications or practice of physician assistants. All jurisdictions require physician assistants to pass the Physician Assistant National Certifying Examination, administered by the National Commission on Certification of Physician Assistants (NCCPA) and open only to graduates of accredited PA education programs. Only those successfully completing the examination may use the credential "Physician Assistant-Certified." In order to remain certified, PAs must complete 100 hours of continuing medical education every 2 years. Every 6 years, they must pass a recertification examination or complete an alternative program combining learning experiences and a take-home examination.

Some PAs pursue additional education in a specialty such as surgery, neonatology, or emergency medicine. PA postgraduate educational programs are available in areas such as internal medicine, rural primary care, emergency medicine, surgery, pediatrics, neonatology, and occupational medicine. Candidates must be graduates of an accredited program and be certified by the NCCPA.

Physician assistants need leadership skills, self-confidence, and emotional stability. They must be willing to continue studying throughout their career to keep up with medical advances.

As they attain greater clinical knowledge and experience, PAs can advance to added responsibilities and higher earnings. However, by the very nature of the profession, clinically practicing PAs always are supervised by physicians.

Employment

Physician assistants held about 62,000 jobs in 2004. The number of jobs is greater than the number of practicing PAs because some hold two or more jobs. For example, some PAs work with a supervising physician, but also work in another practice, clinic, or hospital. According to the American Academy of Physician Assistants, about 15 percent of actively practicing PAs worked in more than one clinical job concurrently in 2004.

More than half of jobs for PAs were in the offices of physicians. About a quarter were in hospitals, public or private. The rest were mostly in outpatient care centers, including health maintenance organizations; the federal government; and public or private colleges, universities, and professional schools. A few were self-employed.

Job Outlook

Employment of PAs is expected to grow much faster than the average for all occupations through the year 2014, ranking among the fastest-growing occupations, due to anticipated expansion of the health care industry and an emphasis on cost containment, resulting in increasing utilization of PAs by physicians and health care institutions.

Physicians and institutions are expected to employ more PAs to provide primary care and to assist with medical and surgical procedures because PAs are cost-effective and productive members of the health care team. Physician assistants can relieve physicians of routine duties and procedures. Telemedicine—using technology to facilitate interactive consultations between physicians and physician assistants—also will expand the use of physician assistants. Job opportunities for PAs should be good, particularly in rural and inner-city clinics, because those settings have difficulty attracting physicians.

Besides the traditional office-based setting, PAs should find a growing number of jobs in institutional settings such as hospitals, academic medical centers, public clinics, and prisons. Additional PAs may be needed to augment medical staffing in inpatient teaching hospital settings as the number of hours physician residents are permitted to work is reduced, encouraging hospitals to use PAs to supply some physician resident services. Opportunities will be best in states that allow PAs a wider scope of practice.

Earnings

Median annual earnings of physician assistants were $69,410 in May 2004. The middle 50 percent earned between $57,110 and $83,560. The lowest 10 percent earned less than $37,320, and the highest 10 percent earned more than $94,880. Median annual earnings of physician assistants in 2004 were $70,310 in general medical and surgical hospitals and $69,210 in offices of physicians.

According to the American Academy of Physician Assistants, median income for physician assistants in full-time clinical practice in 2004 was $74,264; median income for first-year graduates was $64,536. Income varies by specialty, practice setting, geographical location, and years of experience. Employers often pay for their employees' liability insurance, registration fees with the Drug Enforcement Administration, state licensing fees, and credentialing fees.

Related Occupations

Other health care workers who provide direct patient care that requires a similar level of skill and training include audiologists, occupational therapists, physical therapists, registered nurses, and speech-language pathologists.

Sources of Additional Information

For information on a career as a physician assistant, including a list of accredited programs, contact

▶ American Academy of Physician Assistants Information Center, 950 North Washington St., Alexandria, VA 22314-1552. Internet: http://www.aapa.org

For eligibility requirements and a description of the Physician Assistant National Certifying Examination, contact

▶ National Commission on Certification of Physician Assistants, Inc., 12000 Findley Rd., Suite 200, Duluth, GA 30097. Internet: http://www.nccpa.net

Physicians and Surgeons

(O*NET 29-1061.00, 29-1062.00, 29-1063.00, 29-1064.00, 29-1065.00, 29-1066.00, 29-1067.00, and 29-1069.99)

Significant Points

■ Many physicians and surgeons work long, irregular hours; over one-third of full-time physicians worked 60 or more hours a week in 2004.

■ Formal education and training requirements are among the most demanding of any occupation, but earnings are among the highest.

■ Job opportunities should be very good, particularly in rural and low-income areas.

■ New physicians are much less likely to enter solo practice and more likely to work as salaried employees of group medical practices, clinics, hospitals, or health networks.

Nature of the Work

Physicians and surgeons serve a fundamental role in our society and have an effect upon all our lives. They diagnose illnesses and prescribe and administer treatment for people suffering from injury or disease. Physicians examine patients; obtain medical histories; and order, perform, and interpret diagnostic tests. They counsel patients on diet, hygiene, and preventive health care.

There are two types of physicians: M.D.—*Doctor of Medicine*—and D.O.—*Doctor of Osteopathic Medicine.* M.D.s also are known as *allopathic physicians.* While both M.D.s and D.O.s may use all accepted methods of treatment, including drugs and surgery, D.O.s place special emphasis on the body's musculoskeletal system, preventive medicine, and holistic patient care. D.O.s are more likely than M.D.s to be primary care specialists, although they can be found in all specialties. About half of D.O.s practice general or family medicine, general internal medicine, or general pediatrics.

Physicians work in one or more of several specialties, including, but not limited to, anesthesiology, family and general medicine, general internal medicine, general pediatrics, obstetrics and gynecology, psychiatry, and surgery.

Anesthesiologists. Anesthesiologists focus on the care of surgical patients and pain relief. Like other physicians, they evaluate and treat patients and direct the efforts of those on their staffs. Anesthesiologists confer with other physicians and surgeons about appropriate treatments and procedures before, during, and after operations. These critical-care specialists are responsible for maintenance of the patient's vital life functions—heart rate, body temperature, blood pressure, breathing—through continual monitoring and assessment during surgery. They often work outside of the operating room, providing pain relief in the intensive care unit, during labor and delivery, and for those who suffer from chronic pain.

Family and general practitioners. Family and general practitioners are often the first point of contact for people seeking health care, acting as the traditional family doctor. They assess and treat a wide range of conditions, ailments, and injuries, from sinus and respiratory infections to broken bones and scrapes. Family and general practitioners typically have a patient base of regular, long-term visitors. Patients with more serious conditions are referred to specialists or other health care facilities for more intensive care.

General internists. General internists diagnose and provide non-surgical treatment for diseases and injuries of internal organ systems. They provide care mainly for adults who have a wide range of problems associated with the internal organs, such as the stomach, kidneys, liver, and digestive tract. Internists use a variety of diagnostic techniques to treat patients through medication or hospitalization. Like general practitioners, general internists are commonly looked upon as primary care specialists. They have patients referred to them by other specialists, in turn referring patients to those and yet other specialists when more complex care is required.

General pediatricians. Providing care from birth to early adulthood, pediatricians are concerned with the health of infants, children, and teenagers. They specialize in the diagnosis and treatment of a variety of ailments specific to young people and track their patients' growth to adulthood. Like most physicians, pediatricians work with different health care workers, such as nurses and other physicians, to assess and treat children with various ailments, such as muscular dystrophy. Most of the work of pediatricians, however, involves treating day-to-day illnesses that are common to children—minor injuries, infectious diseases, and immunizations—much as a general practitioner treats adults. Some pediatricians specialize in serious medical conditions and pediatric surgery, treating autoimmune disorders or serious chronic ailments.

Obstetricians and gynecologists. Obstetricians and gynecologists (ob/gyns) are specialists whose focus is women's health. They are responsible for general medical care for women, but also provide care related to pregnancy and the reproductive system. Like general practitioners, ob/gyns are concerned with the prevention, diagnosis, and treatment of general health problems, but they focus on ailments specific to the female anatomy, such as breast and cervical cancer, urinary tract and pelvic disorders, and hormonal disorders. Ob/gyns also specialize in childbirth, treating and counseling women throughout their pregnancy, from giving prenatal diagnoses to delivery and postpartum care. Ob/gyns track the health of, and treat, both mother and fetus as the pregnancy progresses.

Psychiatrists. Psychiatrists are the primary caregivers in the area of mental health. They assess and treat mental illnesses through a combination of psychotherapy, psychoanalysis, hospitalization, and medication. Psychotherapy involves regular discussions with patients about their problems; the psychiatrist helps them find solutions through changes in their behavioral patterns, the exploration of their past experiences, and group and family therapy sessions. Psychoanalysis involves long-term psychotherapy and counseling for patients. In many cases, medications are administered to correct chemical imbalances that may be causing emotional problems. Psychiatrists may also administer electroconvulsive therapy to those of their patients who do not respond to, or who cannot take, medications.

Surgeons. Surgeons are physicians who specialize in the treatment of injury, disease, and deformity through operations. Using a variety of instruments, and with patients under general or local anesthesia, a surgeon corrects physical deformities, repairs bone and tissue after injuries, or performs preventive surgeries on patients with debilitating diseases or disorders. Although a large number perform general surgery, many surgeons choose to specialize in a specific area. One of the most prevalent specialties is orthopedic surgery: the treatment of the musculoskeletal system. Others include neurological surgery (treatment of the brain and nervous system), cardiovascular surgery, otolaryngology (treatment of the ear, nose, and throat), and plastic or reconstructive surgery. Like primary care and other specialist physicians, surgeons also examine patients, perform and interpret diagnostic tests, and counsel patients on preventive health care.

A number of other medical specialists, including allergists, cardiologists, dermatologists, emergency physicians, gastroenterologists, ophthalmologists, pathologists, and radiologists, also work in clinics, hospitals, and private offices.

Working Conditions

Many physicians—primarily general and family practitioners, general internists, pediatricians, ob/gyns, and psychiatrists—work in small private offices or clinics, often assisted by a small staff of nurses and other administrative personnel. Increasingly, physicians are practicing in groups or health care organizations that provide backup coverage and allow for more time off. These physicians often work as part of a team coordinating care for a population of patients; they are less independent than solo practitioners of the past.

Surgeons and anesthesiologists typically work in well-lighted, sterile environments while performing surgery and often stand for long periods. Most work in hospitals or in surgical outpatient centers. Many physicians and surgeons work long, irregular hours. Over one-third of full-time physicians and surgeons worked 60 hours or more a week in 2004. Only 8 percent of all physicians and surgeons worked part time, compared with 16 percent for all occupations. Physicians and surgeons must travel frequently between office and hospital to care for their patients. Those who are on call deal with many patients' concerns over the phone and may make emergency visits to hospitals or nursing homes.

Training, Other Qualifications, and Advancement

Formal education and training requirements for physicians are among the most demanding of any occupation—4 years of undergraduate school, 4 years of medical school, and 3 to 8 years of internship and residency, depending on the specialty selected. A few medical schools offer combined undergraduate and medical school programs that last 6 rather than the customary 8 years.

Premedical students must complete undergraduate work in physics, biology, mathematics, English, and inorganic and organic chemistry. Students also take courses in the humanities and the social sciences. Some students volunteer at local hospitals or clinics to gain practical experience in the health professions.

The minimum educational requirement for entry into a medical school is 3 years of college; most applicants, however, have at least a bachelor's degree, and many have advanced degrees. There are 146 medical schools in the United States—126 teach allopathic medicine and award a Doctor of Medicine (M.D.) degree; 20 teach osteopathic medicine and award the Doctor of Osteopathic Medicine (D.O.) degree. Acceptance to medical school is highly competitive. Applicants must submit transcripts, scores from the Medical College Admission Test, and letters of recommendation. Schools also consider an applicant's character, personality, leadership qualities, and participation in extracurricular activities. Most schools require an interview with members of the admissions committee.

Students spend most of the first 2 years of medical school in laboratories and classrooms, taking courses such as anatomy, biochemistry, physiology, pharmacology, psychology, microbiology, pathology, medical ethics, and laws governing medicine. They also learn to take medical histories, examine patients, and diagnose illnesses. During their last 2 years, students work with patients under the supervision of experienced physicians in hospitals and clinics, learning acute, chronic, preventive, and rehabilitative care. Through rotations in internal medicine, family practice, obstetrics and gynecology, pediatrics, psychiatry, and surgery, they gain experience in the diagnosis and treatment of illness.

Following medical school, almost all M.D.s enter a residency—graduate medical education in a specialty that takes the form of paid on-the-job training, usually in a hospital. Most D.O.s serve a 12-month rotating internship after graduation and before entering a residency, which may last 2 to 6 years.

All states, the District of Columbia, and U.S. territories license physicians. To be licensed, physicians must graduate from an accredited medical school, pass a licensing examination, and complete 1 to 7 years of graduate medical education. Although physicians licensed in one state usually can get a license to practice in another without further examination, some states limit reciprocity. Graduates of foreign medical schools generally can qualify for licensure after passing an examination and completing a U.S. residency.

M.D.s and D.O.s seeking board certification in a specialty may spend up to 7 years in residency training, depending on the specialty. A final examination immediately after residency or after 1 or 2 years of practice also is necessary for certification by a member board of the American Board of Medical Specialists (ABMS) or the American Osteopathic Association (AOA). The ABMS represents 24 specialty boards, ranging from allergy and immunology to urology. The AOA has approved 18 specialty boards, ranging from anesthesiology to surgery. For certification in a subspecialty, physicians usually need another 1 to 2 years of residency.

A physician's training is costly. According to the Association of American Medical Colleges, in 2004 more than 80 percent of medical school graduates were in debt for educational expenses.

People who wish to become physicians must have a desire to serve patients, be self-motivated, and be able to survive the pressures and long hours of medical education and practice. Physicians also must have a good bedside manner, emotional stability, and the ability to make decisions in emergencies. Prospective physicians must be willing to study throughout their career in order to keep up with medical advances.

Employment

Physicians and surgeons held about 567,000 jobs in 2004; approximately 1 out of 7 was self-employed and not incorporated. About 60 percent of salaried physicians and surgeons were in office of physicians, and 16 percent were employed by private hospitals. Others practiced in federal, state, and local governments, including hospitals, colleges, universities, and professional schools; private colleges, universities, and professional schools; and outpatient care centers.

According to the American Medical Association (AMA), in 2003 about 2 out 5 physicians in patient care were in primary care, but not in a subspecialty of primary care (table 1).

Table 1. Percent distribution of physicians by specialty, 2003

	Percent
Total	100.0
Primary care	40.8
Family medicine and general practice	12.8
Internal medicine	15.1
Obstetrics & gynecology	5.3
Pediatrics	7.6
Specialties	59.2
Anesthesiology	5.4
Psychiatry	5.4
Surgical specialties, selected	14.6
All other specialties	33.9

SOURCE: American Medical Association, Physician Characteristics and Distribution in the US, 2005.

A growing number of physicians are partners or salaried employees of group practices. Organized as clinics or as associations of physicians, medical groups can afford expensive medical equipment and realize other business advantages.

According to the AMA, the New England and Middle Atlantic states have the highest ratio of physicians to population; the South Central and Mountain states have the lowest. D.O.s are more likely than M.D.s to practice in small cities and towns and in rural areas. M.D.s tend to locate in urban areas, close to hospital and education centers.

Job Outlook

Employment of physicians and surgeons is projected to grow faster than the average for all occupations through the year 2014 due to the continued expansion of health care industries. The growing and aging population will drive overall growth in the demand for physician services as consumers continue to demand high levels of care using the latest technologies, diagnostic tests, and therapies. In addition to employment growth, job openings will result from the need to replace physicians and surgeons who retire over the 2004–2014 period.

Demand for physicians' services is highly sensitive to changes in consumer preferences, health care reimbursement policies, and legislation. For example, if changes to health coverage result in consumers facing higher out-of-pocket costs, they may demand fewer physician services. Demand for physician services may also be tempered by patients relying more on other health care providers—such as physician assistants, nurse practitioners, optometrists, and nurse anesthetists—for some health care services. In addition, new technologies will increase physician productivity. Telemedicine will allow physicians to treat patients or consult with other providers remotely. Increasing use of electronic medical records, test and prescription orders, billing, and scheduling will also improve physician productivity.

Opportunities for individuals interested in becoming physicians and surgeons are expected to be very good. Reports of shortages in some specialties or geographic areas should attract new entrants, encouraging schools to expand programs and hospitals to expand available residency slots. However, because physician training is so lengthy, employment change happens gradually. In the short term, to meet increased demand, experienced physicians may work longer hours; delay retirement; or take measures to increase productivity, such as using more support staff to provide services. Opportunities should be particularly good in rural and low-income areas because some physicians find these areas unattractive due to less control over work hours, isolation from medical colleagues, or other reasons.

Unlike their predecessors, newly trained physicians face radically different choices of where and how to practice. New physicians are much less likely to enter solo practice and more likely to take salaried jobs in group medical practices, clinics, and health networks.

Earnings

Earnings of physicians and surgeons are among the highest of any occupation. According to the Medical Group Management Association's Physician Compensation and Production Survey, median total compensation for physicians in 2004 varied by specialty, as shown in table 2. Total compensation for physicians reflects the amount reported as direct compensation for tax purposes, plus all voluntary salary reductions. Salary, bonus and/or incentive payments, research stipends, honoraria, and distribution of profits were included in total compensation.

Table 2. Median total compensation of physicians by specialty, 2004

	Less than two years in specialty	More than one year in specialty
Anesthesiology	$259,948	$321,686
Surgery: General	228,839	282,504
Obstetrics/gynecology:		
General	203,270	247,348
Psychiatry: General	173,922	180,000
Internal medicine:		
General	141,912	166,420
Pediatrics: General	132,953	161,331
Family practice (without obstetrics)	137,119	156,010

SOURCE: Medical Group Management Association, Physician Compensation and Production Report, 2005.

Self-employed physicians—those who own or are part owners of their medical practice—generally have higher median incomes than salaried physicians. Earnings vary according to number of years in practice; geographic region; hours worked; and skill, personality, and professional reputation. Self-employed physicians and surgeons must provide for their own health insurance and retirement.

Related Occupations

Physicians work to prevent, diagnose, and treat diseases, disorders, and injuries. Other health care practitioners who need similar skills and who exercise critical judgment include chiropractors, dentists, optometrists, physician assistants, podiatrists, registered nurses, and veterinarians.

Sources of Additional Information

For a list of medical schools and residency programs, as well as general information on premedical education, financial aid, and medicine as a career, contact

▶ Association of American Medical Colleges, Section for Student Services, 2450 N St. NW, Washington, DC 20037-1126. Internet: http://www.aamc.org

▶ American Association of Colleges of Osteopathic Medicine, 5550 Friendship Blvd., Suite 310, Chevy Chase, MD 20815-7231. Internet: http://www.aacom.org

For general information on physicians, contact

▶ American Medical Association, 515 N. State St., Chicago, IL 60610. Internet: http://www.ama-assn.org

▶ American Osteopathic Association, Division of Communications, 142 East Ontario St., Chicago, IL 60611. Internet: http://www.osteopathic.org

For information about various medical specialties, contact

▶ American Board of Medical Specialties, 1007 Church St., Suite 404, Evanston, IL 60201-5913. Internet: http://www.abms.org

▶ American Society of Anesthesiologists, 520 N. Northwest Hwy., Park Ridge, IL 60068-2573. Internet: http://www.asahq.org

▶ American Academy of Family Physicians, Resident Student Activities Department, 11400 Tomahawk Creek Pkwy., Leawood, KS 66211-2672. Internet: http://fmignet.aafp.org

▶ American College of Physicians, 190 North Independence Mall West, Philadelphia, PA 19106. Internet: http://www.acponline.org

▶ American College of Obstetricians and Gynecologists, 409 12th St. SW, P.O. Box 96920, Washington, DC 20090-6920. Internet: http://www.acog.org

▶ American Academy of Pediatrics, 141 Northwest Point Blvd., Elk Grove Village, IL 60007-1098. Internet: http://www.aap.org

▶ American Psychiatric Association, 1000 Wilson Blvd., Suite 1825, Arlington, VA 22209-3901. Internet: http://www.psych.org

▶ American College of Surgeons, Division of Education, 633 North Saint Clair St., Chicago, IL 60611-3211. Internet: http://www.facs.org

Information on federal scholarships and loans is available from the directors of student financial aid at schools of medicine.

Information on licensing is available from state boards of examiners.

Physicists and Astronomers

(O*NET 19-2011.00 and 19-2012.00)

Significant Points

- Scientific research and development services firms and the federal government employ 3 out of 5 physicists and astronomers.

- Most jobs are in basic research and development, usually requiring a doctoral degree; master's degree holders qualify for many jobs in applied research and development, while bachelor's degree holders often qualify as technicians, research assistants, or other types of jobs.

- Employment is expected to grow more slowly than average.

- Competition for jobs is expected; however, graduates with a physics or astronomy degree at any level will find their knowledge of science and mathematics useful for entry to many other occupations.

Nature of the Work

Physicists explore and identify basic principles and laws governing motion and gravitation; the macroscopic and microscopic behavior of gases; and the structure and behavior of matter, the generation and transfer between energy, and the interaction of matter and energy. Some physicists use these principles in theoretical areas, such as the nature of time and the origin of the universe; others apply their knowledge of physics to practical areas, such as the development of advanced materials, electronic and optical devices, and medical equipment.

Physicists design and perform experiments with lasers, particle accelerators, telescopes, mass spectrometers, and other equipment. On the basis of their observations and analysis, they attempt to discover and explain laws describing the forces of nature, such as gravity, electromagnetism, and nuclear interactions. Physicists also find ways to apply physical laws and theories to problems in nuclear energy, electronics, optics, materials, communications, aerospace technology, and medical instrumentation.

Astronomy is sometimes considered a subfield of physics. *Astronomers* use the principles of physics and mathematics to learn about the fundamental nature of the universe, including the sun, moon, planets, stars, and galaxies. They also apply their knowledge to solve problems in navigation, space flight, and satellite communications and to develop the instrumentation and techniques used to observe and collect astronomical data.

Most physicists work in research and development. Some do basic research to increase scientific knowledge. Physicists who conduct applied research build upon the discoveries made through basic research and work to develop new devices, products, and processes. For example, basic research in solid-state physics led to the development of transistors and then integrated circuits used in computers.

Physicists also design research equipment, which often has additional unanticipated uses. For example, lasers are used in surgery, microwave devices function in ovens, and measuring instruments can analyze blood or the chemical content of foods. A small number of physicists work in inspection, testing, quality control, and other production-related jobs in industry.

Much physics research is done in small or medium-sized laboratories. However, experiments in plasma, nuclear, and high-energy physics, as well as in some other areas of physics, require extremely large, expensive equipment, such as particle accelerators. Physicists in these subfields often work in large teams. Although physics research may require extensive experimentation in laboratories, research physicists still spend time in offices planning, recording, analyzing, and reporting on research.

Almost all astronomers do research. Some are theoreticians, working on the laws governing the structure and evolution of astronomical objects. Others analyze large quantities of data gathered by observatories and satellites and write scientific papers or reports on their findings. Some astronomers actually operate large space- or ground-based telescopes, usually as part of a team. However, astronomers may spend only a few weeks each year making observations with optical telescopes, radio telescopes, and other instruments. For many years, satellites and other space-based instruments, such as the Hubble space telescope, have provided prodigious amounts of astronomical data. New technology resulting in improvements in analytical techniques and instruments, such as computers and optical telescopes and mounts, is leading to a resurgence in ground-based research. A small number of astronomers work in museums housing planetariums. These astronomers develop and revise programs presented to the public and may direct planetarium operations.

Physicists generally specialize in one of many subfields: elementary particle physics, nuclear physics, atomic and molecular physics, physics of condensed matter (solid-state physics), optics, acoustics, space physics, plasma physics, or the physics of fluids. Some specialize in a subdivision of one of these subfields. For example, within condensed-matter physics, specialties include superconductivity, crystallography, and semiconductors. However, all physics involves the same fundamental principles, so specialties may overlap and physicists may switch from one subfield to another. Also, growing numbers of physicists work in interdisciplinary fields, such as biophysics, chemical physics, and geophysics.

Working Conditions

Physicists often work regular hours in laboratories and offices. At times, however, those who are deeply involved in research may work long or irregular hours. Most do not encounter unusual hazards in their work. Some physicists temporarily work away from home at national or international facilities with unique equipment, such as particle accelerators. Astronomers who make observations with ground-based telescopes may spend long periods in observatories; this work usually involves travel to remote locations and may require long hours, including night work.

Physicists and astronomers whose work depends on grant money often are under pressure to write grant proposals to keep their work funded.

Training, Other Qualifications, and Advancement

Because most jobs are in basic research and development, a doctoral degree is the usual educational requirement for physicists and astronomers. Additional experience and training in a postdoctoral research appointment, although not required, is important for physicists and astronomers aspiring to permanent positions in basic research in universities and government laboratories. Many physics and astronomy Ph.D. holders ultimately teach at the college or university level.

Master's degree holders usually do not qualify for basic research positions, but do qualify for many kinds of jobs requiring a physics background, including positions in manufacturing and applied research and development. Increasingly, many master's degree programs are specifically preparing students for physics-related research and development that does not require a Ph.D. degree. These programs teach students specific research skills that can be used in private-industry jobs. In addition, a master's degree coupled with state certification usually qualifies one for teaching jobs in high schools or at 2-year colleges.

Those with bachelor's degrees in physics are rarely qualified to fill positions in research or in teaching at the college level. They are, however, usually qualified to work as technicians or research assistants in engineering-related areas, in software development and other scientific fields, or in setting up computer networks and sophisticated laboratory equipment. Increasingly, some may qualify for applied research jobs in private industry or take on nontraditional physics roles, often in computer science, such as a systems analyst or database administrator. Some become science teachers in secondary schools. Holders of a bachelor's or master's degree in astronomy often enter an unrelated field. In addition, they are qualified to work in planetariums running science shows, to assist astronomers doing research, and to operate space-based and ground-based telescopes and other astronomical instrumentation. (See the descriptions of engineers, geoscientists, computer programmers, computer scientists and database administrators, computer software engineers, and computer systems analysts elsewhere in this book.)

About 510 colleges and universities offer a bachelor's degree in physics. Undergraduate programs provide a broad background in the natural sciences and mathematics. Typical physics courses include electromagnetism, optics, thermodynamics, atomic physics, and quantum mechanics.

Approximately 185 colleges and universities have departments offering Ph.D. degrees in physics; an additional 68 colleges offer a master's as their highest degree in physics. Graduate students usually concentrate in a subfield of physics, such as elementary particles or condensed matter. Many begin studying for their doctorate immediately after receiving their bachelor's degree.

About 80 universities grant degrees in astronomy, either through an astronomy, physics, or combined physics-astronomy department. Currently, about 40 departments are combined with the physics department and the same number are administered separately. With fewer than 40 doctoral programs in astronomy, applicants face considerable competition for available slots. Those planning a career in the subject should have a very strong physics background. In fact, an undergraduate degree in either physics or astronomy is excellent preparation, followed by a Ph.D. in astronomy.

Mathematical ability, problem-solving and analytical skills, an inquisitive mind, imagination, and initiative are important traits for anyone planning a career in physics or astronomy. Prospective physicists who hope to work in industrial laboratories applying physics knowledge to practical problems should broaden their educational background to include courses outside of physics, such as economics, information technology, and business management. Good oral and written communication skills also are important because many physicists work as part of a team, write research papers or proposals, or have contact with clients or customers with nonphysics backgrounds.

Many physics and astronomy Ph.D. holders begin their careers in a postdoctoral research position, in which they may work with experienced physicists as they continue to learn about their specialty and develop ideas and results to be used in later work. Initial work may be under the close supervision of senior scientists. After some experience, physicists perform increasingly complex tasks and work more independently. Those who develop new products or processes sometimes form their own companies or join new firms to exploit their own ideas. Experience, either in academic laboratories or through internships, fellowships, or work-study programs in industry, also is useful. Some employers of research physicists, particularly in the information technology industry, prefer to hire individuals with several years of postdoctoral experience.

Employment

Physicists and astronomers held about 16,000 jobs in 2004. Jobs for astronomers accounted for only 5 percent of the total. About 33 percent of physicists and astronomers worked for scientific research and development services firms. The federal government employed 25 percent, mostly in the U.S. Department of Defense, but also in the National Aeronautics and Space Administration (NASA) and in the U.S. Departments of Commerce, Health and Human Services, and Energy. Other physicists and astronomers worked in colleges and universities in nonfaculty—usually research—positions or for state governments, information technology companies, pharmaceutical and medicine manufacturing companies, or electronic equipment manufacturers.

In 2004, many physicists and astronomers held faculty positions in colleges and universities. (See the description of teachers—postsecondary elsewhere in this book.)

Although physicists and astronomers are employed in all parts of the country, most work in areas in which universities, large research and development laboratories, or observatories are located.

Job Outlook

Employment of physicists and astronomers is expected to grow more slowly than average for all occupations through 2014. Federal research expenditures are the major source of physics-related and astronomy-related research funds, especially for basic research. Although these expenditures are expected to increase over the 2004–2014 projection period, resulting in some growth in employment and opportunities, the limited science research funds available still will result in competition for basic research jobs among Ph.D. holders. The need to replace physicists and astronomers who retire or otherwise leave the occupation permanently will account for most expected job openings.

Although research and development expenditures in private industry will continue to grow, many research laboratories in private industry are expected to continue to reduce basic research, which includes much physics research, in favor of applied or manufacturing research and product and software development. Nevertheless, persons with a physics background continue to be in demand in the areas of information technology, semiconductor technology, and other applied sciences. This trend is expected to continue; however, many of the new workers will have job titles such as computer software engineer, computer programmer, or systems analyst or developer rather than physicist.

Throughout the 1990s, the number of doctorates granted in physics was much greater than the number of job openings for physicists, resulting in keen competition, particularly for research positions in colleges and universities and in research and development centers. Recent increases in undergraduate physics enrollments, however, may lead to growth in enrollments in graduate physics programs so that toward the end of the projection period, there may be an increase in the number of doctoral degrees granted that will intensify the competition for job openings.

Opportunities may be more numerous for those with a master's degree, particularly graduates from programs preparing students for applied research and development, product design, and manufacturing positions in private industry. Many of these positions, however, will have titles other than physicist, such as engineer or computer scientist.

Persons with only a bachelor's degree in physics or astronomy are not qualified to enter most physicist or astronomer research jobs, but may qualify for a wide range of positions related to engineering; mathematics; computer science; environmental science; and—for those with the appropriate background—some nonscience fields, such as finance. Those who meet state certification requirements can become high school physics teachers, an occupation in strong demand in many school districts. Most states require new teachers to obtain a master's degree in education within a certain time. Despite competition for traditional physics and astronomy research jobs, graduates with a physics or astronomy degree at any level will find their knowledge of science and mathematics useful for entry into many other occupations.

Earnings

Median annual earnings of physicists were $87,450 in May 2004. The middle 50 percent earned between $66,590 and $109,420. The lowest 10 percent earned less than $49,450, and the highest 10 percent earned more than $132,780.

Median annual earnings of astronomers were $97,320 in May 2004. The middle 50 percent earned between $66,190 and $120,350, the lowest 10 percent less than $43,410, and the highest 10 percent more than $137,860.

According to a 2005 National Association of Colleges and Employers survey, the average annual starting salary offer to physics doctoral degree candidates was $56,070.

The American Institute of Physics reported a median annual salary of $104,000 in 2004 for its full-time members with Ph.D.s (excluding those in postdoctoral positions); the median was $94,000 for those with master's degrees and $72,000 for bachelor's degree holders. Those working in temporary postdoctoral positions earned significantly less.

The average annual salary for physicists employed by the federal government was $104,917 in 2005; for astronomy and space scientists, it was $110,195.

Related Occupations

The work of physicists and astronomers relates closely to that of engineers, chemists and materials scientists, atmospheric scientists, environmental scientists, geoscientists, computer systems analysts, computer scientists and database administrators, computer programmers, and mathematicians.

Sources of Additional Information

General information on career opportunities in physics is available from the following organizations:

▸ American Institute of Physics, Career Services Division and Education and Employment Division, One Physics Ellipse, College Park, MD 20740-3843. Internet: http://www.aip.org

▸ The American Physical Society, One Physics Ellipse, College Park, MD 20740-3844. Internet: http://www.aps.org

Podiatrists

(O*NET 29-1081.00)

Significant Points

■ Despite increasing demand for podiatric care, job openings for podiatrists are expected to be limited because the occupation is small and most podiatrists remain in it until they retire.

■ Opportunities for newly trained podiatrists will be better in group medical practices, clinics, and health networks than in traditional, solo practices.

■ Podiatrists need a state license that requires the completion of at least 90 hours of undergraduate study; a 4-year post-graduate program at a college of podiatric medicine; and, in most states, a postdoctoral residency program lasting at least 2 years.

■ Podiatrists enjoy very high earnings.

Nature of the Work

Americans spend a great deal of time on their feet. As the nation becomes more active across all age groups, the need for foot care will become increasingly important to maintaining a healthy lifestyle.

The human foot is a complex structure. It contains 26 bones—plus muscles, nerves, ligaments, and blood vessels—and is designed for balance and mobility. The 52 bones in the feet make up about one-fourth of all the bones in the human body. Podiatrists, also known as *doctors of podiatric medicine* (DPMs), diagnose and treat disorders, diseases, and injuries of the foot and lower leg.

Podiatrists treat corns, calluses, ingrown toenails, bunions, heel spurs, and arch problems; ankle and foot injuries, deformities, and infections; and foot complaints associated with diseases such as diabetes. To treat these problems, podiatrists prescribe drugs, order physical therapy, set fractures, and perform surgery. They also fit corrective inserts called orthotics, design plaster casts and strappings to correct deformities, and design custom-made shoes. Podiatrists may use a force plate or scanner to help design the orthotics: Patients walk across a plate connected to a computer that "reads" their feet, picking up pressure points and weight distribution. From the computer readout, podiatrists order the correct design or recommend another kind of treatment.

To diagnose a foot problem, podiatrists also order X rays and laboratory tests. The foot may be the first area to show signs of serious conditions such as arthritis, diabetes, and heart disease. For example, patients with diabetes are prone to foot ulcers and infections due to poor circulation. Podiatrists consult with and refer patients to other health practitioners when they detect symptoms of these disorders.

Most podiatrists have a solo practice, although more are forming group practices with other podiatrists or health practitioners. Some specialize in surgery, orthopedics, primary care, or public health. Besides these board-certified specialties, podiatrists may practice other specialties, such as sports medicine, pediatrics, dermatology, radiology, geriatrics, or diabetic foot care.

Podiatrists who are in private practice are responsible for running a small business. They may hire employees, order supplies, and keep records, among other tasks. In addition, some educate the community on the benefits of foot care through speaking engagements and advertising.

Working Conditions

Podiatrists usually work in their own offices. They also may spend time visiting patients in nursing homes or performing surgery at hospitals or ambulatory surgical centers, but usually have fewer after-hours emergencies than other doctors have. Those with private practices set their own hours, but may work evenings and weekends to accommodate their patients.

Training, Other Qualifications, and Advancement

All states and the District of Columbia require a license for the practice of podiatric medicine. Each state defines its own licensing requirements, although many states grant reciprocity to podiatrists who are licensed in another state. Applicants for licensure must be graduates of an accredited college of podiatric medicine and must pass written and oral examinations. Some states permit applicants to substitute the examination of the National Board of Podiatric Medical Examiners, given in the second and fourth years of podiatric medical college, for part or all of the written state examination. Most states also require the completion of a postdoctoral residency program of at least 2 years and continuing education for license renewal.

Prerequisites for admission to a college of podiatric medicine include the completion of at least 90 semester hours of undergraduate study, an acceptable grade point average, and suitable scores on the Medical College Admission Test (some colleges also may accept the Dental Admission Test or the Graduate Record Exam). All of the colleges require 8 semester hours each of biology, inorganic chemistry, organic chemistry, and physics, as well as 6 hours of English. The science courses should be those designed for premedical students. Potential podiatric medical students also are evaluated on the basis of extracurricular and community activities, personal interviews, and letters of recommendation. About 95 percent of podiatric students have at least a bachelor's degree.

In 2005, there were seven colleges of podiatric medicine accredited by the Council on Podiatric Medical Education. Colleges of podiatric medicine offer a 4-year program whose core curriculum is similar to that in other schools of medicine. During the first 2 years, students receive classroom instruction in basic sciences, including anatomy, chemistry, pathology, and pharmacology. Third- and fourth-year students have clinical rotations in private practices, hospitals, and clinics. During these rotations, they learn how to take general and podiatric histories, perform routine physical examinations, interpret tests and findings, make diagnoses, and perform therapeutic procedures. Graduates receive the degree of Doctor of Podiatric Medicine (DPM).

Most graduates complete a hospital-based residency program after receiving a DPM. Residency programs last from 2 to 4 years. Residents receive advanced training in podiatric medicine and surgery and serve clinical rotations in anesthesiology, internal medicine, pathology, radiology, emergency medicine, and orthopedic and general surgery. Residencies lasting more than 1 year provide more extensive training in specialty areas.

There are a number of certifying boards for the podiatric specialties of orthopedics, primary medicine, and surgery. Certification means that the DPM meets higher standards than those required for licensure. Each board requires advanced training, the completion of written and oral examinations, and experience as a practicing podiatrist. Most managed-care organizations prefer board-certified podiatrists.

People planning a career in podiatry should have scientific aptitude, manual dexterity, interpersonal skills, and good business sense.

Podiatrists may advance to become professors at colleges of podiatric medicine, department chiefs in hospitals, or general health administrators.

Employment

Podiatrists held about 10,000 jobs in 2004. About 23 percent of podiatrists are self-employed. Most podiatrists were solo practitioners, although more are entering group practices with other podiatrists or other health practitioners. Solo practitioners primarily were unincorporated self-employed workers, although some also were incorporated wage and salary workers in offices of other health practitioners. Other podiatrists are employed in hospitals and by the federal government.

Job Outlook

Employment of podiatrists is expected to grow about as fast as the average for all occupations through 2014. More people will turn to podiatrists for foot care because of the rising number of injuries sustained by a more active and increasingly older population. Additional job openings will result from podiatrists who retire from the occupation, particularly members of the baby-boom generation. However, relatively few job openings from this source are expected because the occupation is small and most podiatrists remain in it until they retire.

Medicare and most private health insurance programs cover acute medical and surgical foot services, as well as diagnostic X rays and leg braces. Details of such coverage vary among plans. However, routine foot care, including the removal of corns and calluses, ordinarily is not covered unless the patient has a systemic condition that has resulted in severe circulatory problems or areas of desensitization in the legs or feet. Like dental services, podiatric care is often discretionary and, therefore, more dependent on disposable income than some other medical services.

Employment of podiatrists would grow even faster were it not for continued emphasis on controlling the costs of specialty health care. Insurers will balance the cost of sending patients to podiatrists against the cost and availability of substitute practitioners, such as physicians and physical therapists. Opportunities will be better for board-certified podiatrists because many managed-care organizations require board certification. Opportunities for newly trained podiatrists will be better in group medical practices, clinics, and health networks than in traditional solo practices. Establishing a practice will be most difficult in the areas surrounding colleges of podiatric medicine, where podiatrists are concentrated.

Earnings

Podiatrists enjoy very high earnings. Median annual earnings of salaried podiatrists were $94,400 in 2004. Additionally, a survey by *Podiatry Management Magazine* reported median net income of $113,000 in 2004. Podiatrists in partnerships tended to earn higher net incomes than those in solo practice. Self-employed podiatrists must provide for their own health insurance and retirement.

Related Occupations

Other workers who apply medical knowledge to prevent, diagnose, and treat lower-body muscle and bone disorders and injuries include athletic trainers, chiropractors, massage therapists, occupational therapists, physical therapists, and physicians and surgeons. Workers who specialize in developing orthopedic shoe inserts, braces, and prosthetic limbs are orthotists and prosthetists.

Sources of Additional Information

For information on a career in podiatric medicine, contact

▶ American Podiatric Medical Association, 9312 Old Georgetown Rd., Bethesda, MD 20814-1621. Internet: http://www.apma.org

Information on the colleges of podiatric medicine and their entrance requirements, curricula, and student financial aid is available from

▶ American Association of Colleges of Podiatric Medicine, 15850 Crabbs Branch Way, Suite 320, Rockville, MD 20855-2622. Internet: http://www.aacpm.org

Power Plant Operators, Distributors, and Dispatchers

(O*NET 51-8011.00, 51-8012.00, 51-8013.01, and 51-8013.02)

Significant Points

■ Keen competition for jobs is expected; opportunities will be best for operators with training in computers and automated equipment.

■ Employment is projected to decline.

■ Most entry-level workers start as helpers or laborers, and several years of training and experience are required to become fully qualified.

Nature of the Work

Electricity is vital for most everyday activities. From the moment you flip the first switch each morning, you are connecting to a huge network of people, electric lines, and generating equipment. Power plant operators control the machinery that generates electricity. Power plant distributors and dispatchers control the flow of electricity from the power plant over a network of transmission lines to industrial plants and substations, and, finally, over distribution lines to residential users.

Power plant operators control and monitor boilers, turbines, generators, and auxiliary equipment in power-generating plants. Operators distribute power demands among generators, combine the current from several generators, and monitor instruments to maintain voltage and regulate electricity flows from the plant. When power requirements change, these workers start or stop generators and connect or disconnect them from circuits. They often use computers to keep records of switching operations and loads on generators, lines, and transformers. Operators also may use computers to prepare reports of unusual incidents, malfunctioning equipment, or maintenance performed during their shift.

Operators in plants with automated control systems work mainly in a central control room and usually are called *control room operators* or *control room operator trainees* or *assistants*. In older plants, the controls for the equipment are not centralized, and *switchboard operators* control the flow of electricity from a central point, whereas *auxiliary equipment operators* work throughout the plant, operating and monitoring valves, switches, and gauges.

The Nuclear Regulatory Commission (NRC) licenses operators of nuclear power plants. *Reactor operators* are authorized to control equipment that affects the power of the reactor in a nuclear power plant. In addition, an NRC-licensed *senior reactor operator* must be on duty during each shift to act as the plant supervisor and supervise the operation of all controls in the control room.

Power distributors and dispatchers, also called *load dispatchers* or *systems operators*, control the flow of electricity through transmission lines to industrial plants and substations that supply residential needs for electricity. They monitor and operate current converters, voltage transformers, and circuit breakers. Dispatchers also monitor other distribution equipment and record readings at a pilot board—a map of the transmission grid system showing the status of transmission circuits and connections with substations and industrial plants.

Dispatchers also anticipate power needs, such as those caused by changes in the weather. They call control room operators to start or stop boilers and generators in order to bring production into balance with needs. Dispatchers handle emergencies such as transformer or transmission line failures and route current around affected areas. In substations, they also operate and monitor equipment that increases or decreases voltage, and they operate switchboard levers to control the flow of electricity in and out of the substations.

Working Conditions

Because electricity is provided around the clock, operators, distributors, and dispatchers usually work one of three daily 8-hour shifts or one of two 12-hour shifts on a rotating basis. Shift assignments may change periodically so that all operators can share duty on less desirable shifts. Work on rotating shifts can be stressful and fatiguing because of the constant change in living and sleeping patterns. Operators, distributors, and dispatchers who work in control rooms generally sit or stand at a control station. This work is not physically strenuous, but it does require constant attention. Operators who work outside the control room may be exposed to danger from electric shock, falls, and burns.

Nuclear power plant operators are subject to random drug and alcohol tests, as are most workers at such plants.

Training, Other Qualifications, and Advancement

Employers often seek high school graduates for entry-level operator, distributor, and dispatcher positions. Candidates with strong mathematics and science skills are preferred. College-level courses and prior experience in a mechanical or technical job are becoming increasingly helpful in a competitive job market. With computers now used to keep records, generate reports, and track maintenance, employers are increasingly requiring computer proficiency. Most entry-level workers start as helpers or laborers. Depending on the results of aptitude tests, their own preferences, and the availability of openings, workers may be assigned to train for one of many utility positions.

Workers selected for training as a fossil-fueled power plant operator or distributor undergo extensive on-the-job and classroom instruction. Several years of training and experience are required for a worker to become a fully qualified control room operator or power plant distributor. With further training and experience, workers may advance to shift supervisor. Utilities generally promote from within; therefore, opportunities to advance by moving to another employer are limited.

Extensive training and experience are necessary to pass the NRC examinations for reactor operators and senior reactor operators. To maintain their license, licensed reactor operators must pass an annual practical plant operation exam and a biennial written exam administered by their employers. Training may include simulator and on-the-job training, classroom instruction, and individual study. Entrants to nuclear power plant operator trainee jobs must have strong mathematics and science skills. Experience in other power plants or with Navy nuclear propulsion plants also is helpful. With further training and experience, reactor operators may advance to senior reactor operator positions.

In addition to receiving preliminary training as a power plant operator, distributor, or dispatcher, most workers are given periodic refresher training—frequently in the case of nuclear power plant operators. Refresher training usually is taken on plant simulators designed specifically to replicate procedures and situations that might be encountered at the trainee's plant.

Employment

Power plant operators, distributors, and dispatchers held about 47,000 jobs in 2004. Jobs were located throughout the country. About 64 percent of jobs were in electric power generation, transmission, and distribution. About 20 percent worked in government, mainly in local government. Others worked for manufacturing establishments that produced electricity for their own use.

Job Outlook

People who want to become power plant operators, distributors, and dispatchers are expected to encounter keen competition for these relatively high-paying jobs. While demand for electricity will increase, the slow pace of construction of new plants will limit opportunities for these workers. In addition, the increasing use of automatic controls and more computerized equipment should boost productivity and decrease the demand for operators. As a result, individuals with training in computers and automated equipment will have the best job prospects. Some job opportunities will arise from the need to replace workers who retire or leave the occupation. However, cost considerations may restrict the number of workers who are replaced, with the job duties instead being given to other workers.

A decline in employment of power plant operators, distributors, and dispatchers is projected through the year 2014 as the utilities industry continues to restructure in response to deregulation and increasing competition. Independent producers are now allowed to sell power directly to industrial and other wholesale customers. Consequently, some utilities that historically operated as regulated local monopolies have restructured their operations in order to reduce costs and compete effectively. While much of this restructuring is complete, the focus on reducing costs persists. This new focus is present in regulated utilities as well as those that have been deregulated. As a result, the number of jobs is expected to decline.

Earnings

Median annual earnings of power plant operators were $52,530 in May 2004. The middle 50 percent earned between $43,310 and $62,030. The lowest 10 percent earned less than $34,550, and the highest 10 percent earned more than $70,330. Median annual earnings of power plant operators in May 2004 were $53,820 in electric power generation, transmission, and distribution.

Median annual earnings of nuclear power reactor operators were $64,090 in May 2004. The middle 50 percent earned between $56,890 and $71,160. The lowest 10 percent earned less than $49,690, and the highest 10 percent earned more than $82,220.

Median annual earnings of power distributors and dispatchers were $57,330 in May 2004. The middle 50 percent earned between $48,010 and $69,100. The lowest 10 percent earned less than $38,220, and the highest 10 percent earned more than $83,030.

Related Occupations

Other workers who monitor and operate plant and system equipment include chemical plant and system operators; petroleum pump system operators, refinery operators, and gaugers; stationary engineers and boiler operators; and water and liquid waste treatment plant and system operators.

Sources of Additional Information

For information about employment opportunities, contact local electric utility companies, locals of unions, and state employment service offices.

For general information about power plant operators, nuclear power reactor operators, and power plant distributors and dispatchers, contact

▸ American Public Power Association, 2301 M St. NW, Washington, DC 20037-1484. Internet: http://www.appanet.org

▸ International Brotherhood of Electrical Workers, 1125 15th St. NW, Washington, DC 20005.

Precision Instrument and Equipment Repairers

(O*NET 49-9061.00, 49-9062.00, 49-9063.01, 49-9063.02, 49-9063.03, 49-9063.04, 49-9064.00, and 49-9069.99)

Significant Points

■ Training requirements include a high school diploma and, in most cases, postsecondary education, coupled with significant on-the-job training.

■ Good opportunities are expected for most types of jobs.

■ Overall employment is expected to grow about as fast as average, but projected growth varies by detailed occupation.

■ About 1 out of 6 are self-employed.

Nature of the Work

Repairing and maintaining watches, cameras, musical instruments, medical equipment, and other precision instruments requires a high level of skill and attention to detail. For example, some devices contain tiny gears that must be manufactured to within one one-hundredth of a millimeter of design specifications, and other devices contain sophisticated electronic controls.

Camera and photographic equipment repairers work through a series of steps in fixing a camera. The first step is determining whether a repair should be attempted, because many inexpensive cameras cost more to repair than to replace. Of the problems for which repair seems worthwhile, the most complicated or expensive are referred back to the manufacturer or to a large repair center. If the repairers decide to proceed with the job themselves, they diagnose the problem, often by disassembling numerous small parts in order to reach the source. They then make needed adjustments or replace a defective part. Many problems are caused by the electronic circuits used in cameras, and fixing these circuits requires an understanding of electronics. Camera repairers also maintain cameras by removing and replacing broken or worn parts and cleaning and lubricating gears and springs. Because many of the components involved are extremely small, repairers must have a great deal of manual dexterity. Frequently, older camera parts are no longer available, requiring repairers to build replacement parts or to strip junked cameras. When machining new parts, workers often use a small lathe, a grinding wheel, and other metalworking tools.

Repairs on digital cameras are similar to those on conventional cameras, but because digital cameras have no film to wind, they have fewer moving parts. Digital cameras rely on software, so any repair to the lens requires that it be calibrated with the use of software and by connecting the camera to a personal computer.

Watch and clock repairers work almost exclusively on expensive and antique timepieces, because moderately priced timepieces are cheaper to replace than to repair. Electrically powered clocks and quartz watches and clocks function with almost no moving parts, limiting necessary maintenance to replacing the battery. Many expensive timepieces still employ old-style mechanical movements and a manual or automatic winding mechanism. This type of timepiece must be regularly adjusted and maintained. Repair and maintenance work on a mechanical timepiece requires using hand tools to disassemble many fine gears and components. Each part is inspected for signs of wear. Some gears or springs may need to be replaced or machined. Exterior portions of the watch may require polishing and buffing. Specialized machines are used to clean all of the parts with ultrasonic waves and a series of baths in cleaning agents. Reassembling a watch requires lubricating key parts.

As with older cameras, replacement parts are frequently unavailable for antique watches or clocks. In such cases, watch repairers must machine their own parts. They employ small lathes and other machines in creating tiny parts.

Musical instrument repairers and tuners combine their love of music with a highly skilled craft. Often referred to as technicians, these artisans work in four specialties: band instruments, pianos and organs, violins, and guitars. (Repairers and tuners who work on electronic organs are discussed in this book's description of electronic home entertainment equipment installers and repairers.)

Band instrument repairers, brass and wind instrument repairers, and percussion instrument repairers focus on woodwind, brass, reed, and percussion instruments damaged through deterioration or by accident. They move mechanical parts or play scales to find problems. They may unscrew and remove rod pins, keys, worn cork pads, and pistons and remove soldered parts by means of gas torches. Using filling techniques or a mallet, they repair dents in metal and wood. These repairers use gas torches, grinding wheels, lathes, shears, mallets, and small hand tools and are skilled in metalworking and woodworking. Percussion instrument repairers often must install new drumheads, which formerly were cut from animal skin, but now are made exclusively from Mylar and other synthetic materials.

Violin and guitar repairers adjust and repair stringed instruments. Some repairers work on both stringed and band instruments. Initially, repairers play and inspect the instrument to find any defects. They replace or repair cracked or broken sections and damaged parts. They also restring the instruments and repair damage to their finish. Because the specifications of all types of instruments vary greatly, custom parts machining is considered an essential skill.

Piano tuners and repairers use similar techniques, skills, and tools. Most workers in this group are piano tuners, tuning and making minor repairs. Tuning involves tightening and loosening different strings to achieve the proper tone or pitch. Because pianos are difficult to transport, tuners normally make house calls. Some repairers specialize in restoring older pianos. Restoration is complicated work, often involving replacing many of the parts, which number more than 12,000 in some pianos. With proper maintenance and restoration, pianos often survive more than 100 years.

Pipe organ repairers do work similar to that of piano repairers, but on a larger scale. In addition, they assemble new organs. Because pipe organs are too large to transport, they must be assembled onsite. Even with repairers working in teams or with assistants, the organ assembly process can take several weeks or even months, depending upon the size of the organ.

Medical equipment repairers and *other precision instrument and equipment repairers* maintain, adjust, calibrate, and repair electronic, electromechanical, and hydraulic equipment. They use various tools, including multimeters, specialized software, and computers designed to communicate with specific pieces of hardware. Among their specialized tools is equipment designed to simulate water or air pressure. These repairers use hand tools, soldering irons, and other electronic tools to repair and adjust equipment. Faulty circuit boards and other parts are normally removed and replaced. Medical equipment repairers and other precision instrument repairers must maintain careful, detailed logs of all maintenance and repair that they perform on each piece of equipment they work with.

Medical equipment repairers, often called *biomedical equipment technicians,* work on medical equipment such as defibrillators, heart monitors, medical imaging equipment (X rays, CAT scanners, and ultrasound equipment), voice-controlled operating tables, and electric wheelchairs.

Other precision instrument and equipment repairers service, repair, and replace a wide range of equipment associated with automated or instrument-controlled manufacturing processes. A precision instrument repairer working at an electric powerplant, for example, would repair and maintain instruments that monitor the operation of the plant, such as pressure and temperature gauges. Replacement parts are not always available, so repairers sometimes machine or fabricate a new part. Preventive maintenance involves regular lubrication, cleaning, and adjustment of many measuring devices. Increasingly, it also involves solving computer software problems as more control devices, such as valves, are controlled by or linked to computer networks. To adjust a control device, a technician may need to connect a laptop computer to the control device's computer and make adjustments through changes to the software commands.

Working Conditions

Camera, watch, and musical instrument repairers work under fairly similar solitary, low-stress conditions with minimal supervision. A quiet, well-lighted workshop or repair shop is typical, while a few of these repairers travel to the instrument being repaired, such as a piano, an organ, or a grandfather clock. Often, these workers can adjust their schedules, allowing for second jobs as needed. Musical instrument repairer jobs are attractive to many professional musicians because the flexible hours common to repair work allow musicians to do the work while still maintaining a regular performing schedule.

Medical equipment and precision instrument and equipment repairers normally work daytime hours, but are often expected to be on call. Still, like other hospital and factory employees, some repairers work irregular hours. Precision instrument repairers work under a wide array of conditions, from hot, dirty, noisy factories to air-conditioned workshops to the outdoors on fieldwork. Attention to safety is essential, as the work sometimes involves dangerous machinery or toxic chemicals. Due to the individualized nature of the work, supervision is fairly minimal.

Training, Other Qualifications, and Advancement

Most employers require at least a high school diploma for beginning precision instrument and equipment repairers. Many employers prefer applicants with some postsecondary education. Much training takes place on the job. The ability to read and understand technical manuals is important. Necessary physical qualities include good fine-motor skills and acute vision. Also, precision equipment repairers must be able to pay close attention to details, enjoy problem solving, and have the desire to disassemble machines to see how they work. Most precision equipment repairers must be able to work alone with minimal supervision.

The educational background required for camera and photographic equipment repairers varies, but some knowledge of electronics is necessary. A number of workers complete postsecondary training, such as an associate degree, in electronics. The job requires the ability to read electronic schematic diagrams and comprehend other technical information in addition to manual dexterity. New employees are trained on the job in two stages over about a year. First, they learn to repair a single product over a couple of weeks. Then, they learn to repair other products and refine their skills for 6–12 months while working under the close supervision of an experienced repairer. Finally, repairers continually teach themselves through studying manuals and attending manufacturer-sponsored seminars on the specifics of new models.

Training also varies for watch and clock repairers. Several associations, including the American Watchmakers-Clockmakers Institute and the National Association of Watch and Clock Collectors, offer certifications. Some certifications can be completed in a few months; others require simply passing an examination; the most demanding certifications require 3,000 hours, taken over 2 years, of classroom time in technical institutes or colleges. Those who have earned the most demanding certifications are usually the most sought after by employers. Clock repairers generally require less training than do watch repairers, because watches have smaller components and require greater precision. Some repairers opt to learn through assisting a master watch repairer. Nevertheless, developing proficiency in watch or clock repair requires several years of education and experience.

For musical instrument repairers and tuners, employers prefer people with post–high school training in music repair technology. According to a Piano Technicians Guild membership survey, the overwhelming majority of respondents had completed at least some college work; most had a bachelor's or higher degree, although not always in music repair technology. Almost all repairers have a strong musical background; many are musicians themselves. Also, a basic ability to play the instruments being repaired is normally required. Courses in instrument repair are offered only at a few technical schools and colleges. Correspondence courses are common for piano tuners. Graduates of these programs normally receive additional training on the job, working with an experienced repairer. Many musical instrument repairers and tuners begin learning their trade on the job as assistants or apprentices. Trainees perform a variety of tasks around the shop. Full qualification usually requires 2 to 5 years of training and practice. Musical instrument repair and tuning requires good manual dexterity, an "ear" for pitch and tone, and good hand-eye coordination. While piano tuning requires good hearing, it can be performed by the blind.

Medical equipment repairers' training includes on-the-job training, manufacturer training classes, and associate degree programs. While an associate degree in electronics or medical technology is normally required, training varies by specialty. For those with a background in electronics, on-the-job training is more common for workers repairing less critical equipment, such as hospital beds or electric wheelchairs. An associate or even a bachelor's degree, often in medical technology or engineering, and a passing grade on a certification exam is likely to be required of persons repairing more critical equipment, such as CAT scanners and defibrillators. Some repairers are trained in the military. New repairers begin by observing and assisting an experienced worker over a period of 3 to 6 months, learning a single piece of equipment at a time. Gradually, they begin working independently while still under close supervision. Biomedical equipment repairers are constantly learning new technologies and equipment through seminars, self-study, and certification exams.

Educational requirements for other precision instrument and equipment repair jobs also vary, but include a high school diploma with a focus on mathematics and science courses. Because repairers need to understand blueprints; electrical schematic diagrams; and electrical, hydraulic, and electromechanical systems, most employers require an associate or sometimes a bachelor's degree in instrumentation and control, electronics, or a related engineering field. In addition to formal education, a year or two of on-the-job training is required before a repairer is considered fully qualified. Many instrument and equipment repairers begin by working in a factory in another capacity, such as repairing electrical equipment. As companies seek to improve efficiency, other types of repair workers are trained to repair precision measuring equipment. Some advancement opportunities exist, but many supervisory positions require a bachelor's degree.

Employment

Precision instrument and equipment repairers held 62,000 jobs in 2004. Employment was distributed among the detailed occupations as follows:

Medical equipment repairers 29,000
Precision instrument and equipment repairers,
    all other 17,000
Musical instrument repairers and tuners 6,100
Camera and photographic equipment repairers..........5,100
Watch repairers...4,300

Medical equipment repairers often work for hospitals or wholesale equipment suppliers, while those in the occupation "all other precision instrument repairers" frequently work for manufacturing companies and wholesalers of durable goods. About 1 out of 6 precision instrument and equipment repairers was self-employed—they may own jewelry, camera, medical equipment, or music stores.

Job Outlook

Good opportunities are expected for most types of precision instrument and equipment repairer jobs. Overall employment growth is projected to be about as fast as the average for all occupations over the 2004–2014 period; however, projected growth varies by detailed occupation.

Job growth among medical equipment repairers should be about as fast as the average for all occupations over the projection period. The rapidly expanding health care industry and elderly population should spark demand for increasingly sophisticated medical equipment and, in turn, create good employment opportunities in this occupation.

By contrast, employment of musical instrument repairers is expected to increase more slowly than the average. Replacement needs are expected to provide the most job opportunities as many repairers and tuners retire. School budget cuts to music programs—specifically, stringed-instrument programs—should hurt the outlook for musical repairers. With fewer new musicians, there will be a slump in instrument rentals, purchases, and repairs. Because training in the repair of musical instruments is difficult to obtain—there are only a few schools that offer training programs, and few experienced workers are willing to take on apprentices—opportunities should be good for those who receive training. Schools report that their graduates easily find employment.

Employment of camera and photographic equipment repairers is expected to decline. The popularity of inexpensive cameras adversely affects employment in this occupation, as most point-and-shoot cameras are cheaper to replace than repair. When a camera breaks, not only is replacing the camera often not much more expensive than repairing it, but the new model is also far more advanced than the old one. However, consumers are spending more on high-end digital cameras than they did on conventional cameras in the past, which should make repairing the cameras more economical.

Employment of watch repairers is expected to increase more slowly than the average. Over the past few decades, changes in technology, including the invention of digital and quartz watches that need few repairs, caused a significant decline in the demand for watch repairers. In recent years, this trend was somewhat reversed as the growing popularity of expensive mechanical watches increased the need for these repairers. Nonetheless, few new repairers entered the field. Thus, the small number of entrants, coupled with the fact that a large proportion of watch and clock repairers are approaching retirement age, should result in very good job opportunities in this field.

The projected slower-than-average employment growth of other precision instrument and equipment repairers reflects the expected lack of employment growth in manufacturing and other industries in which they are employed. Nevertheless, good employment opportunities are expected for these workers due to the relatively small number of people entering the occupation and the need to replace repairers who retire.

Earnings

The following tabulation shows median hourly earnings for various precision instrument and equipment repairers in May 2004:

Precision instrument and equipment repairers, all other	$21.25
Medical equipment repairers	17.90
Camera and photographic equipment repairers	15.54
Watch repairers	13.87
Musical instrument repairers and tuners	13.47

Earnings ranged from less than $7.94 for the lowest 10 percent of musical instrument repairers and tuners to more than $32.32 for the highest 10 percent in the occupation "all other precision instrument and equipment repairers."

Earnings within the different occupations vary significantly depending upon skill levels. For example, a lesser-skilled watch and clock repairer may simply change batteries and replace worn wrist straps, while a highly skilled watch and clock repairer with years of training and experience may rebuild and replace worn parts.

Related Occupations

Many precision instrument and equipment repairers work with precision mechanical and electronic equipment. Other workers who repair precision mechanical and electronic equipment include computer, automated teller, and office machine repairers and coin, vending, and amusement machine servicers and repairers. Other workers who make precision items include dental laboratory technicians and ophthalmic laboratory technicians. Some precision instrument and equipment repairers work with a wide array of industrial equipment. Their work environment and responsibilities are similar to those of industrial machinery installation, maintenance, and repair workers. Much of the work of watch repairers is similar to that of jewelers and precious stone and metal workers. Camera repairers' work is similar to that of electronic home entertainment equipment installers and repairers; both occupations work with consumer electronics that are based around a circuit board but that also involve numerous moving mechanical parts.

Sources of Additional Information

For more information about camera repair careers, contact

▸ National Association of Photographic Equipment Technicians (NAPET), 3000 Picture Pl., Jackson, MI 49201.

For information on musical instrument repair, including schools offering training, contact

▸ National Association of Professional Band Instrument Repair Technicians (NAPBIRT), P.O. Box 51, Normal, IL 61761. Internet: http://www.napbirt.org

For additional information on piano tuning and repair work, contact

▸ Piano Technicians Guild, 4444 Forest Ave., Kansas City, MO 66106. Internet: http://www.ptg.org

For information about training, mentoring programs, employers, and schools with programs in precision instrumentation, automation, and control, contact

▸ ISA—The Instrumentation, Systems, and Automation Society, 67 Alexander Dr, Research Triangle Park, NC 27709. Internet: http://www.isa.org

For information about watch and clock repair and a list of schools with related programs of study, contact

▸ American Watchmakers-Clockmakers Institute (AWI), 701 Enterprise Dr., Harrison, OH 45030-1696. Internet: http://www.awi-net.org

For information about medical equipment technicians and a list of schools with related programs of study, contact

▸ Association for the Advancement of Medical Instrumentation (AAMI), 1110 North Glebe Rd., Arlington, VA 22201-4795. Internet: http://www.aami.org

Prepress Technicians and Workers

(O*NET 51-5021.00, 51-5022.01, 51-5022.02, 51-5022.03, 51-5022.04, 51-5022.05, 51-5022.06, 51-5022.07, 51-5022.08, 51-5022.09, 51-5022.10, 51-5022.11, 51-5022.12, and 51-5022.13)

Significant Points

■ Most prepress technician jobs now require formal postsecondary graphic communications training in the various types of computer software used in digital imaging.

■ Employment is projected to decline as the increased use of computers in typesetting and page layout requires fewer prepress technicians.

Nature of the Work

The printing process has three stages—prepress, press, and binding or postpress. In small print shops, *job printers* are usually responsible for all three stages. They check proofs for errors and print clarity and correct mistakes, print the job, and attach each copy's pages together. In most printing firms, however, each of the stages is the responsibility of a specialized group of workers. *Prepress technicians and workers* are responsible for the first stage, preparing the material for printing presses. They perform a variety of tasks involved with transforming text and pictures into finished pages and making printing plates of the pages.

Advances in computer software and printing technology continue to change prepress work. Most customers today are able to provide printers with pages of material that look like the desired finished product they want printed and bound in volume. Using a process called "desktop publishing," customers are increasingly using their own computers to do much of the typesetting and page layout work formerly done by designers on artboards. Much of this work is now done by desktop publishers or graphic designers with knowledge of publishing software. (A description of desktop publishers appears elsewhere in this book.) It is increasingly common for prepress technicians or other printing workers to receive files from the customer on a computer disk or submitted electronically via e-mail or file transfer protocol, known as FTP, that contains typeset material already laid out in pages.

Prepress work is now done with the use of digital imaging technology by prepress technicians known as "preflight technicians" or production coordinators. Using this technology, these technicians take the electronic files received from customers, check it for completeness, and format it into pages using electronic page layout systems. Even though the pages may already be laid out, they still may have to be formatted to fit the dimensions of the paper stock to be used. When color printing is required, the technicians use digital color page-makeup systems to electronically produce an image of the printed pages and then use off-press color proofing systems to print a copy, or "proof," of the pages as they will appear when printed. The technician then has the proofs delivered or mailed to the customer for a final check. Once the customer gives the "OK to print," technicians use laser "imagesetters" to expose digital images of the pages directly onto thin aluminum printing plates.

Platemakers for a long time used a photographic process to make printing plates. The flat, a layout sheet onto which a negative has been attached, was placed on top of a thin metal plate coated with a light-sensitive resin. Exposure to ultraviolet light activated the chemical in parts of the plate not protected by the film's dark areas. The plate was then developed in a solution that removes the unexposed nonimage area, exposing bare metal. The chemical on areas of the plate exposed to the light hardened and became water repellent. The hardened parts of the plate form the text and images to be printed. Now, the printing industry has largely moved to technology known as "direct-to-plate," by which the prepress technicians send the data directly to a plating system, bypassing the need for stripping film onto a flat.

During the printing process, the plate is first covered with a thin coat of water. The water adheres only to the bare metal nonimage areas and is repelled by the hardened areas that were exposed to light. Next, the plate comes in contact with a rubber roller covered with oil-based ink. Because oil and water do not mix, the ink is repelled by the water-coated area and sticks to the hardened areas. The ink covering the hardened text is transferred to paper.

Working Conditions

Prepress technicians and workers usually work in clean, air-conditioned areas with little noise. Some workers may develop eyestrain from working in front of a video display terminal or musculoskeletal problems such as backaches. Those platemakers who still work with toxic chemicals face the hazard of skin irritations. Workers are often subject to stress and the pressures of short deadlines and tight work schedules.

Prepress employees usually work an 8-hour day. Some workers—particularly those employed by newspapers—work night shifts, weekends, and holidays.

Training, Other Qualifications, and Advancement

Digital imaging technology has largely replaced cold type print technology. Instead of painstakingly taping pieces of photographic negatives to flats, today's prepress technicians use computer software skills to electronically modify and lay out the material; in some cases, the first time the material appears on paper is when the final product rolls off the printing press. Traditionally, prepress technicians and workers started as helpers and were trained on the job, with some jobs requiring years of experience performing the detailed handwork to become skillful enough to perform even difficult tasks quickly. Today, persons seeking to enter prepress technician jobs require formal postsecondary graphic communications training in the various types of computer software used in digital imaging.

Postsecondary graphic communications programs are available from a variety of sources. For beginners, 2-year associate degree programs offered by community and junior colleges and technical schools and some 4-year bachelor's degree programs in graphic design colleges teach the latest prepress skills and allow students to practice applying them. However, bachelor's programs usually are intended for students who may eventually move into management positions in printing or design jobs. Community and junior colleges, 4-year colleges and universities, vocational-technical institutes, industry-sponsored update and retraining programs, and private trade and technical schools all also offer prepress-related courses for workers who do not wish to enroll in a degree program. Many workers with experience in other printing jobs take a few college graphic communications courses to upgrade their skills and qualify for prepress jobs. Prepress training designed to train skilled workers already employed in the printing industry also is offered through unions in the printing industry. Many employers view individuals with a combination of experience in the printing industry and formal training in the new digital technology as the best candidates for prepress jobs. The experience of these applicants in printing press operator or other jobs provides them with an understanding of how printing plants operate, familiarizes them with basic prepress functions, and demonstrates their reliability and interest in advancing in the industry.

Employers prefer workers with good communication skills, both oral and written, for prepress jobs. Prepress technicians and workers should be able to deal courteously with people because, when prepress problems arise, they sometimes have to contact the customer to resolve them. Also, in small shops, they may take customer orders. Persons interested in working for firms using advanced printing technology need to know the basics of electronics and computers. Mathematical skills also are essential for operating many of the software packages used to run modern, computerized prepress equipment. At times, prepress personnel may have to perform computations in order to estimate job costs.

Prepress technicians and workers need good manual dexterity, and they must be able to pay attention to detail and work independently.

Good eyesight, including visual acuity, depth perception, field of view, color vision, and the ability to focus quickly, is also a needed asset. Artistic ability is often a plus. Employers also seek persons who possess an even temperament and an ability to adapt, important qualities for workers who often must meet deadlines and learn how to use new software or operate new equipment.

Employment

Prepress technicians and workers overall held about 141,000 jobs in 2004. Of these, approximately 63,000 were employed as job printers; the remainder was employed as prepress technicians and other prepress workers. Most prepress jobs are found in the printing industry, while newspaper publishing employs the second-largest number of prepress technicians and workers.

The printing and publishing industries are two of the most geographically dispersed in the United States, and prepress jobs are found throughout the country. However, jobs are concentrated in large metropolitan areas such as Chicago, Los Angeles–Long Beach, New York City, Minneapolis–St. Paul, Philadelphia, Boston, and Washington, DC.

Job Outlook

Overall employment of prepress technicians and workers is expected to decline through 2014. Demand for printed material should continue to grow, spurred by rising levels of personal income, increasing school enrollments, higher levels of educational attainment, and expanding markets. But the use of computers and publishing software—often by the clients of the printing company—will result in rising productivity of prepress technicians.

Computer software now allows office workers to specify text typeface and style and to format pages at a desktop computer terminal, shifting many prepress functions away from the traditional printing plants into advertising and public relations agencies, graphic design firms, and large corporations. Many companies are turning to in-house desktop publishing as page layout and graphic design capabilities of computer software have improved and become less expensive and more user-friendly. Some firms are finding it less costly to prepare their own newsletters and other reports than to send them out to trade shops. At newspapers, writers and editors also are doing more composition using publishing software. Rapid growth in the use of desktop publishing software already has eliminated most prepress typesetting and composition technician jobs associated with the older technologies, such as cold type. However, opportunities will be favorable for prepress technicians with strong computer skills, such as preflight technicians, who are employed to check materials prepared by clients and adapt it for printing.

In order to compete in the desktop publishing environment, commercial printing companies are adding desktop publishing and electronic prepress work to the list of services they provide. Electronic prepress technicians, digital proofers, platemakers, and graphic designers are using new equipment and ever-changing software to design and lay out publications and complete their printing more quickly. The increasing range of services offered by printing companies using new digital technologies mean that opportunities in prepress work will be best for those with computer backgrounds who

have completed postsecondary programs in printing technology or graphic communications. Workers with this background will be better able to adapt to the continuing evolution of publishing and printing technology.

Earnings

Median hourly earnings of prepress technicians and workers were $15.30 in May 2004. The middle 50 percent earned between $11.69 and $20.01 an hour. The lowest 10 percent earned less than $9.06, and the highest 10 percent earned more than $24.82 an hour.

For job printers, median hourly earnings were $15.41 in May 2004. The middle 50 percent earned between $12.00 and $20.04 an hour. The lowest 10 percent earned less than $9.57, while the highest 10 percent earned more than $24.05 an hour.

Median hourly earnings in commercial printing, the industry employing the largest number of prepress technicians and workers, were $15.91 in May 2004, while the figure for these workers in the newspaper, periodical, and book publishing industry was $14.22 an hour. For job printers, median hourly earnings in commercial printing in May 2004 were $15.67, while in the newspaper, periodical, and book publishing industry, median hourly earnings were $15.63.

Wage rates for prepress technicians and workers vary according to occupation, level of experience, training, location, size of firm, and union membership status.

Related Occupations

Prepress technicians and workers use artistic skills in their work. These skills also are essential for artists and related workers, graphic designers, and desktop publishers. Moreover, many of the skills used in Web site design also are employed in prepress technology.

In addition to typesetters, other workers who operate machines equipped with keyboards include data entry and information processing workers. Prepress technicians' work also is tied in closely with that of printing machine operators, including job printers.

Sources of Additional Information

Details about training programs may be obtained from local employers such as newspapers and printing shops or from local offices of the state employment service.

For information on careers and training in printing and the graphic arts, write to

▸ Graphic Arts Education and Research Foundation, 1899 Preston White Dr., Reston, VA 20191-5468. Internet: http://www.makeyourmark.org

▸ Graphic Communications Conference of the International Brotherhood of Teamsters, 1900 L St. NW, Washington, DC 20036-5007. Internet: http://www.gciu.org

▸ Printing Industries of America/Graphic Arts Technical Foundation, 200 Deer Run Rd., Sewickley, PA 15143-2324.

Printing Machine Operators

(O*NET 51-5023.01, 51-5023.02, 51-5023.03, 51-5023.04, 51-5023.05, 51-5023.06, 51-5023.07, 51-5023.08, and 51-5023.09)

Significant Points

■ Most printing machine operators are trained on the job.

■ Those skilled in digital printing operations will have the best job opportunities as more printing firms convert to this printing process because of the rising demand for customized print jobs.

■ The expected retirements of skilled press operators will create openings for workers with the proper training.

Nature of the Work

Printing machine operators, also known as press operators, prepare, operate, and maintain the printing presses in a pressroom. Duties of printing machine operators vary according to the type of press they operate—offset lithography, gravure, flexography, screen printing, letterpress, and digital. Offset lithography, which transfers an inked impression from a rubber-covered cylinder to paper or other material, is the dominant printing process. With gravure, the recesses on an etched plate or cylinder are inked and pressed to paper. Flexography is a form of rotary printing in which ink is applied to a surface by a flexible rubber printing plate with a raised image area. Use of flexography should increase over the next decade, but letterpress, in which an inked, raised surface is pressed against paper, remains in existence only as specialty printing. In addition to the major printing processes, plateless or nonimpact processes are coming into general use. Plateless processes—including digital, electrostatic, and ink-jet printing—are used for copying, duplicating, and document and specialty printing, usually by quick and in-house printing shops, and increasingly by commercial printers for short-run jobs and variable-data printing.

To prepare presses for printing, machine operators install and adjust the printing plate, adjust pressure, ink the presses, load paper, and adjust the press to the paper size. Press operators ensure that paper and ink meet specifications and adjust margins and the flow of ink to the inking rollers accordingly. They then feed paper through the press cylinders and adjust feed and tension controls. However, new technology becoming available skips these steps and sends the files directly to the press.

While printing presses are running, press operators monitor their operation and keep the paper feeders well stocked. They make adjustments to correct uneven ink distribution, speed, and temperatures in the drying chamber, if the press has one. If paper jams or tears and the press stops, which can happen with some offset presses, operators quickly correct the problem to minimize downtime. Similarly, operators working with other high-speed presses constantly look for problems, making quick corrections to avoid expensive losses of paper and ink. Throughout the run, operators must regularly pull sheets to check for any printing imperfections, though much of this checking for quality is now being done by computers.

In most shops, press operators also perform preventive maintenance. They oil and clean the presses and make minor repairs.

Machine operators' jobs differ from one shop to another because of differences in the kinds and sizes of presses. Small commercial shops are operated by one person and tend to have relatively small presses, which print only one or two colors at a time. Operators who work with large presses have assistants and helpers. Large newspaper, magazine, and book printers use giant "in-line web" presses that require a crew of several press operators and press assistants. These presses are fed paper in big rolls up to 50 inches or more in width. Presses print the paper on both sides; trim, assemble, score, and fold the pages; and count the finished sections as they come off the press.

Most plants have or will soon have installed printing presses with computers and sophisticated instruments to control press operations, making it possible to set up for jobs in less time. Computers allow press operators to perform many of their tasks electronically. With this equipment, press operators monitor the printing process on a control panel or computer monitor, which allows them to adjust the press electronically.

Working Conditions

Operating a press can be physically and mentally demanding and sometimes tedious. Printing machine operators are on their feet most of the time. Often, operators work under pressure to meet deadlines. Most printing presses are capable of high printing speeds, and adjustments must be made quickly to avoid waste. Pressrooms are noisy, and workers in certain areas wear ear protectors. Working with press machinery can be hazardous, but accidents can be avoided when press operators follow safe work practices. The threat of accidents has decreased with newer computerized presses because operators make most adjustments from a control panel. Many press operators, particularly those who work for newspapers, work weekends, nights, and holidays. They also may work overtime to meet deadlines.

Training, Other Qualifications, and Advancement

Although completion of a formal apprenticeship or a postsecondary program in printing equipment operation continues to be the best way to learn the trade, most printing machine operators are trained on the job while they work as assistants or helpers to experienced operators. Beginning press operators load, unload, and clean presses. With time and training, they may move up to become fully qualified press operators on the type of equipment on which they trained. Some operators gain experience on many kinds of printing presses during the course of their career.

Apprenticeships for press operators, once the dominant method for preparing for this occupation, are becoming less prevalent. When they are offered by the employer, they usually include on-the-job instruction and some related classroom training or correspondence school courses. Apprenticeships used to be for a fixed period of time, but now completion is based on ability to demonstrate competencies.

In contrast, formal postsecondary programs in printing equipment operation offered by technical and trade schools, community colleges, and universities are growing in importance. Some postsecondary school programs require 2 years of study and award an associate degree. Postsecondary courses in printing are increasingly important because they provide the theoretical and technical knowledge needed to operate advanced equipment.

Persons who wish to become printing machine operators need mechanical aptitude to make press adjustments and repairs. Oral and writing skills also are required. Operators should possess the mathematical skills necessary to compute percentages, weights, and measures and to calculate the amount of ink and paper needed to do a job. Because of technical developments in the printing industry, courses in chemistry, electronics, color theory, and physics are helpful.

Technological changes have had a tremendous effect on the skills needed by printing machine operators. New presses now require operators to possess basic computer skills. Even experienced operators periodically receive retraining and skill updating. For example, printing plants that change from sheet-fed offset presses to digital presses have to retrain the entire press crew because skill requirements for the two types of presses are different.

Printing machine operators may advance in pay and responsibility by working on a more complex printing press. Through experience and demonstrated ability, for example, a one-color sheet-fed press operator may become a four-color sheet-fed press operator. Others may advance to pressroom supervisor and become responsible for an entire press crew. Press operators can also draw on their knowledge of press operations to become cost estimators, providing estimates of printing jobs to potential customers.

Employment

Printing machine operators held about 191,000 jobs in 2004. Nearly half of all operator jobs were in the printing industry. Paper manufacturers and newspaper publishers were also large employers. Additional jobs were in the "in-plant" section of organizations and businesses that do their own printing—such as banks, insurance companies, government agencies, and universities.

The printing and newspaper publishing industries are two of the most geographically dispersed in the United States, and press operators can find jobs throughout the country. However, jobs are concentrated in large printing centers such as Chicago, Los Angeles–Long Beach, New York, Minneapolis–St. Paul, Philadelphia, Boston, and Washington, DC.

Job Outlook

Employment of printing machine operators is expected to grow more slowly than average through 2014 as the output of printed materials is expected to keep going up, but increasing automation of the printing industry and the outsourcing of production to foreign countries will moderate the increase. Looming retirements of printing machine operators and the need for workers trained on increasingly computerized printing equipment will also create many job openings over the next decade, particularly for those persons who qualify for formal apprenticeship training or who complete postsecondary training programs in printing.

Demand for books and magazines will increase as school enrollments rise and information proliferates. Additional growth will also come from the increasing ability of the printing industry to profitably print shorter runs—smaller quantities—which should widen the market for printed materials as production costs decline. However, small printing jobs will increasingly be run on sophisticated

high-speed digital printing equipment that requires a more complex set of operator skills, such as database management.

Demand for commercial printing also will continue to be driven by increased expenditures for print advertising materials. New market research techniques are leading advertisers to increase spending on messages targeted to specific audiences and should continue to require the printing of a wide variety of catalogs, direct mail enclosures, newspaper inserts, and other kinds of print advertising. Newspaper printing also will continue to provide jobs.

Employment will not grow in line with output, however, because increased use of new computerized printing equipment will require fewer operators. This will especially be true with the increasing automation of the large printing presses used in the newspaper industry. In addition, more companies are having their work printed out of the country when time sensitivity of the material is not an issue. Also, new business practices within the publishing industry, such as printing-on-demand and electronic publishing, will cut into the production of printed materials. Printing-on-demand refers to the printing of materials as they are requested by customers, in contrast to printing thousands of copies of a publication prior to purchase, many of which are subsequently discarded.

Earnings

Median hourly earnings of printing machine operators were $14.38 in May 2004. The middle 50 percent earned between $10.73 and $18.83 an hour. The lowest 10 percent earned less than $8.54, and the highest 10 percent earned more than $23.06 an hour. Median hourly earnings in the industries employing the largest numbers of printing machine operators in May 2004 were

Newspaper, periodical, book, and directory publishers	$16.46
Converted paper product manufacturing	15.72
Printing and related support activities	15.16
Plastics product manufacturing	13.76
Advertising and related services	12.68

The basic wage rate for a printing machine operator depends on the geographic area in which the work is located and on the type of press being run: Pay varies by the complexity of the press and its size. Workers covered by union contracts usually have higher earnings in the newspaper industry.

Related Occupations

Other workers who set up and operate production machinery include machine setters, operators, and tenders—metal and plastic; and bookbinders and bindery workers.

Sources of Additional Information

Details about apprenticeships and other training opportunities may be obtained from local employers, such as newspapers and printing shops, local offices of the Graphic Communications Conference of the International Brotherhood of Teamsters, local affiliates of Printing Industries of America/Graphic Arts Technical Foundation, or local offices of the state employment service.

For general information about press operators, write to

▸ Graphic Communications Conference of the International Brotherhood of Teamsters, 1900 L St. NW, Washington, DC 20036-5007. Internet: http://www.gciu.org

For information on careers and training in printing and the graphic arts, write to

▸ NPES The Association for Suppliers of Printing Publishing, and Converting Technologies, 1899 Preston White Dr., Reston, VA 20191-4367. Internet: http://www.npes.org/education/index.html

▸ Printing Industry of America/Graphic Arts Technical Foundation, 200 Deer Run Rd., Sewickley, PA 15143.

▸ Graphic Arts Education and Research Foundation, 1899 Preston White Dr., Reston, VA 20191-5468. Internet: http://www.makeyourmark.org

Psychologists

(O*NET 19-3031.01, 19-3031.02, 19-3031.03, 19-3032.00, and 19-3039.99)

Significant Points

■ About 4 out of 10 psychologists are self-employed, compared with less than 1 out of 10 among all professional workers.

■ Most specialists, including clinical and counseling psychologists, need a doctoral degree; school psychologists need an educational specialist degree, and industrial-organizational psychologists need a master's degree.

■ Competition for admission to graduate psychology programs is keen.

■ Overall employment of psychologists is expected to grow faster than the average for all occupations through 2014.

Nature of the Work

Psychologists study the human mind and human behavior. Research psychologists investigate the physical, cognitive, emotional, or social aspects of human behavior. Psychologists in health service provider fields provide mental health care in hospitals, clinics, schools, or private settings. Psychologists employed in applied settings, such as business, industry, government, or nonprofits, provide training, conduct research, design systems, and act as advocates for psychology.

Like other social scientists, psychologists formulate hypotheses and collect data to test their validity. Research methods vary with the topic under study. Psychologists sometimes gather information through controlled laboratory experiments or by administering personality, performance, aptitude, or intelligence tests. Other methods include observation, interviews, questionnaires, clinical studies, and surveys.

Psychologists apply their knowledge to a wide range of endeavors, including health and human services, management, education, law, and sports. In addition to working in a variety of settings, psychologists usually specialize in one of a number of different areas.

Clinical psychologists—who constitute the largest specialty—work most often in counseling centers, independent or group practices, hospitals, or clinics. They help mentally and emotionally disturbed clients adjust to life and may assist medical and surgical patients in dealing with illnesses or injuries. Some clinical psychologists work in physical rehabilitation settings, treating patients with spinal cord injuries, chronic pain or illness, stroke, arthritis, and neurological conditions. Others help people deal with times of personal crisis, such as divorce or the death of a loved one.

Clinical psychologists often interview patients and give diagnostic tests. They may provide individual, family, or group psychotherapy and may design and implement behavior modification programs. Some clinical psychologists collaborate with physicians and other specialists to develop and implement treatment and intervention programs that patients can understand and comply with. Other clinical psychologists work in universities and medical schools, where they train graduate students in the delivery of mental health and behavioral medicine services. Some administer community mental health programs.

Areas of specialization within clinical psychology include health psychology, neuropsychology, and geropsychology. *Health psychologists* promote good health through health maintenance counseling programs designed to help people achieve goals, such as stopping smoking or losing weight. *Neuropsychologists* study the relation between the brain and behavior. They often work in stroke and head injury programs. *Geropsychologists* deal with the special problems faced by the elderly. The emergence and growth of these specialties reflects the increasing participation of psychologists in providing direct services to special patient populations.

Often, clinical psychologists will consult with other medical personnel regarding the best treatment for patients, especially treatment that includes medication. Clinical psychologists generally are not permitted to prescribe medication to treat patients; only psychiatrists and other medical doctors may prescribe certain medications. (See the description of physicians and surgeons elsewhere in this book.) However, two states—Louisiana and New Mexico—currently allow clinical psychologists to prescribe medication with some limitations, and similar proposals have been made in other states.

Counseling psychologists use various techniques, including interviewing and testing, to advise people on how to deal with problems of everyday living. They work in settings such as university counseling centers, hospitals, and individual or group practices.

School psychologists work with students in elementary and secondary schools. They collaborate with teachers, parents, and school personnel to create safe, healthy, and supportive learning environments for all students; address students' learning and behavior problems; improve classroom management strategies or parenting skills; counter substance abuse; assess students with learning disabilities and gifted and talented students to help determine the best way to educate them; and improve teaching, learning, and socialization strategies. They also may evaluate the effectiveness of academic programs, prevention programs, behavior management procedures, and other services provided in the school setting.

Industrial-organizational psychologists apply psychological principles and research methods to the workplace in the interest of improving productivity and the quality of work life. They also are involved in research on management and marketing problems. They screen, train, and counsel applicants for jobs, as well as perform organizational development and analysis. An industrial psychologist might work with management to reorganize the work setting in order to improve productivity or quality of life in the workplace. Industrial psychologists frequently act as consultants brought in by management to solve a particular problem.

Developmental psychologists study the physiological, cognitive, and social development that takes place throughout life. Some specialize in behavior during infancy, childhood, and adolescence or changes that occur during maturity or old age. Developmental psychologists also may study developmental disabilities and their effects. Increasingly, research is developing ways to help elderly people remain independent as long as possible.

Social psychologists examine people's interactions with others and with the social environment. They work in organizational consultation, marketing research, systems design, or other applied psychology fields. Prominent areas of study include group behavior, leadership, attitudes, and perception.

Experimental or *research psychologists* work in university and private research centers and in business, nonprofit, and governmental organizations. They study the behavior of both human beings and animals, such as rats, monkeys, and pigeons. Prominent areas of study in experimental research include motivation, thought, attention, learning and memory, sensory and perceptual processes, effects of substance abuse, and genetic and neurological factors affecting behavior.

Working Conditions

A psychologist's subfield and place of employment determine his or her working conditions. Clinical, school, and counseling psychologists in private practice have their own offices and set their own hours. However, they often offer evening and weekend hours to accommodate their clients. Those employed in hospitals, nursing homes, and other health care facilities may work shifts that include evenings and weekends, while those who work in schools and clinics generally work regular hours.

Psychologists employed as faculty by colleges and universities divide their time between teaching and research and also may have administrative responsibilities; many have part-time consulting practices. Most psychologists in government and industry have structured schedules.

Increasingly, many psychologists are working as part of a team, consulting with other psychologists and professionals. Many experience pressures because of deadlines, tight schedules, and overtime. Their routine may be interrupted frequently. Travel may be required in order to attend conferences or conduct research.

Training, Other Qualifications, and Advancement

A doctoral degree usually is required for employment as an independent licensed clinical or counseling psychologist. Psychologists with a Ph.D. qualify for a wide range of teaching, research, clinical, and counseling positions in universities, health care services, elementary and secondary schools, private industry, and government. Psychologists with a Doctor of Psychology (Psy.D.) degree usually

work in clinical positions or in private practices, but they also sometimes teach, conduct research, or carry out administrative responsibilities.

A doctoral degree generally requires 5 to 7 years of graduate study. The Ph.D. degree culminates in a dissertation based on original research. Courses in quantitative research methods, which include the use of computer-based analysis, are an integral part of graduate study and are necessary to complete the dissertation. The Psy.D. may be based on practical work and examinations rather than a dissertation. In clinical or counseling psychology, the requirements for the doctoral degree include at least a 1-year internship.

A specialist degree is required in most states for an individual to work as a school psychologist, although a few states still credential school psychologists with master's degrees. A specialist (Ed.S.) degree in school psychology requires a minimum of 3 years of full-time graduate study (at least 60 graduate semester hours) and a 1-year internship. Because their professional practice addresses educational and mental health components of students' development, school psychologists' training includes coursework in both education and psychology.

Persons with a master's degree in psychology may work as industrial-organizational psychologists. They also may work as psychological assistants under the supervision of doctoral-level psychologists and may conduct research or psychological evaluations. A master's degree in psychology requires at least 2 years of full-time graduate study. Requirements usually include practical experience in an applied setting and a master's thesis based on an original research project.

Competition for admission to graduate psychology programs is keen. Some universities require applicants to have an undergraduate major in psychology. Others prefer only coursework in basic psychology with courses in the biological, physical, and social sciences and in statistics and mathematics.

A bachelor's degree in psychology qualifies a person to assist psychologists and other professionals in community mental health centers, vocational rehabilitation offices, and correctional programs. Bachelor's degree holders may work as research or administrative assistants for psychologists. Some work as technicians in related fields, such as marketing research. Many find employment in other areas, such as sales or business management.

In the federal government, candidates having at least 24 semester hours in psychology and one course in statistics qualify for entry-level positions. However, competition for these jobs is keen because this is one of the few areas in which one can work as a psychologist without an advanced degree.

The American Psychological Association (APA) presently accredits doctoral training programs in clinical, counseling, and school psychology, as well as accrediting institutions that provide internships for doctoral students in school, clinical, and counseling psychology. The National Association of School Psychologists, with the assistance of the National Council for Accreditation of Teacher Education, also is involved in the accreditation of advanced-degree programs in school psychology.

Psychologists in independent practice or those who offer any type of patient care—including clinical, counseling, and school psychologists—must meet certification or licensing requirements in all states and the District of Columbia. Licensing laws vary by state and by type of position and require licensed or certified psychologists to limit their practice to areas in which they have developed professional competence through training and experience. Clinical and counseling psychologists usually require a doctorate in psychology, the completion of an approved internship, and 1 to 2 years of professional experience. In addition, all states require that applicants pass an examination. Most state licensing boards administer a standardized test, and many supplement that with additional oral or essay questions. Some states require continuing education for renewal of the license.

The National Association of School Psychologists (NASP) awards the Nationally Certified School Psychologist (NCSP) designation, which recognizes professional competency in school psychology at a national, rather than state, level. Currently, 26 states recognize the NCSP and allow those with the certification to transfer credentials from one state to another without taking a new certification exam. In states that recognize the NCSP, the requirements for certification or licensure and those for the NCSP often are the same or similar. Requirements for the NCSP include the completion of 60 graduate semester hours in school psychology; a 1,200-hour internship, 600 hours of which must be completed in a school setting; and a passing score on the National School Psychology Examination.

The American Board of Professional Psychology (ABPP) recognizes professional achievement by awarding specialty certification, primarily in clinical psychology; clinical neuropsychology; and counseling, forensic, industrial-organizational, and school psychology. Candidates for ABPP certification need a doctorate in psychology, postdoctoral training in their specialty, five years of experience, professional endorsements, and a passing grade on an examination.

Aspiring psychologists who are interested in direct patient care must be emotionally stable, mature, and able to deal effectively with people. Sensitivity, compassion, good communication skills, and the ability to lead and inspire others are particularly important qualities for persons wishing to do clinical work and counseling. Research psychologists should be able to do detailed work both independently and as part of a team. Patience and perseverance are vital qualities because achieving results in the psychological treatment of patients or in research may take a long time.

Employment

Psychologists held about 179,000 jobs in 2004. Educational institutions employed about 1 out of 4 psychologists in positions other than teaching, such as counseling, testing, research, and administration. Almost 2 out of 10 were employed in health care, primarily in offices of mental health practitioners, physicians' offices, outpatient mental health and substance abuse centers, and private hospitals. Government agencies at the state and local levels employed psychologists in public hospitals, clinics, correctional facilities, and other settings.

After several years of experience, some psychologists—usually those with doctoral degrees—enter private practice or set up private research or consulting firms. About 4 out of 10 psychologists were self-employed in 2004, compared with less than 1 out of 10 among all professional workers.

In addition to the previously mentioned jobs, many psychologists held faculty positions at colleges and universities and as high school psychology teachers. (See the description of teachers—postsecondary elsewhere in this book.)

Job Outlook

Employment of psychologists is expected to grow faster than average for all occupations through 2014 because of increased demand for psychological services in schools, hospitals, social service agencies, mental health centers, substance abuse treatment clinics, consulting firms, and private companies.

Among the specialties in this field, school psychologists—especially those with a specialist degree or higher—may enjoy the best job opportunities. Growing awareness of how students' mental health and behavioral problems, such as bullying, affect learning is increasing demand for school psychologists to offer student counseling and mental health services. Clinical and counseling psychologists will be needed to help people deal with depression and other mental disorders, marriage and family problems, job stress, and addiction. The rise in health care costs associated with unhealthy lifestyles, such as smoking, alcoholism, and obesity, has made prevention and treatment more critical. An increase in the number of employee assistance programs, which help workers deal with personal problems, also should spur job growth in clinical and counseling specialties. Industrial-organizational psychologists will be in demand to help to boost worker productivity and retention rates in a wide range of businesses. Industrial-organizational psychologists will help companies deal with issues such as workplace diversity and antidiscrimination policies. Companies also will use psychologists' expertise in survey design, analysis, and research to develop tools for marketing evaluation and statistical analysis.

Demand should be particularly strong for persons holding doctorates from leading universities in applied specialties, such as counseling, health, and school psychology. Psychologists with extensive training in quantitative research methods and computer science may have a competitive edge over applicants without background.

Master's degree holders in fields other than industrial-organizational psychology will face keen competition for jobs because of the limited number of positions that require only a master's degree. Master's degree holders may find jobs as psychological assistants or counselors, providing mental health services under the direct supervision of a licensed psychologist. Still others may find jobs involving research and data collection and analysis in universities, government, or private companies.

Opportunities directly related to psychology will be limited for bachelor's degree holders. Some may find jobs as assistants in rehabilitation centers or in other jobs involving data collection and analysis. Those who meet state certification requirements may become high school psychology teachers.

Earnings

Median annual earnings of wage and salary clinical, counseling, and school psychologists in May 2004 were $54,950. The middle 50 percent earned between $41,850 and $71,880. The lowest 10 percent earned less than $32,280, and the highest 10 percent earned more than $92,250. Median annual earnings in the industries employing the largest numbers of clinical, counseling, and school psychologists in May 2004 were

Offices of other health practitioners	$64,460
Elementary and secondary schools	58,360
Outpatient care centers	46,850
Individual and family services	42,640

Median annual earnings of wage and salary industrial-organizational psychologists in May 2004 were $71,400. The middle 50 percent earned between $56,880 and $93,210. The lowest 10 percent earned less than $45,620, and the highest 10 percent earned more than $125,560.

Related Occupations

Psychologists are trained to conduct research and teach, evaluate, counsel, and advise individuals and groups with special needs. Others who do this kind of work include clergy, counselors, physicians and surgeons, social workers, sociologists, and special education teachers.

Sources of Additional Information

For information on careers, educational requirements, financial assistance, and licensing in all fields of psychology, contact

▶ American Psychological Association, Research Office and Education Directorate, 750 1st St. NE, Washington, DC 20002-4242. Internet: http://www.apa.org/students

For information on careers, educational requirements, certification, and licensing of school psychologists, contact

▶ National Association of School Psychologists, 4340 East West Hwy., Suite 402, Bethesda, MD 20814. Internet: http://www.nasponline.org

Information about state licensing requirements is available from

▶ Association of State and Provincial Psychology Boards, P.O. Box 241245, Montgomery, AL 36124-1245. Internet: http://www.asppb.org

Information about psychology specialty certifications is available from

▶ American Board of Professional Psychology, Inc., 300 Drayton St., 3rd Floor, Savannah, GA 31401. Internet: http://www.abpp.org

Radiation Therapists

(O*NET 29-1124.00)

Significant Points

■ Good job opportunities are expected; applicants who are certified and who possess a bachelor's or an associate degree or a certificate in radiation therapy should have the best prospects.

■ Employment is projected to grow faster than average.

■ Radiation therapists need good communication skills because their work involves a great deal of patient interaction.

Nature of the Work

Radiation therapy is the use of radiation to treat cancer in the human body. As part of a medical radiation oncology team, radiation therapists use machines—called linear accelerators—to administer radiation treatment to patients. Linear accelerators, used in a procedure called external beam therapy, project high-energy X rays at targeted cancer cells. As the X rays collide with human tissue, they produce highly energized ions that can shrink and eliminate cancerous tumors. Radiation therapy sometimes is used as the sole treatment for cancer, but usually is used in conjunction with chemotherapy or surgery.

The first step in the radiation treatment process is called simulation. During simulation, a radiation therapist uses an X-ray imaging machine to pinpoint the location of the tumor. The therapist also may use a computerized tomography or CT scan to help determine how best to direct the radiation to minimize damage to healthy tissue. The therapist then positions the patient and adjusts the linear accelerator so that, during treatment, radiation exposure is concentrated on the tumor cells. The radiation therapist then develops a treatment plan in conjunction with a radiation oncologist (a physician who specializes in therapeutic radiology) and a dosimetrist (a technician who calculates the dose of radiation that will be used for treatment). The therapist later explains the treatment plan to the patient and answers any questions that the patient may have.

After simulation, the radiation therapist positions the patient and adjusts the linear accelerator to mirror the conditions that were established in simulation. Then the therapist leaves the room to administer the radiation treatment. From a separate room that is protected from the X-ray radiation, the therapist operates the linear accelerator and monitors the patient's condition through a TV monitor and an intercom system. Treatment can take anywhere from 10 to 30 minutes and is usually administered once a day, 5 days a week, for a period of 2 to 9 weeks.

During the treatment phase, the radiation therapist monitors the patient's physical condition to determine if any adverse side effects are taking place. In addition, the therapist must be aware of the patient's emotional condition. Because many patients are under stress and are emotionally fragile, it is important for the therapist to maintain a positive attitude and provide emotional support. Radiation therapists also must keep detailed records of their patients' treatments. These records include information such as the dose of radiation used for each treatment, the total amount of radiation used to date, the area treated, and the patient's reactions. Radiation oncologists and dosimetrists review these records to ensure that the treatment plan is working, to monitor the amount of radiation exposure that the patient has received, and to keep unwanted side effects to a minimum.

Radiation therapists also assist medical radiation physicists, who keep the linear accelerator working. Because radiation therapists often work alone during the treatment phase, they need to be able to check the linear accelerator for problems and make any adjustments that are needed. Therapists also may assist dosimetrists, who calculate the amount of radiation for each treatment. Therapists may perform the routine aspects of this process, called dosimetry, which involves complex mathematical computations.

Working Conditions

Radiation therapists work in hospitals or in cancer treatment centers. These places are clean, well lighted, and well ventilated. Therapists do a considerable amount of lifting and must be able to help disabled patients get on and off treatment tables. Therapists also work on their feet most of the time. Therapists generally work 40 hours a week, and, unlike other health care occupations, they normally work only during the day. However, because radiation therapy emergencies do occur, some therapists are required to be on call and may have to work outside of their normal hours.

Because they work around radioactive materials, radiation therapists take great care to ensure that they are not exposed to dangerous levels of radiation. Following standard safety procedures can prevent overexposure.

Training, Other Qualifications, and Advancement

Employers generally require applicants to complete an associate or a bachelor's degree program in radiation therapy. Individuals also may become qualified by completing an associate or a bachelor's degree program in radiography, which is the study of radiological imaging, and then completing a 12-month certificate program in radiation therapy. Radiation therapy programs have core courses on radiation therapy procedures and the scientific theories behind these procedures. In addition, such programs often include courses on human anatomy, human physiology, physics, algebra, precalculus, writing, public speaking, computer science, and research methodology.

Some states require that radiation therapists be licensed by a state accrediting board. Some states, as well as many employers, also require that radiation therapists be certified by the American Registry of Radiologic Technologists (ARRT). In order to become ARRT-certified, an applicant needs to complete an accredited radiation therapy program, adhere to ARRT ethical standards, and pass the ARRT certification examination. In 2005, there were 94 accredited radiation therapy programs. While enrolled in an accredited radiation therapy program, students who wish to become ARRT-certified must take classes that are related to the subject matter of the certification examination. The certification examination covers radiation protection and quality assurance, clinical concepts in radiation oncology, treatment planning, treatment delivery, and patient care and education. Candidates also must demonstrate competency in several clinical practices, which include patient care activities; simulation procedures; dosimetry calculations; fabrication of beam modification devices; low-volume, high-risk procedures; and radiation treatment procedures.

AART certification is valid for 1 year, after which therapists must renew their certification. Requirements for renewal include abiding by the ARRT ethical standards, paying the annual dues, and satisfying the continuing education requirements. Continuing education requirements must be met every 2 years and include either the completion of 24 credits of radiation therapy–related courses or the successful attainment of ARRT certification in a discipline other than radiation therapy. Renewed certification, however, may not be required by all states or employers that require initial certification.

Individuals interested in becoming radiation therapists should be psychologically capable of working with cancer patients. They should be caring and empathetic because they work with patients who are ill and under stress. Individuals also need good communication skills because their work involves a great deal of patient interaction. They should be able to keep accurate, detailed records. They also should be physically fit because they work on their feet for long periods and lift and move disabled patients.

Experienced radiation therapists may advance to manage radiation therapy programs in treatment centers or other health care facilities. Managers generally continue to treat patients while taking on management responsibilities. Other advancement opportunities include teaching, technical sales, and research. With additional training and certification, therapists also can become dosimetrists, who use complex mathematical formulas to calculate proper radiation doses.

Employment

Radiation therapists held about 15,000 jobs in 2004. About 84 percent worked in the health care industry, primarily in hospitals and in physicians' offices. Another 13 percent worked for state and local governments.

Job Outlook

Good job opportunities are expected. Applicants who are certified and who possess a bachelor's or an associate degree or a certificate in radiation therapy should have the best prospects.

Employment of radiation therapists is projected to grow faster than average for all occupations during the 2004–2014 period. As the U.S. population grows and ages, demand will increase for radiation treatment. As radiation technology advances, radiation treatment will be prescribed for an increasing proportion of cancer patients. In addition to new jobs created over the projection period, a number of job openings will result as experienced radiation therapists retire or leave the occupation for other reasons.

Earnings

The median annual earnings of radiation therapists in May 2004 were $57,700. The middle 50 percent earned between $47,380 and $69,650. The lowest 10 percent earned less than $38,550, and the highest 10 percent earned more than $83,340. Some employers also reimburse their employees for the cost of continuing education.

Related Occupations

Radiation therapists use advanced machinery to administer medical treatment to patients. Other occupations that perform similar duties include radiation technologists and technicians, diagnostic medical sonographers, nuclear medicine technicians, dental hygienists, respiratory therapists, physical therapy assistants and aides, registered nurses, and physicians and surgeons.

Besides radiation therapists, occupations that build relationships with patients and provide them with emotional support include nursing, psychiatric, and home health aides; counselors; psychologists; social workers; and social and human service assistants.

Sources of Additional Information

Information on certification by the American Registry of Radiologic Technologists and on accredited radiation therapy programs may be obtained from

▶ American Registry of Radiologic Technologists, 1255 Northland Dr., St. Paul, MN 55120-1155. Internet: http://www.arrt.org/web

Information on careers in radiation therapy may be obtained from

▶ American Society of Radiologic Technologists, 15000 Central Ave. SE, Albuquerque, NM 87123-3917. Internet: http://www.asrt.org

Radio and Telecommunications Equipment Installers and Repairers

(O*NET 49-2021.00, 49-2022.01, 49-2022.02, 49-2022.03, 49-2022.04, and 49-2022.05)

Significant Points

■ Employment is projected to decline.

■ Job opportunities will vary by specialty; for example, good opportunities should be available for central office and PBX installers and repairers experienced in current technology, while station installers and repairers can expect keen competition.

■ Applicants with computer skills and postsecondary electronics training should have the best opportunities.

■ Weekend and holiday hours are common; repairers may be on call around the clock in case of emergencies.

Nature of the Work

Telephones and radios depend on a variety of equipment to transmit communications signals. From electronic switches that route telephone signals to their destinations to radio transmitters and receivers that relay signals from wireless phones, the workers who set up and maintain this sophisticated equipment are called radio and telecommunications equipment installers and repairers. These workers no longer just work on equipment that transmits voice signals, but also transmissions such as data, graphics, and video.

Central office installers set up switches, cables, and other equipment in central offices. These locations are the hubs of a telecommunications network—they contain the switches and routers that direct packets of information to their destinations. Although most telephone lines connecting houses to central offices and switching stations are still copper, the lines connecting these central hubs are fiber optic. Fiber-optic lines have led to a revolution in switching equipment. The greatly increased transmission capacity of each line has allowed a few fiber-optic lines to replace many copper lines. Packet switching equipment is evolving rapidly, ever increasing the amount of information that a single fiber-optic line can carry. These switches and routers have the ability to transmit, process, amplify, and direct a massive amount of information. Installing and maintaining this equipment requires a high level of technical knowledge.

The increasing reliability of telephone switches and routers has simplified maintenance. New self-monitoring telephone switches alert repairers to malfunctions. Some switches allow repairers to diagnose and correct problems from remote locations. When faced with a malfunction, the repairer may refer to manufacturers' manuals that provide maintenance instructions.

When problems with telecommunications equipment arise, telecommunications equipment repairers diagnose the source of the problem by testing each of the different parts of the equipment, which requires an understanding of how the software and hardware interact. Repairers often use spectrum and/or network analyzers to locate the problem. A network analyzer sends a signal through the equipment to detect any distortion in the signal. The nature of the signal distortion often directs the repairer to the source of the problem. To fix the equipment, repairers may use small hand tools, including pliers and screwdrivers, to remove and replace defective components such as circuit boards or wiring. Newer equipment is easier to repair because whole boards and parts are designed to be quickly removed and replaced. Repairers also may install updated software or programs that maintain existing software.

Cable television companies employ technicians to install and maintain their distribution centers, called head ends. Their work is similar to central office installers.

PBX installers and repairers set up private branch exchange (PBX) switchboards, which relay incoming, outgoing, and interoffice calls within a single location or organization. To install switches and switchboards, installers first connect the equipment to power lines and communications cables and install frames and supports. They test the connections to ensure that adequate power is available and that the communication links function. They also install equipment such as power systems, alarms, and telephone sets. New switches and switchboards are computerized; workers install software or program the equipment to provide specific features. For example, as a cost-cutting feature, an installer may program a PBX switchboard to route calls over different lines at different times of the day. However, other workers, such as computer support specialists, generally handle complex programming. (The work of computer support specialists is outlined in this book's description of computer support specialists and systems administrators.) Finally, the installer performs tests to verify that the newly installed equipment functions properly. If a problem arises, PBX repairers determine whether it is located within the PBX system or originates in the telephone lines maintained by the local phone company.

Due to rapidly developing technologies, PBX installers must adapt and learn new technologies. Instead of installing PBX systems, companies are choosing to install voice-over Internet protocol (VoIP) systems. VoIP systems operate like a PBX system, but they use a company's computer wiring to run Internet access, network applications, and telephone communications. Specialized phones have their own Internet protocol (IP) addresses. The phones can be plugged into any port in the system and still use the same number.

Station installers and repairers, telephone—commonly known as *telephone installers and repairers* or *telecommunications service technicians*—install and repair telephone wiring and equipment on customers' premises. They install telephone or digital subscriber line (DSL) service by connecting customers' telephone wires to outside service lines. These lines run on telephone poles or in underground conduits. The installer may climb poles or ladders to make the connections. Once the connection is made, the line is tested. When a maintenance problem occurs, repairers test the customers' lines to determine if the problem is located in the customers' premises or in the outside service lines. When onsite procedures fail to resolve installation or maintenance problems, repairers may request support from their technical service center. Line installers and repairers install the wires and cables that connect customers with central offices.

Radio mechanics install and maintain radio transmitting and receiving equipment. This includes stationary equipment mounted on transmission towers and mobile equipment, such as radio communications systems in service and emergency vehicles. Radio mechanics do not work on cellular communications towers and equipment. Newer radio equipment is self-monitoring and may alert mechanics to potential malfunctions. When malfunctions occur, these mechanics examine equipment for damaged components and loose or broken wires. They use electrical measuring instruments to monitor signal strength, transmission capacity, interference, and signal delay, as well as hand tools to replace defective components and parts and to adjust equipment so that it performs within required specifications.

Working Conditions

Radio and telecommunications equipment installers and repairers generally work in clean, well-lighted, air-conditioned surroundings, such as a telephone company's central office, a customer's location, or an electronic repair shop or service center. Telephone installers and repairers work on rooftops, ladders, and telephone poles. Telephone, PBX, and VoIP installers must travel to a customer's location. Radio mechanics may maintain equipment located on the tops of transmissions towers. While working outdoors, these workers are subject to a variety of weather conditions.

Nearly all radio and telecommunications equipment installers and repairers work full time. Many work regular business hours to meet the demand for repair services during the workday. Schedules are more irregular at companies that need repair services 24 hours a day or where installation and maintenance must take place after business hours. At these locations, mechanics work a variety of shifts, including weekend and holiday hours. Repairers may be on call around the clock, in case of emergencies, and may have to work overtime.

The work of most repairers involves lifting, reaching, stooping, crouching, and crawling. Adherence to safety precautions is important in order to guard against work hazards. These hazards include falls, minor burns, electrical shock, and contact with hazardous materials.

Training, Other Qualifications, and Advancement

Most employers seek applicants with postsecondary training in electronics and a familiarity with computers. Training sources include 2-year and 4-year college programs in electronics or communications,

trade schools, and equipment and software manufacturers. Military experience with communications equipment is valued by many employers. Some equipment repairers begin working in telecommunications companies as line installers or telephone installers before moving up to the job of central office installer and other more complex work.

Newly hired repairers usually receive some training from their employers. This may include formal classroom training in electronics, communications systems, or software and informal hands-on training assisting an experienced repairer. Large companies may send repairers to outside training sessions to keep them informed about new equipment and service procedures. As networks have become more sophisticated—often including equipment from a variety of companies—the knowledge needed for installation and maintenance also has increased.

Telecommunications equipment companies provide much of the training on specific equipment. With the rapid advances in switches, routers, and other equipment, repairers need to continually take courses and work to obtain manufacturers' certifications on the latest technology.

Repairers must be able to distinguish colors, because wires are color-coded, and they must be able to hear distinctions in the various tones on a telephone system. For positions that require climbing poles and towers, workers must be in good physical shape. Repairers who handle assignments alone at a customer's site must be able to work without close supervision. For workers who frequently contact customers, a pleasant personality, neat appearance, and good communications skills also are important.

Experienced repairers with advanced training may become specialists or troubleshooters who help other repairers diagnose difficult problems or may work with engineers in designing equipment and developing maintenance procedures. Because of their familiarity with equipment, repairers are particularly well qualified to become manufacturers' sales workers. Workers with leadership ability also may become maintenance supervisors or service managers. Some experienced workers open their own repair services or shops or become wholesalers or retailers of electronic equipment.

Employment

Radio and telecommunications equipment installers and repairers held about 222,000 jobs in 2004. About 215,000 were telecommunications equipment installers and repairers, except line installers, mostly working in the telecommunications industry, and the rest were radio mechanics. Radio mechanics worked in electronic and precision equipment repair and maintenance, telecommunications, electronics and appliance stores, and many other industries.

Job Outlook

Employment of radio and telecommunications equipment installers and repairers is expected to decline through 2014. Although the need for installation work will remain as companies seek to upgrade their telecommunications networks, there will be a declining need for maintenance work—performed by telecommunications equipment installers and repairers, except line installers—because of increasingly reliable self-monitoring and self-diagnosing equipment and because installation of higher-capacity equipment will reduce the amount of equipment needed. The replacement of two-way radio systems with wireless systems, especially in service vehicles, will eliminate the need in many companies for onsite radio mechanics. The increased reliability of wireless equipment and the use of self-monitoring systems also will continue to lessen the need for radio mechanics. Applicants with computer skills and postsecondary electronics training should have the best opportunities for radio and telecommunications equipment installer and repairer jobs.

Job opportunities will vary by specialty. For example, good opportunities should be available for central office and PBX installers and repairers experienced in current technology as the growing popularity of VoIP, expanded multimedia offerings such as video on demand, and other telecommunications services continue to place additional demand on telecommunications networks. These new services require high data transfer rates, which can be achieved only by installing new optical switching and routing equipment. Extending high-speed communications from central offices to customers also will require the installation of more advanced switching and routing equipment. Whereas increased reliability and automation of switching equipment will limit opportunities, these effects will be somewhat offset by the demand for installation and upgrading of switching equipment.

Station installers and repairers can expect keen competition. Prewired buildings and the increasing reliability of telephone equipment will reduce the need for installation and maintenance of customers' telephones. Upgrading internal lines in businesses and the wiring of new homes and businesses with fiber-optic lines should offset some of these losses. As cellular telephones have increased in popularity, the number of pay phones is declining, which also will adversely affect employment of station installers and repairers, as pay phone installation and maintenance is one of their major functions.

Earnings

In May 2004, median hourly earnings of telecommunications equipment installers and repairers, except line installers were $23.96. The middle 50 percent earned between $19.46 and $27.07. The bottom 10 percent earned less than $14.65, whereas the top 10 percent earned more than $30.85. The median hourly earnings of these workers in the wired telecommunications carriers (telephone) industry were $24.92 in May 2004.

Median hourly earnings of radio mechanics in May 2004 were $17.65. The middle 50 percent earned between $13.59 and $21.90. The bottom 10 percent earned less than $10.42, whereas the top 10 percent earned more than $27.62.

Related Occupations

Related occupations that involve work with electronic equipment include broadcast and sound engineering technicians and radio operators; computer, automated teller, and office machine repairers; electronic home entertainment equipment installers and repairers; and electrical and electronics installers and repairers. Line installers and repairers also set up and install telecommunications equipment. Engineering technicians also may repair electronic equipment as part of their duties.

Sources of Additional Information

For information on career and training opportunities, contact

▸ International Brotherhood of Electrical Workers, Telecommunications Department, 1125 15th St. NW, Room 807, Washington, DC 20005.

▸ Communications Workers of America, 501 3rd St. NW, Washington, DC 20001.

For information on training and professional certifications for those already employed by cable telecommunications firms, contact

▸ Society of Cable Telecommunications Engineers, Certification Department, 140 Phillips Rd., Exton, PA 19341-1318. Internet: http://www.scte.org

Radiologic Technologists and Technicians

(O*NET 29-2034.01 and 29-2034.02)

Significant Points

■ Job opportunities are expected to be favorable; some employers report difficulty hiring sufficient numbers of radiologic technologists and technicians.

■ Formal training programs in radiography range in length from 1 to 4 years and lead to a certificate, an associate degree, or a bachelor's degree.

■ Although hospitals will remain the primary employer, a greater number of new jobs will be found in physicians' offices and diagnostic imaging centers.

Nature of the Work

Radiologic technologists and technicians take X rays and administer nonradioactive materials into patients' bloodstreams for diagnostic purposes. Some specialize in diagnostic imaging technologies, such as computerized tomography (CT) and magnetic resonance imaging (MRI).

In addition to radiologic technologists and technicians, others who conduct diagnostic imaging procedures include cardiovascular technologists and technicians and nuclear medicine technologists. (Each is discussed elsewhere in this book.)

Radiologic technologists and technicians, also referred to as *radiographers*, produce X-ray films (radiographs) of parts of the human body for use in diagnosing medical problems. They prepare patients for radiologic examinations by explaining the procedure, removing articles such as jewelry, through which X rays cannot pass, and positioning patients so that the parts of the body can be appropriately radiographed. To prevent unnecessary exposure to radiation, these workers surround the exposed area with radiation protection devices, such as lead shields, or limit the size of the X-ray beam. Radiographers position radiographic equipment at the correct angle and height over the appropriate area of a patient's body. Using instruments similar to a measuring tape, they may measure the thickness of the section to be radiographed and set controls on the X-ray machine to produce radiographs of the appropriate density, detail, and contrast. They place the X-ray film under the part of the patient's body to be examined and make the exposure. They then remove the film and develop it.

Experienced radiographers may perform more complex imaging procedures. For fluoroscopies, radiographers prepare a solution of contrast medium for the patient to drink, allowing the radiologist (a physician who interprets radiographs) to see soft tissues in the body. Some radiographers, called *CT technologists,* operate CT scanners to produce cross-sectional images of patients. Radiographers who operate machines that use strong magnets and radio waves, rather than radiation, to create an image are called *MRI technologists.*

Radiologic technologists and technicians must follow physicians' orders precisely and conform to regulations concerning the use of radiation to protect themselves, their patients, and their co-workers from unnecessary exposure.

In addition to preparing patients and operating equipment, radiologic technologists and technicians keep patient records and adjust and maintain equipment. They also may prepare work schedules, evaluate purchases of equipment, or manage a radiology department.

Working Conditions

Most full-time radiologic technologists and technicians work about 40 hours a week. They may, however, have evening, weekend, or on-call hours. Opportunities for part-time and shift work also are available.

Physical stamina is important, because technologists and technicians are on their feet for long periods and may lift or turn disabled patients. Technologists and technicians work at diagnostic machines, but also may perform some procedures at patients' bedsides. Some travel to patients in large vans equipped with sophisticated diagnostic equipment.

Although radiation hazards exist in this occupation, they are minimized by the use of lead aprons, gloves, and other shielding devices, as well as by instruments monitoring exposure to radiation. Technologists and technicians wear badges measuring radiation levels in the radiation area, and detailed records are kept on their cumulative lifetime dose.

Training, Other Qualifications, and Advancement

Preparation for this profession is offered in hospitals, colleges and universities, vocational-technical institutes, and the U.S. Armed Forces. Hospitals, which employ most radiologic technologists and technicians, prefer to hire those with formal training.

Formal training programs in radiography range in length from 1 to 4 years and lead to a certificate, an associate degree, or a bachelor's degree. Two-year associate degree programs are most prevalent.

Some 1-year certificate programs are available for experienced radiographers or individuals from other health occupations, such as medical technologists and registered nurses, who want to change fields or specialize in CT or MRI. A bachelor's or master's degree in one of the radiologic technologies is desirable for supervisory, administrative, or teaching positions.

The Joint Review Committee on Education in Radiologic Technology accredits most formal training programs for the field. The committee accredited 606 radiography programs in 2005. Radiography programs require, at a minimum, a high school diploma or the equivalent. High school courses in mathematics, physics, chemistry, and biology are helpful. The programs provide both classroom and clinical instruction in anatomy and physiology, patient care procedures, radiation physics, radiation protection, principles of imaging, medical terminology, positioning of patients, medical ethics, radiobiology, and pathology.

Federal legislation protects the public from the hazards of unnecessary exposure to medical and dental radiation by ensuring that operators of radiologic equipment are properly trained. Under this legislation, the federal government sets voluntary standards that the states may use for accrediting training programs and certifying individuals who engage in medical or dental radiography.

In 2005, 38 states certified radiologic technologists and technicians. Certification, which is voluntary, is offered by the American Registry of Radiologic Technologists. To be eligible for certification, technologists generally must graduate from an accredited program and pass an examination. Many employers prefer to hire certified radiographers. To be recertified, radiographers must complete 24 hours of continuing education every two years.

Radiologic technologists and technicians should be sensitive to patients' physical and psychological needs. They must pay attention to detail, follow instructions, and work as part of a team. In addition, operating complicated equipment requires mechanical ability and manual dexterity.

With experience and additional training, staff technologists may become specialists, performing CT scanning, angiography, and magnetic resonance imaging. Experienced technologists also may be promoted to supervisor, chief radiologic technologist, and, ultimately, department administrator or director. Depending on the institution, courses or a master's degree in business or health administration may be necessary for the director's position. Some technologists progress by leaving the occupation to become instructors or directors in radiologic technology programs; others take jobs as sales representatives or instructors with equipment manufacturers.

Employment

Radiologic technologists and technicians held about 182,000 jobs in 2004. More than half of all jobs were in hospitals. Most of the rest were in offices of physicians; medical and diagnostic laboratories, including diagnostic imaging centers; and outpatient care centers.

Job Outlook

Job opportunities are expected to be favorable. Some employers report difficulty hiring sufficient numbers of radiologic technologists and technicians. Imbalances between the demand for, and supply of, radiologic technologists and technicians should spur efforts to attract and retain qualified workers, such as improved compensation and working conditions. Radiologic technologists who also are experienced in more complex diagnostic imaging procedures, such as CT and MRI, will have better employment opportunities, brought about as employers seek to control costs by using multiskilled employees.

Employment of radiologic technologists and technicians is expected to grow faster than the average for all occupations through 2014 as the population grows and ages, increasing the demand for diagnostic imaging. Although health care providers are enthusiastic about the clinical benefits of new technologies, the extent to which they are adopted depends largely on cost and reimbursement considerations. For example, digital imaging technology can improve the quality of the images and the efficiency of the procedure, but remains expensive. Some promising new technologies may not come into widespread use because they are too expensive and third-party payers may not be willing to pay for their use.

Hospitals will remain the principal employer of radiologic technologists and technicians. However, a greater number of new jobs will be found in offices of physicians and diagnostic imaging centers. Health facilities such as these are expected to grow rapidly through 2014 due to the strong shift toward outpatient care encouraged by third-party payers and made possible by technological advances that permit more procedures to be performed outside the hospital. Some job openings also will arise from the need to replace technologists and technicians who leave the occupation.

Earnings

Median annual earnings of radiologic technologists and technicians were $43,350 in May 2004. The middle 50 percent earned between $36,170 and $52,430. The lowest 10 percent earned less than $30,020, and the highest 10 percent earned more than $60,210. Median annual earnings in the industries employing the largest numbers of radiologic technologists and technicians in May 2004 were

Medical and diagnostic laboratories $46,620
General medical and surgical hospitals 43,960
Offices of physicians 40,290

Related Occupations

Radiologic technologists and technicians operate sophisticated equipment to help physicians, dentists, and other health practitioners diagnose and treat patients. Workers in related occupations include cardiovascular technologists and technicians, clinical laboratory technologists and technicians, diagnostic medical sonographers, nuclear medicine technologists, radiation therapists, and respiratory therapists.

Sources of Additional Information

For career information, send a stamped, self-addressed business-size envelope with your request to

▶ American Society of Radiologic Technologists, 15000 Central Ave. SE, Albuquerque, NM 87123-3917. Internet: http://www.asrt.org

For the current list of accredited education programs in radiography, write to

▶ Joint Review Committee on Education in Radiologic Technology, 20 N. Wacker Dr., Suite 2850, Chicago, IL 60606-3182. Internet: http://www.jrcert.org

For information on certification, contact

▶ American Registry of Radiologic Technologists, 1255 Northland Dr., St. Paul, MN 55120-1155. Internet: http://www.arrt.org

Registered Nurses

(O*NET 29-1111.00)

Significant Points

■ Registered nurses constitute the largest health care occupation, with 2.4 million jobs.

■ About 3 out of 5 jobs are in hospitals.

■ The three major educational paths to registered nursing are a bachelor's degree, an associate degree, and a diploma from an approved nursing program.

■ Registered nurses are projected to create the second-largest number of new jobs among all occupations; job opportunities in most specialties and employment settings are expected to be excellent, with some employers reporting difficulty in attracting and retaining enough RNs.

Nature of the Work

Registered nurses (RNs), regardless of specialty or work setting, perform basic duties that include treating patients, educating patients and the public about various medical conditions, and providing advice and emotional support to patients' family members. RNs record patients' medical histories and symptoms, help to perform diagnostic tests and analyze results, operate medical machinery, administer treatment and medications, and help with patient follow-up and rehabilitation.

RNs teach patients and their families how to manage their illness or injury, including post-treatment home care needs, diet and exercise programs, and self-administration of medication and physical therapy. Some RNs also are trained to provide grief counseling to family members of critically ill patients. RNs work to promote general health by educating the public on various warning signs and symptoms of disease and where to go for help. RNs also might run general health screening or immunization clinics, blood drives, and public seminars on various conditions.

RNs can specialize in one or more patient care specialties. The most common specialties can be divided into roughly four categories—by work setting or type of treatment; disease, ailment, or condition; organ or body system type; or population. RNs may combine specialties from more than one area—for example, pediatric oncology or cardiac emergency—depending on personal interest and employer needs.

RNs may specialize by work setting or by type of care provided. For example, *ambulatory care nurses* treat patients with a variety of illnesses and injuries on an outpatient basis, either in physicians' offices or in clinics. Some ambulatory care nurses are involved in telehealth, providing care and advice through electronic communications media such as videoconferencing or the Internet. *Critical care nurses* work in critical or intensive care hospital units and provide care to patients with cardiovascular, respiratory, or pulmonary failure. *Emergency,* or *trauma, nurses* work in hospital emergency departments and treat patients with life-threatening conditions caused by accidents, heart attacks, and strokes. Some emergency nurses are flight nurses, who provide medical care to patients who must be flown by helicopter to the nearest medical facility. *Holistic nurses* provide care such as acupuncture, massage therapy and aromatherapy, and biofeedback, which are meant to treat patients' mental and spiritual health in addition to their physical health. *Home health care nurses* provide at-home care for patients who are recovering from surgery, accidents, and childbirth. *Hospice and palliative care nurses* provide care for, and help ease the pain of, terminally ill patients outside of hospitals. *Infusion nurses* administer medications, fluids, and blood to patients through injections into patients' veins. *Long-term care nurses* provide medical services on a recurring basis to patients with chronic physical or mental disorders. *Medical-surgical nurses* provide basic medical care to a variety of patients in all health settings. *Occupational health nurses* provide treatment for job-related injuries and illnesses and help employers to detect workplace hazards and implement health and safety standards. *Perianesthesia nurses* provide preoperative and postoperative care to patients undergoing anesthesia during surgery. *Perioperative nurses* assist surgeons by selecting and handling instruments, controlling bleeding, and suturing incisions. Some of these nurses also can specialize in plastic and reconstructive surgery. *Psychiatric nurses* treat patients with personality and mood disorders. *Radiologic nurses* provide care to patients undergoing diagnostic radiation procedures such as ultrasounds and magnetic resonance imaging. *Rehabilitation nurses* care for patients with temporary and permanent disabilities. *Transplant nurses* care for both transplant recipients and living donors and monitor signs of organ rejection.

RNs specializing in a particular disease, ailment, or condition are employed in virtually all work settings, including physicians' offices, outpatient treatment facilities, home health care agencies, and hospitals. For instance, *addictions nurses* treat patients seeking help with alcohol, drug, and tobacco addictions. *Developmental disabilities nurses* provide care for patients with physical, mental, or behavioral disabilities; care may include help with feeding, controlling bodily functions, and sitting or standing independently. *Diabetes management nurses* help diabetics to manage their disease by teaching them proper nutrition and showing them how to test blood sugar levels and administer insulin injections. *Genetics nurses* provide early detection screenings and treatment of patients with genetic disorders, including cystic fibrosis and Huntington's disease. *HIV/AIDS nurses* care for patients diagnosed with HIV and AIDS. *Oncology nurses* care for patients with various types of cancer and may administer radiation and chemotherapies. Finally, *wound, ostomy, and continence nurses* treat patients with wounds caused by traumatic injury, ulcers, or arterial disease; provide postoperative care for patients with openings that allow for alternative methods of bodily waste elimination; and treat patients with urinary and fecal incontinence.

RNs specializing in treatment of a particular organ or body system usually are employed in specialty physicians' offices or outpatient care facilities, although some are employed in hospital specialty or critical care units. For example, *cardiac and vascular nurses* treat patients with coronary heart disease and those who have had heart surgery, providing services such as postoperative rehabilitation. *Dermatology nurses* treat patients with disorders of the skin, such as

skin cancer and psoriasis. *Gastroenterology nurses* treat patients with digestive and intestinal disorders, including ulcers, acid reflux disease, and abdominal bleeding. Some nurses in this field also specialize in endoscopic procedures, which look inside the gastrointestinal tract using a tube equipped with a light and a camera that can capture images of diseased tissue. *Gynecology nurses* provide care to women with disorders of the reproductive system, including endometriosis, cancer, and sexually transmitted diseases. *Nephrology nurses* care for patients with kidney disease caused by diabetes, hypertension, or substance abuse. *Neuroscience nurses* care for patients with dysfunctions of the nervous system, including brain and spinal cord injuries and seizures. *Ophthalmic nurses* provide care to patients with disorders of the eyes, including blindness and glaucoma, and to patients undergoing eye surgery. *Orthopedic nurses* care for patients with muscular and skeletal problems, including arthritis, bone fractures, and muscular dystrophy. *Otorhinolaryngology nurses* care for patients with ear, nose, and throat disorders, such as cleft palates, allergies, and sinus disorders. *Respiratory nurses* provide care to patients with respiratory disorders such as asthma, tuberculosis, and cystic fibrosis. *Urology nurses* care for patients with disorders of the kidneys, urinary tract, and male reproductive organs, including infections, kidney and bladder stones, and cancers.

Finally, RNs may specialize by providing preventive and acute care in all health care settings to various segments of the population, including newborns (neonatology), children and adolescents (pediatrics), adults, and the elderly (gerontology or geriatrics). RNs also may provide basic health care to patients outside of health care settings in such venues as correctional facilities, schools, summer camps, and the military. Some RNs travel around the United States and abroad providing care to patients in areas with shortages of medical professionals.

Most RNs work as staff nurses, providing critical health care services along with physicians, surgeons, and other health care practitioners. However, some RNs choose to become advanced practice nurses, who often are considered primary health care practitioners and work independently or in collaboration with physicians. For example, *clinical nurse specialists* provide direct patient care and expert consultations in one of many of the nursing specialties listed above. *Nurse anesthetists* administer anesthesia, monitor patient's vital signs during surgery, and provide post-anesthesia care. *Nurse-midwives* provide primary care to women, including gynecological exams, family planning advice, prenatal care, assistance in labor and delivery, and neonatal care. *Nurse practitioners* provide basic preventive health care to patients and increasingly serve as primary and specialty care providers in mainly medically underserved areas. The most common areas of specialty for nurse practitioners are family practice, adult practice, women's health, pediatrics, acute care, and gerontology; however, there are many other specialties. In most states, advanced practice nurses can prescribe medications.

Some nurses have jobs that require little or no direct patient contact. Most of these positions still require an active RN license. *Case managers* ensure that all of the medical needs of patients with severe injuries and illnesses are met, including the type, location, and duration of treatment. *Forensics nurses* combine nursing with law enforcement by treating and investigating victims of sexual assault, child abuse, or accidental death. *Infection control nurses* identify, track, and control infectious outbreaks in health care facilities; develop methods of outbreak prevention and biological terrorism responses; and staff immunization clinics. *Legal nurse consultants* assist lawyers in medical cases by interviewing patients and witnesses, organizing medical records, determining damages and costs, locating evidence, and educating lawyers about medical issues. *Nurse administrators* supervise nursing staff, establish work schedules and budgets, and maintain medical supply inventories. *Nurse educators* teach student nurses and also provide continuing education for RNs. *Nurse informaticists* collect, store, and analyze nursing data in order to improve efficiency, reduce risk, and improve patient care. RNs also may work as health care consultants, public policy advisors, pharmaceutical and medical supply researchers and salespersons, and medical writers and editors.

Working Conditions

Most RNs work in well-lighted, comfortable health care facilities. Home health and public health nurses travel to patients' homes, schools, community centers, and other sites. RNs may spend considerable time walking and standing. Patients in hospitals and nursing care facilities require 24-hour care; consequently, nurses in these institutions may work nights, weekends, and holidays. RNs also may be on call—available to work on short notice. Nurses who work in office settings are more likely to work regular business hours. About 23 percent of RNs worked part time in 2004, and 7 percent held more than one job.

Nursing has its hazards, especially in hospitals, nursing care facilities, and clinics, where nurses may care for individuals with infectious diseases. RNs must observe rigid, standardized guidelines to guard against disease and other dangers, such as those posed by radiation, accidental needle sticks, chemicals used to sterilize instruments, and anesthetics. In addition, they are vulnerable to back injury when moving patients, shocks from electrical equipment, and hazards posed by compressed gases. RNs who work with critically ill patients also may suffer emotional strain from observing patient suffering and from close personal contact with patients' families.

Training, Other Qualifications, and Advancement

In all states and the District of Columbia, students must graduate from an approved nursing program and pass a national licensing examination, known as the NCLEX-RN, in order to obtain a nursing license. Nurses may be licensed in more than one state, either by examination or by the endorsement of a license issued by another state. Currently 18 states participate in the Nurse Licensure Compact Agreement, which allows nurses to practice in member states without recertifying. All states require periodic renewal of licenses, which may involve continuing education.

There are three major educational paths to registered nursing: A bachelor's of science degree in nursing (BSN), an associate degree in nursing (ADN), and a diploma. BSN programs, offered by colleges and universities, take about 4 years to complete. In 2004, 674 nursing programs offered degrees at the bachelor's level. ADN programs, offered by community and junior colleges, take about 2 to 3 years to complete. About 846 RN programs in 2004 granted associate degrees. Diploma programs, administered in hospitals, last about

3 years. Only 69 programs offered diplomas in 2004. Generally, licensed graduates of any of the three types of educational programs qualify for entry-level positions as staff nurses.

Many RNs with an ADN or diploma later enter bachelor's programs to prepare for a broader scope of nursing practice. Often, they can find a staff nurse position and then take advantage of tuition reimbursement benefits to work toward a BSN by completing an RN-to-BSN program. In 2004, there were 600 RN-to-BSN programs in the United States. Accelerated master's degree programs in nursing also are available. These programs combine 1 year of an accelerated BSN program with 2 years of graduate study. In 2004, there were 137 RN-to-MSN programs.

Accelerated BSN programs also are available for individuals who have a bachelor's or higher degree in another field and who are interested in moving into nursing. In 2004, more than 165 of these programs were available. Accelerated BSN programs last 12 to 18 months and provide the fastest route to a BSN for individuals who already hold a degree.

Individuals considering nursing should carefully weigh the advantages and disadvantages of enrolling in a BSN program, because if they do, their advancement opportunities usually are broader. In fact, some career paths are open only to nurses with a bachelor's or master's degree. A bachelor's degree often is necessary for administrative positions and is a prerequisite for admission to graduate nursing programs in research, consulting, and teaching and all four advanced practice nursing specialties—clinical nurse specialists, nurse anesthetists, nurse-midwives, and nurse practitioners. Individuals who complete a bachelor's receive more training in areas such as communication, leadership, and critical thinking, all of which are becoming more important as nursing care becomes more complex. Additionally, bachelor's degree programs offer more clinical experience in nonhospital settings. In 2004, 417 nursing schools offered master's degrees, 93 offered doctoral degrees, and 46 offered accelerated BSN-to-doctoral programs.

All four advanced practice nursing specialties require at least a master's degree. Most programs last about 2 years and require a BSN degree, and some programs require at least 1 to 2 years of clinical experience as an RN for admission. In 2004, there were 329 master's and post-master's programs offered for nurse practitioners, 218 master's and post-master's programs for clinical nurse specialists, 92 programs for nurse anesthetists, and 45 programs for nurse-midwives. Upon completion of a program, most advanced practice nurses become nationally certified in their area of specialty. In some states, certification in a specialty is required in order to practice that specialty.

All nursing education programs include classroom instruction and supervised clinical experience in hospitals and other health care facilities. Students take courses in anatomy, physiology, microbiology, chemistry, nutrition, psychology and other behavioral sciences, and nursing. Coursework also includes the liberal arts for ADN and BSN students.

Supervised clinical experience is provided in hospital departments such as pediatrics, psychiatry, maternity, and surgery. A growing number of programs include clinical experience in nursing care facilities, public health departments, home health agencies, and ambulatory clinics.

Nurses should be caring, sympathetic, responsible, and detail oriented. They must be able to direct or supervise others, correctly assess patients' conditions, and determine when consultation is required. They need emotional stability to cope with human suffering, emergencies, and other stresses.

Some RNs start their careers as licensed practical nurses or nursing aides and then go back to school to receive their RN degree. Most RNs begin as staff nurses, and with experience and good performance often are promoted to more responsible positions. In management, nurses can advance to assistant head nurse or head nurse and, from there, to assistant director, director, and vice president. Increasingly, management-level nursing positions require a graduate or an advanced degree in nursing or health services administration. They also require leadership, negotiation skills, and good judgment.

Some nurses move into the business side of health care. Their nursing expertise and experience on a health care team equip them to manage ambulatory, acute, home-based, and chronic care. Employers—including hospitals, insurance companies, pharmaceutical manufacturers, and managed care organizations, among others—need RNs for health planning and development, marketing, consulting, policy development, and quality assurance. Other nurses work as college and university faculty or conduct research.

Foreign-educated nurses wishing to work in the United States must obtain a work visa. Applicants are required to undergo a review of their education and licensing credentials and pass a nursing certification and English proficiency exam, both conducted by the Commission on Graduates of Foreign Nursing Schools. (The commission is an immigration-neutral, nonprofit organization that is recognized internationally as an authority on credentials evaluation in the health care field.) Applicants from Australia, Canada (except Quebec), Ireland, New Zealand, and the United Kingdom are exempt from the language proficiency exam. In addition to these national requirements, most states have their own requirements.

Employment

As the largest health care occupation, registered nurses held about 2.4 million jobs in 2004. About 3 out of 5 jobs were in hospitals, in inpatient and outpatient departments. Others worked in offices of physicians, nursing care facilities, home health care services, employment services, government agencies, and outpatient care centers. The remainder worked mostly in social assistance agencies and educational services, public and private. About 1 in 4 RNs worked part time.

Job Outlook

Job opportunities for RNs in all specialties are expected to be excellent. Employment of registered nurses is expected to grow much faster than average for all occupations through 2014, and, because the occupation is very large, many new jobs will result. In fact, registered nurses are projected to create the second-largest number of new jobs among all occupations. Thousands of job openings also will result from the need to replace experienced nurses who leave the occupation, especially as the median age of the registered nurse population continues to rise.

Much-faster-than-average growth will be driven by technological advances in patient care, which permit a greater number of medical problems to be treated, and by an increasing emphasis on preventive care. In addition, the number of older people, who are much more likely than younger people to need nursing care, is projected to grow rapidly.

Employers in some parts of the country and in certain employment settings are reporting difficulty in attracting and retaining an adequate number of RNs, primarily because of an aging RN workforce and a lack of younger workers to fill positions. Enrollments in nursing programs at all levels have increased more rapidly in the past couple of years as students seek jobs with stable employment. However, many qualified applicants are being turned away because of a shortage of nursing faculty to teach classes. The need for nursing faculty will only increase as a large number of instructors nears retirement. Many employers also are relying on foreign-educated nurses to fill open positions.

Even though employment opportunities for all nursing specialties are expected to be excellent, they can vary by employment setting. For example, employment is expected to grow more slowly in hospitals—which comprise health care's largest industry—than in most other health care industries. While the intensity of nursing care is likely to increase, requiring more nurses per patient, the number of inpatients (those who remain in the hospital for more than 24 hours) is not likely to grow by much. Patients are being discharged earlier, and more procedures are being done on an outpatient basis, both inside and outside hospitals. Rapid growth is expected in hospital outpatient facilities, such as those providing same-day surgery, rehabilitation, and chemotherapy.

Despite the slower employment growth in hospitals, job opportunities should still be excellent because of the relatively high turnover of hospital nurses. RNs working in hospitals frequently work overtime and night and weekend shifts and also treat seriously ill and injured patients, all of which can contribute to stress and burnout. Hospital departments in which these working conditions occur most frequently—critical care units, emergency departments, and operating rooms—generally will have more job openings than other departments.

To attract and retain qualified nurses, hospitals may offer signing bonuses, family-friendly work schedules, or subsidized training. A growing number of hospitals also are experimenting with online bidding to fill open shifts, in which nurses can volunteer to fill open shifts at premium wages. This can decrease the amount of mandatory overtime that nurses are required to work.

More and more sophisticated procedures, once performed only in hospitals, are being performed in physicians' offices and in outpatient care centers, such as freestanding ambulatory surgical and emergency centers. Accordingly, employment is expected to grow much faster than average in these places as health care in general expands. However, RNs may face greater competition for these positions because they generally offer regular working hours and more comfortable working environments.

Employment in nursing care facilities is expected to grow faster than average because of increases in the number of elderly, many of whom require long-term care. In addition, the financial pressure on hospitals to discharge patients as soon as possible should produce more admissions to nursing care facilities. Job growth also is expected in units that provide specialized long-term rehabilitation for stroke and head injury patients, as well as units that treat Alzheimer's victims.

Employment in home health care is expected to increase rapidly in response to the growing number of older persons with functional disabilities, consumer preference for care in the home, and technological advances that make it possible to bring increasingly complex treatments into the home. The type of care demanded will require nurses who are able to perform complex procedures.

Generally, RNs with at least a bachelor's degree will have better job prospects than those without a bachelor's. In addition, all four advanced practice specialties—clinical nurse specialists, nurse practitioners, midwives, and anesthetists—will be in high demand, particularly in medically underserved areas such as inner cities and rural areas. Relative to physicians, these RNs increasingly serve as lower-cost primary care providers.

Earnings

Median annual earnings of registered nurses were $52,330 in May 2004. The middle 50 percent earned between $43,370 and $63,360. The lowest 10 percent earned less than $37,300, and the highest 10 percent earned more than $74,760. Median annual earnings in the industries employing the largest numbers of registered nurses in May 2004 were as follows:

Employment services	$63,170
General medical and surgical hospitals	53,450
Home health care services	48,990
Offices of physicians	48,250
Nursing care facilities	48,220

Many employers offer flexible work schedules, child care, educational benefits, and bonuses.

Related Occupations

Workers in other health care occupations with responsibilities and duties related to those of registered nurses are cardiovascular technologists and technicians; diagnostic medical sonographers; dietitians and nutritionists; emergency medical technicians and paramedics; licensed practical and licensed vocational nurses; massage therapists; medical and health services managers; nursing, psychiatric, and home health aides; occupational therapists; physical therapists; physician assistants; physicians and surgeons; radiologic technologists and technicians; respiratory therapists; and surgical technologists.

Sources of Additional Information

For information on a career as a registered nurse and nursing education, contact

▸ National League for Nursing, 61 Broadway, New York, NY 10006. Internet: http://www.nln.org

For information on nursing career options; financial aid; and listings of BSN, graduate, and accelerated nursing programs, contact

▸ American Association of Colleges of Nursing, 1 Dupont Circle NW, Suite 530, Washington, DC 20036. Internet: http://www.aacn.nche.edu

For additional information on registered nurses, including credentialing, contact

▸ American Nurses Association, 8515 Georgia Ave., Suite 400, Silver Spring, MD 20910. Internet: http://nursingworld.org

For information on the NCLEX-RN exam and a list of individual states' boards of nursing, contact

▸ National Council of State Boards of Nursing, 111 E. Wacker Dr., Suite 2900, Chicago, IL 60611. Internet: http://www.ncsbn.org

For information on obtaining U.S. certification and work visas for foreign-educated nurses, contact

▸ Commission on Graduates of Foreign Nursing Schools, 3600 Market St., Suite 400, Philadelphia, PA 19104. Internet: http://www.cgfns.org

For a list of accredited clinical nurse specialist programs, contact

▸ National Association of Clinical Nurse Specialists, 2090 Linglestown Rd., Suite 107, Harrisburg, PA 17110. Internet: http://www.nacns.org/cnsdirectory.shtml

For information on nurse anesthetists, including a list of accredited programs, contact

▸ American Association of Nurse Anesthetists, 222 Prospect Ave., Park Ridge, IL 60068.

For information on nurse-midwives, including a list of accredited programs, contact

▸ American College of Nurse-Midwives, 8403 Colesville Rd., Suite 1550, Silver Spring, MD 20910. Internet: http://www.midwife.org

For information on nurse practitioners, including a list of accredited programs, contact

▸ American Academy of Nurse Practitioners, P.O. Box 12846, Austin, TX 78711. Internet: http://www.aanp.org

Respiratory Therapists

(O*NET 29-1126.00 and 29-2054.00)

Significant Points

- Job opportunities will be very good, especially for therapists with cardiopulmonary care skills or experience working with infants.

- All states (except Alaska and Hawaii), the District of Columbia, and Puerto Rico require respiratory therapists to obtain a license.

- Hospitals will continue to employ the vast majority of respiratory therapists, but a growing number of therapists will work in other settings.

Nature of the Work

Respiratory therapists and *respiratory therapy technicians*—also known as *respiratory care practitioners*—evaluate, treat, and care for patients with breathing or other cardiopulmonary disorders. Practicing under the direction of a physician, respiratory therapists assume primary responsibility for all respiratory care therapeutic treatments and diagnostic procedures, including the supervision of respiratory therapy technicians. Respiratory therapy technicians follow specific, well-defined respiratory care procedures under the direction of respiratory therapists and physicians. In clinical practice, many of the daily duties of therapists and technicians overlap; furthermore, the two have the same education and training requirements. However, therapists generally have greater responsibility than technicians. For example, respiratory therapists will consult with physicians and other health care staff to help develop and modify individual patient care plans. Respiratory therapists also are more likely to provide complex therapy requiring considerable independent judgment, such as caring for patients on life support in intensive-care units of hospitals. In this description, the term *respiratory therapists* includes both respiratory therapists and respiratory therapy technicians.

Respiratory therapists evaluate and treat all types of patients, ranging from premature infants whose lungs are not fully developed to elderly people whose lungs are diseased. Respiratory therapists provide temporary relief to patients with chronic asthma or emphysema, as well as emergency care to patients who are victims of a heart attack, stroke, drowning, or shock.

To evaluate patients, respiratory therapists interview them, perform limited physical examinations, and conduct diagnostic tests. For example, respiratory therapists test patients' breathing capacity and determine the concentration of oxygen and other gases in patients' blood. They also measure patients' pH, which indicates the acidity or alkalinity of the blood. To evaluate a patient's lung capacity, respiratory therapists have the patient breathe into an instrument that measures the volume and flow of oxygen during inhalation and exhalation. By comparing the reading with the norm for the patient's age, height, weight, and sex, respiratory therapists can provide information that helps determine whether the patient has any lung deficiencies. To analyze oxygen, carbon dioxide, and pH levels, therapists draw an arterial blood sample, place it in a blood gas analyzer, and relay the results to a physician, who then may make treatment decisions.

To treat patients, respiratory therapists use oxygen or oxygen mixtures, chest physiotherapy, and aerosol medications. When a patient has difficulty getting enough oxygen into his or her blood, therapists increase the patient's concentration of oxygen by placing an oxygen mask or nasal cannula on the patient and set the oxygen flow at the level prescribed by a physician. Therapists also connect patients who cannot breathe on their own to ventilators that deliver pressurized oxygen into the lungs. The therapists insert a tube into the patient's trachea, or windpipe; connect the tube to the ventilator; and set the rate, volume, and oxygen concentration of the oxygen mixture entering the patient's lungs.

Therapists perform regular assessments of patients and equipment. If the patient appears to be having difficulty breathing or if the oxygen, carbon dioxide, or pH level of the blood is abnormal, therapists change the ventilator setting according to the doctor's orders or check the equipment for mechanical problems. In home care, therapists teach patients and their families to use ventilators and other life-support systems. In addition, therapists visit patients several times a month to inspect and clean equipment and to ensure its proper use. Therapists also make emergency visits if equipment problems arise.

Respiratory therapists perform chest physiotherapy on patients to remove mucus from their lungs and make it easier for them to breathe. For example, during surgery, anesthesia depresses respiration, so chest physiotherapy may be prescribed to help get the patient's lungs back to normal and to prevent congestion. Chest physiotherapy also helps patients suffering from lung diseases, such as cystic fibrosis, that cause mucus to collect in the lungs. Therapists place patients in positions that help drain mucus and then vibrate the patients' rib cages and instruct the patients to cough.

Respiratory therapists also administer aerosols—liquid medications suspended in a gas that forms a mist which is inhaled—and teach patients how to inhale the aerosol properly to ensure its effectiveness.

In some hospitals, therapists perform tasks that fall outside their traditional role. Therapists' tasks are expanding into areas such as pulmonary rehabilitation, smoking cessation counseling, disease prevention, case management, and polysomnography—the diagnosis of breathing disorders during sleep, such as apnea. Respiratory therapists also increasingly treat critical care patients, either as part of surface and air transport teams or as part of rapid-response teams in hospitals.

Working Conditions

Respiratory therapists generally work between 35 and 40 hours a week. Because hospitals operate around the clock, therapists may work evenings, nights, or weekends. They spend long periods standing and walking between patients' rooms. In an emergency, therapists work under a great deal of stress. Respiratory therapists employed in home health care must travel frequently to the homes of patients.

Respiratory therapists are trained to work with hazardous gases stored under pressure. Adherence to safety precautions and regular maintenance and testing of equipment minimize the risk of injury. As in many other health occupations, respiratory therapists run the risk of catching an infectious disease, but carefully following proper procedures minimizes this risk.

Training, Other Qualifications, and Advancement

Formal training is necessary for entry into this field. Training is offered at the postsecondary level by colleges and universities, medical schools, vocational-technical institutes, and the Armed Forces. An associate's degree is required for entry into the field. Most programs award associate's or bachelor's degrees and prepare graduates for jobs as advanced respiratory therapists. A limited number of associate's degree programs lead to jobs as entry-level respiratory therapists. According to the Commission on Accreditation of Allied Health Education Programs (CAAHEP), 51 entry-level and 329 advanced respiratory therapy programs were accredited in the United States, including Puerto Rico, in 2005.

Among the areas of study in respiratory therapy are human anatomy and physiology, pathophysiology, chemistry, physics, microbiology, pharmacology, and mathematics. Other courses deal with therapeutic and diagnostic procedures and tests, equipment, patient assessment, cardiopulmonary resuscitation, the application of clinical practice guidelines, patient care outside of hospitals, cardiac and pulmonary rehabilitation, respiratory health promotion and disease prevention, and medical recordkeeping and reimbursement.

The National Board for Respiratory Care (NBRC) offers certification and registration to graduates of programs accredited by CAA-HEP or the Committee on Accreditation for Respiratory Care (CoARC). Two credentials are awarded to respiratory therapists who satisfy the requirements: Registered Respiratory Therapist (RRT) and Certified Respiratory Therapist (CRT). Graduates from accredited entry-level or advanced-level programs in respiratory therapy may take the CRT examination. CRTs who were graduated from advanced-level programs and who meet additional experience requirements can take two separate examinations leading to the award of the RRT credential.

All states (except Alaska and Hawaii), the District of Columbia, and Puerto Rico require respiratory therapists to obtain a license. Passing the CRT exam qualifies respiratory therapists for state licenses. Also, most employers require respiratory therapists to maintain a cardiopulmonary resuscitation (CPR) certification. Supervisory positions and intensive-care specialties usually require the RRT or at least RRT eligibility.

Therapists should be sensitive to patients' physical and psychological needs. Respiratory care practitioners must pay attention to detail, follow instructions, and work as part of a team. In addition, operating advanced equipment requires proficiency with computers.

High school students interested in a career in respiratory care should take courses in health, biology, mathematics, chemistry, and physics. Respiratory care involves basic mathematical problem solving and an understanding of chemical and physical principles. For example, respiratory care workers must be able to compute dosages of medication and calculate gas concentrations.

Respiratory therapists advance in clinical practice by moving from general care to the care of critically ill patients who have significant problems in other organ systems, such as the heart or kidneys. Respiratory therapists, especially those with bachelor's or master's degrees, also may advance to supervisory or managerial positions in a respiratory therapy department. Respiratory therapists in home health care and equipment rental firms may become branch managers. Some respiratory therapists advance by moving into teaching positions.

Employment

Respiratory therapists held about 118,000 jobs in 2004. More than 4 out of 5 jobs were in hospital departments of respiratory care, anesthesiology, or pulmonary medicine. Most of the remaining jobs were in offices of physicians or other health practitioners, consumer-goods rental firms that supply respiratory equipment for home use, nursing care facilities, and home health care services. Holding a second job is relatively common for respiratory therapists. About 13 percent held another job, compared with 5 percent of workers in all occupations.

Job Outlook

Job opportunities are expected to be very good, especially for respiratory therapists with cardiopulmonary care skills or experience working with infants. Employment of respiratory therapists is expected to increase faster than average for all occupations through the year 2014 because of substantial growth in the numbers of the middle-aged and elderly population—a development that will heighten the incidence of cardiopulmonary disease—and because of the expanding role of respiratory therapists in the early detection of pulmonary disorders, case management, disease prevention, and emergency care.

Older Americans suffer most from respiratory ailments and cardiopulmonary diseases such as pneumonia, chronic bronchitis, emphysema, and heart disease. As their numbers increase, the need for respiratory therapists will increase as well. In addition, advances in inhalable medications and in the treatment of lung transplant patients, heart attack and accident victims, and premature infants (many of whom are dependent on a ventilator during part of their treatment) will increase the demand for the services of respiratory care practitioners.

Although hospitals will continue to employ the vast majority of therapists, a growing number can expect to work outside of hospitals in home health care services, offices of physicians or other health practitioners, or consumer-goods rental firms.

Earnings

Median annual earnings of respiratory therapists were $43,140 in May 2004. The middle 50 percent earned between $37,650 and $50,860. The lowest 10 percent earned less than $32,220, and the highest 10 percent earned more than $57,580. In general medical and surgical hospitals, median annual earnings of respiratory therapists were $43,140 in May 2004.

Median annual earnings of respiratory therapy technicians were $36,740 in May 2004. The middle 50 percent earned between $30,490 and $43,830. The lowest 10 percent earned less than $24,640, and the highest 10 percent earned more than $52,280. Median annual earnings of respiratory therapy technicians employed in general medical and surgical hospitals were $36,990 in May 2004.

Related Occupations

Under the supervision of a physician, respiratory therapists administer respiratory care and life support to patients with heart and lung difficulties. Other workers who care for, treat, or train people to improve their physical condition include registered nurses, occupational therapists, physical therapists, and radiation therapists.

Sources of Additional Information

Information concerning a career in respiratory care is available from

▸ American Association for Respiratory Care, 9425 N. MacArthur Blvd., Suite 100, Irving, TX 75063-4706. Internet: http://www.aarc.org

For a list of accredited educational programs for respiratory care practitioners, contact either of the following organizations:

▸ Commission on Accreditation for Allied Health Education Programs, 35 East Wacker Dr., Suite 1970., Chicago, IL 60601. Internet: http://www.caahep.org

Information on gaining credentials in respiratory care and a list of state licensing agencies can be obtained from

▶ National Board for Respiratory Care, Inc., 8310 Nieman Rd., Lenexa, KS 66214-1579. Internet: http://www.nbrc.org

Sales Engineers

(O*NET 41-9031.00)

Significant Points

■ A bachelor's degree in engineering typically is required; many sales engineers have previous work experience in an engineering specialty.

■ Projected employment growth stems from the increasing number and technical nature of products and services to be sold.

■ More job opportunities are expected in independent sales agencies.

■ Earnings are based on a combination of salary and commissions.

Nature of the Work

Many products and services, especially those purchased by large companies and institutions, are highly complex. Sales engineers—who also may be called *manufacturers' agents, sales representatives,* or *technical sales support workers*—work with the production, engineering, or research and development departments of their companies or with independent sales firms to determine how products and services could be designed or modified to suit customers' needs. They also may advise customers on how best to use the products or services provided.

Selling, of course, is an important part of the job. Sales engineers use their technical skills to demonstrate to potential customers how and why the products or services they are selling would suit the customer better than competitors' products. Often, there may not be a directly competitive product. In these cases, the job of the sales engineer is to demonstrate to the customer the usefulness of the product or service—for example, how much money new production machinery would save.

Most sales engineers have a bachelor's degree in engineering, and many have previous work experience in an engineering specialty. Engineers apply the theories and principles of science and mathematics to technical problems. Their work is the link between scientific discoveries and commercial applications. Many sales engineers specialize in an area related to an engineering specialty. For example, sales engineers selling chemical products may have chemical engineering backgrounds, while those selling business software or information systems may have degrees in computer engineering. Information on engineers, including 17 engineering specialties, appears elsewhere in this book.

Many of the duties of sales engineers are similar to those of other salespersons. They must interest the client in purchasing their products, many of which are durable manufactured products such as turbines. Sales engineers often are teamed with other salespersons who concentrate on the marketing and sales, enabling the sales engineer to concentrate on the technical aspects of the job. By working on a sales team, each member is able to focus on his or her strengths and knowledge.

Sales engineers tend to employ selling techniques that are different from those used by most other sales workers. They generally use a "consultative" style; that is, they focus on the client's problem and show how it could be solved or mitigated with their product or service. This selling style differs from the "benefits and features" method, whereby the salesperson describes the product and leaves the customer to decide how it would be useful.

In addition to maintaining current clients and attracting new ones, sales engineers help clients solve any problems that arise when the product is installed. Afterward, they may continue to serve as a liaison between the client and their company. Increasingly, sales engineers are asked to undertake tasks related to sales, such as market research, because of their familiarity with clients' purchasing needs. Drawing on this same familiarity, sales engineers may help identify and develop new products.

Sales engineers may work directly for manufacturers or service providers, or they may work in small independent sales firms. In an independent firm, they may sell complementary products from several different suppliers and be paid entirely on commission.

Working Conditions

Many sales engineers work more than 40 hours per week to meet sales goals and their clients' needs. Selling can be stressful because sales engineers' income and job security often directly depend on their success in sales and customer service.

Some sales engineers have large territories and travel extensively. Because sales regions may cover several states, sales engineers may be away from home for several days or even weeks at a time. Others work near their home base and travel mostly by car. International travel, to secure contracts with foreign clients, is becoming more common.

Although the hours may be long and often are irregular, many sales engineers have the freedom to determine their own schedule. Consequently, they often can arrange their appointments so that they can have time off when they want it. However, most independent sales engineers do not earn any income while on vacation.

Training, Other Qualifications, and Advancement

A bachelor's degree in engineering usually is required to become a sales engineer. However, some workers with previous experience in sales combined with technical experience or training sometimes hold the title of sales engineer. Also, workers who have a degree in a science, such as chemistry, or even a degree in business with little or no previous sales experience, may be termed sales engineers.

Admissions requirements for undergraduate engineering schools include a solid background in mathematics (algebra, geometry, trigonometry, and calculus) and the physical sciences (biology, chemistry, and physics), as well as basic courses in English, social studies, humanities, and computer science. University programs vary in content, though all require the development of computer skills. For example, some programs emphasize industrial practices, preparing students for a job in industry, whereas others are more theoretical and prepare students for graduate school. Therefore, students should investigate curriculums and check accreditations carefully before making a selection. Once a university has been selected, a student must choose an area of engineering in which to specialize. Some programs offer a general engineering curriculum; students then specialize on the job or in graduate school. Most engineering degrees are granted in electrical, mechanical, or civil engineering. However, engineers trained in one branch may work in related branches.

Many sales engineers first work as engineers. For some, the engineering experience is necessary to obtain the technical background needed to sell their employers' products or services effectively. Others move into the occupation because it offers better earnings and advancement potential or because they are looking for a new challenge.

New graduates with engineering degrees may need sales experience and training before they can work directly as sales engineers. Training may involve teaming with a sales mentor who is familiar with the employer's business practices, customers, procedures, and company culture. After the training period has been completed, sales engineers may continue to partner with someone who lacks technical skills, yet excels in the art of sales.

Promotion may include a higher commission rate, larger sales territory, or elevation to the position of supervisor or marketing manager. Alternatively, sales engineers may leave their companies and form independent firms that may offer higher commissions and more freedom. Independent firms tend to be small, although relatively few sales engineers are self-employed.

It is important for sales engineers to continue their engineering and sales education throughout their careers because much of their value to their employers depends on their knowledge of the latest technology and their ability to sell that technology. Sales engineers in high-technology areas, such as information technology or advanced electronics, may find that technical knowledge rapidly becomes obsolete.

Employment

Sales engineers held about 74,000 jobs in 2004. About 35 percent were employed in wholesale trade and another 27 percent were employed in the manufacturing industries. Smaller numbers of sales engineers worked in information industries, such as software publishers and telecommunications; professional, scientific, and technical services, such as computer systems designs and related services and architectural, engineering, and related services; and other industries. Unlike workers in many other sales occupations, very few sales engineers are self-employed.

Job Outlook

Employment of sales engineers is expected to grow about as fast as the average for all occupations through the year 2014. Projected employment growth stems from the increasing variety and technical nature of goods and services to be sold. Competitive pressures and advancing technology will force companies to improve and update

product designs more frequently and to optimize their manufacturing and sales processes. In addition to new positions created as companies expand their sales forces, some openings will arise each year from the need to replace sales engineers who transfer to other occupations or leave the labor force.

Manufacturers, especially foreign manufacturers that sell their products in the United States, are expected to continue outsourcing more of their sales functions to independent sales agencies in an attempt to control costs. This should result in more job opportunities for sales engineers in independent agencies.

In wholesale trade, both outsourcing to independent sales agencies and the use of information technology are expected to affect employment opportunities for sales engineers. Although outsourcing should lead to more jobs in independent agencies, employment growth for sales engineers in wholesale trade likely will be dampened by the increasing ability of businesses to find, order, and track shipments directly from wholesalers through the Internet without assistance from sales engineers. Since direct purchases from wholesalers are more likely to be of commodity products, their impact on sales engineers should remain somewhat limited.

Employment opportunities and earnings may fluctuate from year to year because sales are affected by changing economic conditions, legislative issues, and consumer preferences. Prospects will be best for those with the appropriate knowledge or technical expertise, as well as the personal traits necessary for successful sales work.

Earnings

Compensation varies significantly by the type of firm and the product sold. Most employers offer a combination of salary and commission payments or a salary plus a bonus. Commissions usually are based on the amount of sales, whereas bonuses may depend on individual performance, on the performance of all workers in the group or district, or on the company's performance. Earnings from commissions and bonuses may vary greatly from year to year, depending on sales ability, the demand for the company's products or services, and the overall economy.

Median annual earnings of sales engineers, including commissions, were $70,620 in May 2004. The middle 50 percent earned between $53,270 and $91,500 a year. The lowest 10 percent earned less than $41,430, and the highest 10 percent earned more than $117,260 a year. Median annual earnings of those employed by firms in the computer systems design and related services industry were $86,980.

In addition to their earnings, sales engineers who work for manufacturers usually are reimbursed for expenses such as transportation, meals, hotels, and customer entertainment. In addition to typical benefits, sales engineers often get personal use of a company car and frequent-flyer mileage. Some companies offer incentives such as free vacation trips or gifts for outstanding performance. Sales engineers who work in independent firms may have higher but less stable earnings and, often, relatively few benefits.

Related Occupations

Sales engineers must have sales ability and knowledge of the products and services they sell, as well as technical and analytical skills.

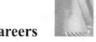
Other occupations that require similar skills include advertising, marketing, promotions, public relations, and sales managers; engineers; insurance sales agents; purchasing managers, buyers, and purchasing agents; real estate brokers and sales agents; sales representatives, wholesale and manufacturing; and securities, commodities, and financial services sales agents.

Sources of Additional Information

Information on careers for manufacturers' representatives and agents is available from

- ▶ Manufacturers' Agents National Association, P.O. Box 3467, Laguna Hills, CA 92654-3467. Internet: http://www.manaonline.org
- ▶ Manufacturers' Representatives Educational Research Foundation, P.O. Box 247, Geneva, IL 60134. Internet: http://www.mrerf.org

Science Technicians

(O*NET 19-4011.01, 19-4011.02, 19-4021.00, 19-4031.00, 19-4041.01, 19-4041.02, 19-4051.01, 19-4051.02, 19-4091.00, 19-4092.00, and 19-4093.00)

Significant Points

- ■ Science technicians in production jobs can be employed on day, evening, or night shifts; some other technicians work outdoors, sometimes in remote locations.

- ■ Many employers prefer applicants who have at least 2 years of specialized training or an associate's degree.

- ■ Projected job growth varies among occupational specialties; for example, forensic science technicians will grow much faster than average, while chemical technicians will grow more slowly than average.

- ■ Job opportunities are expected to be best for graduates of applied science technology programs.

Nature of the Work

Science technicians use the principles and theories of science and mathematics to solve problems in research and development and to help invent and improve products and processes. However, their jobs are more practically oriented than those of scientists. Technicians set up, operate, and maintain laboratory instruments; monitor experiments; make observations; calculate and record results; and often develop conclusions. They must keep detailed logs of all of their work-related activities. Those who perform production work monitor manufacturing processes and may be involved in ensuring quality by testing products for proper proportions of ingredients, for purity, or for strength and durability.

As laboratory instrumentation and procedures have become more complex, the role of science technicians in research and development has expanded. In addition to performing routine tasks, many technicians now develop and adapt laboratory procedures to achieve the best results, interpret data, and devise solutions to problems under the direction of scientists. Moreover, technicians must master the laboratory equipment so that they can adjust settings when necessary and recognize when equipment is malfunctioning.

The increasing use of robotics to perform many routine tasks has freed technicians to operate more sophisticated laboratory equipment. Science technicians make extensive use of computers, computer-interfaced equipment, robotics, and high-technology industrial applications such as biological engineering.

Most science technicians specialize, learning skills and working in the same disciplines in which scientists work. Occupational titles, therefore, tend to follow the same structure as those for scientists. *Agricultural technicians* work with agricultural scientists in food, fiber, and animal research, production, and processing. Some conduct tests and experiments to improve the yield and quality of crops or to increase the resistance of plants and animals to disease, insects, or other hazards. Other agricultural technicians breed animals for the purpose of investigating nutrition. *Food science technicians* assist food scientists and technologists in research and development, production technology, and quality control. For example, food science technicians may conduct tests on food additives and preservatives to ensure compliance with Food and Drug Administration regulations regarding color, texture, and nutrients. These technicians analyze, record, and compile test results; order supplies to maintain laboratory inventory; and clean and sterilize laboratory equipment.

Biological technicians work with biologists studying living organisms. Many assist scientists who conduct medical research—helping to find a cure for cancer or AIDS, for example. Those who work in pharmaceutical companies help develop and manufacture medicinal and pharmaceutical preparations. Those working in the field of microbiology generally work as laboratory assistants, studying living organisms and infectious agents. Biological technicians also analyze organic substances, such as blood, food, and drugs, and some examine evidence in a forensic science laboratory. Biological technicians working in biotechnology laboratories use the knowledge and techniques gained from basic research by scientists, including gene splicing and recombinant DNA, and apply them in product development.

Chemical technicians work with chemists and chemical engineers, developing and using chemicals and related products and equipment. Generally, there are two types of chemical technicians: research and development technicians, who work in experimental laboratories, and process control technicians, who work in manufacturing or other industrial plants. Many research and development chemical technicians conduct a variety of laboratory procedures, from routine process control to complex research projects. For example, they may collect and analyze samples of air and water to monitor pollution levels, or they may produce compounds through complex organic synthesis. Most process technicians work in manufacturing, testing packaging for design, integrity of materials, and environmental acceptability. Often, process technicians who work in plants also focus on quality assurance, monitoring product quality or production processes and developing new production techniques. A few work in shipping to provide technical support and expertise for these functions.

Environmental science and protection technicians perform laboratory and field tests to monitor environmental resources and determine the contaminants and sources of pollution in the environm[ent.] They may collect samples for testing or be involved in abatin[g,] [con]trolling, or remediating sources of environmental polluti[on.] are responsible for waste management operations, cont[rol,] agement of hazardous materials inventory, or general activities involving regulatory compliance. Many environmental science technicians employed at private consulting firms work directly under the supervision of an environmental scientist.

Forensic science technicians investigate crimes by collecting and analyzing physical evidence. Often, they specialize in areas such as DNA analysis or firearm examination, performing tests on weapons or on substances such as fiber, glass, hair, tissue, and body fluids to determine their significance to the investigation. Proper collection and storage methods are important to protect the evidence. Forensic science technicians also prepare reports to document their findings and the laboratory techniques used, and they may provide information and expert opinion to investigators. When criminal cases come to trial, forensic science technicians often give testimony, as expert witnesses, on specific laboratory findings by identifying and classifying substances, materials, and other evidence collected at the scene of a crime. Some forensic science technicians work closely with other experts or technicians. For example, a forensic science technician may consult either a medical expert about the exact time and cause of a death or a technician who specializes in DNA typing in hopes of matching a DNA type to a suspect.

Forest and conservation technicians compile data on the size, content, and condition of forest land tracts. These workers usually work in a forest under the supervision of a forester, conducting specific tasks such as measuring timber, supervising harvesting operations, assisting in roadbuilding operations, and locating property lines and features. They also may gather basic information, such as data on species and populations of trees, disease and insect damage, tree seedling mortality, and conditions that may pose a fire hazard. In addition, forest and conservation technicians train and lead forest and conservation workers in seasonal activities, such as planting tree seedlings, putting out forest fires, and maintaining recreational facilities. Increasing numbers of forest and conservation technicians work in urban forestry—the study of individual trees in cities—and other nontraditional specialties, rather than in forests or rural areas.

Geological and petroleum technicians measure and record physical and geologic conditions in oil or gas wells, using advanced instruments lowered into the wells or analyzing the mud from the wells. In oil and gas exploration, these technicians collect and examine geological data or use scanning electron microscopes to test geological samples to determine their petroleum content and their mineral and element composition. Some petroleum technicians, called *scouts*, collect information about oil and gas well-drilling operations, geological and geophysical prospecting, and land or lease contracts.

Nuclear technicians operate nuclear test and research equipment, monitor radiation, and assist nuclear engineers and physicists in research. Some also operate remote control equipment to manipulate radioactive materials or materials to be exposed to radioactivity.

Other science technicians collect weather information or assist oceanographers.

Working Conditions

Science technicians work under a wide variety of conditions. Most work indoors, usually in laboratories, and have regular hours. Some occasionally work irregular hours to monitor experiments that cannot be completed during regular working hours. Production technicians often work in 8-hour shifts around the clock. Others, such as agricultural, forest and conservation, geological and petroleum, and environmental science and protection technicians, perform much of their work outdoors, sometimes in remote locations.

Some science technicians may be exposed to hazards from equipment, chemicals, or toxic materials. Chemical technicians sometimes work with toxic chemicals or radioactive isotopes, nuclear technicians may be exposed to radiation, and biological technicians sometimes work with disease-causing organisms or radioactive agents. Forensic science technicians often are exposed to human body fluids and firearms. However, these working conditions pose little risk if proper safety procedures are followed. For forensic science technicians, collecting evidence from crime scenes can be distressing and unpleasant.

Training, Other Qualifications, and Advancement

There are several ways to qualify for a job as a science technician. Many employers prefer applicants who have at least 2 years of specialized training or an associate's degree in applied science or science-related technology. Because employers' preferences vary, however, some science technicians have a bachelor's degree in chemistry, biology, or forensic science or have taken several science and math courses at 4-year colleges.

Many technical and community colleges offer associate's degrees in a specific technology or a more general education in science and mathematics. A number of 2-year associate's degree programs are designed to provide easy transfer to a 4-year college or university. Technical institutes usually offer technician training, but provide less theory and general education than do technical or community colleges. The length of programs at technical institutes varies, although 1-year certificate programs and 2-year associate's degree programs are common.

Approximately 20 colleges or universities offer a bachelor's degree program in forensic science; about another 20 schools offer a bachelor-of-science degree in chemistry, biochemistry, or genetic engineering with an emphasis on forensic science or criminology; and a few additional schools offer a bachelor-of-science degree with an emphasis in a specialty area, such as criminology, pathology, jurisprudence, investigation, odontology, toxicology, or forensic accounting. In contrast to some other science technician positions that require only a 2-year degree, forensic science positions usually require a 4-year degree to work in the field. Knowledge and understanding of legal procedures also can be helpful. Prospective forestry and conservation technicians can choose from more than 20 associate's degree programs in forest technology accredited by the Society of American Foresters.

Most chemical process technicians have a 2-year degree, usually an associate's degree in process technology, although in some cases a high school diploma is sufficient. These workers usually receive additional on-the-job training. Entry-level workers whose college training encompasses extensive hands-on experience with a variety of diagnostic laboratory equipment generally require less on-the-job training. Those with a high school diploma typically begin work as trainees under the direct supervision of a more experienced process technician. Many with only a high school diploma eventually earn a 2-year degree in process technology, often paid for by their employer.

Some schools offer cooperative-education or internship programs, allowing students the opportunity to work at a local company or some other workplace while attending classes during alternate terms. Participation in such programs can significantly enhance a student's employment prospects.

Persons interested in careers as science technicians should take as many high school science and math courses as possible. Science courses taken beyond high school, in an associate's or bachelor's degree program, should be laboratory oriented, with an emphasis on bench skills. A solid background in applied basic chemistry, physics, and math is vital. Because computers often are used in research and development laboratories, technicians should have strong computer skills, especially in computer modeling. Communication skills also are important: Technicians often are required to report their findings both orally and in writing. In addition, technicians should be able to work well with others, because teamwork is common. Organizational ability, an eye for detail, and skill in interpreting scientific results are important as well. A high mechanical aptitude, attention to detail, and analytical thinking are all important characteristics of science technicians.

Prospective science technicians can acquire good career preparation through 2-year formal training programs that combine the teaching of scientific principles and theory with practical hands-on application in a laboratory setting with up-to-date equipment. Graduates of 4-year bachelor's degree programs in science who have considerable experience in laboratory-based courses, have completed internships, or have held summer jobs in laboratories also are well qualified for science technician positions and are preferred by some employers. However, those with a bachelor's degree who accept technician jobs generally cannot find employment that uses their more advanced academic education.

Technicians usually begin work as trainees in routine positions under the direct supervision of a scientist or a more experienced technician. Job candidates whose training or educational background encompasses extensive hands-on experience with a variety of laboratory equipment, including computers and related equipment, usually require a short period of on-the-job training. As they gain experience, technicians take on more responsibility and carry out assignments under only general supervision, and some eventually become supervisors. However, technicians employed at universities often have their fortunes tied to those of particular professors; when those professors retire or leave, these technicians face uncertain employment prospects.

Employment

Science technicians held about 324,000 jobs in 2004. As indicated by the following tabulation, chemical and biological technicians accounted for 39 percent of all jobs:

Biological technicians 64,000
Chemical technicians 62,000
Forest and conservation technicians.....................33,000
Environmental science and protection
   technicians, including health 31,000
Agricultural and food science technicians 23,000
Geological and petroleum technicians...................11,000
Forensic science technicians 9,800
Nuclear technicians 7,300

Chemical technicians held jobs in a wide range of manufacturing and service-providing industries. Thirty-five percent worked in chemical manufacturing and another 26 percent worked in professional, scientific, or technical services firms. About 27 percent of biological technicians also worked in professional, scientific, or technical services firms; most other biological technicians worked in pharmaceutical and medicine manufacturing or for federal, state, or local governments. Significant numbers of environmental science and protection technicians also worked for state and local governments and professional, scientific, and technical services firms. About 75 percent of forest and conservation technicians held jobs in the federal government; another 13 percent worked for state governments. Around 18 percent of agricultural and food science technicians worked for food-processing companies; most of the rest worked for scientific research and development services firms and state governments. Approximately 23 percent of all geological and petroleum technicians worked for oil and gas extraction companies, and forensic science technicians worked primarily for state and local governments.

Job Outlook

Job opportunities are expected to be best for graduates of applied science technology programs who are well trained on equipment used in industrial and government laboratories and production facilities. As the instrumentation and techniques used in industrial research, development, and production become increasingly more complex, employers are seeking individuals with highly developed technical and communication skills.

Overall employment of science technicians is expected to increase about as fast as the average for all occupations through the year 2014. The continued growth of scientific and medical research—particularly research related to biotechnology—as well as the development and production of technical products should stimulate demand for science technicians in many industries. The increase in the number of biological technicians will be about as fast as average, as the growing number of agricultural and medicinal products developed with the use of biotechnology techniques will boost demand for these workers. Also, stronger competition among pharmaceutical companies and an aging population are expected to contribute to the need for innovative and improved drugs, further spurring demand for biological technicians. The fastest employment growth of biological technicians should occur in the pharmaceutical and medicine manufacturing industry and educational services.

Job growth for chemical technicians is projected to be slower than average. The chemical manufacturing industry, the major employer of chemical technicians, is anticipated to experience a decline in overall employment as companies downsize and turn to outside contractors to provide specialized services. Job opportunities are expected to be more plentiful in pharmaceutical and medicine manufacturing as the public continues to demand newer and better pharmaceuticals. To meet this demand, pharmaceutical manufacturing firms are expected to continue to devote money to research and development, either through in-house teams or, increasingly, by contracting to professional, scientific, and technical services firms, spurring employment growth of chemical technicians in that industry. An increasing focus on quality assurance will require a greater number of process technicians, further stimulating demand for these workers.

Employment of environmental science and protection technicians should grow about as fast as the average; these workers will be needed to help regulate waste products; to collect air, water, and soil samples for measuring levels of pollutants; to monitor compliance with environmental regulations; and to clean up contaminated sites.

Limited demand for forest and conservation technicians within the federal government will lead to slower-than-average growth in this occupation, due to general downsizing and continued reductions in timber management on federal lands. Opportunities at state and local governments within specialties such as urban forestry and geographic information systems (GIS)—a locator system that uses satellites—may, however, provide some new jobs. In addition, an increased emphasis on specific conservation issues, such as environmental protection, preservation of water resources, and control of exotic and invasive pests, may provide some employment opportunities. Few opportunities will be available in the private sector.

Employment of agricultural and food science technicians is projected to grow about as fast as the average. Best opportunities will be in specific segments of the food-processing industry and in agricultural biotechnology, specifically in scientific research and development services. Research—particularly biotechnological research—will be necessary as it becomes increasingly important to balance greater agricultural output with protection and preservation of soil, water, and the ecosystem. In particular, research will be needed to combat insects and diseases as they further adapt to pesticides and as soil fertility and water quality continue to need improvement. State and local government also should provide many opportunities due to projected increases in employment and as the need to replace retiring workers is expected to accelerate.

Jobs for forensic science technicians are expected to increase much faster than average. Crime scene technicians who work for state public safety departments should experience favorable employment prospects. Jobseekers with a 4-year degree in a forensic science will enjoy much better opportunities than those with only a 2-year degree.

Slower-than-average employment growth is expected for geological and petroleum technicians because employment in the oil and gas extraction and mining industries, among the largest employers of geological and petroleum technicians, is expected to decline. Due to a lack of qualified candidates, however, prospective jobseekers should experience little competition for positions, especially in energy-related fields. Job opportunities also will be favorable in professional, scientific, and technical services firms because geological

and petroleum technicians will be needed to assist environmental scientists and geoscientists as they provide consultation services for companies regarding environmental policy and federal government mandates, such as those requiring lower sulfur emissions.

Along with opportunities created by growth, many job openings should arise from the need to replace technicians who retire or leave the labor force for other reasons. During periods of economic recession, science technicians may be laid off.

Earnings

Median hourly earnings of science technicians in May 2004 were as follows:

Nuclear technicians	$28.46
Forensic science technicians	21.16
Geological and petroleum technicians	19.35
Chemical technicians	18.35
Environmental science and protection technicians, including health	16.99
Biological technicians	15.97
Agricultural and food science technicians	14.29
Forest and conservation technicians	13.14

In 2005, the average annual salary in nonsupervisory, supervisory, and managerial positions in the federal government was $38,443 for biological science technicians, $50,264 for physical science technicians, $62,854 for geodetic technicians, $48,238 for hydrologic technicians, and $58,725 for meteorological technicians.

Related Occupations

Other technicians who apply scientific principles at a level usually acquired in 2-year associate's degree programs include engineering technicians, broadcast and sound engineering technicians and radio operators, drafters, and health technologists and technicians, especially clinical laboratory technologists and technicians, diagnostic medical sonographers, and radiologic technologists and technicians.

Sources of Additional Information

For information about a career as a chemical technician, contact

▸ American Chemical Society, Education Division, Career Publications, 1155 16th St. NW, Washington, DC 20036. Internet: http://www.acs.org

For career information and a list of undergraduate, graduate, and doctoral programs in forensic sciences, contact

▸ American Academy of Forensic Sciences, P.O. Box 669, Colorado Springs, CO, 80901. Internet: http://www.aafs.org

For general information on forestry technicians and a list of schools offering education in forestry, send a self-addressed, stamped business envelope to

▸ Society of American Foresters, 5400 Grosvenor Ln., Bethesda, MD 20814. Internet: http://www.safnet.org

Semiconductor Processors

(O*NET 51-9141.00)

Significant Points

■ Employment is expected to decline over the next 10 years because of increasing automation of fabrication plants in this country and the building of many of the new plants abroad.

■ An associate degree in a relevant curriculum is increasingly required.

Nature of the Work

Electronic semiconductors—also known as computer chips, microchips, or integrated circuits—are the miniature but powerful brains of high-technology equipment. Semiconductors are composed of a myriad of tiny aluminum or copper lines and electric switches, which manipulate the flow of electrical current. Semiconductor processors are responsible for many of the steps necessary in the manufacture of each semiconductor that goes into personal computers, missile guidance systems, and a host of other electronic equipment.

Semiconductor processors are the production workers who manufacture semiconductors in disks of varying sizes, generally eight to twelve inches wide. These disks, called wafers, are thin slices of silicon on which the circuitry of the microchips is layered. Each wafer is eventually cut into dozens or scores of individual chips.

Semiconductor processors make wafers by means of photolithography, a printing process for creating patterns from photographic images. Operating automated equipment, workers imprint precise microscopic patterns of the circuitry on the wafers, etch out the patterns with acids, and replace the patterns with metals that conduct electricity. Then, the wafers receive a chemical bath to make them smooth, and the imprint process begins again on a new layer with the next pattern. Wafers usually have from 8 to 20 such layers of microscopic, three-dimensional circuitry.

Semiconductors are produced in semiconductor-fabricating plants, or "fabs." Within fabs, the manufacturing and cutting of wafers to create semiconductors takes place in "cleanrooms"—production areas that must be kept free of any airborne matter, because even extremely small particles can damage a semiconductor. All semiconductor processors working in cleanrooms—both operators and technicians—must wear special lightweight outer garments known as "bunny suits." These garments fit over clothing to prevent lint and other particles from contaminating semiconductor-processing worksites.

Operators, who make up the majority of the workers in cleanrooms, start and monitor the sophisticated equipment that performs the various tasks during the many steps of the semiconductor production sequence. They spend a great deal of time at computer terminals, monitoring the operation of the equipment to ensure that each of the tasks in the production of the wafer is performed correctly. Operators also may transfer wafer carriers from one development station to the next; in newer fabs, the lifting of heavy wafer carriers and the constant monitoring for quality control are increasingly being automated.

Once begun, the production of semiconductor wafers is continuous. Operators work to the pace of the machinery that has largely automated the production process. Operators are responsible for keeping the automated machinery within proper operating parameters.

Technicians account for a smaller percentage of the workers in cleanrooms, but they troubleshoot production problems and make equipment adjustments and repairs. They also take the lead in assuring quality control and in maintaining equipment. To keep equipment repairs to a minimum, technicians perform diagnostic analyses and run computations. For example, technicians may determine if a flaw in a chip is due to contamination, and peculiar to that wafer, or if the flaw is inherent in the manufacturing process.

Working Conditions

The work pace in cleanrooms is deliberately slow. Limited movement keeps the air in cleanrooms as free as possible of dust and other particles, which can destroy semiconductors during their production. Because the machinery sets the operators' rate of work in the largely automated production process, workers maintain an easygoing pace. Although workers spend some time alone monitoring equipment, operators and technicians spend much of their time working in teams.

Technicians are on their feet most of the day, walking through the cleanroom to oversee production activities. Operators spend a great deal of time sitting or standing at workstations, monitoring computer readouts and gauges. Sometimes they must retrieve wafers from one station and take them to another.

The temperature in the cleanrooms must be kept within a narrow range: usually, it is set at a comfortable 72 degrees Fahrenheit. Although bunny suits cover virtually the entire body, except perhaps the eyes (over which workers wear protective glasses), their lightweight fabric keeps the temperature inside fairly comfortable as well. Entry and exit of workers in bunny suits from the cleanroom are controlled to minimize contamination, and workers must be reclothed in a clean suit and decontaminated each time they return to the cleanroom.

Several highly toxic chemicals are used at various points in the process of manufacturing semiconductors. Workers who are exposed to such chemicals can be seriously harmed. However, semiconductor fabrication plants are designed with safeguards to ensure that these chemicals are handled, used, and disposed of without exposure to workers or the surrounding environment. Toxic chemicals are applied to wafers by computer-controlled machine tools in sealed chambers, and there is normally little risk of workers coming into contact with them.

Semiconductor-fabricating plants operate around the clock. For this reason, night and weekend work is common. In some plants, workers maintain standard 8-hour shifts, 5 days a week. In other plants, employees are on duty for 12-hour shifts to minimize the disruption of cleanroom operations brought about by changes in shift. In some plants, managers allow workers to alternate schedules, thereby distributing the overnight shift equitably.

Training, Other Qualifications, and Advancement

People interested in becoming semiconductor processors—either operators or technicians—need a solid background in mathematics and the physical sciences. In addition to applying these disciplines to the complex manufacturing processes performed in fabs, math and science knowledge are essentials for pursuing higher education in semiconductor technology—and knowledge of both subjects is one of the best ways to advance in the semiconductor fabricating field.

Semiconductor processor workers must also be able to think analytically and critically to anticipate problems and avoid costly mistakes. Communication skills also are vital, as workers must be able to convey their thoughts and ideas both orally and in writing.

For semiconductor processor jobs, employers prefer persons who have completed associate degree programs. However, completion of a 1-year certificate program in semiconductor technology offered by some community colleges, supplemented by experience, may also be sufficient; Some semiconductor technology programs at community colleges include internships at a semiconductor fabricating plants. Other persons also may qualify by completing a degree in high-tech manufacturing, a new degree offered by some community colleges that prepares graduates to work in the semiconductor industry as well as other industries, such as pharmaceuticals, aerospace, or automotive. Degree or certificate program graduates who get hands-on training while attending school should have the best prospects.

To ensure that operators and technicians keep their skills current, many employers provide 40 hours of formal training annually. Some employers also provide financial assistance to employees who want to earn associate and bachelor's degrees to further their career or to work towards becoming a technician.

Summer and part-time employment provide another option for getting started in the field for those who are at least 18 years old and live near a semiconductor processing plant. Students often are hired to work during the summer, and some students are allowed to continue working part time during the school year. Students in summer and part-time semiconductor processor jobs learn what education they need to prosper in the field. They also gain valuable experience that may lead to full-time employment after graduation.

Some semiconductor processing technicians transfer to sales engineer jobs with suppliers of the machines that manufacture the semiconductors or become field support personnel.

Employment

Electronic semiconductor processors held approximately 45,000 jobs in 2004. Nearly all of them were employed in facilities that manufacture semiconductors and other electronic components and accessories, though a small percentage worked in plants that primarily manufacture computers and office equipment.

Job Outlook

Employment of semiconductor processors is projected to decline between 2004 and 2014. The two main reasons for this are increasing automation and the construction of many newer fabs in other countries. Semiconductor manufacturers are shifting production to larger 12" wafers, which produce twice as many chips as fabs making 8" wafers. Plants that make 12" wafers are more automated, allowing them to sharply increase production with the same number of workers. Additionally, a number of domestic companies are building more fabs overseas, where costs are lower. Imports of semiconductors from non-U.S. companies also are growing and may continue to increase throughout the decade. In spite of the decline in employment, some jobs will open up due to the need to replace workers who leave the occupation.

Despite the expected decline in employment of semiconductor processors, the demand for semiconductor chips remains very high, stemming from the many existing and future applications for semiconductors in computers, appliances, machinery, biotechnology, vehicles, cell phones and other telecommunications devices, and other equipment. Moreover, the advent of the new 64-bit microchip and "dual-core" chips is expected to provide the power of computer servers or workstations onto desktop computers and open up a wealth of new applications, particularly in medical devices.

Industry development of semiconductors made from better materials means that semiconductors will become even smaller, more powerful, and more durable. For example, the industry has begun producing a new generation of microchips made with copper rather than aluminum wires, which will better conduct electricity. Also, technology now exists to make chips for wireless connections to the Internet possible over a range of several miles, while another company will soon be producing chips that will save massive amounts of energy in many kinds of electric products.

Job prospects will be best for people with postsecondary education in electronics or semiconductor technology.

Earnings

Median hourly earnings of electronic semiconductor processors were $13.85 in May 2004. The middle 50 percent earned between $11.44 and $16.90 an hour. The lowest 10 percent earned less than $9.53, and the top 10 percent earned more than $20.46 an hour.

Technicians with an associate degree in electronics or semiconductor technology generally start at higher salaries than those with less education. About 15 percent of all electronic semiconductor processors belonged to a union.

Related Occupations

Electronic semiconductor processors do production work that resembles the work of precision assemblers and fabricators of electrical and electronic equipment. Also, many electronic semiconductor processors have academic training in semiconductor technology, which emphasizes scientific and engineering principles. Other occupations that require some college or postsecondary vocational training emphasizing such principles are engineering technicians, electrical and electronics engineers, and science technicians.

Sources of Additional Information

For more information on semiconductor processor careers, contact

▶ Maricopa Advanced Technology Education Center (MATEC), 2323 West 14th St., Suite 540, Tempe, AZ 85281. Internet: http://matec.org/ops/career.shtml

Small Engine Mechanics

(O*NET 49-3051.00, 49-3052.00, and 49-3053.00)

Significant Points

- Employment is expected to grow as fast as the average for all occupations, and persons with formal training as a mechanic should enjoy good job prospects.

- Use of motorcycles, motorboats, and outdoor power equipment is seasonal in many areas, so mechanics may service other types of equipment or work reduced hours in the winter.

Nature of the Work

Small engines powering motorcycles, motorboats, and outdoor power equipment share many characteristics with their larger counterparts, including breakdowns. Small engine mechanics repair and service power equipment ranging from racing motorcycles to chain saws. Mechanics usually specialize in the service and repair of one type of equipment, although they may work on closely related products.

Motorcycle mechanics repair and overhaul motorcycles, motor scooters, mopeds, dirt bikes, and all-terrain vehicles. Besides repairing engines, they may work on transmissions, brakes, and ignition systems and make minor body repairs. Mechanics often service just a few makes and models of motorcycles, because most work for dealers that service only the products they sell.

Motorboat mechanics, or *marine equipment mechanics*, repair and adjust the electrical and mechanical equipment of inboard and outboard boat engines. Most small boats have portable outboard engines that are removed and brought into the repair shop. Larger craft, such as cabin cruisers and commercial fishing boats, are powered by diesel or gasoline inboard or inboard-outboard engines, which are removed only for major overhauls. Most of these repairs are performed at the docks or marinas. Motorboat mechanics also may work on propellers, steering mechanisms, marine plumbing, and other boat equipment.

Outdoor power equipment and other small engine mechanics service and repair outdoor power equipment, such as lawn mowers, garden tractors, edge trimmers, and chain saws. They also may occasionally work on portable generators and go-carts. In addition, small engine mechanics in certain parts of the country may work on snowblowers and snowmobiles, but demand for this type of repair is both seasonal and regional.

Like large engines, small engines require periodic service to minimize the chance of breakdowns and to keep them operating at peak performance. During routine equipment maintenance, mechanics follow a checklist that includes the inspection and cleaning of brakes, electrical systems, fuel injection systems, plugs, carburetors, and other parts. Following inspection, mechanics usually repair or adjust parts that do not work properly or replace unfixable parts.

Routine maintenance is normally a major part of the mechanic's work.

When a piece of equipment breaks down, mechanics use various techniques to diagnose the source and extent of the problem. The mark of a skilled mechanic is the ability to diagnose mechanical, fuel, and electrical problems and to make repairs in a minimal amount of time. Quick and accurate diagnosis requires problem-solving ability and a thorough knowledge of the equipment's operation.

In larger repair shops, mechanics may use special computerized diagnostic testing equipment as a preliminary tool in analyzing equipment. This computerized equipment provides a systematic performance report of various components to compare against normal ratings. After pinpointing the problem, the mechanic makes the needed adjustments, repairs, or replacements. Some jobs require minor adjustments or the replacement of a single item, while a complete engine overhaul requires a number of hours to disassemble the engine and replace worn valves, pistons, bearings, and other internal parts.

Small engine mechanics use common hand tools, such as wrenches, pliers, and screwdrivers. They also utilize power tools, such as drills and grinders, when customized repairs warrant their use. Computerized engine analyzers, compression gauges, ammeters and voltmeters, and other testing devices help mechanics locate faulty parts and tune engines. Some highly skilled mechanics use specialized components and the latest computerized equipment to customize and tune motorcycles and motorboats for racing.

Working Conditions

Small engine mechanics usually work in repair shops that are well lighted and ventilated, but are sometimes noisy when engines are tested. Motorboat mechanics may work outdoors at docks or marinas, as well as in all weather conditions, when making repairs aboard boats. They may work in cramped or awkward positions to reach a boat's engine.

During the winter months in the northern United States, mechanics may work fewer than 40 hours a week because the amount of repair and service work declines when lawn mowers, motorboats, and motorcycles are not in use. Many mechanics work only during the busy spring and summer seasons. However, many schedule time-consuming engine overhauls or work on snowmobiles and snowblowers during winter downtime. Mechanics may work considerably more than 40 hours a week when demand is strong.

Training, Other Qualifications, and Advancement

Due to the increasing complexity of motorcycles and motorboats, most employers prefer to hire mechanics who have graduated from formal training programs for small engine mechanics. Because the number of these specialized postsecondary programs is limited, most mechanics learn their skills on the job or while working in related occupations. For trainee jobs, employers hire persons with mechanical aptitude who are knowledgeable about the fundamentals of small two- and four-stroke engines. Many trainees develop an interest in mechanics and acquire some basic skills through working on automobiles, motorcycles, motorboats, or outdoor power equipment as a hobby. Others may be introduced to mechanics through vocational automotive training in high school or one of many post-secondary institutions.

Trainees learn routine service tasks under the guidance of experienced mechanics by replacing ignition points and spark plugs or by taking apart, assembling, and testing new equipment. As they gain experience and proficiency, trainees progress to more difficult tasks, such as advanced computerized diagnosis and engine overhauls. Anywhere from 3 to 5 years of on-the-job training may be necessary before a novice worker becomes competent in all aspects of the repair of motorcycle and motorboat engines.

Employers often send mechanics and trainees to special courses conducted by motorcycle, motorboat, and outdoor power equipment manufacturers or distributors. These courses, which last as long as 2 weeks, upgrade workers' skills and provide information on repairing new models. They also may be used as a refresher for employees. They are usually a prerequisite for any mechanic who performs warranty work for manufacturers or insurance companies.

Most employers prefer to hire high school graduates for trainee mechanic positions, but will accept applicants with less education if they possess adequate reading, writing, and arithmetic skills. Many equipment dealers employ students part time and during the summer to help assemble new equipment and perform minor repairs. Helpful high school courses include small engine repair, automobile mechanics, science, and business arithmetic.

Knowledge of basic electronics is essential for small engine mechanics because electronic components control an engine's performance; the vehicle's instrument displays; and a variety of other functions of motorcycles, motorboats, and outdoor power equipment.

The most important work possessions of mechanics are their hand tools. Mechanics usually provide their own tools, and many experienced mechanics have invested thousands of dollars in them. Employers typically furnish expensive power tools, computerized engine analyzers, and other diagnostic equipment, but mechanics accumulate hand tools with experience.

The skills used as a small engine mechanic generally transfer to other occupations, such as automobile, diesel, or heavy vehicle and mobile equipment mechanics. Experienced mechanics with leadership ability may advance to shop supervisor or service manager jobs. Mechanics with sales ability sometimes become sales representatives or open their own repair shops.

Employment

Small engine mechanics held about 73,000 jobs in 2004. Motorcycle mechanics held around 19,000 jobs. Motorboat mechanics held approximately 23,000 and outdoor power equipment and other small engine mechanics about 31,000. Almost half worked for other motor vehicle dealers, an industry that includes retail dealers of motorcycles, boats, and miscellaneous vehicles, or for retail hardware, lawn, and garden stores. Most of the remainder were employed by independent repair shops, marinas and boatyards, equipment rental companies, wholesale distributors, and landscaping services. About 20 percent were self-employed, compared to about 7 percent of workers in all installation, maintenance, and repair occupations.

Job Outlook

Employment of small engine mechanics is expected to grow about as fast as the average for all occupations through the year 2014. Most of the job openings are expected to be due to the need to replace many experienced small engine mechanics that are expected to transfer to other occupations, retire, or stop working for other reasons. Job prospects should be especially favorable for persons who complete mechanic training programs.

Motorcycle usage should continue to be popular with persons between 18 and 24 years, an age group that historically has had the greatest proportion of motorcycle enthusiasts. Motorcycles also are becoming increasingly popular with persons over the age of 40. Traditionally, this group has more disposable income to spend on recreational equipment such as motorcycles and motorboats.

Over the next decade, more people will be entering the 40-and-older age group, the group responsible for the largest segment of marine craft purchases. These potential buyers will help expand the market for motorboats while maintaining the demand for qualified mechanics.

The construction of new single-family houses will result in an increase in the lawn and garden equipment in operation, increasing the need for mechanics. However, equipment growth will be slowed by trends toward smaller lawns and the contracting out of maintenance to lawn service firms. Small engine mechanics' growth will also be tempered by the tendency of many consumers to dispose of and replace relatively inexpensive items rather than have them repaired.

Employers will increasingly prefer mechanics to have knowledge of both two- and four-stroke engines, as well as other emissions-reducing technology, as the government increases regulation over the emissions produced by small engines. While advancements in technology will lengthen the interval between checkups, the need for qualified mechanics to perform services on motorcycles, motorboats, and lawn and garden equipment will increase.

Earnings

Median hourly earnings of motorcycle mechanics were $13.70 in May 2004. The middle 50 percent earned between $10.58 and $17.53. The lowest 10 percent earned less than $8.48, and the highest 10 percent earned more than $21.95. Median hourly earnings in May 2004 in other motor vehicle dealers, the industry employing the largest number of motorcycle mechanics, were $13.60.

Median hourly earnings of motorboat mechanics were $14.74. The middle 50 percent earned between $11.46 and $18.11. The lowest 10 percent earned less than $9.21, and the highest 10 percent earned more than $21.90. Median hourly earnings in May 2004 in other motor vehicle dealers, the industry employing the largest number of motorboat mechanics, were $14.29.

Median hourly earnings of outdoor power equipment and other small engine mechanics were $11.98 in May 2004. The middle 50 percent earned between $9.44 and $15.25. The lowest 10 percent earned less than $7.53, and the highest 10 percent earned more than $19.19. Median hourly earnings in lawn and garden equipment and supplies stores, the industry employing the largest number of outdoor power equipment and other small engine mechanics, were $11.40.

Small engine mechanics tend to receive few benefits in small shops, but those employed in larger shops often receive paid vacations, sick leave, and health insurance. Some employers also pay for work-related training and provide uniforms.

Related Occupations

Mechanics and repairers who work on mobile equipment other than small engines include automotive service technicians and mechanics, diesel service technicians and mechanics, and heavy vehicle and mobile equipment service technicians and mechanics.

Sources of Additional Information

For more details about work opportunities, contact local motorcycle, motorboat, and lawn and garden equipment dealers, boatyards, and marinas. Local offices of the state employment service also may have information about employment and training opportunities.

For a list of accredited private trade and technical schools that offer programs in small engine servicing and repair, contact

▸ Accrediting Commission of Career Schools and Colleges of Technology, 2101 Wilson Blvd., Suite 302, Arlington, VA 22201. Internet: http://www.accsct.org

Social Scientists, Other

(O*NET 19-3041.00, 19-3091.01, 19-3091.02, 19-3092.00, 19-3093.00, and 19-3094.00)

Significant Points

■ About half work for federal, state, and local governments, mostly for the federal government.

■ The educational attainment of social scientists is among the highest of all occupations.

■ Anthropologists and archaeologists will experience average growth, but slower-than-average employment growth is expected for geographers, historians, political scientists, and sociologists because they enjoy fewer opportunities outside of government and academic settings.

■ Competition for jobs will remain keen for all specialties because many of these social scientists compete for jobs with other workers, such as psychologists, statisticians, and market and survey researchers.

Nature of the Work

The major social science occupations covered in this job description include anthropologists, archaeologists, geographers, historians, political scientists, and sociologists. (Economists, market and survey researchers, psychologists, and urban and regional planners are covered elsewhere in this book.)

Social scientists study all aspects of society—from past events and achievements to human behavior and relationships among groups. Their research provides insights that help us understand different ways in which individuals and groups make decisions, exercise power, and respond to change. Through their studies and analyses, social scientists suggest solutions to social, business, personal, governmental, and environmental problems.

Research is a major activity of many social scientists, who use a variety of methods to assemble facts and construct theories. Applied research usually is designed to produce information that will enable people to make better decisions or manage their affairs more effectively. Collecting information takes many forms, including interviews and questionnaires to gather demographic and opinion data, living and working among the population being studied, performing field investigations, analyzing historical records and documents, experimenting with human or animal subjects in a laboratory, and preparing and interpreting maps and computer graphics. The work of specialists in social science varies greatly, although specialists in one field may find that their research overlaps work being conducted in another discipline.

Anthropologists study the origin and the physical, social, and cultural development and behavior of humans. They may examine the way of life, archaeological remains, language, or physical characteristics of people in various parts of the world. Some compare the customs, values, and social patterns of different cultures. Anthropologists usually concentrate in sociocultural anthropology, archaeology, linguistics, or biophysical anthropology. Sociocultural anthropologists study the customs, cultures, and social lives of groups in settings that range from unindustrialized societies to modern urban centers. Linguistic anthropologists investigate the role of, and changes to, language over time in various cultures. Biophysical anthropologists research the evolution of the human body, look for the earliest evidences of human life, and analyze how culture and biology influence one another. Physical anthropologists examine human remains found at archaeological sites in order to understand population demographics and factors that affected these populations, such as nutrition and disease.

Archaeologists examine and recover material evidence such as the ruins of buildings, tools, pottery, and other objects remaining from past human cultures in order to determine the chronology, history, customs, and living habits of earlier civilizations. Most anthropologists and archaeologists specialize in a particular region of the world.

Geographers analyze distributions of physical and cultural phenomena on local, regional, continental, and global scales. Economic geographers study the distribution of resources and economic activities. Political geographers are concerned with the relationship of geography to political phenomena, whereas cultural geographers study the geography of cultural phenomena. Physical geographers examine variations in climate, vegetation, soil, and landforms and their implications for human activity. Urban and transportation geographers study cities and metropolitan areas, while regional geographers study the physical, economic, political, and cultural characteristics of regions ranging in size from a congressional district to entire continents. Medical geographers investigate health care delivery systems, epidemiology (the study of the causes and control of epidemics), and the effect of the environment on health.

Most geographers use geographic information systems (GIS) technology to assist with their work. For example, they may use GIS to create computerized maps that can track information such as population growth, traffic patterns, environmental hazards, natural resources, and weather patterns, after which they use the information to advise governments on the development of houses, roads, or landfills.

Historians research, analyze, and interpret the past. They use many sources of additional information in their research, including government and institutional records, newspapers and other periodicals, photographs, interviews, films, and unpublished manuscripts such as personal diaries and letters. Historians usually specialize in a country or region; a particular period; or a particular field, such as social, intellectual, cultural, political, or diplomatic history. Biographers collect detailed information on individuals. Other historians help study and preserve archival materials, artifacts, and historic buildings and sites.

Political scientists study the origin, development, and operation of political systems and public policy. They conduct research on a wide range of subjects, such as relations between the United States and other countries, the institutions and political life of nations, the politics of small towns or a major metropolis, and the decisions of the U.S. Supreme Court. Studying topics such as public opinion, political decision making, ideology, and public policy, they analyze the structure and operation of governments, as well as various political entities. Depending on the topic, a political scientist might conduct a public-opinion survey, analyze election results or public documents, or interview public officials.

Sociologists study society and social behavior by examining the groups and social institutions people form, as well as various social, religious, political, and business organizations. They also study the behavior of and interaction among groups, trace their origin and growth, and analyze the influence of group activities on individual members. Sociologists are concerned with the characteristics of social groups, organizations, and institutions; the ways individuals are affected by each other and by the groups to which they belong; and the effect of social traits such as gender, age, or race on a person's daily life. The results of sociological research aid educators, lawmakers, administrators, and others who are interested in resolving social problems and formulating public policy.

Most sociologists work in one or more specialties, such as social organization, stratification, and mobility; racial and ethnic relations; education; the family; social psychology; urban, rural, political, and comparative sociology; gender relations; demography; gerontology; criminology; and sociological practice.

Working Conditions

Most social scientists have regular hours. Generally working behind a desk, either alone or in collaboration with other social scientists, they read and write research articles or reports. Many experience the pressures of writing and publishing, as well as those associated with deadlines and tight schedules. Sometimes they must work overtime, for which they usually are not compensated. Social scientists often work as an integral part of a research team, among whose members good communications skills are important. Travel may be necessary to collect information or attend meetings. Social scientists on foreign assignment must adjust to unfamiliar cultures, climates, and languages.

Some social scientists do fieldwork. For example, anthropologists, archaeologists, and geographers may travel to remote areas, live among the people they study, learn their languages, and stay for long periods at the site of their investigations. They may work under rugged conditions, and their work may involve strenuous physical exertion.

Social scientists employed by colleges and universities usually have flexible work schedules, often dividing their time among teaching, research, writing, consulting, and administrative responsibilities.

Training, Other Qualifications, and Advancement

The educational attainment of social scientists is among the highest of all occupations. The Ph.D. or an equivalent degree is a minimum requirement for most positions in colleges and universities and is important for advancement to many top-level nonacademic research and administrative posts. Graduates with master's degrees in applied specialties usually have better opportunities outside of colleges and universities, although the situation varies by field. Graduates with a master's degree in a social science may qualify for teaching positions in community colleges. Bachelor's degree holders have limited opportunities and, in most social science occupations, do not qualify for "professional" positions. The bachelor's degree does, however, provide a suitable background for many different kinds of entry-level jobs, such as research assistant, administrative aide, or management or sales trainee. With the addition of sufficient education courses, social science graduates also can qualify for teaching positions in secondary and elementary schools.

Training in statistics and mathematics is essential for many social scientists. Mathematical and quantitative research methods increasingly are being used in geography, political science, and other fields. The ability to utilize computers for research purposes is mandatory in most disciplines. Most geographers—and increasing numbers of archaeologists—also will need to be familiar with GIS technology.

Many social science students find that internships or field experience is beneficial. Numerous local museums, historical societies, government agencies, and other organizations offer internships or volunteer research opportunities. Archaeological field schools instruct future anthropologists, archaeologists, and historians in how to excavate, record, and interpret historical sites.

Depending on their jobs, social scientists may need a wide range of personal characteristics. Intellectual curiosity and creativity are fundamental personal traits because social scientists constantly seek new information about people, things, and ideas. The ability to think logically and methodically is important to a political scientist comparing, for example, the merits of various forms of government. Objectivity, having an open mind, and systematic work habits are important in all kinds of social science research. Perseverance is essential for an anthropologist, who might have to spend years studying artifacts from an ancient civilization before making a final analysis and interpretation. Excellent written and oral communication skills also are necessary for all these professionals.

Employment

Social scientists held about 18,000 jobs in 2004. Many worked as researchers, administrators, and counselors for a wide range of employers. About half worked for federal, state, and local governments, mostly in the federal government. Other employers included scientific research and development services; management, scientific, and technical consulting services; business, professional, labor, political, and similar organizations; and architectural, engineering, and related firms.

Many individuals with training in a social science discipline teach in colleges and universities and in secondary and elementary schools. (For more information, see teachers—postsecondary elsewhere in this book.) The proportion of social scientists who teach varies by specialty: For example, the academic world usually is a more important source of jobs for graduates in history than for graduates in most other social science fields.

Job Outlook

Overall employment of social scientists is expected to grow more slowly than average for all occupations through 2014. However, projected growth rates vary by specialty. Anthropologists and archaeologists will experience average employment growth. Employment of geographers, historians, political scientists, and sociologists will grow more slowly than average, mainly because these workers enjoy fewer opportunities outside of government and academic settings.

Competition will remain keen for social science positions. Many jobs in policy, research, or marketing for which social scientists qualify are not advertised exclusively as social scientist positions. Because of the wide range of skills and knowledge possessed by the social scientists discussed here, many compete for jobs with other workers, such as market and survey researchers, psychologists, engineers, urban and regional planners, and statisticians.

A few social scientists will find opportunities as university faculty, although competition for these jobs also will remain keen. Usually, there are more graduates than available faculty positions, although retirements among faculty are expected to rise in the next few years. The growing importance and popularity of social science subjects in secondary schools is strengthening the demand for social science teachers at that level.

Anthropologists and archaeologists will see the majority of their employment growth in the management, scientific, and technical consulting services industry. Anthropologists who work as consultants often apply anthropological knowledge and methods to problems ranging from economic development issues to forensics. Also, as construction projects increase, archaeologists will be needed to perform preliminary excavations in order to preserve historical sites and artifacts.

Geographers will have opportunities to utilize their skills to advise government, real estate developers, utilities, and telecommunications firms on where to build new roads, buildings, power plants, and cable lines. Geographers also will advise on environmental matters, such as where to build a landfill or preserve wetland habitats. Geographers with a background in GIS will find numerous job opportunities applying GIS technology in nontraditional areas, such

as emergency assistance, where GIS can track locations of ambulances, police, and fire rescue units and their proximity to the emergency. Workers in these jobs may not necessarily be called "geographers," but instead may be referred to by a different title, such as "GIS analyst" or "GIS specialist." GIS technology also will be utilized in areas of growing importance, such as homeland security and defense.

Historians, political scientists, and sociologists will find jobs in policy or research. Historians may find opportunities with historic preservation societies as public interest in preserving and restoring historical sites increases. Political scientists will be able to utilize their knowledge of political institutions to further the interests of nonprofit, political lobbying, and social organizations. Sociologists may find work conducting policy research for consulting firms and nonprofit organizations, and their knowledge of society and social behavior may be used by a variety of companies in product development, marketing, and advertising. Job growth will be very slow in the federal government, a key employer of social scientists.

Earnings

In May 2004, anthropologists and archaeologists had median annual earnings of $43,890; geographers, $58,970; historians, $44,490; political scientists, $86,750; and sociologists, $57,870.

In the federal government, social scientists with a bachelor's degree and no experience could start at a yearly salary of $24,677 or $30,567 in 2005, depending on their college records. Those with a master's degree could start at $37,390, and those with a Ph.D. degree could begin at $45,239, while some individuals with experience and an advanced degree could start at $54,221. Beginning salaries were slightly higher in selected areas of the country where the prevailing local pay level was higher.

Related Occupations

Social scientists' duties and training outlined in this job description are similar to those of other occupations covered elsewhere in this book, including other social science occupations: economists, market and survey researchers, psychologists, and urban and regional planners. Many social scientists conduct surveys, study social problems, teach, and work in museums, performing tasks similar to those of statisticians; counselors; social workers; teachers—postsecondary; teachers—preschool, kindergarten, elementary, middle, and secondary; and archivists, curators, and museum technicians.

Political scientists are concerned with the function of government, including the legal system, as are lawyers; paralegals and legal assistants; and judges, magistrates, and other judicial workers. Many political scientists analyze and report on current events, much as do news analysts, reporters, and correspondents.

Along with conservation scientists and foresters, atmospheric scientists, and environmental scientists and hydrologists, geographers are concerned with the earth's environment and natural resources. Geographers also use GIS computer technology to make maps. Other occupations with similar duties are surveyors, cartographers, photogrammetrists, and surveying technicians; computer systems analysts; and computer scientists and database administrators.

Detailed information about economists, market and survey researchers, psychologists, and urban and regional planners is presented elsewhere in this book.

Sources of Additional Information

For information about careers in anthropology, contact

▸ American Anthropological Association, 2200 Wilson Blvd., Suite 600, Arlington, VA 22201. Internet: http://www.aaanet.org

For information about careers in archaeology, contact

▸ Society for American Archaeology, 900 2nd St. NE, Suite 12, Washington, DC 20002-3560. Internet: http://www.saa.org

▸ Archaeological Institute of America, 656 Beacon St., 6th Floor, Boston, MA 02215-2006. Internet: http://www.archaeological.org

For information about careers in geography, contact

▸ Association of American Geographers, 1710 16th St. NW, Washington, DC 20009-3198. Internet: http://www.aag.org

Information on careers for historians is available from

▸ American Historical Association, 400 A St. SE, Washington, DC 20003-3889. Internet: http://www.historians.org

For information about careers in political science, contact

▸ American Political Science Association, 1527 New Hampshire Ave. NW, Washington, DC 20036-1206. Internet: http://www.apsanet.org

▸ National Association of Schools of Public Affairs and Administration, 1120 G St. NW, Suite 730, Washington, DC 20005-3869. Internet: http://www.naspaa.org

Information about careers in sociology is available from

▸ American Sociological Association, 1307 New York Ave. NW, Suite 700, Washington, DC 20005-4712. Internet: http://www.asanet.org

Speech-Language Pathologists

(O*NET 29-1127.00)

Significant Points

■ About half work in educational services, and most others are employed by health care and social assistance facilities.

■ A master's degree in speech-language pathology is the standard credential required for licensing in most states.

■ Employment is expected to grow because the expanding population in older age groups is prone to medical conditions that result in speech, language, and swallowing problems.

■ Excellent job opportunities are expected.

Nature of the Work

Speech-language pathologists, sometimes called *speech therapists*, assess, diagnose, treat, and help to prevent speech, language, cognitive-communication, voice, swallowing, fluency, and other related disorders.

Speech-language pathologists work with people who cannot produce speech sounds or cannot produce them clearly; those with speech rhythm and fluency problems, such as stuttering; people with voice disorders, such as inappropriate pitch or harsh voice; those

with problems understanding and producing language; those who wish to improve their communication skills by modifying an accent; and those with cognitive communication impairments, such as attention, memory, and problem-solving disorders. They also work with people who have swallowing difficulties.

Speech, language, and swallowing difficulties can result from a variety of causes, including stroke, brain injury or deterioration, developmental delays or disorders, learning disabilities, cerebral palsy, cleft palate, voice pathology, mental retardation, hearing loss, or emotional problems. Problems can be congenital, developmental, or acquired. Speech-language pathologists use qualitative and quantitative assessment methods, including standardized tests, as well as special instruments, to analyze and diagnose the nature and extent of speech, language, and swallowing impairments. Speech-language pathologists develop an individualized plan of care tailored to each patient's needs. For individuals with little or no speech capability, speech-language pathologists may select augmentative or alternative communication methods, including automated devices and sign language, and teach their use. They teach these individuals how to make sounds, improve their voices, or increase their oral or written language skills to communicate more effectively. They also teach individuals how to strengthen muscles or use compensatory strategies to swallow without choking or inhaling food or liquid. Speech-language pathologists help patients develop, or recover, reliable communication and swallowing skills so patients can fulfill their educational, vocational, and social roles.

Speech-language pathologists keep records on the initial evaluation, progress, and discharge of clients. This helps pinpoint problems, tracks client progress, and justifies the cost of treatment when applying for reimbursement. They counsel individuals and their families concerning communication disorders and how to cope with the stress and misunderstanding that often accompany them. They also work with family members to recognize and change behavior patterns that impede communication and treatment and show them communication-enhancing techniques to use at home.

Most speech-language pathologists provide direct clinical services to individuals with communication or swallowing disorders. In medical facilities, they may perform their job in conjunction with physicians, social workers, psychologists, and other therapists. Speech-language pathologists in schools collaborate with teachers, special educators, interpreters, other school personnel, and parents to develop and implement individual or group programs, provide counseling, and support classroom activities. Some speech-language pathologists conduct research on how people communicate. Others design and develop equipment or techniques for diagnosing and treating speech problems.

Working Conditions

Speech-language pathologists usually work at a desk or table in clean comfortable surroundings. In medical settings, they may work at the patient's bedside and assist in positioning the patient. In school settings, they may work with students in an office or classroom. Some deliver services in the client's home. While the job is not physically demanding, it requires attention to detail and intense concentration. The emotional needs of clients and their families may be demanding. Most full-time speech-language pathologists work 40 hours per week; about 1 in 5 work part time. Those who work on a contract basis may spend a substantial amount of time traveling between facilities.

Training, Other Qualifications, and Advancement

In 2005, 47 states required speech-language pathologists to be licensed if they worked in a health care setting, and all states required a master's degree or equivalent. A passing score on the national examination on speech-language pathology, offered through the Praxis Series of the Educational Testing Service, is needed as well. Other requirements typically are 300 to 375 hours of supervised clinical experience and 9 months of postgraduate professional clinical experience. Forty-one states have continuing education requirements for licensure renewal. Medicaid, Medicare, and private health insurers generally require a practitioner to be licensed to qualify for reimbursement.

Only 11 states require this same license to practice in the public schools. The other states issue a teaching license or certificate that typically requires a master's degree from an approved college or university. Some states will grant a temporary teaching license or certificate to bachelor's degree applicants, but a master's degree must be earned in 3 to 5 years. A few states grant a full teacher's certificate or license to bachelor's degree applicants.

In 2004, 239 colleges and universities offered graduate programs in speech-language pathology that are accredited by the Council on Academic Accreditation in Audiology and Speech-Language Pathology. While graduation from an accredited program is not always required to become a speech-language pathologist, it may be helpful in obtaining a license or may be required to obtain a license in some states. Courses cover the anatomy, physiology, and development of the areas of the body involved in speech, language, and swallowing; the nature of disorders; acoustics; and psychological aspects of communication. Graduate students also learn to evaluate and treat speech, language, and swallowing disorders and receive supervised clinical training in communication disorders.

Speech-language pathologists can acquire the Certificate of Clinical Competence in Speech-Language Pathology (CCC-SLP) offered by the American Speech-Language-Hearing Association. To earn a CCC, a person must have a graduate degree and 400 hours of supervised clinical experience, complete a 36-week postgraduate clinical fellowship, and pass the Praxis Series examination in speech-language pathology administered by the Educational Testing Service (ETS).

Speech-language pathologists should be able to effectively communicate diagnostic test results, diagnoses, and proposed treatment in a manner easily understood by their patients and their families. They must be able to approach problems objectively and be supportive. Because a patient's progress may be slow, patience, compassion, and good listening skills are necessary.

As speech-language pathologists gain clinical experience and engage in continuing professional education, many develop expertise with certain populations, such as preschoolers and adolescents, or disorders, such as aphasia and learning disabilities. Some may obtain board recognition in a specialty area, such as child language,

fluency, or feeding and swallowing. Experienced clinicians may become mentors or supervisors of other therapists or be promoted to administrative positions.

Employment

Speech-language pathologists held about 96,000 jobs in 2004. About half were employed in educational services, primarily in preschools and elementary and secondary schools. Others were employed in hospitals; offices of other health practitioners, including speech-language pathologists; nursing care facilities; home health care services; individual and family services; outpatient care centers; and child day care centers.

A few speech-language pathologists are self-employed in private practice. They contract to provide services in schools, offices of physicians, hospitals, or nursing care facilities or work as consultants to industry.

Job Outlook

Employment of speech-language pathologists is expected to grow about as fast as the average for all occupations through the year 2014. As the members of the baby boom generation continue to age, the possibility of neurological disorders and associated speech, language, and swallowing impairments increases. Medical advances are also improving the survival rate of premature infants and trauma and stroke victims, who then need assessment and possible treatment. An increased emphasis also has been placed on early identification of speech and language problems in young children. The combination of growth in the occupation and an expected increase in retirements over the coming years should create excellent job opportunities for speech-language pathologists. Opportunities should be particularly favorable for those with the ability to speak a second language, such as Spanish.

In health care facilities, restrictions on reimbursement for therapy services may limit the growth of speech-language pathologists in the near term. However, over the long run, the demand for therapists should continue to rise as growth in the number of individuals with disabilities or limited function spurs demand for therapy services.

Employment in educational services will increase along with growth in elementary and secondary school enrollments, including enrollment of special education students. Federal law guarantees special education and related services to all eligible children with disabilities. Greater awareness of the importance of early identification and diagnosis of speech and language disorders will also increase employment.

The number of speech-language pathologists in private practice will rise due to the increasing use of contract services by hospitals, schools, and nursing care facilities.

Earnings

Median annual earnings of speech-language pathologists were $52,410 in May 2004. The middle 50 percent earned between $42,090 and $65,750. The lowest 10 percent earned less than $34,720, and the highest 10 percent earned more than $82,420.

Median annual earnings in the industries employing the largest numbers of speech-language pathologists in May 2004 were

Offices of other health practitioners	$57,240
General medical and surgical hospitals	55,900
Elementary and secondary schools	48,320

According to a 2003 survey by the American Speech-Language-Hearing Association, the median annual salary for full-time certified speech-language pathologists who worked on a calendar-year basis, generally 11 or 12 months annually, was $48,000. Certified speech-language pathologists who worked 25 or fewer hours per week had a median hourly salary of $40.00. Starting salaries for certified speech-language pathologists with one to three years of experience were $42,000 for those who worked on a calendar-year basis. According to a 2004 survey by the American Speech-Language-Hearing Association, the median annual salary for speech-language pathologists in schools was $50,000 for those employed on an academic-year basis (usually 9 or 10 months).

Related Occupations

Speech-language pathologists specialize in the prevention, diagnosis, and treatment of speech and language problems. Workers in related occupations include audiologists, occupational therapists, optometrists, physical therapists, psychologists, and recreational therapists. Speech-language pathologists in school systems often work closely with special education teachers in assisting students with disabilities.

Sources of Additional Information

State licensing boards can provide information on licensure requirements. State departments of education can supply information on certification requirements for those who wish to work in public schools.

For information on careers in speech-language pathology, a description of the CCC-SLP credential, and a listing of accredited graduate programs in speech-language pathology, contact

▸ American Speech-Language-Hearing Association, 10801 Rockville Pike, Rockville, MD 20852. Internet: http://www.asha.org

Stationary Engineers and Boiler Operators

(O*NET 51-8021.01 and 51-8021.02)

Significant Points

- Workers usually acquire their skills through a formal apprenticeship program or through on-the-job training supplemented by courses at a trade or technical school.

- Most states and cities have licensing requirements.

- Employment is expected to show little or no growth through the year 2014.

- Applicants may face competition for jobs; opportunities will be best for workers with training in computerized controls and instrumentation.

Nature of the Work

Heating, air-conditioning, refrigeration, and ventilation systems keep large buildings and other commercial facilities comfortable all year long. Industrial plants often have facilities to provide electrical power, steam, or other services. Stationary engineers and boiler operators operate and maintain these systems, which include boilers, air-conditioning and refrigeration equipment, diesel engines, turbines, generators, pumps, condensers, and compressors. The equipment that stationary engineers and boiler operators control is similar to equipment operated by locomotive or marine engineers, except that it is not in a moving vehicle.

Stationary engineers and boiler operators start up, regulate, repair, and shut down equipment. They ensure that the equipment operates safely, economically, and within established limits by monitoring meters, gauges, and computerized controls. Stationary engineers and boiler operators control equipment manually and, if necessary, make adjustments. They also record relevant events and facts concerning the operation and maintenance of the equipment. With regard to steam boilers, for example, they observe, control, and record the steam pressure, temperature, water level, chemistry, power output, fuel consumption, and emissions from the vessel. They watch and listen to machinery and routinely check safety devices, identifying and correcting any trouble that develops. They use hand and power tools to perform repairs and maintenance ranging from a complete overhaul to replacing defective valves, gaskets, or bearings. Servicing, troubleshooting, repairing, and monitoring modern systems all require the use of sophisticated electrical and electronic test equipment.

Stationary engineers typically use computers to operate the mechanical, electrical, and fire safety systems of new buildings and plants. Engineers monitor, adjust, and diagnose these systems from a central location, using a computer linked into the buildings' communications network.

Routine maintenance, such as lubricating moving parts, replacing filters, and removing soot and corrosion that can reduce the boiler's operating efficiency, is a regular part of the work of stationary engineers and boiler operators. They test the water in the boiler and add chemicals to prevent corrosion and harmful deposits. In most facilities, stationary engineers are responsible for the maintenance and balancing of air systems, as well as hydronic systems that heat or cool buildings by circulating fluid (such as water or water vapor) in a closed system of pipes. They also may check the air quality of the ventilation system and make adjustments to keep the operation of the boiler within mandated guidelines.

In a large building or industrial plant, a stationary engineer may be in charge of all mechanical systems in the building. Engineers may supervise the work of assistant stationary engineers, turbine operators, boiler tenders, and air-conditioning and refrigeration operators and mechanics. Most stationary engineers perform other maintenance duties, such as carpentry, plumbing, locksmithing, and electrical repairs. In a small building or industrial plant, there may be only one stationary engineer.

Working Conditions

Stationary engineers and boiler operators generally have steady, year-round employment. The average workweek is 40 hours. In facilities that operate around the clock, engineers and operators usually work one of three daily 8-hour shifts on a rotating basis. Weekend and holiday work often is required.

Engine rooms, power plants, boiler rooms, mechanical rooms, and electrical rooms usually are clean and well lighted. Even under the most favorable conditions, however, some stationary engineers and boiler operators are exposed to high temperatures, dust, dirt, and high noise levels from the equipment. General maintenance duties also may require contact with oil, grease, or smoke. Workers spend much of the time on their feet. They also may have to crawl inside boilers and work in crouching or kneeling positions to inspect, clean, or repair equipment.

Stationary engineers and boiler operators work around hazardous machinery, such as low- and high-pressure boilers and electrical equipment. They must follow procedures to guard against burns, electric shock, noise, danger from moving parts, and exposure to hazardous materials such as asbestos or certain chemicals.

Training, Other Qualifications, and Advancement

Stationary engineers and boiler operators usually acquire their skills through a formal apprenticeship program or through on-the-job training supplemented by courses at a trade or technical school. In addition, valuable experience can be obtained in the Navy or the merchant marine because marine engineering plants are similar to many stationary power and heating plants. Most employers prefer to hire persons with at least a high school diploma or the equivalent. However, continuing education—such as college courses—is becoming increasingly important, in part because of the growing complexity of the equipment with which engineers and operators now work. Mechanical aptitude, manual dexterity, and good physical condition also are important.

The International Union of Operating Engineers sponsors apprenticeship programs and is the principal union for stationary engineers and boiler operators. In selecting apprentices, most local labor-management apprenticeship committees prefer applicants with education or training in mathematics, computers, mechanical drawing, machine shop practice, physics, and chemistry. An apprenticeship usually lasts 4 years and includes 8,000 hours of on-the-job training. In addition, apprentices receive 600 hours of classroom instruction in subjects such as boiler design and operation, elementary physics, pneumatics, refrigeration, air conditioning, electricity, and electronics.

Those who acquire their skills on the job usually start as boiler tenders or helpers to experienced stationary engineers and boiler operators. This practical experience may be supplemented by postsecondary vocational training in computerized controls and instrumentation. However, becoming an engineer or operator without completing a formal apprenticeship program usually requires many years of work experience.

Most large and some small employers encourage and pay for skill-improvement training for their employees. Training almost always is provided when new equipment is introduced or when regulations concerning some aspect of the workers' duties change.

Most states and cities have licensing requirements for stationary engineers and boiler operators. Applicants usually must be at least 18 years of age, reside for a specified period in the state or locality in which they wish to work, meet experience requirements, and pass a written examination. A stationary engineer or boiler operator who moves from one state or city to another may have to pass an examination for a new license due to regional differences in licensing requirements.

There are several classes of stationary engineer licenses. Each class specifies the type and size of equipment the engineer is permitted to operate without supervision. A licensed first-class stationary engineer is qualified to run a large facility, supervise others, and operate equipment of all types and capacities. An applicant for this license may be required to have a high school education, apprenticeship or on-the-job training, and several years of experience. Licenses below first class limit the types or capacities of equipment the engineer may operate without supervision.

Stationary engineers and boiler operators advance by being placed in charge of larger, more powerful, or more varied equipment. Generally, engineers advance to these jobs as they obtain higher-class licenses. Some stationary engineers and boiler operators advance to boiler inspectors, chief plant engineers, building and plant superintendents, or building managers. A few obtain jobs as examining engineers or technical instructors.

Employment

Stationary engineers and boiler operators held about 50,000 jobs in 2004. Jobs were dispersed throughout a variety of industries. The majority of jobs were in state and local government facilities; hospitals; educational services; electric power generation, transmission, and distribution facilities; and manufacturing firms, such as pulp, paper, and paperboard mills. Other jobs were in architectural, engineering, and related services and real estate firms. Some were employed as contractors to a building or plant.

Stationary engineers and boiler operators worked throughout the country, generally in the more heavily populated areas in which large industrial and commercial establishments are located.

Job Outlook

Applicants may face competition for jobs as stationary engineers and boiler operators. Employment opportunities will be best for those with apprenticeship training or vocational school courses covering systems that are operated by computerized controls and instrumentation.

Employment of stationary engineers and boiler operators is expected to grow more slowly than the average for all occupations through the year 2014. Continuing commercial and industrial development will increase the amount of equipment to be operated and maintained. However, automated systems and computerized controls are making newly installed equipment more efficient, thus reducing the number of jobs needed for its operation. Furthermore, relatively few job openings will arise from the need to replace experienced workers who transfer to other occupations or leave the labor force. The low replacement rate in this occupation reflects its relatively high wages.

Earnings

Median annual earnings of stationary engineers and boiler operators were $44,150 in May 2004. The middle 50 percent earned between $34,500 and $55,460. The lowest 10 percent earned less than $27,010, and the highest 10 percent earned more than $66,570. Median annual earnings of stationary engineers and boiler operators in May 2004 were $48,340 in local government and $43,710 in general medical and surgical hospitals.

Related Occupations

Workers who monitor and operate stationary machinery include chemical plant and system operators; gas plant operators; petroleum pump system operators, refinery operators, and gaugers; power plant operators, distributors, and dispatchers; and water and liquid waste treatment plant and system operators. Other workers who maintain the equipment and machinery in a building or plant are industrial machinery mechanics and maintenance workers, as well as millwrights.

Sources of Additional Information

Information about apprenticeships, vocational training, and work opportunities is available from state employment service offices, locals of the International Union of Operating Engineers, vocational schools, and state and local licensing agencies.

Specific questions about this occupation should be addressed to

▸ International Union of Operating Engineers, 1125 17th St. NW, Washington, DC 20036. Internet: http://www.iuoe.org

▸ National Association of Power Engineers, Inc., 1 Springfield St., Chicopee, MA 01013.

▸ Building Owners and Managers Institute International, 1521 Ritchie Hwy., Arnold, MD 21012. Internet: http://www.bomi-edu.org

Statisticians

(O*NET 15-2041.00)

Significant Points

■ About 41 percent of statisticians work for federal, state, and local governments; other employers include scientific research and development services and finance and insurance firms.

■ A master's degree in statistics or mathematics is the minimum educational requirement for most jobs as a statistician.

■ Employment of statisticians is projected to grow more slowly than average because many jobs that require a degree in statistics will not carry the title "statistician."

■ Individuals with a degree in statistics should have favorable job opportunities in a variety of disciplines.

Nature of the Work

Statistics is the scientific application of mathematical principles to the collection, analysis, and presentation of numerical data. Statisticians contribute to scientific inquiry by applying their mathematical and statistical knowledge to the design of surveys and experiments; the collection, processing, and analysis of data; and the interpretation of the results. Statisticians may apply their knowledge of statistical methods to a variety of subject areas, such as biology, economics, engineering, medicine, public health, psychology, marketing, education, and sports. Many economic, social, political, and military decisions cannot be made without statistical techniques, such as the design of experiments to gain federal approval of a newly manufactured drug.

One technique that is especially useful to statisticians is sampling—obtaining information about a population of people or group of things by surveying a small portion of the total. For example, to determine the size of the audience for particular programs, television-rating services survey only a few thousand families rather than all viewers. Statisticians decide where and how to gather the data, determine the type and size of the sample group, and develop the survey questionnaire or reporting form. They also prepare instructions for workers who will collect and tabulate the data. Finally, statisticians analyze, interpret, and summarize the data, using computer software.

In business and industry, statisticians play an important role in quality control and in product development and improvement. In an automobile company, for example, statisticians might design experiments to determine the failure time of engines exposed to extreme weather conditions by running individual engines until failure and breakdown. Working for a pharmaceutical company, statisticians might develop and evaluate the results of clinical trials to determine the safety and effectiveness of new medications. And, at a computer software firm, statisticians might help construct new statistical software packages to analyze data more accurately and efficiently. In addition to product development and testing, some statisticians also are involved in deciding what products to manufacture, how much to charge for them, and to whom the products should be marketed. Statisticians also may manage assets and liabilities, determining the risks and returns of certain investments.

Statisticians also are employed by nearly every government agency. Some government statisticians develop surveys that measure population growth, consumer prices, or unemployment. Other statisticians work for scientific, environmental, and agricultural agencies and may help determine the level of pesticides in drinking water, the number of endangered species living in a particular area, or the number of people afflicted with a particular disease. Statisticians also are employed in national defense agencies, determining the accuracy of new weapons and the likely effectiveness of defense strategies.

Because statistical specialists are employed in so many work areas, specialists who use statistics often have different professional designations. For example, a person using statistical methods to analyze economic data may have the title econometrician, while statisticians in public health and medicine may hold titles such as biostatistician, biometrician, or epidemiologist.

Working Conditions

Statisticians usually work regular hours in comfortable offices. Some statisticians travel to provide advice on research projects, supervise and set up surveys, or gather statistical data. While advanced communications devices such as e-mail and teleconferencing are making it easier for statisticians to work with clients in different areas, there still are situations that require the statistician to be present, such as during meetings or while gathering data. Some in this occupation may have duties that vary widely, such as designing experiments or performing fieldwork in various communities. Statisticians who work in academia generally have a mix of teaching and research responsibilities.

Training, Other Qualifications, and Advancement

Although employment opportunities exist for individuals with a bachelor's degree, a master's degree in statistics or mathematics is usually the minimum educational requirement for most statistician jobs. Research and academic positions in institutions of higher education, for example, require at least a master's degree, and usually a Ph.D., in statistics. Beginning positions in industrial research often require a master's degree combined with several years of experience.

The training required for employment as an entry-level statistician in the federal government, however, is a bachelor's degree, including at least 15 semester hours of statistics or a combination of 15 hours of mathematics and statistics if at least 6 semester hours are in statistics. Qualifying as a mathematical statistician in the federal government requires 24 semester hours of mathematics and statistics, with a minimum of 6 semester hours in statistics and 12 semester hours in an area of advanced mathematics, such as calculus, differential equations, or vector analysis.

In 2004, approximately 230 universities offered a degree program in statistics, biostatistics, or mathematics. Many other schools also offered graduate-level courses in applied statistics for students majoring in biology, business, economics, education, engineering, psychology, and other fields. Acceptance into graduate statistics programs does not require an undergraduate degree in statistics, although good training in mathematics is essential.

Many schools also offered degrees in mathematics, operations research, and other fields that include a sufficient number of courses in statistics to qualify graduates for some entry-level positions with the federal government. Required subjects for statistics majors include differential and integral calculus, statistical methods, mathematical modeling, and probability theory. Additional courses that undergraduates should take include linear algebra, design and analysis of experiments, applied multivariate analysis, and mathematical statistics.

Because computers are used extensively for statistical applications, a strong background in computer science is highly recommended. For positions involving quality and productivity improvement, training in engineering or physical science is useful. A background in biological, chemical, or health science is important for positions involving the preparation and testing of pharmaceutical or agricultural products. Courses in economics and business administration are helpful for many jobs in market research, business analysis, and forecasting.

Good communications skills are important for prospective statisticians in industry, who often need to explain technical matters to persons without statistical expertise. An understanding of business and the economy also is valuable for those who plan to work in private industry.

Beginning statisticians generally are supervised by an experienced statistician. With experience, they may advance to positions with more technical responsibility and, in some cases, supervisory duties. However, opportunities for promotion are greater for persons with advanced degrees. Master's and Ph.D. degree holders usually enjoy independence in their work and may become qualified to engage in research; develop statistical methods; or, after a number of years of experience in a particular area, become statistical consultants.

Employment

Statisticians held about 19,000 jobs in 2004. Twenty percent of these jobs were in the federal government, where statisticians were concentrated in the Departments of Commerce, Agriculture, and Health and Human Services. Another 20 percent were found in state and local governments, including state colleges and universities. Most of the remaining jobs were in private industry, especially in scientific research and development services, insurance carriers, and pharmaceutical and medicine manufacturing. In addition, many professionals with a background in statistics were among the 53,000 postsecondary mathematical science teachers. (See the description of teachers—postsecondary elsewhere in this book.)

Job Outlook

Employment of statisticians is projected to grow more slowly than the average for all occupations over the 2004–2014 period because many jobs that require a degree in statistics will not carry the title "statistician." However, job opportunities should remain favorable for individuals with a degree in statistics. For example, many jobs involve the analysis and interpretation of data from economics, biological science, psychology, computer software engineering, and other disciplines. Despite the limited number of jobs resulting from growth, a number of openings will become available as statisticians transfer to other occupations or retire or leave the workforce for other reasons.

The use of statistics is widespread and growing. Among graduates with a master's degree in statistics, those with a strong background in an allied field, such as finance, biology, engineering, or computer science, should have the best prospects of finding jobs related to their field of study. Federal agencies will hire statisticians in many fields, including demography, agriculture, consumer and producer surveys, Social Security, health care, and environmental quality. Because the federal government is one of the few employers that considers a bachelor's degree an adequate entry-level qualification, competition for entry-level positions in the federal government is expected to be strong for persons just meeting the minimum qualifications for statisticians. Those who meet state certification requirements may become high school statistics teachers.

Manufacturing firms will hire statisticians with master's and doctoral degrees for quality control of various products, including pharmaceuticals, motor vehicles, aircraft, chemicals, and food. For example, pharmaceutical firms will employ statisticians to assess the effectiveness and safety of new drugs, to decide whether to market them, and to make sure they comply with federal standards. To address global product competition, motor vehicle manufacturers will need statisticians to improve the quality of automobiles, trucks, and their components by developing and testing new designs. Statisticians with knowledge of engineering and the physical sciences will find jobs in research and development, working with teams of scientists and engineers to help improve design and production processes to ensure consistent quality of newly developed products. Many statisticians also will find opportunities developing statistical software for computer software manufacturing firms.

Firms will rely heavily on workers with a background in statistics to forecast sales, analyze business conditions, and help to solve management problems to maximize profits. In addition, consulting firms increasingly will offer sophisticated statistical services to other businesses. Because of the widespread use of computers in this field and the growing number of widely used software packages, statisticians in all industries should have good computer programming skills and knowledge of statistical software.

Earnings

Median annual earnings of statisticians were $58,620 in May 2004. The middle 50 percent earned between $42,770 and $80,690. The lowest 10 percent earned less than $32,870, while the highest 10 percent earned more than $100,500.

The average annual salary for statisticians in the federal government in nonsupervisory, supervisory, and managerial positions was $81,262 in 2005, while mathematical statisticians averaged $91,446. According to a 2005 survey by the National Association of Colleges and Employers, starting salary offers for mathematics/statistics graduates with a bachelor's degree averaged $43,448 a year.

Related Occupations

People in a wide range of occupations work with statistics. Among these are actuaries, mathematicians, operations research analysts, computer scientists and database administrators, computer systems analysts, computer programmers, computer software engineers, engineers, economists, market and survey researchers, and financial analysts and personal financial advisors. Some statisticians also work as secondary or postsecondary teachers.

Sources of Additional Information

For information about career opportunities in statistics, contact

▸ American Statistical Association, 1429 Duke St., Alexandria, VA 22314-3415. Internet: http://www.amstat.org

For more information on doctoral-level careers and training in mathematics, a field closely related to statistics, contact

▸ American Mathematical Society, 201 Charles St., Providence, RI 02904-2213. Internet: http://www.ams.org

Information on obtaining positions as statisticians with the federal government is available from the Office of Personnel Management through USAJOBS, the federal government's official employment information system. This resource for locating and applying for job opportunities can be accessed through the Internet at http://www.usajobs.opm.gov or through an interactive voice response telephone system at (703) 724-1850 or TDD (978) 461-8404. These numbers are not toll free, and charges may result.

Surgical Technologists

(O*NET 29-2055.00)

Significant Points

■ Employment is expected to grow much faster than the average for all occupations through the year 2014.

■ Job opportunities are expected to be good.

■ Training programs last 9 to 24 months and lead to a certificate, diploma, or associate degree.

■ Hospitals will continue to be the primary employer, although much faster employment growth is expected in offices of physicians and in outpatient care centers, including ambulatory surgical centers.

Nature of the Work

Surgical technologists, also called *scrubs* and *surgical* or *operating room technicians,* assist in surgical operations under the supervision of surgeons, registered nurses, or other surgical personnel. Surgical technologists are members of operating room teams, which most commonly include surgeons, anesthesiologists, and circulating nurses. Before an operation, surgical technologists help prepare the operating room by setting up surgical instruments and equipment, sterile drapes, and sterile solutions. They assemble both sterile and nonsterile equipment, as well as adjust and check it to ensure it is working properly. Technologists also get patients ready for surgery by washing, shaving, and disinfecting incision sites. They transport patients to the operating room, help position them on the operating table, and cover them with sterile surgical "drapes." Technologists also observe patients' vital signs, check charts, and assist the surgical team with putting on sterile gowns and gloves.

During surgery, technologists pass instruments and other sterile supplies to surgeons and surgeon assistants. They may hold retractors, cut sutures, and help count sponges, needles, supplies, and instruments. Surgical technologists help prepare, care for, and dispose of specimens taken for laboratory analysis and help apply dressings. Some operate sterilizers, lights, or suction machines and help operate diagnostic equipment.

After an operation, surgical technologists may help transfer patients to the recovery room and clean and restock the operating room.

Working Conditions

Surgical technologists work in clean, well-lighted, cool environments. They must stand for long periods and remain alert during operations. At times they may be exposed to communicable diseases and unpleasant sights, odors, and materials.

Most surgical technologists work a regular 40-hour week, although they may be on call or work nights, weekends, and holidays on a rotating basis.

Training, Other Qualifications, and Advancement

Surgical technologists receive their training in formal programs offered by community and junior colleges, vocational schools, universities, hospitals, and the military. In 2005, the Commission on Accreditation of Allied Health Education Programs (CAAHEP) recognized more than 400 accredited programs. Programs last from 9 to 24 months and lead to a certificate, diploma, or associate degree. High school graduation normally is required for admission. Recommended high school courses include health, biology, chemistry, and mathematics.

Programs provide classroom education and supervised clinical experience. Students take courses in anatomy, physiology, microbiology, pharmacology, professional ethics, and medical terminology. Other studies cover the care and safety of patients during surgery, sterile techniques, and surgical procedures. Students also learn to sterilize instruments; prevent and control infection; and handle special drugs, solutions, supplies, and equipment.

Most employers prefer to hire certified technologists. Technologists may obtain voluntary professional certification from the Liaison Council on Certification for the Surgical Technologist by graduating from a CAAHEP-accredited program and passing a national certification examination. They may then use the Certified Surgical Technologist (CST) designation. Continuing education or reexamination is required to maintain certification, which must be renewed every 4 years.

Certification also may be obtained from the National Center for Competency Testing. To qualify to take the exam, candidates follow one of three paths: complete an accredited training program; undergo a 2-year hospital on-the-job training program; or acquire seven years of experience working in the field. After passing the exam, individuals may use the designation Tech in Surgery-Certified, TS-C (NCCT). This certification may be renewed every 5 years through either continuing education or reexamination.

Surgical technologists need manual dexterity to handle instruments quickly. They also must be conscientious, orderly, and emotionally stable to handle the demands of the operating room environment. Technologists must respond quickly and must be familiar with operating procedures in order to have instruments ready for surgeons without having to be told. They are expected to keep abreast of new developments in the field.

Technologists advance by specializing in a particular area of surgery, such as neurosurgery or open heart surgery. They also may work as circulating technologists. A circulating technologist is the "unsterile" member of the surgical team who prepares patients; helps with anesthesia; obtains and opens packages for the "sterile" persons to remove the sterile contents during the procedure; interviews the patient before surgery; keeps a written account of the surgical procedure; and answers the surgeon's questions about the patient during the surgery. With additional training, some technologists advance to first assistants, who help with retracting, sponging, suturing, cauterizing bleeders, and closing and treating wounds. Some surgical technologists manage central supply departments in hospitals or take positions with insurance companies, sterile supply services, and operating equipment firms.

Employment

Surgical technologists held about 84,000 jobs in 2004. About 7 out of 10 jobs for surgical technologists were in hospitals, mainly in operating and delivery rooms. Other jobs were in offices of physicians or dentists who perform outpatient surgery and in outpatient care centers, including ambulatory surgical centers. A few, known as private scrubs, are employed directly by surgeons who have special surgical teams, like those for liver transplants.

Job Outlook

Employment of surgical technologists is expected to grow much faster than the average for all occupations through the year 2014 as the volume of surgery increases. Job opportunities are expected to be good. The number of surgical procedures is expected to rise as the population grows and ages. The number of older people, including the baby boom generation, who generally require more surgical procedures will account for a larger portion of the general population. Technological advances, such as fiber optics and laser technology, will permit an increasing number of new surgical procedures to be performed and also will allow surgical technologists to assist with a greater number of procedures.

Hospitals will continue to be the primary employer of surgical technologists, although much faster employment growth is expected in offices of physicians and in outpatient care centers, including ambulatory surgical centers.

Earnings

Median annual earnings of surgical technologists were $34,010 in May 2004. The middle 50 percent earned between $28,560 and $40,750. The lowest 10 percent earned less than $23,940, and the highest 10 percent earned more than $45,990. Median hourly earnings in the industries employing the largest numbers of surgical technologists in May 2004 were

Offices of dentists	$37,510
Offices of physicians	36,570
General medical and surgical hospitals	33,130

Related Occupations

Other health occupations requiring approximately 1 year of training after high school include dental assistants, licensed practical and licensed vocational nurses, clinical laboratory technologists and technicians, and medical assistants.

Sources of Additional Information

For additional information on a career as a surgical technologist and a list of CAAHEP-accredited programs, contact

▸ Association of Surgical Technologists, 6 West Dry Creek Circle, Littleton, CO 80120. Internet: http://www.ast.org

For information on becoming a Certified Surgical Technologist, contact

▸ Liaison Council on Certification for the Surgical Technologist, 6 West Dry Creek Circle, Suite 100, Littleton, CO 80120. Internet: http://www.lcc-st.org

For information on becoming a Tech in Surgery-Certified, contact

▸ National Center for Competency Testing, 7007 College Blvd., Suite 250, Overland Park, KS 66211.

Surveyors, Cartographers, Photogrammetrists, and Surveying Technicians

(O*NET 17-1021.00, 17-1022.00, 17-3031.01, and 17-3031.02)

Significant Points

- About 2 out of 3 jobs are in architectural, engineering, and related services.

- Opportunities will be best for surveyors, cartographers, and photogrammetrists who have a bachelor's degree and strong technical skills.

- Applicants for jobs as technicians may face competition.

Nature of the Work

Surveyors, cartographers, and photogrammetrists are responsible for measuring and mapping the earth's surface. Traditionally, *surveyors* establish official land, airspace, and water boundaries. They write descriptions of land for deeds, leases, and other legal documents; define airspace for airports; and take measurements of construction and mineral sites. Other surveyors provide data relevant to the shape, contour, location, elevation, or dimension of land or land features. *Cartographers* compile geographic, political, and cultural information and prepare maps of large areas. *Photogrammetrists* measure and analyze aerial photographs that are subsequently used to prepare detailed maps and drawings. *Surveying and mapping technicians* assist these professionals in their duties by collecting data in the field and using it to calculate mapmaking information for use in performing computations and computer-aided drafting.

Surveyors measure distances, directions, and angles between points and elevations of points, lines, and contours on, above, and below the earth's surface. In the field, they select known survey reference points and determine the precise location of important features in the survey area. Surveyors research legal records, look for evidence of previous boundaries, and analyze the data to determine the location of boundary lines. They also record the results of surveys; verify the accuracy of data; and prepare plots, maps, and reports. Surveyors who establish boundaries must be licensed by the state in which they work. Surveyors are sometimes called to provide expert testimony in court cases concerning matters pertaining to surveying.

Cartographers measure, map, and chart the earth's surface. Their work involves everything from performing geographical research and compiling data to actually producing maps. Cartographers col-

lect, analyze, and interpret both spatial data—such as latitude, longitude, elevation, and distance—and nonspatial data—for example, population density, land-use patterns, annual precipitation levels, and demographic characteristics. Their maps may give both physical and social characteristics of the land. They prepare maps in either digital or graphic form, using information provided by geodetic surveys, aerial photographs, and satellite data.

Photogrammetrists prepare detailed maps and drawings from aerial photographs, usually of areas that are inaccessible, difficult, or more costly to survey by other methods. *Map editors* develop and verify the contents of maps, using aerial photographs and other reference sources. Some states require photogrammetrists to be licensed as surveyors.

Some surveyors perform specialized functions closer to those of cartographers than to those of traditional surveyors. For example, *geodetic surveyors* use high-accuracy techniques, including satellite observations (remote sensing), to measure large areas of the earth's surface. *Geophysical prospecting surveyors* mark sites for subsurface exploration, usually in relation to petroleum. *Marine or hydrographic surveyors* survey harbors, rivers, and other bodies of water to determine shorelines, the topography of the bottom, water depth, and other features.

There is more to surveying and cartography than meets the eye. Chains, transits, theodolites, and plumb lines have given way to cutting-edge technology such as the Global Positioning System (GPS), laptops, and robotic total stations as the preferred tools of surveyors. Advanced computer software known as Geographic Information Systems (GIS) has become an invaluable tool to booth surveyors and cartographers.

Surveyors are able to use GPS to locate reference points with a high degree of precision. To use this system, a surveyor places a satellite signal receiver—a small instrument mounted on a tripod—on a desired point and another receiver on a point for which the geographic position is known. The receiver simultaneously collects information from several satellites to establish a precise position. The receiver also can be placed in a vehicle for tracing out road systems. Because receivers now come in different sizes and shapes, and because the cost of receivers has fallen, much more surveying work can be done with GPS. Surveyors then must interpret and check the results produced by the new technology.

Fieldwork is done by a survey party that gathers the information needed by the surveyor. A typical survey party consists of a party chief and one or more surveying technicians and helpers. The party chief, who may be either a surveyor or a senior surveying technician, leads day-to-day work activities. Surveying technicians assist the party chief by adjusting and operating surveying instruments such as the total station, which measures and records angles and distances simultaneously. Surveying technicians or assistants position and hold the vertical rods, or targets, that the operator sights on to measure angles, distances, or elevations. In addition, they may hold measuring tapes if electronic distance-measuring equipment is not used. Surveying technicians compile notes, make sketches, and enter the data obtained from surveying instruments into computers either in the field or at the office. Survey parties also may include laborers or helpers who perform less-skilled duties, such as clearing brush from sight lines, driving stakes, or carrying equipment.

GIS software is capable of assembling, integrating, analyzing, and displaying data identified according to location and compiled from previous surveys and mappings. GIS software has become an important tool of both surveyors and cartographers. A GIS typically is used to handle maps that combine information that is useful for environmental studies, geology, engineering, planning, business marketing, and other disciplines. As more of these systems are developed, a new type of mapping scientist is emerging from the older specialties of photogrammetrist and cartographer: The *geographic information specialist* combines the functions of mapping science and surveying into a broader field concerned with the collection and analysis of geographic data.

Working Conditions

Surveyors and surveying technicians usually work an 8-hour day, 5 days a week, and may spend a lot of time outdoors. Sometimes they work longer hours during the summer, when weather and light conditions are most suitable for fieldwork. Seasonal demands for longer hours are related to demand for specific surveying services. For example, construction-related work may be limited during times of inclement weather and aerial photography is most effective when the leaves are off the trees.

Surveyors and technicians engage in active, sometimes strenuous, work. They often stand for long periods, walk considerable distances, and climb hills with heavy packs of instruments and other equipment. They also can be exposed to all types of weather. Traveling is sometimes part of the job, and land surveyors and technicians may commute long distances, stay away from home overnight, or temporarily relocate near a survey site.

Although surveyors can spend considerable time indoors while planning surveys, searching court records for deed information, analyzing data, and preparing reports and maps, cartographers and photogrammetrists spend virtually all of their time in offices using computers and seldom visit the sites they are mapping.

Training, Other Qualifications, and Advancement

Most people prepare for a career as a licensed surveyor by combining postsecondary school courses in surveying with extensive on-the-job training. However, as technology advances, a 4-year college degree is increasingly becoming a prerequisite. A number of universities now offer 4-year programs leading to a bachelor's degree in surveying. Junior and community colleges, technical institutes, and vocational schools offer 1-year, 2-year, and 3-year programs in both surveying and surveying technology.

All 50 states and all U.S. territories license surveyors. For licensure, most state licensing boards require that individuals pass a written examination given by the National Council of Examiners for Engineering and Surveying (NCEES). Most states also require surveyors to pass a written examination prepared by the state licensing board. In addition, candidates must meet varying standards of formal education and work experience in the field.

In the past, many with little formal training in surveying started as members of survey crews and worked their way up to become licensed surveyors. Currently, the route to licensure is most often a combination of 4 years of college followed by passage of the Fundamentals of Surveying Exam. After passing this exam, most candidates continue to work under the supervision of an experienced surveyor for another 4 years and then take the Principles and Practice of Surveyors Exam for licensure. Specific requirements for training and education vary among the states. An increasing number of states require a bachelor's degree in surveying or in a closely related field, such as civil engineering or forestry (with courses in surveying), regardless of the number of years of experience. Some states require the degree to be from a school accredited by the Accreditation Board for Engineering and Technology (ABET). Many states also have a continuing education requirement.

High school students interested in surveying should take courses in algebra, geometry, trigonometry, drafting, mechanical drawing, and computer science. High school graduates with no formal training in surveying usually start as apprentices. Beginners with postsecondary school training in surveying usually can start as technicians or assistants. With on-the-job experience and formal training in surveying—either in an institutional program or from a correspondence school—workers may advance to senior survey technician and then to party chief and, in some cases, to licensed surveyor (depending on state licensing requirements). However, it is becoming increasingly difficult to gain licensure without a formal education in surveying.

The National Society of Professional Surveyors, a member organization of the American Congress on Surveying and Mapping, has a voluntary certification program for surveying technicians. Technicians are certified at four levels requiring progressive amounts of experience in addition to the passing of written examinations. Although not required for state licensure, many employers require certification for promotion to positions with greater responsibilities.

Surveyors should have the ability to visualize objects, distances, sizes, and abstract forms. They must work with precision and accuracy, because mistakes can be costly. Members of a survey party must be in good physical condition, because they work outdoors and often carry equipment over difficult terrain. They need good eyesight, coordination, and hearing to communicate verbally and manually (using hand signals). Surveying is a cooperative operation, so good interpersonal skills and the ability to work as part of a team are important. Good office skills also are essential, because surveyors must be able to research old deeds and other legal papers and prepare reports that document their work.

Cartographers and photogrammetrists usually have a bachelor's degree in cartography; geography; or a related field such as surveying, engineering, forestry, or a physical science. Although it is possible to enter these positions through previous experience as a photogrammetric or cartographic technician, nowadays most cartographic and photogrammetric technicians have had some specialized postsecondary school training. With the development of GIS, cartographers and photogrammetrists need additional education and stronger technical skills—including more experience with computers—than in the past.

The American Society for Photogrammetry and Remote Sensing has a voluntary certification program for photogrammetrists. To qualify for this professional distinction, individuals must meet work experience standards and pass an oral or a written examination.

Employment

Surveyors, cartographers, photogrammetrists, and surveying technicians held about 131,000 jobs in 2004. The following tabulation shows the distribution of employment by occupational specialty:

Surveying and mapping technicians 65,000

Surveyors 56,000

Cartographers and photogrammetrists....................11,000

The architectural, engineering, and related services industry—including firms that provided surveying and mapping services to other industries on a contract basis—provided 2 out of 3 jobs for these workers. Federal, state, and local governmental agencies provided almost 1 in 6 jobs. Major federal government employers are the U.S. Geological Survey (USGS), the Bureau of Land Management (BLM), the National Geodetic Survey, and the Army Corps of Engineers. Most surveyors in state and local government work for highway departments or urban planning and redevelopment agencies. Construction, mining, and utility companies also employ surveyors, cartographers, photogrammetrists, and surveying technicians. Only a small number were self-employed in 2004.

Job Outlook

Overall employment of surveyors, cartographers, photogrammetrists, and surveying technicians is expected to grow about as fast as average for all occupations through the year 2014. The widespread availability and use of advanced technologies, such as GPS, GIS, and remote sensing, will continue to increase both the accuracy and productivity of these workers, limiting job growth to some extent. However, job openings will continue to arise from the need to replace workers who transfer to other occupations or who leave the labor force altogether. Many of the workers in these occupations are approaching retirement age.

Opportunities for surveyors, cartographers, and photogrammetrists should remain concentrated in architectural, engineering, and related services firms. Areas such as urban planning, emergency preparedness, and natural resource exploration and mapping also should provide employment growth, particularly with regard to producing maps for the management of emergencies and updating maps with the newly available technology. However, employment may fluctuate from year to year as a function of construction activity or with mapping needs for land and resource management.

Opportunities should be stronger for professional surveyors than for surveying and mapping technicians. Advancements in technology, such as total stations and GPS, have made surveying parties smaller than they were in the past. Opportunities for technicians should be available in basic GIS-related data-entry work. However, many persons possess the basic skills needed to qualify for these jobs, so applicants for technician jobs may face competition.

As technologies become more complex, opportunities will be best for surveyors, cartographers, and photogrammetrists who have a bachelor's degree and strong technical skills. Increasing demand for geographic data, as opposed to traditional surveying services, will mean better opportunities for cartographers and photogrammetrists who are involved in the development and use of geographic and land information systems. New technologies, such as GPS and GIS, also may enhance employment opportunities for surveyors and for surveying technicians who have the educational background and who have acquired technical skills that enable them to work with the new systems. At the same time, upgraded licensing requirements will continue to limit opportunities for professional advancement for those without a bachelor's degree.

Earnings

Median annual earnings of cartographers and photogrammetrists were $46,080 in May 2004. The middle 50 percent earned between $35,160 and $59,830. The lowest 10 percent earned less than $28,210 and the highest 10 percent earned more than $74,440.

Median annual earnings of surveyors were $42,980 in May 2004. The middle 50 percent earned between $31,940 and $57,190. The lowest 10 percent earned less than $24,640 and the highest 10 percent earned more than $71,640. Median hourly earnings of surveyors employed in architectural, engineering, and related services were $41,710 in May 2004.

Median annual earnings of surveying and mapping technicians were $30,380 in May 2004. The middle 50 percent earned between $23,600 and $40,100. The lowest 10 percent earned less than $19,140, and the highest 10 percent earned more than $51,070. Median annual earnings of surveying and mapping technicians employed in architectural, engineering, and related services were $28,610 in May 2004, while those employed by local governments had median annual earnings of $34,810.

Related Occupations

Surveying is related to the work of civil engineers, architects, and landscape architects because an accurate survey is the first step in land development and construction projects. Cartography and geodetic surveying are related to the work of environmental scientists and hydrologists and geoscientists, who study the earth's internal composition, surface, and atmosphere. Cartography also is related to the work of geographers and urban and regional planners, who study and decide how the earth's surface is to be used.

Sources of Additional Information

For career information on surveyors, cartographers, photogrammetrists, and surveying technicians, contact

▸ American Congress on Surveying and Mapping, Suite 403, 6 Montgomery Village Ave., Gaithersburg, MD 20879. Internet: http://www.acsm.net

Information about career opportunities, licensure requirements, and the surveying technician certification program is available from

▸ National Society of Professional Surveyors, Suite 403, 6 Montgomery Village Ave., Gaithersburg, MD 20879. Internet: http://www.acsm.net/nsps

For information on a career as a geodetic surveyor, contact

▸ American Association of Geodetic Surveying (AAGS), Suite 403, 6 Montgomery Village Ave., Gaithersburg, MD 20879. Internet: http://www.acsm.net/aags

General information on careers in photogrammetry and remote sensing is available from

▸ ASPRS: Imaging and Geospatial Information Society, 5410 Grosvenor Ln., Suite 210, Bethesda, MD 20814-2160. Internet: http://www.asprs.org

Teachers—Postsecondary

(O*NET 25-1011.00, 25-1021.00, 25-1022.00, 25-1031.00, 25-1032.00, 25-1041.00, 25-1042.00, 25-1043.00, 25-1051.00, 25-1052.00, 25-1053.00, 25-1054.00, 25-1061.00, 25-1062.00, 25-1063.00, 25-1064.00, 25-1065.00, 25-1066.00, 25-1067.00, 25-1069.99, 25-1071.00, 25-1072.00, 25-1081.00, 25-1082.00, 25-1111.00, 25-1112.00, 25-1113.00, 25-1121.00, 25-1122.00, 25-1123.00, 25-1124.00, 25-1125.00, 25-1126.00, 25-1191.00, 25-1192.00, 25-1193.00, 25-1194.00, and 25-1199.99)

Significant Points

■ Opportunities for postsecondary teaching jobs are expected to be good, but many new openings will be for part-time or non-tenure-track positions.

■ Prospects for teaching jobs will be better and earnings higher in academic fields in which many qualified teachers opt for nonacademic careers, such as health specialties, business, and computer science, for example.

■ Educational qualifications for postsecondary teacher jobs range from expertise in a particular field to a Ph.D., depending on the subject being taught and the type of educational institution.

Nature of the Work

Postsecondary teachers instruct students in a wide variety of academic and vocational subjects beyond the high school level that may lead to a degree or to improvement in one's knowledge or career skills. These teachers include college and university faculty, postsecondary career and technical education teachers, and graduate teaching assistants.

College and university faculty make up the majority of postsecondary teachers. They teach and advise more than 16 million full- and part-time college students and perform a significant part of our nation's research. Faculty also keep up with new developments in their field and may consult with government, business, nonprofit, and community organizations.

Faculty usually are organized into departments or divisions, based on academic subject or field. They usually teach several different related courses in their subject—algebra, calculus, and statistics, for example. They may instruct undergraduate or graduate students or both. College and university faculty may give lectures to several hundred students in large halls, lead small seminars, or supervise students in laboratories. They prepare lectures, exercises, and laboratory experiments; grade exams and papers; and advise and work with students individually. In universities, they also supervise graduate students' teaching and research. College faculty work with an increasingly varied student population made up of growing shares of part-time, older, and culturally and racially diverse students.

Faculty keep abreast of developments in their field by reading current literature, talking with colleagues, and participating in professional conferences. They may also do their own research to expand knowledge in their field. They may perform experiments; collect and analyze data; and examine original documents, literature, and other source material. From this process, they arrive at conclusions and publish their findings in scholarly journals, books, and electronic media.

Most college and university faculty extensively use computer technology, including the Internet; e-mail; CD-ROMs; and software programs, such as statistical packages. They may use computers in the classroom as teaching aids and may post course content, class notes, class schedules, and other information on the Internet. The use of e-mail, chat rooms, and other techniques has greatly improved communications between students and teachers and among students.

Some faculty use the Internet to teach courses to students at remote sites. These so-called "distance learning" courses are an increasingly popular option for non-traditional students such as working adults. While the courses are more convenient for students, faculty who teach these courses must be able to adapt existing courses to make them successful online or design a new course that takes advantage of the format.

Most faculty members serve on academic or administrative committees that deal with the policies of their institution, departmental matters, academic issues, curricula, budgets, equipment purchases, and hiring. Some work with student and community organizations. Department chairpersons are faculty members who usually teach some courses but have heavier administrative responsibilities.

The proportion of time spent on research, teaching, administrative, and other duties varies by individual circumstance and type of institution. Faculty members at universities normally spend a significant part of their time doing research; those in 4-year colleges, somewhat less; and those in 2-year colleges, relatively little. The teaching load, however, often is heavier in 2-year colleges and somewhat lighter at 4-year institutions. Full professors at all types of institutions usually spend a larger portion of their time conducting research than do assistant professors, instructors, and lecturers.

In addition to traditional 2- and 4-year institutions, an increasing number of faculty work in alternative schools or in programs that are aimed at providing career-related education for working adults. Courses are usually offered online or on nights and weekends. Faculty at these programs generally work part time and are only responsible for teaching, with little to no administrative and research responsibilities.

Postsecondary vocational education teachers, also known as *postsecondary career and technical education teachers,* provide instruction for occupations that require specialized training but may not require a 4-year degree, such as welder, dental hygienist, X-ray technician, auto mechanic, and cosmetologist. Classes often are taught in an industrial or laboratory setting where students are provided hands-on experience. For example, welding instructors show students various welding techniques and essential safety practices, watch them use tools and equipment, and have them repeat procedures until they meet the specific standards required by the trade. Increasingly, career and technical education teachers are integrating academic and vocational curriculums so that students obtain a variety of skills that can be applied to the "real world."

Career and technical education teachers have many of the same responsibilities that other college and university faculty have. They must prepare lessons, grade papers, attend faculty meetings, and keep abreast of developments in their field. Career and technical education teachers at community colleges and career and technical schools also often play a key role in students' transition from school to work by helping to establish internship programs for students and by facilitating contact between students and prospective employers.

Graduate teaching assistants, often referred to as *graduate TAs*, assist faculty, department chairs, or other professional staff at colleges and universities by performing teaching or teaching-related duties. In addition to their work responsibilities, assistants have their own school commitments, as they are also students who are working towards earning a graduate degree, such as a Ph.D. Some teaching assistants have full responsibility for teaching a course—usually one that is introductory in nature—which can include preparation of lectures and exams and assigning final grades to students. Others provide assistance to faculty members, which may consist of a variety of tasks such as grading papers, monitoring exams, holding office hours or help-sessions for students, conducting laboratory sessions, or administering quizzes to the class. Teaching assistants generally meet initially with the faculty member whom they are going to assist in order to determine exactly what is expected of them, as each faculty member may have his or her own needs. For example, some faculty members prefer assistants to sit in on classes, while others assign them other tasks to do during class time. Graduate teaching assistants may work one-on-one with a faculty member or, for large classes, they may be one of several assistants.

Working Conditions

Postsecondary teachers who work full time usually have flexible schedules. They must be present for classes, usually 12 to 16 hours per week, and for faculty and committee meetings. Most establish regular office hours for student consultations, usually 3 to 6 hours per week. Otherwise, teachers are free to decide when and where they will work and how much time to devote to course preparation, grading, study, research, graduate student supervision, and other activities.

Some teach night and weekend classes. This is particularly true for teachers at 2-year community colleges or institutions with large enrollments of older students who have full-time jobs or family responsibilities. Most colleges and universities require teachers to work 9 months of the year, which allows them the time to teach additional courses, do research, travel, or pursue nonacademic interests during the summer and school holidays. Colleges and universities usually have funds to support research or other professional development needs of full-time faculty, including travel to conferences and research sites.

About 3 out of 10 college and university faculty worked part time in 2004. Some part-timers, known as "adjunct faculty," have primary jobs outside of academia—in government, private industry, or nonprofit research—and teach "on the side." Others prefer to work part-time hours or seek full-time jobs but are unable to obtain them due to intense competition for available openings. Some work part time in more than one institution. Some adjunct faculty are not qualified for tenure-track positions because they lack a doctoral degree.

University faculty may experience a conflict between their responsibilities to teach students and the pressure to do research and publish their findings. This may be a particular problem for young faculty seeking advancement in 4-year research universities. Also, recent cutbacks in support workers and the hiring of more part-time faculty have put a greater administrative burden on full-time faculty. Requirements to teach online classes also have added greatly to the workloads of postsecondary teachers. Many find that developing the courses to put online, plus learning how to operate the technology and answering large amounts of e-mail, is very time-consuming.

Graduate TAs usually have flexibility in their work schedules like college and university faculty, but they also must spend a considerable amount of time pursuing their own academic coursework and studies. The number of hours that TAs work varies, depending on their assignments. Work may be stressful, particularly when assistants are given full responsibility for teaching a class; however, these types of positions allow graduate students the opportunity to gain valuable teaching experience. This experience is especially helpful for those graduate teaching assistants who seek to become faculty members at colleges and universities after completing their degree.

Training, Other Qualifications, and Advancement

The education and training required of postsecondary teachers varies widely, depending on the subject taught and educational institution employing them. Educational requirements for teachers are generally the highest at 4-year research universities while experience and expertise in a related occupation is the principal qualification at career and technical institutes.

Postsecondary teachers should communicate and relate well with students, enjoy working with them, and be able to motivate them. They should have inquiring and analytical minds and a strong desire to pursue and disseminate knowledge. Additionally, they must be self-motivated and able to work in an environment in which they receive little direct supervision.

Training requirements for postsecondary career and technical education teachers vary by state and by subject. In general, teachers need a bachelor's or higher degree plus at least 3 years of work experience in their field. In some fields, a license or certificate that demonstrates one's qualifications may be all that is required. Teachers update their skills through continuing education in order to maintain certification. They must also maintain ongoing dialogue with businesses to determine the most current skills needed in the workplace.

Four-year colleges and universities usually consider doctoral degree holders for full-time, tenure-track positions, but may hire master's degree holders or doctoral candidates for certain disciplines, such as the arts, or for part-time and temporary jobs. Most college and university faculty are in four academic ranks—professor, associate professor, assistant professor, and instructor. These positions usually are considered to be tenure-track positions. Most faculty members are hired as instructors or assistant professors. A smaller number of additional faculty members, called lecturers, are usually employed on contracts for a single academic term and are not on the tenure track.

In 2-year colleges, master's degree holders fill most full-time positions. However, in certain fields where there may be more applicants than available jobs, institutions can be more selective in their hiring practices. In these fields, master's degree holders may be passed over in favor of candidates holding Ph.Ds. Many 2-year institutions increasingly prefer job applicants to have some teaching experience or experience with distance learning. Preference also may be given to those holding dual master's degrees, especially at smaller institutions, because they can teach more subjects.

Schools and programs that provide education and training for working adults generally hire people who are experienced in the field to teach part time. A master's degree is also usually required.

Doctoral programs take an average of 6 years of full-time study beyond the bachelor's degree, including time spent completing a master's degree and a dissertation. Some programs, such as those in the humanities, may take longer to complete; others, such as those in engineering, usually are shorter. Candidates specialize in a subfield of a discipline—for example, organic chemistry, counseling psychology, or European history—but also take courses covering the entire discipline. Programs typically include 20 or more increasingly specialized courses and seminars plus comprehensive examinations on all major areas of the field. Candidates also must complete a dissertation—a written report on original research in the candidate's major field of study. The dissertation sets forth an original hypothesis or proposes a model and tests it. Students in the natural sciences and engineering usually do laboratory work; in the humanities, they study original documents and other published material. The dissertation is done under the guidance of one or more faculty advisors and usually takes 1 or 2 years of full-time work.

Some students, particularly those who studied in the natural sciences, spend additional years after earning their degree on postdoctoral research and study before taking a faculty position. Some Ph.D.s are able to extend postdoctoral appointments, or take new ones, if they are unable to find a faculty job. Most of these appointments offer a nominal salary.

Obtaining a position as a graduate teaching assistant is a good way to gain college teaching experience. To qualify, candidates must be enrolled in a graduate school program. In addition, some colleges and universities require teaching assistants to attend classes or take some training prior to being given responsibility for a course.

Although graduate teaching assistants usually work at the institution and in the department where they are earning their degree, teaching or internship positions for graduate students at institutions that do not grant a graduate degree have become more common in recent years. For example, a program called Preparing Future Faculty, administered by the Association of American Colleges and Universities and the Council of Graduate Schools, has led to the creation of many now-independent programs that offer graduate students at research universities the opportunity to work as teaching assistants at other types of institutions, such as liberal arts or community colleges. Working with a mentor, the graduate students teach classes and learn how to improve their teaching techniques. They may attend faculty and committee meetings; develop a curriculum; and learn how to balance the teaching, research, and administrative roles that faculty play. These programs provide valuable learning opportunities for graduate students interested in teaching at the postsec-

ondary level and also help to make these students aware of the differences among the various types of institutions at which they may someday work.

For faculty, a major step in the traditional academic career is attaining tenure. New tenure-track faculty usually are hired as instructors or assistant professors and must serve a period—usually 7 years—under term contracts. At the end of the period, their record of teaching, research, and overall contribution to the institution is reviewed; tenure is granted if the review is favorable. Those denied tenure usually must leave the institution. Tenured professors cannot be fired without just cause and due process. Tenure protects the faculty's academic freedom—the ability to teach and conduct research without fear of being fired for advocating controversial or unpopular ideas. It also gives both faculty and institutions the stability needed for effective research and teaching and provides financial security for faculty. Some institutions have adopted post-tenure review policies to encourage ongoing evaluation of tenured faculty.

The number of tenure-track positions is declining as institutions seek flexibility in dealing with financial matters and changing student interests. Institutions rely more heavily on limited term contracts and part-time, or adjunct, faculty, thus shrinking the total pool of tenured faculty. Limited-term contracts—typically 2 to 5 years, may be terminated or extended when they expire, but generally do not lead to the granting of tenure. In addition, some institutions have limited the percentage of faculty who can be tenured.

For most postsecondary teachers, advancement involves a move into administrative and managerial positions, such as departmental chairperson, dean, and president. At 4-year institutions, such advancement requires a doctoral degree. At 2-year colleges, a doctorate is helpful but not usually required, except for advancement to some top administrative positions.

Employment

Postsecondary teachers held nearly 1.6 million jobs in 2004. Most were employed in public and private 4-year colleges and universities and in 2-year community colleges. Other postsecondary teachers are employed by schools and institutes that specialize in training people in a specific field, such as technology centers or culinary schools, or work for businesses that provide professional development courses to employees of companies. Some career and technical education teachers work for state and local governments and job training facilities. The following tabulation shows postsecondary teaching jobs in specialties having 20,000 or more jobs in 2004:

Health specialties teachers	150,000
Graduate teaching assistants	143,000
Vocational education teachers	127,000
Business teachers	85,000
Art, drama, and music teachers	78,000
Biological science teachers	76,000
English language and literature teachers	69,000
Education teachers	60,000
Mathematical science teachers	53,000
Computer science teachers	45,000
Engineering teachers	42,000

Nursing instructors and teachers 41,000

Psychology teachers...37,000

Foreign language and literature teachers...............27,000

Communications teachers 26,000

History teachers 24,000

Chemistry teachers 23,000

Philosophy and religion teachers 23,000

Job Outlook

Overall, employment of postsecondary teachers is expected to grow much faster than the average for all occupations through 2014. A significant proportion of these new jobs will be part-time positions. Job opportunities are generally expected to be very good—although they will vary somewhat from field to field—as numerous openings for all types of postsecondary teachers result from retirements of current postsecondary teachers and continued increases in student enrollments.

Projected growth in college and university enrollment over the next decade stems mainly from the expected increase in the population of 18- to 24-year-olds, who constitute the majority of students at postsecondary institutions, and from the increasing number of high school graduates who choose to attend these institutions. Adults returning to college to enhance their career prospects or to update their skills also will continue to create new opportunities for postsecondary teachers, particularly at community colleges and for-profit institutions that cater to working adults. However, many postsecondary educational institutions receive a significant portion of their funding from state and local governments, so expansion of public higher education will be limited by state and local budgets. Nevertheless, in addition to growth in enrollments, the need to replace the large numbers of postsecondary teachers who are likely to retire over the next decade will also create a significant number of openings. Many postsecondary teachers were hired in the late 1960s and the 1970s to teach members of the baby boom generation, and they are expected to retire in growing numbers in the years ahead.

Ph.D. recipients seeking jobs as postsecondary teachers will experience favorable job prospects over the next decade. While competition will remain tight for tenure-track positions at 4-year colleges and universities, there will be a considerable number of part-time or renewable term appointments at these institutions and positions at community colleges available to them. Opportunities for master's degree holders are also expected to be favorable, as community colleges and other institutions that employ them, such as professional career education programs, are expected to experience considerable growth.

Opportunities for graduate teaching assistants are expected to be very good due to prospects for much higher undergraduate enrollments coupled with more modest graduate enrollment increases. Constituting almost 9 percent of all postsecondary teachers, graduate teaching assistants play an integral role in the postsecondary education system, and they are expected to continue to do so in the future.

One of the main reasons why students attend postsecondary institutions is to prepare themselves for careers, so the best job prospects for postsecondary teachers are likely to be in fields where job growth is expected to be strong over the next decade. These will include fields such as business, health specialties, nursing, and biological sciences. Community colleges and other institutions offering career and technical education have been among the most rapidly growing, and these institutions are expected to offer some of the best opportunities for postsecondary teachers.

Earnings

Median annual earnings of all postsecondary teachers in May 2004 were $51,800. The middle 50 percent earned between $36,590 and $72,490. The lowest 10 percent earned less than $25,460, and the highest 10 percent earned more than $99,980.

Earnings for college faculty vary according to rank and type of institution, geographic area, and field. According to a 2004–2005 survey by the American Association of University Professors, salaries for full-time faculty averaged $68,505. By rank, the average was $91,548 for professors, $65,113 for associate professors, $54,571 for assistant professors, $39,899 for instructors, and $45,647 for lecturers. Faculty in 4-year institutions earn higher salaries, on average, than do those in 2-year schools. In 2004–2005, faculty salaries averaged $79,342 in private independent institutions, $66,851 in public institutions, and $61,103 in religiously affiliated private colleges and universities. In fields with high-paying nonacademic alternatives—medicine, law, engineering, and business, among others—earnings exceed these averages. In other fields—such as the humanities and education—they are lower.

Many faculty members have significant earnings in addition to their base salary from consulting, teaching additional courses, research, writing for publication, or other employment. In addition, many college and university faculty enjoy some unique benefits, including access to campus facilities, tuition waivers for dependents, housing and travel allowances, and paid sabbatical leaves. Part-time faculty usually have fewer benefits than full-time faculty.

Earnings for postsecondary career and technical education teachers vary widely by subject, academic credentials, experience, and region of the country. Part-time instructors usually receive few benefits.

Related Occupations

Postsecondary teaching requires the ability to communicate ideas well, motivate students, and be creative. Workers in other occupations that require these skills are teachers—preschool, kindergarten, elementary, middle, and secondary; education administrators; librarians; counselors; writers and editors; public relations specialists; and management analysts. Faculty research activities often are similar to those of scientists, as well as to those of managers and administrators in industry, government, and nonprofit research organizations.

Sources of Additional Information

Professional societies related to a field of study often provide information on academic and nonacademic employment opportunities. Names and addresses of many of these societies appear in job descriptions elsewhere in this book.

Special publications on higher education, such as *The Chronicle of Higher Education*, list specific employment opportunities for faculty. These publications are available in libraries.

For information on the Preparing Future Faculty program, contact

▸ Council of Graduate Schools, One Dupont Circle NW, Suite 430, Washington, DC 20036-1173. Internet: http://www.preparing-faculty.org

For information on postsecondary career and technical education teaching positions, contact state departments of career and technical education. General information on adult and career and technical education is available from

▸ Association for Career and Technical Education, 1410 King St., Alexandria, VA 22314. Internet: http://www.acteonline.org

Television, Video, and Motion Picture Camera Operators and Editors

(O*NET 27-4031.00 and 27-4032.00)

Significant Points

■ Workers acquire their skills through on-the-job or formal postsecondary training.

■ Technical expertise, a good eye, imagination, and creativity are essential.

■ Keen competition for job openings is expected because many talented peopled are attracted to the field.

Nature of the Work

Television, video, and motion picture camera operators produce images that tell a story, inform or entertain an audience, or record an event. *Film and video editors* edit soundtracks, film, and video for the motion picture, cable, and broadcast television industries. Some camera operators do their own editing.

Making commercial-quality movies and video programs requires technical expertise and creativity. Producing successful images requires choosing and presenting interesting material, selecting appropriate equipment, and applying a good eye and a steady hand to ensure smooth, natural movement of the camera.

Camera operators use television, video, or motion picture cameras to shoot a wide range of material, including television series, studio programs, news and sporting events, music videos, motion pictures, documentaries, and training sessions. Some camera operators film or videotape private ceremonies and special events, such as weddings and conference program sessions. Those who record images on videotape are often called *videographers*. Many are employed by independent television stations; local affiliate stations of television networks; large cable and television networks; or smaller, independent production companies. *Studio camera operators* work in a broadcast studio and usually videotape their subjects from a fixed position. *News camera operators*, also called *electronic news gathering (ENG) operators*, work as part of a reporting team, following

newsworthy events as they unfold. To capture live events, they must anticipate the action and act quickly. ENG operators sometimes edit raw footage on the spot for relay to a television affiliate for broadcast.

Camera operators employed in the entertainment field use motion picture cameras to film movies, television programs, and commercials. Those who film motion pictures also are known as *cinematographers*. Some specialize in filming cartoons or special effects. Cinematographers may be an integral part of the action, using cameras in any of several different mounts. For example, the camera operator can be stationary and shoot whatever passes in front of the lens, or the camera can be mounted on a track, with the camera operator responsible for shooting the scene from different angles or directions. Wider use of digital cameras has enhanced the number of angles and the clarity that a camera operator can provide. Other camera operators sit on cranes and follow the action while crane operators move them into position. *Steadicam operators* mount a harness and carry the camera on their shoulders to provide a clear picture while they move about the action. Camera operators who work in the entertainment field often meet with directors, actors, editors, and camera assistants to discuss ways of filming, editing, and improving scenes.

Working Conditions

Working conditions for camera operators and editors vary considerably. Those employed by television and cable networks and advertising agencies usually work a 5-day, 40-hour week; however, they may work longer hours to meet production schedules. ENG operators often work long, irregular hours and must be available to work on short notice. Camera operators and editors working in motion picture production also may work long, irregular hours.

ENG operators and those who cover major events, such as conventions or sporting events, frequently travel locally and stay overnight or travel to distant places for longer periods. Camera operators filming television programs or motion pictures may travel to film on location.

Some camera operators—especially ENG operators covering accidents, natural disasters, civil unrest, or military conflicts—work in uncomfortable or even dangerous surroundings. Many camera operators must wait long hours in all kinds of weather for an event to take place and must stand or walk for long periods while carrying heavy equipment. ENG operators often work under strict deadlines.

Training, Other Qualifications, and Advancement

Employers usually seek applicants with a good eye, imagination, and creativity, as well as a good technical understanding of how the camera operates. Television, video, and motion picture camera operators and editors usually acquire their skills through on-the-job training or formal postsecondary training at vocational schools, colleges, universities, or photographic institutes. Formal education may be required for some positions.

Many universities, community and junior colleges, vocational-technical institutes, and private trade and technical schools offer courses in camera operation and videography. Basic courses cover equipment, processes, and techniques. Bachelor's degree programs, especially those including business courses, provide a well-rounded education. Film schools also may provide training on the artistic or aesthetic aspects of filmmaking.

Individuals interested in camera operations should subscribe to videographic newsletters and magazines, join audio-video clubs, and seek summer or part-time employment in cable and television networks, motion picture studios, or camera and video stores.

Camera operators in entry-level jobs learn to set up lights, cameras, and other equipment. They may receive routine assignments requiring adjustments to their cameras or decisions on what subject matter to capture. Camera operators in the film and television industries usually are hired for a project on the basis of recommendations from individuals such as producers, directors of photography, and camera assistants from previous projects or through interviews with the producer. ENG and studio camera operators who work for television affiliates usually start in small markets to gain experience.

Camera operators need good eyesight, artistic ability, and hand-eye coordination. They should be patient, accurate, and detail oriented. Camera operators also should have good communication skills and, if needed, the ability to hold a camera by hand for extended periods.

Camera operators who run their own businesses, or freelance, need business skills as well as talent. These individuals must know how to submit bids, write contracts, get permission to shoot on locations that normally are not open to the public, obtain releases to use film or tape of people, price their services, secure copyright protection for their work, and keep financial records.

With experience, operators may advance to more demanding assignments or to positions with larger or network television stations. Advancement for ENG operators may mean moving to larger media markets. Other camera operators and editors may become directors of photography for movie studios, advertising agencies, or television programs. Some teach at technical schools, film schools, or universities.

Employment

Television, video, and motion picture camera operators held about 28,000 jobs in 2004, and film and video editors held about 20,000. Many are employed by independent television stations, local affiliate stations of television networks or broadcast groups, large cable and television networks, or smaller independent production companies. About 1 in 5 camera operators were self-employed. Some self-employed camera operators contracted with television networks, documentary or independent filmmakers, advertising agencies, or trade show or convention sponsors to work on individual projects for a set fee, often at a daily rate.

Most of the salaried camera operators were employed by television broadcasting stations or motion picture studios. More than half of the salaried film and video editors worked for motion picture studios. Most camera operators and editors worked in large metropolitan areas.

Job Outlook

Television, video, and motion picture camera operators and editors can expect keen competition for job openings because the work is attractive to many people. The number of individuals interested in positions as videographers and movie camera operators usually is much greater than the number of openings. Those who succeed in landing a salaried job or attracting enough work to earn a living by freelancing are likely to be the most creative and highly motivated people, able to adapt to rapidly changing technologies and adept at operating a business. Related work experience or job-related training also can benefit prospective camera operators.

Employment of camera operators and editors is expected to grow about as fast as the average for all occupations through 2014. Rapid expansion of the entertainment market, especially motion picture production and distribution, will spur growth of camera operators. In addition, computer and Internet services will provide new outlets for interactive productions. Growth will be tempered, however, by the increased off-shore production of motion pictures. Camera operators will be needed to film made-for-the-Internet broadcasts, such as live music videos, digital movies, sports features, and general information or entertainment programming. These images can be delivered directly into the home either on compact discs or as streaming video over the Internet. Job growth in radio and television broadcasting will be tempered by the use of robocams and Parkervision systems for studio broadcasts; cameras in these systems are automated and under the control of a single person working either on the studio floor or in a director's booth.

Earnings

Median annual earnings for television, video, and motion picture camera operators were $37,610 in May 2004. The middle 50 percent earned between $22,640 and $56,400. The lowest 10 percent earned less than $15,730, and the highest 10 percent earned more than $76,100. Median annual earnings were $48,900 in the motion picture and video industries and $29,560 in radio and television broadcasting.

Median annual earnings for film and video editors were $43,590 in May 2004. The middle 50 percent earned between $29,310 and $63,890. The lowest 10 percent earned less than $21,710, and the highest 10 percent earned more than $93,950. Median annual earnings were $44,710 in the motion picture and video industries, which employed the largest numbers of film and video editors.

Many camera operators who work in film or video are freelancers, whose earnings tend to fluctuate each year. Because most freelance camera operators purchase their own equipment, they incur considerable expense acquiring and maintaining cameras and accessories. Some camera operators belong to unions, including the International Alliance of Theatrical Stage Employees and the National Association of Broadcast Employees and Technicians.

Related Occupations

Related arts and media occupations include artists and related workers; broadcast and sound engineering technicians; and radio operators, designers, and photographers.

Sources of Additional Information

For information about careers as a camera operator, contact

▸ International Cinematographer's Guild, 80 Eighth Avenue, 14th Floor, New York, NY 10011.

▸ National Association of Broadcast Employees and Technicians, 501 Third Street NW, 6th Floor, Washington, DC 20001. Internet: http://www.nabetcwa.org/

Information about career and employment opportunities for camera operators and film and video editors also is available from local offices of state employment service agencies, local offices of the relevant trade unions, and local television and film production companies that employ these workers.

Tool and Die Makers

(O*NET 51-4111.00)

Significant Points

■ Most tool and die makers train for 4 or 5 years in apprenticeships or postsecondary programs; employers typically recommend apprenticeship training.

■ Employment is projected to decline because of strong foreign competition and advancements in automation.

■ Excellent job opportunities are expected; employers in certain parts of the country report difficulty attracting well-trained applicants.

Nature of the Work

Tool and die makers are among the most highly skilled workers in manufacturing. These workers produce tools, dies, and special guiding and holding devices that enable machines to manufacture a variety of products we use daily—from clothing and furniture to heavy equipment and parts for aircraft.

Toolmakers craft precision tools and machines that are used to cut, shape, and form metal and other materials. They also produce jigs and fixtures (devices that hold metal while it is bored, stamped, or drilled) and gauges and other measuring devices. Die makers construct metal forms (dies) that are used to shape metal in stamping and forging operations. They also make metal molds for diecasting and for molding plastics, ceramics, and composite materials. Some tool and die makers craft prototypes of parts and then, working with engineers and designers, determine how best to manufacture the part. In addition to developing, designing, and producing new tools and dies, these workers also may repair worn or damaged tools, dies, gauges, jigs, and fixtures.

To perform these functions, tool and die makers employ many types of machine tools and precision measuring instruments. They also must be familiar with the machining properties, such as hardness and heat tolerance, of a wide variety of common metals, alloys, plastics, ceramics, and other composite materials. As a result, tool and die makers are knowledgeable in machining operations, mathematics, and blueprint reading. In fact, tool and die makers often are considered highly specialized machinists. The main difference between tool and die makers and machinists is that machinists normally make a single part during the production process, while tool and die makers make parts and assemble and adjust machines used in the production process. (See the description of machinists elsewhere in this book.)

Traditionally, tool and die makers, working from blueprints, first must plan the sequence of operations necessary to manufacture the tool or die. Next, they measure and mark the pieces of metal that will be cut to form parts of the final product. At this point, tool and die makers cut, drill, or bore the part as required, checking to ensure that the final product meets specifications. Finally, these workers assemble the parts and perform finishing jobs such as filing, grinding, and polishing surfaces. While manual machining has declined, companies still employ it for some simple and low-quantity parts.

Most tool and die makers today use computer-aided design (CAD) to develop products and parts. Specifications entered into computer programs can be used to electronically develop blueprints for the required tools and dies. Numerical tool and process control programmers use computer-aided design or computer-aided manufacturing (CAD/CAM) programs to convert electronic drawings into CAM-based computer programs that contain instructions for a sequence of cutting tool operations. (See the description of computer control programmers and operators elsewhere in this book.) After these programs are developed, computer numerically controlled (CNC) machines follow the set of instructions contained in the program to produce the part. Computer-controlled machine tool operators or machinists normally operate CNC machines; however, tool and die makers are trained in both operating CNC machines and writing CNC programs, and they may perform either task. CNC programs are stored electronically for future use, saving time and increasing worker productivity.

After machining the parts, tool and die makers carefully check the accuracy of the parts, using many tools, including coordinate measuring machines (CMM), which use software and sensor arms to compare the dimensions of the part to electronic blueprints. Next, they assemble the different parts into a functioning machine. They file, grind, shim, and adjust the different parts to properly fit them together. Finally, the tool and die makers set up a test run using the tools or dies they have made to make sure that the manufactured parts meet specifications. If problems occur, they compensate by adjusting the tools or dies.

Working Conditions

Tool and die makers usually work in toolrooms. These areas are quieter than the production floor because there are fewer machines in use at one time. They also are generally kept clean and cool to minimize heat-related expansion of metal workpieces and to accommodate the growing number of computer-operated machines. To minimize the exposure of workers to moving parts, machines have guards and shields. Most computer-controlled machines are totally enclosed, minimizing the exposure of workers to noise, dust, and the lubricants used to cool workpieces during machining. Tool and die makers also must follow safety rules and wear protective equipment, such as safety glasses to shield against bits of flying metal, earplugs to protect against noise, and gloves and masks to reduce exposure to hazardous lubricants and cleaners. These workers also need stamina because they often spend much of the day on their feet and may do moderately heavy lifting.

Companies employing tool and die makers have traditionally operated only one shift per day. Overtime and weekend work are common, especially during peak production periods.

Training, Other Qualifications, and Advancement

Most tool and die makers learn their trade through 4 or 5 years of education and training in formal apprenticeships or postsecondary programs. Apprenticeship programs include a mix of classroom instruction and on-the-job-training. According to most employers, these apprenticeship programs are the best way to learn all aspects of tool and die making. A number of tool and die makers receive most of their formal classroom training from community and technical colleges, often in conjunction with an apprenticeship program.

Traditional apprenticeship programs allowed workers to advance by completing a set number of hours of on-the-job training and successfully completing specific courses. The National Institute of Metalworking Skills (NIMS) is developing new standards that would replace the required number of hours with competency-based tests. Whether competency tests will change the length of the traditional training process will probably depend upon the apprentice's prior experience, dedication, and natural ability. However, the required training courses for a journeyman tool and die maker will continue to take 4 to 5 years to complete.

Even after completing the apprenticeship, tool and die makers still need years of experience to become highly skilled. Most specialize in making certain types of tools, molds, or dies.

Tool and die maker trainees learn to operate milling machines, lathes, grinders, wire electrical discharge machines, and other machine tools. They also learn to use hand tools for fitting and assembling gauges and other mechanical and metal-forming equipment. In addition, they study metalworking processes, such as heat treating and plating. Classroom training usually consists of tool designing, tool programming, blueprint reading, and, if needed, mathematics courses, including algebra, geometry, trigonometry, and basic statistics. Tool and die makers increasingly must have good computer skills to work with CAD/CAM technology, CNC machine tools, and computerized measuring machines.

Workers who become tool and die makers without completing formal apprenticeships generally acquire their skills through a combination of informal on-the-job training and classroom instruction at a vocational school or community college. They often begin as machine operators and gradually take on more difficult assignments. Many machinists become tool and die makers.

Because tools and dies must meet strict specifications—precision to one ten-thousandth of an inch is common—the work of tool and die makers requires skill with precision measuring devices and a high degree of patience and attention to detail. Good eyesight is essential. Persons entering this occupation also should be mechanically inclined, be able to work and solve problems independently, have strong mathematical skills, and be capable of doing work that requires concentration and physical effort.

Employers generally look for someone with a strong educational background as an indication that the person can more easily adapt to change, which is a constant in this occupation. As automation continues to change the way tools and dies are made, workers regularly need to update their skills in order to learn how to operate new equipment. Also, as materials such as alloys, ceramics, polymers, and plastics are increasingly used, tool and die makers need to learn new machining techniques to deal with the new materials.

There are several ways for skilled workers to advance. Some move into supervisory and administrative positions in their firms, or they may start their own shop. Others may take computer courses and become computer-controlled machine tool programmers. With a college degree, a tool and die maker can go into engineering or tool design.

Employment

Tool and die makers held about 103,000 jobs in 2004. Most worked in industries that manufacture metalworking machinery, transportation equipment (such as motor vehicle parts and aerospace products), and fabricated metal products, as well as plastics product manufacturing. Although they are found throughout the country, jobs are most plentiful in the Midwest, Northeast, and West, where many of the metalworking industries are located.

Job Outlook

Despite declining employment, excellent job opportunities are expected. Employers in certain parts of the country report difficulty attracting qualified applicants. The number of workers receiving training in this occupation is expected to continue to be fewer than the number of openings created each year by tool and die makers who retire or transfer to other occupations. A major factor limiting the number of people entering the occupation is that many young people who have the educational and personal qualifications necessary to learn tool and die making may prefer to attend college or may not wish to enter production occupations.

Employment of tool and die makers is projected to decline over the 2004–2014 period because of strong foreign competition and advancements in automation, including CNC machine tools and computer-aided design, that should improve worker productivity. On the other hand, tool and die makers play a key role in building and maintaining advanced automated manufacturing equipment. As firms invest in new equipment, modify production techniques, and implement product design changes more rapidly, they will continue to rely heavily on skilled tool and die makers for retooling.

Earnings

Median hourly earnings of tool and die makers were $20.55 in May 2004. The middle 50 percent earned between $16.70 and $25.93. The lowest 10 percent had earnings of less than $13.57, while the top 10 percent earned more than $31.19. Median hourly earnings in the manufacturing industries employing the largest numbers of tool and die makers in May 2004 were

Motor vehicle parts manufacturing	$26.93
Plastics product manufacturing	20.17
Forging and stamping	20.09

Metalworking machinery manufacturing 19.82

Machine shops; turned product; and screw, nut,
and bolt manufacturing 18.84

Apprentices' pay is tied to their skill level. As they gain more skills and reach specific levels of performance and experience, their pay increases.

Related Occupations

The occupations most closely related to the work of tool and die makers are other machining occupations. These include machinists; computer control programmers and operators; and machine setters, operators, and tenders—metal and plastic. Another occupation that requires precision and skill in working with metal is welding, soldering, and brazing workers.

Like tool and die makers, assemblers and fabricators assemble complex machinery. When measuring parts, tool and die makers use some of the same tools and equipment that inspectors, testers, sorters, samplers, and weighers use in their jobs.

Sources of Additional Information

For career information and to have inquiries on training and employment referred to member companies, contact

▸ Precision Machine Products Association, 6700 West Snowville Rd., Brecksville, OH 44141-3292. Internet: http://www.pmpa.org

For lists of schools and employers with tool and die apprenticeship and training programs, contact

▸ National Tooling and Machining Association, 9300 Livingston Rd., Ft. Washington, MD 20744. Internet: http://www.ntma.org

For information on careers, education and training, earnings, and apprenticeship opportunities in metalworking, contact

▸ Precision Metalforming Association Educational Foundation, 6363 Oak Tree Blvd., Independence, OH 44131-2500.

Urban and Regional Planners

(O*NET 19-3051.00)

Significant Points

■ Local governments employ 7 out of 10 urban and regional planners.

■ Most entry-level jobs require a master's degree; bachelor's-degree holders may find some entry-level positions, but advancement opportunities are limited.

■ Most new jobs will be in affluent, rapidly growing urban and suburban communities.

Nature of the Work

Planners develop long- and short-term plans to use land for the growth and revitalization of urban, suburban, and rural communities while helping local officials make decisions concerning social, economic, and environmental problems. Because local governments employ the majority of urban and regional planners, they often are referred to as community, regional, or city planners.

Planners promote the best use of a community's land and resources for residential, commercial, institutional, and recreational purposes. Planners may be involved in various other activities, including making decisions relating to establishing alternative public transportation systems, developing resources, and protecting ecologically sensitive regions. Urban and regional planners address issues such as traffic congestion, air pollution, and the effects of growth and change on a community. They may formulate plans relating to the construction of new school buildings, public housing, or other kinds of infrastructure. Some planners are involved in environmental issues ranging from pollution control to wetland preservation, forest conservation, and the location of new landfills. Planners also may be involved in drafting legislation on environmental, social, and economic issues, such as sheltering the homeless, planning a new park, or meeting the demand for new correctional facilities.

Planners examine proposed community facilities, such as schools, to be sure that these facilities will meet the changing demands placed upon them over time. They keep abreast of economic and legal issues involved in zoning codes, building codes, and environmental regulations. They ensure that builders and developers follow these codes and regulations. Planners also deal with land-use issues created by population movements. For example, as suburban growth and economic development create more new jobs outside cities, the need for public transportation that enables workers to get to those jobs increases. In response, planners develop transportation models and explain their details to planning boards and the general public.

Before preparing plans for community development, planners report on the current use of land for residential, business, and community purposes. Their reports include information on the location and capacity of streets, highways, airports, water and sewer lines, schools, libraries, and cultural and recreational sites. They also provide data on the types of industries in the community, the characteristics of the population, and employment and economic trends. Using this information, along with input from citizens' advisory committees, planners design the layout of land uses for buildings and other facilities, such as subway lines and stations. Planners prepare reports showing how their programs can be carried out and what they will cost.

Planners use computers to record and analyze information and to prepare reports and recommendations for government executives and others. Computer databases, spreadsheets, and analytical techniques are utilized to project program costs and forecast future trends in employment, housing, transportation, or population. Computerized geographic information systems enable planners to map land areas, to overlay maps with geographic variables such as population density, and to combine or manipulate geographic information to produce alternative plans for land use or development.

Urban and regional planners often confer with land developers, civic leaders, and public officials and may function as mediators in community disputes, presenting alternatives that are acceptable to opposing parties. Planners may prepare material for community relations programs, speak at civic meetings, and appear before legislative committees and elected officials to explain and defend their proposals.

In large organizations, planners usually specialize in a single area, such as transportation, demography, housing, historic preservation, urban design, environmental and regulatory issues, or economic development. In small organizations, planners do various kinds of planning.

Working Conditions

Urban and regional planners often travel to inspect the features of land under consideration for development or regulation, including its current use and the types of structures on it. Some local government planners involved in site development inspections spend most of their time in the field. Although most planners have a scheduled 40-hour workweek, they frequently attend evening or weekend meetings or public hearings with citizens' groups. Planners may experience the pressure of deadlines and tight work schedules, as well as political pressure generated by interest groups affected by proposals related to urban development and land use.

Training, Other Qualifications, and Advancement

For jobs as urban and regional planners, employers prefer workers who have advanced training. Most entry-level jobs in federal, state, and local government agencies require a master's degree from an accredited program in urban or regional planning or a master's degree in a related field, such as urban design or geography. A bachelor's degree from an accredited planning program, coupled with a master's degree in architecture, landscape architecture, or civil engineering, is good preparation for entry-level planning jobs in various areas, including urban design, transportation, and the environment. A master's degree from an accredited planning program provides the best training for a wide range of planning fields. Although graduates from one of the limited number of accredited bachelor's degree programs qualify for some entry-level positions, their advancement opportunities often are limited unless they acquire an advanced degree.

Courses in related disciplines, such as architecture, law, earth sciences, demography, economics, finance, health administration, geographic information systems, and management, are highly recommended. Because familiarity with computer models and statistical techniques is important, courses in statistics and computer science also are recommended.

In 2005, 68 colleges and universities offered an accredited master's degree program, and 15 offered an accredited bachelor's degree program, in urban or regional planning. Accreditation for these programs is from the Planning Accreditation Board, which consists of representatives of the American Institute of Certified Planners, the American Planning Association, and the Association of Collegiate Schools of Planning. Most graduate programs in planning require a minimum of 2 years of study.

Specializations most commonly offered by planning schools are environmental planning, land use and comprehensive planning, economic development, housing, historic preservation, and social planning. Other popular offerings include community development, transportation, and urban design. Graduate students spend consider-able time in studios, workshops, and laboratory courses learning to analyze and solve planning problems. They often are required to work in a planning office part time or during the summer. Local government planning offices frequently offer students internships, providing experience that proves invaluable in obtaining a full-time planning position after graduation.

The American Institute of Certified Planners, a professional institute within the American Planning Association, grants certification to individuals who have the appropriate combination of education and professional experience and who pass an examination. Certification may be helpful for promotion.

Planners must be able to think in terms of spatial relationships and visualize the effects of their plans and designs. They should be flexible and be able to reconcile different viewpoints and make constructive policy recommendations. The ability to communicate effectively, both orally and in writing, is necessary for anyone interested in this field.

After a few years of experience, planners may advance to assignments requiring a high degree of independent judgment, such as designing the physical layout of a large development or recommending policy and budget options. Some public-sector planners are promoted to community planning director and spend a great deal of time meeting with officials, speaking to civic groups, and supervising a staff. Further advancement occurs through a transfer to a larger jurisdiction with more complex problems and greater responsibilities or into related occupations, such as director of community or economic development.

Employment

Urban and regional planners held about 32,000 jobs in 2004. About 7 out of 10 were employed by local governments. Companies involved with architectural, engineering, and related services, as well as management, scientific, and technical consulting services, employ an increasing proportion of planners in the private sector. Others are employed in state government agencies dealing with housing, transportation, or environmental protection, and a small number work for the federal government.

Job Outlook

Employment of urban and regional planners is expected to grow about as fast as average for all occupations through 2014. Employment growth will be driven by the need for state and local governments to provide public services such as regulation of commercial development, the environment, transportation, housing, and land use and development for an expanding population. Nongovernmental initiatives dealing with historic preservation and redevelopment will provide additional openings. Some job openings also will arise from the need to replace experienced planners who transfer to other occupations, retire, or leave the labor force for other reasons. Graduates with a master's degree from an accredited program should have an advantage in the job market.

Most new jobs for urban and regional planners will be in local government, as planners will be needed to address an array of problems associated with population growth, especially in affluent, rapidly expanding communities. For example, new housing developments require roads, sewer systems, fire stations, schools, libraries, and recreation facilities that must be planned for in the midst of a consideration of budgetary constraints. Small-town chambers of commerce, economic development authorities, and tourism bureaus may hire planners, preferably with some background in marketing and public relations.

The fastest job growth for urban and regional planners will occur in the private sector, primarily in professional, scientific, and technical services. For example, planners may be employed by these firms to help design security measures for a building that meet a desired security level but that also are subtle and blend in with the surrounding area. However, because the private sector employs fewer than 2 out of 10 urban and regional planners, not as many new jobs will be created in the private sector as in government.

Earnings

Median annual earnings of urban and regional planners were $53,450 in May 2004. The middle 50 percent earned between $41,950 and $67,530. The lowest 10 percent earned less than $33,840, and the highest 10 percent earned more than $82,610. Median annual earnings in local government, the industry employing the largest number of urban and regional planners, were $52,520.

Related Occupations

Urban and regional planners develop plans for the growth of urban, suburban, and rural communities. Others whose work is similar include architects, civil engineers, environmental engineers, landscape architects, and geographers.

Sources of Additional Information

Information on careers, salaries, and certification in urban and regional planning is available from

▸ American Planning Association, 1776 Massachusetts Ave. NW, Washington, DC 20036-1904. Internet: http://www.planning.org

Information on accredited urban and regional planning programs is available from

▸ Association of Collegiate Schools of Planning, 6311 Mallard Trace, Tallahassee, FL 32312. Internet: http://www.acsp.org

Veterinarians

(O*NET 29-1131.00)

Significant Points

■ Veterinarians should have an affinity for animals and the ability to get along with their owners.

■ Graduation from an accredited college of veterinary medicine and a state license are required.

■ Competition for admission to veterinary school is keen; however, graduates should have very good job opportunities.

■ About 1 out of 5 veterinarians is self-employed; self-employed veterinarians usually have to work hard and long to build a sufficient client base.

Nature of the Work

Veterinarians play a major role in the health care of pets; livestock; and zoo, sporting, and laboratory animals. Some veterinarians use their skills to protect humans against diseases carried by animals and conduct clinical research on human and animal health problems. Others work in basic research, broadening the scope of fundamental theoretical knowledge, and in applied research, developing new ways to use knowledge.

Most veterinarians perform clinical work in private practices. More than 50 percent of these veterinarians predominantly or exclusively treat small animals. Small-animal practitioners usually care for companion animals, such as dogs and cats, but also treat birds, reptiles, rabbits, and other animals that can be kept as pets. About one-fourth of all veterinarians work in mixed animal practices, where they see pigs, goats, sheep, and some nondomestic animals in addition to companion animals. Veterinarians in clinical practice diagnose animal health problems; vaccinate against diseases, such as distemper and rabies; medicate animals suffering from infections or illnesses; treat and dress wounds; set fractures; perform surgery; and advise owners about animal feeding, behavior, and breeding.

A small number of private-practice veterinarians work exclusively with large animals, mostly horses or cows; some also care for various kinds of food animals. These veterinarians usually drive to farms or ranches to provide veterinary services for herds or individual animals. Much of this work involves preventive care to maintain the health of the animals. These veterinarians test for and vaccinate against diseases and consult with farm or ranch owners and managers regarding animal production, feeding, and housing issues. They also treat and dress wounds; set fractures; and perform surgery, including cesarean sections on birthing animals. Veterinarians euthanize animals when necessary. Other veterinarians care for zoo, aquarium, or laboratory animals.

Veterinarians who treat animals use medical equipment such as stethoscopes; surgical instruments; and diagnostic equipment, including radiographic and ultrasound equipment. Veterinarians working in research use a full range of sophisticated laboratory equipment.

Veterinarians can contribute to human as well as animal health. A number of veterinarians work with physicians and scientists as they research ways to prevent and treat various human health problems. For example, veterinarians contributed greatly in conquering malaria and yellow fever; solved the mystery of botulism; produced an anticoagulant used to treat some people with heart disease; and defined and developed surgical techniques for humans, such as hip and knee joint replacements and limb and organ transplants. Today, some determine the effects of drug therapies, antibiotics, or new surgical techniques by testing them on animals.

Some veterinarians are involved in food safety at various levels. Veterinarians who are livestock inspectors check animals for transmissible diseases, advise owners on the treatment of their animals, and may quarantine animals. Veterinarians who are meat, poultry, or egg product inspectors examine slaughtering and processing plants, check live animals and carcasses for disease, and enforce government regulations regarding food purity and sanitation.

Working Conditions

Veterinarians often work long hours. Those in group practices may take turns being on call for evening, night, or weekend work; solo practitioners may work extended and weekend hours, responding to emergencies or squeezing in unexpected appointments. The work setting often can be noisy.

Veterinarians in large-animal practices spend time driving between their office and farms or ranches. They work outdoors in all kinds of weather and may have to treat animals or perform surgery under unsanitary conditions. When working with animals that are frightened or in pain, veterinarians risk being bitten, kicked, or scratched.

Veterinarians working in nonclinical areas, such as public health and research, have working conditions similar to those of other professionals in those lines of work. In these cases, veterinarians enjoy clean, well-lit offices or laboratories and spend much of their time dealing with people rather than animals.

Training, Other Qualifications, and Advancement

Prospective veterinarians must graduate with a Doctor of Veterinary Medicine (D.V.M. or V.M.D.) degree from a 4-year program at an accredited college of veterinary medicine and must obtain a license to practice. There are 28 colleges in 26 states that meet accreditation standards set by the Council on Education of the American Veterinary Medical Association (AVMA). The prerequisites for admission vary. Many of these colleges do not require a bachelor's degree for entrance, but all require a significant number of credit hours—ranging from 45 to 90 semester hours—at the undergraduate level. However, most of the students admitted have completed an undergraduate program. Applicants without a bachelor's degree face a difficult task gaining admittance.

Preveterinary courses emphasize the sciences. Veterinary medical colleges typically require classes in organic and inorganic chemistry, physics, biochemistry, general biology, animal biology, animal nutrition, genetics, vertebrate embryology, cellular biology, microbiology, zoology, and systemic physiology. Some programs require calculus; some require only statistics, college algebra and trigonometry, or precalculus. Most veterinary medical colleges also require core courses, including some in English or literature, the social sciences, and the humanities. Increasingly, courses in practice management and career development are becoming a standard part of the curriculum to provide a foundation of general business knowledge for new graduates.

In addition to satisfying preveterinary course requirements, applicants must submit test scores from the Graduate Record Examination (GRE), the Veterinary College Admission Test (VCAT), or the Medical College Admission Test (MCAT), depending on the preference of the college to which they are applying. Currently, 22 schools require the GRE, 4 require the VCAT, and 2 accept the MCAT.

In admittance decisions, some veterinary medical colleges place heavy consideration on a candidate's veterinary and animal experience. Formal experience, such as work with veterinarians or scientists in clinics, agribusiness, research, or some area of health science, is particularly advantageous. Less formal experience, such as working with animals on a farm or ranch or at a stable or animal shelter, also is helpful. Students must demonstrate ambition and an eagerness to work with animals.

There is keen competition for admission to veterinary school. The number of accredited veterinary colleges has remained largely the same since 1983, whereas the number of applicants has risen significantly. Only about 1 in 3 applicants was accepted in 2004. AVMA-recognized veterinary specialties—such as pathology, internal medicine, dentistry, nutrition, ophthalmology, surgery, radiology, preventive medicine, and laboratory animal medicine—are usually in the form of a 2-year internship. Interns receive a small salary but usually find that their internship experience leads to a higher beginning salary relative to those of other starting veterinarians. Veterinarians who seek board certification in a specialty also must complete a 3- to 4-year residency program that provides intensive training in specialties such as internal medicine, oncology, radiology, surgery, dermatology, anesthesiology, neurology, cardiology, ophthalmology, and exotic small-animal medicine.

All states and the District of Columbia require that veterinarians be licensed before they can practice. The only exemptions are for veterinarians working for some federal agencies and some state governments. Licensing is controlled by the states and is not strictly uniform, although all states require the successful completion of the D.V.M. degree—or equivalent education—and a passing grade on a national board examination. The Educational Commission for Foreign Veterinary Graduates (ECFVG) grants certification to individuals trained outside the United States who demonstrate that they meet specified requirements for the English language and for clinical proficiency. ECFVG certification fulfills the educational requirement for licensure in all states. Applicants for licensure satisfy the examination requirement by passing the North American Veterinary Licensing Exam (NAVLE), an 8-hour computer-based examination consisting of 360 multiple-choice questions covering all aspects of veterinary medicine. Administered by the National Board of Veterinary Medical Examiners (NBVME), the NAVLE includes visual materials designed to test diagnostic skills and constituting 10 percent of the total examination.

The majority of states also require candidates to pass a state jurisprudence examination covering state laws and regulations. Some states do additional testing on clinical competency as well. There are few reciprocal agreements between states, making it difficult for a veterinarian to practice in a different state without first taking that state's examination.

Nearly all states have continuing education requirements for licensed veterinarians. Requirements differ by state and may involve attending a class or otherwise demonstrating knowledge of recent medical and veterinary advances.

Most veterinarians begin as employees in established practices. Despite the substantial financial investment in equipment, office space, and staff, many veterinarians with experience set up their own practice or purchase an established one.

Newly trained veterinarians can become U.S. Government meat and poultry inspectors, disease-control workers, animal welfare and safety workers, epidemiologists, research assistants, or commissioned officers in the U.S. Public Health Service or various branches of the U.S. Armed Forces. A state license may be required.

Prospective veterinarians must have good manual dexterity. They should have an affinity for animals and the ability to get along with their owners, especially pet owners, who tend to form a strong bond with their pet. Veterinarians who intend to go into private practice should possess excellent communication and business skills because they will need to manage their practice and employees successfully and promote, market, and sell their services.

Employment

Veterinarians held about 61,000 jobs in 2004. About 1 out of 5 veterinarians was self-employed in a solo or group practice. Most others were salaried employees of another veterinary practice. The federal government employed about 1,200 civilian veterinarians, chiefly in the U.S. Departments of Agriculture, Health and Human Services, and, increasingly, Homeland Security. Other employers of veterinarians are state and local governments, colleges of veterinary medicine, medical schools, research laboratories, animal food companies, and pharmaceutical companies. A few veterinarians work for zoos, but most veterinarians caring for zoo animals are private practitioners who contract with the zoos to provide services, usually on a part-time basis.

In addition, many veterinarians hold veterinary faculty positions in colleges and universities. (See the description of teachers—postsecondary elsewhere in this book.)

Job Outlook

Employment of veterinarians is expected to increase as fast as average for all occupations over the 2004–2014 projection period. Despite this average growth, very good job opportunities are expected because the 28 schools of veterinary medicine, even at full capacity, result in a limited number of graduates each year. However, as mentioned earlier, there is keen competition for admission to veterinary school. As pets are increasingly viewed as a member of the family, pet owners will be more willing to spend on advanced veterinary medical care, creating further demand for veterinarians.

Most veterinarians practice in animal hospitals or clinics and care primarily for companion animals. Recent trends indicate particularly strong interest in cats as pets. Faster growth of the cat population is expected to increase the demand for feline medicine and veterinary services, while demand for veterinary care for dogs should continue to grow at a more modest pace.

Pet owners are becoming more aware of the availability of advanced care and are more willing to pay for intensive veterinary care than in the past because many pet owners are more affluent and because they consider their pet part of the family. More pet owners even purchase pet insurance, increasing the likelihood that a considerable amount of money will be spent on veterinary care for their pets. More pet owners also will take advantage of nontraditional veterinary services, such as preventive dental care.

New graduates continue to be attracted to companion-animal medicine because they prefer to deal with pets and to live and work near heavily populated areas. This situation will not necessarily limit the ability of veterinarians to find employment or to set up and maintain a practice in a particular area. Rather, beginning veterinarians may take positions requiring evening or weekend work to accommodate the extended hours of operation that many practices are offering. Some veterinarians take salaried positions in retail stores offering veterinary services. Self-employed veterinarians usually have to work hard and long to build a sufficient client base.

The number of jobs for large-animal veterinarians is likely to grow more slowly than that for veterinarians in private practice who care for companion animals. Nevertheless, job prospects may be better for veterinarians who specialize in farm animals than for companion-animal practitioners because of low earnings in the former specialty and because many veterinarians do not want to work in rural or isolated areas.

Continued support for public health and food safety, national disease control programs, and biomedical research on human health problems will contribute to the demand for veterinarians, although positions in these areas of interest are few in number. Homeland security also may provide opportunities for veterinarians involved in efforts to minimize animal diseases and prevent them from entering the country. Veterinarians with training in food safety, animal health and welfare, and public health and epidemiology should have the best opportunities for a career in the federal government.

Earnings

Median annual earnings of veterinarians were $66,590 in May 2004. The middle 50 percent earned between $51,420 and $88,060. The lowest 10 percent earned less than $39,020, and the highest 10 percent earned more than $118,430.

According to a survey by the American Veterinary Medical Association, average starting salaries of veterinary medical college graduates in 2004 varied by type of practice as follows:

Small animals, predominantly	$50,878
Small animals, exclusively	50,703
Large animals, exclusively	50,403
Private clinical practice	49,635
Large animals, predominantly	48,529
Mixed animals	47,704
Equine (horses)	38,628

The average annual salary for veterinarians in the federal government in nonsupervisory, supervisory, and managerial positions was $78,769 in 2005.

Related Occupations

Veterinarians prevent, diagnose, and treat diseases, disorders, and injuries in animals. Those who do similar work for humans include chiropractors, dentists, optometrists, physicians and surgeons, and podiatrists. Veterinarians have extensive training in physical and life sciences, and some do scientific and medical research, similar to the work of biological scientists and medical scientists.

Animal care and service workers and veterinary technologists and technicians work extensively with animals. Like veterinarians, they must have patience and feel comfortable with animals. However, the level of training required for these occupations is substantially less than that needed by veterinarians.

Sources of Additional Information

For additional information on careers in veterinary medicine, a list of U.S. schools and colleges of veterinary medicine, and accreditation policies, send a letter-size, self-addressed, stamped envelope to

▸ American Veterinary Medical Association, 1931 N. Meacham Rd., Suite 100, Schaumburg, IL 60173-4360. Internet: http://www.avma.org

For information on veterinary education, write to

▸ Association of American Veterinary Medical Colleges, 1101 Vermont Ave. NW, Suite 710, Washington, DC 20005. Internet: http://www.aavmc.org

For information on scholarships, grants, and loans, contact the financial aid officer at the veterinary schools to which you wish to apply.

Information on obtaining a veterinary position with the federal government is available from the Office of Personnel Management through USAJOBS, the federal government's official employment information system. This resource for locating and applying for job opportunities can be accessed through the Internet at http://www.usajobs.opm.gov or through an interactive voice response telephone system at (703) 724-1850 or TDD (978) 461-8404. These numbers are not toll free, and charges may result.

Veterinary Technologists and Technicians

(O*NET 29-2056.00)

Significant Points

- Animal lovers get satisfaction in this occupation, but aspects of the work can be unpleasant, physically and emotionally demanding, and sometimes dangerous.

- Entrants generally complete a 2-year or 4-year veterinary technology program and must pass a state examination.

- Employment is expected to grow much faster than average.

- Keen competition is expected for jobs in zoos.

Nature of the Work

Owners of pets and other animals today expect state-of-the-art veterinary care. To provide this service, veterinarians use the skills of veterinary technologists and technicians, who perform many of the same duties for a veterinarian that a nurse would for a physician, including routine laboratory and clinical procedures. Although specific job duties vary by employer, there often is little difference between the tasks carried out by technicians and by technologists, despite some differences in formal education and training. As a result, most workers in this occupation are called technicians.

Veterinary technologists and technicians typically conduct clinical work in a private practice under the supervision of a veterinarian—often performing various medical tests along with treating and diagnosing medical conditions and diseases in animals. For example,

they may perform laboratory tests such as urinalysis and blood counts, assist with dental prophylaxis, prepare tissue samples, take blood samples, or assist veterinarians in a variety of tests and analyses in which they often utilize various items of medical equipment, such as test tubes and diagnostic equipment. While most of these duties are performed in a laboratory setting, many are not. For example, some veterinary technicians obtain and record patients' case histories, expose and develop X rays, and provide specialized nursing care. In addition, experienced veterinary technicians may discuss a pet's condition with its owners and train new clinic personnel. Veterinary technologists and technicians assisting small-animal practitioners usually care for companion animals, such as cats and dogs, but can perform a variety of duties with mice, rats, sheep, pigs, cattle, monkeys, birds, fish, and frogs. Very few veterinary technologists work in mixed animal practices where they care for both small companion animals and larger, nondomestic animals.

Besides working in private clinics and animal hospitals, veterinary technologists and technicians may work in research facilities, where they may administer medications orally or topically; prepare samples for laboratory examinations; and record information on an animal's genealogy, diet, weight, medications, food intake, and clinical signs of pain and distress. Some may be required to sterilize laboratory and surgical equipment and provide routine postoperative care. At research facilities, veterinary technologists typically work under the guidance of veterinarians, physicians, and other laboratory technicians. Some veterinary technologists vaccinate newly admitted animals and occasionally are required to euthanize seriously ill, severely injured, or unwanted animals.

While the goal of most veterinary technologists and technicians is to promote animal health, some contribute to human health as well. Veterinary technologists occasionally assist veterinarians as they work with other scientists in medical-related fields such as gene therapy and cloning. Some find opportunities in biomedical research, wildlife medicine, the military, livestock management, or pharmaceutical sales.

Working Conditions

People who love animals get satisfaction from working with and helping them. However, some of the work may be unpleasant, physically and emotionally demanding, and sometimes dangerous. At times, veterinary technicians must clean cages and lift, hold, or restrain animals, risking exposure to bites or scratches. These workers must take precautions when treating animals with germicides or insecticides. The work setting can be noisy.

Veterinary technologists and technicians who witness abused animals or who euthanize unwanted, aged, or hopelessly injured animals may experience emotional stress. Those working for humane societies and animal shelters often deal with the public, some of whom might react with hostility to any implication that the owners are neglecting or abusing their pets. Such workers must maintain a calm and professional demeanor while they enforce the laws regarding animal care. In some animal hospitals, research facilities, and animal shelters, a veterinary technician is on duty 24 hours a day, which means that some may work night shifts. Most full-time veterinary technologists and technicians work about 40 hours a week, although some work 50 or more hours a week.

Training, Other Qualifications, and Advancement

There are primarily two levels of education and training for entry to this occupation: a 2-year program for veterinary technicians and a 4-year program for veterinary technologists. Most entry-level veterinary technicians have a 2-year degree, usually an associate's degree, from an accredited community college program in veterinary technology in which courses are taught in clinical and laboratory settings using live animals. About 15 colleges offer veterinary technology programs that are longer and that culminate in a 4-year bachelor's degree in veterinary technology. These 4-year colleges, in addition to some vocational schools, also offer 2-year programs in laboratory animal science. Approximately 5 schools offer distance learning.

In 2004, 116 veterinary technology programs in 43 states were accredited by the American Veterinary Medical Association (AVMA). Graduation from an AVMA-accredited veterinary technology program allows students to take the credentialing exam in any state in the country. Each state regulates veterinary technicians and technologists differently; however, all states require them to pass a credentialing exam following coursework. Passing the state exam assures the public that the technician or technologist has sufficient knowledge to work in a veterinary clinic or hospital. Candidates are tested for competency through an examination that includes oral, written, and practical portions and that is regulated by the State Board of Veterinary Examiners or the appropriate state agency. Depending on the state, candidates may become registered, licensed, or certified. Most states, however, use the National Veterinary Technician (NVT) exam. Prospects usually can have their passing scores transferred from one state to another as long as both states utilize the same exam.

Employers recommend American Association for Laboratory Animal Science (AALAS) certification for those seeking employment in a research facility. AALAS offers certification for three levels of technician competence, with a focus on three principal areas—animal husbandry, facility management, and animal health and welfare. Those who wish to become certified must satisfy a combination of education and experience requirements prior to taking an exam. Work experience must be directly related to the maintenance, health, and well-being of laboratory animals and must be gained in a laboratory animal facility as defined by AALAS. Candidates who meet the necessary criteria can begin pursuing the desired certification on the basis of their qualifications. The lowest level of certification is Assistant Laboratory Animal Technician (ALAT), the second level is Laboratory Animal Technician (LAT), and the highest level of certification is Laboratory Animal Technologist (LATG). The examination consists of multiple-choice questions and is longer and more difficult for higher levels of certification, ranging from 2 hours for the ALAT to 3 hours for the LATG.

Persons interested in careers as veterinary technologists and technicians should take as many high school science, biology, and math courses as possible. Science courses taken beyond high school, in an associate's or bachelor's degree program, should emphasize practical skills in a clinical or laboratory setting. Because veterinary technologists and technicians often deal with pet owners, communication skills are very important. In addition, technologists and technicians should be able to work well with others, because teamwork with veterinarians is common. Organizational ability and the ability to pay attention to detail also are important.

Technologists and technicians usually begin work as trainees in routine positions under the direct supervision of a veterinarian. Entry-level workers whose training or educational background encompasses extensive hands-on experience with a variety of laboratory equipment, including diagnostic and medical equipment, usually require a shorter period of on-the-job training. As they gain experience, technologists and technicians take on more responsibility and carry out more assignments under only general veterinary supervision. Some eventually may become supervisors.

Employment

Veterinary technologists and technicians held about 60,000 jobs in 2004. Most worked in veterinary services. The remainder worked in boarding kennels; animal shelters; stables; grooming salons; zoos; and local, state, and federal agencies.

Job Outlook

Employment of veterinary technologists and technicians is expected to grow much faster than the average for all occupations through the year 2014. Job openings also will stem from the need to replace veterinary technologists and technicians who leave the occupation over the 2004–2014 period. Keen competition is expected for veterinary technologist and technician jobs in zoos due to expected slow growth in zoo capacity, low turnover among workers, the limited number of positions, and the fact that the occupation attracts many candidates.

Pet owners are becoming more affluent and more willing to pay for advanced care because many of them consider their pet to be part of the family. This growing affluence and view of pets will spur employment growth for veterinary technologists and technicians. The number of dogs used as companion pets, which also drives employment growth, is expected to increase more slowly during the projection period than in the previous decade. However, the rapidly growing number of cats utilized as companion pets is expected to boost the demand for feline medicine and services, offsetting any reduced demand for veterinary care for dogs. The availability of advanced veterinary services, such as preventive dental care and surgical procedures, may provide opportunities for workers specializing in those areas. Biomedical facilities, diagnostic laboratories, wildlife facilities, humane societies, animal control facilities, drug or food manufacturing companies, and food safety inspection facilities will provide additional jobs for veterinary technologists and technicians. Furthermore, demand for these workers will stem from the desire to replace veterinary assistants with more highly skilled technicians and technologists in animal clinics and hospitals, shelters, kennels, and humane societies.

Employment of veterinary technicians and technologists is relatively stable during periods of economic recession. Layoffs are less likely to occur among veterinary technologists and technicians than in some other occupations because animals will continue to require medical care.

Earnings

Median hourly earnings of veterinary technologists and technicians were $11.99 in May 2004. The middle 50 percent earned between $9.88 and $14.56. The bottom 10 percent earned less than $8.51, and the top 10 percent earned more than $17.12.

Related Occupations

Others who work extensively with animals include animal care and service workers, veterinary assistants, and laboratory animal caretakers. Like veterinary technologists and technicians, they must have patience and feel comfortable with animals. However, the level of training required for these occupations is less than that needed by veterinary technologists and technicians. Veterinarians, who need much more formal education, also work extensively with animals, preventing, diagnosing, and treating their diseases, disorders, and injuries.

Sources of Additional Information

For information on certification as a laboratory animal technician or technologist, contact

▸ American Association for Laboratory Animal Science, 9190 Crestwyn Hills Dr., Memphis, TN 38125. Internet: http://www.aalas.org

For information on careers in veterinary medicine and a listing of AVMA-accredited veterinary technology programs, contact

▸ American Veterinary Medical Association, 1931 N. Meacham Rd., Suite 100, Schaumburg, IL 60173-4360. Internet: http://www.avma.org

Water and Liquid Waste Treatment Plant and System Operators

(O*NET 51-8031.00)

Significant Points

- Employment is concentrated in local government and private water, sewage, and other systems utilities.

- Completion of an associate degree or a 1-year certificate program increases an applicant's chances for employment and promotion.

- Because the number of applicants in this field is normally low, job prospects will be good for qualified individuals, particularly those with training in all aspects of water and wastewater treatment.

Nature of the Work

Clean water is essential for everyday life. *Water treatment plant and system operators* treat water so that it is safe to drink. *Liquid waste treatment plant and system operators*, also known as wastewater treatment plant and system operators, remove harmful pollutants from domestic and industrial liquid waste so that it is safe to return to the environment.

Water is pumped from wells, rivers, streams, and reservoirs to water treatment plants, where it is treated and distributed to customers. Wastewater travels through customers' sewer pipes to wastewater treatment plants, where it is either treated and returned to streams, rivers, and oceans or reused for irrigation and landscaping. Operators in both types of plants control equipment and processes that remove or destroy harmful materials, chemical compounds, and microorganisms from the water. They also control pumps, valves, and other equipment that moves the water or wastewater through the various treatment processes, after which they dispose of the removed waste materials.

Operators read, interpret, and adjust meters and gauges to make sure that plant equipment and processes are working properly. Operators operate chemical-feeding devices; take samples of the water or wastewater; perform chemical and biological laboratory analyses; and adjust the amounts of chemicals, such as chlorine, in the water. They use a variety of instruments to sample and measure water quality, and they utilize common hand and power tools to make repairs to valves, pumps, and other equipment.

Water and wastewater treatment plant and system operators increasingly rely on computers to help monitor equipment, store the results of sampling, make process-control decisions, schedule and record maintenance activities, and produce reports. When equipment malfunctions, operators also may use computers to determine the cause of the malfunction and seek its solution.

Occasionally, operators must work during emergencies. A heavy rainstorm, for example, may cause large amounts of wastewater to flow into sewers, exceeding a plant's treatment capacity. Emergencies also can be caused by conditions inside a plant, such as chlorine gas leaks or oxygen deficiencies. To handle these conditions, operators are trained to make an emergency management response and use special safety equipment and procedures to protect public health and the facility. During these periods, operators may work under extreme pressure to correct problems as quickly as possible. Because working conditions may be dangerous, operators must be extremely cautious.

The specific duties of plant operators depend on the type and size of the plant. In smaller plants, one operator may control all of the machinery, perform tests, keep records, handle complaints, and perform repairs and maintenance. A few operators may handle both a water treatment and a wastewater treatment plant. In larger plants with many employees, operators may be more specialized and monitor only one process. The staff also may include chemists, engineers, laboratory technicians, mechanics, helpers, supervisors, and a superintendent.

Water pollution standards are largely set by two major federal environmental statutes: the Clean Water Act, which regulates the discharge of pollutants, and the Safe Drinking Water Act, which specifies standards for drinking water. Industrial facilities that send their wastes to municipal treatment plants must meet certain minimum standards to ensure that the wastes have been adequately pretreated and will not damage municipal treatment facilities. Municipal water treatment plants also must meet stringent standards for drinking water. The list of contaminants regulated by these statutes has grown over time. As a result, plant operators must be familiar with the guidelines established by federal regulations and how they affect their plant. In addition, operators must be aware of any guidelines imposed by the state or locality in which the plant operates.

Working Conditions

Water and wastewater treatment plant and system operators work both indoors and outdoors and may be exposed to noise from machinery and to unpleasant odors. Operators' work is physically demanding and often is performed in unclean locations. Operators must pay close attention to safety procedures because of the presence of hazardous conditions, such as slippery walkways, dangerous gases, and malfunctioning equipment. Plants operate 24 hours a day, 7 days a week; therefore, operators work one of three 8-hour shifts, including weekends and holidays, on a rotational basis. Operators may be required to work overtime.

Training, Other Qualifications, and Advancement

A high school diploma usually is required for an individual to become a water or wastewater treatment plant operator. Operators need mechanical aptitude and should be competent in basic mathematics, chemistry, and biology. They must have the ability to apply data to formulas prescribing treatment requirements, flow levels, and concentration levels. Some basic familiarity with computers also is necessary because of the trend toward computer-controlled equipment and more sophisticated instrumentation. Certain positions—particularly in larger cities and towns—are covered by civil service regulations. Applicants for these positions may be required to pass a written examination testing their mathematics skills, mechanical aptitude, and general intelligence.

The completion of an associate degree or a 1-year certificate program in water quality and wastewater treatment technology increases an applicant's chances for employment and promotion because plants are becoming more complex. Offered throughout the country, these programs provide a good general knowledge of water and wastewater treatment processes, as well as basic preparation for becoming an operator.

Trainees usually start as attendants or operators-in-training and learn their skills on the job under the direction of an experienced operator. They learn by observing and doing routine tasks such as recording meter readings; taking samples of wastewater and sludge; and performing simple maintenance and repair work on pumps, electric motors, valves, and other plant equipment. Larger treatment plants generally combine this on-the-job training with formal classroom or self-paced study programs.

The Safe Drinking Water Act Amendments of 1996, enforced by the U.S. Environmental Protection Agency, specify national minimum standards for certification and recertification of operators of community and nontransient, noncommunity water systems. As a result, operators must pass an examination certifying that they are capable of overseeing wastewater treatment plant operations. There are different levels of certification, depending on the operator's experience and training. Higher levels qualify the operator for overseeing a wider variety of treatment processes. Certification requirements vary by state and by size of the treatment plant. Although relocation may mean having to become certified in a new jurisdiction, many states accept other states' certifications.

Most state drinking water and water pollution control agencies offer courses to improve operators' skills and knowledge. The courses cover principles of treatment processes and process control, laboratory procedures, maintenance, management skills, collection systems, safety, chlorination, sedimentation, biological treatment, sludge treatment and disposal, and flow measurements. Some operators take correspondence courses on subjects related to water and wastewater treatment, and some employers pay part of the tuition for related college courses in science or engineering.

As operators are promoted, they become responsible for more-complex treatment processes. Some operators are promoted to plant supervisor or superintendent; others advance by transferring to a larger facility. Postsecondary training in water and wastewater treatment, coupled with increasingly responsible experience as an operator, may be sufficient to qualify a worker for becoming superintendent of a small plant, where a superintendent also serves as an operator. However, educational requirements are rising as larger, more complex treatment plants are built to meet new drinking water and water pollution control standards. With each promotion, the operator must have greater knowledge of federal, state, and local regulations. Superintendents of large plants generally need an engineering or science degree.

A few operators get jobs as technicians with state drinking water or water pollution control agencies. In that capacity, they monitor and provide technical assistance to plants throughout the state. Vocational-technical school or community college training generally is preferred for technician jobs. Experienced operators may transfer to related jobs with industrial liquid waste treatment plants, water or liquid waste treatment equipment and chemical companies, engineering consulting firms, or vocational-technical schools.

Employment

Water and wastewater treatment plant and system operators held about 94,000 jobs in 2004. Almost 4 in 5 operators worked for local governments. Others worked primarily for private water, sewage, and other systems utilities and for private waste treatment and disposal and waste management services companies. Private firms are increasingly providing operation and management services to local governments on a contract basis.

Water and wastewater treatment plant and system operators were employed throughout the country, but most jobs were in larger towns and cities. Although nearly all operators worked full time, those in small towns may work only part time at the treatment plant, with the remainder of their time spent handling other municipal duties.

Job Outlook

Employment of water and wastewater treatment plant and system operators is expected to grow about as fast as the average for all occupations through the year 2014. Job prospects will be good for qualified individuals because the number of applicants in this field is normally low, due primarily to the unclean and physically demanding nature of the work. Workers who have training in all aspects of water and wastewater treatment and who can handle multiple duties will have the best opportunities.

The increasing population and the growth of the economy are expected to boost demand for essential water and wastewater treatment services. As new plants are constructed to meet this demand, employment of water and wastewater treatment plant and system operators will increase. In addition, many job openings will occur as experienced operators leave the labor force or transfer to other occupations.

Local governments are the largest employers of water and wastewater treatment plant and system operators. However, federal certification requirements have increased utilities' reliance on private firms specializing in the operation and management of water and wastewater treatment facilities. As a result, employment in privately owned facilities will grow faster than the average.

Earnings

Median annual earnings of water and wastewater treatment plant and system operators were $34,960 in May 2004. The middle 50 percent earned between $27,180 and $43,720. The lowest 10 percent earned less than $21,700, and the highest 10 percent earned more than $53,540. Median annual earnings of water and liquid waste treatment plant and systems operators in May 2004 were $34,990 in local government and $32,350 in water, sewage, and other systems.

In addition to their annual salaries, water and wastewater treatment plant and system operators usually receive benefits that may include health and life insurance, a retirement plan, and educational reimbursement for job-related courses.

Related Occupations

Other workers whose main activity consists of operating a system of machinery to process or produce materials include chemical plant and system operators; gas plant operators; petroleum pump system operators, refinery operators, and gaugers; power plant operators, distributors, and dispatchers; and stationary engineers and boiler operators.

Sources of Additional Information

For information on employment opportunities, contact state or local water pollution control agencies, state water and liquid waste operator associations, state environmental training centers, or local offices of the state employment service.

For information on certification, contact

▸ Association of Boards of Certification, 208 Fifth St., Ames, IA 50010-6259. Internet: http://www.abccert.org

For educational information related to a career as a water or liquid waste treatment plant and system operator, contact

▸ American Water Works Association, 6666 West Quincy Ave., Denver, CO 80235. Internet: http://www.awwa.org

▸ Water Environment Federation, 601 Wythe St., Alexandria, VA 22314-1994. Internet: http://www.wef.org

QUICK JOB SEARCH

Seven Steps to Getting a Good Job in Less Time

The Complete Text of a Results-Oriented Minibook by Michael Farr

Millions of job seekers have found better jobs faster using the techniques in the *Quick Job Search*. So can you! The *Quick Job Search* covers the essential steps proven to cut job search time in half and is used widely by job search programs throughout North America. Topics include how to identify your key skills, define your ideal job, write a great resume quickly, use the most effective job search methods, get more interviews, and much more.

If you completed "Using the Job-Match Grid to Choose a Career" earlier in this book, the activities in this section will complement those efforts by helping you to define other skills you possess, focus your resume, and get a job quickly.

While it is a section in this book, the *Quick Job Search* is available from JIST Publishing as a separate booklet and in an expanded form as *Seven-Step Job Search*.

Quick Job Search Is Short, But It May Be All You Need

While *Quick Job Search* is short, it covers the basics on how to explore career options and conduct an effective job search. While these topics can seem complex, I have found some simple truths about looking for a job:

- If you are going to work, you might as well look for what you really want to do and are good at.

- If you are looking for a job, you might as well use techniques that will reduce the time it takes to find one—and that help you get a better job than you might otherwise.

That's what I emphasize in *Quick Job Search*.

Trust Me—Do the Worksheets. I know you will resist completing the worksheets. But trust me. They are worth your time. Doing them will give you a better sense of what you are good at, what you want to do, and how to go about getting it. You will also most likely get more interviews and present yourself better. Is this worth giving up a night of TV? Yes, I think so.

Once you finish this minibook and its activities, you will have spent more time planning your career than most people do. And you will know more than the average job seeker about finding a job.

Why Such a Short Book? I've taught job seeking skills for many years, and I've written longer and more detailed books than this one. Yet I have often been asked to tell someone, in a few minutes or hours, the most important things they should do in their career planning or job search. Instructors and counselors also ask the same question because they have only a short time to spend with folks they're trying to help. I've given this a lot of thought, and the seven topics in this book are the ones I think are most important to know.

This minibook is short enough to scan in a morning and conduct a more effective job search that afternoon. Granted, doing all the activities would take more time, but they will prepare you far better than scanning the book. Of course, you can learn more about all the topics it covers, but this minibook, *Quick Job Search,* may be all you need.

You can't just read about getting a job. The best way to get a job is to go out and get interviews! And the best way to get interviews is to make a job out of getting a job.

After many years of experience, I have identified just seven basic things you need to do that make a big difference in your job search. Each will be covered and expanded on in this minibook.

1. Identify your key skills.
2. Define your ideal job.
3. Learn the two most effective job search methods.
4. Create a superior resume and a portfolio.
5. Organize your time to get two interviews a day.
6. Dramatically improve your interviewing skills.
7. Follow up on all leads.

So, without further delay, let's get started!

STEP 1: Identify Your Key Skills and Develop a "Skills Language" to Describe Yourself

One survey of employers found that about 90 percent of the people they interviewed might have the required job skills, but they could not describe those skills and thereby prove that they could do the job they sought. They could not answer the basic question "Why should I hire you?"

Knowing and describing your skills is essential to doing well in interviews. This same knowledge is important to help you decide what type of job you will enjoy and do well. For these reasons, I consider identifying your skills a necessary part of a successful career plan or job search.

The Three Types of Skills

Most people think of their skills as job-related skills, such as using a computer. But we all have other types of skills that are important for success on a job—and that are important to employers. The following triangle arranges skills in three groups, and I think that this is a very useful way to consider skills.

Let's look at these three types of skills—self-management, transferable, and job-related—and identify those that are most important to you.

Quip

We all have thousands of skills. Consider the many skills required to do even a simple thing like ride a bike or bake a cake. But, of all the skills you have, employers want to know those key skills you have for the job they need done. You must clearly identify these key skills and then emphasize them in interviews.

Self-Management Skills

To begin identifying your skills, answer the question in the box that follows.

YOUR GOOD WORKER TRAITS

Write down three things about yourself that you think make you a good worker. Think about what an employer might like about you or the way you work.

1. _____

2. _____

3. _____

You just wrote down the most important things for an employer to know about you! They describe your basic personality and your ability to adapt to new environments. They are some of the most important skills to emphasize in interviews, yet most job seekers don't realize their importance—and don't mention them.

Review the Self-Management Skills Checklist that follows and put a check mark beside any skills you have. The key self-management skills listed first cover abilities that employers find particularly important. If one or more of the key self-management skills apply to you, mentioning them in interviews can help you greatly.

SELF-MANAGEMENT SKILLS CHECKLIST

Following are the key self-management skills that employers value highly. Place a check by those you already have.

❏ Have good attendance   ❏ Arrive on time

❏ Get work done on time   ❏ Get along with co-workers

❏ Am honest   ❏ Follow instructions

❏ Get along with supervisor   ❏ Am hard working/productive

(continued)

(continued)

Place a check by other self-management skills you have.

❏ Ambitious	❏ Discreet	❏ Helpful
❏ Mature	❏ Physically strong	❏ Sincere
❏ Assertive	❏ Eager	❏ Humble
❏ Methodical	❏ Practical	❏ Spontaneous
❏ Capable	❏ Efficient	❏ Humorous
❏ Modest	❏ Problem-solving	❏ Steady
❏ Cheerful	❏ Energetic	❏ Imaginative
❏ Motivated	❏ Proud of work	❏ Tactful
❏ Competent	❏ Enthusiastic	❏ Independent
❏ Natural	❏ Quick to learn	❏ Team player
❏ Conscientious	❏ Expressive	❏ Industrious
❏ Open-minded	❏ Reliable	❏ Tenacious
❏ Creative	❏ Flexible	❏ Informal
❏ Optimistic	❏ Resourceful	❏ Thrifty
❏ Culturally tolerant	❏ Formal	❏ Intelligent
❏ Original	❏ Responsible	❏ Trustworthy
❏ Decisive	❏ Friendly	❏ Intuitive
❏ Patient	❏ Results-oriented	❏ Versatile
❏ Dependable	❏ Good-natured	❏ Loyal
❏ Persistent	❏ Self-confident	❏ Well-organized

List the other self-management skills you have that have not been mentioned but you think are important to include.

_____

_____

_____

After you finish checking the list, circle the five skills you feel are most important and write them in the box that follows.

YOUR TOP FIVE SELF-MANAGEMENT SKILLS

1. _____

2. _____

3. _____

4. _____

5. _____

 When thinking about their skills, some people find it helpful to complete the Essential Job Search Data Worksheet that starts on page 326. It organizes skills and accomplishments from previous jobs and other life experiences. Take a look at it and decide whether to complete it now or later.

Transferable Skills

We all have skills that can transfer from one job or career to another. For example, the ability to organize events could be used in a variety of jobs and may be essential for success in certain occupations. Your mission is to find a job that requires the skills you have and enjoy using.

It's not bragging if it's true. Using your new skills language may be uncomfortable at first, but employers need to learn about your skills. So practice saying positive things about the skills you have for the job. If you don't, who will?

TRANSFERABLE SKILLS CHECKLIST

Following are the key transferable skills that employers value highly. Place a check by those you already have. You may have used them in a previous job or in some non-work setting.

❏ Managing money/budgets
❏ Speaking in public
❏ Managing people
❏ Organizing/managing projects
❏ Meeting deadlines

❏ Using computers
❏ Meeting the public
❏ Writing well
❏ Negotiating

Place a check by the skills you have for working with data.

❏ Analyzing data
❏ Counting/taking inventory
❏ Auditing/checking for accuracy
❏ Investigating
❏ Budgeting
❏ Keeping financial records
❏ Calculating/computing

❏ Observing/inspecting
❏ Classifying data
❏ Paying attention to details
❏ Comparing/evaluating
❏ Researching/locating information
❏ Compiling/recording facts
❏ Synthesizing

Place a check by the skills you have for working with people.

❏ Administering
❏ Counseling people
❏ Being diplomatic
❏ Demonstrating

❏ Being kind
❏ Having insight
❏ Being outgoing
❏ Helping others

❏ Being patient
❏ Instructing others
❏ Being pleasant
❏ Interviewing people

(continued)

(continued)

❑ Being sensitive	❑ Being tactful	❑ Caring for others
❑ Listening	❑ Supervising	❑ Trusting
❑ Being sociable	❑ Being tough	❑ Coaching
❑ Persuading	❑ Tolerating	❑ Understanding
		❑ Confronting others

Place a check by your skills in working with words and ideas.

❑ Being articulate	❑ Being logical
❑ Creating new ideas	❑ Remembering information
❑ Being ingenious	❑ Communicating verbally
❑ Designing	❑ Speaking publicly
❑ Being inventive	❑ Corresponding with others
❑ Editing	❑ Writing clearly

Place a check by the leadership skills you have.

❑ Being competitive	❑ Having self-confidence
❑ Mediating problems	❑ Planning events
❑ Delegating	❑ Influencing others
❑ Motivating people	❑ Running meetings
❑ Directing others	❑ Making decisions
❑ Motivating yourself	❑ Solving problems
❑ Getting results	❑ Making explanations
❑ Negotiating agreements	❑ Taking risks

Place a check by your creative or artistic skills.

❑ Appreciating music	❑ Dancing
❑ Expressing yourself	❑ Playing instruments
❑ Being artistic	❑ Drawing
❑ Performing/acting	❑ Presenting artistic ideas

Place a check by your skills for working with things.

❑ Assembling things	❑ Operating tools/machines
❑ Driving or operating vehicles	❑ Constructing or repairing things
❑ Building things	

Add the other transferable skills you have that have not been mentioned but you think are important to include.

_____

_____

_____

When you are finished, circle the five transferable skills you feel are most important for you to use in your next job and list them below.

YOUR TOP FIVE TRANSFERABLE SKILLS

1. _____

2. _____

3. _____

4. _____

5. _____

Job-Related Skills

Job content or job-related skills are those you need to do a particular occupation. A carpenter, for example, needs to know how to use various tools. Before you select job-related skills to emphasize, you must first have a clear idea of the jobs you want. So let's put off developing your job-related skills list until you have defined the job you want—the topic that is covered next.

STEP 2: Define Your Ideal Job

Too many people look for a job without clearly knowing what they are looking for. Before you go out seeking a job, I suggest that you first define exactly what you want—not *just a job* but *the job*.

Most people think that a job objective is the same as a job title, but it isn't. You need to consider other elements of what makes a job satisfying for you. Then, later, you can decide what that job is called and what industry it might be in. You can compromise on what you consider your ideal job later if you need to.

EIGHT FACTORS TO CONSIDER IN DEFINING YOUR IDEAL JOB

As you try to define your ideal job, consider the following eight important questions. When you know what you want, your task then becomes finding a position that is as close to your ideal job as possible.

1. **What skills do you want to use?** From the skills lists in Step 1, select the top five skills that you enjoy using and most want to use in your next job.

    a._____

    b._____

    c._____

    d._____

    e._____

(continued)

(continued)

2. **What type of special knowledge do you have?** Perhaps you know how to fix radios, keep accounting records, or cook food. Write down the things you know from schooling, training, hobbies, family experiences, and other sources. One or more of these knowledge areas could make you a very special applicant in the right setting._____

_____

_____

3. **With what types of people do you prefer to work?** Do you like to work with competitive people, or do you prefer hardworking folks, creative personalities, relaxed people, or some other types?_____

_____

_____

4. **What type of work environment do you prefer?** Do you want to work inside, outside, in a quiet place, in a busy place, or in a clean or messy place; or do you want to have a window with a nice view? List the types of environments you prefer._____

_____

_____

5. **Where do you want your next job to be located—in what city or region?** If you are open to living and working anywhere, what would your ideal community be like? Near a bus line? Close to a childcare center?_____

_____

_____

6. **What benefits or income do you hope to have in your next job?** Many people will take less money or fewer benefits if they like a job in other ways—or if they need a job quickly to survive. Think about the minimum you would take as well as what you would eventually like to earn. Your next job will probably pay somewhere in between._____

_____

_____

7. **How much and what types of responsibility are you willing to accept?** Usually, the more money you want to make, the more responsibility you must accept. Do you want to work by yourself, be part of a group, or be in charge? If you want to be in charge, how many people are you willing to supervise?

_____

_____

_____

8. **What values are important or have meaning to you?** Do you have important values you would prefer to include in considering the work you do? For example, some people want to work to help others, clean up the environment, build structures, make machines work, gain power or prestige, or care for animals or plants. Think about what is important to you and how you might include this in your next job._____

_____

_____

_____

Is It Possible to Find Your Ideal Job?

Can you find a job that meets all the criteria you just defined? Perhaps. Some people do. The harder you look, the more likely you are to find it. But you will likely need to compromise, so it is useful to know what is *most* important to include in your next job. Go back over your responses to the eight factors and mark a few of those that you would most like to have or include in your ideal job.

FACTORS I WANT IN MY IDEAL JOB

Write a brief description of your ideal job. Don't worry about a job title, or whether you have the experience, or other practical matters yet._____

_____

_____

_____

How Can You Explore Specific Job Titles and Industries?

You might find your ideal job in an occupation you haven't considered yet. And, even if you are sure of the occupation you want, it may be in an industry that is unfamiliar to you. This combination of occupation and industry forms the basis for your job search, and you should consider a variety of options.

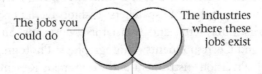

The jobs you could do — The industries where these jobs exist

Your ideal job exists in the overlap of those jobs that interest you most *and* in those industries that best meet your needs and interests!

There are thousands of job titles, and many jobs are highly specialized, employing just a few people. While one of these more specialized jobs may be just what you want, most work falls within more general job titles that employ large numbers of people.

REVIEW THE TOP JOBS IN THE WORKFORCE

The list of job titles that follows was based on a list developed by the U.S. Department of Labor. It contains approximately 270 major jobs that employ about 90 percent of the U.S. workforce.

The job titles are organized within 16 major groupings called interest areas, presented in bold type. These groupings will help you quickly identify fields most likely to interest you. Job titles are presented in regular type within these groupings.

Begin with the interest areas that appeal to you most, and underline any job title that interests you. (Don't worry for now about whether you have the experience or credentials to do these jobs.) Then quickly review the remaining interest areas, underlining any job titles there that interest you. Note that some job titles are listed more than once because they fit into more than one interest area. When you have gone through all 16 interest areas, go back and circle the 5 to 10 job titles that interest you most. These are the ones you will want to research in more detail.

1. **Agriculture and Natural Resources:** Agricultural and Food Scientists; Agricultural Workers; Biological Scientists; Conservation Scientists and Foresters; Engineers; Farmers, Ranchers, and Agricultural Managers; Fishers and Fishing Vessel Operators; Forest, Conservation, and Logging Workers; Grounds Maintenance Workers; Material Moving Occupations; Pest Control Workers; Purchasing Managers, Buyers, and Purchasing Agents; Science Technicians.

2. **Architecture and Construction:** Architects, except Landscape and Naval; Boilermakers; Brickmasons, Blockmasons, and Stonemasons; Carpenters; Carpet, Floor, and Tile Installers and Finishers; Cement Masons, Concrete Finishers, Segmental Pavers, and Terrazzo Workers; Construction and Building Inspectors; Construction Equipment Operators; Construction Laborers; Construction Managers; Drafters; Drywall Installers, Ceiling Tile Installers, and Tapers; Electrical and Electronics Installers and Repairers; Electricians; Elevator Installers and Repairers; Glaziers; Hazardous Materials Removal Workers; Heating, Air-Conditioning, and Refrigeration Mechanics and Installers; Home Appliance Repairers; Insulation Workers; Landscape Architects; Line Installers and Repairers; Maintenance and Repair Workers, General; Material Moving Occupations; Painters and Paperhangers; Pipelayers, Plumbers, Pipefitters, and Steamfitters; Plasterers and Stucco Masons; Radio and Telecommunications Equipment Installers and Repairers; Roofers; Sheet Metal Workers; Structural and Reinforcing Iron and Metal Workers; Surveyors, Cartographers, Photogrammetrists, and Surveying Technicians.

3. **Arts and Communication:** Actors, Producers, and Directors; Advertising, Marketing, Promotions, Public Relations, and Sales Managers; Air Traffic Controllers; Announcers; Artists and Related Workers; Barbers, Cosmetologists, and Other Personal Appearance Workers; Broadcast and Sound Engineering Technicians and Radio Operators; Commercial and Industrial Designers; Communications Equipment Operators; Dancers and Choreographers; Dispatchers; Fashion Designers; Floral Designers; Graphic Designers; Interior Designers; Interpreters and Translators; Musicians, Singers, and Related Workers; News Analysts, Reporters, and Correspondents; Photographers; Photographic Process Workers and Processing Machine Operators; Precision Instrument and Equipment Repairers; Public Relations Specialists; Television, Video, and Motion Picture Camera Operators and Editors; Writers and Editors.

4. **Business and Administration:** Accountants and Auditors; Administrative Services Managers; Billing and Posting Clerks and Machine Operators; Bookkeeping, Accounting, and Auditing Clerks; Brokerage Clerks; Budget Analysts; Building Cleaning Workers; Communications Equipment Operators; Data Entry and Information Processing Workers; Engineering Technicians; File Clerks; Human Resources Assistants, except Payroll and Timekeeping; Human Resources, Training, and Labor Relations Managers

and Specialists; Management Analysts; Meeting and Convention Planners; Meter Readers, Utilities; Office and Administrative Support Worker Supervisors and Managers; Office Clerks, General; Operations Research Analysts; Payroll and Timekeeping Clerks; Postal Service Workers; Procurement Clerks; Production, Planning, and Expediting Clerks; Secretaries and Administrative Assistants; Shipping, Receiving, and Traffic Clerks; Stock Clerks and Order Fillers; Top Executives; Weighers, Measurers, Checkers, and Samplers, Recordkeeping.

5. **Education and Training:** Archivists, Curators, and Museum Technicians; Counselors; Education Administrators; Fitness Workers; Instructional Coordinators; Librarians; Library Assistants, Clerical; Library Technicians; Teacher Assistants; Teachers—Adult Literacy and Remedial Education; Teachers— Postsecondary; Teachers—Preschool, Kindergarten, Elementary, Middle, and Secondary; Teachers—Self-Enrichment Education; Teachers—Special Education.

6. **Finance and Insurance:** Advertising Sales Agents; Appraisers and Assessors of Real Estate; Bill and Account Collectors; Claims Adjusters, Appraisers, Examiners, and Investigators; Cost Estimators; Credit Authorizers, Checkers, and Clerks; Financial Analysts and Personal Financial Advisors; Financial Managers; Insurance Sales Agents; Insurance Underwriters; Interviewers; Loan Officers; Market and Survey Researchers; Securities, Commodities, and Financial Services Sales Agents; Tellers.

7. **Government and Public Administration:** Agricultural Workers; Court Reporters; Fire Fighting Occupations; Inspectors, Testers, Sorters, Samplers, and Weighers; Occupational Health and Safety Specialists and Technicians; Police and Detectives; Science Technicians; Tax Examiners, Collectors, and Revenue Agents; Top Executives; Urban and Regional Planners.

8. **Health Science:** Agricultural Workers; Animal Care and Service Workers; Athletic Trainers; Audiologists; Cardiovascular Technologists and Technicians; Chiropractors; Clinical Laboratory Technologists and Technicians; Dental Assistants; Dental Hygienists; Dentists; Diagnostic Medical Sonographers; Dietitians and Nutritionists; Licensed Practical and Licensed Vocational Nurses; Massage Therapists; Medical and Health Services Managers; Medical Assistants; Medical Records and Health Information Technicians; Medical Transcriptionists; Nuclear Medicine Technologists; Nursing, Psychiatric, and Home Health Aides; Occupational Therapist Assistants and Aides; Occupational Therapists; Opticians, Dispensing; Optometrists; Pharmacists; Pharmacy Aides; Pharmacy Technicians; Physical Therapist Assistants and Aides; Physical Therapists; Physician Assistants; Physicians and Surgeons; Podiatrists; Radiation Therapists; Radiologic Technologists and Technicians; Recreational Therapists; Registered Nurses; Respiratory Therapists; Science Technicians; Speech-Language Pathologists; Surgical Technologists; Veterinarians; Veterinary Technologists and Technicians.

9. **Hospitality, Tourism, and Recreation:** Athletes, Coaches, Umpires, and Related Workers; Barbers, Cosmetologists, and Other Personal Appearance Workers; Building Cleaning Workers; Chefs, Cooks, and Food Preparation Workers; Flight Attendants; Food and Beverage Serving and Related Workers; Food Processing Occupations; Food Service Managers; Gaming Services Occupations; Hotel, Motel, and Resort Desk Clerks; Lodging Managers; Recreation Workers; Reservation and Transportation Ticket Agents and Travel Clerks; Travel Agents.

10. **Human Service:** Child Care Workers; Counselors; Interviewers; Personal and Home Care Aides; Probation Officers and Correctional Treatment Specialists; Psychologists; Social and Human Service Assistants; Social Workers.

(continued)

(continued)

11. **Information Technology:** Coin, Vending, and Amusement Machine Servicers and Repairers; Computer and Information Systems Managers; Computer Operators; Computer Programmers; Computer Scientists and Database Administrators; Computer Software Engineers; Computer Support Specialists and Systems Administrators; Computer Systems Analysts; Computer, Automated Teller, and Office Machine Repairers.

12. **Law and Public Safety:** Correctional Officers; Emergency Medical Technicians and Paramedics; Fire Fighting Occupations; Job Opportunities in the Armed Forces; Judges, Magistrates, and Other Judicial Workers; Lawyers; Paralegals and Legal Assistants; Police and Detectives; Private Detectives and Investigators; Science Technicians; Security Guards and Gaming Surveillance Officers.

13. **Manufacturing:** Agricultural Workers; Aircraft and Avionics Equipment Mechanics and Service Technicians; Assemblers and Fabricators; Automotive Body and Related Repairers; Automotive Service Technicians and Mechanics; Bookbinders and Bindery Workers; Computer Control Programmers and Operators; Desktop Publishers; Diesel Service Technicians and Mechanics; Electrical and Electronics Installers and Repairers; Electronic Home Entertainment Equipment Installers and Repairers; Food Processing Occupations; Heavy Vehicle and Mobile Equipment Service Technicians and Mechanics; Home Appliance Repairers; Industrial Machinery Mechanics and Maintenance Workers; Industrial Production Managers; Inspectors, Testers, Sorters, Samplers, and Weighers; Jewelers and Precious Stone and Metal Workers; Machine Setters, Operators, and Tenders—Metal and Plastic; Machinists; Material Moving Occupations; Medical, Dental, and Ophthalmic Laboratory Technicians; Millwrights; Painting and Coating Workers, except Construction and Maintenance; Photographic Process Workers and Processing Machine Operators; Power Plant Operators, Distributors, and Dispatchers; Precision Instrument and Equipment Repairers; Prepress Technicians and Workers; Printing Machine Operators; Radio and Telecommunications Equipment Installers and Repairers; Semiconductor Processors; Small Engine Mechanics; Stationary Engineers and Boiler Operators; Textile, Apparel, and Furnishings Occupations; Tool and Die Makers; Water and Liquid Waste Treatment Plant and System Operators; Water Transportation Occupations; Welding, Soldering, and Brazing Workers; Woodworkers.

14. **Retail and Wholesale Sales and Service:** Advertising, Marketing, Promotions, Public Relations, and Sales Managers; Cashiers; Counter and Rental Clerks; Customer Service Representatives; Demonstrators, Product Promoters, and Models; Funeral Directors; Order Clerks; Property, Real Estate, and Community Association Managers; Purchasing Managers, Buyers, and Purchasing Agents; Real Estate Brokers and Sales Agents; Receptionists and Information Clerks; Retail Salespersons; Sales Engineers; Sales Representatives, Wholesale and Manufacturing; Sales Worker Supervisors.

15. **Scientific Research, Engineering, and Mathematics:** Actuaries; Atmospheric Scientists; Biological Scientists; Chemists and Materials Scientists; Drafters; Economists; Engineering and Natural Sciences Managers; Engineering Technicians; Engineers; Environmental Scientists and Hydrologists; Geoscientists; Mathematicians; Medical Scientists; Photographers; Physicists and Astronomers; Psychologists; Science Technicians; Social Scientists, Other; Statisticians; Surveyors, Cartographers, Photogrammetrists, and Surveying Technicians.

16. **Transportation, Distribution, and Logistics:** Aircraft Pilots and Flight Engineers; Bus Drivers; Cargo and Freight Agents; Couriers and Messengers; Material Moving Occupations; Postal Service Workers; Rail Transportation Occupations; Taxi Drivers and Chauffeurs; Truck Drivers and Driver/Sales Workers; Water Transportation Occupations.

You can find thorough descriptions for the job titles in the preceding list in the Occupational Outlook Handbook, *published by the U.S. Department of Labor. Its descriptions include infomation on earnings, training and education needed to hold specific jobs, working conditions, advancement opportunities, projected growth, and sources for additional information. Most libraries have this book.*

You also can find descriptions of these jobs on the Internet. Go to www.bls.gov/oco/.

The New Guide for Occupational Exploration, *Fourth Edition, also provides more information on the interest areas used in this list. This book is published by JIST Works and describes about 1,000 major jobs, arranged within groupings of related jobs.*

Finally, "A Short List of Additional Resources" at the end of this minibook gives you resources for more job information.

CONSIDER MAJOR INDUSTRIES

What industry you work in is often as important as the career field. For example, some industries pay much better than others, and others may simply be more interesting to you. A book titled *40 Best Fields for Your Career* contains very helpful reviews for each of the major industries mentioned in the following list. Many libraries and bookstores carry this book, as well as the U.S. Department of Labor's *Career Guide to Industries,* or you can find the information on the Internet at www.CareerOINK.com or at www.bls.gov/oco/cg/.

Underline industries that interest you, and then learn more about the opportunities they present. Jobs in most careers are available in a variety of industries, so consider what industries fit you best and focus your job search in these.

Agriculture and natural resources: Agriculture, forestry, and fishing; mining; oil and gas extraction.

Manufacturing, construction, and utilities: Aerospace product and parts manufacturing; chemical manufacturing, except drugs; computer and electronic product manufacturing; construction; food manufacturing; machinery manufacturing; motor vehicle and parts manufacturing; pharmaceutical and medicine manufacturing; printing; steel manufacturing; textile, textile products, and apparel manufacturing; utilities.

Trade: Automobile dealers, clothing, accessories, and general merchandise stores; grocery stores; wholesale trade.

Transportation: Air transportation; truck transportation and warehousing.

Information: Broadcasting; Internet service providers, Web search portals, and data processing services; motion picture and video industries; publishing, except software; software publishing; telecommunications.

Financial activities: Banking; insurance; securities, commodities, and other investments.

Professional and business services: Advertising and public relations; computer systems design and related services; employment services; management, scientific, and technical consulting services; scientific research and development services.

Education, health care, and social services: Child daycare services; educational services; health care; social assistance, except child care.

(continued)

(continued)

> **Leisure and hospitality:** Art, entertainment, and recreation; food services and drinking places; hotels and other accommodations.
>
> **Government and advocacy, grantmaking, and civic organizations:** Advocacy, grantmaking, and civic organizations; federal government; state and local government, except education and health care.

THE TOP JOBS AND INDUSTRIES THAT INTEREST YOU

Go back over the lists of job titles and industries. For numbers 1 and 2 below, list the jobs that interest you most. Then select the industries that interest you most, and list them below in number 3. These are the jobs and industries you should research most carefully. Your ideal job is likely to be found in some combination of these jobs and industries, or in more specialized but related jobs and industries.

1. The five job titles that interest you most

    a._____

    b._____

    c._____

    d._____

    e._____

2. The five next most interesting job titles

    a._____

    b._____

    c._____

    d._____

    e._____

3. The industries that interest you most

    a._____

    b._____

    c._____

    d._____

    e._____

Is Self-Employment or Starting a Business an Option?

More than one in 10 workers are self-employed or own their own businesses. If these options interest you, consider them as well. Talk to people in similar roles to gather information and look for books and Web sites that provide information on options that are similar to those that interest you. A book titled *Best Jobs for the 21st*

Century (JIST Works) includes lists and descriptions of jobs with high percentages of self-employed. Also, the Small Business Administration's Web site at www.sba.gov is a good source of basic information on related topics.

SELF-EMPLOYMENT AREAS OF INTEREST

In the following space, write your current interest in self-employment or starting a business in an area related to your general job objective.

_____

_____

_____

Can You Identify Your Job-Related Skills Now That You've Defined Your Ideal Job?

Earlier, I suggested that you should first define the job you want and then identify key job-related skills you have that support your ability to do that job. These are the job-related skills to emphasize in interviews.

So, now that you have determined your ideal job, you can pinpoint the job-related skills it requires. If you haven't done so, complete the Essential Job Search Data Worksheet on pages 326–330. Completing it will give you specific skills and accomplishments to highlight.

Yes, completing that worksheet requires time, but doing so will help you clearly define key skills to emphasize in interviews—when what you say matters so much. People who complete that worksheet will do better in their interviews than those who don't. After you complete the Essential Job Search Data Worksheet, you are ready to list your top five job-related skills.

Quip

It's a hassle, but... Completing the Essential Job Search Data Worksheet that starts on page 326 will help you define what you are good at—and remember examples of when you did things well. This information will help you define your ideal job and will be of great value in interviews. Look at the worksheet now, and promise to do it later today.

YOUR TOP FIVE JOB-RELATED SKILLS

List the top five job-related skills you think are most important. Include the job-related skills you have that you would most like to use in your next job.

1. _____

2. _____

3. _____

4. _____

5. _____

STEP 3: Use the Most Effective Methods to Find a Job in Less Time

Employer surveys have found that most employers don't advertise their job openings. They most often hire people they already know, people who find out about the jobs through word of mouth, or people who happen to be in the right place at the right time. Although luck plays a part in finding job openings, you can use the tips in this step to increase your luck.

Let's look at the job search methods that people use. The U.S. Department of Labor conducts a regular survey of unemployed people actively looking for work. Following are the results of their most recent findings.

Percentage of Unemployed People Who Use Various Job Search Methods

- Contacted employer directly: 62.7%
- Sent out resumes/filled out applications: 54.5%
- Contacted public employment agency: 19.9%
- Placed or answered help wanted ads: 16.4%
- Contacted friends or relatives: 18%
- Contacted private employment agency: 7.7%
- Used other active search methods: 11.8%

Source: U.S. Department of Labor, Current Population Survey

> **Note**
> *This step covers a number of job search methods. Most of the material is presented as information, with a few interactive activities. While each topic is short and reasonably interesting, taking a break now and then will help you absorb it all.*

The survey shows that most people use more than one job search technique. For example, one person might read want ads, fill out applications, and ask friends for job leads. Others might send out resumes, contact everyone they know through previous jobs, and sign up at employment agencies.

But the survey covered only seven job search methods and asked only whether the job seeker did or did not use each method. The survey did not cover Internet job searches, nor did it ask whether a method actually worked in getting job offers.

Unfortunately, there hasn't been much conclusive recent research on the effectiveness of various job search methods. Most of what we know is based on older research and the observations of people who work directly with job seekers, such as professional resume writers and career counselors. I'll share what we do know about the effectiveness of job search methods in the content that follows.

Get the Most Out of Less Effective Job Search Methods

>
> **Quip**
> **Your job search objective.** Almost everyone finds a job eventually, so your objective should be to find a good job in less time. The job search methods I emphasize in this minibook will help you do just that.

The truth is that every job search method works for someone. But experience and research show that some methods are more effective than others are. Your task in the job search is to spend more of your time using more effective methods—and increase the effectiveness of all the methods you use.

So let's start by looking at some traditional job search methods and how you can increase their effectiveness. Only about one-third of all job seekers get their jobs using one of these methods, but you should still consider using them to some extent in your search. Later in the step, you'll read about the most effective methods, the ones you should devote the most time to in your search.

Newspaper and Internet Help Wanted Ads

Most jobs are never advertised, and only about 16 percent of all people get their jobs through the want ads. Everyone who reads the paper knows about these openings, so competition is fierce for the few advertised jobs.

The Internet also lists many job openings. But, as happens with newspaper ads, enormous numbers of people view these postings. Many job seekers make direct contact with employers via a company's Web site. Some people do get jobs through the bigger sites, so go ahead and apply. Just be sure to spend most of your time using more effective methods.

Filling Out Applications

Most employers require job seekers to complete an application form. Applications are designed to collect negative information, and employers use applications to screen people out. If, for example, your training or work history is not the best, you will often never get an interview, even if you can do the job.

Completing applications is a more effective approach for young and entry-level job seekers. The reason is that there is a shortage of workers for the relatively low-paying jobs typically sought by less-experienced job seekers. As a result, when trying to fill those positions, employers are more willing to accept a lack of experience or fewer job skills. Even so, you will get better results by filling out the application, if asked to do so, and then requesting an interview with the person in charge.

When you complete an application, make it neat and error-free, and do not include anything that could get you screened out. If necessary, leave a problem section blank. You can always explain situations in an interview.

Employment Agencies

There are three types of employment agencies. One is operated by the government and is free. The others, private employment agencies and temp agencies, are run as for-profit businesses and charge a fee to either you or an employer. Following are the advantages and disadvantages to using each.

The government employment service and One-Stop centers. Each state and province has a network of local offices to pay unemployment compensation, provide job leads, and offer other services—at no charge to you or to employers. The service's name varies by region. It may be called Job Service, Department of Labor, Unemployment Office, Workforce Development, or another name. Many of these offices are now also online, and some even require their users to sign up with a login and password to search for job leads and use other services on the Internet.

The Employment and Training Administration Web site at www.doleta.gov/uses gives you information on the programs provided by the government employment service, plus links to other useful sites. Canada's government employment Web site is at www.jobbank.gc.ca.

The government employment service lists only 5 to 10 percent of the available openings nationally, and only about 6 percent of all job seekers get their jobs there. Even so, visit your local office early in your job search. Find out whether you qualify for unemployment compensation and learn more about its services. Look into it—the price is right.

Private employment agencies. Private employment agencies are businesses that charge a fee either to you or to the employer who hires you. Fees can be from less than one month's pay to 15 percent or more of your annual salary. You will often see these agencies' ads in the help wanted section of the newspaper. Many have Web sites.

Be careful about using fee-based employment agencies. Recent research indicates that more people use and benefit from fee-based agencies than in the past. However, relatively few people who register with private agencies get a job through them.

If you use a private employment agency, ask for interviews with the employers who agree to pay the agency's fee. Do not sign an exclusive agreement or be pressured into accepting a job. Also, continue to actively look for your own leads. You can find these agencies in the phone book's yellow pages, and many state- or province-government Web sites offer lists of the private employment agencies in their states.

Temporary agencies. Temporary agencies offer jobs that last from several days to many months. They charge the employer an hourly fee, and then pay you a bit less and keep the difference. You pay no direct fee to the agency. Many private employment agencies now provide temporary jobs as well.

Temp agencies have grown rapidly for good reason. They provide employers with short-term help, and employers often use them to find people they might want to hire later. If the employers are dissatisfied, they can just ask the agency for different temp workers.

Temp agencies can help you survive between jobs and get experience in different work settings. Temp jobs provide a very good option while you look for long-term work, and you might get a job offer while working in a temp job. Holding a temporary job might even lead to a regular job with the same or a similar employer.

School and Other Employment Services

Only a small percentage of job seekers use school and other special employment services, probably because few job seekers have the service available to them. If you are a student or graduate, find out about any employment services at your school. Some schools provide free career counseling, resume-writing help, referrals to job openings, career interest tests, reference materials, Web sites listing job openings, and other services. Special career programs work with veterans, people with disabilities, welfare recipients, union members, professional groups, and many others. So check out these services and consider using them.

Mailing Versus Posting Resumes on the Internet

Many job search experts used to suggest that sending out lots of resumes was a great technique. That advice probably helped sell their resume books, but mailing resumes to people you do not know was never an effective approach. It very rarely works. A recent survey of 1,500 successful job seekers showed that only 2 percent found their positions through sending an unsolicited resume. The same is true for the Internet.

Although mailing your resume to strangers doesn't make much sense, posting it on the Internet might because

- It doesn't take much time.

- Many employers have the potential of finding your resume.

- You can post your resume on niche sites that attract only employers in your field.

- Your Internet resume is easily updated, allowing you to post your current accomplishments.

- You can easily link your resume to projects and Web sites that highlight your accomplishments.

Job searching on the Internet has its limitations, just like other methods. I'll cover resumes in more detail later and provide tips on using the Internet throughout this minibook.

Use the Two Job Search Methods That Work Best

The fact is that most jobs are not advertised, so how do *you* find them? The same way that about two-thirds of all job seekers do: networking with people you know (which I call making warm contacts) and directly contacting employers (which I call making cold contacts). Both of these methods are based on the job search rule you should know above all:

The Most Important Job Search Rule: Don't wait until the job opens before contacting the employer!

Employers fill most jobs with people they meet before a job is formally open. The trick is to meet people who can hire you before a job is formally available. Instead of asking whether the employer has any jobs open, I suggest that you say, *"I realize you may not have any openings now, but I would still like to talk to you about the possibility of future openings."*

Most Effective Job Search Method 1: Develop a Network of Contacts in Five Easy Stages

Studies find that 60 percent of all people located their jobs through a lead provided by a friend, a relative, or an acquaintance. That makes the people you know your number one source of job leads—more effective than all the traditional methods combined! Developing and using your contacts is called *networking*, and here's how it works:

1. **Make lists of people you know.** Make a thorough list of anyone you are friendly with. Then make a separate list of all your relatives. These two lists alone often add up to 25 to 100 people or more. Next, think of other groups of people that you have something in common with, such as former co-workers or classmates, members of your social or sports groups, members of your professional association, former employers, neighbors, and other groups. You might not know many of these people personally or well, but most will help you if you ask them.

2. **Contact each person in your list in a systematic way.** Obviously, some people will be more helpful than others, but any one of them might help you find a job lead.

3. **Present yourself well.** Begin with your friends and relatives. Call and tell them you are looking for a job and need their help. Be as clear as possible about the type of employment you want and the skills and qualifications you have. Look at the sample JIST Card and phone script later in this step for good presentation ideas.

4. **Ask your contacts for leads.** It is possible that your contacts will know of a job opening that interests you. If so, get the details and get right on it! More likely, however, they will not, so you should ask each person the Three Magic Networking Questions.

> **Quip**
>
> **Most jobs are never advertised because employers don't need to advertise or don't want to.** Employers trust people referred to them by someone they know far more than they trust strangers. And most jobs are filled by referrals and people that the employer knows, eliminating the need to advertise. So, your job search must involve more than looking at ads.

The Three Magic Networking Questions

● **Do you know of any openings for a person with my skills?**

If the answer is "No" (which it usually is), then ask...

● **Do you know of someone else who might know of such an opening? If your contact does, get that name and ask for another one.**

If he or she doesn't, ask...

(continued)

(continued)

- **Do you know of anyone who might know of someone else who might know of a job opening?**

  Another good way to ask this is "Do you know someone who knows lots of people?" If all else fails, this will usually get you a name.

5. **Contact these referrals and ask them the same questions.** From each person you contact, try to get two names of other people you might contact. Doing this consistently can extend your network of acquaintances by hundreds of people. Eventually, one of these people will hire you or refer you to someone who will!

If you are persistent in following these five steps, networking might be the only job search method you need. It works.

Dialing for dollars. The phone can get you more interviews per hour than any other job search tool. But it won't work unless you use it actively.

The phone book's yellow pages provide the most complete, up-to-date listing of potential job search targets you can get. It organizes them into categories that are very useful for job seekers. Just find a category that interests you, evaluate each listing, and then contact employers that interest you. All it takes is a 30-second phone call. Ask to speak with the hiring authority.

Most Effective Job Search Method 2: Contact Employers Directly

It takes more courage, but making direct contact with employers is a very effective job search technique. I call these cold contacts because people you don't know in advance will need to warm up to your inquiries. Two basic techniques for making cold contacts follow.

Use the yellow pages to find potential employers. Begin by looking at the index in the front of your phone book's yellow pages. For each entry, ask yourself, *"Would an organization of this kind need a person with my skills?"* If you answer *"Yes,"* then that organization or business type is a possible target. You can also rate "Yes" entries based on your interest, writing a "1" next to those that seem very interesting, a "2" next to those that you are not sure of, and a "3" next to those that aren't interesting at all.

Next, select a type of organization that got a "Yes" response and turn to that section of the yellow pages. Call each organization listed there and ask to speak to the person who is most likely to hire or supervise you—typically the manager of the business or a department head—not the personnel or human resources manager. A sample telephone script is included later in this section to give you ideas about what to say.

You can easily adapt this approach for use on the Internet by using sites such as www.yellowpages.com to get contacts anywhere in the world, or you can find phone and e-mail contacts on an employer's own Web site.

Drop in without an appointment. Another effective cold contact method is to just walk into a business or organization that interests you and ask to speak to the person in charge. Although dropping in is particularly effective in small businesses, it also works surprisingly well in larger ones. Remember to ask for an interview even if there are no openings now. If your timing is inconvenient, ask for a better time to come back for an interview.

Most Jobs Are with Small Employers

Businesses and organizations with fewer than 250 employees employ about 72 percent of all U.S. workers. Small organizations are also the source for around 75 percent of the new jobs created each year. They are simply too important to overlook in your job search! Many of them don't have personnel departments, which makes direct contacts even easier and more effective.

Create a Powerful Job Search Tool—the JIST Card®

Look at the sample cards that follow—they are JIST Cards, and they get results. Computer printed or even neatly written on a 3-by-5–inch card, JIST Cards include the essential information employers want to know.

A JIST Card Is a Mini Resume

JIST Cards have been used by thousands of job search programs and millions of people. Employers like their direct and timesaving format, and they have been proven as an effective tool to get job leads. Attach one to your resume. Give them to friends, relatives, and other contacts and ask them to pass them along to others who might know of an opening. Enclose them in thank-you notes after interviews. Leave one with employers as a business card. However you get them in circulation, you may be surprised at how well they work.

You can easily create JIST Cards on a computer and print them on card stock you can buy at any office supply store. Or have a few hundred printed cheaply by a local quick print shop. While they are often done as 3-by-5 cards, they can be printed in any size or format.

Sandy Nolan

Position: General Office/Clerical

Cell phone: (512) 232-9213

Email: snolan@aol.com

More than two years of work experience plus one year of training in office practices. Type 55 wpm, trained in word processing, post general ledger, have good interpersonal skills, and get along with most people. Can meet deadlines and handle pressure well.

Willing to work any hours.

Organized, honest, reliable, and hardworking.

Richard Straightarrow   **Home: (602) 253-9678**
                                           Message: (602) 257-6643
                                             E-mail: RSS@email.com

Objective: Electronics installation, maintenance, and sales

Four years of work experience plus a two-year A.S. degree in Electronics Engineering Technology. Managed a $360,000/year business while going to school full time, with grades in the top 25%. Familiar with all major electronic diagnostic and repair equipment. Hands-on experience with medical, consumer, communication, and industrial electronics equipment and applications. Good problem-solving and communication skills. Customer service oriented.

Willing to do what it takes to get the job done.

Self motivated, dependable, learn quickly.

A JIST Card Can Lead to an Effective Phone Script

The phone is an essential job search tool that can get you more interviews per hour than any other job search tool. But the technique won't work unless you use it actively throughout your search. After you have created your JIST Card, you can use it as the basis for a phone script to make warm or cold calls. Revise your JIST Card content so that it sounds natural when spoken, and then edit it until you can read it out loud in about 30 seconds. The sample phone script that follows is based on the content of a JIST Card. Use it to help you modify your own JIST Card into a phone script.

Overcome phone phobia! Making cold calls takes guts, but most people can get one or more interviews an hour using cold calls. Start by calling people you know and people they refer you to. Then try calls to businesses that don't sound very interesting. As you get better, call more desirable targets.

"Hello. My name is Pam Nykanen. I am interested in a position in hotel management. I have four years' experience in sales, catering, and accounting with a 300-room hotel. I also have an associate degree in hotel management, plus one year of experience with the Brady Culinary Institute. During my employment, I helped double revenues from meetings and conferences and increased bar revenues by 46 percent. I have good problem-solving skills and am good with people. I am also well-organized, hardworking, and detail-oriented. When may I come in for an interview?"

With your script in hand, make some practice calls to warm or cold contacts. If making cold calls, contact the person most likely to supervise you. Then present your script just as you practiced it—without stopping.

Although the sample script assumes that you are calling someone you don't know, you can change it to address warm contacts and referrals. Making cold calls takes courage but works very well for many who are willing to do it.

Use the Internet in Your Job Search

The Internet has limitations as a job search tool. While many have used it to get job leads, it has not worked well for far more. Too many assume they can simply add their resume to resume databases, and employers will line up to hire them. Just like the older approach of sending out lots of resumes, good things sometimes happen, but not often.

I recommend two points that apply to all job search methods, including using the Internet:

- It is unwise to rely on just one or two methods in conducting your job search.

- It is essential that you use an active rather than a passive approach in your job search.

Use More Than One Job Search Method

I encourage you to use the Internet in your job search, but I suggest that you use it along with other techniques. Use the same sorts of job search techniques online as you do offline, including contacting employers directly and building up a network of personal contacts that can help you with your search.

Tips to Increase Your Effectiveness in Internet Job Searches

The following tips can increase the effectiveness of using the Internet in your job search:

- **Be as specific as possible in the job you seek.** This is important in using any job search method, and it's even more important in using the Internet in your job search. The Internet is enormous, so it is essential to be as focused as possible in your search. Narrow your job title or titles to be as specific as possible. Limit your search to specific industries or areas of specialization. Locate and use specialized job banks in your area of interest.

- **Have reasonable expectations.** Success on the Internet is more likely if you understand its limitations and strengths. For example, employers trying to find someone with skills in high demand, such as nurses, are more likely to use the Internet to recruit job candidates.

- **Limit your geographic options.** If you don't want to move or would move only to certain areas, state this preference on your resume and restrict your search to those areas. Many Internet sites allow you to view or search for only those jobs that meet your location criteria.

- **Create an electronic resume.** With few exceptions, resumes submitted on the Internet end up as simple text files with no graphic elements. Employers search databases of many resumes for those that include key words or meet other searchable criteria. So create a simple text resume for Internet use and include words that are likely to be used by employers searching for someone with your abilities. (See Step 4 for more on creating an electronic resume.)

- **Get your resume into the major resume databases.** Most Internet employment sites let you add your resume for free and then charge employers to advertise openings or to search for candidates. Although adding your resume to these databases is not likely to result in job offers, doing so allows you to use your stored resume to easily apply for positions that are posted at these sites. These easy-to-use sites often provide all sorts of useful information for job seekers.

- **Make direct contacts.** Visit the Web sites of organizations that interest you and learn more about them. Many post openings, allow you to apply online, offer information on benefits and work environment, or even provide access to staff who can answer your questions. Even if they don't, you can always search the site or e-mail a request for the name of the person in charge of the work that interests you and then communicate with that person directly.

- **Network.** You can network online, too, finding names and e-mail addresses of potential employer contacts or of other people who might know someone with job openings. Look at and participate in interest groups, professional association sites, alumni sites, chat rooms, e-mail discussion lists, and employer sites—these are just some of the many creative ways to network and interact with people via the Internet.

Check Out Career-Specific Sites First

Thousands of Internet sites provide lists of job openings and information on careers or education. Many have links to other sites that they recommend. Service providers such as America Online (www.aol.com) and the Microsoft Network (www.msn.com) have partnered with sites such as Careerbuilder.com to include career information and job listings plus links to other sites. Also check out www.jist.com and www.CareerOINK.com. Two additional career-related sites are Riley Guide at www.rileyguide.com and Monster.com at www.monster.com.

STEP 4: Write a Simple Resume Now and a Better One Later

Sending out resumes and waiting for responses is not an effective job-seeking technique. But, many employers *will* ask you for a resume, and it can be a useful tool in your job search. I suggest that you begin with a simple resume you can complete quickly. I've seen too many people spend weeks working on a resume when they could have been out getting interviews instead. If you want a better resume, you can work on it on weekends and evenings. So let's begin with the basics.

Tips for Creating a Superior Resume

The following tips make sense for any resume format:

- **Write it yourself.** It's okay to look at other resumes for ideas, but write yours yourself. Doing so will force you to organize your thoughts and background.
- **Make it error-free.** One spelling or grammar error will create a negative impressionist (see what I mean?). Get someone else to review your final draft for any errors. Then review it again because these rascals have a way of slipping in.
- **Make it look good.** Poor copy quality, cheap paper, bad type quality, or anything else that creates a poor appearance will turn off employers to even the best resume content. Get professional help with design and printing if necessary. Many professional resume writers and even print shops offer writing and desktop design services if you need help.
- **Be brief, be relevant.** Many good resumes fit on one page, and few justify more than two. Include only the most important points. Use short sentences and action words. If it doesn't relate to and support the job objective, cut it!
- **Be honest.** Don't overstate your qualifications. If you end up getting a job you can't handle, who does it help? And a lie can result in your being fired later.
- **Be positive.** Emphasize your accomplishments and results. A resume is no place to be too humble or to display your faults.
- **Be specific.** Instead of saying, "I am good with people," say, "I supervised four people in the warehouse and increased productivity by 30 percent." Use numbers whenever possible, such as the number of people served, percentage of sales increase, or amount of dollars saved.

You should also know that everyone feels that he or she is a resume expert. Whatever you do, someone will tell you that it's wrong. Remember that a resume is simply a job search tool.

You should never delay or slow down your job search because your resume is not good enough. The best approach is to create a simple and acceptable resume as quickly as possible and then use it. As time permits, create a better one if you feel you must.

Avoid the resume pile. Resume experts often suggest that a dynamite resume will jump out of the pile. This is old-fashioned advice. It assumes that you are applying to large organizations and for advertised jobs. Today most jobs are with small employers and are not advertised. To avoid joining that stack of resumes in the first place, look for job openings that others overlook.

Writing Chronological Resumes

Most resumes use a chronological format where the most recent experience is listed first, followed by each previous job. This arrangement works fine for someone with work experience in several similar jobs, but not as well for those with limited experience or for career changers.

Look at the two resumes for Judith Jones that follow. Both use the chronological approach.

The first resume would work fine for most job search needs. It could be completed in about an hour.

Notice that the second one includes some improvements. The first resume is good, but most employers would like the additional positive information in the improved resume.

Basic Chronological Resume Example

Judith J. Jones

115 South Hawthorne Avenue
Chicago, Illinois 66204
(312) 653-9217 (home)
email: jj@earthlink.net

Leaves lots of options open by not using one job title.

Everything supports her job objective.

JOB OBJECTIVE

Desire a position in the office management, accounting, or administrative assistant area. Prefer a position requiring responsibility and a variety of tasks.

EDUCATION AND TRAINING

Acme Business College, Lincoln, Illinois
Graduate of a one-year business program.

John Adams High School, South Bend, Indiana
Diploma, business education.

U.S. Army
Financial procedures, accounting functions.

Emphasis on all related education is important because it helps overcome her lack of "work" experience.

Other: Continuing-education classes and workshops in business communication, computer spreadsheet and database programs, scheduling systems, and customer relations.

EXPERIENCE

Uses her education in this section to add credentials.

2003–present—Claims Processor, Blue Spear Insurance Co., Willmette, Illinois. Handle customer medical claims, develop management reports based on spreadsheets I created, exceed productivity goals.

2002–2003—Returned to school to upgrade my business and computer skills. Took courses in advanced accounting, spreadsheet and database programs, office management, human relations, and new office techniques.

1999–2002—E4, U.S. Army. Assigned to various stations as a specialist in financial operations. Promoted prior to honorable discharge.

1998–1999—Sandy's Boutique, Wilmette, Illinois. Responsible for counter sales, display design, cash register, and other tasks.

1996–1998—Held part-time and summer jobs throughout high school.

PERSONAL

I am reliable, hardworking, and good with people.

I give some tips you can use when you write your simple chronological resume. Use the preceding resume as your guide.

Improved Chronological Resume Example

Judith J. Jones

115 South Hawthorne Avenue
Chicago, Illinois 66204

jj@earthlink.net
(312) 653-9217

Adds lots of details to reinforce skills throughout.

Provides more details here.

JOB OBJECTIVE

Seeking a position requiring excellent business management expertise in an office environment. Position should require a variety of skills, including office management, word processing, and spreadsheet and database application use.

EDUCATION AND TRAINING

Acme Business College, Lincoln, IL
Completed one-year program in Professional Office Management. Achieved GPA in top 30% of class. Courses included word processing, accounting theory and systems, advanced spreadsheet and database applications, graphics design, time management, and supervision.

John Adams High School, South Bend, IN
Graduated with emphasis on business courses. Earned excellent grades in all business topics and won top award for word-processing speed and accuracy.

Other: Continuing-education programs at own expense, including business communications, customer relations, computer applications, and sales techniques.

EXPERIENCE

Uses numbers to reinforce results.

2003–present—Claims Processor, Blue Spear Insurance Company, Wilmette, IL. Process 50 complex medical insurance claims per day, almost 20% above department average. Created a spreadsheet report process that decreased department labor costs by more than $30,000 a year. Received two merit raises for performance.

2002–2003—Returned to business school to gain advanced office skills.

1999–2002—Finance Specialist (E4), U.S. Army. Systematically processed more than 200 invoices per day from commercial vendors. Trained and supervised eight employees. Devised internal system allowing 15% increase in invoices processed with a decrease in personnel. Managed department with a budget equivalent of more than $350,000 a year. Honorable discharge.

1998–1999—Sales Associate promoted to Assistant Manager, Sandy's Boutique, Wilmette, IL. Made direct sales and supervised four employees. Managed daily cash balances and deposits, made purchasing and inventory decisions, and handled all management functions during owner's absence. Sales increased 26% and profits doubled during tenure.

1996–1998—Held various part-time and summer jobs through high school while maintaining GPA 3.0/4.0. Earned enough to pay all personal expenses, including car insurance. Learned to deal with customers, meet deadlines, work hard, and handle multiple priorities.

STRENGTHS AND SKILLS

Reliable, with strong work ethic. Excellent interpersonal, written, and oral communication and math skills. Accept supervision well, effectively supervise others, and work well as a team member. General ledger, accounts payable, and accounts receivable expertise. Proficient in Microsoft Word, Excel, and Outlook; WordPerfect.

Tips for Writing a Simple Chronological Resume

Follow these tips as you write a basic chronological resume:

- **Name.** Use your formal name (not a nickname).

- **Address and contact information.** Avoid abbreviations in your address and include your ZIP code. If you may move, use a friend's address or include a forwarding address. Most employers will not write to you, so provide reliable phone numbers and other contact options. Always include your area code in your phone number because you never know where your resume might travel. Make sure that you have an answering machine or voice mail, and record a professional-sounding message. Include alternative ways to reach you, such as a cell phone and e-mail address.

- **Job objective.** You should almost always have one, even if it is general. Notice how Judith Jones keeps her options open with her broad job objective in her basic resume on page 311. Writing "secretary" or "clerical" might limit her from being considered for other jobs.

- **Education and training.** Include any training or education you've had that supports your job objective. If you did not finish a formal degree or program, list what you did complete and emphasize accomplishments. If your experience is not strong, add details here such as related courses and extracurricular activities. In the two examples, Judith Jones puts her business schooling in both the education and experience sections. Doing this fills a job gap and allows her to present her training as equal to work experience.

- **Previous experience.** Include the basics such as employer name, job title, dates employed, and responsibilities—but emphasize specific skills, results, accomplishments, superior performance, and so on.

- **Personal data.** Do not include irrelevant details such as height, weight, and marital status or a photo. Current laws do not allow an employer to base hiring decisions on these points. Providing this information can cause some employers to toss your resume. You can include information about hobbies or leisure activities in a special section that directly supports your job objective. The first sample includes a Personal section in which Judith lists some of her strengths, which are often not included in a resume.

- **References.** Make sure that each reference will make nice comments about you and ask each to write a letter of recommendation that you can give to employers. You do not need to list your references on your resume. List them on a separate page and give it to employers who ask. If your references are particularly good, however, you can mention this somewhere—the last section is often a good place.

When you have a simple, errorless, and eye-pleasing resume, get on with your job search. There is no reason to delay! If you want to create a better resume in your spare time (evenings or weekends), use the name and contact information you currently have and improve the other sections of the resume.

Tips for an Improved Chronological Resume

Use these tips to improve your simple resume:

- **Job objective.** A poorly written job objective can limit the jobs an employer might consider you for. Think of the skills you have and the types of jobs you want to do; describe them in general terms. Instead of using a narrow job title such as "restaurant manager," you might write "manage a small to mid-sized business."

- **Education and training.** New graduates should emphasize their recent training and education more than those with a few years of related work experience would. A more detailed education and training section might include specific courses you took, and activities or accomplishments that support your job objective or reinforce your key skills. Include other details that reflect how hard you work, such as working your way through school or handling family responsibilities.

- **Skills and accomplishments.** Include those that support your ability to do well in the job you seek now. Even small details count. Maybe your attendance was perfect, you met a tight deadline, or you did the work of others during vacations. Be specific and include numbers—even if you have to estimate them. Judith's improved chronological resume example features more accomplishments and skills. Notice the impact of the numbers to reinforce results.

- **Job titles.** Past job titles may not accurately reflect what you did. For example, your job title may have been "cashier," but you also opened the store, trained new staff, and covered for the boss on vacations. Perhaps "head cashier and assistant manager" would be more accurate. Check with your previous employer if you are not sure.

(continued)

(continued)

- **Promotions.** If you were promoted or got good evaluations, say so—"cashier, promoted to assistant manager," for example. You can list a promotion to a more responsible job as a separate job if doing so results in a stronger resume.

- **Gaps in employment and other problem areas.** Employee turnover is expensive, so few employers want to hire people who won't stay or who won't work out. Gaps in employment, jobs held for short periods, or a lack of direction in the jobs you've held are all concerns for employers. So consider your situation and try to give an explanation of a problem area. Here are a few examples:

  2007—Continued my education at...   2006 to present—Self-employed as barn painter and...

  2007—Traveled extensively throughout...   2006—Took year off to have first child

  Use entire years to avoid displaying employment gaps you can't explain easily. If you had a few months of unemployment at the beginning of 2006 and then began a job in mid-2006, for example, you can list the job as "2006 to 2007."

Writing Skills and Combination Resumes

Quip

Skip the negatives. Remember that a resume can get you screened out, but it is up to you to get the interview and the job. Cut out anything negative in your resume!

The skills resume emphasizes your most important skills, supported by specific examples of how you have used them. This type of resume allows you to use any part of your life history to support your ability to do the job you want.

While skills resumes can be very effective, creating them requires more work. And some employers don't like them because they can hide a job seeker's faults (such as job gaps, lack of formal education, or little related work experience) better than can a chronological resume. Still, a skills resume may make sense for you.

Look over the sample resumes that follow for ideas. Notice that one resume includes elements of a skills *and* a chronological resume. This so-called combination resume makes sense if your previous job history or education and training are positive.

More Resume Examples

Quip

A resume is not the most effective tool for getting interviews. A better approach is to make direct contact with those who hire or supervise people with your skills and ask them for an interview, even if no openings exist now. Then send a resume.

Find resume layout and presentation ideas in the four samples that follow.

The chronological resume sample on page 315 focuses on accomplishments through the use of numbers. While Jon's resume does not say so, it is obvious that he works hard and that he gets results.

The skills resume on page 316 is for a recent high school graduate whose only work experience was at a school office!

The combination resume on page 317 emphasizes Grant's relevant education and transferable skills because he has little work experience in the field.

The electronic resume on page 318 is appropriate for scanning or e-mail submission. It has a plain format that is easily read by scanners. It also has lots of key words that increase its chances of being selected when an employer searches a database.

Use the information from your completed Essential Job Search Data Worksheet to write your resume.

The Chronological Resume to Emphasize Results

This simple chronological resume has few but carefully chosen words. It has an effective summary at the beginning, and every word supports his job objective.

Jon Feder

2140 Beach Road
Pompano Beach, Florida 20000

Phone: (222) 333-4444
E-mail: jfeder@com.com

Objective: Management position in a major hotel *He emphasizes results!*

Summary of Experience: Three years of experience in sales, catering banquet services, and guest relations in a 75-room hotel. Doubled sales revenues from conferences and meetings. Increased dining room and bar revenues by 40%. Won prestigious national and local awards for increased productivity and services.

Experience: Beachcomber Hotel, Pompano Beach, Florida
Assistant Manager
20XX to Present

Notice his use of numbers to increase the impact of the statements.

- Oversee a staff of 24, including dining room and bar, housekeeping, and public relations operations.
- Introduced new menus and increased dining room revenues by 40%. Awarded *Saveur* magazine's prestigious first place Hotel Cuisine award as a result of my selection of chefs.
- Attracted 58% more bar patrons by implementing Friday night Jazz at the Beach.

Beachcombers' Suites, Hollywood Beach, Florida
Sales and Public Relations
20XX to 20XX

Bullets here and above improve readability and emphasize key points.

- Doubled venues per month from weddings, conferences, and meetings.
- Chosen Chamber of Commerce Newcomer of the Year 20XX for the increase in business within the community.

Education: Associate Degree in Hotel Management from Sullivan Technical Institute
Certificate in Travel Management from Phoenix University

While Jon had only a few years of related work experience, he used this resume to help him land a very responsible job in a large resort hotel.

The Skills Resume for Those with Limited Work Experience

In this skills resume, each skill directly supports the job objective of this recent high school graduate with very limited work experience.

Catalina A. Garcia

2340 N. Delaware Street · Denver, Colorado 81613
Home: (413) 643-2173 (Leave Message)
Cell phone: (413) 345-2189
E-mail: cagarcia@net.net

Position Desired
Office assistant in a fast-paced business

Support for her key skills comes from her activities: school, clubs, and volunteer work.

Skills and Abilities

Note her key skills.

Communications — Excellent written and verbal presentation skills. Use proper grammar and have a good speaking voice.

Interpersonal — Able to get along well with all types of people. Accept supervision. Received positive evaluation from previous supervisors.

Flexible — Willing to try new things and am interested in improving efficiency on assigned tasks.

Notice the emphasis on adaptive skills.

Attention to Detail — Maintained confidential student records accurately and efficiently. Uploaded 500 student records in one day without errors.

Hard Working — Worked 30 hours per week throughout high school and maintained above-average grades.

She makes good use of numbers.

This statement is very strong.

Student Contact — Cordially dealt with as many as 150 students a day in Dean's office.

Dependable — Never absent or tardy in four years.

Awards — English Department Student of the Year, April 20XX
20XX Outstanding Student Newspaper, Newspaper Association of America

Education

Denver North High School. Took advanced English and communication classes. Member of student newspaper staff and FCCLA for four years. Graduated in top 30% of class.

Other

Girls' basketball team for four years. This taught me discipline, teamwork, how to follow instructions, and hard work. I am ambitious, outgoing, reliable, and willing to work.

Catalina's resume makes it clear that she is talented and hard working.

The Combination Resume for Those Changing Careers

Grant just finished computer programming school and has no work experience in the field. After listing the topics covered in the course, he summarized his employment experience, specifying that he earned promotions quickly. This would be attractive to any employer.

Grant Thomas

717 Carlin Court • Mendelein, IL 60000 • (555) 555-3333
E-mail: gthomas@com.com

Profile

- Outstanding student and tutor
- Winner of international computer software design competition three years
- Capable of being self-directed and independent, but also a team player
- Effective communicator, both orally and written
- Creative problem solver

Education and Training

M.S. in Software Engineering, Massachusetts Institute of Technology, Cambridge, MA
B.S. in Computer Engineering, California State University, Fullerton, CA
A rigorous education that focuses on topics such as

He includes important information that specifies topics he studied.

- Structure and interpretation of computer programs
- Circuits and electronics
- Signals and systems
- Computation structures
- Microelectronic devices and circuits
- Computer system engineering
- Computer language engineering
- Mathematics for computer science
- Analog electronics laboratory
- Digital systems laboratory

The work experiences support the job objective.

Highlights of Experience and Abilities

- Develop, create, and modify general computer applications software.
- Analyze user needs and develop software solutions.
- Confer with system analysts, computer programmers, and others.
- Modify existing software to correct errors.
- Coordinate software system installation and monitor equipment functioning to ensure specifications are met.
- Supervise work of programmers and technicians.
- Train customers and employees to use new and modified software.

Employment History

Software Specialist, First Rate Computers, Mendelein, IL 20XX – Present
- Technician and Customer and Employee Trainer throughout high school
- Promoted to software specialist and worked as a full-time telecommuting employee while completing the B.S. and M.S. degrees

References available on request

The Electronic Resume

William Brown
409 S. Maish Road
Phoenix, AZ 50000

Because this electronic format is to be scanned or e-mailed, it has no bold, bullets, or italics.

Phone message: (300) 444-5567

E-mail: wbrown@email.com

The many key words ensure that the employers' computer searches will select this resume.

OBJECTIVE

Store management career track in car audio store

==
SUMMARY OF SKILLS

Strategic planning, time management, team building,
leadership, problem solving, quality customer service,
conflict resolution, increasing productivity, confident,
outgoing, high performing, aggressive sales

==
EXPERIENCE   *Note the results statements and numbers used below.*

Total of three years in sales

* SHIFT SUPERVISOR, Tech World, Audio Department, Phoenix,
AZ, April 20XX to present: Promoted to Shift Supervisor of
nine salespeople in three months. Responsible for strategic
planning, time management, team building, leadership,
problem solving, quality customer service, conflict
resolution, and increasing productivity. Highest-selling
team for three years.

* AUDIO SALESPERSON, Tech World, Audio Department, Phoenix,
AZ, January 20XX to April 20XX: Arranged display, organized
stockroom, sales to customers, and tracked inventory.
Highest-selling staff member for three months.

==
EDUCATION AND TRAINING

Phoenix High School, top 40% of class

Additional training: Team Building, Franklin Time Management
seminar, Team Building seminar

==
OTHER

* Installed audio systems in 10 cars: family, friends, and
my own.

* Member of United States Autosound Association (USAA)

Use a Career Portfolio to Support Your Resume

Your resume is impressive, but there is another way that you can show prospective employers evidence of who you are and what you can do—a career portfolio.

What Is a Career Portfolio?

Unlike a resume, a career portfolio is a collection of documents that can include a variety of items. Here are some items you may want to place in your portfolio:

- Resume
- School transcripts
- Summary of skills
- Credentials, such as diplomas and certificates of recognition
- Reference letters from school officials and instructors, former employers, or co-workers
- List of accomplishments: Describe hobbies and interests that are not directly related to your job objective and are not included on your resume.
- Examples of your work: Depending on your situation, you can include samples of your art, photographs of a project, audiotapes, videotapes, images of Web pages you developed, and other media that can provide examples of your work.

Place each item on a separate page when you assemble your career portfolio.

Create a Digital Portfolio

A digital portfolio, also known as an electronic portfolio, contains all the information from your career portfolio in an electronic format. This material is then copied onto a CD-ROM or published on a Web site. With a digital portfolio, you can present your skills to a greater number of people than you can your paper career portfolio.

YOUR CAREER PORTFOLIO

On the following lines, list the items you want to include in your career portfolio. Think specifically of those items that show your skills, education, and personal accomplishments.

_____

_____

_____

_____

_____

_____

_____

_____

_____

STEP 5: Redefine What Counts as an Interview, and Then Get Two a Day

The average job seeker gets about five interviews a month—fewer than two a week. Yet many job seekers use the methods in this *Quick Job Search* to get two interviews a day. Getting two interviews a day equals 10 a week and 40 a month. That's 800 percent more interviews than the average job seeker gets. Who do you think will get a job offer quicker?

However, getting two interviews a day is nearly impossible unless you redefine what counts as an interview. If you define an interview in a different way, getting two a day is quite possible.

The New Definition of an Interview: Any face-to-face contact with someone who has the authority to hire or supervise a person with your skills—even if no opening exists at the time you talk with them.

If you use this new definition, it becomes *much* easier to get interviews. You can now interview with all sorts of potential employers, not just those who have job openings now. While most other job seekers look for advertised or actual openings, you can get interviews before a job opens up or before it is advertised and widely known. You will be considered for jobs that may soon be created but that others will not know about. And, of course, you can also interview for existing openings just as everyone else does.

Spending as much time as possible on your job search and setting a job search schedule are important parts of this Step.

Make Your Search a Full-Time Job

Job seekers average fewer than 15 hours a week looking for work. On average, unemployment lasts three or more months, with some people out of work far longer (for example, older workers and higher earners). My many years of experience researching job seeking indicate that the more time you spend on your job search each week, the less time you will likely remain unemployed.

Of course, using the more effective job search methods presented in this minibook also helps. Many job search programs that teach job seekers my basic approach of using more effective methods and spending more time looking have proven that these seekers often find a job in half the average time. More importantly, many job seekers also find better jobs using these methods.

So, if you are unemployed and looking for a full-time job, you should plan to look on a full-time basis. It just makes sense to do so, although many do not, or they start out well but quickly get discouraged. Most job seekers simply don't have a structured plan—they have no idea what they are going to do next Thursday. The plan that follows will show you how to structure your job search like a job.

Decide How Much Time You Will Spend Looking for Work Each Week and Day

First and most importantly, decide how many hours you are willing to spend each week on your job search. You should spend a minimum of 25 hours a week on hard-core job search activities with no goofing around. The following worksheet walks you through a simple but effective process to set a job search schedule for each week.

PLAN YOUR JOB SEARCH WEEK
1. How many hours are you willing to spend each week looking for a job?_____
2. Which days of the week will you spend looking for a job?_____
3. How many hours will you look each day?_____
4. At what times will you begin and end your job search on each of these days?_____
_____

Create a Specific Daily Job Search Schedule

Having a specific daily schedule is essential because most job seekers find it hard to stay productive each day. The sample daily schedule that follows is the result of years of research into what schedule gets the best results. I tested many schedules in job search programs I ran, and this particular schedule worked best.

Consider using a schedule like this sample daily schedule. Why? Because it works.

A Sample Daily Schedule That Works

Time	Activity
7–8 a.m.	Get up, shower, dress, eat breakfast
8–8:15 a.m.	Organize work space, review schedule for today's interviews and promised follow-ups, check e-mail, update schedule as needed
8:15–9 a.m.	Review old leads for follow-up needed today; develop new leads from want ads, yellow pages, the Internet, warm contact lists, and other sources; complete daily contact list
9–10 a.m.	Make phone calls and set up interviews
10–10:15 a.m.	Take a break
10:15–11 a.m.	Make more phone calls, set up more interviews
11 a.m.–Noon	Send follow-up notes and do other office activities as needed
Noon–1 p.m.	Lunch break, relax
1–3 p.m.	Go on interviews, make cold contacts in the field
Evening	Read job search books, make calls to warm contacts not reachable during the day, work on a better resume, spend time with friends and family, exercise, relax

If you are not accustomed to using a daily schedule book or electronic planner, promise yourself to get a good one tomorrow. Choose one that allows for each day's plan on an hourly basis, plus daily to-do lists. Record your daily schedule in advance, and then add interviews as they come. Get used to carrying your planner with you and use it!

You can find a variety of computer programs or pocket-sized electronic schedulers to help organize your job search. If you don't use electronic tools, a simple schedule book and other paper systems will work just fine.

STEP 6: Dramatically Improve Your Interviewing Skills

Interviews are where the job search action is. You have to get them; then you have to do well in them. According to surveys of employers, most job seekers do not effectively present the skills they have to do the job. Even worse, most job seekers can't answer one or more problem questions.

This lack of performance in interviews is one reason why employers will often hire a job seeker who does well in the interview over someone with better credentials. The good news is that you can do simple things to dramatically improve your interviewing skills. This section will emphasize interviewing tips and techniques that make the most difference.

Your First Impression May Be the Only One You Make

Some research suggests that if the interviewer forms a negative impression in the first five minutes of an interview, your chances of getting a job offer approach zero. I know from experience that many job seekers can create a lasting negative impression within seconds.

Tips for Interviewing

Because a positive first impression is so important, I share these suggestions to help you get off to a good start:

- **Make a good impression before you arrive.** Your resume, e-mails, applications, and other written correspondence create an impression before the interview, so make them professional and error-free.

- **Do some homework on the organization before you go.** You can often get information on a business and on industry trends from the Internet or a library.

- **Dress and groom the same way the interviewer is likely to be dressed—but cleaner!** Employer surveys find that almost half of all people's dress or grooming creates an initial negative impression. So this is a big problem. If necessary, get advice on your interviewing outfits from someone who dresses well. Pay close attention to your grooming, too—little things do count.

- **Be early.** Leave in plenty of time to be a few minutes early to an interview.

- **Be friendly and respectful with the receptionist.** Doing otherwise will often get back to the interviewer and result in a quick rejection.

- **Follow the interviewer's lead in the first few minutes.** It's often informal small talk but very important for that person to see how you interact. This is a good time to make a positive comment on the organization or even something you see in the office.

- **Understand that a traditional interview is not a friendly exchange.** In a traditional interview situation, there is a job opening, and you will be one of several applicants for it. In this setting, the employer's task is to eliminate all applicants but one. The interviewer's questions are designed to elicit information that can be used to screen you out. And your objective is to avoid getting screened out. It's hardly an open and honest interaction, is it?

  Setting up interviews before an opening exists eliminates the stress of a traditional interview. In pre-interviews, employers are not trying to screen you out, and you are not trying to keep them from finding out stuff about you. Having said that, knowing how to answer questions that might be asked in a traditional interview is good preparation for any interview you face.

- **Be prepared to answer the tough interview questions.** Your answers to a few key problem questions may determine whether you get a job offer. There are simply too many possible interview questions to cover one by one. Instead, 10 basic questions cover variations of most other interview questions. So, if you can learn to answer the Top 10 Problem Interview Questions well, you will know how to answer most others.

- **Be prepared for the most important interview question of all.** "Why should I hire you?" is the most important question of all to answer well. Do you have a convincing argument why someone should hire you over someone else? If you don't, you probably won't get that job you really want. So think carefully about why someone should hire you and practice your response. Then make sure you communicate this in the interview, even if the interviewer never asks the question in a clear way.

> ### Top 10 Problem Interview Questions
> 1. Why should I hire you?
> 2. Why don't you tell me about yourself?
> 3. What are your major strengths?
> 4. What are your major weaknesses?
> 5. What sort of pay do you expect to receive?
> 6. How does your previous experience relate to the jobs we have here?
> 7. What are your plans for the future?
> 8. What will your former employer (or references) say about you?
> 9. Why are you looking for this type of position, and why here?
> 10. Why don't you tell me about your personal situation?

Follow the Three-Step Process for Answering Interview Questions

I've developed a three-step process for answering interview questions. I know this might seem too simple, but the three-step process is easy to remember and can help you create a good answer to most interview questions. The technique has worked for thousands of people, so consider trying it.

1. **Understand what is really being asked.**

   Most questions are designed to find out about your self-management skills and personality, but interviewers are rarely this blunt. The employer's *real* question is often one or more of the following:

   - Can I depend on you?

   - Are you easy to get along with?

   - Are you a good worker?

   - Do you have the experience and training to do the job if we hire you?

   - Are you likely to stay on the job for a reasonable period of time and be productive?

   Ultimately, if you don't convince the employer that you will stay and be a good worker, it won't matter if you have the best credentials—he or she won't hire you.

2. **Answer the question briefly in a nondamaging way.** Present the facts of your particular work experience as advantages, not disadvantages. Many interview questions encourage you to provide negative information. One classic question I included in my list of Top 10 Problem Interview Questions was "What are your major weaknesses?" This is obviously a trick question, and many people are just not prepared for it.

   A good response is to mention something that is not very damaging, such as *"I have been told that I am a perfectionist, sometimes not delegating as effectively as I might."*

   But your answer is not complete until you continue with the next step.

3. **Answer the real question by presenting your related skills.** Base your answer on the key skills you have that support the job, and give examples to support these skills. For example, an employer might say to a recent graduate, *"We were looking for someone with more experience in this field. Why should we consider you?"* Here is one possible answer:

"I'm sure there are people who have more experience, but I do have more than six years of work experience, including three years of advanced training and hands-on experience using the latest methods and techniques. Because my training is recent, I am open to new ideas and am used to working hard and learning quickly."

In the previous example (about your need to delegate), a good skills statement might be

"I've been working on this problem and have learned to let my staff do more, making sure that they have good training and supervision. I've found that their performance improves, and it frees me up to do other things."

Whatever your situation, learn to answer questions that present you well. It's essential to communicate your skills during an interview, and the three-step process can help you answer problem questions and dramatically improve your responses. It works!

How to Earn a Thousand Dollars a Minute

What do you do when the employer asks, "How much money would it take to get you to join our company?"

Tips on Negotiating Pay

Remember these few essential tips when it comes time to negotiate your pay:

- **The Number 1 Salary Negotiation Rule: The person who names a specific amount first loses.**
- **The only time to negotiate is after you have been offered the job.** Employers want to know how much you want to be paid so that they can eliminate you from consideration. They figure if you want too much, you won't be happy with their job and won't stay. And if you will take too little, they may think you don't have enough experience. So never discuss your salary expectations until an employer offers you the job.
- **If pressed, speak in terms of wide pay ranges.** If you are pushed to reveal your pay expectations early in an interview, ask the interviewer what the normal pay range is for this job. Interviewers will often tell you, and you can say that you would consider offers in this range.

  If you are forced to be more specific, speak in terms of a wide pay range. If you figure that the company will likely pay from $20,000 to $25,000 a year, for example, say that you would consider "any fair offer in the low to mid-twenties." This statement covers the employer's range and goes a bit higher. If all else fails, tell the interviewer that you would consider any reasonable offer.

  For this tip to work, you must know in advance what the job is likely to pay. You can get this information by asking people who do similar work, or from a variety of books and Internet sources of career information.

- **If you want the job, you should say so.** This is no time to be playing games.
- **Don't say "no" too quickly.** Never, ever turn down a job offer during an interview! Instead, thank the interviewer for the offer and ask to consider the offer overnight. You can turn it down tomorrow, saying how much you appreciate the offer and asking to be considered for other jobs that pay better or whatever. And it is okay to ask for additional pay or other concessions. But if you simply can't accept the offer, say why and ask the interviewer to keep you in mind for future opportunities. You just never know.

STEP 7: Follow Up on all Job Leads

It's a fact: People who follow up with potential employers and with others in their network get jobs more quickly than those who do not.

Thank-You Notes Make a Difference

Although thank-you notes can be e-mailed, most people appreciate and are more impressed by a mailed note. Here are some tips about mailed thank-you notes that you can easily adapt to e-mail use:

- You can handwrite or type thank-you notes on quality paper and matching envelopes.

- Keep the notes simple, neat, and error-free.

- Make sure to include a few copies of your JIST Card in the envelope.

Here is an example of a simple thank-you note.

April 5, XXXX

Mr. Kijek,

Thanks so much for your willingness to see me next Wednesday at 9 a.m. I know that I am one of many who are interested in working with your organization. I appreciate the opportunity to meet you and learn more about the position.

I've enclosed a JIST Card that presents the basics of my skills for this job and will bring my resume to the interview. Please call me if you have any questions at all.

Sincerely,

Bruce Vernon

Use Job Lead Cards to Follow Up

If you use contact management software, use it to schedule follow-up activities. But the simple paper system I describe here can work very well or can be adapted for setting up your contact management software.

- Use a simple 3-by-5–inch card to record essential information about each person in your network.

- Buy a 3-by-5–inch card file box and tabs for each day of the month.

- File the cards under the date you want to contact the person.

- Follow through by contacting the person on that date.

I've found that staying in touch with a good contact every other week can pay off big. Here's a sample card to give you ideas about creating your own.

> ORGANIZATION: ___Mutual Health Insurance___
>
> CONTACT PERSON: ___Anna Tomey___   PHONE: ___317-355-0216___
>
> SOURCE OF LEAD: ___Aunt Ruth___
>
> NOTES: ___4/10 Called. Anna on vacation. Call back 4/15. 4/15 Interview set___
> ___4/20 at 1:30. 4/20 Anna showed me around. They use the same computers___
> ___we used in school! (Friendly people.) Sent thank-you note and JIST___
> ___Card, call back 5/1. 5/1 Second interview 5/8 at 9 a.m.!___

In Closing

This is a short book, but it may be all you need to get a better job in less time. I hope this will be true for you, and I wish you well in your search. Remember this: You won't get a job offer because someone knocks on your door and offers one. Job seeking does involve luck, but you are more likely to have good luck if you are out getting interviews.

I'll close this minibook with a few final tips:

- **Approach your job search as if it were a job itself.** Create and stick to a daily schedule, and spend at least 25 hours a week looking.

- **Follow up on each lead you generate and ask each contact for referrals.**

- **Set out each day to schedule at least two interviews.** Remember the new definition of an interview—an interview includes talking to potential employers who don't have an opening now.

- **Send out lots of thank-you notes and JIST Cards.**

- **When you want the job, tell the employer that you want it and why you should be hired over everyone else.**

Don't get discouraged. There are lots of jobs out there, and someone needs an employee with your skills—your job is to find that someone.

I wish you luck in your job search and in your life.

ESSENTIAL JOB SEARCH DATA WORKSHEET

Take some time to complete this worksheet carefully. It will help you write your resume and answer interview questions. You can also photocopy it and take it with you to help complete applications and as a reference throughout your job search. Use an erasable pen or pencil to allow for corrections. Whenever possible, emphasize skills and accomplishments that support your ability to do the job you want. Use extra sheets as needed.

Your name_____

Date completed _____

Job objective _____

Key Accomplishments

List three accomplishments that best prove your ability to do the kind of job you want.

1. _____

2. _____

3. _____

Education and Training

Name of high school(s) and specific years attended _____

Subjects related to job objective _____

_____

Related extracurricular activities/hobbies/leisure activities _____

_____

Accomplishments/things you did well _____

_____

Specific things you can do as a result _____

_____

Schools you attended after high school, specific years attended, and degrees/certificates earned _____

_____

Courses related to job objective _____

_____

Related extracurricular activities/hobbies/leisure activities _____

_____

Accomplishments/things you did well _____

_____

Specific things you can do as a result _____

_____

Other Training

Include formal or informal learning, workshops, military training, skills you learned on the job or from hobbies—anything that will help support your job objective. Include specific dates, certificates earned, or other details as needed. _____

_____

(continued)

(continued)

Work and Volunteer History

List your most recent job first, followed by each previous job. Military experience, unpaid or volunteer work, and work in a family business should be included here, too. If needed, use additional sheets to cover *all* significant paid or unpaid work experiences. Emphasize details that will help support your new job objective. Include numbers to support what you did: the number of people served over one or more years, number of transactions processed, percentage of sales increased, total inventory value you were responsible for, payroll of the staff you supervised, total budget responsible for, and so on. Emphasize results you achieved, using numbers to support them whenever possible. Mentioning these things on your resume and in an interview will help you get the job you want.

Job 1

Dates employed_____

Name of organization_____

Supervisor's name and job title_____

Address_____

Phone number/e-mail address/Web site_____

What did you accomplish and do well?_____

_____

Things you learned; skills you developed or used_____

_____

Raises, promotions, positive evaluations, awards_____

_____

Computer software, hardware, and other equipment you used_____

_____

Other details that might support your job objective_____

_____

Job 2

Dates employed_____

Name of organization_____

Supervisor's name and job title_____

Address_____

Phone number/e-mail address/Web site_____

What did you accomplish and do well?_____

_____

Things you learned; skills you developed or used_____

_____

Raises, promotions, positive evaluations, awards_____

_____

Computer software, hardware, and other equipment you used_____

_____

Other details that might support your job objective_____

_____

Job 3

Dates employed_____

Name of organization_____

Supervisor's name and job title_____

Address_____

Phone number/e-mail address/Web site_____

What did you accomplish and do well?_____

_____

Things you learned; skills you developed or used_____

_____

Raises, promotions, positive evaluations, awards_____

_____

Computer software, hardware, and other equipment you used_____

_____

Other details that might support your job objective_____

_____

References

Think of people who know your work well and will be positive about your work and character. Past supervisors are best. Contact them and tell them what type of job you want and your qualifications, and ask what they will say about you if contacted by a potential employer. Some employers will not provide references by phone, so ask them for a letter of reference in advance. If a past employer may say negative things, negotiate what they will say or get written references from others you worked with there.

Reference name_____

Position or title_____

Relationship to you_____

Contact information (complete address, phone number, e-mail address)_____

_____

(continued)

(continued)

Reference name_____

Position or title_____

Relationship to you_____

Contact information (complete address, phone number, e-mail address)_____

_____

Reference name_____

Position or title_____

Relationship to you_____

Contact information (complete address, phone number, e-mail address)_____

_____

A Short List of Additional Resources

Thousands of books and countless Internet sites provide information on career subjects. Space limitations do not permit me to describe the many good resources available, so I list here some of the most useful ones. Because this is my list, I've included books I've written or that JIST publishes. You should be able to find these and many other resources at libraries, bookstores, and Web bookselling sites.

Resume and Cover Letter Books

My books. *The Quick Resume & Cover Letter Book* is one of the top-selling resume books at various large bookstore chains. It is very simple to follow, is inexpensive, has good design, and has good sample resumes written by professional resume writers. For more in-depth but still quick help, check out my two books in the *Help in a Hurry* series: *Same-Day Resume* (with advice on creating a simple resume in an hour and a better one later) and *15-Minute Cover Letter*, co-authored with Louise Kursmark (offering sample cover letters and tips for writing them fast and effectively).

Other books published by JIST. The following titles include many sample resumes written by professional resume writers, as well as good advice: *Amazing Resumes* by Jim Bright and Joanne Earl; *Cover Letter Magic* by Wendy S. Enelow and Louise M. Kursmark; the entire *Expert Resumes* series by Enelow and Kursmark; *Federal Resume Guidebook* by Kathryn Kraemer Troutman; *Gallery of Best Resumes, Gallery of Best Cover Letters,* and other books by David F. Noble; and *Résumé Magic* by Susan Britton Whitcomb.

Job Search and Interviewing Books

My books. You may want to check out my two books in the *Help in a Hurry* series: *Seven-Step Job Search* (even more tips and step-by-step guidance to cut your job search time in half) and *Next-Day Job Interview* (quick tips for preparing for a job interview at the last minute). *The Very Quick Job Search* is a thorough book with detailed advice and a "quick" section of key tips you can finish in a few hours. *Getting the Job You Really Want* includes many in-the-book activities and good career decision-making and job search advice.

Other books published by JIST. Titles include *Inside Secrets of Finding a Teaching Job* by Warner, Bryan, and Warner; *Insider's Guide to Finding a Job* by Wendy S. Enelow and Shelly Goldman; *Job Search Handbook for People with Disabilities* by Daniel J. Ryan; *Job Search Magic* and *Interview Magic* by Susan Britton Whitcomb; *Ultimate Job Search* by Richard H. Beatty; and *Over-40 Job Search Guide* by Gail Geary.

Books with Information on Jobs

The primary reference books. The *Occupational Outlook Handbook* is the source of job titles listed in this book. Published by the U.S. Department of Labor and updated every other year, the *OOH* covers about 90 percent of the workforce. The *O*NET Dictionary of Occupational Titles* book has descriptions for more than 1,000 jobs based on the O*NET (Occupational Information Network) database developed by the Department of Labor. The *Enhanced Occupational Outlook Handbook* includes the *OOH* descriptions plus more than 7,000 additional descriptions of related jobs from the O*NET and other sources. The *New Guide for Occupational Exploration* allows you to explore major jobs based on your interests.

Other books published by JIST. Here are a few good books that include job descriptions and helpful details on career options: *Overnight Career Choice, Best Jobs for the 21st Century, 50 Best Jobs for Your Personality, 40 Best Fields for Your Career, 200 Best Jobs for College Graduates,* and *300 Best Jobs Without a Four-Year Degree.*

Internet Resources

There are too many Web sites to list, but here are a few places you can start. A book by Anne Wolfinger titled *Best Career and Education Web Sites* gives unbiased reviews of the most helpful sites and ideas on how to use them. *Job Seeker's Online Goldmine,* by Janet Wall, lists the extensive free online job search tools from government and other sources. This book's job descriptions also include Internet addresses for related organizations. And www.jist.com lists recommended sites for career, education, and related topics, along with comments on each. Be aware that some Web sites provide poor advice, so ask your librarian, instructor, or counselor for suggestions on those best for your needs.

Other Resources

Libraries. Most libraries have the books mentioned here, as well as many other resources. Many also provide Internet access so that you can research online information. Ask the librarian for help finding what you need.

People. People who hold the jobs that interest you are one of the best career information sources. Ask them what they like and don't like about their work, how they got started, and the education or training needed. Most people are helpful and will give advice you can't get any other way.

Career Counseling. A good vocational counselor can help you explore career options. Take advantage of this service if it is available to you! Also consider a career-planning course or program, which will encourage you to be more thorough in your thinking.

Sample Resumes for Some of the Top Computer and Technical Careers

If you read the previous information, you know that I believe you should not depend on a resume alone in your job search. Even so, you will most likely need one, and you should have a good one.

Unlike some career authors, I do not preach that there is only one right way to do a resume. I encourage you to be an individual and to do what you think will work well for you. But I also know that some resumes are clearly better than others. The following pages contain some resumes that you can use as examples when preparing your own resume.

Each resume was written by a professional resume writer who is a member of one or more professional associations. These writers are highly qualified and hold various credentials. Most will provide help (for a fee) and welcome your contacting them (although this is not a personal endorsement).

The resumes appear in books published by JIST Works, including the following:

- *100 Fastest-Growing Careers* by Michael Farr

- *Best Resumes for College Students and New Grads* by Louise M. Kursmark

- *Expert Resumes for Computer and Web Jobs* by Wendy S. Enelow and Louise M. Kursmark

- *Expert Resumes for Health Care Careers* by Wendy S. Enelow and Louise M. Kursmark

- *Gallery of Best Resumes* by David F. Noble
- *Gallery of Best Resumes for People Without a Four-Year Degree* by David F. Noble

Contact Information for Resume Contributors

The following professional resume writers contributed resumes to this section. Their names are listed in alphabetical order. Each entry indicates which resume that person contributed.

Arnold G. Boldt, CPRW, JCTC
Arnold-Smith Associates
625 Panorama Trail, Building One,
Ste. 120C
Rochester, NY 14625
Phone: (585) 383-0350
Fax: (585) 387-0516
E-mail: Arnie@ResumeSOS.com
Web site: www.ResumeSOS.com
Resume on page 342

Kristie Cook, CPRW
Absolutely Write
Olathe, KS
Resume on page 335

Debbie Ellis, CPRW, MRW
Phoenix Career Group
Toll-free phone: (800) 876-5506
Fax: (859) 236-3900
E-mail:
debbie@phoenixcareergroup.com
Web site:
www.phoenixcareergroup.com
Resume on page 340

**Louise Garver, CEIP, CMP,
CPRW, JCTC, MCDP**
Career Directions, LLC
115 Elm Street, Ste. 203
Enfield, CT 06082
Phone: (860) 623-9476
Fax: (860) 623-9473
E-mail: careerpro@cox.net
Web site: www.resumeimpact.com
Resume on page 336

**Rosemarie Ginsberg, CEIP,
CPRW**
Employment Recruiter
Creative Staffing Associates, Inc.
15 Michael Road
Framingham, MA 01701
Phone: (508) 877-5100
Fax: (508) 877-3511
E-mail: csadirecthire@aol.com
Resume on page 341

**Nancy Karvonen, CCM, CEIP,
CPRW, IJCTC**
Executive Director, A Better Word
& Resume
4490 Count Rd. HH
Orland, CA 95963
Phone: (209) 745-5107
Toll-free: (877) 973-7863
Fax: (209) 745-7114
E-mail: careers@aresumecoach.com
Resume on pages 343–344

Jeanne Knight, JCTC
Career and Job Search Coach
P.O. Box 828
Melrose, MA 02176
Phone: (617) 968-7747
E-mail: Jeanne@careerdesigns.biz
Web site: www.careerdesigns.biz
Resume on page 339

**Rolande L. LaPointe, CCM,
CIPC, CPC, CPRW, CRW, CSS,
IJCTC**
President, RO-LAN Associates,
Inc.
725 Sabattus St.
Lewiston, ME 04240
Phone: (207) 784-1010
Fax: (207) 782-3446
E-mail: RLapointe@aol.com
Resume on pages 337–338

**Wanda McLaughlin, CPRW,
CEIP**
President, Execuwrite
Chandler, AZ 85226
Phone: (480) 732-7966
Toll-free: (866) 732-7966
E-mail: wanda@execuwrite.com
Web site: www.execuwrite.com
Resume on page 334

Rich Porter
CareerWise Communications, LLC
332 Magellan Ct.
Portage, MI 49002-7000
Phone: (269) 321-0183
Fax: (269) 321-0191
E-mail:
careerwise_resumes@yahoo.com
Resume on page 345–346

**Vivian VanLier, CCMC, CEIP,
CPRW, JCTC, CPRC**
Advantage Resume & Career
Services
6701 Murietta Ave.
Valley Glen, CA 91405
Phone: (818) 994-6655
Fax: (818) 994-6620
E-mail: VivianVanLier@
CareerCoach4U.com
Web site:
www.CuttingEdgeResumes.com
Resume on page 333

Computer Programmers

JOHN STRONG

555 South Lynn Road
Pasadena, California 55555

(626) 555-5555
jstrong@email.com

APPLICATIONS PROGRAMMER—VISUAL BASIC

❑ Technical training plus more than 2 years of experience in program design, development, documentation, implementation and debugging.

❑ Able to understand and interpret needs of end user to design quality software. Consistent attention to detail with an ability to analyze and interpret the implications of decisions to minimize bugs and create user-friendly programs. Skilled in troubleshooting and problem solving.

❑ Quick learner who enjoys challenges and possesses a high level of energy and motivation. Dedicated to seeing projects through to completion.

❑ Experienced collaborating with clients and team members. Ability to convey technical information at all levels.

Computer Applications: Visual Basic... ADO... SQL... Crystal Reports... Windows... Word... Excel... Access... Outlook... FoxPro... Citrix... PC Anywhere... HTML (basic knowledge)... Internet

---

PROFESSIONAL EXPERIENCE

Application Programmer • 2001 to Present
APPLICATION LEADERS, INC., Pasadena, CA
Write programs in Visual Basic for company providing software solutions to manufacturing industry.
Representative Projects:
- Created, debugged and perfected entry screens for new release of company's main product.
- Produced reports providing critical information on gross profit, inventory transactions/projections, sales forecasts and purchase requirements.
- Wrote program to read EDI documents and generate sales-related reports.
- Collaborated on development of program that enables manufacturer to directly transfer orders to banks for approval using FTP.
- Developed customized programs to meet customer needs.

EDUCATION

PASADENA CITY COLLEGE, Pasadena, CA
Associate of Arts, Social Science May 2003
Honors: Deans List, Honors for Superior Achievement in Economics Award

COMPUTER LEARNING CENTER, Los Angeles, CA
Certificate in Client/Server Programming 2001
Relevant Course Work: Visual Basic, Integrating a Visual Basic Front-End with a SQL Server Back-End, Access, C, C++, Oracle, Client/Server Architecture
Honors: Awarded National Vocational Technical Honors Society Membership

UCLA EXTENSION, Los Angeles, CA, 2002
ActiveX Component Development with Visual Basic 6

Computer Software Engineers

MARY G. RODRIGUEZ

4411 East Maryland Avenue — Gilbert, AZ 85234
(480) 781-0710 — MRodriguez@aol.com

FOCUS Position as **Software Engineer** where B.S. Degree in Computer Science, experience in Object-Oriented Programming, and knowledge of Internet technology are desirable.

TECHNICAL EXPERTISE

Program Design / Development / Maintenance

Database & Network Administration

System Upgrades & Enhancements

Hardware & Software Evaluation / Support

Programming Languages / Platforms:
Java 1.2, C++, Visual C++, HTML, JCL, CICS, SQL, COBOL, Pascal, BASIC, NATURAL, FORTRAN, MS-DOS, Windows, UNIX

Software:
MS Office, CorelDRAW, Harvard Graphics, PageMaker, WordPerfect, Quattro Pro, Novell Network

RELATED EXPERIENCE

Programmer / Analyst   STATE OF ARIZONA, Phoenix, AZ — 2002–2004
Used 4GL programming languages to develop interdepartmental programs. Analyzed data and wrote basic requirements documentation to create databases and programs. Assisted in training end users.
  Achievements:
  — Assisted in upgrading 20-system linked network in Novell.

Programmer   ANALYTICAL RESEARCH, INC., Sacramento, CA — 2001–2002
Directly accountable for all facets of programming and system maintenance for market research company providing services for major travel and leisure accounts throughout the world, including America West Airlines, Lufthansa, United Airlines, and Ritz-Carlton Hotels.

Developed and implemented custom marketing research programs; administered 30,000+ database; coordinated user additions, deletions, and system back-up functions for Novell network. Participated in all phases of hardware and software upgrades, enhancements, and maintenance. Occasionally supervised temporary employees.
  Achievements:
  — Developed presentations for visual aids and company books utilizing a variety of graphic packages, including Harvard Graphics, CorelDRAW, ACROSS, and Windows.
  — Managed 200+ slide presentations to major clients.
  — Member of team that brought existing system, programs, and databases successfully into Y2K compliance.

Desktop Publisher   ARTISTRY, INC., Los Angeles, CA — 1997–2000
Assisted customers in the development of visual graphic presentations for custom brochures and marketing materials. Determined client requirements, assisted in selection of special graphic designs and programs, and designed and processed orders.
  Achievements:
  — Developed strong skills in computer operations and creative design.

EDUCATION / TRAINING

B.S. in Computer Science, 2001   CALIFORNIA STATE UNIVERSITY, Northridge, CA
Emphasis: Software Engineering & Computer Mathematics

Java, Intermediate Java, C++, Visual C++   SCOTTSDALE COLLEGE, Scottsdale, AZ
— Currently attending
— Developed Mortgage Calculator utilizing Java applets

Computer Support Specialists and System Administrators

PENELOPE S. RICHARDS

4601 Arlington Drive, Baltimore, MD 21111
Home: (410) 521-4690
E-mail: oraclepro@hotmail.com

SUMMARY OF QUALIFICATIONS

- Computer Specialist with more than 8 years of experience in IT/IS.
- Praised by superiors for Oracle expertise, ability to work as a team member, and customer responsiveness.
- Proven oral and written communication skills; comfortable delivering presentations to large groups and training both technical and non-technical people in group settings as well as one-on-one.

TECHNICAL SKILLS

Oracle	Delphi	Enterprise Technologies 4.0	Telnet
PMRS	Windows 98/NT/XP	MS IIS	ARCserve
HP900	Novell NetWare	UNIX	TM1 Database
SunSPARC	Banyan	FTP	ADP
JAM	TCP/IP		

EXPERIENCE

COMPUTER SPECIALIST   2002–Present
Web Hosts Unlimited—Baltimore, MD
Perform system accounts maintenance; change TCP/IP protocols for security purposes and manage IP address changes under Internet Information Server (IIS); maintain active server pages (ASP); provide user support; back up TM1 database using ARCserve software; and monitor and install Microsoft security patches.

- Served as trouble desk coordinator, traveling on a moment's notice when necessary to provide onsite assistance.
- Wrote a database manual for onsite users to easily enhance the system and troubleshoot/solve problems.
- Recognized for outstanding performance.

COMPUTER SPECIALIST   1998–2002
Market Researchers, Inc.—Washington, DC
Served as Lead Senior Computer Specialist for design, development, and implementation of two customized, complex database systems; worked as Lead Database Administrator (DBA) on and off site and trained Assistant DBAs; provided onsite user support in all areas of client/server software installation and upgrades.

- Designed, developed, tested, and maintained four Oracle Version 8 databases on a SunSPARC 2.0 server.
- Created, implemented, and maintained forms, reports, and program modules using JYACC JAM 6.3.
- Received Outstanding Performance award two years straight.
- Commended by the director for going the extra mile to troubleshoot and debug customized software for offsite operations systems.

COMPUTER SPECIALIST   1995–1998
Onsite Marketing, Inc.—Washington, DC
Provided application software and database support; supervised 16 personnel; installed patches; verified nightly database changes were run and synchronized with Honolulu location; and assisted switching stations with transmission validity.

- Conducted application software training classes for new personnel.
- Participated on the qualification board for personnel as the senior software engineer.
- Recognized with outstanding performance award.

EDUCATION

Northern Virginia Community College—Alexandria, Virginia
Computer Technology, Effective Presentation

Dental Hygienists

Juanita P. Morales

3482 McCandlish Road
Grand Blanc, MI 48439
810-555-2396 • jpmsmiles@home.net

Profile

- ❖ Certification and training as **Dental Hygienist.**
- ❖ Experience as chair-side **Dental Assistant** in general and periodontal practices.
- ❖ Ability to earn **trust** and develop **rapport** with patients.
- ❖ Strong patient **assessment** and **education** skills.
- ❖ Training and experience in using **Prophy Jet** and **ultrasonic scalers.**

Dental Experience

CARO PERIODONTAL ASSOCIATES • Caro, MI	2005–Present
FAMILY DENTAL • Clarkston, MI	2001–2005
DR. ROGER ANDERSON • Rochester, MI	2000–2001
MACKIN ROAD DENTAL CLINIC • Lapeer, MI	1996–2000

Education

MOTT COMMUNITY COLLEGE • Flint, MI
Certificate in Dental Hygiene   2005
  — Graduated in Top 10% of class
  — Passed state and national exams
  — Past President, MCC Dental Students Association

Selected Classes & Training

- ❖ "Infection Control in a Changing World"
- ❖ "Advanced Techniques in Root Planing and Instrument Sharpening"
- ❖ "AIDS: Oral Signs, Symptoms, and Treatments"
- ❖ "Periodontal Diseases in Children and Adolescents"
- ❖ "Periodontal Screening Record"
- ❖ "Strategies for Teamwork and Communication Skills"

Community Involvement

- ❖ International Institute — Event Assistant
- ❖ Spanish-Speaking Information Center — Volunteer Tutor
- ❖ Big Brothers/Big Sisters of Greater Flint — Big Sister

References available on request

Dieticians and Nutritionists

Paulette A. Turcotte, R.D.

357 Clearview Drive, #200   (207) 942-5555 (Home)
Bangor, Maine 04401   paturcotte@hotmail.com   (207) 942-4444 (Work)

Career Profile

Registered Dietitian with many years of combined experience in food service management and supervision (including clinical and community dietetics). Documented record of success having earned recognition as a results-oriented manager. Highest satisfaction derived from solving dietetic management problems. Skilled in evaluating food service activities, counseling, and professional presentations.

Education

B.S. Foods & Nutrition   University of New Hampshire (Durham, NH)
Dietetic Internship   University of Minnesota Hospital (Minneapolis, MN)
— Earned Registered Dietitian Status

Experience Highlights

Dietetic Food Service Management & Supervision

Direct activities of a 600-bed medical center staffed by four subordinate registered dietitians, two registered dietetic technicians, and 65 food-service employees. Responsibilities and skills:

- Administer all areas of personnel management, including interviewing, hiring, scheduling, evaluating, and monitoring.
- Conceptualize and administer all in-service orientation training for staff and employees.
- Develop and implement policies and procedures.
- Provide administrative direction to nutritional care for patients.
- Administer the A.A. and M.S. degree affiliation programs for dietetic students.
- Oversee all food service, purchasing, and sanitation functions.
- Administer related performance assessments/improvement programs and safety practices.
- Coordinate inter-departmental professional activities.
- Serve as a consultant to medical staff on dietetic matters.
- Attend and participate in hospital staff meetings.
- Write/endorse evaluation reports, letters, memos, statistical dietetic reports, and medical records.
- Conduct facility inspections; plan, evaluate, and implement departmental renovations.
- Oversee dining room, dish room, storeroom, kitchen, and office facilities and equipment.
- Plan, organize, and direct special meals for holidays and special functions.
- Consistently earn satisfactory reports from visiting inspectors.

Clinical Dietetics

Plan, develop, and implement nutritional programs for patients and their families as follows:

- Programs: Nutrition Principles, Dietary Plans, Food Selection, and Preparation.
- Develop and write regular and modified diets; conduct ward rounds.
- Recommend nutritional products and subsistence items.
- Advise/assist personnel in public dining facilities and food service systems.
- Plan, organize, and implement National Nutrition Month activities.

Community Dietetics

Work with community groups concerning nutritional needs, including (but not limited to) the following:

- Write nutrition articles for local newspapers and for local and state dietetic bulletins.
- Inspect community nursing homes, personal-care homes, and residential-care homes.

          (continued)

(continued)

Employment

Bangor VA Medical Center (Bangor, ME)   1990–Present
Assistant Chief, Dietetic Service (1990–1996)
Clinical Nutrition Manager (April 1996–Present) Due to Department Restructuring
- Serve on the VA Homeless Working Group Committee
- Member, Bangor Medical Center Fitness Committee, 1996
- President, Bangor Employee Association, 1996
- Member, Patient Education Committee, 1996
- Member, Station Safety Committee, 1996
- Member, Common Data Base Committee, 1996
  — Assist in Clinical Pathways & Interdisciplinary Computerized Assessment Processing

VA Medical Centers   1979–1990
Hampton VA Medical Center (Hampton, VA)   1984–1990
Chief, Clinical Section, Dietetic Service (1985–1990)
Chief, Administrative Section, Dietetic Service (1984–1985)

Des Moines VA Medical Center (Des Moines, IA)   1980–1984
Section Chief, Clinical Section, Dietetic Service

Kansas City VA Medical Center (Kansas City, MO)   1979–1980
Clinical Dietitian, Dietetic Service

U.S. Air Force   1970–1979
Ehrling Bergquist USAF Regional Hospital (Offutt AFB, NE)   1976–1979
Administrator, Food Service Management (Captain USAF)

Homestead USAF Regional Hospital (Homestead AFB, FL)   1972–1976
Administrator, Food Service Management

Sheppard USAF Regional Hospital (Sheppard AFB, TX)   1970–1972
Clinical Dietitian

Professional Affiliations

American Cancer Society Board Member   1995–Present
American Heart Association Board Member   1995–Present
President, Tidewater Dietetic Association   1989
Executive Board, Virginia Dietetic Association   1988–1990
Chairman, Federal Women's Program, Des Moines VAMC (Des Moines, IA)   1981
Equal Employment Opportunity, Co-Chairman, Des Moines VAMC (Des Moines, IA)   1980

Volunteer Work

Board Member—United Valley Chapter of the American Red Cross   1990–1995
Augusta Symphony Chorus   1990–1991
Board Member—Habitat for Humanity (1989), Club Member (1991)   1989–1991
Friendship Force, Treasurer (1988), News Editor (1987)   1987–1988
(Organization that promotes world peace)

Personal Data

Available for work-related travel; willing to relocate.
Traveled extensively utilizing effective communication skills with people of varied cultures.
Served for 9 years as Captain in the USAF; Honorably Discharged.
Separate listing of personal and professional references is available upon request.

Engineers

SEAN L. STEEPER

17 Woodcliff Road
Westboro, MA 01581

Home: 333-333-3333
slsteeper@hotmail.com

INDUSTRIAL ENGINEER
New Product Design • Manufacturing Process Redesign • Project Management

EDUCATION

University of Massachusetts ~ Amherst, MA
B.S. Industrial Engineering ~ Graduated with Honors ~ May 2003

RELEVANT COURSEWORK

Engineering Design • Systems Engineering • Computer Integrated Manufacturing • Production Systems
Production Engineering • Operations Research • Oral and Visual Communications
Industrial Psychology • Ergonomics • Quality Management

ACADEMIC PROJECTS

- Researched and recommended alternative methods for coating coronary stents for a leading manufacturer of cardiovascular products. Designed and manufactured prototype for spray-coating each stent, as opposed to the current practice of dipping them, which resulted in a 25% reduction in defects.
- Designed a facility and assembly-line layout to optimize production for an electronics products company.
- Generated a comprehensive Safety and Development Plan for a medical devices company.
- Created an ergonomically efficient material-handling trolley.

ENGINEERING EXPERIENCE

ABC Cardiovascular, Amherst, MA   5/02–10/02
Industrial Engineer, Co–Op

- Designed, developed, and implemented a unique device for facilitating the movement of coronary stent and catheter products from one workstation to another, resulting in a 20% decrease in scrapped product.
- Revised and simplified the Standard Operating Procedure for a label-printing machine that included detailed, easy-to-follow troubleshooting procedures and digital photographs.
- Analyzed production reports associated with a crimping machine and successfully identified one product that was consistently more prone to defects than others. Recommended machine adjustments to alleviate defects.
- Optimized floor space by rearranging and redesigning four production cells within a tightly constricted space.
- Member of a team to prepare for a critical FDA audit. Ensured machines were fully validated and safety guards were properly and securely in place.

ADDITIONAL EXPERIENCE

Albright Roofing and Painting, Framingham, MA   9/03–Present
Construction Laborer—Contribute to roofing and home painting projects.

Dunmore Plastering, Southboro, MA   Summers 01 and 03
Plasters Foreman—Organized and monitored building materials and inventory levels.

Independently Employed, Amherst, MA   1/99–5/01
Agricultural Contractor—Performed agricultural contract work for farmers.

Paralegals and Legal Assistants

Lydia C. Hendricks

65 Thorn Hill Court
Greenville, South Carolina 29607
Mobile (828) 516-4548 · Residence (828) 236-9925 · Email lydiac@earthlink.net

PARALEGAL / LEGAL SECRETARY

Dedicated to providing superior, uninterrupted administrative support to legal and non-legal staff.

Confident, articulate, and results-oriented legal-support professional offering a strong foundation of education and experience. Creative and enthusiastic with proven record of success in prioritizing and processing heavy workflow without supervision. Superior organization and communication skills; committed to personal and professional growth. Looking to join an established team that rewards hard work and personal achievement with stability and the opportunity for increased responsibility.

IMMEDIATE VALUES OFFERED

- Highly proficient in word processing, data entry, and Dictaphone transcription using Microsoft application software; noticed for maintaining consistently superior levels of accuracy.
- Organized, efficient, and thorough; maintain flexibility in changing work assignments.
- Perform well under stress, taking pressure off superiors and peers.
- Proficient in the planning and execution of projects in time-critical environments.
- Dependable and successful problem-resolution and time-management solutions.
- Creative and cooperative, working equally well individually or as part of a team.
- Outstanding record of performance, reliability, confidentiality, and ethical business standards.
- Computer skills include Microsoft Word 97/2000 and Windows 95/98, and WordPerfect; familiarity with Microsoft Excel, PowerPoint, and Access. Typing rate approximately 80 WPM.

LEGAL EXPERIENCE

Criminal / Civil	Powers of Attorney	Complaints
Domestic Relations	Divorce	Exhibits / Witness Lists
Affidavits	Adoption	QDRO
Subpoenas	Probate	Personal Injury
Motions	Wills	Client Interviewing
Orders	Estates	Real Estate
Research	Worker's Compensation	Mortgages / Deeds

SUMMER INTERNSHIP EXPERIENCE

Paralegal, **Tranter & Tranter, Attorneys and Counselors At Law** Greenville, SC 2004
(Temporary Replacement) Legal Secretary, **Elmer George, Attorney At Law** Spartanburg, SC 2003–04

EDUCATION AND SPECIAL CERTIFICATIONS

Associate of Science Degree, Paralegal Studies — Sullivan College, Greenville, SC
Magna Cum Laude Distinction
Dean's List
Degree Awarded 6/2005

Attended South Carolina Business College, 19 credit hours accumulated, Legal Writing
Attended Hutchinson Community College, 24 credit hours accumulated, Criminal Justice

Commissioned Notary Public, South Carolina State-at-Large — Status, current

---

Photographers

Margo L. Kramer

2520 Main Street • Townsville, MA 01583 • 508/555-1234 • pixperfect@cs.com

Objective

To apply photography education along with freelance and internship experience in a studio or fine-arts institution.

Education

Bachelor of Fine Arts, May 2002   The Art Institute of Boston, Boston, MA
     Photography major
     Portfolio scholarship award for Rail Series, 1999

Internships

The Image Maker, Boston, MA   A non-profit photography gallery
     Assistant to Director during auction and member selection for exhibits. Independently built and maintained an accurate mailing list.

The Art of Life, Inc., Boston, MA   A custom black-and-white photofinishing, matting, and framing studio
     Applied photography techniques to assist with retouching/spotting of finished fine-art photographs for gallery inventory and professional darkroom clients. Acquired experience and became proficient in matting and framing fine-art photographs. Utilizing computer skills, scanned photographs, and entered pertinent data relative to individual photographs into database, creating a foundation for the existing photographic database.

Exhibits

     Gallery 601, "Behind the Scenes Portfolio"
     Equinox Grille, "Mixed Media"
     Water Street Café, "Thanksgiving Parade"
     Kougeaus Gallery, "Waiting" (from "Rails" series; selected photography)
     First Impression Gallery, "Student Exhibit"

Publications

     Old House Interiors ....Stylist/Photo Assistant, "Bates Mansion 2001"
     Gallery Guide...Advertisement for Kougeaus Gallery Exhibition
     Art Institute of Boston ....Awards Brochure, "Connections"

Additional

Experienced with medium-format photography and digital photography for portraits, documentaries, and special events, including weddings, birthdays, anniversaries. Additional experience includes extensive knowledge of textures and patterns for visual display.

Funded education working in local restaurant and as freelance photographer, stylist, and garden planner.

Portfolio available   www.margosart.com/portfolio

Physician Assistants

Lawrence A. Timmons

585-334-7305   24 Leonardo Drive, Rochester, New York 14624   latpa@webtv.net

SUMMARY: *Physician's Assistant and Licensed Paramedic. Extensive training and field experience in Advanced Life Support and critical care. Twenty years' experience in active duty and management roles with suburban ambulance service.*

EDUCATION:

May 2002   **Bachelor of Science, Physician's Assistant**
University of Rochester; Rochester, New York
GPA: 3.6 / Dean's List

Clinical Rotations:

– Critical Care Medicine	– Emergency Medicine	– OB/Gyn	– Psychiatry
– Orthopaedics	– General Surgery	– Cardiology	– Pediatrics
– Internal Medicine	– Family Medicine		

May 1998   **Associate of Applied Science, Liberal Arts,**
Monroe Community College; Rochester, New York

CERTIFICATIONS:

Licensed Physician's Assistant (NYS)—1 yr.   Licensed Paramedic (NYS)—7 yrs.
Pediatric Advanced Life Support—7 yrs.   Advanced Cardiac Life Support—7 yrs.
Advanced Trauma Life Support—3 yrs.

RELEVANT EXPERIENCE:

2002–Present   **Park Ridge Hospital Emergency Department; Rochester, New York**
Physician's Assistant
Treat acute and non-acute patients in emergency department setting.
- Examine and evaluate incoming patients; diagnose and assess treatment options.
- Provide treatment and prescribe medications as necessary and appropriate.
- Admit patients to the hospital for further care as required.
- Suture lacerations and treat orthopedic injuries.
- Address needs of patients ranging from pediatric to geriatric.

1985–2001   **Mendon Volunteer Ambulance Corps; Rochester, New York**
Vice President / General Manager (2000–2001)
Directed day-to-day operations for suburban ambulance service responding to more than 4,500 calls per year. Responsibility for 130 paid and volunteer active-duty members.
- Appointed department heads responsible for Basic Life Support, Advanced Life Support, Logistics, Training, and Safety.
- Managed $450,000 operations budget.
EMT / Paramedic (1985–2001)
- Personally logged more than 5,000 hours of active duty time over 16 years.
- Served as Monroe/Livingston County Paramedic Preceptor for five years.

1994–2000   **Flight Paramedic, Mercy Flight; Canandaigua, New York**
Administered critical care to patients for air medical service covering 11-county region and responding to 500 calls per year.
- Responded to accident scenes in remote locations.
- Provided Advanced Life Support to patients as only care-giver aboard flight.

1993–Present   **Trainer / Guest Lecturer**
University of Buffalo and Monroe Community College Paramedic Training Programs.

Prepress Technicians and Workers

TAMURA YAMAGUCHI

400 Woodruff Lane
Oakwood, Kansas 66022

tyamaguchi@southernbell.net
(883) 109-9743

DIGITAL PRE-PRESS OPERATOR

PROFESSIONAL PROFILE

Talented print production specialist with impressive experience in digital imaging pre-press operations. Fast, accurate, and willing to work long hours to meet deadlines. Communicate with customers and vendors. Develop customer awareness of color and file format preparation.

SOFTWARE PACKAGES

- Illustrator
- Photoshop
- PageMaker
- FrameMaker
- QuarkXpress
- FileMaker Pro
- Acrobat Distiller and Exchange
- Preps
- Trapwise
- PressTouch
- PowerPoint Mac & PC

WORKFLOW

- Delta Workstation
- Scitex PS and PS Ripping

EQUIPMENT

- AgfaSelect Set 7000
- AgfaAvantra 44 Imagesetter
- Creo Platesetter and Lodum (CTP) Output

FILE MANAGEMENT

- Manual Trapping
- Print Files to Disk
- Color Manipulation
- Troubleshooting Postscript and PDF Files
- Pre-Flight for Digital Imaging

VALUE OFFERED

Premier Printing, Inc., Oakwood, Kansas   2000–Present
Senior Desktop Operator

Produce complex metallic-on-metallic printing for one of state's largest sheetfed printing firms, serving software clients.

- Print Scitex workflow to Brisque Workstation, rip and trap, and impose files with Preps.
- Print ICF file to Brisque and output Iris 43 wide-digital Dylux or Iris4Print for Kodak approval.

Oakwood Printing Inc., Oakwood, Kansas   1999–2000
Desktop Operator

Accomplished digital pre-press operation for commercial printing firm.

- Reproduced jobs on Delta Workstation, ripped and trapped, imposed file with Signastation, and output with Epson Digital Dylux.
- Implemented Delta Workflow and directed to plate.

(Continued)

(continued)

TAMURA YAMAGUCHI
PAGE TWO

**VALUE
OFFERED
(CONTINUED)**

MidWest Lithographer, Oakwood, Kansas   1997–1999
Digital Imaging Technician/Lead
Led crew in digital pre-press for one of oldest printing companies in Kansas.

- Instrumental in setting up on-site processing team at Cisco.
- Completed and uploaded complex rush FTP website project in 3 hours. Instructed client on file preparation.

AMP Graphic Services, Kansas City, Kansas   1993–1997
Pre-Press Foreman
Oversaw 3 shifts for turnkey and fulfillment house utilizing web press. As qualified digital pre-press operator, prepared files for digital printing.

- Collected data and created 3000-record FileMaker Pro database for easy archival and retrieval of complete job histories including photos.
- Set company production record for 3-day turnaround of 8-book set of 50,000 prints to Europe. Worked crews in 3 shifts to finish 750 plates within 24 hours.
- Directed, trained, and evaluated desktop operator, stripper, proofer, and plater.
- Coordinated daily operations with pressroom foreman.
- Wrote and instituted detailed procedures in compliance with ISO Certification.

Advanced Publishing, Ltd., Tokyo, Japan   1986–1993
Production Manager/Photographer/Graphic Artist

Rapidly progressed from graphic artist to production manager for this fast-paced firm. Published monthly and weekly architectural publications within tight time frames.

- Supervised 9-person production team consisting of graphic designers, artists, and photographers.
- Produced business cards, letterhead, 4-color brochures, and flyers for commercial-art customers.
- Interacted with customers to correct errors and identify potential color and preparation problems.

**SPECIALIZED
TRAINING**

University of Wisconsin—Madison, Wisconsin
First Institute of Art & Design—Tokyo, Japan

- Graphic Arts   • Graphic Design   • Delta System   • Color Production
- Applescript   • Commercial Photography
- Fingerprint Press Device Calibration to Ensure Color Accuracy

Speech-Language Pathologists

JANIS F. MAYER, MA, CCC-SLP
SPEECH-LANGUAGE PATHOLOGIST

1128 WRIGHTS WAY
HOLLAND, MI 49422
HOME: 616.563.1794
MOBILE: 616.323.1409
speakwell@yahoo.com

PROFILE

Dynamic, results-oriented therapist with 15 years' experience and outstanding qualifications in treating preprimary and school-aged children in public schools, private schools, charter schools, private practice, and clinic settings. Deeply committed to enriching the lives of impaired children; recognized for sensitivity to the needs of special-needs students and for the ability to effectively balance professionalism with empathy. Establish excellent interpersonal relations with students, parents, school administrators, and other healthcare professionals. Acknowledged by peers as an extremely proficient therapist with strong organizational and leadership skills. Proven ability to independently handle significant responsibilities and large caseloads due to in-depth knowledge of disorder types and various therapeutic techniques. Exceptional teacher and mentor. Supervisory instructor to intern graduate students from Grand Valley State University and Ohio State University.

AREAS OF EXPERTISE

- Articulation, Language, Voice, and Fluency Disorders
- Adult Voice and Fluency Disorders
- Oral Motor Training
- ADD/ADHD
- Myofunctional Therapy

- Reading and Writing Disorders
- Apraxia Therapy
- Specific Learning Disability/Dyslexia
- Auditory Processing Disorders
- Fast Forward Computer Language Program

Extensive expertise in managing the therapy programs for all disorder types, including pervasive developmental disorders (e.g., autism, Asperger Syndrome, and hyperlexia); learning disabilities; developmental aphasia/apraxia; mental impairments, including Down Syndrome; hearing impairments; and physical impairments, including cerebral palsy, brain injury, and myofunctional disorders.

PROFESSIONAL EXPERIENCE

HOLLAND PUBLIC SCHOOLS, Holland, Michigan   **1987–Present**

<u>Teacher of the Speech and Language Impaired.</u> Effectively serve the Preprimary Impaired (PPI) population at Central Elementary, a large elementary school in this incorporated public school district. Caseload currently includes more than 35 special-needs students.

Notable Achievements:

- Designed and implemented an innovative treatment program for the preschool-aged population that is currently in use in this public school district.

- Effectively administer all phases of therapy from diagnosis to treatment planning, intervention, case management, and coordination of services with other therapy and healthcare professionals.

- Instrumental in creating a strong spirit of collaboration with parents and making them an integral part of the treatment process. Along with a comprehensive approach to treatment, parental involvement is also credited with rapid and extensive progress made by special-needs students.

- Proven expertise in interpreting diagnostic data to plan and implement appropriate treatment and assembling and organizing relevant data to document results, especially related to the preparation of MET reports and IEPC plans.

- Initiate frequent meetings with teachers and the director of special education regarding quality-of-care improvement and service-delivery options.

(continued)

JANIS F. MAYER   *Page 2*

PROFESSIONAL EXPERIENCE (CONT.)

CENTRAL MICHIGAN SPEECH CENTER, Mount Pleasant, Michigan   1991–Present

<u>Speech-Language Pathologist.</u> Part-time private practice providing individual therapy for children and group social skills training. Accomplished therapist emphasizing early intervention in treatment. Research medical cause/etiology for presenting problem, and develop and design therapy plans that are tailored to the individual client. Manage the day-to-day operations of the practice (i.e., appointment scheduling, billing, report writing, etc.). Caseload consists of approximately 20 clients.

Notable Achievements:

- Manage a very successful speech program during the school year that complements therapies performed for the school district. In addition, developed and maintain an innovative summer treatment program for students during summer vacation.

- Foster spirit of collaboration and involvement in treatment process with parents and other family members.

- Successfully incorporate technology into treatment, using a wide range of educational software including the Fast Forward Language/Reading Program.

- Actively consult with medical personnel, teachers, and other speech therapists regarding treatment strategies, when necessary.

- Keenly familiar with Medicaid and insurance billing practices.

- As a result of excellent professional reputation, the practice was featured in a segment broadcast on WWFT channel 8. A piece on the practice was also run in the "Health" section of the *Mount Pleasant Press.*

EDUCATION

Master of Arts, Speech-Language Pathology
CENTRAL MICHIGAN UNIVERSITY, Mount Pleasant, **1986**

Bachelor of Science, Speech Pathology and Audiology
CENTRAL MICHIGAN UNIVERSITY, **1985**

CERTIFICATIONS & AFFILIATIONS

Certificate of Clinical Competence, ASHA

Certificate of Continuing Education in Elementary Education (Certified K–8)

American Speech-Language Hearing Association (ASHA)

Michigan Speech-Language Hearing Association (MSHA)

Michigan Education Association (MEA)

International Association of Orofacial Myologists (IAOM)

AWARDS & HONORS

ACE Award for Continuing Education, ASHA

Clinician of the Year, Central Michigan University

Graduate Fellowship Award, Central Michigan University

Robert Wood Johnson Internship Award, Central Michigan University

Important Trends in Jobs and Industries

In putting this section together, my objective was to give you a quick review of major labor market trends. To accomplish this, I included three excellent articles that originally appeared in U.S. Department of Labor publications.

The first article is "Tomorrow's Jobs." It provides a superb—and short—review of the major trends that will affect your career in the years to come. Read it for ideas on selecting a career path for the long term.

The second article is "Employment Trends in Major Industries." While you may not have thought much about it, the industry you work in is just as important as your occupational choice. This great article will help you learn about major trends affecting various industries.

The third article, "Training for Techies," covers a multitude of education and training options that can lead to jobs in computer-related and technical fields. Its charts and real-world examples show you that you may already have the training you need to get a job in your chosen field.

Tomorrow's Jobs

Making informed career decisions requires reliable information about opportunities in the future. Opportunities result from the relationships between the population, the labor force, and the demand for goods and services.

Population ultimately limits the size of the labor force—individuals working or looking for work—which constrains how much can be produced. Demand for various goods and services determines employment in the industries providing them. Occupational employment opportunities, in turn, result from demand for skills needed within specific industries. Opportunities for medical assistants and other healthcare occupations, for example, have surged in response to rapid growth in demand for health services.

Examining the past and projecting changes in these relationships is the foundation of the U.S. Department of Labor's Occupational Outlook Program. "Tomorrow's Jobs" presents highlights of Bureau of Labor Statistics projections of the labor force and occupational and industry employment that can help guide your career plans.

Population

Population trends affect employment opportunities in a number of ways. Changes in population influence the demand for goods and services. For example, a growing and aging population has increased the demand for health services. Equally important, population changes produce corresponding changes in the size and demographic composition of the labor force.

The U.S. civilian noninstitutional population is expected to increase by 23.9 million over the 2004–2014 period, at a slower rate of growth than during both the 1994–2004 and 1984–1994 periods (Chart 1). Continued growth will mean more consumers of goods and services, spurring demand for workers in a wide range of occupations and industries. The effects of population growth on various occupations will differ. The differences are partially accounted for by the age distribution of the future population.

The youth population, aged 16 to 24, will grow 2.9 percent over the 2004–2014 period. As the baby boomers

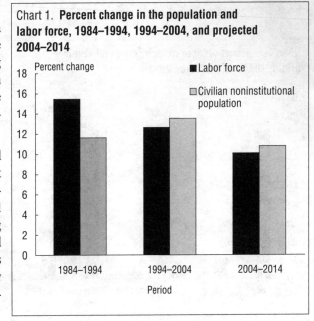

Chart 1. **Percent change in the population and labor force, 1984–1994, 1994–2004, and projected 2004–2014**

continue to age, the group aged 55 to 64 will increase by 36 percent or 10.4 million persons, more than any other group. The group aged 35 to 44 will decrease in size, reflecting the birth dearth following the baby boom generation.

Minorities and immigrants will constitute a larger share of the U.S. population in 2014. The number of Hispanics is projected to continue to grow much faster than those of all other racial and ethnic groups.

Labor Force

Population is the single most important factor in determining the size and composition of the labor force—that is, people who are either working or looking for work. The civilian labor force is projected to increase by 14.7 million, or 10 percent, to 162.1 million over the 2004–2014 period.

The U.S. workforce will become more diverse by 2014. White, non-Hispanic persons will continue to make up a decreasing share of the labor force, falling from 70 percent in 2004 to 65.6 percent in 2014 (Chart 2). However, despite relatively slow growth, white, non-Hispanics will remain the largest group in the labor force in 2014. Asians are projected to account for an increasing share of the labor force by 2014, growing from 4.3 to 5.1 percent. Hispanics are projected to be the fastest growing of the four labor force groups, growing by 33.7 percent. By 2014, Hispanics will continue to constitute a larger proportion of the labor force than will blacks, whose share will grow from 11.3 percent to 12.0 percent.

The numbers of men and women in the labor force will grow, but the number of women will grow at a faster rate than the number of men. The male labor force is projected to grow by 9.1 percent from 2004 to 2014, compared with 10.9 percent for women. As a result, men's share of the labor force is expected to decrease from 53.6 to 53.2 percent, while women's share is expected to increase from 46.4 to 46.8 percent.

The youth labor force, aged 16 to 24, is expected to slightly decrease its share of the labor force to 13.7 percent by 2014. The primary working age group, between 25 and 54 years old, is projected to decline from 69.3 percent of the labor force in 2004 to 65.2 percent by 2014. Workers 55 and older, on the other hand, are projected to increase from 15.6 percent to 21.2 percent of the labor force between 2004 and 2014, due to the aging of the baby-boom generation (Chart 3).

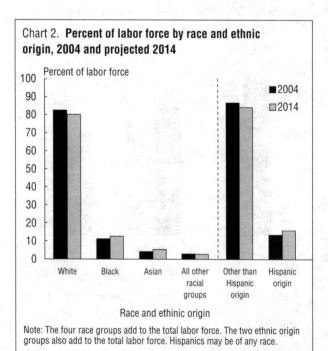

Chart 2. **Percent of labor force by race and ethnic origin, 2004 and projected 2014**

Note: The four race groups add to the total labor force. The two ethnic origin groups also add to the total labor force. Hispanics may be of any race.

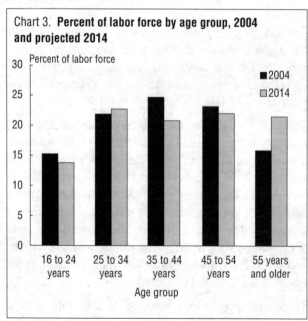

Chart 3. **Percent of labor force by age group, 2004 and projected 2014**

Part IV: Important Trends in Jobs and Industries 351

Employment

Total employment is expected to increase from 145.6 million in 2004 to 164.5 million in 2014, or by 13 percent. The 18.9 million jobs that will be added by 2014 will not be evenly distributed across major industrial and occupational groups. Changes in consumer demand, technology, and many other factors will contribute to the continually changing employment structure in the U.S. economy.

The following two sections examine projected employment change from both industrial and occupational perspectives. The industrial profile is discussed in terms of primary wage and salary employment. Primary employment excludes secondary jobs for those who hold multiple jobs. The exception is employment in agriculture, which includes self-employed and unpaid family workers in addition to wage and salary workers.

The occupational profile is viewed in terms of total employment—including primary and secondary jobs for wage and salary, self-employed, and unpaid family workers. Of the nearly 146 million jobs in the U.S. economy in 2004, wage and salary workers accounted for 133.5 million; self-employed workers accounted for 12.1 million; and unpaid family workers accounted for about 141,000. Secondary employment accounted for 1.7 million jobs. Self-employed workers held 9 out of 10 secondary jobs; wage and salary workers held most of the remainder.

Industry

Service-providing industries. The long-term shift from goods-producing to service-providing employment is expected to continue. Service-providing industries are expected to account for approximately 18.7 million of the 18.9 million new wage and salary jobs generated over the 2004–2014 period (Chart 4).

Education and health services. This industry supersector is projected to grow faster, 30.6 percent, and add more jobs than any other industry supersector. About 3 out of every 10 new jobs created in the U.S. economy will be in either the healthcare and social assistance or private educational services sectors.

Healthcare and social assistance—including private hospitals, nursing and residential care facilities, and individual and family services—will grow by 30.3 percent and add 4.3 million new jobs. Employment growth will be driven by increasing demand for healthcare and social assistance because of an aging population and longer life expectancies. Also, as more women enter the labor force, demand for childcare services is expected to grow. Private educational services will grow by 32.5 percent and add 898,000 new jobs through 2014. Rising student enrollments at all levels of education will create demand for educational services.

Professional and business services. This industry supersector, which includes some of the fastest-growing industries in the U.S. economy, will grow by 27.8 percent and add more than 4.5 million new jobs.

Employment in administrative and support and waste management and remediation services will grow by 31 percent and add 2.5 million new jobs to the economy by 2014. The fastest-growing industry in this sector will be employment services, which will grow by 45.5 percent and will contribute almost two-thirds of all new jobs in

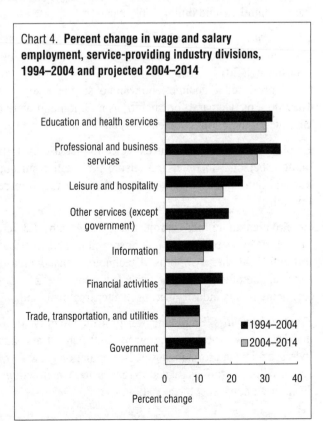

Chart 4. **Percent change in wage and salary employment, service-providing industry divisions, 1994–2004 and projected 2004–2014**

administrative and support and waste management and remediation services. Employment services ranks among the fastest-growing industries in the nation and is expected to be among those that provide the most new jobs.

Employment in professional, scientific, and technical services will grow by 28.4 percent and add 1.9 million new jobs by 2014. Employment in computer systems design and related services will grow by 39.5 percent and add almost one-fourth of all new jobs in professional, scientific, and technical services. Employment growth will be driven by the increasing reliance of businesses on information technology and the continuing importance of maintaining system and network security. Management, scientific, and technical consulting services also will grow very rapidly, by 60.5 percent, spurred by the increased use of new technology and computer software and the growing complexity of business.

Management of companies and enterprises will grow by 10.6 percent and add 182,000 new jobs.

Information. Employment in the information supersector is expected to increase by 11.6 percent, adding 364,000 jobs by 2014. Information contains some of the fast-growing computer-related industries such as software publishers; Internet publishing and broadcasting; and Internet service providers, Web search portals, and data processing services. Employment in these industries is expected to grow by 67.6 percent, 43.5 percent, and 27.8 percent, respectively. The information supersector also includes telecommunications; broadcasting; and newspaper, periodical, book, and directory publishers. Increased demand for residential and business land-line and wireless services, cable service, high-speed Internet connections, and software will fuel job growth among these industries.

Leisure and hospitality. Overall employment will grow by 17.7 percent. Arts, entertainment, and recreation will grow by 25 percent and add 460,000 new jobs by 2014. Most of these new job openings will come from the amusement, gambling, and recreation sector. Job growth will stem from public participation in arts, entertainment, and recreation activities—reflecting increasing incomes, leisure time, and awareness of the health benefits of physical fitness.

Accommodation and food services is expected to grow by 16.5 percent and add 1.8 million new jobs through 2014. Job growth will be concentrated in food services and drinking places, reflecting increases in population, dual-income families, and dining sophistication.

Trade, transportation, and utilities. Overall employment in this industry supersector will grow by 10.3 percent between 2004 and 2014. Transportation and warehousing is expected to increase by 506,000 jobs, or by 11.9 percent through 2014. Truck transportation will grow by 9.6 percent, adding 129,000 new jobs, while rail transportation is projected to decline. The warehousing and storage sector is projected to grow rapidly at 24.8 percent, adding 138,000 jobs. Demand for truck transportation and warehousing services will expand as many manufacturers concentrate on their core competencies and contract out their product transportation and storage functions.

Employment in retail trade is expected to increase by 11 percent, from 15 million to 16.7 million. Increases in population, personal income, and leisure time will contribute to employment growth in this industry, as consumers demand more goods. Wholesale trade is expected to increase by 8.4 percent, growing from 5.7 million to 6.1 million jobs.

Employment in utilities is projected to decrease by 1.3 percent through 2014. Despite increased output, employment in electric power generation, transmission, and distribution and natural gas distribution is expected to decline through 2014 due to improved technology that increases worker productivity. However, employment in water, sewage, and other systems is expected to increase 21 percent by 2014. Jobs are not easily eliminated by technological gains in this industry because water treatment and waste disposal are very labor-intensive activities.

Financial activities. Employment is projected to grow 10.5 percent over the 2004–2014 period. Real estate and rental and leasing is expected to grow by 16.9 percent and add 353,000 jobs by 2014. Growth will be due, in part, to increased demand for housing as the population grows. The fastest-growing industry in the financial activities supersector will be activities related to real estate, which will grow by 32.1 percent, reflecting the housing boom that persists throughout most of the nation.

Finance and insurance is expected to increase by 496,000 jobs, or 8.3 percent, by 2014. Employment in securities, commodity contracts, and other financial investments and related activities is expected to grow 15.8 percent by 2014, reflecting the increased number of baby boomers in their peak savings years, the growth of tax-favorable retirement plans, and the globalization of the securities markets. Employment in credit intermediation and related services, including banks, will grow by 5.4 percent and add about one-third of all new jobs within finance and insurance. Insurance carriers and related activities is expected to grow by 9.5 percent and add 215,000 new jobs by 2014. The number of jobs within agencies, brokerages, and other insurance-related activities is expected to grow about 19.4 percent, as many insurance carriers downsize their sales staffs and as agents set up their own businesses.

Government. Between 2004 and 2014, government employment, including that in public education and hospitals, is expected to increase by 10 percent, from 21.6 million to 23.8 million jobs. Growth in government employment will be fueled by growth in state and local educational services and the shift of responsibilities from the federal government to the state and local governments. Local government educational services is projected to increase 10 percent, adding 783,000 jobs. State government educational services is projected to grow by 19.6 percent, adding 442,000 jobs. Federal government employment, including the postal service, is expected to increase by only 1.6 percent as the federal government continues to contract out many government jobs to private companies.

Other services (except government). Employment will grow by 14 percent. More than 1 out of every 4 new jobs in this supersector will be in religious organizations, which is expected to grow by 11.9 percent. Other automotive repair and maintenance will be the fastest-growing industry at 30.7 percent. Also included among other services is personal care services, which is expected to increase by 19.5 percent.

Goods-producing industries. Employment in the goods-producing industries has been relatively stagnant since the early 1980s. Overall, this sector is expected to decline 0.4 percent over the 2004–2014 period. Although employment is expected to decline or increase more slowly than in the service-providing industries, projected growth among goods-producing industries varies considerably (Chart 5).

Construction. Employment in construction is expected to increase by 11.4 percent, from 7 million to 7.8 million. Demand for new housing and an increase in road, bridge, and tunnel construction will account for the bulk of job growth in this supersector.

Manufacturing. Employment change in manufacturing will vary by individual industry, but overall employment in this supersector will decline by 5.4 percent or 777,000 jobs. For example, employment in transportation equipment manufacturing is expected to grow by 95,000 jobs. Due to an aging population and increasing life expectancies, pharmaceutical and medicine manufacturing is expected to grow by 26.1 percent and add 76,000 jobs through 2014. However, productivity gains, job automation, and international competition will adversely affect employment in many other manufacturing industries. Employment in textile mills and apparel manufacturing will decline by 119,000 and 170,000 jobs, respectively. Employment in computer and electronic product manufacturing also will decline by 94,000 jobs through 2014.

Agriculture, forestry, fishing, and hunting. Overall employment in agriculture, forestry, fishing, and hunting is expected to decrease by 5.2 percent. Employment is expected to continue to decline due to advancements in technology. The only industry within this supersector

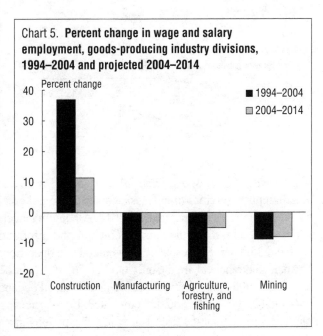

Chart 5. **Percent change in wage and salary employment, goods-producing industry divisions, 1994–2004 and projected 2004–2014**

expected to grow is support activities for agriculture and forestry, which includes farm labor contractors and farm management services. This industry is expected to grow by 18.2 percent and add 19,000 new jobs.

Mining. Employment in mining is expected to decrease 8.8 percent, or by some 46,000 jobs, by 2014. Employment in coal mining and metal ore mining is expected to decline by 23.3 percent and 29.3 percent, respectively. Employment in oil and gas extraction also is projected to decline by 13.1 percent through 2014. Employment decreases in these industries are attributable mainly to technology gains that boost worker productivity, growing international competition, restricted access to federal lands, and strict environmental regulations that require cleaning of burning fuels.

Occupation

Expansion of service-providing industries is expected to continue, creating demand for many occupations. However, projected job growth varies among major occupational groups (Chart 6).

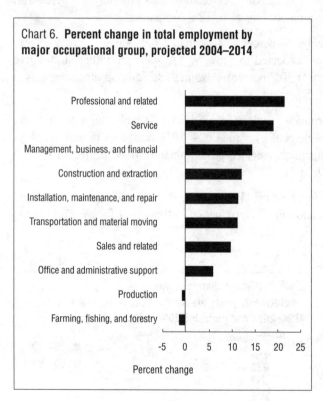

Chart 6. **Percent change in total employment by major occupational group, projected 2004–2014**

Professional and related occupations. Professional and related occupations will grow the fastest and add more new jobs than any other major occupational group. Over the 2004–2014 period, a 21.2-percent increase in the number of professional and related jobs is projected, which translates into 6 million new jobs. Professional and related workers perform a wide variety of duties, and are employed throughout private industry and government. About three-quarters of the job growth will come from three groups of professional occupations—computer and mathematical occupations; healthcare practitioners and technical occupations; and education, training, and library occupations—which will add 4.5 million jobs combined.

Service occupations. Service workers perform services for the public. Employment in service occupations is projected to increase by 5.3 million, or 19 percent, the second largest numerical gain and second highest rate of growth among the major occupational groups. Food preparation and serving related occupations are expected to add the most jobs among the service occupations, 1.7 million by 2014. However, healthcare support occupations are expected to grow the fastest, 33.3 percent, adding 1.2 million new jobs.

Management, business, and financial occupations. Workers in management, business, and financial occupations plan and direct the activities of business, government, and other organizations. Their employment is expected to increase by 2.2 million, or 14.4 percent, by 2014. Among managers, the numbers of preschool and childcare center/program educational administrators and of computer and information systems managers will grow the fastest, by 27.9 percent and 25.9 percent, respectively. General and operations managers will add the most new jobs, 308,000, by 2014. Farmers and ranchers are the only workers in this major occupational group whose numbers are expected to decline, losing 155,000 jobs. Among business and financial occupations, accountants and auditors and management analysts will add the most jobs, 386,000 combined. Employment, recruitment, and placement specialists and personal financial advisors will be the fastest-growing occupations in this group, with job increases of 30.5 percent and 25.9 percent, respectively.

Construction and extraction occupations. Construction and extraction workers construct new residential and commercial buildings, and also work in mines, quarries, and oil and gas fields. Employment of these workers is expected to grow 12 percent, adding 931,000 new jobs. Construction trades and related workers will account for more than three-fourths of these new jobs, 699,000, by 2014. Many extraction occupations will decline, reflecting overall employment losses in the mining and oil and gas extraction industries.

Installation, maintenance, and repair occupations. Workers in installation, maintenance, and repair occupations install new equipment and maintain and repair older equipment. These occupations will add 657,000 jobs by 2014, growing by 11.4 percent. Automotive service technicians and mechanics and general maintenance and repair workers will account for half of all new installation, maintenance, and repair jobs. The fastest growth rate will be among security and fire alarm systems installers, an occupation that is expected to grow 21.7 percent over the 2004–2014 period.

Transportation and material moving occupations. Transportation and material moving workers transport people and materials by land, sea, or air. The number of these workers should grow 11.1 percent, accounting for 1.1 million additional jobs by 2014. Among transportation occupations, motor vehicle operators will add the most jobs, 629,000. Material moving occupations will grow 8.3 percent and will add 405,000 jobs. Rail transportation occupations are the only group in which employment is projected to decline, by 1.1 percent, through 2014.

Sales and related occupations. Sales and related workers transfer goods and services among businesses and consumers. Sales and related occupations are expected to add 1.5 million new jobs by 2014, growing by 9.6 percent. The majority of these jobs will be among retail salespersons and cashiers, occupations that will add 849,000 jobs combined.

Office and administrative support occupations. Office and administrative support workers perform the day-to-day activities of the office, such as preparing and filing documents, dealing with the public, and distributing information. Employment in these occupations is expected to grow by 5.8 percent, adding 1.4 million new jobs by 2014. Customer service representatives will add the most new jobs, 471,000. Desktop publishers will be among the fastest-growing occupations in this group, increasing by 23.2 percent over the decade. However, due to rising productivity and increased automation, office and administrative support occupations also account for 11 of the 20 occupations with the largest employment declines.

Farming, fishing, and forestry occupations. Farming, fishing, and forestry workers cultivate plants, breed and raise livestock, and catch animals. These occupations will decline 1.3 percent and lose 13,000 jobs by 2014. Agricultural workers, including farmworkers and laborers, accounted for the overwhelming majority of new jobs in this group. The number of fishing and hunting workers is expected to decline, by 16.6 percent, while the number of logging workers is expected to increase by less than 1 percent.

Production occupations. Production workers are employed mainly in manufacturing, where they assemble goods and operate plants. Production occupations are expected to decline less than 1 percent, losing 79,000 jobs by 2014. Jobs will be created for many production occupations, including food processing workers; machinists; and welders, cutters, solderers, and brazers. Textile, apparel, and furnishings occupations, as well as assemblers and fabricators, will account for much of the job losses among production occupations.

Among all occupations in the economy, computer and healthcare occupations are expected to grow the fastest over the projection period (Chart 7). In fact, healthcare occupations make up 12 of the 20 fastest-growing occupations, while computer occupations account for 5 out of the 20 fastest-growing occupations in the economy. In addition to high growth rates, these 17 computer and healthcare occupations combined will add more than 1.8 million new jobs. High growth rates among computer and healthcare occupations reflect projected rapid growth in the computer and data processing and health services industries.

The 20 occupations listed in Chart 8 will account for 7.1 million jobs combined, over the 2004–2014 period. The occupations with the largest numerical increases cover a wider range of occupational categories than do those occupations with the fastest growth rates. Health occupations will account for some of these increases in employment,

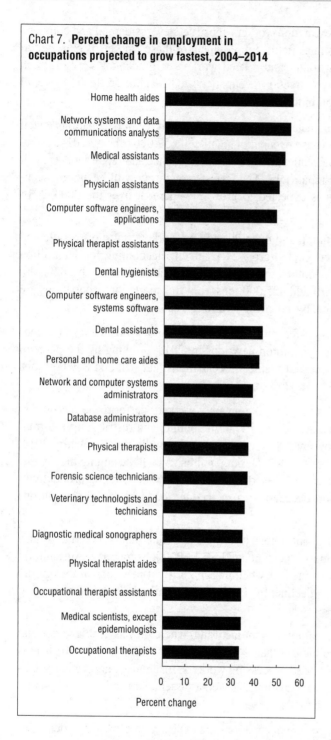

Chart 7. **Percent change in employment in occupations projected to grow fastest, 2004–2014**

- Home health aides
- Network systems and data communications analysts
- Medical assistants
- Physician assistants
- Computer software engineers, applications
- Physical therapist assistants
- Dental hygienists
- Computer software engineers, systems software
- Dental assistants
- Personal and home care aides
- Network and computer systems administrators
- Database administrators
- Physical therapists
- Forensic science technicians
- Veterinary technologists and technicians
- Diagnostic medical sonographers
- Physical therapist aides
- Occupational therapist assistants
- Medical scientists, except epidemiologists
- Occupational therapists

0 10 20 30 40 50 60

Percent change

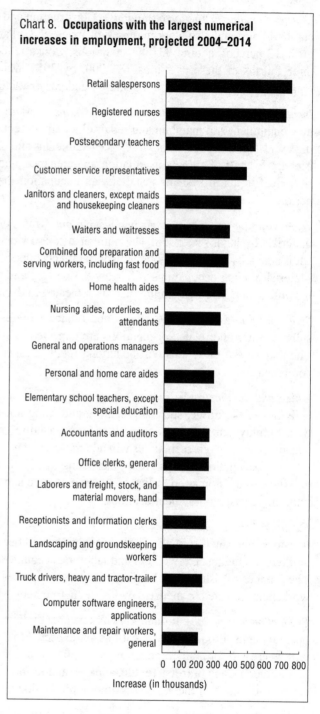

Chart 8. **Occupations with the largest numerical increases in employment, projected 2004–2014**

- Retail salespersons
- Registered nurses
- Postsecondary teachers
- Customer service representatives
- Janitors and cleaners, except maids and housekeeping cleaners
- Waiters and waitresses
- Combined food preparation and serving workers, including fast food
- Home health aides
- Nursing aides, orderlies, and attendants
- General and operations managers
- Personal and home care aides
- Elementary school teachers, except special education
- Accountants and auditors
- Office clerks, general
- Laborers and freight, stock, and material movers, hand
- Receptionists and information clerks
- Landscaping and groundskeeping workers
- Truck drivers, heavy and tractor-trailer
- Computer software engineers, applications
- Maintenance and repair workers, general

0 100 200 300 400 500 600 700 800

Increase (in thousands)

as well as occupations in education, sales, transportation, office and administrative support, and food service. Many of these occupations are very large, and will create more new jobs than will those with high growth rates. Only 3 out of the 20 fastest-growing occupations—home health aides, personal and home care aides, and computer software application engineers—also are projected to be among the 20 occupations with the largest numerical increases in employment.

Declining occupational employment stems from declining industry employment, technological advancements, changes in business practices, and other factors. For example, increased productivity and farm consolidations are expected to result in a decline of 155,000 farmers and ranchers over the 2004–2014 period (Chart 9).

The majority of the 20 occupations with the largest numerical decreases are office and administrative support and production occupations, which are affected by increasing plant and factory automation and the implementation of office technology that reduces the needs for these workers. For example, employment of word processors and typists is expected to decline due to the proliferation of personal computers, which allows other workers to perform duties formerly assigned to word processors and typists.

Education and Training

Among the 20 fastest-growing occupations, a bachelor's or associate degree is the most significant source of postsecondary education or training for 12 of them—network systems and data communications analysts; physician assistants; computer software engineers, applications; physical therapist assistants; dental hygienists; computer software engineers, systems software; network and computer systems administrators; database administrators; forensic science technicians; veterinary technologists and technicians; diagnostic medical sonographers; and occupational therapists assistants.

On-the-job training is the most significant source of postsecondary education or training for another 5 of the 20 fastest-growing occupations—physical therapist aides, medical assistants, home health aides, dental assistants, and personal and home care aides.

In contrast, on-the-job training is the most significant source of postsecondary education or training for 13 of the 20 occupations with the largest numerical increases; 6 of these 20 occupations have an associate or higher degree as the most significant source of postsecondary education or training. On-the-job training also is the most significant source of postsecondary education or training for all 20 of the occupations with the largest numerical decreases.

Chart 9. **Job declines in occupations with the largest numerical decreases in employment, projected 2004–2014**

Decrease (in thousands)

Total Job Openings

Job openings stem from both employment growth and replacement needs (Chart 10). Replacement needs arise as workers leave occupations. Some transfer to other occupations while others retire, return to school, or quit to assume household responsibilities. Replacement needs are projected to account for more than 60 percent of the

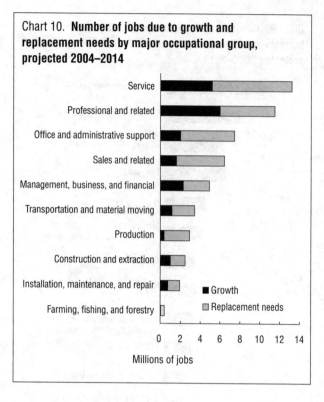

Chart 10. **Number of jobs due to growth and replacement needs by major occupational group, projected 2004–2014**

approximately 55 million job openings between 2004 and 2014. Thus, even occupations projected to experience slower-than-average growth or to decline in employment still may offer many job openings.

Professional and related occupations are projected to grow faster and add more jobs than any other major occupational group, with 6 million new jobs by 2014. Three-fourths of the job growth in professional and related occupations is expected among computer and mathematical occupations; healthcare practitioners and technical occupations; and education, training, and library occupations. With 5.5 million job openings due to replacement needs, professional and related occupations are the only major group projected to generate more openings from job growth than from replacement needs.

Service occupations are projected to have the largest number of total job openings, 13.2 million, reflecting high replacement needs. A large number of replacements will be necessary as young workers leave food preparation and service occupations. Replacement needs generally are greatest in the largest occupations and in those with relatively low pay or limited training requirements.

Office automation will significantly affect many individual office and administrative support occupations. Overall, these occupations are projected to grow more slowly than average, while some are projected to decline. Office and administrative support occupations are projected to create 7.5 million job openings over the 2004–2014 period, ranking third behind service and professional and related occupations.

Farming, fishing, and forestry occupations are projected to have the fewest job openings, approximately 286,000. Because job growth is expected to be slow, and levels of retirement and job turnover high, more than 95 percent of these projected job openings are due to replacement needs.

Editor's Note: This section, with minor changes, came from the *Occupational Outlook Handbook* and was written by the U.S. Department of Labor staff. Much of this section uses 2004 data, the most recent available at press time. By the time it is carefully collected and analyzed, data used by the U.S. Department of Labor is typically several years old. Because market trends tend to be gradual, this delay does not affect the material's usefulness.

Employment Trends in Major Industries

The U.S. economy can be broken down into numerous industries, each with its own set of characteristics. The Department of Labor has identified 45 industries that account for three-quarters of all workers. This section provides an overview of these industries and the economy as a whole.

Nature of the Industry

Industries are defined by the processes they use to produce goods and services. Workers in the United States produce and provide a wide variety of products and services and, as a result, the types of industries in the U.S. economy range widely—from agriculture, forestry, and fishing to aerospace manufacturing. Each industry has a unique combination of occupations, production techniques, inputs and outputs, and business characteristics. Understanding the nature of industries that interest you is important because it is this unique combination that determines working conditions, educational requirements, and the job outlook.

Industries consist of many different places of work, called establishments. Establishments are physical locations in which people work, such as the branch office of a bank, a gasoline service station, a school, a department store, or a plant that manufactures machinery. Establishments range from large factories and corporate office complexes employing thousands of workers to small community stores, restaurants, professional offices, and service businesses employing only a few workers. Establishments should not be confused with companies or corporations, which are legal entities. Thus, a company or corporation may have a single establishment or more than one establishment. Establishments that use the same or similar processes to produce goods or services are organized together into industries. Industries are, in turn, organized together into industry groups such as Information and Trade. These are further organized into industry subsectors and then ultimately into industry sectors. For the purposes of labor market analysis, the Bureau of Labor Statistics organizes industry sectors into industry supersectors. A company or corporation could own establishments classified in more than one industry, industry sector, or even industry supersector.

Each industry subsector is made up of a number of industry groups, which are, as mentioned, determined by differences in production processes. An easily recognized example of these distinctions is in the food manufacturing subsector, which is made up of industry groups that produce meat products, preserved fruits and vegetables, bakery items, and dairy products, among others. Each of these industry groups requires workers with varying skills and employs unique production techniques. Another example of these distinctions is found in utilities, which employs workers in establishments that provide electricity, natural gas, and water.

There are slightly more than 8 million private business establishments in the United States. Business establishments in the United States are predominantly small; 59.9 percent of all establishments employed fewer than 5 workers.

However, the medium-sized to large establishments employ a greater proportion of all workers. For example, establishments that employed 50 or more workers accounted for only 4.6 percent of all establishments, yet employed 56.3 percent of all workers. The large establishments—those with more than 500 workers—accounted for only 0.2 percent of all establishments, but employed 17.3 percent of all workers. Table 1 presents the percent distribution of employment according to establishment size.

The average size of these establishments varies widely across industries. Most establishments in the construction, wholesale trade, retail trade, finance and insurance, real estate and rental and leasing, and professional, scientific, and technical services industries are small, averaging fewer than 20 employees per establishment. However, wide differences within industries can exist. Hospitals, for example, employ an average of 724.9 workers, while physicians' offices employ an average of 10.1. Similarly, although there is an average of 14.3 employees per establishment for all of retail trade, department stores employ an average of 124.1 people but jewelry stores employ an average of only 5.8.

Establishment size can play a role in the characteristics of each job. Large establishments generally offer workers greater occupational mobility and advancement potential, whereas small establishments may provide their employees with broader experience by requiring them to assume a wider range of responsibilities. Also, small establishments are distributed throughout the nation—every locality has a few small businesses. Large establishments, in contrast, employ more workers and are less common, but they play a much more prominent role in the economies of the areas in which they are located.

Table 1. Percent distribution of nongovernment establishments and employment by establishment size

Establishment size (number of workers)	Establishments	Employment
Total	100.0	100.0
1 to 4	59.9	6.8
5 to 9	16.9	8.4
10 to 19	11.1	11.2
20 to 49	7.6	17.3
50 to 99	2.6	13.3
100 to 249	1.4	16.4
250 to 499	0.4	9.3
500 to 999	0.1	6.6
1,000 or more	0.1	10.7

Working Conditions

Just as the goods and services produced in each industry are different, working conditions vary significantly among industries. In some industries, the work setting is quiet, temperature-controlled, and virtually hazard-free, while other industries are characterized by noisy, uncomfortable, and sometimes dangerous work environments. Some industries require long workweeks and shift work, but standard 40-hour workweeks are common in many other industries. In still other industries, a lot of the jobs can be seasonal, requiring long hours during busy periods and abbreviated schedules during slower months. Production processes, establishment size, and the physical location of work usually determine these varying conditions.

One of the most telling indicators of working conditions is an industry's injury and illness rate. Overexertion, being struck by an object, and falls on the same level are among the most common incidents causing work-related injury or illness. In 2003, approximately 5.0 million nonfatal injuries and illnesses were reported across the various nongovernment industries. Among major industry divisions, manufacturing and construction tied for the highest rate of injury and illness—6.8 cases for every 100 full-time workers—while financial activities had the lowest rate—1.7 cases. About 5,700 work-related fatalities were reported in 2004; the most common events resulting in fatal injuries were transportation incidents, contact with objects and equipment, assaults and violent acts, and falls.

Work schedules are another important reflection of working conditions, and the operational requirements of each industry lead to large differences in hours worked and in part-time versus full-time status. In food services and drinking places, for example, fully 41.1 percent of employees worked part time in 2005 compared with only 1.7 percent in motor vehicles and motor vehicle equipment manufacturing. Table 2 presents industries having relatively high and low percentages of part-time workers.

Table 2. Part-time workers as a percent of total employment, selected industries

Industry	Percent part-time
All industries	17.4
Many part-time workers	
Food services and drinking places	41.1
Grocery stores	35.3
Clothing, accessory, and general merchandise stores	33.8
Arts, entertainment, and recreation	32.0
Child day care services	28.7
Motion picture and video industries	27.1
Social assistance	24.6
Educational services	21.9
Few part-time workers	
Pharmaceutical and medicine manufacturing	3.6
Utilities	3.2
Oil and gas extraction	3.2
Computer and electronic product manufacturing	2.8
Steel manufacturing	2.4
Mining	2.3
Aerospace product and parts manufacturing	1.9
Motor vehicles and parts manufacturing	1.7

The low proportion of part-time workers in some manufacturing industries often reflects the continuous nature of the production processes that makes it difficult to adapt the volume of production to short-term fluctuations in product demand. Once these processes are begun, it is costly to halt them; machinery must be tended and materials must be moved continuously. For example, the chemical manufacturing industry produces many different chemical products through controlled chemical reactions. These processes require chemical operators to monitor and adjust the flow of materials into and out of the line of production. Because production may continue 24 hours a day, 7 days a week under the watchful eyes of chemical operators who work in shifts, full-time workers are more likely to be employed. Retail trade and service industries, on the other hand, have seasonal cycles marked by various events that affect the hours worked, such as school openings or important holidays. During busy times of the year, longer hours are common, whereas slack periods lead to cutbacks in work hours and shorter workweeks. Jobs in these industries are generally appealing to students and others who desire flexible, part-time schedules.

Employment

The total number of jobs in the United States in 2004 was 145.6 million. This included 12.1 million self-employed workers, 141,000 unpaid workers in family businesses, and 133.5 million wage and salary jobs—including primary and secondary job holders. The total number of jobs is projected to increase to 164.5 million by 2014, and wage and salary jobs are projected to account for more than 152.1 million of them.

As shown in table 3, wage and salary jobs are the vast majority of all jobs, but they are not evenly divided among the various industries. Education, health, and social services had the largest number of jobs in 2004 with almost 28 million. Manufacturing, construction, and utilities had almost 21.9 million jobs, including 14.3 million manufacturing and 7.0 million construction jobs. The trade supersector was nearly as large, with about 20.7 million jobs, followed by professional and business services with 16.4 million jobs in 2004. Among the 45 industries, wage and salary employment ranged from only 156,200 in steel manufacturing to over 13 million in health services. The three largest industries—education services, health services, and food services and drinking places—together accounted for 34.7 million jobs, over one-quarter of the nation's wage and salary employment.

Table 3. Wage and salary employment, 2004, and projected change, 2004–14 (Employment in thousands)

Industry	2004		2014		2004–2014	
	Employment	Percent distribution	Employment	Percent distribution	Percent change	Employment change
All industries	133,478	100.0	152,093	100.0	13.9	18,615
Agriculture and natural resources	1,672	1.3	1,567	1.0	–6.3	–105
Agriculture, forestry, and fishing	1,149	0.9	1,090	0.7	–5.2	–60
Mining	207	0.2	180	0.1	–12.9	–27
Oil and gas extraction	316	0.2	297	0.2	–6.1	–19
Manufacturing, construction, and utilities	21,864	16.4	21,872	14.4	0.0	8
Aerospace product and parts manufacturing	444	0.3	480	0.3	8.2	36
Chemical manufacturing, except drugs	596	0.5	510	0.3	–14.4	–86
Computer and electronic product manufacturing	1,326	1.0	1,232	0.8	–7.1	–94
Construction	6,964	5.2	7,757	5.1	11.4	792
Food manufacturing	1,498	1.1	1,555	1.0	3.8	57
Machinery manufacturing	1,142	0.9	995	0.7	–12.8	–146
Motor vehicle and parts manufacturing	1,109	0.8	1,171	0.8	5.6	62
Pharmaceutical and medicine manufacturing	291	0.2	367	0.2	26.1	76
Printing	665	0.5	600	0.4	–9.8	–65
Steel manufacturing	156	0.1	135	0.1	–13.4	–21
Textile, textile product, and apparel manufacturing	701	0.5	380	0.2	–44.6	–321
Utilities	570	0.4	563	0.4	–1.3	–8
Trade	20,689	15.5	22,814	15.0	10.3	2,125
Automobile dealers	1,254	0.9	1,407	0.9	12.2	153
Clothing, accessory, and general merchandise stores	4,205	3.1	4,628	3.0	10.1	423
Grocery stores	2,447	1.8	2,607	1.7	6.6	160
Wholesale trade	5,655	4.2	6,131	4.0	8.4	476
Transportation	4,250	3.2	4,756	3.1	11.9	506
Air transportation	515	0.4	560	0.4	8.8	45
Truck transportation and warehousing	1,907	1.4	2,174	1.4	14.0	267

Industry	2004		2014		2004–2014	
	Employment	Percent distribution	Employment	Percent distribution	Percent change	Employment change
Information	3,138	2.4	3,502	2.3	11.6	364
Broadcasting	327	0.2	362	0.2	10.7	35
Motion picture and video industries	368	0.3	430	0.3	17.1	63
Publishing, except software	671	0.5	715	0.5	6.5	44
Software publishers	239	0.2	400	0.3	67.6	161
Telecommunications	1,043	0.8	975	0.6	–6.5	–68
Internet service providers, Web search portals, and data processing services	388	0.3	496	0.3	27.8	108
Financial activities	8,052	6.0	8,901	5.9	10.5	849
Banking	1,783	1.3	1,751	1.2	–1.8	–31
Insurance	2,260	1.7	2,476	1.6	9.5	215
Securities, commodities, and other investments	767	0.6	888	0.6	15.8	121
Professional and business services	16,414	12.3	20,980	13.8	27.8	4,566
Advertising and public relations services	425	0.3	520	0.3	22.4	95
Computer systems design and related services	1,147	0.9	1,600	1.1	39.5	453
Employment services	3,470	2.6	5,050	3.3	45.5	1,580
Management, scientific, and technical consulting services	779	0.6	1,250	0.8	60.5	471
Scientific research and development services	548	0.4	613	0.4	11.9	65
Education, health, and social services	27,973	21.0	34,399	22.6	23.0	6,426
Child day care services	767	0.6	1,062	0.7	38.4	295
Educational services	12,778	9.6	14,901	9.8	16.6	2,123
Health services	13,062	9.8	16,626	10.9	27.3	3,564
Social assistance, except child day care	1,365	1.0	1,810	1.2	32.6	445
Leisure and hospitality	12,479	9.3	14,694	9.7	17.7	2,215
Arts, entertainment, and recreation	1,833	1.4	2,293	1.5	25.1	460
Food services and drinking places	8,850	6.6	10,301	6.8	16.4	1,451
Hotels and other accommodations	1,796	1.3	2,100	1.4	16.9	304
Government and advocacy, grantmaking, and civic organizations	11,047	8.3	12,170	8.0	10.2	1,123
Advocacy, grantmaking, and civic organizations	1,231	0.9	1,410	0.9	14.5	179
Federal government	1,943	1.5	1,993	1.3	2.5	50
State and local government, except education and health	7,872	5.9	8,767	5.8	11.4	895

Note: May not add to totals due to omission of industries not covered.

Although workers of all ages are employed in each industry, certain industries tend to possess workers of distinct age groups. For the previously mentioned reasons, retail trade employs a relatively high proportion of younger workers to fill part-time and temporary positions. The manufacturing sector, on the other hand, has a relatively high median age because many jobs in the sector require a number of years to learn and perfect specialized skills that do not easily transfer to other firms. Also, manufacturing employment has been declining, providing fewer opportunities for younger workers to get jobs. As a result, one-fourth of the workers in retail trade were 24 years of age or younger in 2004, compared with only 8.2 percent of workers in manufacturing. Table 4 contrasts the age distribution of workers in all industries with the distributions in five very different industries.

Table 4. Percent distribution of wage and salary workers by age group, selected industries

Industry	Age group			
	16 to 24	25 to 44	45 to 64	65 and older
All industries	14	47	36	4
Computer systems design and related services	7	63	29	1
Educational services	9	42	45	3
Food services and drinking places	44	39	15	2
Telecommunications	8	56	34	2
Utilities	5	43	50	2

Employment in some industries is concentrated in one region of the country. Such industries often are located near a source of raw or unfinished materials upon which the industry relies. For example, oil and gas extraction jobs are concentrated in Texas, Louisiana, and Oklahoma; many textile mills and products manufacturing jobs are found in North Carolina, South Carolina, and Georgia; and a significant proportion of motor vehicle manufacturing jobs are located in Michigan and Ohio. On the other hand, some industries—such as grocery stores and educational services—have jobs distributed throughout the nation, reflecting the general population density.

Occupations in the Industry

The occupations found in each industry depend on the types of services provided or goods produced. For example, because construction companies require skilled trades workers to build and renovate buildings, these companies employ large numbers of carpenters, electricians, plumbers, painters, and sheet metal workers. Other occupations common to construction include construction equipment operators and mechanics, installers, and repairers. Retail trade, on the other hand, displays and sells manufactured goods to consumers. As a result, retail trade employs numerous retail salespersons and other workers, including more than three-fourths of all cashiers. Table 5 shows the industry sectors and the occupational groups that predominate in each.

Table 5. Industry sectors and their largest occupational group

Industry sector	Largest occupational group	Percent of industry wage and salary jobs
Agriculture, forestry, fishing, and hunting	Farming, fishing, and forestry occupations	61.1
Mining	Construction and extraction occupations	33.3
Construction	Construction and extraction occupations	66.2
Manufacturing	Production occupations	52.1
Wholesale trade	Sales and related occupations	24.7
Retail trade	Sales and related occupations	52.5
Transportation and warehousing	Transportation and material moving occupations	56.0
Utilities	Installation, maintenance, and repair occupations	25.6
Information	Professional and related occupations	29.1
Finance and insurance	Office and administrative support occupations	51.4
Real estate and rental and leasing	Sales and related occupations	22.7

Industry sector	Largest occupational group	Percent of industry wage and salary jobs
Professional, scientific, and technical services	Professional and related occupations	42.6
Management of companies and enterprises	Office and administrative support occupations	33.6
Administrative and support and waste management and remediation services	Office and administrative support occupations	23.2
Educational services, private	Professional and related occupations	59.6
Health care and social assistance	Professional and related occupations	42.6
Arts, entertainment, and recreation	Service occupations	57.2
Accommodation and food services	Service occupations	84.0
Government	Professional and related occupations	43.7

The occupational distribution clearly is influenced by the structure of its industries, yet there are many occupations, such as general managers or secretaries, that are found in all industries. In fact, some of the largest occupations in the U.S. economy are dispersed across many industries. For example, the group of professional and related occupations is among the largest in the nation while also experiencing the fastest growth rate. (See table 6.) Other large occupational groups include service occupations; office and administrative support occupations; sales and related occupations; and management, business, and financial occupations.

Table 6. Total employment and projected change by broad occupational group, 2004–14 (Employment in thousands)

Occupational group	Employment, 2004	Percent change, 2004–2014
Total, all occupations	145,612	13.0
Professional and related occupations	28,544	21.2
Service occupations	27,673	19.0
Office and administrative support occupations	23,907	5.8
Sales and related occupations	15,330	9.6
Management, business, and financial occupations	14,987	14.4
Production occupations	10,562	–0.1
Transportation and material moving occupations	10,098	11.1
Construction and extraction occupations	7,738	12.0
Installation, maintenance, and repair occupations	5,747	11.4
Farming, fishing, and forestry occupations	1,026	–1.3

Training and Advancement

Workers prepare for employment in many ways, but the most fundamental form of job training in the United States is a high school education. Better than 88 percent of the nation's workforce possessed a high school diploma or its equivalent in 2004. However, many occupations require more training, so growing numbers of workers pursue additional training or education after high school. In 2004, 28.7 percent of the nation's workforce reported having completed some college or an associate's degree as their highest level of education, while an additional 29.5 percent continued in their studies and attained a bachelor's or higher degree. In addition to these types of formal education, other sources of qualifying training include formal company-provided training, apprenticeships, informal on-the-job training, correspondence courses, Armed Forces vocational training, and non-work-related training.

The unique combination of training required to succeed in each industry is determined largely by the industry's production process and the mix of occupations it requires. For example, manufacturing employs many machine operators who generally need little formal education after high school, but sometimes complete considerable on-the-job training. In contrast, the educational services industry employs many types of teachers, most of whom require a bachelor's or higher degree. Training requirements by industry sector are shown in table 7.

Table 7. Percent distribution of workers by highest grade completed or degree received, by industry sector

Industry sector	High school diploma or less	Some college or associate degree	Bachelor's or higher degree
All industries	41.6	28.7	29.5
Agriculture, forestry, fishing, and hunting	64.3	21.4	14.2
Mining	60.4	21.8	17.8
Construction	64.7	24.5	10.8
Manufacturing	51.5	25.1	23.4
Wholesale trade	42.7	29.0	28.3
Retail trade	50.6	32.3	17.1
Transportation and warehousing	52.6	31.7	15.6
Utilities	38.7	34.1	27.0
Information	26.7	31.3	42.0
Finance and insurance	24.9	31.6	43.4
Real estate and rental and leasing	36.2	31.7	32.2
Professional, scientific, and technical services	14.4	25.1	60.6
Administrative and support and waste management services	55.3	28.4	16.3
Educational services	17.8	19.0	63.2
Health care and social assistance	30.6	34.8	34.7
Arts, entertainment, and recreation	39.5	31.8	28.6
Accommodation and food services	60.7	28.4	11.0

Persons with no more than a high school diploma accounted for about 64.7 percent of all workers in construction; 64.3 in agriculture, forestry, fishing, and hunting; 60.7 percent in accommodation and food services; 60.4 percent in mining; 51.5 percent in manufacturing; and 50.6 in retail trade. On the other hand, those who had acquired a bachelor's or higher degree accounted for 63.2 percent of all workers in private educational services; 60.6 percent in professional, scientific, and technical services; 43.4 percent in finance and insurance; and 42.0 percent in information.

Education and training also are important factors in the variety of advancement paths found in different industries. Each industry has some unique advancement paths, but workers who complete additional on-the-job training or education generally help their chances of being promoted. In much of the manufacturing sector, for example, production workers who receive training in management and computer skills increase their likelihood of being promoted to supervisory positions. Other factors that impact advancement and that may figure prominently in industries include the size of the establishments, institutionalized career tracks, and the mix of occupations. As a result, persons who seek jobs in particular industries should be aware of how these advancement paths and other factors may later shape their careers.

Earnings

Like other characteristics, earnings differ by industry, the result of a highly complicated process that reflects a number of factors. For example, earnings may vary due to the nature of occupations in the industry, average hours worked, geographical location, workers' average age, educational requirements, profits, and the degree of union representation of the workforce. In general, wages are highest in metropolitan areas to compensate for the higher cost of living. Also, as would be expected, industries that employ a large proportion of unskilled minimum-wage or part-time workers tend to have lower earnings.

The difference in earnings between the industries of software publishers and of food services and drinking places illustrates how various characteristics of industries can result in great differences in earnings. In software publishers, earnings of all wage and salary workers averaged $1,342 a week in 2004, while in food service and drinking places, earnings of all wage and salary workers averaged only $194 weekly. The difference is large primarily because software publishing establishments employ more higher-skilled, full-time workers, while food services and drinking places employ many lower-skilled workers on a part-time basis. In addition, most workers in software publishing are paid an annual salary, while many workers in food service and drinking places are paid a low hourly wage that is supplemented with money the workers receive as tips. Table 8 highlights the industries with the highest and lowest average weekly earnings.

Table 8. Average weekly earnings of production or nonsupervisory workers on private nonfarm payrolls, selected industries

Industry	Earnings
All industries	$529
Industries with high earnings	
Software publishers	1,342
Computer systems design and related services	1,136
Aerospace product and parts manufacturing	1,019
Scientific research and development services	1,006
Motor vehicle and parts manufacturing	925
Mining	909
Industries with low earnings	
Food manufacturing	510
Grocery stores	332
Arts, entertainment, and recreation	313
Hotels and other accommodations	302
Child day care services	299
Food services and drinking places	194

Employee benefits, once a minor addition to wages and salaries, continue to grow in diversity and cost. In addition to traditional benefits—paid vacations, life and health insurance, and pensions—many employers now offer various benefits to accommodate the needs of a changing labor force. Such benefits sometimes include childcare; employee assistance programs that provide counseling for personal problems; and wellness programs that encourage exercise, stress management, and self-improvement. Benefits vary among occupational groups, full- and part-time workers, public and private sector workers, regions, unionized and nonunionized workers, and small and large establishments. Data indicate that full-time workers and those in medium-sized and large establishments—those with 100 or more workers—usually receive better benefits than do part-time workers and those in smaller establishments.

Union representation of the workforce varies widely by industry, and it also may play a role in determining earnings and benefits. In 2004, about 13.8 percent of workers throughout the nation were union members or covered by union contracts. As table 9 demonstrates, union affiliation of workers varies widely by industry. Fully 50.0 percent of the workers in air transportation were union members, the highest rate of all the industries, followed by 37.6 percent in educational services, and 33.0 percent in iron and steel mills and steel product manufacturing. Industries with the lowest unionization rate include computer systems design and related services, 1.3 percent; food services and drinking places, 1.7 percent; and advertising and related services, 1.7 percent.

Table 9. Union members and other workers covered by union contracts as a percent of total employment, selected industries

Industry	Percent union members or covered by union contract
All industries	13.8
Industries with high unionization rates	
Air transportation	50.0
Educational services	37.6
Iron and steel mills and steel product manufacturing	33.0
Motor vehicles and motor vehicle equipment manufacturing	30.2
Industries with low unionization rates	
Banking and related activities	1.9
Advertising and related services	1.7
Food services and drinking places	1.7
Computer systems design and related services	1.3

Outlook

Total employment in the United States is projected to increase by about 14 percent over the 2004–2014 period. Employment growth, however, is only one source of job openings. The total number of openings in any industry also depends on the industry's current employment level and its need to replace workers who leave their jobs. Throughout the economy, replacement needs will create more job openings than will employment growth. Employment size is a major determinant of job openings—larger industries generally have larger numbers of workers who must be replaced and provide more openings. The occupational composition of an industry is another factor. Industries with high concentrations of professional, technical, and other jobs that require more formal education—occupations in which workers tend to leave their jobs less frequently—generally have fewer openings resulting from replacement needs. On the other hand, more replacement openings generally occur in industries with high concentrations of service, laborer, and other jobs that require little formal education and have lower wages because workers in these jobs are more likely to leave their occupations.

Employment growth is determined largely by changes in the demand for the goods and services provided by an industry, worker productivity, and foreign competition. Each industry is affected by a different set of variables that determines the number and composition of jobs that will be available. Even within an industry, employment may grow at different rates in different occupations. For example, changes in technology, production methods, and business practices in an industry might eliminate some jobs, while creating others. Some industries may be growing rapidly overall, yet opportunities for workers in occupations within those industries could be stagnant or even declining because they are adversely affected by technological change. Similarly, employment of some occupations may be declining in the economy as a whole, yet may be increasing in a rapidly growing industry.

Employment growth rates over the next decade will vary widely among industries. Agriculture and natural resources is the only sector in which all of the industries are expected to experience employment declines. Consolidation of farm land, increasing worker productivity, and depletion of wild fish stocks should continue to decrease employment in agriculture, forestry, and fishing. Employment in mining is expected to decline due to labor-saving technology while jobs in oil and gas extraction are expected to decrease with the continued reliance on foreign sources of energy.

Employment in manufacturing, construction, and utilities is expected to remain nearly unchanged as growth in construction is partially offset by declines in utilities and selected manufacturing industries. Growth in construction employment will stem from new factory construction as existing facilities are modernized; from new school construction, reflecting growth in the school-age population; and from infrastructure improvements, such as road and bridge construction. Employment declines are expected in chemical manufacturing, except drugs; machinery manufacturing; computer and electronic product manufacturing; printing; steel manufacturing; and textile, textile product, and apparel manufacturing. Textile, textile product, and apparel manufacturing is projected to lose about 321,200 jobs over the 2004–2014 period—more than any other manufacturing industry—due primarily to increasing imports replacing domestic products.

Employment gains are expected in some manufacturing industries. Small employment gains in food manufacturing are expected, as a growing and ever more diverse population increases the demand for manufactured food products. Employment growth in pharmaceutical and medicine manufacturing is expected, as sales of pharmaceuticals increase with growth in the population, particularly among the elderly, and with the introduction of new medicines to the market. Both food and pharmaceutical and medicine manufacturing also have growing export markets. Aerospace product and parts manufacturing and motor vehicle and parts manufacturing are both expected to have modest employment increases.

Growth in overall employment will result primarily from growth in service-providing industries over the 2004–2014 period, almost all of which are expected to have increasing employment. Job growth is expected to be led by health services and educational services, with large numbers of new jobs also in employment services, food services and drinking places, state and local government, and wholesale trade. When combined, these sectors will account for almost half of all new wage and salary jobs across the nation. Employment growth is expected in many other service-providing industries, but they will result in far fewer numbers of new jobs.

Health services will account for the most new wage and salary jobs, about 3.6 million over the 2004–2014 period. Population growth, advances in medical technologies that increase the number of treatable diseases, and a growing share of the population in older age groups will drive employment growth. Offices of physicians, the largest health care industry group, is expected to account for about 760,000 of these new jobs as patients seek more healthcare outside of the traditional inpatient hospital setting.

The educational services industry is expected to grow by nearly 17 percent over the 2004–2014 period, adding about 2.1 million new jobs. A growing emphasis on improving education and making it available to more children and young adults will be the primary factors contributing to employment growth. Employment growth at all levels of education is expected, particularly at the postsecondary level, as children of the baby boomers continue to reach college age, and as more adults pursue continuing education to enhance or update their skills.

Employment in one of the nation's fastest-growing industries—employment services—is expected to increase by more than 45 percent, adding another 1.6 million jobs over the 2004–2014 period. Employment will increase, particularly in temporary help services and professional employer organizations, as businesses seek new ways to make their workforces more specialized and responsive to changes in demand.

The food services and drinking places industry is expected to add almost 1.5 million new jobs over the 2004–2014 projection period. Increases in population, dual-income families, and dining sophistication will contribute to job growth. In addition, the increasing diversity of the population will contribute to job growth in food services and drinking places that offer a wider variety of ethnic foods and drinks.

Over 890,000 new jobs are expected to arise in state and local government, adding more than 11 percent over the 2004–2014 period. Job growth will result primarily from growth in the population and its demand for public services. Additional job growth will result as state and local governments continue to receive greater responsibility for administering federally funded programs from the federal government.

Wholesale trade is expected to add almost 480,000 new jobs over the coming decade, reflecting growth both in trade and in the overall economy. Most new jobs will be for sales representatives at the wholesale and manufacturing levels. However, industry consolidation and the growth of electronic commerce using the Internet are expected to limit job growth to 8.4 percent over the 2004–2014 period, less than the 14 percent projected for all industries.

Continual changes in the economy have far-reaching and complex effects on employment in industries. Job seekers should be aware of these changes, keeping alert for developments that can affect job opportunities in industries and the variety of occupations that are found in each industry.

Editor's Note: The preceding article was adapted from the Career Guide to Industries, *a publication of the U.S. Department of Labor. A book titled* 40 Best Fields for Your Career *(JIST Publishing) includes information from the* Career Guide to Industries *plus useful "best fields" lists and other helpful insights.*

Training for Techies: Career Preparation in Information Technology

Maria and Spencer are both in their early twenties. Maria recently completed her bachelor's degree in English; Spencer dropped out of college after a few semesters. If asked to speculate on Maria's and Spencer's occupations, perhaps you would guess writer and waiter.

But it might surprise you to learn that Maria is a computer systems analyst and Spencer is a computer programmer. While majoring in English, Maria took several computer-related courses and gained experience working in a computer lab. Spencer, although not formally enrolled in a degree program, took courses at a community college and earned certification in a programming language. Both benefited from the flexible training requirements for individuals hoping to work in information technology, often identified as IT.

The Bureau of Labor Statistics (BLS) projects that 5 of the 12 fastest-growing occupations between 2004 and 2014 will be computer related. For this reason, future jobseekers need to know about the variety of ways to prepare for a career in information technology. Following a discussion of how these workers are defined, this article focuses on the available training, which ranges from certificates to advanced degrees.

What Is an Information Technology Worker?

The information technology workforce is defined differently by trade organizations and government sources.

The Information Technology Association of America defines an information technology worker by using the eight career clusters developed by the National Workforce Center for Emerging Technologies. Those career clusters include programming and software engineering, technical support, enterprise systems, database development and administration, Web development and administration, network design and administration, digital media, and technical writing. According to its latest study, "Bouncing Back: Jobs, Skills, and the Continuing Demand for IT Workers," the Association notes that 92 percent of all information technology workers are in non-information technology companies, 80 percent of them in small companies outside the information technology industry.

The U.S. Department of Commerce identifies information technology workers more broadly as those who design, manufacture, operate, maintain, and repair information technology products and provide related services across all industries.

For purposes of this article, information technology workers are considered to be those employed in 12 computer-related Standard Occupational Classification System (SOC) occupations. These occupations are

★ Computer and information systems managers

★ Computer programmers

- ★ Computer and information scientists, research

- ★ Computer systems analysts

- ★ Computer hardware engineers

- ★ Computer software engineers, applications

- ★ Computer software engineers, systems software

- ★ Computer support specialists

- ★ Database administrators

- ★ Network and computer systems administrators

- ★ Network systems and data communications analysts

- ★ All other computer specialists, a residual category of workers

Using this definition, BLS data shows that about 3.4 million information technology workers were employed in the United States in 2004. However, that number excludes marketing and sales workers employed by information technology companies.

What Type of Training Do I Need?

As Maria's and Spencer's backgrounds suggest, there is considerable interest in the topic of education and training required for information technology workers. This interest stems from the U.S. economy's demand for such workers and a presumption that the current educational system is not producing enough of them for the workforce. Rita Caldwell, director of the National Science Foundation, notes that there are many pathways for becoming an information technology worker. Training ranges from a few months for certification to 6 years for a doctoral degree.

BLS data shows that in 2004, most information technology workers—about 58 percent—had a bachelor's or higher degree, although the number who had some college but no degree is rapidly increasing and accounted for almost 20 percent of these workers. (See Chart 1.) In fact, anecdotal information suggests that many people attend community colleges not to earn degrees but to take computer-related courses in hopes of getting a job or as a way to retrain and update their skills. And according to the National Science Foundation, two-thirds of workers who had a bachelor's degree and worked in a computer-related occupation had majored in subjects other than computer and information sciences. (See Chart 2.)

Clearly, earning a postsecondary degree in a computer-related field is not the only way to prepare for a job in information technology. But learning the technical skills necessary to work in these occupations remains paramount. Specialized certification and degree programs—associate, bachelor's, and graduate-level ones—are the primary ways workers train for information technology occupations.

Certification

Technical or professional certification demonstrates that an individual has achieved a level of competency in a particular field. There are various certifications available for information technology workers. Spencer, for example, earned certification that qualified him for a computer programming job. Product vendors and industry organizations offer different types of certification, providing a training niche that is expected to continue.

Growth of certification. According to the Information Technology Association of America's study on the information technology workforce, the significance of certification has grown in each of its job categories in the last year.

More than 100 vendors and organizations offer certifications in information technology, and certification is growing more popular.

When international trends are considered, the impact of certification is even more dramatic. In his report "The Certification System in Information Technology," author Clifford Adelman describes a "parallel universe" outside conventional educational routes for potential information technology workers to develop skills. The report notes that about 1.6 million people worldwide have earned roughly 2.4 million information technology certifications.

Vendor and organization certification. Product vendors and software firms—including Microsoft, Cisco, and Oracle—offer certification and may require individuals who work with their products to be certified. And industry organizations, such as the Institute for the Certification of Computing Professionals, offer voluntary certification. The Institute's certification is available to those who have a college degree and at least 2 years of experience and have passed a series of examinations.

Vendor certification evolved from the difficulty employers had finding skilled workers to fill the rising number of high-tech jobs created by the Internet boom in the mid- to late 1990s. Because certification is faster, cheaper, and more focused than traditional educational tracks, vendor certification soon emerged as a solution to the problem of worker shortages.

One example of the rapid growth in vendor certification is the increase in the number of Microsoft Certified Professional awards over recent years: 427,086 in January 2000; 593,462 in January 2001; 718,372 in January 2002; and 853,791 in January 2003.

Future of certification. Certification has become an increasingly important standard in the information technology industry in the last decade. However, it has also become more controversial. Although it enables workers to demonstrate a specific set of skills, some employers say that certification is not a viable substitute for practical experience. Others prefer that workers have formal education and practical experience, predicting that certifications will diminish in importance. But as the following example illustrates, certification should continue to play a role in training information technology workers.

The growing importance of network security in information technology has led to an increased demand for computer security professionals. Someone who wants to work in information security can get one of a variety of certifications instead of a 2- or 4-year degree. Employers interested in securing their organizations' computer networks seek individuals with expertise in information security—which a specialized certification presumably demonstrates.

In an era in which new technology may become obsolete in a few years, acquiring skills quickly is important to both employers and workers.

Chart 1

Distribution of workers in computer-related occupations by highest level of educational attainment, 2005

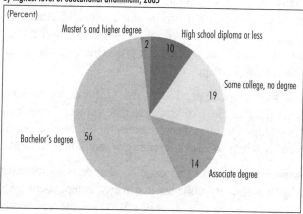

Chart 2

Field of study distribution for all degree holders in computer-related occupations

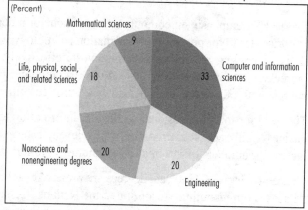

Source: National Science Foundation. SESTAT Integrated Data System. The SESTAT Web site is sestat.nsf.gov.

Degrees

Many employers of information technology workers require applicants to have a degree, which they perceive as proof of a worker's ability to think logically. And there are plenty of options for students interested in earning a degree in information technology. According to the National Center for Education Statistics, computer and information sciences include computer programming, data processing, information science and systems, computer systems analysis, and computer science.

But, as mentioned previously, most information technology workers who have a degree do not have one in a computer field. Some, like Maria, studied subjects completely unrelated to information technology and gained computer knowledge through other coursework and related experience. Associate, bachelor's, and graduate degree programs have different focuses in training workers for information technology jobs.

Associate degrees. The associate degree is an increasingly attractive option for information technology workers. Most community colleges and many independent technical institutes and proprietary schools offer an associate degree in computer science or related information technology fields. Because many of these programs are designed to meet the needs of local businesses, they are more occupation-specific than are those of a 4-year degree. Some jobs may be better suited to the level of training these programs offer. Many students who earn an associate degree seek employment as computer support specialists or as computer programmers. There has been a steady rise in the number of associate degrees granted in the computer and information sciences over the last decade.

Bachelor's degrees. As previously indicated, most information technology workers have at least a bachelor's degree. In his report for the National Research Center for Career and Technical Education, "The Perceived Influence of Industry-Sponsored Credentials," Kenneth Bartlett points out that employers still prefer a 4-year college degree as preparation for information technology jobs. And in a tight job market, preference for a bachelor's degree rises as employers attempt to differentiate among potential jobseekers. But the degree concentration and relevant experience required may vary by occupation.

For computer software engineers, most employers prefer that applicants have at least a bachelor's degree and broad knowledge and experience with computer systems and technologies. The usual degree concentrations for applications software engineers are computer science and software engineering; for systems software engineers, usual concentrations are computer science and computer information systems.

There is no universally accepted way to prepare for a job as a systems analyst or database administrator, network administrator, or network systems and data communications analyst. However, most employers place a premium on some formal college education; a bachelor's degree is a prerequisite for many jobs. Some workers in these occupations have a degree in either computer science, mathematics, or information systems.

The lack of emphasis on computer-related bachelor's degrees in information technology occupations points to an important trend for prospective information technology workers. Employers still demand technical skills, but "soft" skills—including the ability to communicate effectively, both orally and in writing—also are important for these jobseekers to have. Knowing how to write a computer program or administer a database is critical, but ability to interact with other computer specialists, clients, customers, and users continues to gain importance.

The need for multidimensional workers in information technology means that employers prefer workers who have business skills and acumen along with relevant and up-to-date technical expertise. Thus, it is not surprising that increasing numbers of information technology workers do not have computer-related degrees.

Graduate degrees. Graduate degrees are preferred for some of the more complex jobs in software engineering and database administration. According to the National Center for Education Statistics, the number of master's degrees conferred in computer and information sciences has risen sharply, while the number of doctoral degrees in computer science has grown slightly.

Many computer and information systems mangers have a master's degree in business administration (MBA) with technology as a core component. This so-called techno-MBA degree differs from a traditional MBA because of its heavy emphasis on information technology in addition to the standard business curriculum. And because computer and information systems managers make not only technology decisions but also business decisions for their organizations, techno-MBA programs are becoming increasingly popular.

Information technology workers interested in becoming a computer or information scientist usually need a doctoral degree in computer science or computer engineering because of the highly innovative and technical nature of the work. Some computer and information systems managers may have a doctoral degree in a computer-related field, demonstrating thorough technical knowledge.

Flexible Pathways

The discussion about career preparation for information technology occupations reveals that there is no universal education and training requirement for jobseekers in information technology. A computer-related degree may be the easiest and most direct route to take, but it is by no means the only one. There is a variety of ways in which workers can demonstrate the computer knowledge and skills necessary to get a job in one of several computer-related occupations. Practical experience, although difficult to measure and quantify, is important and allows jobseekers flexibility—especially for those who do not have a computer-related degree.

Information technology workers must continually acquire new skills to remain in this dynamic field. To this end, the role of community colleges in educating and retraining information technology workers should continue to grow in the coming years. An Urban Institute report, "The Role of Community Colleges in Expanding the Supply of Information Technology Workers," says that these schools conduct a large amount of information technology training and contribute to retraining both veteran workers and those from other fields.

Technology changes at such a rapid pace that retraining and updating information technology skills is essential, even for workers already in their jobs. The emphasis on nondegree programs, such as employer training and self-study, also will rise in importance. And just as colleges and universities are increasingly using distance education as an efficient and cost-saving measure, organizations are using it to train and retrain their employees in information technology.

There are several ways that individuals may prepare to become an information technology worker. At first glance, the tracks that Maria and Spencer took to get jobs in their respective computer-related occupations might seem unorthodox. Yet with rapidly changing technology and increasingly flexible training requirements, the routes they took should remain commonplace.

For More Information

Consult the *Occupational Outlook Handbook* to learn more about specific information technology occupations. Along with training requirements, the *Handbook* provides details about the nature of the work, working conditions, earnings, employment, and job outlook for the following information technology occupations: computer and information systems managers; computer hardware engineers; computer programmers; computer software engineers; computer support specialists and systems administrators; and systems analysts, computer scientists, and database administrators.

The following organizations also provide information for computer-related careers:

Association for Computing Machinery (ACM)
1515 Broadway
New York, NY 10036-5701
(800) 342-6626
(212) 626-0500
www.acm.org

IEEE Computer Society
Headquarters Office
1730 Massachusetts Ave. NW
Washington, DC 20036-1992
(800) 678-4333
(202) 371-0101
www.computer.org

National Workforce Center for Emerging Technologies
3000 Landerholm Circle SE, N258
Bellevue, WA 98007-6484
(425) 564-4215
www.nwcet.org

Information about the designation of Certified Computing Professional is available from
Institute for Certification of Computer Professionals (ICCP)
2350 E. Devon Ave., Suite 115
Des Plaines, IL 60018-4610
(800) U-GET-CCP (843-8227)
(847) 229-4227
www.iccp.org

Information about training leading to a CompTIA certification is available from
Computing Technology Industry Association (CompTIA)
1815 S. Meyers Rd., Suite 300
Oakbrook Terrace, IL 60181-5228
(630) 678-8300
www.comptia.org

For information about training for Microsoft certification, contact
Microsoft Corporation
One Microsoft Way
Redmond, WA 98052-6399
(800) MICROSOFT (642-7676)
www.microsoft.com/learning/default.mspx

Information about training for Oracle certification is available from
Oracle Corporation
500 Oracle Parkway
Redwood Shores, CA 94065
(800) 633-0738
(800) ORACLE1 (672-2531)
(650) 506-7000
education.oracle.com

For information about training for Cisco certification, contact
Cisco Systems, Inc.
170 W. Tasman Dr.
San Jose, CA 95134
(800) 553-NETS (6387)
(408) 526-4000
http://www.cisco.com/web/learning/

Information about training for Novell certification is available from
Novell, Inc.
2211 N. First St.
San Jose, CA 95131
(800) 233-3382
www.novell.com/training/index.html

From the Occupational Outlook Quarterly by the U.S. Department of Labor. Written by Roger Moncarz, an economist in the Office of Occupational Statistics and Employment Projections, BLS.

Index